dBASE III® Plus
Applications Library

Thomas W. Carlton

with

Charles O. Stewart III

dBASE III® Plus Applications Library

Copyright 1986 © by Que™ Corporation

Library of Congress Catalog No.: LC 85-63880
ISBN 0-88022-228-X

90   89   88   87   9   8   7   6   5   4   3   2

Interpretation of the printing code: the rightmost double-digit number is the year of the book's printing; the rightmost single-digit number, the number of the book's printing. For example, a printing code of 87-4 shows that the fourth printing of the book occurred in 1987.

Screen reproductions were produced with Inset, a graphics-and-text-integrator program from American Programmers Guild, Ltd.

Dedications

To my wife, Susan,
who encouraged and supported this undertaking.
—T.W.C.

To Mary, Peter, and Molly.
—C.O.S.

Product Director
David P. Ewing, M.A.

Editorial Director
David F. Noble, Ph.D.

Managing Editor
Gregory Croy

Production Editor
Bill Nolan

Technical Editors
Allen L. Wyatt
Doug Ferris
Tim Stanley

Production Foreman
Dennis Sheehan

Production
Joe Ramon
Mae Louise Shinault
Peter Tocco
Lynne Tone

About the Authors

Thomas W. Carlton

As an independent consultant and as corporate business analyst for CF Industries, Inc., in Long Grove, Illinois, Thomas W. Carlton has used dBASE extensively in accounting and financial-analysis applications. He is a graduate of Kalamazoo College, with a major in physics and a minor in economics and mathematics. He graduated from the University of Chicago's Graduate School of Business, with a concentration in accounting and statistics.

Mr. Carlton is the author of *1-2-3 Financial Macros* (Que Corporation, 1985) and the contributor of several articles to *IBM PC Update: New Techniques for Professionals* and *Absolute Reference: The Journal for 1-2-3 and Symphony Users*.

Charles O. Stewart III

Charles O. Stewart III is a staff writer in the Product Development Department at Que Corporation. He was a production editor for many Que books, including *Using WordPerfect*, *Using 1-2-3* (2nd Edition), *R:base 5000 User's Guide*, *Using Reflex*, and *Using Javelin*.

Mr. Stewart received a B.A. in English from Indiana University and an M.A. in English from the University of Illinois, where he studied literature and critical theory and taught composition and business communication.

Before joining Que, Mr. Stewart was a technical editor in the Engineering Publications Department at Allison Gas Turbine Operations, General Motors Corporation.

Contents

3   Tips and Techniques

4   Personnel System

5 Sales-Tracking System

6   Fixed-Asset Manager

7 Customer-Account System

9   Linking Stand-Alone Applications

Acknowledgments

Chapter 5 was developed and written by Bill Hatfield, MIS manager for Que Corporation and president of Hatfield and Associates, a data-processing and consulting firm in Indianapolis.

Portions of Chapters 1 and 2 were adapted with permission from the *dBASE III Plus Handbook*, 2nd Edition, by George Tsu-der Chou (Que Corporation, 1986).

I want to thank Dave Ewing, product development director, Que Corporation, for his comments and suggestions during the writing of this book, and Bill Nolan, production editor, Que Corporation, for his valuable comments and suggestions during the editing of the book. Both made significant contributions to the end result.

I also want to thank the people at CF Industries for their encouragement and support in this undertaking.

—T.W.C.

Trademark Acknowledgments

Introduction

Over the years, dBASE® in its various releases has earned a reputation as a potent and versatile tool that is well suited to complex business applications. Developing a business application in dBASE III® Plus is considerably less difficult than developing the same application in a programming language such as BASIC, COBOL, or Pascal, with no sacrifice in power.

The full power of dBASE III Plus derives from its combination of a relational database, interactive query commands, and a powerful applications-development language. With dBASE III Plus, you can develop user-friendly applications that allow someone with limited computer experience to enter data and generate reports in a routine manner. When a special need arises, you can use the interactive command mode to update, analyze, and summarize the data. And as your business grows, you can reorganize your data files and revise or add programs to your dBASE applications to keep them current with your needs.

Why An Applications Library?

The applications library presented in this book is intended primarily for those who are familiar with dBASE and have had some experience with applications development. This practical book contains six complete business applications with a description of each application from the application developer's view. By studying these applications and combining the relevant portions with your own code, you can get started developing applications that will meet your particular needs—or the needs of others.

And why develop business applications in dBASE III Plus? There are three primary reasons. First, you may find that no commercially available programs meet your needs. Second, you may not like the way the available programs operate. Third, you may find that commercial programs are too general to perform your applications efficiently.

If yours is a general business application and your (or your client's) business is similar to many other small- or medium-sized businesses, then you may find a considerable selection of commercial programs that are suitable. But if your application is unique, then a custom-designed program may be the only choice.

Even if commercially available packages can perform your application, you may find that they require you to change the way you run your business, or at least the way you collect and record your data. Or such packages may require data that is difficult to collect in your business. The fact that an application *could* be done with a commercial program doesn't mean that it *should* be.

Finally, commercially available programs are, of necessity, designed as general-purpose packages. In some cases, this means that they do more than your application requires, or that they require you to enter data that you don't really need for the operation of your business. In other cases, the general-purpose programs produce output that is difficult for you to use. You shouldn't have to change the way you do business just to meet the demands of a program!

A rule of thumb is that custom applications are much more expensive to develop than "canned" programs are to purchase. Depending on your business and application, however, the extra expense can be a wise investment.

Who Should Use This Book?

If you've had some experience with applications development but want to learn how to build business applications using dBASE III Plus, then you should use this book. The dBASE III Plus Applications Library provides many examples that illustrate techniques for applications development and patterns to follow in developing your own dBASE business applications.

If you plan to develop one or more of these applications, all the dBASE III Plus code is provided. All you need to do is read the appropriate chapters and either enter the code from the listings or purchase the optional disk (see the back of this book for an order form).

If you are developing a different application, you can use portions of the dBASE III Plus code in this book as the core for developing your own application. By not having to "reinvent the wheel," you save valuable time and effort. In addition, this book provides you with many helpful ideas on how to develop applications that are well-structured, efficient, and accurate.

If you are not yet experienced in using dBASE III Plus at the dot prompt, or if you would like a more detailed explanation of the fundamentals of dBASE programming, you should read George Tsu-der Chou's *dBASE III Plus Handbook*, 2nd Edition, also published by Que Corporation. Dr. Chou's book contains a complete and very readable discussion of using dBASE III Plus interactively and of the fundamentals of dBASE III Plus programming.

What Is in This Book?

Chapter 1, "An Overview of dBASE III Plus," begins with a brief history of dBASE, and then discusses the features of dBASE III Plus. The chapter also talks about the difference between using dBASE interactively and developing business applications with dBASE.

Chapter 2, "Applications Development with dBASE III Plus," discusses the process of developing applications. dBASE III users with limited programming experience should read this chapter before reading the application chapters.

Chapter 3, "Tips and Techniques," discusses elements common to all the applications in the book, such as using memory variables in subroutines, using memory files to store key system parameters, entering data, designing a consistent user interface, accomplishing database queries, and printing reports. The chapter also includes a brief discussion of the RUN command, which allows you to include DOS commands in a dBASE application, and of importing and exporting data with dBASE.

Chapters 4 through 8 present the applications library, one application for each chapter. The applications are presented roughly in order of increasing complexity. Besides presenting the code and explaining how it accomplishes the application, each chapter summarizes the steps of development that lead up to the actual writing of the code. Furthermore, most of the chapters suggest possible extensions to the applications.

Chapter 4, "Personnel System," shows how to set up a master file containing basic information on a company's employees. The application creates reports, mailing lists, and labels based on the employee information, and enables the user to perform simple queries.

Chapter 5, "Sales-Tracking System," presents a system for tracking product sales and calculating monthly commissions and inventory requirements. The system also provides up to date information about a particular customer or about a particular salesperson's performance.

Chapter 6, "Fixed-Asset Manager," introduces an application that records all of a company's fixed assets and calculates depreciation for book purposes using either straight-line or accelerated depreciation. This application has a query mode for looking up specific assets and their depreciation, and a flexible report generator that prints asset reports and depreciation reports in a variety of formats.

Chapter 7, "Customer-Account System," discusses a simple system for managing accounts receivable. The system records charges and payments, automatically bills accounts, creates monthly statements and management reports, and flags past-due accounts.

Chapter 8, "General-Ledger and Financial-Reporting System," treats the most complex application in the book, a computerized replacement for a manual accounting system. The chapter discusses the general ledger, the financial-reporting system, and methods for linking the general ledger to other accounting modules to develop a complete accounting system.

Chapter 9, "Linking Stand-Alone Applications," discusses how to tie together dBASE III applications with other applications developed both with dBASE III and with other programs. The chapter discusses four techniques for tying applications together:

common data files, common data-entry programs, programs to summarize data from one system and transfer it to the other, and data transfer from non-dBASE applications by reading data from a report that was saved to disk. Each technique is described and illustrated with an example.

How To Use This Book

Read the first three chapters to get an overview of applications development with dBASE III Plus and the approach used in this book. Before attempting one of the more complex applications, you might work with one of the simpler applications, such as the personnel system or the sales-tracking system.

I suggest that you enter essentially as shown the application or portion of an application that you are interested in, and that you get it working before you substantially modify it. Working with a tested "known quantity" prevents the confusion that would ensue if you first modified the application, then attempted to run it and encountered a problem. You wouldn't know whether the source of the problem was your modifications or a mistake made while entering the unmodified parts of the application. If you want to avoid typing errors and the tedium of keying in the applications code, purchase Que's *dBASE III Plus Applications Disk and Software Guide*. The applications disk contains all the code published in this book. For pricing and ordering information, see the form in the back of this book.

If you are not already doing so, I suggest that you make use of dBASE III Plus's capability of substituting an external program editor for the one supplied with the software. I have my copy of dBASE III Plus set up to use the Norton Editor™ as the program editor when I issue a MODIFY COMMAND statement from the dot prompt. I have also used the IBM Professional Editor™ and the IBM Personal Editor™. Any of these third-party editors is far superior to the program editor built into dBASE. For information on setting up your copy of dBASE III Plus to use an external editor, see the section "Using Another Editor with dBASE III Plus" in Chapter 3.

Other Sources of dBASE Knowledge

Que's *dBASE III Plus Handbook*, 2nd Edition, by George Tsu-der Chou, is an excellent companion to this book. The last five chapters of the *Handbook*— "Fundamentals of Command-File Programming," "Programming Input and Output Operations," "Conditional Branching and Program Loops," "Modular Programming," and "An Integrated Database System"—contain information you will find particularly useful in developing applications from scratch or adapting those presented here.

If you want to learn tricks and techniques from an experienced dBASE applications developer, consult Joseph-David Carrabis' *dBASE III Advanced Programming*, also from Que Corporation. That book offers a wealth of practical advice on writing applications in dBASE, along with useful observations on ways to approach applications development.

1

An Overview of dBASE III Plus

Before we consider the applications developed in this book, we ought to look at the evolution of dBASE, which for some time now has been the most widely used database manager on the IBM® PC. dBASE has evolved through several versions from the original dBASE II® to the current dBASE III Plus. Each new version of dBASE has offered more power and capability to both the application developer and the user.

This chapter begins with a brief history of dBASE, and then moves to an overview of dBASE III Plus. We look at system limitations, such as the maximum number of open files or the maximum number of records; hardware requirements; and networking capabilities. This chapter also covers some of the enhancements with dBASE III Plus for using the program interactively, such as the Assistant. Finally, we consider the boon that batch processing with dBASE III Plus is to the applications developer.

A Brief History of dBASE

The original dBASE program, dBASE II, was developed several years ago; it originally ran on 8-bit microcomputers using the CP/M-80™ disk operating system. That version of dBASE II was used on various microcomputers, such as the TRS-80®, the Osborne™, the Kaypro™ portable, and the Apple® II (with a CP/M® card installed). dBASE II later was rewritten for the IBM personal computer and compatible machines. Version 2.4 was released in September, 1983, for IBM PCs running under PC DOS V1.1, 2.0, or 2.1.

Before the introduction of dBASE II, database management systems were used mainly on large computers because the systems then available required powerful processors and huge amounts of computer memory. ("Huge" compared to microcomputers available in the 1970s. The IBM personal computer AT compares favorably with a small mainframe computer of the late 1960s or early 1970s.) The processing languages for these database management systems were foreign to most nonprogrammers; processing data with those systems required programs written by professionally trained programmers. Because of the high costs of purchasing and operating database management systems, the power of database management could be enjoyed only by users of larger computer systems.

The release of dBASE II represented a bold attempt to tap the power of recently developed microcomputers for database management applications. Since its release, the program has become the best-known microcomputer software for database management. Although the limited processing power and memory capacity of the early microcomputers often compromised the power of dBASE II, that program nonetheless revolutionized the way information was handled on microcomputers.

Early criticism of dBASE II was directed toward its slow processing speed and the small size of the databases it supported. These problems were due partly to the restricted processing power of the microprocessors available in 1979 and 1980.

Nonprogrammers, furthermore, often complained that the programming language was difficult and time-consuming to master. dBASE II was not user friendly because its design philosophy was largely adapted from that of systems for large computers; database management applications for those systems were written by professional programmers. In addition, the computer language in which dBASE II was developed was not designed for performing the kinds of processing tasks required by a large database management system. As a result, the computational power of dBASE II was not satisfactory for larger database management applications.

Since the introduction of dBASE II, microcomputer technology has advanced rapidly. Most microcomputers now use powerful 16-bit microprocessors, which process data much faster than the 8-bit processors of earlier microcomputers. Large memory capacity also is now readily available at low cost. New and more powerful computer languages, such as the C language, have been developed and perfected for microcomputers.

In response to the technical advances in hardware and software, as well as to competitive pressures, dBASE III was introduced in 1984. Although evolved from dBASE II, dBASE III was drastically different from its predecessor; dBASE III therefore cannot be considered simply an upgraded version of dBASE II. dBASE III was designed for the modern 16-bit microprocessor. It took advantage of the greatly increased memory capacity and processing speed of the IBM PC and compatible computers, offering significant enhancements in both user friendliness and database management capabilities.

The strength of dBASE II lay in its programming features, which provided powerful tools for creating database management applications. However, dBASE II was not designed to support menus, which simplify database management for nonprogrammers. dBASE III corrected many of the deficiencies of dBASE II. With its "help" screens (detailed helpful hints accessed by a single keystroke) and the ASSIST command, dBASE III enabled microcomputer users to start manipulating data in a relatively short time. Because of the program's tremendous power and flexibility, however, considerable time and effort were still required to master dBASE III before serious business applications could be developed.

dBASE III still had shortcomings in the areas of interactive usage and database capability; these shortcomings became apparent as a generation of more user-friendly competitors began to appear. Responding to the demand for an even friendlier and more powerful program, Ashton-Tate introduced dBASE III Plus late in 1985. dBASE III Plus introduces several new features that give users nearly the same capabilities in interactive mode that are available through the programming features. At the same time, several new features improve dBASE III Plus's debugging capabilities and help to reduce the programming effort involved in developing applications.

Ashton-Tate introduced a multiuser version of dBASE several years ago, but it never became widely used. With the introduction of dBASE III Plus, Ashton-Tate now supplies in the same package both a single-user system and a network multiuser system. The network version is upward-compatible from the single-user version; a properly designed single-user application can be modified into a multiuser version with the addition of the appropriate commands for file- and record-locking.

In summary, dBASE III Plus has once again defined a standard of performance that the competition is scrambling to meet.

Features of dBASE III Plus

dBASE III Plus is a relational database management system. The program runs on IBM personal computers and compatible machines, and is designed for creating, maintaining, and manipulating relational databases.

dBASE III Plus stores information in relational data tables. The information in the database can be processed in two ways. One way is interactive command processing. In that method, the information database is manipulated by means of commands entered interactively from the keyboard. After each command is entered, results are displayed on an output device such as a monitor or a printer.

Another method for processing information with dBASE III Plus is batch command processing. Processing tasks are defined in a set of command procedures. The collection of commands is stored in a command file, which can be compared to a computer program. These commands are then executed in a batch. With a batch-command file, a processing menu can be designed so that users can select particular tasks while the program is running.

The batch-command processing capability is the core of dBASE's usefulness for application development. The batch command capabilities have been enhanced with each release of dBASE to the point where the command language is well suited to writing applications using modular, top-down programming techniques.

But the interactive mode remains important for application development. In interactive mode you can manually go through the program steps from the keyboard and examine the results after each command. And if a problem occurs in the application, you can dig into the data files from the keyboard to locate and fix the problem. Interactive mode is an invaluable aid for both application development and system maintenance.

System Limitations

dBASE III Plus has a large but finite database capacity. The database files hold a maximum of:

1 billion records
2 billion bytes (equivalent to 100 20-megabyte hard disks)
4000 bytes per record
128 fields per record
254 bytes per field

The memo files hold a maximum of 512 kilobytes per memo field.

The most severe limitation of dBASE is the maximum of 15 open files. It is very easy to bump into this limit when developing even moderately complex business applications. The larger applications in this book were developed to operate within the 15-file limit. dBASE III Plus allows 10 database files to be open at once, but the total number of open files—including database, index, memo, procedure, and program files—cannot exceed 15. (This is a limitation imposed by PC-DOS, not by dBASE.) There can be a maximum of 7 open index files and 1 open format file per database file.

System Requirements

dBASE III Plus is designed to run on the IBM PC, IBM portable computer, IBM PC XT™, IBM personal computer AT, the COMPAQ®, and other IBM-compatible microcomputers. dBASE III Plus requires MS-DOS® or PC-DOS Version 2.0 or later. The minimum computer memory requirement is 256K under DOS Version 2.0 or 2.1, but more memory offers increased processing speed. dBASE will not run in 256K of memory under DOS 3.0 or above. If you plan to replace the dBASE editor with an external program editor or make use of the RUN command, your computer should have at least 384K of memory and preferably 512K.

For serious application development, your PC should have at least a 360K floppy disk and a 10-megabyte hard disk. You can do development work on a two floppy disk system, but the process is slowed down considerably. If the application that you are developing involves large numbers of transactions or database entries, then the user's system will also require a hard disk to run the application successfully.

As this book was going to press, Ashton-Tate announced the removal of all copy protection from its products and offered for a fee to upgrade all registered users to the non-copy-protected version. But many existing installations of dBASE still are copy protected with Softguard's SuperLok system. If your dBASE program is copy-protected and you are using a floppy disk system, two disks are required to start up dBASE. If you are using a hard disk, you can load on the hard disk all of dBASE except the copy-protection files, and use the copy-protected master disk as a key disk to start dBASE.

The SuperLok copy protection system offers the option of installing the copy protection on your hard disk, but I strongly recommend against it. If something happens to your hard disk (and they do occasionally fail), then the copy of dBASE on the hard disk is GONE! (There is a backup disk, however.) I have a client who had two hard disk failures as a result and lost his $700 SuperLok'd payroll program. When you lose the use of your business applications even for a few days, you're in trouble. Use the key disk or purchase the upgrade!

Networking Capabilities

The dBASE III Plus package includes both a single-user and a multiuser version of dBASE III Plus. The multiuser system supports either the IBM PC Network Program or Novell® Advanced NetWare®/86. The multiuser version of dBASE provides capabilities for file-locking and record-locking, as well as a security system including data encryption and password protection.

The multiuser version is upwardly compatible from the single-user version, with additional commands provided to implement the network functions. You could conceivably set up a single user system as a multiuser system simply by adding the necessary file and record-locking commands, but response time and efficiency will be better if you redesign the application as a multiuser application.

A multiuser system provides a number of advantages over a single-user system. In a multiuser accounting application, for example, one person can be entering receivables while a second person is printing checks from the payables and a third person is looking up an account balance to answer a customer's question. An upwardly-compatible multiuser dBASE gives your single-user applications an expansion path that wasn't available before.

Although this book concentrates on single-user applications, you can consult the network-programming section of the dBASE III Plus user manual to make the transition to a multiuser system after you have mastered the concepts for a single-user system. If you are interested in developing a multiuser application, I suggest that you begin by getting the application to work as a single-user application. Next, add the networking commands necessary to run the application on a multiuser system; finally, monitor the application's performance and redesign those portions of the system that turn out to be bottlenecks.

Using dBASE III Plus Interactively

dBASE III Plus, unlike its predecessors dBASE III and dBASE II, makes most of its power available to the interactive user without requiring the writing of programs or command files. Several high-level commands make it possible for the user to set up and maintain complex relationships between data files and to perform complex queries.

In particular, the MODIFY CATALOG command enables the interactive dBASE user to group together all dBASE files associated with a particular application. The MODIFY VIEW command gives the user the ability to define and maintain relationships between database files. And the SET FIELDS TO command gives the user selective access to the fields in the related files almost as if these fields were together in one file.

Numerous commands support the editing of data and the creation of report and query files. The APPEND, BROWSE, and EDIT commands give the interactive user full-screen data-entry capability. The CREATE/MODIFY SCREEN command lets the user define the screen layout for data-entry and query screens. The CREATE/MODIFY QUERY command provides the user with a full-screen query editor that can be used to define and save a complex query. The CREATE/MODIFY REPORT command makes a report generator with titles, multilevel headings, and two levels of subtotaling available. The report generator in conjunction with the MODIFY QUERY command can produce most of the reports required in a business aplication.

The Dot Prompt

All of the program's interactive features are available from the "dot prompt," dBASE's traditional user interface. dBASE places a period on the screen and waits for the user to enter a command. After the user enters the command, dBASE parses it and either performs the command or issues an error message. The dot-prompt interface is designed for the knowledgeable user who knows dBASE commands and wants to get the job done quickly and with minimum effort. But the dot prompt is poorly suited for the beginning or casual user who has not reached the required level of expertise.

The Assistant

With the release of dBASE III in 1984, Ashton-Tate partially addressed the needs of the beginning or casual user by adding the Assistant, a menu-driven command interface that walks the user through the creation of a dBASE command. The original Assistant was rather limited in its capabilities, and Ashton-Tate has dramatically upgraded the Assistant for dBASE III Plus. Now it is a full-blown menu system, rather than a series of help screens. Figure 1.1 shows the menu for the dBASE III Plus Assistant.

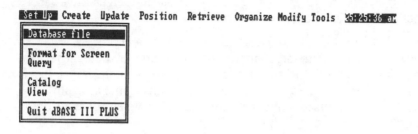

Figure 1.1. The Assistant menu.

Using dBASE III Plus for Applications Development

As mentioned previously, the creators of dBASE III Plus adapted most of its design philosophy from database management systems used on large computers. The predominant mode of processing on large computers is batch processing. Batch processing is an effective method for data management. With its batch-processing capabilities, dBASE III Plus can be considered a highly sophisticated computer programming language for developing database management applications. This applications development feature is not shared by many other user-friendly database software packages designed for micros.

Applications development using dBASE III plus involves developing database file structures to hold the data required for the application plus developing a set of batch-command files to process the data as required by the application. The batch command files, which we refer to in the rest of the book as dBASE programs and subroutines, can perform the entire application, or they can perform portions of the application, leaving the user responsible for performing the rest in interactive mode.

Conclusion

This chapter has covered the history of dBASE and the distinctive features of dBASE III Plus. Although dBASE III Plus can be used interactively, the real power of of the program lies in its built-in programming language, which supports an effective batch processing mode ideal for applications development.

In Chapter 2 we turn our attention to the application-development process. The development steps outlined there represent the distilled wisdom of thousands of programmers, the fruit of much trial and error and many programming hours. By following these steps (or their equivalent) instead of rashly diving into program development, you'll save yourself considerable time and effort when you develop your dBASE applications.

2

Applications Development
with dBASE III Plus

A dBASE III application is merely a set of database files and a collection of dBASE III commands stored in program or procedure files. If you have used dBASE interactively from the dot prompt, you are halfway toward beginning to write applications. If you have used dBASE through the Assistant or a programmed application, then you will have to learn to use dBASE from the dot prompt before making much headway in developing applications.

The border between interactive dBASE use and application development is nebulous. You probably already have one or more business applications set up using interactive dBASE. Typical business applications using dBASE include mailing lists, address books, periodical indexes, and simple personnel databases. These interactive applications are on the border of applications development. To make them work, you have to use dBASE interactively to define database structures and develop procedures for data entry, queries, and reporting.

However, applications development goes well beyond setting up files and procedures using interactive dBASE. As the application becomes more complex and the intended user less competent with dBASE, the role of programming in applications development becomes more dominant. If you are setting up a business information system for a knowledgeable user, the optimum solution may be to develop programs for data entry, routine reports, and system maintenance functions, but to let all *ad hoc* querying and reporting be done interactively. On the other hand, if you are developing an accounting system to record business transactions, and the user is a clerk with little or no dBASE experience, then you would probably want to develop a turnkey application where the user does everything through the application's menus.

This chapter discusses all the steps in developing an application with dBASE III Plus. Topics discussed include identifying the purpose and functions of the system, understanding the needs of users, defining file structures, using "top down" programming and modular design, creating block diagrams and flowcharts, writing and documenting program code, developing menu systems, testing the application, and using procedure files and other techniques to improve system performance.

The Applications-Development Process

You can begin to develop dBASE applications in two ways. One way is to dive in and code the programs without planning. This "brute force" method is successful generally with small dBASE programs that do just one thing. If the program is simple and involves just one or at most two pages of dBASE code, then this method may work for you.

For larger or more complex applications, time spent planning the application and breaking it down into tasks and program modules before coding pays big dividends in time and effort saved. In fact, careful planning and design can make the difference between an application that works and one that is "dead on arrival." (What you are doing is breaking a complex task down into a series of simple ones that you can conquer by brute force.)

The use of two strategies—top-down design and modular programming—results in an application that consists of a series of small programs or subroutines (one to two pages each) that each perform one task in the application. These small programs can be developed and tested individually before being assembled into the completed application. The planning that you do to develop the top-down program design and the list of program modules helps to ensure that everything will work together when the modules are assembled.

Identifying the Purpose and Functions of the Application

The first step in developing any business application is to understand clearly the purpose and functions of the application. Let's assume that you're an applications developer who has just been contacted by a new client. Your first task is to determine what the application should do to satisfy the client's needs. There are several key questions you should ask as you begin your analysis of the problem. What are the problems with the old system (if one exists)? What specific outputs will be produced by the application? What specific data will be entered to produce the outputs? What type of data security, backups, and other safeguards will be required of the system?

For example, suppose your client wants to computerize his or her company's general ledger. A number of questions should be answered in some detail. Does the client want the general ledger to prepare a trial balance or the company's financial statements? Does he or she want the ledger to track balances by general-ledger account or by ledger account and division? Does he or she want the ledger to be stand-alone or to tie into other computerized accounting systems? What do the data-input forms look like? What do the current reports look like? What kind of audit trail will satisfy the auditors?

After you have come to an understanding with your client about the purpose and functions of the application, you must consider the people who will use it. Are they computer literate? Are they familiar with dBASE? Are they cognizant of the business issues involved in using the system? Will different portions of the application be handled by users with varying skill levels? The users' level of knowledge will affect the techniques used for data entry, queries, and reporting. This information will determine also how much of the application will involve interactive dBASE and how much will involve batch processing and menus for users.

Defining the File Structures

After you have met with your client to determine the purpose and functions of the application and who the users will be, you are ready to begin designing the necessary file structures. You do this now because the structure of the data files usually influences how the system functions are implemented in programs and subroutines.

Laying out file structures for a relational database is an art that has to be mastered through practice. However, some useful rules can guide you in developing the file structure for a particular application. The paragraphs that follow examine these rules in the context of laying out file structures for a customer-account system. (Chapter 7 provides a full treatment of this application.)

Keep it simple. The customer-account file in figure 2.1 contains data on one customer per record. There is one record for each customer with an open account, and all the records in the file contain the same customer data. Don't attempt to keep more than one type of database record in the file; keep only the essential information. In general, if the application doesn't use it, don't store it.

Place repeated fields in a separate file. The customer-account system maintains transaction information for each customer. You do not want to include this information in the customer master file CACUST.DBF, because there can be an unlimited number of transaction records for each customer. Instead, you place the transaction information in a separate database, whose structure is shown in figure 2.2. The transaction records are linked with a particular customer by the customer ID number, which is contained in the field CUST_ID. The transaction file can contain many transaction records for each customer. In the jargon of database management, this is known as a one-to-many relationship.

Segregate less commonly used data in a separate database. Your application will run faster with less data in the main database. Because the data you have segregated is used less often, the segregation entails no significant performance penalty.

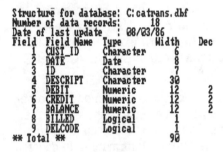

```
Structure for database: C:cacust.dbf
Number of data records:        0
Date of last update   : 07/28/86
Field  Field Name  Type       Width  Dec
    1  CUST_ID     Character      6
    2  COMPANY     Character     26
    3  ADDR1       Character     26
    4  ADDR2       Character     26
    5  CITY        Character     16
    6  STATE       Character      2
    7  ZIP         Character     10
    8  F_NAME      Character     10
    9  L_NAME      Character     16
   10  PHONE       Character     14
   11  STATUS      Character      1
   12  BALANCE     Numeric       12    2
   13  CREDITLIM   Numeric       12    2
   14  AUTOBILL    Logical        1
   15  AUTOFEE     Numeric       12    2
   16  AUTODESCR   Character     30
   17  COMMENT     Character     60
   18  STMTDATE    Date           8
   19  STMTBAL     Numeric       12    2
** Total **                    301
```

Fig. 2.1. Structure of the customer master file from the customer-account application.

```
Structure for database: C:catrans.dbf
Number of data records:       18
Date of last update   : 08/03/86
Field  Field Name  Type       Width  Dec
    1  CUST_ID     Character      6
    2  DATE        Date           8
    3  ID          Character      7
    4  DESCRIPT    Character     30
    5  DEBIT       Numeric       12    2
    6  CREDIT      Numeric       12    2
    7  BALANCE     Numeric       12    2
    8  BILLED      Logical        1
    9  DELCODE     Logical        1
** Total **                     90
```

Fig.2.2. Structure of the transaction data file from the customer-account application.

Don't overlap fields. Use one key field as a bridge between the master file and the subsidiary file, but don't carry the same data redundantly in both files except for the key field.

Plan around the limit of 15 open files. The larger applications in this book were designed around the 15-file limit. Given an unlimited number of open files, I would have designed the applications with more and smaller database files.

Specifying the Function of Each Program

The next step in developing the application is to determine the division of labor among the programs. This step represents a further refinement of the process of describing, defining, and planning the system. The *top-down* analysis involved in this step produces a block diagram that will serve as a guide through the rest of the application development. Indeed, the entire process of refining the design of the application describes what is meant by top-down development.

Using Top-Down Design Principles

Top-down design is a commonly used method of analyzing the requirements of an application and developing a plan of attack. In general terms, this approach involves mapping out a general strategy that breaks the problem down into a series of smaller problems. Then you can work out the details of each smaller problem until you have resolved the business application into a series of small tasks that can each be accomplished with one or two pages of dBASE code.

Creating a Block Diagram for the System

I generally like to begin the top-down analysis of an application by drawing a block diagram of the system. Figure 2.3 shows the block diagram of the fixed-asset manager discussed in Chapter 6. This diagram illustrates how I divided the application into tasks.

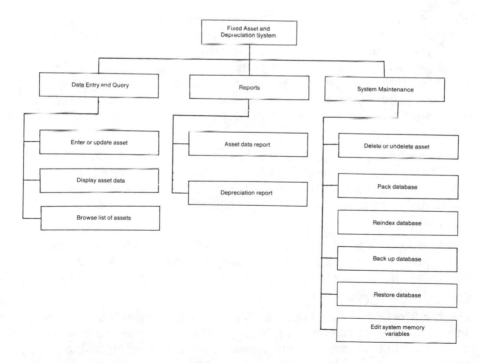

Fig. 2.3. Block diagram of the fixed-asset manager.

You develop the block diagram by recalling the functions identified in your initial analysis of the system. This block diagram fits in nicely with the top-down and modular approaches to applications development. But bear in mind that the purpose of the block diagram is to help you, not constrain you; feel free to change it as needed. You will probably change the block diagram many times as the system specifications change or as you develop the programs and subroutines that implement the tasks specified in the diagram.

The decision of what functions to include in the block diagram, such as the function in figure 2.3 for entering or updating an asset, is influenced partly by what the system has to do (the system specification), partly by the way dBASE operates, and partly by the preferences of the application developer and the end user.

In the fixed-asset application, the system specification determines the functions included in the system, like entering, updating, browsing, and deleting fixed-asset information. Personal preferences and a consideration of how dBASE operates determined that entering and updating data should be combined in one function, with the delete and browse functions handled separately.

Using Modular Programming

The best way to distribute the tasks constituting a function (such as entering and updating assets) among a program and subroutines is to write down the steps that dBASE will take to perform the task and then to divide these steps into logically related groups. Once you have identified the steps that dBASE requires to perform each task, you can determine what steps will be incorporated in the program and what steps will be incorporated in subroutines. The goal of this planning is to reduce the entire system to a set of modules that can each be implemented in one to two pages of code.

There are two rules of thumb for dividing tasks among programs and subroutines. First, have each program or subroutine perform one complete task. Don't have one program stop in the middle of a task and another program pick up where the first left off. Instead, design the program to perform an entire task by having it call subroutines to perform each subtask.

If you observe the principles of top-down programming, you end up with a multilevel block diagram that breaks the application into tasks, and breaks each task into subtasks until the resulting subtasks are small enough to be completed by a dBASE program of one or two pages.

The second rule of thumb is to make certain that each of the programs and subroutines has one entry point and one exit point. This advice is consistent with the "one task per module" philosophy of programming. The dBASE programming language does not always make this easy to do, but it is a goal to strive for.

If you find that the same step or series of steps is required to complete more than one task in the application, these steps should be implemented in "general purpose" subroutines that can be called by any program that needs them. Using common subroutines has two advantages: First, you don't have to enter the same or similar code in several programs; you just enter the subroutine call. Second, if the code needs to be changed, you have to change it in only one place.

One example of using a subroutine to perform a common subtask is the subroutine to open the databases for the fixed-asset manager (Chapter 6). This subroutine is called by every program in the application. A database must be opened with all its indexes by every program that can change the data in a key field. Otherwise, the indexes that are not open during the update will not be updated as the data files are changed, and the database file will have to be reindexed. A subroutine to open all the databases and indexes avoids this problem and makes it easy to add or change a database index without having to change every program in the system.

Using Flowcharts or Pseudocode

After you've created a block diagram of the system and have planned the various modules you think the system will need, you're ready to lay out all the processing steps by drawing flowcharts or writing pseudocode. There are other methods of representing the logic of each program and subroutine, but flowcharts and pseudocode are the most popular.

I have used flowcharts in this book because I find flowcharts' pictorial representation of program logic more helpful than pseudocode's text representation. However, many programmers find pseudocode to be the most effective approach to laying out program logic. Pseudocode is basically a program outline, with program steps described in concise English like statements rather than dBASE commands.

Developing the Programs

After you have used either flowcharts or pseudocode to lay out the logic of the system, you are ready to begin the actual coding. The first consideration is the order of program development. Which programs will you work on first? One approach is to continue with the top-down strategy. You start with the main application program and work down through the system diagram, leaving the programs at the bottom of the chart (the programs that do the actual processing steps) for last. At each point, you can test the programs you have finished by coding dummy subroutines to simulate the presence of the lower-level programs that you have not yet coded.

I have found that I prefer a "bottom-up" approach to program coding. I look at the system diagram and start with one of the detail programs that does not depend on any other program in the system. I develop and test this program, and repeat the process with other independent programs. Then I move to the programs that call the programs that I have already developed and tested. (Note that testing is simplified with the bottom-up approach because no dummy subroutines are necessary.)

Using this approach, I usually begin by coding the system utility programs that open files and those that reindex files when the indexes are damaged. Then I code the data-entry portions of the system. By the time the data-entry programs are coded and tested, there is test data in the database to use with the query and reporting programs. The last thing I develop is the main user menu that controls the entire system (the top level of the system block diagram). You'll find this order of coding in all the applications presented in this book.

Moving from Flowchart to dBASE Code

Your flowcharts or pseudocode listings of each program should include sufficient detail to capture the program logic. The next task is to translate each step in the flowchart or pseudocode into one or more dBASE commands. If you have done your homework before starting to code, the actual coding will be fairly routine.

Testing Individual Programs

Whether you follow either the top-down or the bottom-up approach to program coding, you should test individual programs and subroutines by simulating their use in the application. For example, when testing the data-entry programs, you should enter data similar to what would be entered in practice. You should also test each program and subroutine for its handling of abnormal situations and data-entry errors. This testing helps prevent the end user from destroying data or crashing the system after it's up and running.

If you follow the top-down approach, you will have to create your test data sets using interactive dBASE until you approach the end of program development and have coded the lower-level subroutines. You test the higher-level routines by writing dummy routines that simulate the operation of the lower-level routines.

If you follow the bottom-up approach to program coding, you may have to write a test program to call the subroutine you just coded, but you should be able to enter the test data as you test the programs and subroutines you have developed.

Documenting Your Programs

Trying to correct or modify an application that has little or no program documentation can be incredibly frustrating. Be considerate of those (including yourself) who will have to maintain the application: document the programs as you go. Program documentation starts with the program header and includes comment lines and line-by-line comments adjacent to the dBASE commands and statements.

The Program Header

The program header provides the name of the program, a description of what it does, the date of the last update, and, optionally, the significance of each subroutine parameter. A sample header for the SCROLLER subroutine is shown in Figure 2.4.

```
*************************************************************************
* SCROLLER - Program to accept keystrokes from user to scroll the screen  *
*           PARAMETERS: SCNT    - returns vertical scroll amt to next screen *
*                       CNTR    - number of lines displayed on last screen *
*                       MSCROLL - number of lines that fit on a screen *
*                       SCREEN  - current screen number *
*                       SMAX    - maximum screen number *
*           8/5/86                                                     *
*************************************************************************
```

Fig. 2.4. Sample program header.

Comment Lines

Another important piece of program documentation is comment lines in the program. I generally try to place one comment line in the program for each box in the flowchart. That way, it is easy to examine the program listing alongside the flowchart.

Line-by-Line Comments Using &&

The final piece of documentation within the program is line-by-line comments using the && function. Line-by-line comments are useful for documenting exactly what each line of program code is doing. Figure 2.5 shows a program fragment with comment lines as well as line-by-line comments.

```
* Set environment and open files
SET DELETED ON
DO faopen                            && Open files and indexes
SELECT fixasset
RESTORE FROM famem ADDITIVE          && Restore system memory variables
smax=2                               && Number of browse screens per record
mtitle="BROWSE LIST OF FIXED ASSETS" && Screen title
DO borders WITH fatitle,mtitle
```

Fig. 2.5. Program fragment with comment lines and line-by-line comments.

Creating the Menu System

A menu system ties the programs together and provides the user with easy access to all the system's functions. If you have coded the programs in a top-down manner, the menu system was completed first, and the system is finished when you code the last detail program. If you have coded the programs from the bottom up, coding the the menus completes the system. With either approach, the menu system will probably duplicate the system block diagram.

Testing the System

After all the programs and subroutines have been developed and tested in isolation, it is time to test the entire system. Sit down and try to use the system as the users will. Go through the typical use cycles to make sure that the programs work together as they should. Make data-entry mistakes to ensure that the application handles them appropriately. Check the data files to be certain that the application enters, updates, and removes data properly. It is impossible to do too much testing.

Creating User Documentation

In addition to the developer's documentation, which consists of the system specification, the system block diagram, the program flow charts, and the commented program listings, you will need to develop some documentation that instructs the user how to run the application.

User documentation can range from a simple instruction sheet that merely jogs the user's memory, to a multipage user manual that discusses both the business and the data management aspects of the application and provides examples for the user to follow. The nature of the user documentation should be a subject of negotiation between you and your client.

Enhancing System Performance

After you have developed and tested an application, you will have a collection of dozens of programs and subroutines. You can speed up the execution of the application by consolidating these programs and subroutines into one or more procedure files. You can further increase execution speed by using the utility dBCODE that comes with the dBASE III Plus system to compile your program and procedure files, or by using a third-party dBASE compiler to turn your application into directly executable machine language code.

Using Procedure Files

Breaking down your application into programs and subroutines, each performing one or more related steps in a task, makes it easier to develop and maintain the application. Ideally, your application will consist of many programs and subroutines that are each one to three pages long.

However, an application runs more slowly when it is written as a collection of programs and subroutines instead of as one long program. Each time a subroutine is called, dBASE must open the subroutine file and read in the code from disk. dBASE will run more slowly with subroutines even if you use a hard disk or place all the subroutines in a RAM disk.

Procedure files provide a solution to the slow execution of subroutines. If you place all critical subroutines together in a procedure file, dBASE opens the procedure file only once—when the command SET PROCEDURE TO <file> is encountered in the program—and reads the subroutines from the procedure file into memory. (You probably will not gain any speed from using procedure files unless the PC that runs the application has at least 384K of memory.)

Depending on the amount of memory on the user's PC and the way you use subroutines in your application, using a procedure file may or may not result in a noticeable increase in execution speed. The most dramatic improvement comes when a subroutine is called many times from within a loop. You will witness almost no speed improvement if subroutines are each used just once during the execution.

I said previously that you should not put subroutines in procedure files until the application has been developed and tested. There are four reasons why you wouldn't want to use procedure files during the development phase.

First, it is harder to find a subroutine among 20 or 30 other subroutines in a procedure file. Second, a logic error such as an unterminated IF statement or DO WHILE loop can cause the subroutine to continue executing past its end into the next subroutine in the file. This can cause very unpredictable results. Third, if you edit the procedure file and make a change, you have to close the procedure file and reopen it before dBASE recognizes the change. Fourth, the built-in dBASE editor cannot handle any but the smallest procedure files.

Limitations with Procedure Files

Procedure files have two important limitations. First, a procedure file can contain only 32 subroutines. Second, only one procedure file can be open at once. You can close a procedure file and open another within the application, but you cannot return to a program or subroutine in the first procedure file from a call to a subroutine in a second. Therefore, you must select the subroutines that are used together and include no more than 32 of them in each procedure file.

How to Make a Procedure File

To make a procedure file, use your favorite text editor or word processor to load the selected subroutines into one file. (You cannot use the built-in dBASE program editor because it has a file size limit of 5000 bytes.) You must add the statement PROCEDURE <module name> at the beginning of each subroutine that you include in the procedure file.

To use the procedure file, include the statement SET PROCEDURE TO <procedure file> in the program that calls the subroutines. The statement must occur before the first subroutine call. When the program is finished with the current procedure file, you can close the file with either SET PROCEDURE TO or CLOSE PROCEDURE. This command should *not* be included in a subroutine within the procedure file.

You can have more than one procedure file for an application. Shared subroutines present a problem because they would have to be included in more than one procedure file. It may be best to leave them out of all procedure files so that there is only one place to update them. dBASE looks for subroutines in the procedure file first, then looks for ordinary program files. (Remember the 15-file limit.)

Using dBCODE

A second option for speeding up an application is to use the dBASE utility dBCODE to compress the program and subroutine files. This option also should be used only after the application is developed and tested. The compressed files run faster, but they cannot be edited. To make a change in the program, you have to edit the original code and use dBCODE with the modified original. Before using dBCODE, be sure to read carefully the entire section on RUNTIME+ in your *Programming with dBASE III Plus* manual (volume 2 of the dBASE user's manual).

Using a dBASE Compiler

A third option for speeding up an application is to use one of the third-party dBASE compilers. By compiling your application code, you cut out the interpreter step in running the programs. Execution speed is dramatically increased, especially for programs that contain long loops iterated many times.

Conclusion

Don't let the steps presented in this chapter fool you into thinking that application development is a *linear* process. Application development is an *iterative* process. You proceed through the steps until you reach a point where you have to back up and revise some of your earlier work. Don't be surprised if you have to revise the system block diagram and database layout after you have already started coding the programs. And clients frequently want to make changes or additions when the development process is well along. Application development is a creative process that cannot be laid out neatly beforehand. The best advice is to approach the process in an organized yet flexible manner to minimize inevitable changes.

The next chapter explains those "tips and techniques" that were used to develop the applications in this book and which you can use as you begin applications development.

3

Tips and Techniques

The preceding chapter presented, in broad terms, the steps you follow to design and implement an application with dBASE III Plus. This chapter serves as an effective bridge to the application chapters because it discusses methods for entering data, querying the database, and printing reports. The tips and techniques discussed here will increase your understanding of the chapters that follow and should be useful as you develop your own applications.

The chapter begins with a brief review of memory variables and a look at the use of memory-variable files in applications. The text then discusses tips and techniques for entering data, querying the database, and producing simple as well as complex reports. In addition, the chapter provides tips on interfacing with DOS, importing data from other software, and using alternative program editors with dBASE III Plus.

Using Memory Variables

Memory variables represent temporary memory locations that can hold an alphanumeric string or a numeric value. dBASE III Plus allows two types of memory variables: *public* and *private*. Public variables (sometimes called *global* variables) are available to any program or subroutine until they are released or cleared with the CLEAR ALL command. A memory variable can be declared public with a PUBLIC statement at the dot prompt or in any program or subroutine, and can then be used by any other program or subroutine.

Private memory variables are the "property" of the program or subroutine that creates them. A private variable is created when the variable is first defined in a program or subroutine. The variable is available for use within the defining program and by any subroutine called from the defining program. Private variables are released automatically when the defining program or subroutine exits or returns.

I recommend that you define as PRIVATE those memory variables that are local to a particular subroutine. Doing so prevents puzzling problems that can occur later when your subroutine is called from another program and one of the variable names in the calling program matches the name of a local variable in the subroutine. If this happens and you have not declared the local variable private in the subroutine, the subroutine will change the value in the calling program.

The importance of defining local memory variables as private was underscored for me while I was working on the programs in this book. I tend to use the same variable names to control looping in different programs, and encountered some very strange loop execution because I neglected to declare as private the loop-counter variables in the subroutines.

There are two ways to pass the values stored in memory variables between programs and subroutines. Values are passed *implicitly* by using the same variable name in both the calling program and the subroutine. The subroutine can use or change the value of the variable; any changes will be reflected in the variable for both the subroutine and the calling program. (It was this implicit passing of values that caused the problems I mentioned in the preceding paragraph.) Values are passed *explicitly* by using the statement

    DO <subroutine> WITH <parm1>, <parm2> . . .

in the calling program and using the statement

    PARAMETERS <parm1>, <parm2> . . .

in the subroutine. The parameters must be listed in the same order in both statements.

Explicit parameter-passing has two advantages over implicit passing. First, you can write a general-purpose subroutine that can be called from many other programs and subroutines without having to worry about using the same variable names in the calling program. Second, explicit parameter-passing documents precisely what data from the caller is used by the subroutine. This documentation is important for general-purpose subroutines that are incorporated in a number of different programs. And it helps to demystify the operation of a subroutine should you have to make changes to the application at some later date.

Storing Memory Variables

The values of current memory variables can be saved to a file at any time with the command

    SAVE TO <filename>

In effect, this command makes a "snapshot" of the current memory variables for later use. The memory variables are saved to a memory variable file with the specified filename and the extension .MEM. You can selectively save variables to a memory file with the command

SAVE ALL LIKE <specification> TO <filename>

To restore the saved values, you use the command

RESTORE FROM <filename>

or

RESTORE FROM <filename> ADDITIVE

Without the ADDITIVE modifier, the RESTORE command releases all existing memory variables before restoring the saved values. With the ADDITIVE modifier, the RESTORE command retains the values of all current memory variables except those that have the same names as variables being restored.

Using Memory Files in dBASE III Plus Applications

Memory files provide a simple means of managing the flow of information between programs in an application and between sessions in an application. As such, memory files have many uses in applications development with dBASE III Plus. One of the most important uses is to save values from run to run of the application. For example, a check-writing program can save the number of the last check printed. The next time the program is started up, the number of the last check is restored from the memory file and the check-writing program is ready to go. Sequential invoice numbers or serial numbers could be generated using a memory file to save and restore the last number generated.

You can also use memory files to store printer definitions. The memory file can hold information like the printer setup string, the number of characters per line, escape sequences to switch printer features on and off, number of lines per page, and page margins. All the applications in this book use a memory file to store printer definitions. If you are installing the application on a new system, you can quickly change the printer setup by editing the memory file. If you use two or more printers, such as a letter quality printer and a dot-matrix printer, you can have one memory file for each printer and quickly switch printer definitions by restoring variables from the appropriate memory file.

Another use of memory files is to record or control the execution sequence of the application. For example, an application may include an update or posting operation that should be run only once per day, week, month, quarter, or year, or only after all data entry for the period is finished. A memory variable stored in a memory file can be used as a flag to control the data-entry and posting process. When the required data entry is finished, the flag is set to allow the update. When the update program is run, it resets the flag so that the update cannot be run again until the data entry is done once more. If the flag is still set for update when the next cycle of data entry begins, a warning can be issued indicating that the update program needs to be run before the user begins entering new data.

Memory files can also be used to initialize and reinitialize the values of memory variables in a program. A data-entry program is an excellent application for this use of memory files. If you want to accept values into memory variables using @ . . . SAY . . . GET commands, you have to define or reinitialize each memory variable before it is used for data entry. Complex data-entry screens would require a long list of STORE commands to do this. Program execution is enhanced by restoring the default values from a memory file instead.

Memory files can also be used to debug a program by "saving" program values to memory files at key points during execution. Or you might do this so that you can restart the application later from the point at which it was stopped. This use of memory files is helpful for debugging programs that aren't working right despite the absence of error messages. It is also useful when program execution must be interrupted from time to time, and the user needs to be able to restart the program from the point of interruption.

Using Memory Files in the Applications Library

Each of the applications in this book uses a memory file. The file stores system parameters and printer definitions, as well as values that are passed from one session to the next. You could, of course, maintain the contents of an application's memory file by restoring the variables at the dot prompt and entering the new values, but a simple program makes it easier for an end user to modify the variables. The contents of the memory file CAMEM.MEM for the customer-accounts system (Chapter 7) are shown in figure 3.1. The main program CAMEM is shown in listing 3.1, and subroutine CAME1 is shown in listing 3.2.

Listings are at the end of the chapter.

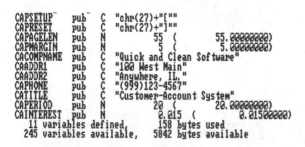

```
CAPSETUP    pub   C   "chr(27)+"["""
CAPRESET    pub   C   "chr(27)+"]"""
CAPAGELEN   pub   N        55 (        55.00000000)
CAPMARGIN   pub   N         5 (         5.00000000)
CACOMPNAME  pub   C   "Quick and Clean Software"
CAADDR1     pub   C   "100 West Main"
CAADDR2     pub   C   "Anywhere, IL."
CAPHONE     pub   C   "(999)123-4567"
CATITLE     pub   C   "Customer-Account System"
CAPERIOD    pub   N        20 (        20.00000000)
CAINTEREST  pub   N     0.015 (         0.01500000)
    11 variables defined,      158 bytes used
   245 variables available,   5842 bytes available
```

Fig. 3.1. Memory file for the customer-accounts system.

CAMEM begins with an IF clause to check whether memory file CAMEM.MEM exists. If the file is found, the program restores memory variables from that memory file. If the file is not found, the program initializes the memory variables with blanks and default values.

The main body of the program is a DO WHILE loop. The code in the loop first calls subroutine CAME1 to display a screen for editing the memory variables. (For discussion of the subroutine BORDERS, which is called from CAME1, see the section "Designing a Consistent User Interface" later in this chapter.) This screen allows the user to enter new values or revise existing ones. The loop is exited if the user presses *Y* in response to the prompt **OK (Y or N)?** at the end of the screen update, or if the user presses *N* and then declines to make further changes.

If the user has pressed *Y* at the **OK** prompt, the TRIM command is used to remove the trailing blanks from memory variables CAPSETUP and CAPRESET; then subroutine CAME1 is called again to display the contents of CAMEM.MEM. This time, a CLEAR GETS command following the call to the subroutine allows the user to view the screen but not to make any changes. The program then asks whether the user wants to save the changes to the CAMEM.MEM file. If the user presses *Y*, the program saves the new values to CAMEM.MEM, clears the screen, and returns control to the calling program.

The programs in each application are developed and tested from the bottom up (after the system has been designed from the top down). This method requires running the programs in stand-alone mode during development and testing. Any program that uses variables from the application's memory file must therefore restore variables from the memory file so that the programs can run in stand-alone mode. Consequently, the command

RESTORE FROM <file> ADDITIVE

is included at the top of each application program. Use of the ADDITIVE parameter prevents the RESTORE command from disturbing any other variables that may have been defined at a higher level in the system.

Commands and Functions for Data Entry

dBASE III Plus has many different data-entry commands and functions that you can use in your application programs. The WAIT, INPUT, and ACCEPT commands display a prompt on the current screen line and store the user's response in a specified memory variable. The @ . . . GET and READ commands can accept data into either a memory variable or directly into fields of the current database record. The READKEY and INKEY functions return the numeric value of the last key pressed. Finally, the interactive dBASE III Plus commands APPEND, BROWSE, and EDIT can be used to accept data into the current database.

Using ACCEPT TO, INPUT TO, and WAIT TO

The ACCEPT TO, INPUT TO, and WAIT TO commands each display a prompt on the current line of the screen and store the user's response in a memory variable. You do not have to initialize the variable before it is used in one of these commands. ACCEPT TO and INPUT TO both accept a word or a line of input from the user and store it in the specified memory variable. ACCEPT TO treats all input as text and stores it in a character variable, whereas INPUT TO treats all input as a dBASE III Plus expression and stores the result of the expression in a variable of the appropriate data type. WAIT TO is useful when you want the user to enter a single-character response, such as a menu selection.

Figure 3.2 shows the differences between ACCEPT and INPUT. A text string needs quotes with INPUT but not with ACCEPT. The ACCEPT command treats the characters 7/15/86 as text, but INPUT treats them as another expression for the number 0.00542636 (7 divided by 15 divided by 86). To enter the date 7/15/86 with INPUT, the user must enter *CTOD('7/15/86')*.

```
. accept 'Enter Text: ' to mem1
Enter Text: It is a very fine day
. accept 'Enter Number: ' to mem2
Enter Number: 123.456
. accept 'Enter Date: ' to mem3
Enter Date: 7/15/86
. input 'Enter Text: ' to mem4
Enter Text: "It is a very fine day"
. input 'Enter Number: ' to mem5
Enter Number: 123.456
. input 'Enter Date: ' to mem6
Enter Date: 7/15/86
. display memory
MEM1        pub  C  "It is a very fine day"
MEM2        pub  C  "123.456"
MEM3        pub  C  "7/15/86"
MEM4        pub  C  "It is a very fine day"
MEM5        pub  N       123.456  (       123.45600000)
MEM6        pub  N         0.01  (         0.00542636)
    6 variables defined,      82 bytes used
  250 variables available,  5918 bytes available
```

Fig. 3.2. Examples of using the ACCEPT TO and INPUT TO commands.

WAIT TO accepts a single keystroke into a character variable without waiting for a carriage return. This command is useful for menu selections or other variables used in decisions.

Using @ . . . SAY . . . GET

The @ . . . SAY . . . GET command is a more powerful and general data-entry command than the ACCEPT TO, INPUT TO, and WAIT TO commands. This command allows you to specify the type of data the user is to enter, its format, and the valid input range if the data is of the numeric or the date type. The applications in this book use @ . . . SAY . . . GET commands to enter data because all the screens are formatted with borders, which are disturbed by ACCEPT TO, INPUT TO, and WAIT TO commands.

The @ . . . SAY portion of the command governs the command's output. This portion of the command can also be used to display or print formatted reports. For data entry, the @ . . . SAY is used to display the prompt. The @ . . . GET portion of the command handles input. This portion of the command displays a data-entry field on the screen, starting at the specified row-and-column location. In an application, you would use a series of @ . . . SAY . . . GET commands to display the screen form and data-entry fields, then use the READ command to insert the user's input into memory variables or the fields of the current database record.

dBASE III Plus's screen generator, MODIFY SCREEN, produces a file of @ . . . SAY . . . GET commands. Using MODIFY SCREEN in an application is a two step process. First, you prepare the basic screen layout with MODIFY SCREEN. Then you change the file extension from from .FRM to .PRG, and use the resulting file as a screen-form subroutine called by the dBASE III Plus statement DO <name of form>.

With the @ . . . SAY . . . GET command, you can specify the format of the data entry with the PICTURE clause. The PICTURE clause is a general-purpose formatting routine that works with @ . . . SAY or @ . . . GET to let you specify the width of the field, the number of decimals for a numeric field, the characters displayed in the field along with the data, and the format of the character or numeric value within the field. Figures 3.3 and 3.4 demonstrate the use of PICTURE clauses for display of numeric and alphanumeric data, respectively.

```
. SSNO=123456789
:
: @ 24, 60 SAY ssno PICTURE '999-99-9999'              123-45-6789
:
: @ 24, 60 SAY ssno/1000                                  123456.79
:
: @ 24, 60 SAY ssno/1000 PICTURE '999,999.99'           123,456.79
:
```

Fig. 3.3. PICTURE clauses control the display format of alphanumeric data.

```
. name='John Q. Public'
.
. @ 24, 60 SAY name PICTURE 'xxxxxxxxxxxxxxxxxxx'          John Q. Public
.
. @ 24, 60 SAY name PICTURE '@!'                          JOHN Q. PUBLIC
.
. @ 24, 60 SAY name PICTURE 'xxxxxxxx'                    John Q.
.
```

Fig. 3.4. Alphanumeric data is displayed in varying formats with PICTURE clauses.

The @ . . . GET command also has a RANGE clause, which allows you to specify valid ranges for input of the numeric and date data types. You can specify an allowable range, as in

RANGE 0, 1

or an upper or lower boundary, as in

RANGE 3,

or

RANGE ,1000

You can specify ranges for dates by using date type memory variables or the CTOD function. An example of a date range is:

update=CTOD('12/31/86')
@ 10, 10 SAY 'Enter date:' GET mdate RANGE CTOD('1/1/80'),update

This @ . . . SAY . . . GET command will allow the user to enter any date between 1/1/80 and 12/31/86.

Using BROWSE, APPEND, and EDIT

The dBASE III Plus interactive commands BROWSE, APPEND, and EDIT can be used to present data-entry screens. These commands are attractive because they require little programming effort. The disadvantage is that they give the user greater latitude than does a custom data-entry program, and you may or may not want to allow the user this much freedom.

Important note: *Some third-party dBASE compilers do not support the BROWSE, APPEND, and EDIT commands. However, this is of concern only if you intend to use one of these compilers with your business applications.*

You won't notice any use of the interactive commands APPEND or EDIT in the applications library. But you will see BROWSE used to present the user with a screen containing multiple records. I have found that it is generally more appropriate to lay out a data-entry screen with MODIFY SCREEN or with MODIFY COMMAND and then to use the resulting file full of @ . . . SAY . . . GET commands as a subroutine than it is to use EDIT or APPEND with a screen file providing the format. Controlling data entry is easier with a set of @ . . . SAY . . . GET commands and a READ command than with EDIT or APPEND.

BROWSE, on the other hand, is quite useful in applications programs. When you want the user to update just one field for many records in the database, you can restrict BROWSE so that the user can view several fields but can change only the specified field. BROWSE executes quickly and requires less programming effort than does writing a custom full-screen editing program for multiple database records. In other situations, the decision whether to use BROWSE or to write a custom equivalent will depend on your assessment of the user's ability to use BROWSE effectively.

Using READKEY and INKEY

READKEY and INKEY are specialized data-entry functions that give your programs the ability to read individual keystrokes from the user's input. The READKEY function returns an integer value representing the key that was pressed to exit from the last full-screen edit operation (READ, APPEND, BROWSE, CHANGE, CREATE, EDIT, INSERT, MODIFY). READKEY also indicates whether any data were changed by the full-screen edit function. Your programs can use this command to find out how the user terminated the full-screen edit operation; the programs then can branch accordingly.

READKEY is used by several programs in those applications to determine whether the user exited from a READ command with the ESC key. If so, these programs exit from the data-entry section of the program.

The INKEY function returns an integer representing the next key in the keyboard buffer. INKEY is used when the program needs to check for keyboard input, but should not pause if there is none. INKEY allows the developer to create full-screen edit and query screens that use the same arrow-key commands used for data entry with EDIT, APPEND, or BROWSE.

In the program SCROLLER, shown in listing 3.3, INKEY is used to read the arrow keys so that the user can move from screen to screen (for more on SCROLLER, see Chapter 6). The program uses a loop that waits for a keypress (DO WHILE I=0), checks the integer representing the keypress (i=INKEY()), and continues if a supported key has been pressed. A DO CASE construction then sets two scroll counters in accordance with the key pressed, and the program returns control to the calling program.

Designing a Consistent User Interface (BORDERS)

A consistent screen interface adds a professional touch to your applications. Used throughout the application library, the BORDERS subroutine is a convenient way to create screen borders, a screen title, an area for display of entry of data, and a command line (see listing 3.4).

The BORDERS subroutine is very simple. First, it clears the screen. Then it uses @ . . . SAY commands to display two title lines, which are centered at the top of the screen. Finally, it uses dBASE III Plus's line-drawing commands to put a border around the screen and divide the screen into three sections (see fig. 3.5).

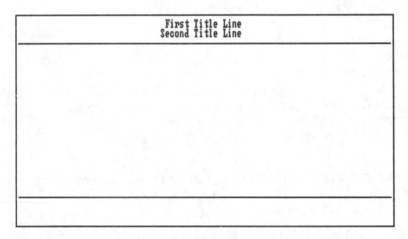

Fig. 3.5. Screen produced by the subroutine BORDERS.

When you use a formatted screen like the one in figure 3.5, you must use the @ . . . SAY and @ . . . GET commands to display data and read user input from the screen. The ? display command and the ACCEPT TO, INPUT TO, or WAIT TO commands erase a portion of the border line around the outside of the screen. This is no disadvantage because the @ . . . SAY and @ . . . GET commands can do everything the ?, ACCEPT TO, INPUT TO, or WAIT TO commands can do, and more. (For further discussion of the ? command, see the section "Printing Titles and Headers.")

Verifying User Data Entry

Regardless of whether the application is designed for a sophisticated dBASE III Plus user or for a clerk with no computer experience, the application should perform as much data validation as possible to detect and correct data-input errors before they corrupt the database.

Fortunately, dBASE III Plus provides you with a number of techniques for data validation. For numeric or date data, the simplest data-entry validation is to use the @ . . . GET command with PICTURE and RANGE clauses, which limit data entries to a specified range. The IIF function can be used within a data-entry loop to verify either numeric or character data by checking an enumerated list, by checking a range, or by looking up data in a file. The sections that follow describe these methods of data validation.

Using @ . . . GET with RANGE To Validate Numeric Values

For numeric or date data, the simplest method of data-entry validation is to use the @ . . . GET command with PICTURE and RANGE clauses to prevent the entry of a number or date outside the specified range. For example, if the user is supposed to enter an integer between 1 and 10, the following commands will only accept an integer in that range:

```
@ 10, 20 SAY "Enter command number" GET no PICTURE '99' RANGE 1,10
READ
```

The upper and lower bounds of the range can be variables or dBASE III Plus expressions. The PICTURE and RANGE clauses give you great flexibility in specifying exactly the right range for each number being entered.

Validating Character Data

The procedure for validating character data or numeric data that does not fall neatly into a range is a little more complicated. The following discussion covers three methods of using the IIF function within a data-entry loop to validate data: to verify an enumerated list, to check a range, and to look up data in a file. The discussion uses character data but applies to numeric data as well.

Verifying Enumerated Choices

The IIF function provides a simple and elegant method for checking an entry against a small list of possible correct entries (an enumerated list). The following program fragment shows the method for checking a character data-entry against an enumerated list:

```
ok=.F.
DO WHILE .not. ok
   name=SPACE(7)
   @ 10, 10 SAY "Enter Name" GET name PICTURE '!!!!!!!'
   READ
   ok=IIF(name$'CCC    ,FFFFFF ,GGGGGGG'.and..not.',','$name,.T.,.F.)
ENDDO
```

The data-entry and validation is performed within a loop that is exited only when the validation line (IIF . . .) returns the logical value TRUE. The @ . . . SAY . . . GET and READ commands get the value of NAME from the user. The next line performs the validation check against the enumerated list whose elements are 'CCC   ' (*CCC* followed by four spaces), 'FFFFFF ' (*FFFFFF* followed by one space), and 'GGGGGGG'.

The $ operator is the substring comparison operator. The first $ operator compares the value in the variable NAME with the string

'CCC   ,FFFFFF ,GGGGGGG'

and returns the value .T. if a match is found. To prevent a garbled entry like

'FF ,GGG'

from being accepted, a second substring comparison is done to make sure that there is no ',' (comma) in the variable NAME. If a match was found in the first substring comparison and a match is not found in the second comparison, then the IIF statement returns the value .T. and the entry is accepted. Otherwise, IIF returns the value .F. and the loop is repeated so that the user can try again. The user must enter one of the correct values to exit this loop.

Checking Ranges

Range checking for character data can be accomplished by a data-entry loop almost identical to the one for an enumerated list. In the following program fragment, IIF is used to make sure that the name entered by the user begins with a letter between C and F, inclusive:

```
ok=.F.
DO WHILE .not. ok
   name=SPACE(7)
   @ 10, 10 SAY "Enter Name" GET name PICTURE '!!!!!!!'
   READ
   ok=IIF(SUBSTR(name,1,1)>='C'.and.SUBSTR(name,1,1)<='F',.T.,.F.)
ENDDO
```

The IIF statement in this code fragment tests the first character of the NAME variable to see whether the character is greater than or equal to 'C' and less than or equal to 'F'. If this is the case, the value .T. is assigned to OK and the loop is exited. If this is not the case, the value .F. is assigned to OK, and the loop is repeated until the user enters a valid name.

Using Lookup Files

The third method of validating data is to look up the data in a database file. In the personnel application in Chapter 4, all employee data is keyed with the Social Security number. When the user enters a Social Security number, the program validates it by checking the file to see whether the corresponding employee record exists. Depending on the task being performed, the Social Security number may be accepted if the record is found or accepted if the record is *not* found.

The entry would be accepted if the entry is not found when, for example, the user is entering new employee records into the system. The entries must be checked to ensure that two employee records are not entered accidentally under the same Social Security number. On the other hand, the entry would be accepted if the entry is found when the user is querying or updating an existing entry.

The following program fragment validates an entry by looking it up in a database file. In this case, we assume that the lookup file is the active file and that it is indexed by the field whose value is being looked up. This data-entry loop is very similar to the loops in the two preceding program fragments:

```
ok=.F.
DO WHILE .not. ok
   mssno=SPACE(9)
   @ 10, 10 SAY "Enter SSN:" GET mssno PICTURE '@R 999-99-9999'
   READ
   SEEK mssno
   ok=IIF(.not.EOF(),.T.,.F.)
ENDDO
```

The data validation requires two lines in this example. First, the SEEK command is used to locate the Social Security number in the file. (Note that MSSNO is a memory variable, not a field in the database!) The Social Security number is accepted if it is found by the SEEK command (if EOF() is false). The Social Security number is rejected and the loop is repeated if the number is not found in the file (if EOF() is true).

Breaking Out of a Data-Entry Loop

In the three preceding code fragments, the data-entry loop is repeated until a correct entry is received. But often you will want the user to be able to terminate data entry without having made a correct entry, or any entry at all. The simplest way to do this is to choose a value of the variable being entered that will cause the program to break out of the loop. I commonly use a blank field in a character variable or a zero field in a numeric variable to perform this action.

The following program fragment shows the data-entry loop for validating data by looking it up in a file, but adds a test for a blank value in the variable MSSNO. The program will break out of the data-entry loop and return control to the calling program if the user enters a blank Social Security number. Otherwise, the loop will proceed with data validation as discussed previously.

```
ok=.F.
DO WHILE .not. ok
   mssno=SPACE(9)          && Initialize the variable
   @ 10, 10 SAY "Enter SSN:" GET mssno PICTURE '@R 999-99-9999'
   READ
   IF mssno=' '            && If the entry is blank,
      EXIT                 &&   then quit
   ENDIF
   SEEK mssno              && Otherwise, look it up
   ok=IIF(.not.EOF(),.T.,.F.)     && ok=.T. if SSN is found
ENDDO
IF .not.ok
    * clean-up statements such as CLOSE DATABASES, CLEAR, etc.
   RETURN
ENDIF
```

After the READ statement, an IF statement tests whether the first character of the Social Security number is a space. (Remember that MSSNO is a character variable in this example.) If the first character is blank, the EXIT statement transfers execution out of the data-entry loop. Another IF statement follows the ENDDO statement to check whether the loop was exited abnormally.

If the loop is exited normally, OK will contain the value .T. The only time OK is ever false is if the program breaks out of the loop with an EXIT statement. *IF .not.ok* tests whether the user broke out of the data-entry loop by leaving the Social Security number blank. (The program could test for the blank social security number again, but the technique of checking the loop variable, OK, is more general. You can readily add other validity checks if needed, without having to change the IF .NOT. OK.)

When the second IF statement detects that the loop was exited abnormally, the program can perform any necessary exit processing and return.

Preserving Data Integrity

The issue of maintaining the integrity of data in an application goes beyond data validation, especially in a complex application such as an accounting system. In a general ledger or other double-entry accounting system, data integrity includes data validation, but it also includes ensuring that the user always completes a double-entry accounting entry. The programs should be designed so that an incomplete entry can never be posted to the accounting system.

The three basic methods of accepting data from the user provide varying degrees of protection for that data. The first is to read data directly from the keyboard into a database file, but this method provides no protection. The second is to read data from the keyboard into memory variables and perform all validations before posting the data to the database. This provides an intermediate level of protection. The third method is to read all data into a temporary file that can be extensively error-checked and corrected before the data is posted in a batch to the database files. This approach provides the highest level of protection against incorrect input data.

Reading Data Directly into a Data File

If the program uses @ . . . SAY . . . GET, EDIT, BROWSE, or APPEND to read data directly to a database file, any incorrect data is entered into the current record before it is error checked. If a program error occurs or the user breaks out of the data-entry program, any incorrect data remains in the database.

If the data is entered into a new record and the user terminates the data entry, then the program can delete the new record. However, this method leaves deleted records scattered throughout the database file. You can pack the file to eliminate deleted records, but that can take a long time with a large database file, and you might inadvertently remove other deleted records that you want to retain. If the data is entered in an existing record and the user terminates the data entry, the program has no way to automatically reconstruct the former contents of the record. The user must go back at a later time and make corrections. For these reasons, it is often appropriate in a business application to use indirect methods of data entry, such as memory variables or temporary files.

Reading Data into Memory Variables

The simplest indirect method of data entry is to read each data entry into a memory variable and to update the appropriate database record with the REPLACE command after the data has been validated. This method is usually the preferred data-entry method in a business application.

The disadvantages of indirect versus direct data entry are that you cannot use the APPEND, EDIT, or BROWSE full-screen editing commands with memory variables. Furthermore, the program must set up the memory variables before data entry and update the database record after data validation. These disadvantages add to the programming effort.

The following block of code shows a simple example of entering data into a memory variable, and then posting the validated data to the database. The program fragment consists of a data-entry and -validation loop followed by APPEND BLANK and REPLACE commands to put the new data into a new database record.

```
ok=.F.
DO WHILE .not. ok
   mssno=SPACE(9)
   @ 10, 10 SAY "Enter SSN:" GET mssno PICTURE '@R 999-99-9999'
   READ
   SEEK mssno
   ok=IIF(.not.EOF(),.T.,.F.)
ENDDO
APPEND BLANK
REPLACE ssno WITH mssno
```

Reading Data into a Temporary File for Batch Update

The technique of indirect data entry using memory variables is suitable for most business applications. But it's not appropriate when the user needs to make a number of related data entries that must be validated as a group before they are posted to the database. This situation is typical of a double-entry accounting system, in which it is absolutely essential that every accounting entry has offsetting debits and credits. Each journal entry, possibly consisting of several debit entries and several credit entries, must be checked to ensure that debits equal credits before the entry is written into the accounting files.

The easiest way to handle this requirement is to read data entries into a temporary file; there, they are segregated from the actual accounting files until the group of entries has been validated. If data entry is cancelled before the data is successfully validated, the accounting file is untouched. You can program the application to post the temporary file to the main database as soon as the data is validated, or you can program the system so that the new data is not posted until a batch data-posting program is run at the end of the day, week, month, or year.

The following block of code shows a simple example of data entry into a temporary file followed by batch update of the main file.

```
* Create an empty database file with the correct structure
USE database
ERASE temp.dbf
COPY STRUCTURE TO temp
USE temp

* Enter account and amount until balance=0
balance=0
ok=.F.
DO WHILE .not. ok
   APPEND BLANK
   @ 10, 10 SAY 'Account Number:' GET account PICTURE '9999'
   @ 10, 30 SAY 'Amount:' GET amount PICTURE '999999.99'
   READ
   balance=balance+amount
   ok=IIF(balance=0,.T.,.F.)
ENDDO
```

```
* Update main database with data just entered
USE database INDEX index
APPEND FROM temp
```

Querying the Database

dBASE III Plus really shines when retrieving data from the databases in an application. The program has a number of commands that select the desired record or subset of the database without further user intervention. The basic commands for searching the database for a desired record are LOCATE, SEEK, and FIND. The powerful command SET FILTER TO <criterion> makes the database file "look" as if it contains only those records that match the specified criterion. Finally, the versatile MODIFY QUERY command invokes a full-screen query editor that gives the user the capability to enter complex, *ad hoc* queries from within the application.

Using LOCATE, SEEK, and FIND

The basic commands to search the database for a desired record are LOCATE, SEEK, and FIND. LOCATE is primarily useful in sequential processing of a database. The command finds the first record in the database that matches the specified criteria. The companion command to LOCATE is CONTINUE, which finds the next record that matches the same criteria as the last LOCATE.

SEEK and FIND both find the first record whose key fields match the specified key. The FIND command is a holdover from dBASE II; In developing new applications, you should always use SEEK, since SEEK does the same job as FIND plus a lot more. However, if you are maintaining an existing application that uses FIND statements, it is not worth changing them to SEEK statements. In an indexed file, if you know the key fields for the record you are searching for, SEEK is the fastest means of locating a specified record.

Using SET FILTER TO <criterion>

The SET FILTER TO <criterion> command is a powerful dBASE III Plus command that makes the database file act as if it contained only records that match the specified criterion or criteria. This command is used widely in the applications library, especially for reporting. The simplest way to create a sophisticated report is often just to print a list of all records in the database after executing a SET FILTER TO command.

The command SET FILTER TO <criterion> is useful in conjunction with the EDIT and BROWSE commands to allow the user to edit certain records in the file without having access to the rest. SET FILTER TO is useful also in conjunction with LOCATE,

SEEK or FIND to locate the first record that meets both the search criteria and the filter criteria.

SET FILTER TO <criterion> is easy to use. You include the SET FILTER TO command followed by the criterion, which can be any valid logical expression involving at least one value that depends on a field in the database. The SET FILTER TO command does not become active until the next time the record pointer is moved in the database, so it is common to include a GO TOP, SKIP, or SEEK command right after the SET FILTER TO command. (The SET FILTER TO command does not become active until the record pointer is moved so that you can always access the current database record, even after setting the filter.)

The following use of SET FILTER TO selects all records in the database with the name field starting with any letter besides *A*:

    SET FILTER TO name#'A'

The next example of SET FILTER TO selects all records in the currently open database with an account number of 100 and with an amount less than the amount in the current record of the budget file:

    SET FILTER TO acct=100.and.amount<=budget–>amount

(We assume that the budget file is open in one of the other nine work areas and that the record pointer has been previously positioned to the correct record in the budget file.)

Using MODIFY QUERY

Application developers will appreciate the invaluable MODIFY QUERY command, which is new with dBASE III Plus. This command invokes a full-screen query editor that can be incorporated into an application to give the user the ability to enter complex, *ad hoc* queries from within the application. Figure 3.6 shows the definition of a fixed-asset query using the MODIFY QUERY command.

The query shown in figure 3.6 selects all fixed-asset records for assets that belong to Division 1 and are located in the office. The ability to include *ad hoc* querying in an application without a lot of programming effort is a real boon to developers. The following program fragment shows how the MODIFY QUERY command can be incorporated in a program.

```
DELETE FILE fasubset.qry     && Delete old query file
MODIFY QUERY fasubset        && Get new query
GO TOP                       && Move record pointer to engage filter
```

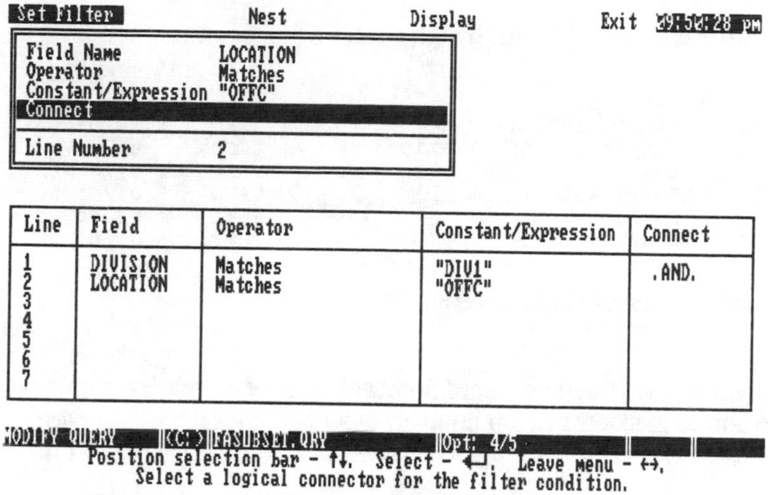

```
 Set Filter          Nest         Display         Exit  09:50:28 PM

┌────────────────────────────────────────────────────┐
│ Field Name          LOCATION                         │
│ Operator            Matches                          │
│ Constant/Expression "OFFC"                           │
│ Connect                                              │
│                                                      │
│ Line Number         2                                │
└────────────────────────────────────────────────────┘
```

Line	Field	Operator	Constant/Expression	Connect
1	DIVISION	Matches	"DIV1"	
2	LOCATION	Matches	"OFFC"	.AND.
3				
4				
5				
6				
7				

```
 MODIFY QUERY      |<C:>|FASUBSET.QRY              |Opt: 4/5
```
Position selection bar - ↑↓, Select - ⏎, Leave menu - ↔,
Select a logical connector for the filter condition.

Fig. 3.6. Fixed-asset query using MODIFY QUERY.

Printing Reports

Generating a printed report from a dBASE III Plus application can be as simple as using the command LIST FOR <condition> TO PRINT or as complex as programming a custom report generator for the report. Report formats can be created with MODIFY REPORT and stored in a format file for printing with the REPORT FORM command. For complex, presentation-quality reports, you can use dBASE III Plus's programming language to design the report to your (or your client's) specification.

Using DISPLAY or LIST To Generate Simple Reports

To print a simple tabular list of data, a DISPLAY or LIST command may be all the code you'll need. DISPLAY or LIST can send to the printer a simple tabular report that contains specified database rows and calculated data. Such a report has no titles and has the field name or dBASE III Plus expression as a column heading. Each column is formatted in accordance with the database structure or the default format for a computed field. There are no control breaks or column totals.

The following program fragment prints out selected fields from the fixed-assets file for records satisfying the condition *LOCATION = 'DIV1'*.

```
USE fixasset

LIST id_number,descript,location,serv_date,cost;
    FOR division ='DIV1' TO PRINT
```

Figure 3.7 shows the printout generated by this program fragment.

```
Record#  id_number  descript                 location serv_date      cost
      1  A-1001     IBM PC COMPUTER          OFFC     06/01/84    3000.00
      2  A-1010     TOYOTA COROLLA 4DR 1984  OFFC     09/08/84    9000.00
      6  A-1100     Desk                     PLT1     01/30/82    1500.00
      9  C-2        File Cabinet             OFFC     01/01/60     150.00
     11  AJ-436     Machine Tool             PLT1     06/30/80   25400.00
     15  S-1001     Shelving                 PLT1     01/01/85    1000.00
```

Fig. 3.7. Report printed with the LIST command.

The assets for Division 1 are listed by record number (order of entry). For each fixed asset, the report shows the identification number, description, location, in-service date, and purchase cost. (For more on the fixed-asset application, see Chapter 6.)

Using REPORT FORM with MODIFY REPORT To Generate Formatted Reports

If the application calls for a formatted, tabular report, then the dBASE III Plus REPORT FORM command may be able to produce the report. REPORT FORM prints a report using a report definition created with the MODIFY REPORT command. MODIFY REPORT and REPORT FORM offer the potential for an *ad hoc* reporting facility from within an application program. If the user is knowledgeable enough to define his or her own reports, you can incorporate both MODIFY REPORT and REPORT FORM into the application.

The MODIFY REPORT command is an interactive, full-screen, report-definition command that allows the developer or the user to define a formatted report with titles, multiline headings, individual column formats, and two-level control breaks and subtotals. MODIFY REPORT can be used to prepare the majority of the reports required for a business application.

Figure 3.8 shows a fixed-asset listing by division and location, which was produced by means of the REPORT FORM command. This report shows the capabilities of MODIFY REPORT and REPORT FORM, including specification of multiline titles and column headings, control breaks and subtotals at two levels, formatting of numeric columns, and printing or suppression of subtotals at control breaks. You can see that this report is attractive and readable, but it lacks fancy formatting features such as underlines before subtotals. The dBASE MODIFY REPORT and REPORT FORM commands are best suited for tabular reports that do not have to be formatted in a particular way.

```
                              Fixed Asset Tracking System
                             List of Fixed Assets by Division
                                     and Location
                             --------------------------------


                                              ASSET IN-SERVICE  ORIGINAL   SALVAGE DEPR   DEPR. END OF
     ID    DESCRIPTION             SERIAL NUMBER   TYPE  DATE       COST    VALUE METHOD   LIFE LIFE
   ------  -----------------------  -----------------  -----  --------  -----------  ----------- ------  ----- ------


   ** Division: CORP

   * Location: OFFC
    1011-1  dBASE III Plus Software   919191        SOFT  03/01/86      695.00      0.00 S         5  2/91
    3434    Ledger book              11323          BOOK  04/22/86       13.95      0.00 S         2  3/88
    C-1     File Cabinet             none           FURN  01/01/60      150.00      0.00 S         8 12/67
    P-1001  Printer                  EPSON FX185    COMP  01/01/86      795.00    100.00 S         5 12/90
   * Subsubtotal *

   ** Subtotal **                                                     1653.95

                                                                      1653.95


   ** Division: DIV1

   * Location: OFFC
    A-1001  IBM PC COMPUTER          900908880332221 COMP  06/01/84     3000.00    300.00 S         5  5/89
    A-1010  TOYOTA COROLLA 4DR 1984  YF9090909AA1    AUTO  09/08/84     9000.00   2000.00 S         3  8/87
    C-2     File Cabinet             none            FURN  01/01/60      150.00      0.00 S         8 12/67
   * Subsubtotal *

                                                                      12150.00

   * Location: PLT1
    A-1100  Desk                                     FURN  01/30/82     1500.00    150.00 S         5 12/86
    AJ-436  Machine Tool             aj-123-6116     MACH  06/30/80    25400.00   2540.00 S         8  5/88
    S-1001  Shelving                                 FURN  01/01/85     1000.00      0.00 S        10 12/94
   * Subsubtotal *

   ** Subtotal **                                                     27900.00

                                                                      40050.00


   ** Division: DIV2

   * Location: OFFC
    C-3     File Cabinet             none            FURN  01/01/60      150.00      0.00 S         8 12/67
   * Subsubtotal *

                                                                        150.00

   * Location: PLT2
    B-77777 Forklift Truck           bd-98989898989  VHCL  02/15/83    35000.00   5000.00 S         5  1/88
   * Subsubtotal *

                                                                      35000.00

   * Location: PLT5
    123     Robot - R2D2             1234567890123   P&E   04/30/86   125345.69  12534.57 S         8  3/94
    KK-11   Typewriter               IBM-10010011001 EQUP  01/01/83     1500.00      0.00 S         5 12/87
```

Fig. 3.8. Fixed-asset listing produced with MODIFY REPORT (continued next page).

```
                                   Fixed Asset Tracking System
                                 List of Fixed Assets by Division
                                           and Location
                                 --------------------------------


                                              ASSET IN-SERVICE   ORIGINAL    SALVAGE DEPR  DEPR. END OF
   ID   DESCRIPTION                SERIAL NUMBER    TYPE   DATE       COST    VALUE METHOD  LIFE LIFE
 ------ --------------------------- ------------------ ----- ---------- ----------- ----------- ------ ----- ------


 KK-112  Copy Machine             112233445566     EQUP  05/01/86    3500.00      0.00 S        5  4/91
 * Subsubtotal *
                                                                   130345.69

 ** Subtotal **
                                                                   165495.69


 ** Division: R&D


 * Location: LAKE
   A-1004  17' rowboat & oars       1121            VHCL  04/08/86    1200.00    120.00 S       10  3/96
   B-0001  Pool Filter             1212121-9999     EQUP  06/01/81    5500.00      0.00 S        5  5/86
 * Subsubtotal *
                                                                     6700.00

 ** Subtotal **
                                                                     6700.00


 ** Division: SALE


 * Location: CHI
   B-1010  Store Building                           BUIL  05/31/80  250000.00      0.00 D       30  4/10
   C-1010  Store Fixtures                           SALE  01/01/80   10000.00      0.00 S        5 12/84
 * Subsubtotal *
                                                                   260000.00

 ** Subtotal **
                                                                   260000.00

 *** Total ***
                                                                   473899.64
```

Fig. 3.8. Fixed-asset listing produced with MODIFY REPORT.

The report in figure 3.8 was created by using the MODIFY REPORT command to enter the report definitions shown in figure 3.9. These definitions include the title, page width, expressions for subtotals and sub-subtotals (first- and second-level control breaks), and the contents of headings and columns. Note that the contents of a column may be either a field in one of the open databases or a dBASE expression combining information from database fields, memory variables, and constants.

The trick to setting up column contents in MODIFY REPORT is preparation: before you go into MODIFY REPORT, open and define all databases and memory variables that are to be used in your report. You cannot define a column to contain a variable that is not presently defined, or a field from a database that is not presently open—even if they will be defined and open when the report is run.

```
Report definitions for report FAREP4.FRM

Page title:      Fixed Asset Tracking System
                 List of Fixed Assets by Division
                 and Location
                 --------------------------------

Page width:      132

Group on expression      division
Group heading            Division:
Summary report only      No
Page eject after group   No
Sub-group on expression  location
Sub-group heading        Location:

COL      Contents                   Heading            W   D Tot
---  -------------------  ---------------------------- --  -- ---
 1   ID_number            ;;   ID;-------              7
 2   descript             ;;DESCRIPTION;---------------30
                          ------------- (30 dashes)
 3   serial_no            ;;SERIAL NUMBER;--------------18
                          ---- (18 dashes)
 4   type                 ;ASSET; TYPE;-----           5
 5   serv_date            ;IN-SERVICE;   DATE;---------- 10
 6   cost                 ;    ORIGINAL;       COST;----- 11  2 Yes
                          ------- (11 dashes)
 7   salvage              ;     SALVAGE;       VALUE;----- 11  2 No
                          ------- (11 dashes)
 8   depr_mthd            ;DEPR;METHOD;------           6
 9   depr_life            ;DEPR.;LIFE;-----             5   0 No
10   STR(IIF(MONTH(       ;END OF;LIFE;------           6
     serv_date)=1,12,
     MONTH(serv_date)-1),2)
     +'/'+SUBSTR(STR(
     YEAR(serv_date)+depr_life
     +IIF(month(serv_date)=1,
     -1,0),4),3,2)
```

Fig. 3.9. Report definitions for the listing in figure 3.8.

Figures 3.10, 3.11, and 3.12 show the three screens used to enter definitions in MODIFY REPORT. Figure 3.10 is the screen used to enter the report-title and page-formatting information (the first two items in figure 3.9).

Figure 3.11 shows the screen used to enter the control-break and subtotal information (items 3 through 9 in figure 3.9). The report has two levels of control breaks and subtotals. For each of those, you enter a database field or a dBASE

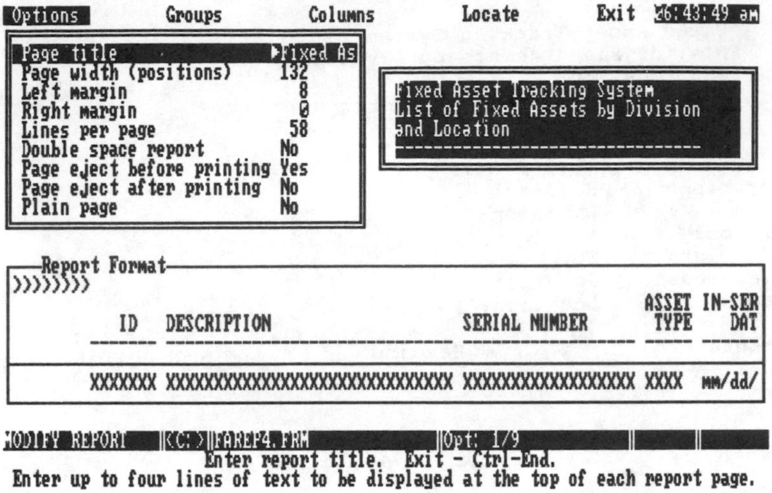

```
 Options        Groups       Columns       Locate       Exit  6:43:49 am
┌──────────────────────────────┐
│Page title          ▶Fixed As │
│Page width (positions)    132 │ ┌────────────────────────────────┐
│Left margin                 8 │ │Fixed Asset Tracking System     │
│Right margin                0 │ │List of Fixed Assets by Division│
│Lines per page             58 │ │and Location                    │
│Double space report        No │ │────────────────────────────────│
│Page eject before printing Yes│ └────────────────────────────────┘
│Page eject after printing  No │
│Plain page                 No │
└──────────────────────────────┘

┌─Report Format────────────────────────────────────────────────────────
│>>>>>>>>
│                                                      ASSET IN-SER
│        ID  DESCRIPTION                 SERIAL NUMBER  TYPE  DAT
│       ─────── ──────────────────────── ─────────────────── ──── ─────
│
│       XXXXXXX XXXXXXXXXXXXXXXXXXXXXXXX XXXXXXXXXXXXXXXXXXX XXXX  mm/dd/
└────────────────────────────────────────────────────────────────────
 MODIFY REPORT   ⟨C: ⟩ FAREF4.FRM            Opt: 1/9
                 Enter report title.  Exit - Ctrl-End.
 Enter up to four lines of text to be displayed at the top of each report page.
```

Fig. 3.10. The Options screen of MODIFY REPORT.

expression. A control break will be generated each time the value of the database field or dBASE expression changes. In this case, the first-level control break occurs when the value of the database field DIVISION changes. The second-level control break occurs when the value of the field LOCATION changes—or when DIVISION changes, even if the value in LOCATION remains the same.

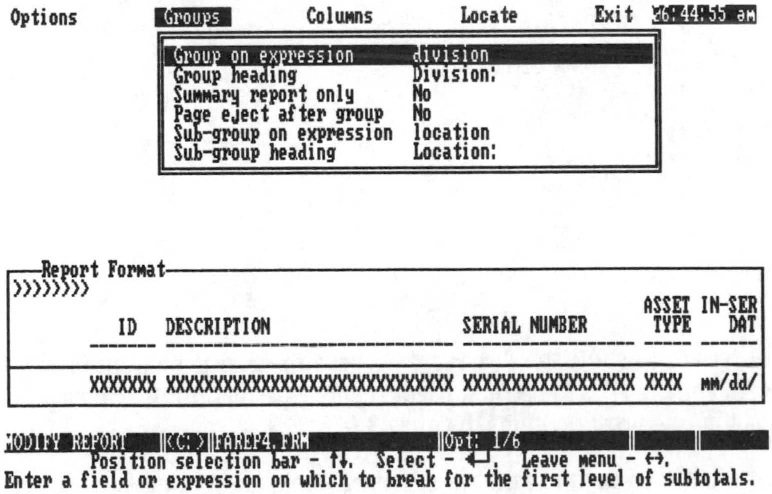

```
 Options        Groups       Columns       Locate       Exit  6:44:55 am
              ┌──────────────────────────────────────────┐
              │Group on expression      division         │
              │Group heading            Division:        │
              │Summary report only      No               │
              │Page eject after group   No               │
              │Sub-group on expression  location         │
              │Sub-group heading        Location:        │
              └──────────────────────────────────────────┘


┌─Report Format────────────────────────────────────────────────────────
│>>>>>>>>
│                                                      ASSET IN-SER
│        ID  DESCRIPTION                 SERIAL NUMBER  TYPE  DAT
│       ─────── ──────────────────────── ─────────────────── ──── ─────
│
│       XXXXXXX XXXXXXXXXXXXXXXXXXXXXXXX XXXXXXXXXXXXXXXXXXX XXXX  mm/dd/
└────────────────────────────────────────────────────────────────────
 MODIFY REPORT   ⟨C: ⟩ FAREF4.FRM            Opt: 1/6
              Position selection bar - ↑↓.  Select - ←┘.  Leave menu - ↔.
 Enter a field or expression on which to break for the first level of subtotals.
```

Fig. 3.11. The Groups screen of MODIFY REPORT.

Figure 3.12 shows the screen for entering the column definitions shown in figure 3.9. The column definitions are entered for one column at a time; the PgUp and PgDn keys are used to move from one column to another. The screen shows the headings selected for entry or updating of the multiline column heading.

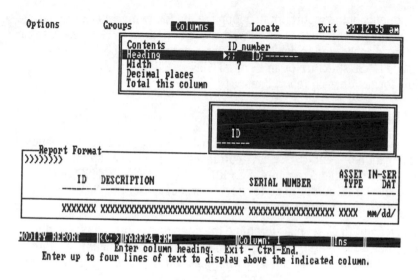

Fig. 3.12. The Columns screen of MODIFY REPORT.

Limitations of REPORT FORM and MODIFY REPORT

Some reports just cannot be handled by REPORT FORM and MODIFY REPORT. For example, presentation-quality reports often require a format different from the default dBASE III Plus format. Reports showing subtotals set off with single and double underlines are difficult to do with REPORT FORM. Another type of report that cannot be produced with REPORT FORM and MODIFY REPORT is one that requires calling a subroutine to calculate one or more items in each report row. Finally, you cannot produce nontabular reports with these commands. These limitations may make it necessary to write code to produce the custom reports you need.

Programming Custom Reports

Code for a programmed report consists generally of a DO WHILE loop that is executed once for each report row. Before the DO WHILE loop is entered, the program sends any setup commands to the printer. During the execution of the loop, a line counter is used to keep track of the printer's position on the page. An IF statement is used to test the value in the counter; if the printer is at the bottom of page, the program prints the page number and ejects the page. A similar IF statement is used to print the title and headings at the top of the next page. Listing 3.5 shows the layout of a typical report-generator program.

The four components of the report-printing loop are the following: check top of page, print next report line, check control break, and check bottom of page. These steps are fairly standard from application to application. Even a nontabular report will probably just involve a DO CASE structure or an IF . . . THEN . . . ELSE structure to print the appropriate line format on each report line.

Printing Titles and Headers

The titles and headers are printed by either ? commands or @ . . . SAY commands. If you use a combination of ? and @ . . . SAY commands to prepare a report, remember that the ? command requires SET PRINT ON and SET CONSOLE OFF commands in order for its output to go to the printer, but the @ . . . SAY command requires a SET DEVICE TO PRINT command.

It is usually convenient to place in a subroutine the code that prints the report titles and headings. Using a subroutine shortens the main printing loop, making it more readable. Use of a subroutine does not significantly slow down printing, because the titles and headings are only printed once per report page.

Printing Report Lines

In a custom report definition, the developer is responsible for laying out the report lines on the page. dBASE III Plus provides two different types of commands to print report lines: ? and @. . . SAY.

The ? and ?? commands evaluate and display the value of the supplied expression. The ? command issues a carriage return and linefeed first, while the ?? command prints the expression at the current line and location on the page. The ? and ?? commands have two drawbacks for printing custom reports. First, they print numbers in dBASE III Plus standard format and print character strings without any extra formatting characters. Second, ? and ?? print their output starting at the beginning of the report line and at the current position in the line, respectively. It takes more programming effort to position a field exactly where you want it on the page with this relative positioning method than with a command that allows absolute positioning on the page.

The @ . . . SAY command is the second alternative for printing report lines. Like ? and ??, @ . . . SAY prints the value of the supplied expression, but the latter command prints that value in the specified row and column, and you can use the

PICTURE clause to format numeric, character, and logical fields. The custom reports in the application library are all programmed with @ . . . SAY.

Printing Nontabular Reports

A nontabular report is a report whose format changes from row to row. The report-printing logic for a nontabular report will probably involve a DO CASE structure or an IF . . . THEN . . . ELSE structure to print different report line formats, depending on the contents of the report line or its place in the report. Within the DO CASE structure or the IF . . . THEN . . . ELSE structure, each type of report line is printed with a different set of ? statements or @. . . SAY statements.

Control Breaks and Subtotals

You can add any number of levels of control breaks by adding control-break sections to the general report structure. Code for a report with one level of subtotals would have a single control-break structure:

```
* if control break, print subtotals
IF <control break>
   <Print subtotals, zero out accumulator variables>
ENDIF
```

The code to produce two levels of subtotals would contain two IF statements:

```
* if subsubtotal break, print subsubtotals
IF <subsubtotal break> (subsubtotal field or subtotal field changes)
   <Print subsubtotals>
   <Reset subsubtotal accumulator variables>
ENDIF

* if subtotal break, print subtotals
IF <subtotal break> (ignore changes in subsubtotal field)
   <Print subtotals>
   <Reset subtotal accumulator variables>
ENDIF
```

You can add as many levels of subtotaling as desired by adding IF clauses. Note that each level of subtotals has its own accumulator variables. Also note that each subtotal level must check for changes not only in its own control field but for changes in all the control fields for the subtotals above it in the control-break hierarchy.

A Custom Replacement for REPORT FORM

Listing 3.6 shows a custom report-generator program, FADLRPT, that produces a report of fixed assets by division and location. The report created by FADLRPT is identical to the report in figure 3.8. FADLRPT (and FADLHEAD, the headings subroutine in listing 3.7) are direct replacements for the REPORT FORM command that generated figure 3.8. The command DO FADLRPT is a direct replacement for the command *REPORT FORM farep4* in the program FAREPORT in Chapter 6 (listing 6.15). (Because FADLRPT is a direct replacement for the REPORT FORM command, the user or the calling program must open files, set indexes, and set up the printer before calling FADLRPT.)

This custom report generator has code for two levels of control breaks to print subtotals and sub-subtotals. The body of the report is generated by the code within a DO WHILE loop that is executed once for each detail line in the report.

The loop begins by checking whether the printer is at the top of a new page. If so, the title and headings are printed by a call to FADLHEAD. Next, the program checks for changes of the value in the DIVISION and LOCATION fields. If so, the program prints the new division or location name; note that a division control break forces a location control break.

Next, the report line for the current database record is printed, the accumulator variables TCOST (grand total), SCOST (subtotal), and SSCOST (sub-subtotal) are updated, and the next database record is retrieved.

If the next record has a new value in DIVISION or LOCATION, a location control break has occurred. In that case, the sub-subtotal is printed and the sub-subtotal accumulator, SSCOST, is reset to zero. If the next record has a new value in DIVISION, a division control break has occurred. The subtotal is printed and the subtotal accumulator, SCOST, is reset to zero.

Finally, the program checks to see whether the printer is at the bottom of a page. Then execution returns to the top of the loop. When the end-of-file is reached, the loop terminates and execution continues after the loop, where the grand total is printed. Then the report generator returns control to the calling program.

As you can see, a lot of custom code is needed to duplicate the function of the REPORT FORM command. It is worthwhile to use REPORT FORM wherever possible in your applications.

Printing Page Numbers

You can print page numbers at the bottom of the page (or at the top of the page, if desired) with a statement like the following:

```
@ pglen+5,(width–8)/2 SAY 'Page '+STR(pageno,2)
```

The variable PGLEN determines the end of the page; that is the page length against which the line counter mentioned previously is tested in an IF statement. A typical value for PGLEN might be 55; WIDTH is the width of the report in characters, including left and right margins. The variable PAGENO is the page counter, which is incremented each time a page is ejected.

Setting Up the Printer

If the report needs to use special printer features such as letter-quality or compressed printing, you will need to issue a printer setup command before the report loop and a printer reset command after the report is completed. Suppose that the printer is an EPSON FX-80 and the report needs to be done in compressed print. The following program fragment shows how the printer setup is accomplished.

```
mok=' '
@ 21, 20 SAY 'Align printer then press any key' GET mok
READ
SET PRINT ON          && Direct ? output to printer
SET CONSOLE OFF
? CHR(15)             && Compressed Print mode is ASCII code 15
SET CONSOLE ON
SET PRINT OFF         && Direct ? output back to console
```

Printing Reports with SET FILTER TO

You can combine any of the preceding reporting techniques with the SET FILTER TO or SET FILTER TO FILE commands to print selected reports from the database. If you incorporate both the MODIFY QUERY command and MODIFY REPORT command in the application program, and use the SET FILTER TO FILE and REPORT FORM commands to print the report, then the user will be able to produce a wide variety of custom reports from within the application.

Using Another Editor with dBASE III Plus

I recommend that you replace dBASE III Plus's built-in program editor with a third-party editor. dBASE's built-in program editor has a number of deficiencies for serious program development, including a limit of 5,000 characters in a program file, somewhat primitive facilities for formatting program lines, and no capability for moving blocks of code around within the program file.

dBASE III Plus allows you to substitute your own editor for the built-in editor. In the same directory as the DBASE.COM file, set up a CONFIG.DB file with the following line:

TE = <editor name>

This line in the CONFIG.DB file tells dBASE III Plus to call the specified editor when you type MODIFY COMMAND at the dot prompt. The name of the editor should include the DOS path and the extension (.COM or .EXE). For example, if your editor program is named EDIT.COM and it is in subdirectory C:\UTILITY, then you would include the following line in the CONFIG.DB file:

TE = C:\UTILITY\EDIT.COM

I have successfully used several editors with dBASE III Plus, including the IBM Professional Editor, The IBM Personal Editor, and The Norton Editor. A good program editor, which can be purchased for $100 or less, is a sound investment if you are doing serious application development with dBASE III Plus. A word processor such as WordPerfect or Microsoft Word could also be used as the dBASE program editor if your system has a hard disk and 640K of memory. However, a word processor is too large and complicated to make a good program editor.

Interfacing with DOS (RUN or !)

The dBASE III Plus RUN command (or its equivalent, !) allows access to operating system functions, which can be very useful within an application. For example, with the RUN command you can have a backup program in your dBASE III Plus application that uses the DOS BACKUP and RESTORE commands to perform system backups and restores from within the application.

The RUN command can also be useful for copying files. There is a dBASE III Plus COPY command to perform this function, but the DOS COPY command is faster. The difference in speed can be significant if the application copies a large file.

Importing Data from Other Software into dBASE III Plus

dBASE III Plus provides several ways of importing data from other software packages. First, and easiest, dBASE III Plus can read data directly from files written by the most popular spreadsheet packages, including Lotus 1-2-3 and Symphony worksheet files. dBASE III Plus can also read data directly from other programs that can store data in DIF files or SYLK files. (Most spreadsheet packages and many other programs can write data in DIF or SYLK file formats.)

dBASE III Plus can also directly load a delimited ASCII text file. A delimited text file is one in which the contents of each field are enclosed in delimiters, usually quotation marks or blanks. This format is not generally useful for loading data from other business applications.

With a little programming, you can make dBASE III Plus read any text file that contains data in columns, such as a tabular report that was saved to disk instead of printed. Listing 3.8 shows the layout of a typical program to import data from a text file. (A further discussion and a detailed example of this type of data-import program can be found in Chapter 9.)

Conclusion

As this chapter has illustrated, dBASE III Plus offers the applications developer a wide range of options for entering data, querying the database, and printing reports. The next five chapters present stand-alone applications for a personnel system, sales-tracking system, fixed-asset manager, accounts-receivable system, and general ledger. In each application you will see applications of the valuable tips and techniques presented here.

Listing 3.1. Main program to maintain the memory file of the system.

```
**********************************************************************
* CAMEM    -        Define customer account system parameters       *
*                   9/9/86                                           *
**********************************************************************

* Restore existing or initialize new entries, depending on whether file exists
IF FILE("camem.mem")
   RESTORE FROM camem ADDITIVE
   capsetup=SUBSTR(capsetup+SPACE(80),1,80)        &&Pad to 80 chars with blanks
   capreset=SUBSTR(capreset+SPACE(80),1,80)        &&Pad to 80 chars with blanks
   cacompname=SUBSTR(cacompname+SPACE(26),1,26) &&Pad company name to 26 chars
   caaddr1=SUBSTR(caaddr1+SPACE(26),1,26)          &&Pad address line 1 to 26 chars
   caaddr2=SUBSTR(caaddr2+SPACE(26),1,26)          &&Pad address line 2 to 26 chars
   caphone=SUBSTR(caphone+SPACE(13),1,13)          &&Pad phone number to 13 chars
ELSE
   STORE "Customer-Account System" TO catitle
   STORE SPACE(80) TO capsetup,capreset
   STORE 0 TO capmargin
   STORE 55 TO capagelen
   STORE SPACE(26) TO cacompname, caaddr1, caaddr2
   STORE SPACE(13) TO caphone
   STORE 30 TO caperiod
   STORE .015 TO cainterest
ENDIF

* get new values
mok=.F.
mok1=.F.
title= "Edit System Memory Variables"
DO WHILE .not.mok
   * Display data entry screen
   DO came1          &&Display memory variable data entry screen
   @ 21, 9 SAY "Enter or revise desired memory variables. Press ESC to end edit"
   READ
   @ 21, 1 SAY SPACE(78)

   * Confirm edit.
   mok=.F.
   @ 21, 33 SAY "OK (Y or N)?" GET mok PICTURE "Y"
   READ
   IF .not. mok
      mok1=.T.
      @ 22, 20 SAY "Want to make further changes (Y or N)? " GET mok1 PICTURE "Y"
      READ
      IF .not. mok1
         EXIT   && Quit loop with mok=.F.
      ENDIF
   ENDIF
ENDDO
```

```
* If ok, Save new memory file
IF mok
   capsetup=TRIM(capsetup)
   capreset=TRIM(capreset)
   cacompname=TRIM(cacompname)
   caaddr1=TRIM(caaddr1)
   caaddr2=TRIM(caaddr2)
   DO came1                              &&Redisplay screen
   CLEAR GETS                            &&but do not read
   mok=.T.
   @ 22,17 SAY "Save changes to new CAMEM file (Y or N) " GET mok PICTURE "Y"
   READ
   IF mok

       SAVE TO camem ALL LIKE ca*
   ENDIF
ENDIF

* Tidy up and return
CLEAR
RETURN
```

Listing 3.2. Screen-definition subroutine used with the CAMEM program.

```
*****************************************************************
* CAME1 -          Display memory variable data entry screen for   *
*                  Customer Accounts System                        *
*                  9/9/86                                          *
*****************************************************************

DO borders WITH catitle,"Edit System Memory Variables"
@  6,  2 SAY "PRINTER LEFT MARGIN:"  GET capmargin PICTURE "999" RANGE 0,132
@  6, 40 SAY "PRINTER PAGE LENGTH:" GET capagelen PICTURE "99" RANGE 1, 99
@  7,  2 SAY "SETUP COMPRESSED PRINT:" GET capsetup FUNCTION "S30"
@  8,  2 SAY "RESET PRINTER TO NORMAL:" GET capreset FUNCTION "S30"
@ 10, 2 SAY "COMPANY NAME:" GET cacompname
@ 11, 2 SAY "ADDRESS:" GET caaddr1
@ 12, 2 SAY "CITY, STATE, ZIP:" GET caaddr2
@ 13, 2 SAY "PHONE NUMBER:" GET caphone
@ 15, 2 SAY "PAYMENT GRACE PERIOD:" GET caperiod PICTURE '99'
@ 16, 2 SAY "MONTHLY INTEREST RATE ON OVERDUE BALANCES:" GET cainterest;
   PICTURE '9.9999'

RETURN
```

Listing 3.3. The SCROLLER program using the INKEY function.

```
*****************************************************************************
* SCROLLER - Program to accept keystrokes from user to scroll the screen   *
*            PARAMETERS: SCNT    - returns vertical scroll amt to next screen *
*                        CNTR    - number of lines displayed on last screen *
*                        MSCROLL - number of lines that fit on a screen    *
*                        SCREEN  - current screen number                   *
*                        SMAX    - maximum screen number                   *
*            8/5/86                                                         *
*****************************************************************************
PARAMETERS scnt,cntr,mscroll,screen,smax
PRIVATE i

* Wait for one of specified keys
@ 22, 2 SAY "PRESS: ARROW KEYS, PGUP ,PGDN, ENTER, HOME ";
        +"(BOF), or END (EOF); ESC to quit"
i=0
SET ESCAPE OFF
DO WHILE .not.STR(i,2)$"13, 5,24,18, 3,27, 4,19, 1, 6"  && List of valid keys
   i=INKEY()                                             && Read keypress
ENDDO
SET ESCAPE ON

* Reset record pointer and cumulative count based on key pressed
DO CASE
    CASE i=27           && ESC key
        * flag to Exit the display loop
        scnt=999

    CASE i=5            && UP arrow key
        * Move record pointer to one line above start
        scnt=-(cntr+1)

    CASE i=24           && DOWN arrow key
        * Move record pointer down one line
        scnt=-(cntr-1)

    CASE i=18           && PGUP key
        * Scroll up one screen
        scnt=-(cntr+mscroll)

    CASE i=3.or.i=13    && PGDN or ENTER key
        * Scroll down one screen
        scnt=0

    CASE i=19           && Left arrow key
        *move one screen left
        scnt=-cntr
        screen=MAX(screen-1,0)

    CASE i=4            && Right arrow key
        * move one screen right
        scnt=-cntr
        screen=MIN(screen+1,smax)
```

```
        CASE i=1                && HOME key
            * Move to beginning of filtered file
            scnt=0
            GO TOP

        CASE i=6                && END key
            * Move to end of filtered file
            scnt=-(mscroll-1)
            、O BOTTOM

    ENDCASE
    RETURN
```

Listing 3.4. The subroutine BORDERS.

```
*********************************************************
* BORDERS   - Clear screen and draw borders and titles *
*            5/18/86                                    *
*********************************************************

PARAMETERS sys_title,scrn_title

CLEAR
@ 2, (80-LEN(sys_title))/2 SAY sys_title
@ 3, (80-LEN(scrn_title))/2 SAY scrn_title
@ 4, 1 TO 4, 78
@ 1, 0 TO 23, 79
@ 20, 1 TO 20, 78
RETURN
```

Listing 3.5. General layout of a report-generator program.

```
<Send printer setup commands to the printer>

* Loop to print report lines
line=0
DO WHILE .not.EOF

    * if line=0, print titles and headings
    IF line=0
       DO headings
    ENDIF

    * Print next report line
    <program code to print report line>
    line=line+1

    * if control break, print subtotals
    IF <control break>
        <Print subtotals, zero out accumulator variables>
    ENDIF

    * if end of page, print page number and eject
    IF line>endofpage.or.EOF()
        <print page number>
        EJECT
        LINE=0
    ENDIF
ENDDO

<Print grand totals>

<Reset printer>
```

Listing 3.6. A custom report program, FADLRPT.

```
***********************************************************************
* FADLRPT -       Custom Report to List Fixed Assets by Division and Location *
*                 This report program replaces the command REPORT FORM FAREP4 *
*                 in the program FAREPORT in chapter 6.                        *
*                 9/29/86                                                      *
***********************************************************************

* Initialize variables
mdate=date()                            && Report date
pageno=1                                && Report page number
pagelen=55                              && Report page length (max report lines)
cntr=0                                  && Report line counter
STORE 0 to sscost,scost,tcost           && Accumulator variables
ssvalue=IIF(location=' ','*',' ')       && Subsubtotal cannot match location
svalue=IIF(division=' ','*',' ')        && Subtotal cannot match division

* Loop to print fixed assets by division and location
DO WHILE .NOT.EOF()

   * Top of page processing
   IF cntr=0
      DO fadlhead WITH cntr,mdate,pageno        && Print title and headings
   ENDIF

   * Print new division and location headings if required
   IF svalue#division                   && If new division
      cntr=cntr+1                        && Increment counter
      IF cntr>pagelen-1                  && Check for end of page
         DO fadlhead WITH cntr,mdate,pageno     && New page if end
      ENDIF
      @ cntr, fapmargin SAY "** Division: "+division    && Print new division
      cntr=cntr+1
      svalue=division                    && Record division in subtotal variable
      ssvalue=IIF(location=' ','*',' ') && Subsubtotal cannot match location
   ENDIF

   IF ssvalue#location                   && If new location
      cntr=cntr+1                        && Increment counter
      IF cntr>pagelen-1                  && Check for end of page
         DO fadlhead WITH cntr,mdate,pageno     && New page if end
      ENDIF
      @ cntr, fapmargin SAY "* Location: "+location     && Print new location
      cntr=cntr+1
      ssvalue=location                   && Record location in subsubtotal variable
   ENDIF

   * Print next database record
   @ cntr, fapmargin+   0 SAY id_number
   @ cntr, fapmargin+   8 SAY descript
   @ cntr, fapmargin+  39 SAY serial_no
   @ cntr, fapmargin+  58 SAY type
   @ cntr, fapmargin+  64 SAY serv_date
   @ cntr, fapmargin+  75 SAY cost PICTURE '99999999.99'
   @ cntr, fapmargin+  87 SAY salvage PICTURE '99999999.99'
   @ cntr, fapmargin+  99 SAY depr_mthd
   @ cntr, fapmargin+ 106 SAY depr_life PICTURE '99999'
   @ cntr, fapmargin+ 112 SAY STR(IIF(MONTH(serv_date)=1,12,MONTH(serv_date)-1);
      ,2)+'/'+SUBSTR(STR(YEAR(serv_date)+depr_life+IIF(MONTH(serv_date)=1,-1,0);
      ,4),3,2)
   cntr=cntr+1
```

(Continued on next page.)

Listing 3.6, continued.

```
    * Update subtotals and total, skip to next record
    tcost=tcost+cost


    scost=scost+cost
    sscost=sscost+cost
    SKIP                                    && Skip to next record

    * Print Subsubtotal if subsubtotal break
    IF ssvalue#location.or.svalue#division.or.EOF()      && Has break occurred?
       IF cntr>pagelen-1                              && Check if need new page
          cntr=0
          DO fadlhead WITH cntr,mdate,pageno
       ENDIF
       @ cntr, fapmargin+0 SAY '* Subsubtotal *'         && Print subsubtotal
       cntr=cntr+1
       @ cntr, fapmargin+75 SAY sscost PICTURE "99999999.99"
       STORE 0 TO sscost                        && Reset subsubtotal accumulator
       cntr=cntr+1
    ENDIF

    * Print subtotal if subtotal break
    IF svalue#division.or.EOF()             && Control break reached?
       IF cntr>pagelen-1                     && Need new page?
          cntr=0
          DO fadlhead WITH cntr,mdate
       ENDIF
       @ cntr, fapmargin+0 SAY "** Subtotal **"          && Print subtotal
       cntr=cntr+1
       @ cntr, fapmargin+75 SAY scost PICTURE "99999999.99"
       STORE 0 TO scost                        && Reset subtotal accumulator
       cntr=cntr+1
    ENDIF

    * Bottom of page processing
    IF cntr>pagelen                         && If bottom of page
       cntr=0                               && Reset line counter
    ENDIF

ENDDO

* Top of page processing
IF cntr=0
   DO fadlhead WITH cntr,mdate,pageno          && Print title and headings
ENDIF

* Print grand totals
@ cntr, fapmargin+0 SAY "*** TOTAL ***"
cntr=cntr+1
@ cntr, fapmargin+75  SAY tcost     PICTURE "99999999.99"
EJECT

RETURN
```

Listing 3.7. The subroutine FADLHEAD.

```
* ****************************************************************
* FADLHEAD - Print title and heading for asset list            *
*            8/31/86                                            *
* ****************************************************************
PARAMETERS cntr,mdate,pageno
PRIVATE i,j
@  1, fapmargin SAY "Page no."+STR(pageno,5)
@  2, fapmargin SAY mdate
@  3, fapmargin+ 49 SAY "Fixed Asset Tracking System"
@  4, fapmargin+ 48 SAY "List of Fixed Assets by Division"
@  5, fapmargin+ 59 SAY "and Location"
@  6, fapmargin+ 48 SAY "--------------------------------"
@  9, fapmargin SAY "                                                          ";
   +" ASSET IN-SERVICE   ORIGINAL     SALVAGE DEPR   DEPR. END OF"
@ 10, fapmargin SAY "  ID   DESCRIPTION                            SERIAL NUMBER        ";
   +"  TYPE    DATE          COST     VALUE METHOD LIFE  LIFE"
@ 11, fapmargin SAY "------- ------------------------------- --------------------";
   +" ----- ---------- ----------- ----------- ------ ----- ------"
cntr=13
RETURN
```

Listing 3.8 Skeleton for a data-import program.

```
* Load buffer file (each line of text is read into one 132-char field)
USE <buffer file>
ZAP
APPEND FROM <text file> SDF

* Find start of import data
start=.F.
DO WHILE .not.start.and..not.EOF()
   <check for start of data>
   SKIP
ENDDO

* Loop to process data into database file
SELECT B              && Work area B will be database file
USE <database file>
SELECT A              && Work area A is buffer file
DO WHILE .not.EOF().and.<valid data>
   <store values from report columns into memory variables>
   SELECT B
   APPEND BLANK
   REPLACE <values with values in memory variables>
   SELECT A
   SKIP
ENDDO
```

4

Personnel System

The staff at Johnson Typesetting increased from 60 to 120 employees when the company acquired Smith Printing. This sudden doubling as well as the company's anticipated future growth made it necessary to devise some new methods for keeping accurate and detailed employee records. Faced with the task of integrating the new employees, owner Bob Johnson hired us to design a database application for keeping employee records on a personal computer.

What Johnson wanted was a system that would, first of all, keep track of basic information for each current employee, such as name, address, Social Security number, job title, department, employment date, and so forth. The system should enable him to print a variety of reports, including mailing lists and labels, based on the information in the employee files. Finally, Johnson wanted to be able someday to run the application on a multiuser system and to provide restricted access to confidential information.

Suppose that we've met with Bob Johnson, have discussed his needs, and have developed with dBASE III Plus a personnel system that can be expanded or modified later. This chapter covers all the stages involved in developing the application. We begin by considering the purpose and functions of the system; then describe the data and index files that are needed before the system is developed.

The first programs we look at are those designed to open and reindex the data files. Next, we look at the programs and subroutines that enable users to enter employee data, query the database, produce a variety of reports, and perform system maintenance. Finally, we look at a menu system for users, consider the use of procedure files, and note possible extensions to the application.

Identifying the Purpose and Function of the System

The purpose of the personnel system is to keep accurate and detailed employee records that can be easily accessed, manipulated, analyzed, and printed. The application developed here provides the following functions:

- maintains basic information about employees such as name, address, department, title, years of service, and anniversary date

- allows employees to be accessed by Social Security number or name for queries and updates

- prints lists of employees based on criteria such as years of service, anniversary date, or department

- prints mailing labels and address lists to disk for the office word-processing package, Microsoft® Word

- can be expanded to provide restricted access to sensitive information such as wages or salary, job classification, and performance rating (additional extensions could include, for example, a record of benefits received by each employee and a career history for each employee)

- runs on a single-user PC, but can be set up for multiuser operation

In addition to the system's input and output functions, there are utility functions to reindex, pack, back up, and restore the databases, and perform other system-maintenance functions, without having to resort to interactive dBASE commands.

Defining the File Structures

The next step in developing the application is to design the data files and any necessary index files. The personnel system uses one data file: an employee master file. The employee master file records nonsensitive information for each employee, such as name, address, Social Security number, anniversary date, job title, department, starting date, and anniversary date. This file is indexed by Social Security number and name. (For more on recording "sensitive" information, see the section "Extensions to the System.")

Employee Master File

The employee master file, PEEMPL.DBF, contains one record for each current employee (see fig. 4.1). Nearly all the fields store character data. The first field in the file is the Social Security number (SSNO), which uniquely identifies each employee. The Social Security number can be kept in either a number field or a character field, but we've chosen to store it in a character field to make it easier to manipulate as a key field.

The next three fields contain the employee's first name (FIRST), middle initial (MI), and last name (LAST), respectively. The employee's name is kept in three fields so that we can index the file by the employee's last name. We can also look up employees or print reports by the contents of the last name field.

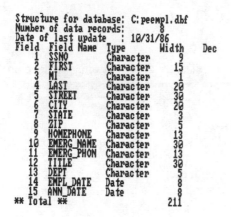

```
Structure for database: C:peempl.dbf
Number of data records:        8
Date of last update   : 10/31/86
Field  Field Name  Type      Width   Dec
    1   SSNO        Character    9
    2   FIRST       Character   15
    3   MI          Character    1
    4   LAST        Character   20
    5   STREET      Character   30
    6   CITY        Character   20
    7   STATE       Character    3
    8   ZIP         Character    5
    9   HOMEPHONE   Character   13
   10   EMERG_NAME  Character   30
   11   EMERG_PHON  Character   13
   12   TITLE       Character   30
   13   DEPT        Character    5
   14   EMPL_DATE   Date         8
   15   ANN_DATE    Date         8
** Total **                   211
```

Fig. 4.1. Structure of employee master file (PEEMPL.DBF).

The next four fields contain the employee's mailing address, including street (STREET), city (CITY), state (STATE), and ZIP code (ZIP). The next field contains the employee's home phone number (HOMEPHONE). The next two fields contain the name (EMERG_NAME) and phone number (EMERG_PHON) of a person to contact in case of an emergency involving the employee.

The next four fields contain nonsensitive information about the employee's job, including job title (TITLE), department (DEPT), employment date (EMPL_DATE), and anniversary date (ANN_DATE). The DEPT field holds a five-character cost-center number that identifies the employee's department.

Index Files

The order of the records in the database file PEEMPL.DBF is determined by the order in which the records are entered. To search the file or display the records in a different order, we need an index file for each order desired. For example, PEEMPL.DBF is accessed by Social Security number during data entry, and by employee name during data entry and report printing. Index keys and index files are listed in table 4.1.

Table 4.1
Indexes Used with the Employee Data File

File	Index Key	Name	Indexed By
PEEMPL	SSNO	PEEMPL1	Social Security number
	LAST+FIRST+MI	PEEMPL2	employee name

Specifying the Function of Each Program

The next step in development is to create a block diagram of the system. We develop the block diagram from the list of functions that the system must perform. This block diagram serves as a road map during the development process.

Figure 4.2 shows the block diagram of the personnel system. In this block diagram, the system has been divided into functions dealing with data entry, queries and reporting, and system maintenance. These divisions become the three submenus of the main menu. The system is built modularly, with each function performed by a separate program. Subroutines perform functions common to more than one program and isolate complex portions of code from the main programs.

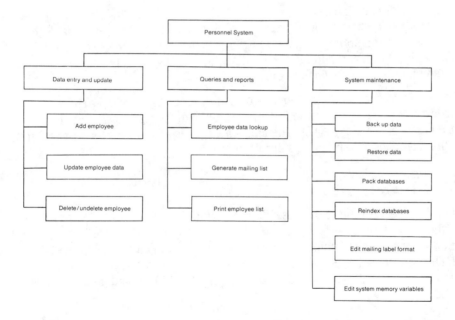

Fig. 4.2. Block diagram for the personnel system.

The system includes programs to add, update, and delete employee data; look up employee information; print mailing lists, labels, and employee lists; and perform a range of maintenance operations.

The menu system designed for this application corresponds to the block diagram in figure 4.2. Users begin at a menu and choose one of three submenus (see figs. 4.3 through 4.6). Consistent with the "bottom-up" approach to programming described in Chapter 2, the menus for the personnel system are not discussed until after we've considered the main programs and subroutines (see the section "Creating a Menu System").

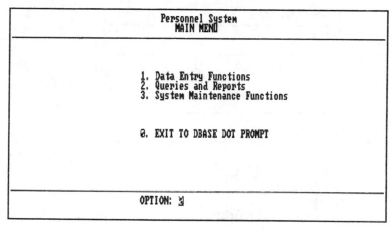

Fig. 4.3. Main menu.

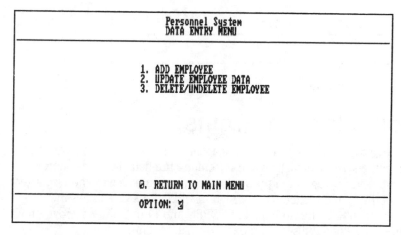

Fig. 4.4. Data-entry menu.

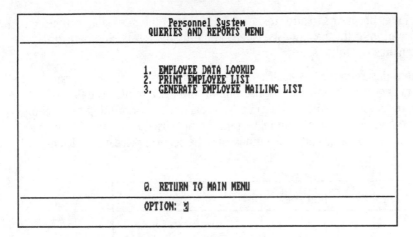

Fig. 4.5. Queries and reports menu.

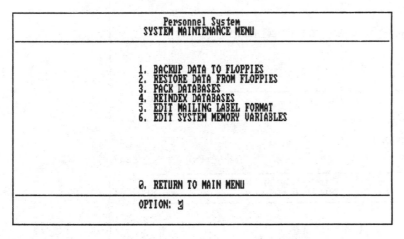

Fig. 4.6. System-maintenance menu.

Developing the Programs

The first step in developing the programs for the application is to write a subroutine to open all the files in the system and a program to reindex the data files. The subroutine PEOPEN is called by every program in the system to open the data files and associated indexes. As one of the system-maintenance programs, PEINDEX establishes the two index files listed in table 4.1. After looking at PEOPEN and PEINDEX, we move on to consider programs for editing the system memory variables, entering and manipulating data, creating several different types of reports, performing a range of system maintenance functions, and creating a menu system.

Opening the Data Files (PEOPEN)

Listings are at the end of the chapter.

The subroutine PEOPEN opens the required data files and indexes for each program in the application (see listing 4.1). This subroutine is called by every program that uses the data file and the indexes. If we add or delete an index file in a later change to the system, we will need only to change PEOPEN and all the programs in the system will open the database with the new indexes.

Reindexing the Data File (PEINDEX)

The subroutine PEINDEX reindexes the data file in the personnel system. We code this routine at the beginning of the development process so that it will be available to rebuild the indexes if the data file gets clobbered during development. Listing 4.2 shows that PEINDEX is merely a list of INDEX ON commands that create the index files for the employee master file (PEEMPL.DBF).

Managing the System Memory File

The last task before developing the main programs is to set up a file to hold the system memory variables. The following sections discuss the structure of the system memory file and a program that allows you or your client to edit the memory variables when the system is set up or when any changes need to be made.

Description of the System Memory File

The system memory file (PEMEM.MEM) holds memory variables that are used by the programs in the personnel system. Figure 4.7 shows the structure of the system memory file. All five of the memory variables defined for the personnel system deal with printing and report titles. These are the system title (PETITLE), the left margin for printed reports (PEPMARGIN), the last print line on the page (PEPAGELEN), the printer setup string for compressed print (PEPSETUP), and the printer setup string to restore the printer to normal print (PEPRESET).

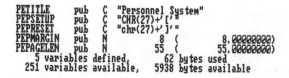

```
PETITLE     pub   C   "Personnel System"
PEPSETUP    pub   C   "CHR(27)+'['"
PEPRESET    pub   C   "chr(27)+']'"
PEPMARGIN   pub   N          8 (          8.00000000)
PEPAGELEN   pub   N         55 (         55.00000000)
    5 variables defined,       62 bytes used
  251 variables available,   5938 bytes available
```

Fig. 4.7. Contents of the system memory file, PEMEM.MEM

Editing the System Memory File (PEMEM)

The PEMEM program provides for adjustment of the system memory variables when the system is installed, a new printer is purchased, or one of the system parameters needs to be changed. You should modify this program whenever you change the contents of the system memory file so that you can easily change the values of the saved memory variables during development and testing.

The PEMEM program begins by using the FILE function to determine whether PEMEM.MEM exists (see listing 4.3). If the file is found, the values are restored and the two printer setup strings are padded to 80 characters with spaces. This padding makes it possible for the user to enter the specified number of characters during the edit. The TRIM function removes these trailing spaces when the edit is finished and before the variables are stored. If PEMEM.MEM does not exist, the memory variables are created and initialized with appropriate values.

Next, the program enters a DO WHILE loop. The loop begins with a call to subroutine PEME1 to display the edit screen. PEME1 consists of a call to the BORDERS subroutine to set up the display screen and a set of @ . . . SAY . . . GET commands that display the data (see listing 4.4). The resulting edit screen is shown in figure 4.8. (For discussion of BORDERS, see the section "Designing a Consistent User Interface" in Chapter 3.)

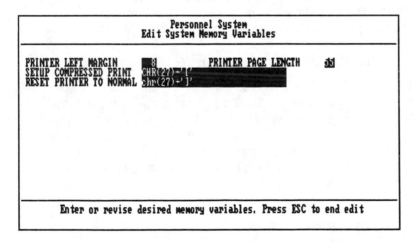

Fig. 4.8. Screen for the user to update the system memory variables.

Note that the subroutine PEME1 can be created in one of two ways. One way is to enter it with your program editor. Another approach is to lay out the @ . . . SAY . . . GET commands with the MODIFY SCREEN command and then use the program editor to enter the rest of the subroutine. (For further discussion of MODIFY SCREEN, see the section "Using @ . . . SAY . . . GET" in Chapter 3.)

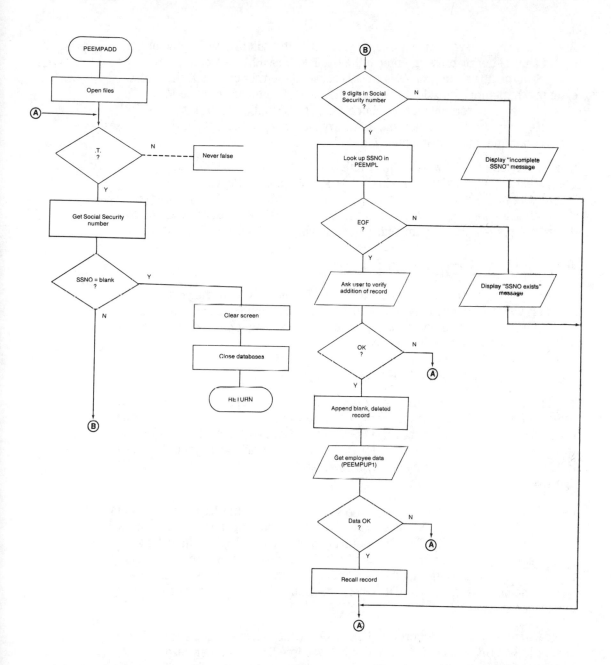

Fig. 4.9. Flowchart for the program PEEMPADD.

After the changes have been entered, the user ends the edit by pressing Esc or Ctrl-End at any field or by pressing Enter at the last field. PEMEM then prompts the user to confirm that the edited variables are acceptable. If the user presses *Y*, the loop is exited with memory variable MOK set to the value .T. If the user presses *N*, the program asks the user whether further changes are desired. If the user presses *Y* in response to this second prompt, the data-entry loop is repeated. But if the user presses *N* a second time, the loop is exited with MOK set to .F.

Finally, PEMEM checks whether the MOK flag is set to .T., which indicates that the user accepted the edited variables in the previous loop. If so, the user is asked whether he or she wants to save these variables to PEMEM.MEM. If the user presses *Y*, the variables are saved. If MOK flag is set to .F. or the user does not want to save the variables, then the program quits without saving the changes.

Entering Employee Data

As you recall from the block diagram in figure 4.2, one portion of the personnel system is devoted to functions for entering and updating employee information. In this section we look at programs and subroutines for adding, updating, deleting, and undeleting (or recalling) employee records.

Adding Employees (PEEMPADD)

The first step in using the personnel system is to enter data for a new employee. The program PEEMPADD allows the user to enter new employees into the system from the keyboard. Briefly, this program consists of a "do forever" loop (DO WHILE .T.) that gets the Social Security number for an employee and calls subroutine PEEMPUP1 to enter the employee information. The flowchart for PEEMPADD is shown in figure 4.9.

PEEMPADD begins by opening files and restoring memory variables from the system memory file (see listing 4.5). The program calls PEOPEN to open the database file and both indexes. A SET DELETED ON command prevents the SEEK command from finding a deleted Social Security number. (SEEK is used later in the program to verify that an active record containing the new Social Security number does not already exist in the file.) Next, PEEMPADD enters a data-entry loop to accept data for an employee from the user.

The data-entry loop is a "do forever" loop (DO WHILE .T.) that accepts and validates the Social Security number for the new employee (see fig. 4.10), then reads the personnel data for the new employee, using a full-screen data-entry form. The loop begins by getting the Social Security number from the user. If the user enters a blank Social Security number, the data-entry loop is exited.

```
┌─────────────────────────────────────────────────────────────────────┐
│                          Personnel System                             │
│                   ADD EMPLOYEE TO PERSONNEL SYSTEM                     │
├─────────────────────────────────────────────────────────────────────┤
│  ENTER SOCIAL SECURITY NUMBER OF NEW EMPLOYEE (blank to exit) 555-55-5555 │
│                                                                       │
│                                                                       │
│                                                                       │
│                                                                       │
│                                                                       │
│                                                                       │
├─────────────────────────────────────────────────────────────────────┤
│      Confirm social security number for new employee (Y or N) N       │
└─────────────────────────────────────────────────────────────────────┘
```

Fig. 4.10. Screen to accept Social Security number for new employees.

Because the Social Security number is the master key for the personnel system, the program has been designed to keep tight control over this number. After accepting the Social Security number, the program verifies that it contains nine digits. If not, a warning message is displayed and the program waits for a keypress before repeating the loop. The program also verifies that the number has not already been entered into the system by using the SEEK command to look for a record containing the number. If the SEEK command does not leave the record pointer at the end of the file, then an existing record already contains the number the user has entered. In that case, an error message is displayed and the loop is repeated. If a valid number has been entered, the program asks the user to confirm this number.

If the number is valid, PEEMPADD appends a blank record to the employee database, fills in the Social Security number, and marks the record as deleted. The new record is marked as deleted so that there won't be an active, blank record in the database if the program is interrupted before the rest of the data is entered. The program can still process the deleted record as long as the record pointer remains on it.

Next, the program calls the subroutine PEEMPUP1 for entry of the data into the employee master file. The flowchart for PEEMPUP1 is shown in figure 4.11; program code is provided in listing 4.6. Note that PEEMPADD passes two parameters to PEEMPUP1: the logical value .T. and the value contained in MOK, which is initialized to .F. before the call. The first value is passed into the parameter EDITFLAG in PEEMPUP1. If EDITFLAG is true, then PEEMPUP1 can be used to enter a new record; otherwise, the subroutine is used to display data without editing. The second parameter has two purposes: it controls execution of the data-entry loop (DO WHILE .NOT. OK), and serves as a status flag that is returned to the calling program (PEEMPADD) to indicate whether a record has been added successfully to the master file and the user has approved the record.

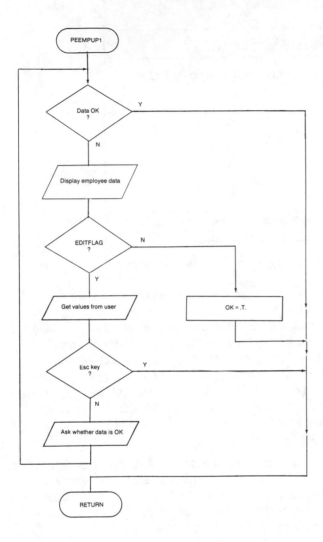

Fig. 4.11. Flowchart for subroutine PEEMPUP1.

If PEEMPADD finds the OK flag set to .T., the program recalls the record, making it active, then repeats the main loop to accept another Social Security number (see fig. 4.10). If the user enters a blank Social Security number at this screen, PEEMPADD exits the main loop, closes the database files, and returns to calling program PEMENU1 (the data-entry menu, which is discussed in the section "Creating a Menu System").

The body of PEEMPUP1 is a DO WHILE loop that uses a series of @ . . . SAY and @ . . . GET commands to display the data-entry screen shown in figure 4.12. The only field that can't be edited is the Social Security number field. Within the loop, the first parameter (EDITFLAG) controls execution of an IF . . . ELSE clause. If EDITFLAG is set to true, as should be the case for a new record, the program accepts full-screen input from the user. If EDITFLAG is false, then a CLEAR GETS command keeps any changes the user might have made from being written into the database.

Fig. 4.12. Screen to enter data in the employee master file.

If PEEMPUP1 has been called for entry or editing of data—if, in other words, the value .T. has been passed to EDITFLAG—the READKEY() function is used to check which key the user presses to finish the edit. If the user presses Esc, the subroutine breaks out of the data-entry loop and returns with the OK flag set to .F., indicating invalid data. If the user presses Ctrl-End to finish the edit of a record, the program responds by asking the user to confirm the data entry. If the user presses *Y* in confirmation, PEEMPUP1 returns control to the calling program with the OK flag set to true, indicating that the data is good. But if the user presses *N*, the program loops back to the top of the data-entry loop so that more changes can be made.

When PEEMPUP1 is used just to display the contents of the record, the @ . . . SAY and @ . . . GET commands are followed by a CLEAR GETS command and a READ command that display the screen until the user presses any key. Then the subroutine returns with the OK flag set true.

Updating Employee Records

Now that we've considered a program to add new employees to the system, we turn to a program and associated subroutines for updating that employee information. The PEEMPUPD program provides the user with the ability to update the employee master file. The next section looks at the main program, PEEMPUPD. Subsequent sections examine in detail the two primary subroutines called by the main program: PEFINDEM and PEEMPUP1.

Main Program for Updating Employee Records (PEEMPUPD)

Updating employee data with the program PEEMPUPD is a two-step process similar to the process involved with PEEMPADD, the program to add an employee record. First, the user identifies the employee to update. This identification step is different from PEEMPADD in that the user can look up the employee record either by last name or by Social Security number. If the user enters a partial Social Security number or employee last name, the identification screen displays each employee record that matches the Social Security number or name in sequence so that the user can select the correct employee record. Second, the user uses a full-screen edit screen to enter changes for the employee.

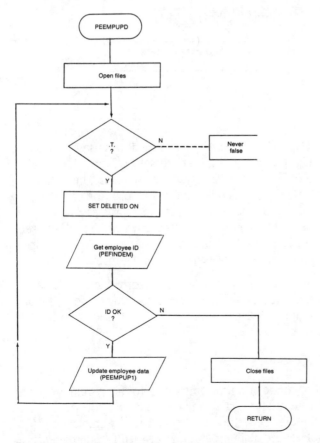

Fig. 4.13. Flowchart for the program PEEMPUPD.

PEEMPUPD calls two subroutines to perform the individual tasks involved in updating the employee master record. The flowchart of PEEMPUPD is shown in figure 4.13; program code is provided in listing 4.7. PEEMPUPD begins by opening the employee master file (PEEMPL.DBF). Then the program enters the main "do forever" update loop.

In the loop, PEEMPUPD first sets DELETED ON to ignore deleted records. Then the program calls subroutine PEFINDEM to identify the employee to update. PEFINDEM allows the user to identify the employee by entering part or all of the Social Security number or name. Figures 4.14 and 4.15 show the two screens produced by

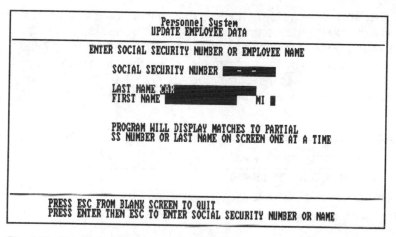

Fig. 4.14. Screen to identify employee by Social Security number or by name.

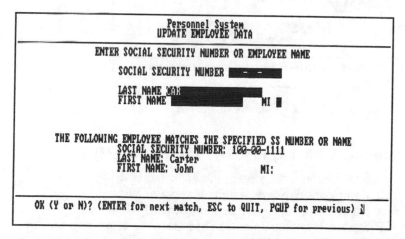

Fig. 4.15. Screen to match partial names or Social Security numbers.

PEFINDEM. (The subroutine is discussed in the following section.) Note in figure 4.14 that *CAR* has been entered in the LAST NAME field; the program finds a partial match with *CARTER*, as shown in the bottom half of figure 4.15. After the call to PEFINDEM, the program tests the OK flag. If the OK flag is false, PEEMPUPD exits the update loop.

If the OK flag is true, PEEMPUPD calls subroutine PEEMPUP1 to update the employee master file record for the specified employee. PEEMPUP1 produces the edit screen shown in figure 4.16. This screen shows the complete employee record for John Carter.

Program control then returns to the top of the loop to identify another employee. If the user leaves both the blank Social Security number and the name blank at this screen (see fig. 4.14), the OK flag is set to false. When the program finds the OK flag set to false, the main loop is exited. The program then closes the databases, sets DELETE OFF, and returns control to the calling program, PEMENU1 (the data-entry menu, which is discussed in the section "Creating a Menu System").

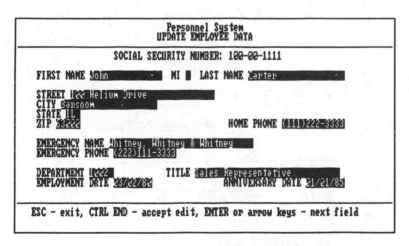

Fig. 4.16. Screen to update data in the employee master file.

Presenting Screens To Identify Employees (PEFINDEM)

The PEFINDEM subroutine presents the screens shown in figures 4.14 and 4.15 for the user to identify the employee by Social Security number or by name. The subroutine begins by setting EXACT OFF so that inexact match will be found, then enters a DO WHILE loop that is executed until the user has selected an employee by Social Security number or by last name and has accepted the results. Figure 4.17 shows a flowchart for PEFINDEM; program code is provided in listing 4.8.

The first step in the loop is to ask the user for the Social Security number or last name of the employee. As the screen in figure 4.14 indicates, the user can choose to enter only part of the Social Security number or the last name. The program will display matching records, one after the other, until the user accepts a record or all the matching records have been displayed. A series of @ . . . SAY and @ . . . GET commands followed by a READ command accept the user's entry. The program then enters a DO CASE structure to process the user's entry.

If the user enters data in the SOCIAL SECURITY number field, the program blanks any entry the user has made in the LAST NAME field and uses the SEEK command to find the first matching Social Security number in the file. If the user has entered the complete Social Security number, the program will find the matching number in the file. If the user has entered the first digits of an incomplete Social Security number, the SEEK command will find the first employee record with initial digits that match the digits entered by the user. If no matching Social Security number is found, the program displays an error message, and control returns to the top of the identification loop.

If the user has left the SOCIAL SECURITY field blank but has entered data in the LAST NAME field, the program sets a filter on the employee file based on any nonblank entries in these fields. (A blank entry in either field is ignored in the SET FILTER command because of the TRIM function.) Then PEFINDEM uses a SEEK command to find the first record that matches the complete or partial LAST NAME entry. Figure 4.19 illustrates a match for part of a last name. If no matching record is found, the program displays an error message and returns to the top of the identification loop.

If the user has entered nothing in the Social Security number or last-name fields, an error message is displayed and the program pauses for a keypress. Then the loop is repeated.

If both the Social Security number and the last name are blank, the OTHERWISE clause in the DO CASE command causes the program to break out of the identification loop.

After executing the DO CASE command, the program enters an inner loop to display the matching employee records in succession until the user selects one or the end of file is reached. As shown in figure 4.19, the loop displays the full Social Security number and name for the matching employee record and prompts the user to verify this record. If the user does not press *Y* to accept the record, the READKEY() function is used to check whether the user has pressed Esc or PgUp. If the user has pressed Esc, the program breaks out of the inner loop and returns to the top of the identification loop. If the user presses PgUp, the inner loop uses the SKIP command to display the previous match. If the user presses any other key, the program uses the SKIP command to display the next match.

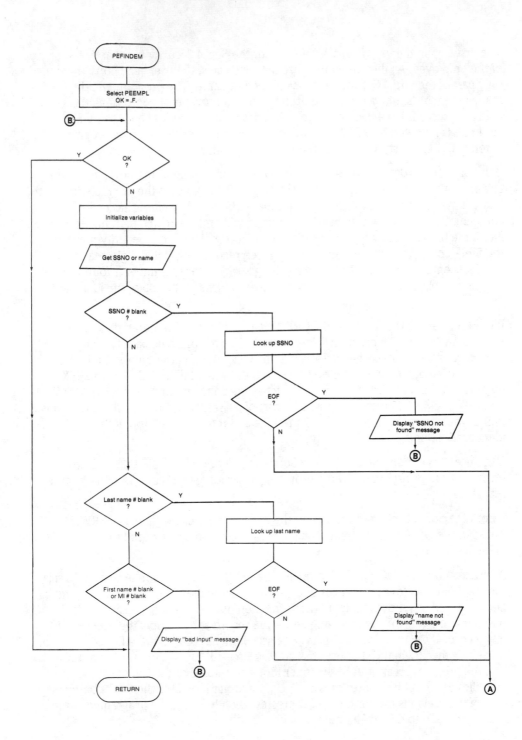

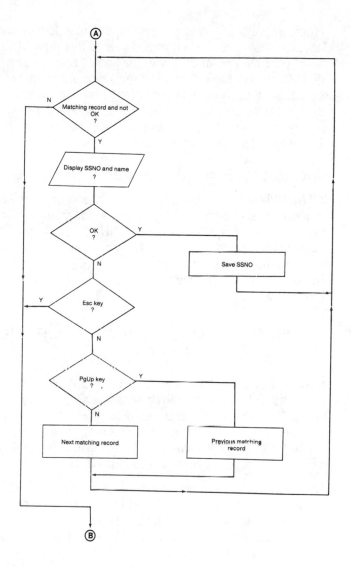

Fig. 4.17. Flowchart for the subroutine PEFINDEM.

If the user presses *Y* to accept a record, the inner loop is exited with OK set to true. The main loop also is exited with OK set to true. PEFINDEM then returns control to calling program PEEMPUPD with the Social Security number in memory variable MSSNO, the OK flag set true, and the file record pointer at the selected employee record. But if the user breaks out of the main loop by entering blank values for both the SOCIAL SECURITY NUMBER and LAST NAME fields, PEFINDEM returns to PEEMPUPD with a blank value in MSSNO, the OK flag set to false, and the file record pointer at an indeterminate location.

Updating the Employee Master Record (PEEMPUP1)

PEEMPUPD uses the PEEMPUP1 subroutine to do the full-screen update of the employee master record. The only field in the master record that this subroutine will not change is the SOCIAL SECURITY NUMBER field and a temporary calculation field that is not accessible to the user. The screen shown in figure 4.16 shows the employee master record for employee John Carter. (For a full discussion of PEEMPUP1 with listing and flowchart, see the preceding section, "Adding Employees To the System.")

Deleting and Undeleting Employee Records (PEEMPDEL)

Now we turn to the last program in the portion of the personnel system that handles data entry and update: a program to delete and undelete employee records. PEEMPDEL allows the user to delete an employee record from the database if the employee resigns or is terminated. This program also makes it possible to recall a record for an employee who was deleted by mistake or who is rehired, but only if the database files have not been packed in the interim.

The program begins by opening the database files with PEOPEN. Next, the program enters a "do forever" loop (DO WHILE .T.) that is executed once for each record to be deleted or undeleted. The loop is exited when the user enters a blank Social Security number at the first screen. Figure 4.18 shows the flowchart for PEEMPDEL; program code is shown in listing 4.9.

The loop begins by displaying a data-entry screen to get the Social Security number for the employee to be deleted or undeleted (see fig. 4.19). After the user enters a Social Security number, the program first checks to see whether the entry is blank. If the entry is blank, PEEMPDEL exits the loop. If a number was entered, the program uses SET DELETED ON to ignore records that are already marked for deletion. Then SEEK is used to find the specified Social Security number in the file.

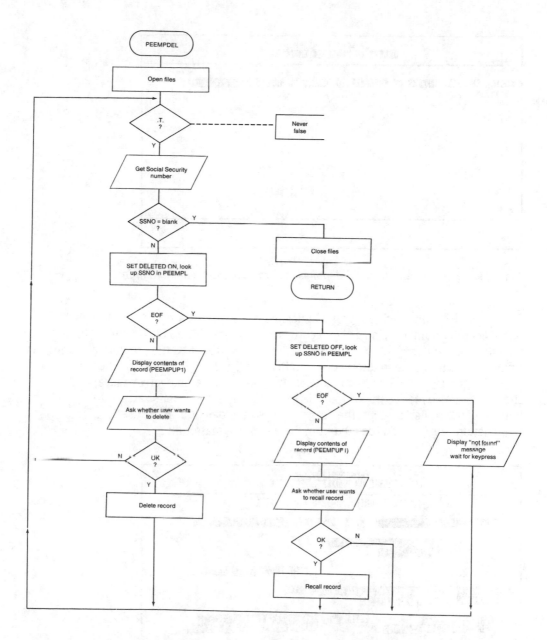

Fig. 4.18. Flowchart for PEEMPDEL.

```
                        Personnel System
                  DELETE OR UNDELETE EMPLOYEE
  ─────────────────────────────────────────────────────────
  SOCIAL SECURITY NUMBER OF EMPLOYEE TO DELETE OR UNDELETE  ███ ─ ██ ─ ████
  (blank to exit)
```

Fig. 4.19. Screen where the user identifies the employee to be deleted or undeleted.

This first SEEK command looks for a undeleted employee record with the specified Social Security number. If an active record is found, then .NOT. EOF(), the control condition in the IF . . . ELSE . . . ENDIF command is true, and the program calls the PEEMPUP1 subroutine in display-only mode (with the first parameter specified as .F.) to display the record. The screen to delete or undelete an employee in figure 4.20 shows the employee record for John Carter. A message in the status area at the bottom of the screen prompts the user to confirm the deletion. If the user confirms the deletion, the record is deleted from the employee master file.

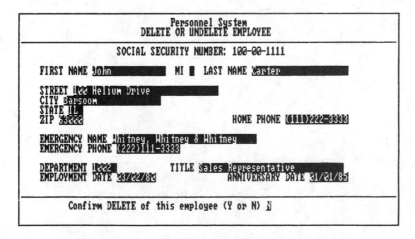

Fig. 4.20. Screen displaying the record to be deleted.

If the first SEEK command did not find a active employee record with the specified Social Security number, then the control condition in the IF . . . ELSE . . . ENDIF command is false, and the program tries again with deleted records included in the search (SET DELETED OFF). Any record found at this point is deleted. The program then calls PEEMPUP1 in display mode to display the deleted record and prompts the user to indicate whether he or she wants to recall the deleted record to active status. If the user presses *Y*, the program recalls the record in the employee master file.

The program can recall only the first record found with a matching Social Security number, even if there is more than one deleted record for that Social Security number. This situation could arise if you add, delete, add again, and delete again the same employee without packing the database. You would have two deleted records for the employee, but only the first one could be recalled. You could address this potential problem by writing a loop like the one to display all matching employees in the PEFINDEM subroutine, but the situation will probably not arise often enough to justify the effort.

Important note: *To minimize the problems that can occur when the database is not packed periodically, you should encourage the user to pack the database files at regular intervals.*

If neither of the SEEK commands locates the Social Security number in the file, PEEMPDEL displays an error message and waits for a keypress before continuing. The program then returns to the top of the loop to identify another employee to delete or undelete (see screen 4.19). The loop continues until the user enters a blank Social Security number at the identification screen. When exiting the loop, the program closes the databases, uses SET DELETED OFF so that deleted records are no longer ignored, and returns.

Querying the Database and Printing Reports

We have now developed programs to enter, update, delete, and restore employee information. The next step is to develop the programs that allow Bob Johnson (or someone else at Johnson Typesetting) to query the personnel database and print a variety of reports. In this section we look at programs that enable the user to review and print information for each employee in the employee master file. We also look at programs to print employee lists sorted in various ways, including mailing lists and mailing labels.

Looking Up Employee Data (PEEMPQY)

The PEEMPQY program enables Bob Johnson to look up data on an employee identified either by name or by Social Security number. The screens presented to the user are similar to the screens produced by PEEMPUPD for the update function, except that the user can only look at the information, not change it.

The PEEMPQY program is a simple "do forever" loop that calls subroutines to allow the user to specify an employee by name or Social Security number and to display the contents of the employee master file record for that employee. The loop is repeated until the subroutine PEFINDEM returns with the OK flag set to false, which indicates that the user entered a blank Social Security number and last name at the identification screen. When the OK flag is set to false, the program exits the loop and returns. The flowchart for PEEMPQY is shown in figure 4.21; program code is provided in listing 4.10.

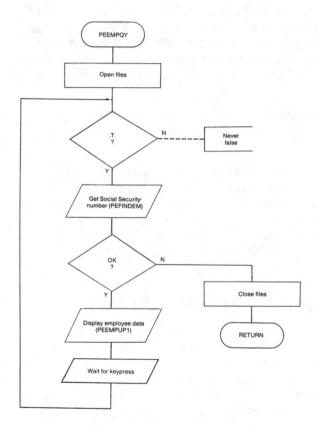

Fig. 4.21. Flowchart for the program PEEMPQY.

The program logic to support the display mode is discussed in more detail in the sections "Adding Employees to the System" and "Updating Employee Records." As listing 4.10 shows, PEEMPQY uses the same subroutines as do the data-entry programs, such as PEEMPUPD. In fact, the programs PEEMPQY and PEEMPUPD are nearly identical.

PEEMPQY calls the subroutine PEFINDEM to identify the employee by Social Security number or name. If a partial Social Security number or name is entered, the program displays one by one on the screen the Social Security number and name for matching employee records. This continues until the user chooses one of the records or until no more matching records are found. The first screen produced by PEFINDEM is shown in figure 4.22. In this screen, complete first and last names have been entered for employee John Carter.

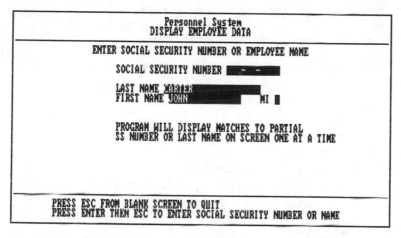

Fig. 4.22. Screen to identify employee for data display function.

After the user has identified the employee, PEEMPQY calls subroutine PEEMPUP1 with the first parameter .F. and the second parameter the variable OK. Calling PEEMPUP1 with the first parameter set to .F. causes PEEMPUP1 to display data for the current employee without allowing the data to be edited (see fig. 4.11 and listing 4.6). After calling PEEMPUP1, PEEMPQY pauses for a keypress so that the user can view the data. Figure 4.23 shows the employee master file data for John Carter, the employee identified in figure 4.22.

The last action of PEEMPQY is to return to the employee identification screen (see fig. 4.22) to begin the display process again. The user exits the program by first verifying that the Social Security number and last name fields are blank; then pressing Esc. PEEMPQY clears the screen, closes the databases, issues the command SET DELETED OFF, and returns.

Fig. 4.23. Screen displaying the employee master record for the selected employee.

Printing Individual Records

To produce "quick and dirty" hardcopy output, Bob Johnson can print each record in the employee master file by using the PrtSc key to "dump" the contents of a screen to the printer. One enhancement to the system would be a program to batch print a record card for each employee. (For more on system enhancements, see "Extensions to the System.")

Printing Employee Lists

The personnel system can print lists of employees sorted in a specified order and selected on the basis of specified criteria. For example, the report shown in figure 4.24 lists employees by department and includes such information as job title, employment and anniversary dates, and important phone numbers. The capability to analyze the composition of his workforce in this manner should be very useful to Bob Johnson, not only during the merger with Smith Printing, but also as Johnson Typesetting continues to grow.

The dBASE III Plus MODIFY QUERY command enables the user to perform these complex queries. Using MODIFY QUERY is more difficult for the user than is simply picking one of several predefined queries from a menu. However, the additional effort pays off when the user needs to generate unusual *ad hoc* reports. (For more on the MODIFY QUERY command, see Chapter 3, "Tips and Techniques.")

The PEEMPLIS program is a simple, straight-line program (no loops) that calls a subroutine to get the sort order and selection criteria for the report; then uses the dBASE REPORT FORM command to send the report to the printer. There is one

```
Page No.    1
10/21/86
                                 Employee List by Department

SOCIAL                                                 EMPLOY- ANNIVER-
SECURITY                                               MENT    SARY     HOME          EMERGENCY
NUMBER    EMPLOYEE NAME            JOB TITLE      DEPT  DATE    DATE     PHONE NUMBER  PHONE NUMBER
--------  -----------------------  -------------  ----- ------- -------- ------------- -------------


** 1001
   123456789 Case Jerome I.        Programmer Analyst  1001  01/01/86 01/01/86 1234567890  0987656789
   555555556 Jones Janet E.        Manager             1001  06/15/74 01/21/84 3345545543  3343434543
   123123123 Smith John A.         Supervisor          1001  02/01/82 06/07/84 2135468790  2233445543

** 1002
   100001111 Carter John           Sales Representative 1002  03/02/80 01/01/85 1112223333  2221113333
   223244344 Johnson Brad E.       Manager             1002  04/21/82 01/01/86 3211234566  3336565656
```

Fig. 4.24. Report showing list of employees by department.

report definition for each of the seven sort orders. The flowchart for PEEMPLIS is
shown in figure 4.25.

PEEMPLIS begins by opening the database files with PEOPEN (see listing 4.11). Then
the program displays a message telling the user to set up the printer; the program
waits for a keypress before continuing. (PEEMPLIS has the user set up the printer first
so that once the report order is chosen, the user can do something else while the
program indexes the database for printing. Indexing a large database can take some
time.) The program next calls the subroutine PEEMPLI1, which displays a menu of
possible list orders, gives the user the option of specifying selection criteria, and
indexes the file in the selected order. The flowchart for PEEMPLI1 is shown in
figure 4.26.

The parameter passed to PEEMPLI1 is memory variable MCHOICE (see listing 4.12).
The subroutine uses that parameter to return the user's choice for the sort order to
the calling program. PEEMPLI1 begins by displaying a menu of report order options
and accepting the user's selection (see fig. 4.27). If the user selects the last option,
option 0, the subroutine exits immediately. If the user selects any of the other
options, the subroutine continues.

The subroutine next asks the user whether he or she wants to enter record-selection
criteria to narrow the list of employees. If the user does not enter selection criteria, all
active employee records are selected. If the user wants to enter selection criteria, the
subroutine displays a screen with instructions, then uses the MODIFY QUERY
command to allow the user to build selection criteria (see fig. 4.28). In the MODIFY
QUERY screen in figure 4.29, selection criteria have been entered to limit the

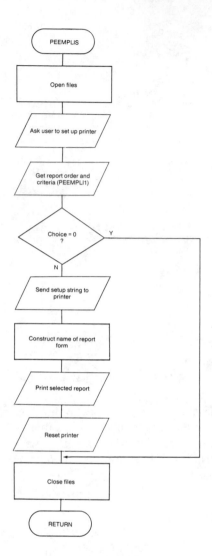

Fig. 4.25. Flowchart of the program PEEMPLIS.

department groupings to those with numbers that do not match 1000. Note in figure 4.24 that employee lists for Departments 1001 and 1002 only are shown.

After the user specifies the selection criteria, the screen displays the message CREATING INDEX while the employee master file PEEMPL.DBF is indexed in the order selected. This indexing order is accomplished by commands within a series of CASE clauses. If the user has selected Social Security number order or name order,

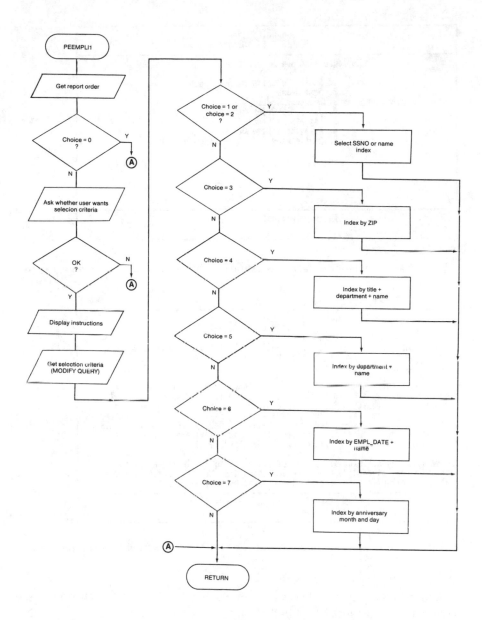

Fig. 4.26. Flowchart of the subroutine PEEMPLI1.

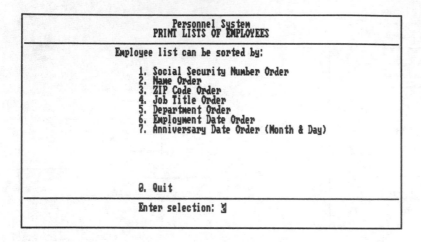

Fig. 4.27. Menu where the user selects the sort option for the employee list report.

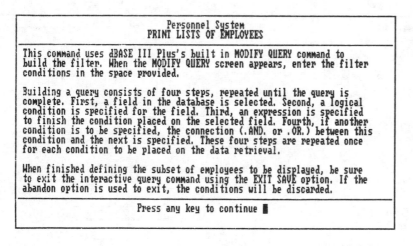

Fig. 4.28. Instructions for entering selection criteria to create a list of employees.

no index files are created, because the index files for those orders already exist and are opened automatically by PEOPEN as the first and second indexes, respectively. The appropriate index is therefore activated by the SET ORDER TO command. The indexes for the remaining choices are not maintained by the system, due to the limit of 15 open files with dBASE III Plus. (For more information on file limitations, see Chapter 3, "Tips and Techniques.") For all but the first two sort choices, PEEMPLI1 first creates the desired index; then activates the index with a SET INDEX TO command.

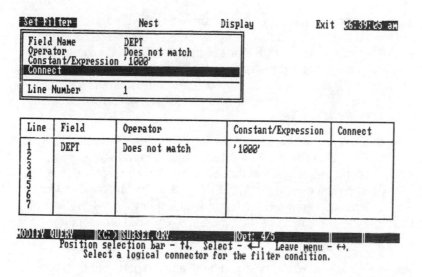

Fig. 4.29. Entering selection criteria with MODIFY QUERY.

After creating and activating the appropriate index files, PEEMPLI1 returns control to the calling program. PEEMPLIS checks the variable MCHOICE to see whether the user pressed *0* (zero) to chose the *Quit* option. If so, the program clears the screen, closes the databases, and returns control to calling program PEMENU2 (the queries and reports menu, discussed in the section "Creating a Menu System").

If the user did not choose the quit option, PEEMPLIS switches the printer on (SET PRINTER ON) and the monitor off (SET CONSOLE OFF), and sends the printer setup string to the printer. Then the program prints the employee list, using the REPORT FORM command and one of seven predefined dBASE report formats corresponding to the sort menu options. (These formats are discussed in the following paragraphs.) After printing the specified report, the program resets the printer and the monitor, closes the databases and returns to the queries and reports menu.

The report formats are named PELIST1, PELIST2, PELIST3, PELIST4, PELIST5, PELIST6, and PELIST7. The digit in each name corresponds to the option number from the sort menu. The program specifies the correct report format by constructing the name in a memory variable and using the & (macro substitution) operator to obtain the name of the report format in the REPORT FORM command.

The correct report format is specified by the following commands:

```
i="pelist"+STR(mchoice,1)
REPORT FORM &1
```

The first line defines a character memory variable containing the report name by concatenating to the character string *pelist* the alphanumeric representation of the value contained in the variable MCHOICE. For example, if MCHOICE contains the value 1, then the variable i is assigned the value *pelist1*. The second line uses the macro substitution operator (&) to substitute the contents of the memory variable i in the REPORT FORM command. For example, with i containing *pelist1*, dBASE reads the second line as *REPORT FORM pelist1*.

In this application, the seven report definitions are defined in interactive dBASE by the developer, using MODIFY REPORT. Table 4.2 shows the titles and group fields, and table 4.3 shows the report fields for each of the seven reports. The report title is entered at the first screen presented in the MODIFY REPORT command, the *Group on expression* at the second screen, and the report field headings and definitions at the third screen. Note that the employee list shown in figure 4.24 uses report definition PELIST5 and illustrates the report format described in table 4.3.

One possible enhancement to the system would be to add a report-definition option to the system-maintenance menu. This option would allow the user to change the report definitions as needed without having to contact the developer or resort to interactive dBASE. Such an option would display a menu of reports corresponding to the sort order menu in figure 4.27. When the user selected a report definition from the menu, the program would execute the REPORT FORM command for the selected report definition.

Table 4.2
Titles and Group Definitions
for the Employee List Reports

Report	Title	Group On
PELIST1	Employee List by Social Security No.	None
PELIST2	Employee List by Employee Name	None
PELIST3	Employee List by ZIP Code	ZIP
PELIST4	Employee List by Job Title	TITLE
PELIST5	Employee List by Department	DEPT
PELIST6	Employee List by Employment Date	YEAR(DATE( ))– YEAR(EMPL_DATE)
PELIST7	Employee List by Anniversary Date	MONTH(ANN_DATE)

Table 4.3
Report Field Headings and Definitions

For all reports except PELIST3:

Field	Heading	Definition	Width
1	SOCIAL;SECURITY;NUMBER ;---------	SSNO	9
2	;;EMPLOYEE NAME ;----------------------------	TRIM(LAST)+' '+TRIM(FIRST)+ IIF(MI#' ',' '+MI+'.',' ')	29
3	;;JOB TITLE ;----------------------------	TITLE	29
4	;;DEPT.;-----	DEPT	5
5	EMPLOY-;MENT;DATE;--------	EMPL_DATE	8
6	ANNIVER-;SARY;DATE;--------	ANN_DATE	8
7	;HOME;PHONE NUMBER ;-------------	HOMEPHONE	13
8	;EMERGENCY;PHONE NUMBER ;-------------	EMERG_PHON	13

For PELIST3:

Field	Heading	Definition	Width
1	SOCIAL;SECURITY;NUMBER ;---------	SSNO	9
2	;;EMPLOYEE NAME ;-----------------------------	TRIM(LAST)+' '+TRIM(FIRST)+ IIF(MI#' ',' '+MI+'.',' ')	29
3	;;DEPT.;-----	DEPT	5
4	;;STREET ADDRESS ;----------------------------	STREET	30
5	;;CITY, STATE, ZIP CODE ;----------------------------	TRIM(CITY)+', '+ TRIM(STATE)+'. '+ZIP	32
6	;HOME;PHONE NUMBER ;-------------	HOMEPHONE	13

Printing Mailing Lists and Address Labels (PEEMPMAI)

In addition to employee lists, Bob Johnson wants to be able to print mailing lists and labels. The steps required are similar to those required to print employee lists. The PEEMPMAI program does the following:

- prints a name and address file that can be used by a word processor such as Microsoft Word to generate form letters (see fig. 4.30)

- prints mailing labels on label stock (see fig. 4.31)

The program enables the user to skip either of these steps.

```
first,mi,last,street,city,state,zip
"Jerome","I","Case","101 E. Main","Littletown","IL","62000"
"Janet","E","Jones","5566 Redlands, Apt B-5","Orkin","IL","63000"
"John","A","Smith","2222 E. West St.","Eastern","IL","61000"
"John"," ","Carter","100 Helium Drive","Barsoom","IL","63000"
"Brad"."E"."Johnson","1234 E. 5th St.","Short Grove","IL","64000"
```

Fig. 4.30. Contents of the sample name and address file (EMPLIST3.TXT).

```
Jerome I. Case              Janet E. Jones
101 E. Main                 5566 Redlands, Apt B-5
Littletown, IL    62000     Orkin, IL    63000



John A. Smith               John  Carter
2222 E. West St.            100 Helium Drive
Eastern, IL    61000        Barsoom, IL    63000



Brad E. Johnson
1234 E. 5th St.
Short Grove, IL     64000
```

Fig. 4.31. Sample mailing labels.

The PEEMPMAI program is a simple, straight-line program that calls a subroutine to get the sort order and selection criteria for the report. Then the program uses the SET ALTERNATE command and ? command to generate a name and address file, and the LABEL command to print mailing labels. The flowchart for PEEMPMAI is shown in figure 4.32.

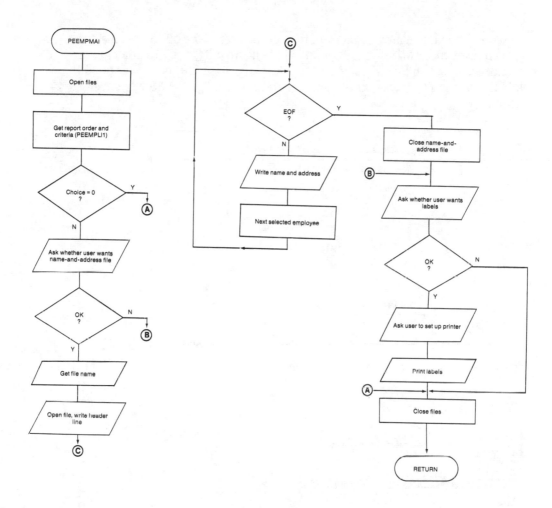

Fig. 4.32. Flowchart of the program PEEMPMAI.

The program begins by calling PEOPEN to open the database files (see listing 4.13). PEEMPMAI then calls subroutine PEEMPLI1, which displays a menu of list orderings, gives the user the option of specifying selection criteria, and indexes the file in the selected order. (The PEEMPLI1 subroutine is discussed in more detail in the preceding section, "Printing Employee Lists.")

Briefly, PEEMPLI1 works in the following manner. The user begins by selecting one of the seven sort orders shown in figure 4.33. PEEMPLI1 then prompts the user to specify selection criteria. If the user does not specify any criteria, the printed mailing list will include all active employees in the employee master file. If the user does want to specify criteria, PEEMPLI1 issues the MODIFY QUERY command, which displays the screen shown in figure 4.34. (You can refer the user to the dBASE manual for detailed instructions on using this command.) In figure 4.34, the selection criteria include a filter set on the ZIP code field to select only those ZIP codes over 60000. Note that all the ZIP codes in the sample report shown in figure 4.30 were over 60000.

```
                         Personnel System
                 GENERATE EMPLOYEE MAILING LIST AND LABELS

             Employee list can be sorted by:

                 1. Social Security Number Order
                 2. Name Order
                 3. ZIP Code Order
                 4. Job Title Order
                 5. Department Order
                 6. Employment Date Order
                 7. Anniversary Date Order (Month & Day)




                 0. Quit

             Enter selection: █
```

Fig. 4.33. Menu to select sort option for printing mailing lists.

```
 Set Filter          Nest          Display          Exit  11:25:28 am
┌──────────────────────────────────────────────────┐
│ Field Name          ZIP                            │
│ Operator            Comes after                    │
│ Constant/Expression '60000'                        │
│ Connect                                            │
├──────────────────────────────────────────────────┤
│ Line Number         1                              │
└──────────────────────────────────────────────────┘
```

Line	Field	Operator	Constant/Expression	Connect
1 2 3 4 5 6 7	ZIP	Comes after	'60000'	

```
MODIFY QUERY     |C:>|SUBSET.QRY              |Opt: 4/5|
       Position selection bar - ↑↓.  Select - ←┘.  Leave menu - ↔.
                 Select a logical connector for the filter condition.
```

Fig. 4.34. Using MODIFY QUERY to enter selection criteria.

PEEMPLI1 then returns control to calling program PEEMPMAI. If the user has entered zero for the sort order, the program exits and returns to the queries and reports menu. If the user chose a valid sort option, a prompt asks whether to generate a name and address list for later use with a word processor. If the user presses *Y*, PEEMPMAI requests a file name, then uses the command SET ALTERNATE TO &FNAME to redirect output of the ? command to the specified file. The screen to enter the file name is shown in figure 4.35. (Note the use of the & operator to specify the file name with the contents of memory variable FNAME.)

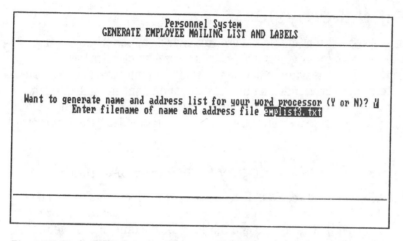

Fig. 4.35. Entering the file name to print the name and address file.

The name and address file produced by the program is in the format required by Microsoft Word (see fig. 4.30). The first line in the list is a header line containing the field names separated by commas. The remaining lines contain the field contents enclosed in double quotation marks and separated by commas. It is necessary to enclose the field contents in quotation marks because some of them have internal commas; see, for example, the line for Janet E. Jones in figure 4.30. Without the quotation marks, Microsoft Word would treat *Apt. B-5* as the contents of the CITY field, when in fact that string is part of the STREET field. The memory variable DELIMIT is used to simplify coding of the program line that produces these lines of the list. DELIMIT is a string containing CHR(34) (the double quotation mark), a comma, and CHR(34) again.

The header line is generated by the first ? command in the program. The name and address lines are generated by a DO WHILE loop that prints each line in index order. To export mailing lists from dBASE III Plus to other word processors, consult the word processor's manual for the correct format.

After finishing the name and address file section, PEEMPMAI prompts the user to indicate whether mailing labels are desired. If so, the program displays a message asking the user to set up the label stock in the printer and pauses until the user presses a key. The first label is a "test" label printed with the SAMPLE option. The SAMPLE option prints sample labels until the user has set up the labels correctly. Then the LABEL command prints the labels in the specified format. After printing labels, the program closes the databases, sets DELETED OFF, and returns to the queries and reports menu.

Maintaining the System

We have looked at programs that enable the user to enter data, perform queries, and print reports. Now we turn to programs that enable the user to perform various system-maintenance operations without having to use dBASE interactively. We have already discussed programs for reindexing the database and maintaining the system memory file. In this section we look at programs for backing up and restoring the data files, changing the format for mailing labels, and packing the database to remove deleted records.

Backing Up Data Files to Floppy Disks (PEBACKUP)

The program PEBACKUP uses three DOS BACKUP commands to save the data files (.DBF), index files (.NDX), and memory file (.MEM) from a hard disk to one or more floppy disks (see listing 4.14). The second and third BACKUP commands have the /A option set so that they will not erase the data written by the first BACKUP command. DOS prompts the user to insert floppy disks as needed. Note that the program is set up to make it easy to change the target disk drive. In addition, PEBACK backs up data from the current drive and directory. If your (or your client's) system has a tape drive, the tape drive's backup and restore commands can be substituted for the DOS commands.

Restoring Data Files from Floppy Disks (PERESTOR)

The program PERESTOR enables users to restore all system data from backup files made with PEBACKUP (see listing 4.15). You would use this command after a hardware failure or an accidental erasure of data. PERESTOR uses the DOS RESTORE command to restore to the current directory the entire contents of the source disk(s). The source drive is stored in a memory variable for easy updating.

Packing the Database (PEPACK)

The program PEPACK permanently removes deleted records from the database (see listing 4.16). Deleted records remain in a file and can be recalled to active status until the PACK command is used. Periodically running the PEPACK program reduces the size of the databases and improves processing speed. Packing the database can take a considerable time, so the program gives the user a chance to cancel the command.

Important note: *Warn the user that employee master records which have been deleted cannot be recovered after the database has been packed.*

Changing the Format for Mailing Labels (PECHGLBL)

The PECHGLBL program enables the user to redefine the mailing label format (see listing 4.17). The program consists of a DO WHILE loop containing a MODIFY LABEL command and a LABEL command with the SAMPLE option. The loop is executed until the user accepts the changes made to the label definition.

The MODIFY LABEL command invokes the text editor so that the user can change the label definitions in the label file (see fig. 4.36). Then the program offers the user a chance to print sample labels to test the changes. If the user does not accept the changes, PECHGLBL returns to the modification screen in figure 4.36 for additional changes.

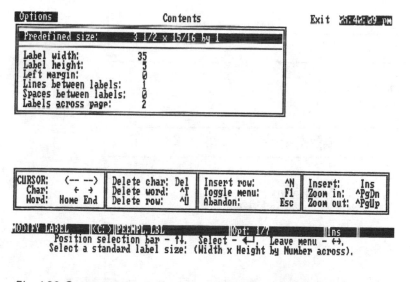

Fig. 4.36. Screen where the user can change mailing-label definitions.

Creating a Menu System

The next stage in the development of the personnel system is to create the menu system. To keep each menu simple, this application uses a main menu and three subsidiary menus. Figures 4.37 through 4.40 show the main menu, data-entry menu, queries and reports menu, and the system-maintenance menu, respectively. Note that the structure of this menu system mirrors the block diagram shown in figure 4.2.

The main menu program, PERSONNL, is the entry point for the system (see listing 4.18). As such, PERSONNL must establish the environment for the entire system. A series of SET commands performs that task.

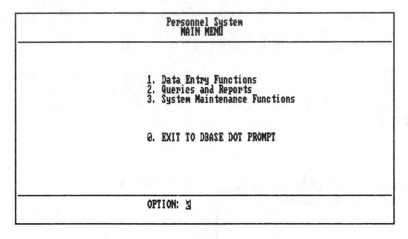

Fig. 4.37. The main menu.

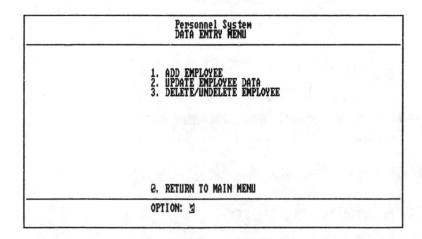

Fig. 4.38. The data-entry menu.

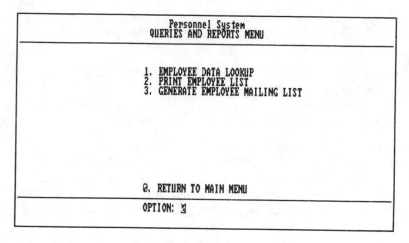

Fig. 4.39. The queries and reports menu.

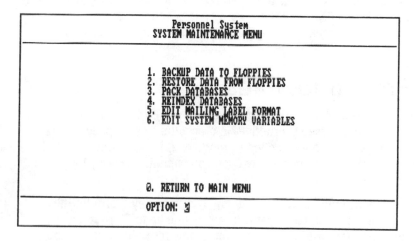

Fig. 4.40. The system-maintenance menu.

The code for PERSONNL is straightforward. After setting the environment, the program enters a main loop to display the menu screen and accept the user's keypress. Because the user must press a numeric key to make a selection, the user's choice is range-checked with the RANGE option of the @ . . . GET command.

A DO CASE structure at the bottom of the listing executes a program corresponding to a menu selection. Any selection from the main menu calls one of the submenu programs, PEMENU1, PEMENU2, or PEMENU3. The menu display and the DO CASE structure are contained in a DO WHILE loop that repeats the menu until the user selects option 0, the EXIT option. PERSONNL exits the main loop, restores the system defaults (SET TALK ON, SET SAFETY OFF), closes all the open files, clears the screen, and returns.

The three submenu programs, PEMENU1, PEMENU2, and PEMENU3, call the programs that perform the major operations of the system. Upon termination of the program, control returns to the submenu for an additional choice. The user may select another function from the submenu or return to the main menu.

The first menu program groups together functions for adding, updating, deleting, and undeleting employee records. The second menu program controls the query and report functions. The third menu program leads to system-maintenance functions for backing up data to floppy disks, restoring data from floppy disks, packing the database, reindexing the database, editing the mailing-label format, and editing the system memory variables. Code for these three submenus is shown in listings 4.19, 4.20, and 4.21. The code for submenu programs PEMENU1, PEMENU2, and PEMENU3 is similar to the code for PERSONNL.

You may want to rearrange the menus to suit your (or your client's) particular needs. You may prefer a single menu with all the system options in one place. Or you may like a multiple-menu arrangement like the one designed here for the personnel system.

Using Procedure Files

The final step in the development of the Personnel system is to test the entire system and to place the most heavily used subroutines in procedure files to speed program execution. Although you should test individual modules as they are developed, the whole system needs to be tested thoroughly upon completion, especially if you are turning it over to a client.

Clients will appreciate the time you will save them by placing key subroutines in procedure files. Recall from Chapter 2 that you can include up to 32 routines in a procedure file. Because there are fewer than 32 programs and subroutines in the personnel system, all the programs and subroutines except the main program can be included in a single procedure file invoked from the main menu program (PERSONNL). For more on testing the system and using procedure files, see Chapter 2, "Applications Development with dBASE III Plus."

Extensions to the System

You can enhance or extend the personnel system in a number of ways. The most important extension would be to add necessary but "sensitive" information like salary, job class, and performance rating to the employee master file. But then you would need a means to control or restrict access to this sensitive information. There are three ways to provide this security.

You can keep all the data for the personnel system on floppy disks handled only by an authorized employee. This solution is the simplest because it entails merely adding the appropriate fields to the employee master file and to the screen and report definitions.

You can put the sensitive information in its own file on a separate floppy disk kept by an authorized employee. The advantage to this approach is that access to nonsensitive information is easily accomplished. But this solution presents problems for the developer. The programs must be modified so that they check for the existence of the special file and use different screen and report definitions if they find the file. You can use the IF EXIST(filename) function to do this, but you'll have to place numerous IF EXIST commands in the programs. You'll also need a second set of screen and report definitions.

Finally, you can provide password security for sensitive data with the security system provided with the multiuser version of dBASE III Plus. This security system provides the ability to control access to individual fields in a database and a function to test the user's access level based on the ID number used to access the system. The multiuser version of dBASE III Plus can be installed on a single-user machine so that the security system can be used. For the developer, this solution involves as much additional work as the second solution, and adds the complexity of managing the security system. However, this approach provides users with the most flexibility and security and partially prepares the personnel application for operation on a multiuser system.

Several additional reports could enhance the reporting function of the system. As you recall from the section on queries and reports, the PrtSc key can be used to print individual records. One enhancement would be a program to print in batch mode a record card for each employee.

Many additional capabilities can be added to the basic personnel system, depending on your (or your client's) needs. You could add career and benefits information for employees, for example. Or you could add information required to satisfy equal opportunity reporting requirements. The system can be expanded with additional fields in the employee master file or with additional files to handle any or all of these capabilities.

Conclusion

This chapter has presented a personnel system that enables users to track basic information for employees. The system can be modified to accommodate a range of additional information about employees. If the system is set up to run in single-user mode on the multiuser version of dBASE III Plus, you (or your client) can have a secure, password-protected application.

Listing 4.1. The subroutine PEOPEN.

```
**************************************************
* PEOPEN -      Open personel database files    *
*              9/21/86                          *
**************************************************

CLOSE DATABASES

* Open employee master
SELECT A
USE peempl INDEX peempl1, peempl2

RETURN
```

Listing 4.2. The program PEINDEX.

```
**************************************************
* PEINDEX -      Reindex personnel databases    *
*              9/21/86                           *
**************************************************

CLOSE DATABASES
RESTORE FROM pemem
title="Reindex Personnel System Files"
DO borders WITH petitle,title

* reindex employee master
@ 6, 25 SAY "REINDEXING EMPLOYEE FILE"
USE peempl
@ 7, 27 SAY 'by social security number'
INDEX ON ssno TO peempl1
@ 8, 27 SAY 'by employee name'
INDEX ON UPPER(last)+UPPER(first)+mi TO peempl2

CLEAR
CLOSE DATABASES
RETURN
```

Listing 4.3. The program PEMEM.

```
*************************************************************
* PEMEM   -        Define Personnel System parameters     *
*                  9/21/86                                 *
*************************************************************

* Restore existing or initialize new entries, depending on whether file exists
IF FILE("pemem.mem")
   RESTORE FROM pemem
   pepsetup=SUBSTR(pepsetup+SPACE(80),1,80)      && Pad to 80 chars with blanks
   pepreset=SUBSTR(pepreset+SPACE(80),1,80)      && Pad to 80 chars with blanks
ELSE
   STORE "Personnel System" TO petitle
   STORE SPACE(80) TO pepsetup,pepreset
   STORE 0 TO pepmargin
   STORE 55 TO pepagelen
ENDIF

* get new values
mok=.F.
mok1=.F.
title= "Edit System Memory Variables"
DO WHILE .not.mok
   * Dipelay data entry screen
   DO peme1            && Display memory variable data entry screen
   @ 21, 9 SAY "Enter or revise desired memory variables. Press ";
       +"ESC to end edit"
   READ
   @ 21, 1 SAY SPACE(78)

   * Confirm edit.
   mok=.F.
   @ 21, 35 SAY "OK (Y or N)? " GET mok PICTURE "Y"
   READ
   IF .not. mok
      mok1=.T.
      @ 22, 20 SAY "Want to make further changes (Y or N)? ";
         GET mok1 PICTURE "Y"
      READ
      IF .not. mok1
         EXIT    &&  Quit loop with mok=.F.
      ENDIF
   ENDIF
ENDDO

* If ok, Save new memory file
IF mok
   pepsetup=TRIM(pepsetup)
   pepreset=TRIM(pepreset)
   DO peme1                              && Redisplay screen
   CLEAR GETS                            && but do not read
   mok=.T.
   @ 22,17 SAY "Save changes to new PEMEM file (Y or N) " GET mok PICTURE "Y"
   READ
   IF mok
      SAVE TO pemem ALL LIKE pe*
   ENDIF
ENDIF

* Tidy up and return
CLEAR
RETURN
```

Listing 4.4. The subroutine PEME1.

```
******************************************************************
* PEME1 -        Display memory variable data entry screen for  *
*                Personnel System                               *
*                9/21/86                                        *
******************************************************************

DO borders WITH petitle,"Edit System Memory Variables"
@  6,  2 SAY "PRINTER LEFT MARGIN    " GET pepmargin PICTURE "999" RANGE 0,132
@  6, 40 SAY "PRINTER PAGE LENGTH    " GET pepagelen PICTURE "99" RANGE 1, 99
@  7,  2 SAY "SETUP COMPRESSED PRINT " GET pepsetup FUNCTION "S30"
@  8,  2 SAY "RESET PRINTER TO NORMAL" GET pepreset FUNCTION "S30"

RETURN
```

Listing 4.5. The program PEEMPADD.

```
*****************************************
* PEEMPADD - Add new employee record   *
*             9/21/86                   *
*****************************************


* Open files
DO peopen
RESTORE FROM pemem ADDITIVE
SET DELETED ON
mtitle='ADD EMPLOYEE TO PERSONNEL SYSTEM'

* Main loop.
DO WHILE .T.                     && Do loop until exited by entering blank ssno

   * get social security number from user
   mssno=SPACE(9)
   DO borders WITH petitle,mtitle
   @  6, 2  SAY "ENTER SOCIAL SECURITY NUMBER OF NEW EMPLOYEE (blank to exit)";
      GET mssno PICTURE '@R 999-99-9999'
   READ

   * Exit on blank ss number
   IF mssno= ' '
      EXIT
   ENDIF

   * Check that ss number has nine digits. LOOP if not.
   IF LEN(trim(mssno))<9
      mok=' '
      @ 21, 10 SAY 'SS Number must have nine digits! Press any key to continue';
        GET mok
      READ
      LOOP
   ENDIF
```

```
* Lookup social security number in employee master file
SEEK mssno
ok=.F.

* If not found, employee with this ssno can be added.
IF EOF()                      && not found means it is a valid new ss no.
    @ 21, 11 SAY 'Confirm social security number for new employee (Y or N)';
      GET ok PICTURE 'Y'
    READ
    @ 21, 1 CLEAR TO 22, 78

    * If user confirmed number, add record to empl master, get data
    IF ok
       APPEND BLANK
       DELETE
       REPLACE ssno WITH mssno
       mok=.F.
       DO borders WITH petitle,mtitle
       DO peempup1 WITH .T.,mok        && Call peempup1 in edit mode

       IF mok            && If data entry ok, recall record to make it active
          RECALL
       ENDIF mok
    ENDIF ok

 ELSE          && Not end of file on seek
    * Display error message that social security number found
    mok=' '
    @ 21, 10 SAY "Social Security number exists in file. ";
             +"Press any key to continue";
       GET mok
    READ
    @ 21, 1 CLEAR TO 22, 78

 ENDIF EOF()
ENDDO

* tidy up and return
CLEAR
CLOSE DATABASES
SET DELETED OFF
RETURN
```

Listing 4.6. The subroutine PEEMPUP1.

```
*********************************************************
* PEEMPUP1 -     Edit screen for employee master file    *
*               2/13/87                                   *
*********************************************************

PARAMETERS editflag,ok

@ 5, 1 CLEAR TO 19, 78
ok=.F.
DO WHILE .not.ok
   * Display record in center portion of screen.
   @  5, 21  SAY "SOCIAL SECURITY NUMBER:"
   @  5, 45  SAY  PEEMPL->SSNO  FUNCTION "R"  PICTURE "999-99-9999"
   @  7,  5  SAY "FIRST NAME" GET  PEEMPL->FIRST
   @  7, 33  SAY "MI" GET  PEEMPL->MI  PICTURE "!"
   @  7, 39  SAY "LAST NAME" GET  PEEMPL->LAST
   @  9,  5  SAY "STREET" GET  PEEMPL->STREET
   @ 10,  5  SAY "CITY" GET  PEEMPL->CITY
   @ 11,  5  SAY "STATE" GET  PEEMPL->STATE  PICTURE "!!!"
   @ 12,  5  SAY "ZIP" GET  PEEMPL->ZIP  PICTURE "99999"
   @ 12, 45  SAY "HOME PHONE" GET  PEEMPL->HOMEPHONE  FUNCTION "R";
     PICTURE "(999)999-9999"
   @ 14,  5  SAY "EMERGENCY NAME" GET  PEEMPL->EMERG_NAME
   @ 15,  5  SAY "EMERGENCY PHONE" GET  PEEMPL->EMERG_PHON  FUNCTION "R";
     PICTURE "(999)999-9999"
   @ 17,  5  SAY "DEPARTMENT" GET  PEEMPL->DEPT  PICTURE "99999"
   @ 17, 32  SAY "TITLE" GET  PEEMPL->TITLE
   @ 18,  5  SAY "EMPLOYMENT DATE" GET  PEEMPL->EMPL_DATE
   @ 18, 44  SAY "ANNIVERSARY DATE" GET  PEEMPL->ANN_DATE

   *Check edit flag
   IF editflag
      * Flag is true, do edit
      @ 21, 4 SAY 'ESC - exit, CTRL END - accept edit, ';
        +'ENTER or arrow keys - next field'
      READ
      @ 21, 1 CLEAR TO 22, 78

      * Check for ESC key
      i=readkey()
      IF i=12            && ESC key code
         EXIT            && Break out of data entry loop with ok=.F.
      ENDIF

      * verify data entry
      @ 21, 33 SAY 'OK (Y or N)?' GET ok PICTURE 'y'
      READ
      @ 21, 1 CLEAR TO 22, 78

   ELSE          && Flag not true, display only
      CLEAR GETS
      mok=' '
      @ 21, 26 SAY 'Press any key to continue' GET mok
      READ
      ok=.T.
   ENDIF

ENDDO

RETURN
```

Listing 4.7. The program PEEMPUPD.

```
**************************************************
* PEEMPUPD - Update employee record              *
*           9/21/86                              *
**************************************************

* Open files
DO peopen
RESTORE FROM pemem ADDITIVE
mtitle='UPDATE EMPLOYEE DATA'

* Main loop.
DO WHILE .T.               && Do loop until exited by entering blank ssno

   * Display screen
   SET DELETED ON
   DO borders WITH petitle,mtitle

   * get social security number from user
   ok=.F.
   mssno=SPACE(9)
   DO pefindem WITH mssno,ok

   * Exit data entry loop on not ok
   IF .not.ok
     EXIT
   ENDIF

   * Allow user to make changes to employee master in full screen edit mode
   DO peempup1 WITH .T.,ok

ENDDO

* tidy up and return
CLEAR
CLOSE DATABASES
SET DELETED OFF
RETURN
```

Listing 4.8. The subroutine PEFINDEM.

```
*******************************************************************
* PEFINDEM - Look up employee by social security number or name  *
*            10/14/86                                            *
*******************************************************************
* Parameters
PARAMETERS mssno,ok

* Initialization
SET EXACT OFF            && Do not want to limit SEEK's to exact matches
ok=.F.

*Data entry loop to get employee by social security number or name
DO WHILE .not.ok
   @  5, 1 CLEAR TO 19, 78
   @ 21, 1 CLEAR TO 22, 78
   mssno=SPACE(9)
   mfirst=SPACE(15)
   mlast=SPACE(20)
   mmi=' '

   * Read social security number or employee name
   @  5, 17  SAY "ENTER SOCIAL SECURITY NUMBER OR EMPLOYEE NAME"
   @  7, 22  SAY "SOCIAL SECURITY NUMBER" GET mssno;
     PICTURE '@R 999-99-9999'
   @  9, 22  SAY "LAST NAME" GET mlast FUNCTION 'A!'
   @ 10, 22  SAY 'FIRST NAME' GET mfirst FUNCTION 'A!'
   @ 10, 52  SAY 'MI' GET mmi FUNCTION 'A!'
   @ 13, 22  SAY 'PROGRAM WILL DISPLAY MATCHES TO PARTIAL'
   @ 14, 22  SAY 'SS NUMBER OR LAST NAME ON SCREEN ONE AT A TIME'
   @ 21, 9   SAY "PRESS ESC FROM BLANK SCREEN TO QUIT"
   @ 22, 9   SAY "PRESS ENTER THEN ESC TO ENTER SOCIAL SECURITY NUMBER OR NAME"
   READ
   @ 13, 1 CLEAR TO 14, 78
   @ 21, 1 CLEAR TO 22, 78

   * determine which was entered, and look up in EMPLOYEE MASTER file
   DO CASE
      * Lookup nonzero social security number
      CASE mssno#' '
           mlast=SPACE(20)             && Make sure last name is empty
           SET ORDER TO 1              && SS number index is #1
           SEEK TRIM(mssno)

           * If not found, display message & loop
           IF EOF()
             mok=' '
             @ 21, 9 SAY "Social Security number not found.  ";
               +"Press any key to continue" GET mok
             READ
             @ 21, 1 CLEAR TO 22, 78
             LOOP
           ENDIF

      * Lookup employee name
      CASE mlast#' '
           SET ORDER TO 2              && last name index is #2

           * Set filter to those records with the indicated first name and MI.
           SET FILTER TO UPPER(first)=TRIM(mfirst).and.mi=TRIM(mmi)

           * Lookup first record with indicated last name
           SEEK TRIM(mlast)

           * Check if found
```

```
        IF EOF()
          mok=' '
          @ 21, 6 SAY "Could not find matching employee name.   ";
            +"Press any key to continue" GET mok
          READ
          @ 21, 1 CLEAR TO 22, 78
          SET FILTER TO
          LOOP
        ENDIF

    * Handle if wrong part of fields entered
    CASE mfirst#' ' .or. mmi#' '
        mok=' '
        @ 21, 12 SAY "Invalid search specification.   ";
          +"Press any key to continue" GET mok
        READ
        @ 21, 1 CLEAR TO 22, 78
        LOOP

    OTHERWISE                       && all fields are empty
        EXIT

ENDCASE

* Browse matching SS numbers or names until user selects employee or EOF
ok=.F.
DO WHILE .not.ok.and..not.EOF().and.;
      ((mlast#' '.and.UPPER(last)=TRIM(mlast)).or.;
      (mssno#' '.and.ssno=TRIM(mssno)))
    @ 14,  9  SAY 'THE FOLLOWING EMPLOYEE MATCHES THE ';
              +'SPECIFIED SS NUMBER OR NAME'
    @ 15, 22  SAY "SOCIAL SECURITY NUMBER:"
    @ 15, 46  SAY ssno PICTURE '@R 999-99-9999'
    @ 16, 22  SAY "LAST NAME: "+last
    @ 17, 22  SAY 'FIRST NAME: '+first
    @ 17, 52  SAY 'MI: '+mi
    @ 21,  5  SAY 'OK (Y or N)? (ENTER for next match, ESC to QUIT, ';
              +'PGDN for next)':
      GET ok PICTURE 'Y'
    READ
    @ 21, 1 CLEAR TO 22, 78
    IF .not.ok
        i=READKEY()
        DO CASE
          CASE i=12             && ESC key
              EXIT              && Break out of display loop
          CASE i=6             && PGUP key
              SKIP -1          && Backup one record
        OTHERWISE
              SKIP
        ENDCASE
    ELSE
        mssno=ssno
    ENDIF
  ENDDO

  SET FILTER TO
ENDDO .not.ok

@  5, 1 CLEAR TO 19, 78
@ 21, 1 CLEAR TO 22, 78
RETURN
```

Listing 4.9. The program PEEMPDEL.

```
***************************************************
* PEEMPDEL - Delete or Undelete employee record *
*            10/15/86                            *
***************************************************

* Open files
DO peopen
RESTORE FROM pemem ADDITIVE
mtitle='DELETE OR UNDELETE EMPLOYEE'
ok=.T.

* Main loop.
DO WHILE .T.              && Do loop until exited by entering blank ssno

    * get social security number from user
    mssno=SPACE(9)
    DO borders WITH petitle,mtitle
    @  6, 2  SAY "SOCIAL SECURITY NUMBER OF EMPLOYEE TO DELETE OR UNDELETE";
       GET mssno PICTURE '@R 999-99-9999'
    @  7, 2  SAY "(blank to exit)"
    READ

    * Exit on blank ss number
    IF mssno= ' '
       EXIT
    ENDIF

    * Lookup social security number in employee master file
    SET DELETED ON              && Want active records only
    SEEK mssno                  && Look for record with matching SS number

    * If not found, check with deleted on
    IF .not.EOF()          && Found record to delete
       DO peempup1 WITH .F.,ok
       ok=.F.
       @ 21, 11 SAY 'Confirm DELETE of this employee (Y or N)';
         GET ok PICTURE 'Y'
       READ
       IF ok
          DELETE
       ENDIF
```

```
ELSE                    && Did not find active record, check for deleted record
    SET DELETED OFF     && Want deleted records now
    SEEK mssno          && Look for SS number again
    IF .not.EOF()       && If found, record is deleted!
        DO peempup1 WITH .F.,ok
        ok=.F.
        @ 21, 11 SAY 'Confirm RECALL of this employee (Y or N)';
            GET ok PICTURE 'Y'
        READ
        IF ok
            RECALL
        ENDIF

    ELSE
        * If SSNO not found, display error message and loop
        mok=' '
        @ 21, 10 SAY 'Social Security number not found! ';
                +'Press any key to continue';
            GET mok
        READ
        @ 21, 1 CLEAR TO 22, 78
    ENDIF
ENDIF

    ENDDO

    * tidy up and return
    CLEAR
    CLOSE DATABASES
    SET DELETED OFF
    RETURN
```

Listing 4.10. The program PEEMPQY.

```
***************************************************
* PEEMPQY - Display Employee Data on Screen      *
*           2/13/87                              *
***************************************************

* Open files
DO peopen
RESTORE FROM pemem ADDITIVE
mtitle='DISPLAY EMPLOYEE DATA'

* Main loop.
DO WHILE .T.              && Do loop until exited by entering blank ssno

   * Display screen
   SET DELETED ON
   DO borders WITH petitle,mtitle

   * get social security number from user
   ok=.F.
   mssno=SPACE(9)
   DO pefindem WITH mssno,ok

   * Exit display loop on not ok
   IF .not.ok
      EXIT
   ENDIF

   * Allow user to view employee master in display-only mode
   DO peempup1 WITH .F.,ok

ENDDO

* tidy up and return
CLEAR
CLOSE DATABASES
SET DELETED OFF
RETURN
```

Listing 4.11. The program PEEMPLIS.

```
************************************************************
* PEEMPLIS -    Generate sorted lists of employees       *
*                  9/21/86                                *
************************************************************

* Open files, restore system memory variables
DO peopen
SET DELETED ON                          && Only want active employees
RESTORE FROM pemem ADDITIVE
mtitle='PRINT LISTS OF EMPLOYEES'
DO borders WITH petitle, mtitle

* Display setup printer message
mok=' '
@ 21, 20 SAY 'Setup printer, then press any key to continue' GET mok
READ
@ 21, 1 CLEAR TO 22, 78

* Get sort option and selection criteria
mchoice=0
DO peempli1 WITH mchoice

* If choice=0, quit
IF mchoice#0

   @ 5, 1 CLEAR TO 19, 78
   @ 5, 35 SAY 'PRINTING...'

   *Send setup string to printer
   SET PRINT ON
   SET CONSOLE OFF
   ? &pepsetup

   * Print employee list using REPORT FORM command
   i="pelist"+STR(mchoice,1)    && Variable I contains the report name
   REPORT FORM &i               && Call the desired report

   * Reset printer, close databases, and return
   ? &pepreset
   SET CONSOLE ON
   SET PRINT OFF

ENDIF

CLEAR
CLOSE DATABASES
RETURN
```

Listing 4.12. The subroutine PEEMPLI1.

```
*****************************************************************
* PEEMPLI1 -    Get information from user for employee lists    *
*                 2/13/87                                        *
*****************************************************************

PARAMETERS mchoice

* Display a menu of sort options
mchoice=0
@ 5, 20 SAY 'Employee list can be sorted by:'
@  7, 25 SAY '1. Social Security Number Order'
@  8, 25 SAY '2. Name Order'
@  9, 25 SAY '3. ZIP Code Order'
@ 10, 25 SAY '4. Job Title Order'
@ 11, 25 SAY '5. Department Order'
@ 12, 25 SAY '6. Employment Date Order'
@ 13, 25 SAY '7. Anniversary Date Order (Month & Day)'
@ 19, 25 SAY '0. Quit'
@ 21, 25 SAY 'Enter selection:' GET mchoice PICTURE '9'
READ
@  5, 1 CLEAR TO 19, 78
@ 21, 1 CLEAR TO 22, 78

* Quit if user selected option 0.
IF mchoice#0

   * Ask user if he wants to specify selection criteria
   mans=.F.
   @  5, 12 SAY 'All employees are selected unless you specify criteria'
   @ 21, 17 SAY 'Want to specify selection criteria (Y or N)?';
      GET mans PICTURE 'Y'
   READ
   @  5, 1 CLEAR TO 19, 78
   @ 21, 1 CLEAR TO 22, 78
   IF mans
      mok=" "
      * Write Instructions
      @ 5, 2 SAY "This command uses dBASE III Plus's built ";
              +"in MODIFY QUERY command to"
      @ 6, 2 SAY "build the filter. When the MODIFY QUERY screen ";
              +"appears, enter the filter"
      @ 7, 2 SAY "conditions in the space provided."
      @ 9, 2 SAY "Building a query consists of four steps, repeated ";
              +"until the query is"
      @ 10, 2 SAY "complete. First, a field in the database is ";
              +"selected. Second, a logical"
      @ 11, 2 SAY "condition is specified for the field. Third, an ";
              +"expression is specified"
      @ 12, 2 SAY "to finish the condition placed on the selected ";
              +"field. Fourth, if another"
      @ 13, 2 SAY "condition is to be specified, the connection ";
              +"(.AND. or .OR.) between this"
      @ 14, 2 SAY "condition and the next is specified. These four ";
              +"steps are repeated once"
      @ 15, 2 SAY "for each condition to be placed on the data retrieval."
      @ 17, 2 SAY "When finished defining the subset of employees to ";
              +"be displayed, be sure"
      @ 18, 2 SAY "to exit the interactive query command using the ";
              +"EXIT SAVE option. If the"
      @ 19, 2 SAY "abandon option is used to exit, the conditions will ";
              +"be discarded."
      @ 21, 26 SAY "Press any key to continue" GET mok
      READ
```

```
          ERASE subset.qry
          MODIFY QUERY subset          && Specify criteria using MODIFY QUERY COMMAND
          DO borders WITH petitle,mtitle
          @ 5, 1 CLEAR TO 19, 78              &&  Clear Screen
          @ 21, 1 CLEAR TO 22, 78
       ENDIF

    * select or create proper index
    @ 5, 33 SAY 'CREATING INDEX'
    DO CASE
       CASE mchoice=1.or.mchoice=2
          SET ORDER TO mchoice    && First two indexes are already open
       CASE mchoice=3
          USE peempl
          INDEX ON zip TO temp
          SET INDEX TO temp
       CASE mchoice=4
          USE peempl
          INDEX ON title+dept+last+first+mi TO temp
          SET INDEX TO temp
       CASE mchoice=5
          USE peempl
          INDEX ON dept+last+first+mi TO temp
          SET INDEX TO temp
       CASE mchoice=6
          USE peempl
          SET DATE ANSI
          INDEX ON DTOC(empl_date)+last+first+mi TO temp
          SET DATE AMER
          SET INDEX TO temp
       CASE mchoice=7
          USE peempl
          INDEX ON STR(10000+100*MONTH(ann_date)+DAY(ann_date),5);
               +last+first+mi TO temp
          SET INDEX TO temp
    ENDCASE
ENDIF choice#0

RETURN
```

Listing 4.13. The program PEEMPMAI.

```
*********************************************************
* PEEMPMAI -    Generate sorted employee mailing lists  *
*              10/15/86                                  *
*********************************************************

* Open files, restore system memory variables
DO peopen
SET DELETED ON                   && Only want active employees
RESTORE FROM pemem ADDITIVE
mtitle='GENERATE EMPLOYEE MAILING LIST AND LABELS'
DO borders WITH petitle, mtitle

* Get sort option and selection criteria
mchoice=0
DO peempli1 WITH mchoice

* If choice#0, continue
IF mchoice#0
   DO borders WITH petitle, mtitle
```

(Continued on next page.)

Listing 4.13, continued.

```
   * Print employee name and address list to text file
   ans=.T.
   @ 10, 3 SAY 'Want to generate name and address list for ';
        +'your word processor (Y or N)?' GET ans PICTURE 'y'
   READ
   IF ans
       fname='emplist'+STR(mchoice,1)+'.txt'
       @ 11, 13 SAY 'Enter filename of name and address file';
                GET fname PICTURE 'xxxxxxxxx.xxx'
       READ
       SET ALTERNATE TO &fname
       SET ALTERNATE ON
       SET CONSOLE OFF
       delimit=CHR(34)+','+CHR(34)
       ? 'first,mi,last,street,city,state,zip'
       GO TOP
       DO WHILE .not.EOF()
          ? CHR(34)+TRIM(first)+delimit+mi+delimit+TRIM(last)+delimit;
            +TRIM(street)+delimit+TRIM(city)+delimit+TRIM(state)+delimit;
            +zip+CHR(34)
          SKIP
       ENDDO
       SET CONSOLE ON
       SET ALTERNATE OFF
       SET ALTERNATE TO
   ENDIF

   * Print mailing labels
   ans=.T.
   @ 14, 20 SAY 'Want to print mailing labels (Y or N)?' GET ans PICTURE 'Y'
   READ
   IF ans
       * Display setup printer message
       mok=' '
       @ 21, 10 SAY 'Insert label stock in printer, then press any key for test';
       GET mok
       READ
       @  21, 1 CLEAR TO 22, 78
       SET PRINT ON
       SET CONSOLE OFF

       * Print labels
       LABEL FORM peempl SAMPLE



       SET CONSOLE ON
       SET PRINT OFF
   ENDIF ans

ENDIF choice#0

* Close databases and return
CLOSE DATABASES
SET DELETED OFF
CLEAR
RETURN
```

Listing 4.14. The program PEBACKUP.

```
**********************************************************************
* PEBACKUP -     Back up personnel data files to backup device    *
*               7/24/86                                           *
**********************************************************************
target="b:"                              && Target drive for backup
CLEAR
files1="*.dbf"
RUN BACKUP &files1 &target
files2="*.ndx"
RUN BACKUP &files2 &target/A
files3="*.mem"
RUN BACKUP &files3 &target/A
CLEAR
RETURN
```

Listing 4.15. The program PERESTOR.

```
**********************************************************************
* PERESTOR -     RESTORE personnel data from backup device        *
*               7/24/86                                           *
**********************************************************************
source="b:"                             && Source drive for restore
target="c:"
files1=target+"*.*"
RUN RESTORE &source &files1
CLEAR
RETURN
```

Listing 4.16. The program PEPACK.

```
**************************************************
* PEPACK -        Pack personnel database files    *
*                 9/21/86                          *
**************************************************

DO peopen
RESTORE FROM pemem
mtitle="Remove Deleted Records from Files"
DO borders WITH petitle,mtitle
@ 12, 25 SAY "This command can run slowly"
mok=.T.
@ 21, 26 SAY "Want to continue (Y or N)?" GET mok PICTURE "Y"
READ
@ 12, 1 SAY SPACE(78)
@ 21, 1 SAY SPACE(78)

IF mok
   * Pack employee file
   @ 13, 28 SAY 'Packing Employee Master File'
   pack
   @ 13, 1 SAY SPACE(78)

ENDIF mok

* Quit
CLEAR
CLOSE DATABASES
RETURN
```

Listing 4.17. The program PECHGLBL.

```
***************************************************
* PECHGLBL -      Change mailing label format    *
*                 10/14/86                        *
***************************************************

DO peopen
RESTORE FROM pemem
mtitle="Change Mailing Label Format"

ok=.F.
DO WHILE .not.ok
    * change label format
    MODIFY LABEL peempl

    * Give user the opportunity to print a sample
    DO borders WITH petitle,mtitle
    mans=.F.
    @ 21, 24 SAY 'Want to print sample (Y or N)?' GET mans PICTURE 'Y'
    READ

    IF mans
        mno=1
        @ 22, 26 SAY 'How many labels in sample?' GET mno PICTURE '9' RANGE 1,9
        READ
        SET CONSOLE OFF
        SET PRINT ON
        SET ORDER TO 0
        GO TOP
        SET FILTER TO RECNO()<=mno
        LABEL FORM peempl
        SET CONSOLE ON
        SET PRINT OFF

        @ 21, 1 CLEAR TO 22, 78
        @ 21, 33 SAY 'OK (Y or N)?' GET ok PICTURE 'Y'
        READ
        @ 21, 1 CLEAR TO 21, 78
    ELSE
        EXIT
    ENDIF
ENDDO

* Quit
CLEAR
CLOSE DATABASES
RETURN
```

Listing 4.18. The program PERSONNL.

```
*********************************************************
* PERSONNL - Personnel System application main menu *
*            7/24/86                                 *
*********************************************************

* Setup environment
SET TALK OFF
SET SAFETY OFF
SET DEVICE TO SCREEN
SET PRINT OFF
CLOSE DATABASES
CLEAR ALL

* Main loop
option=-1
DO WHILE option#0
   RESTORE FROM pemem ADDITIVE
   DO borders WITH petitle, "MAIN MENU"

   * Display Menu
   option=0
   @  8, 28  SAY "1. Data Entry Functions"
   @  9, 28  SAY "2. Queries and Reports"
   @ 10, 28  SAY "3. System Maintenance Functions"
   @ 14, 28  SAY "0. EXIT TO DBASE DOT PROMPT"
   @ 21, 28  SAY "OPTION:" GET option PICTURE "9" RANGE 0,3
   READ
   @ 21, 1 SAY SPACE(78)

   * Do selected option
   DO CASE
      CASE option=1
         DO pemenu1                  && Data Entry Functions
      CASE option=2
         DO pemenu2                  && Queries and Reports
      CASE option=3
         DO pemenu3                  && System Maintenance

      OTHERWISE                      && Confirm option=0 before leaving
         mq=.T.
         @ 21, 20 SAY "Do you really want to quit (Y or N)?";
           GET mq PICTURE 'Y'
         READ
         option=IIF(mq,0,-1)         && Reset option to -1 if (N)o
   ENDCASE
* End of main loop
ENDDO (option#0)

* Restore system defaults and exit
SET TALK ON
SET SAFETY ON
CLEAR ALL
CLEAR
RETURN
```

Listing 4.19. The program PEMENU1.

```
**************************************************
* PEMENU1 - Personnel System Data  Entry menu    *
*              7/24/86                            *
**************************************************

* Main loop
mopt=-1
DO WHILE mopt#0
   RESTORE FROM pemem ADDITIVE
   DO borders WITH petitle,"DATA ENTRY MENU"

   * Display Menu
   mopt=0
   @  7, 27  SAY "1. ADD EMPLOYEE"
   @  8, 27  SAY "2. UPDATE EMPLOYEE DATA"
   @  9, 27  SAY "3. DELETE/UNDELETE EMPLOYEE"
   @ 19, 27  SAY "0. RETURN TO MAIN MENU"
   @ 21, 27  SAY "OPTION:" GET mopt PICTURE "9" RANGE 0,3
   READ
   @ 21, 1 SAY SPACE(78)

   * Do selected option
   DO CASE
      CASE mopt=1
         DO peempadd                     && Add employee & enter data
      CASE mopt=2
         DO peempupd                     && Update employee data
      CASE mopt=3
         DO peempdel                     && Delete/Undelete employee data
   ENDCASE
* End of main loop
ENDDO (mopt#0)

* Restore system defaults and exit
CLEAR
RETURN
```

Listing 4.20. The program PEMENU2.

```
*****************************************************************************
* PEMENU2 -      Personnel System Account Queries and Reports menu       *
*               9/21/86                                                   *
*****************************************************************************

* Main loop
mopt=-1
DO WHILE mopt#0
   RESTORE FROM pemem ADDITIVE
   DO borders WITH petitle,"QUERIES AND REPORTS MENU"

   * Display Menu
   mopt=0
   @  7, 27  SAY "1. EMPLOYEE DATA LOOKUP"
   @  8, 27  SAY "2. PRINT EMPLOYEE LIST"
   @  9, 27  SAY "3. GENERATE EMPLOYEE MAILING LIST"
   @ 19, 27  SAY "0. RETURN TO MAIN MENU"
   @ 21, 27  SAY "OPTION:" GET mopt PICTURE "9" RANGE 0,3
   READ
   @ 21, 1 SAY SPACE(78)

   * Do selected option
   DO CASE
      CASE mopt=1
         DO peempqy                    && employee data query
      CASE mopt=2
         DO peemplis                   && print employee list
      CASE mopt=3
         DO peempmai                   && employee mailing list
   ENDCASE
* End of main loop
ENDDO (mopt#0)

* Restore system defaults and exit
CLEAR
RETURN
```

Listing 4.21. The program PEMENU3.

```
**************************************************
* PEMENU3 - Personnel System Maintenance menu    *
*              7/24/86                            *
**************************************************

* Main loop
mopt=-1
DO WHILE mopt#0
   RESTORE FROM pemem ADDITIVE
   DO borders WITH petitle,"SYSTEM MAINTENANCE MENU"

   * Display Menu
   mopt=0
   @  7, 27  SAY "1. BACKUP DATA TO FLOPPIES"
   @  8, 27  SAY "2. RESTORE DATA FROM FLOPPIES"
   @  9, 27  SAY "3. PACK DATABASES"
   @ 10, 27  SAY "4. REINDEX DATABASES"
   @ 11, 27  SAY "5. EDIT MAILING LABEL FORMAT"
   @ 12, 27  SAY "6. EDIT SYSTEM MEMORY VARIABLES"
   @ 19, 27  SAY "0. RETURN TO MAIN MENU"
   @ 21, 27  SAY "OPTION:" GET mopt PICTURE "9" RANGE 0,7
   READ
   @ 21, 1 SAY SPACE(78)

   * Do selected option
   DO CASE
      CASE mopt=1
           DO pebackup                && Backup database files to floppy
      CASE mopt=2
           DO perestor                && Restore files from floppy
      CASE mopt=3
           DO pepack                  && Pack database files
      CASE mopt=4
           DO peindex                 && Reindex database files
      CASE mopt=5
           DO pechglbl                && Edit mailing label def.
      CASE mopt=6
           DO pemem                   && Edit system memory variables
   ENDCASE
* End of main loop
ENDDO (mopt#0)

* Restore system defaults and exit
CLEAR
RETURN
```

5

Sales-Tracking System

When Fred Adams started his marketing firm three years ago, he had no idea that it would grow so quickly. His original one-man operation soon employed five full-time sales representatives marketing 30 products. Fred became so busy calculating commissions and inventory requirements that he had little time to devote to the management of his company, much less to explore further growth potentials.

Fred's immediate need was for a computerized system that would keep track of all product sales and calculate monthly commissions and inventory requirements. It should also allow quick retrieval of information about a particular customer or salesperson and provide a variety of printed reports for in-depth analysis. Specifically, he needed sales information by product to determine which products to market more aggressively or possibly eliminate altogether.

After looking at "canned" sales-tracking systems available at local computer stores, Fred decided to hire a consultant to develop a customized system using dBASE III Plus. Suppose that we have met with Fred, have discussed his needs, and have developed a sales-tracking system that can be expanded later on as Fred's requirements grow.

This chapter takes you through all the stages involved in developing the application. We begin by considering the purpose and functions of the system, then describe the data and index files you need to create before developing the programs. Next, we look at the programs and subroutines that enable the user to create and maintain records for customers and salespersons, enter sales transactions, print a variety of reports, and perform system maintenance. Finally, we look at a menu system, the use of procedure files, and possible extensions to the system.

Identifying the Purpose and Functions of the System

The main purpose of the sales-tracking system is to record each salesperson's product sales by customer for each month. To support this purpose, information about sales, salespersons, and customers must be available within the system. Custom data-entry screens make it easy for the user to enter sales transactions and add, update, delete, undelete, query, and review records for customers and salespersons.

Additional data-entry screens simplify report printing, as well. Fred can print reports showing commissions, inventory usage, and product sales analysis. The salesperson-commission report lists by salesperson (for each sale) the customer ID, product ID, quantity, sales amount, and commission amount, with totals for the sales and commission amounts. The inventory-usage report, which Fred can use to determine inventory requirements, lists by product the product ID and period sales. Finally, the product sales-analysis report lists by product line the product ID, period sales (quantity and dollars), period cost-of-sales, and gross profit, with subtotals for each product and grand totals at the end.

Three other reports are supplied by the sales-tracking system. The first is a customer master list that simply lists the customer master-file information. The second report is a master listing of the salesperson file. The third report is a customer sales-analysis report, which lists customer ID and period sales.

Defining the File Structures

We've met with Fred to determine what information he needs. The next step in developing the sales-tracking system is to design the required data files and any necessary index files. The sales-tracking system needs a detail file for recording sales transactions and two master files to store information about customers and salespersons.

A product master file could be added to maintain detail information about each individual product, but this option will be left for future enhancement. Another use of the product master file would be to validate product ID numbers during data entry. For now, the product ID number will be limited using a range check (1–30) on entry.

The detail file and two master files are the basis of the sales-tracking system in its current form. The sections that follow discuss these files in detail.

The Transaction File

The transaction file, SPTRAN00.DBF, is the key to the sales-tracking system. This file contains the details about each sale and is used to produce all the reports Fred requires. The transaction file does not, however, contain *all* the information for these reports. As a detail file, it contains only those items that relate to the specific event (sale); the file contains no global or unchanging items such as the customer's address or phone number. These global items are maintained in separate master files and are referenced by a unique identifier in the detail file. The basic data for a sale are customer, salesperson, product, month, quantity, dollar amount, and cost (see fig. 5.1).

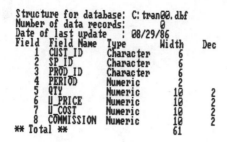

```
Structure for database: C: tran00.dbf
Number of data records:        0
Date of last update   : 08/29/86
Field  Field Name  Type       Width   Dec
    1  CUST_ID     Character     6
    2  SP_ID       Character     6
    3  PROD_ID     Character     6
    4  PERIOD      Numeric       2
    5  QTY         Numeric      10      2
    6  U_PRICE     Numeric      10      2
    7  U_COST      Numeric      10      2
    8  COMMISSION  Numeric      10      2
  ** Total **                  61
```

Fig. 5.1. Structure of the transaction file, TRAN00.DBF.

The CUST_ID and SP_ID fields are keys that link the transaction file to the two master files, which contain data on customers and salespersons. The PROD_ID field identifies the product sold and is also an index into the transaction file. The PERIOD field contains the month of the transaction and is also an index into the transaction file. The four remaining fields—QTY, U_PRICE, U_COST and COMMISSION—contain the quantity, unit price, unit cost, and commission for the sale.

Master Files

Two separate master files are required to support the transaction-detail file. The customer master file and the salesperson master file contain unique information about customers and salespersons, respectively, and play an important role in the reporting function.

The Customer File

The first master file is the customer file, CUST00.DBF, whose structure is shown in figure 5.2. The CUST_ID field is the primary key for the customer file, allowing quick access to a particular customer record. The COMPANY field contains the customer's company name. The next five fields—ADDR_1, ADDR_2, CITY, STATE, ZIP—contain the customer's address information. The PHONE field contains the phone number, including the area code. The last two fields, F_NAME and L_NAME, contain the first and last name of the primary customer contact. This information has been broken down into two fields to simplify production of the direct-mail letters Fred Adams sends to his customers.

The Salesperson File

The salesperson master file contains all the information pertinent to each member of the sales staff (see fig. 5.3). The first field, SP_ID, is the primary key for accessing this file. The next eight fields—S_ADDR1, S_ADDR2, S_CITY, S_STATE, S_ZIP,

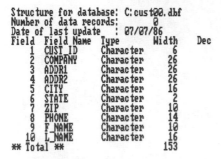

```
Structure for database: C:cust00.dbf
Number of data records:        0
Date of last update   : 07/07/86
Field  Field Name  Type        Width    Dec
    1  CUST_ID     Character       6
    2  COMPANY     Character      26
    3  ADDR1       Character      26
    4  ADDR2       Character      26
    5  CITY        Character      16
    6  STATE       Character       2
    7  ZIP         Character      10
    8  PHONE       Character      14
    9  F_NAME      Character      10
   10  L_NAME      Character      16
** Total **                     153
```

Fig. 5.2. Structure of the customer master file, CUST00.DBF.

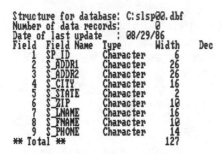

```
Structure for database: C:slsp00.dbf
Number of data records:        0
Date of last update   : 08/29/86
Field  Field Name  Type        Width    Dec
    1  SP_ID       Character       6
    2  S_ADDR1     Character      26
    3  S_ADDR2     Character      26
    4  S_CITY      Character      16
    5  S_STATE     Character       2
    6  S_ZIP       Character      10
    7  S_LNAME     Character      16
    8  S_FNAME     Character      10
    9  S_PHONE     Character      14
** Total **                     127
```

Fig. 5.3. Structure of the salesperson master file, SLSM00.DBF.

S_LNAME, S_FNAME, and S_PHONE—record the same information as the corresponding fields in the customer file.

Index Files

The sales-tracking system maintains a number of index files. Each database file (the transaction file, the customer file, and the salesperson file) uses one index as a primary index for data retrievals during execution of the programs. In addition, each file has additional indexes that are used in printing reports sorted in various orders. The indexes for each file are shown in table 5.1.

Specifying the Function of Each Program

The next step in developing the application is to create a block diagram showing the programs needed for the system. This block diagram should reflect the functions that the system must perform, and serve as a road map during development.

Table 5.1
Indexes Used in the Sales-Tracking System

File	Index Key	Index Name	Description
TRAN00	CUST_ID+PROD_ID+STR(PERIOD,2)	TRAN01	Index by customer ID (primary index)
	SP_ID+CUST_ID+PROD_ID	TRAN02	Index by salesperson (sales-by-salesperson report)
	PROD_ID+CUST_ID+STR(PERIOD,2)	TRAN03	Index by product (sales-by-product-report)
	STR(PERIOD,2)+PROD_ID+CUST_ID	TRAN04	Index by period (sales-by-period report)
CUST00	CUST_ID	CUST01	Index by customer ID (primary index)
	COMPANY	CUST02	Company index (customer list)
	L_NAME+F_NAME	CUST03	Name index (customer list)
	ZIP+COMPANY	CUST04	ZIP code index (customer mailings)
SLSP00	SP_ID	SLSP01	Index by salesperson ID (primary index)
	SP_LNAME+SP_FNAME	SLSP02	Index by salesperson name (salesperson list)

In the block diagram shown in figure 5.4, the sales-tracking system has been divided into on-line functions (data entry and query), reporting, and system maintenance. The system is modular, with a separate program performing each function. Subroutines perform functions that are common to more than one program, and are used to isolate complex portions of code from the main programs. Figure 5.5 shows functions and subroutines for the sales-tracking system.

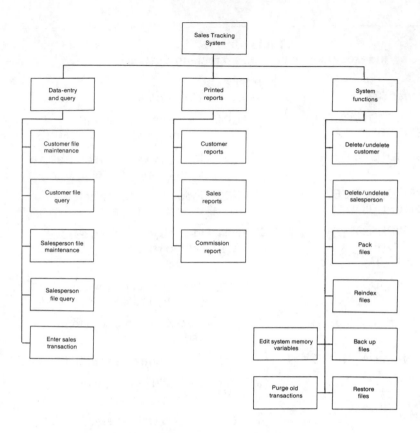

Fig. 5.4. Block diagram of the sales-tracking system.

The menu system designed for this application corresponds to the block diagram. Users begin at a main menu and choose one of three submenus for entering, changing, deleting, and reviewing data; printing reports; and performing a range of system-maintenance activities (see figs. 5.6–5.9). Consistent with the "bottom up" approach to programming described in Chapter 2, the menu system for the sales-tracking system will not be discussed until we've considered the main programs and subroutines (see the "Creating a Menu System" section).

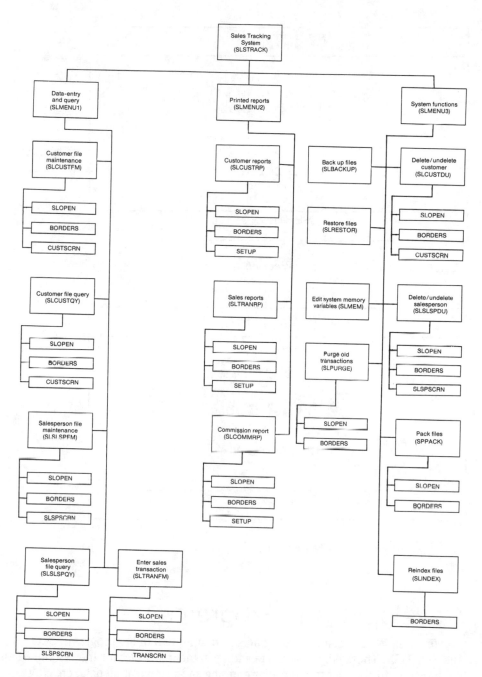

Fig. 5.5. Detailed block diagram with subroutines.

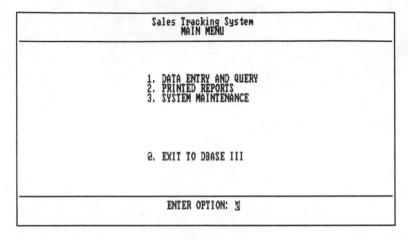

Fig. 5.6. Main menu for the sales-tracking system.

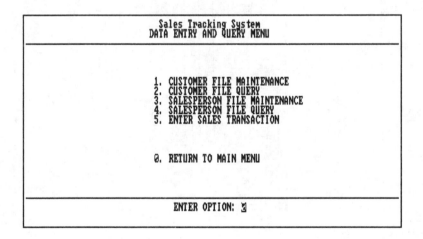

Fig. 5.7. Data-entry and -query menu.

Developing the Programs

The first step in developing the programs is to write two utility programs, SLOPEN and SLINDEX. These programs create and open the index files for the system. Then we move on to consider programs for entering and manipulating data, creating several types of reports, performing various system maintenance tasks, and creating a menu system to guide users through the application.

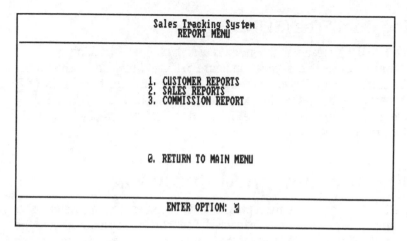

Fig. 5.8. Report menu.

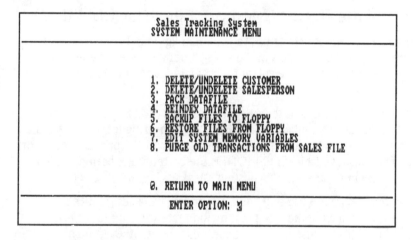

Fig. 5.9. System-maintenance menu.

Opening Data Files (SLOPEN)

Listings are
at the end of
the chapter.

Every program in the system calls the subroutine SLOPEN to open the data files and
associated indexes (see listing 5.1). This routine sets up work areas for all the files
used by the system, and uses the SELECT command to choose the work area
containing the customer file and its indexes.

Reindexing Data Files (SLINDEX)

The subroutine SLINDEX creates all the indexes used by the sales-tracking system. The flowchart for the subroutine is shown in figure 5.10, and the code is shown in listing 5.2. The current index files are erased and then rebuilt using the INDEX ON command. This program deletes the index files and then rebuilds them. SLINDEX also displays a message (`Working . . .`) as it begins activity in each of the three files used by the sales-tracking system.

Managing the System Memory File

The last task before developing the main programs for the sales-tracking system is to set up a file to hold the system memory variables. The following sections discuss the structure of the system memory file and the program that allows the user to edit the memory variables when the system is set up or when any changes need to be made.

Description of the System Memory File (SLMEM.MEM)

The system memory file, whose contents are shown in figure 5.11, holds memory variables that are used by the programs in the sales-tracking system. The file holds variables for a printer setup string, the current sales period, and commission-calculation constants.

The first variable (SLTITLE) contains the system title. The second and third variables (SLPSETUP and SLPRESTOR) contain, respectively, a setup string that initializes the printer before reports are printed and a setup string that resets the printer after reports are completed. The fourth variable (SLPERIOD) is the current sales period, which corresponds to the month of the year for posting sales.

The programs in this application use two "quantity-break" variables (SLBRK2 and SLBRK3) to determine which of the three commission-rate variables (SLCOMM1, SLCOMM2, or SLCOMM3) is used. The first commission rate (0.01), the base commission, is used for any sales in which the quantity is less than the first quantity break (10). The second commission rate (0.03) is used for sales in which the quantity is greater than the first quantity break (10) but less than the second quantity break (20). The third commission rate (0.05) is used for any sales in which the quantity is higher than the second quantity break.

Program To Edit the System Memory File (SLMEM)

The program SLMEM enables the user to adjust the system memory variables when the system is installed, a new printer is purchased, or one of the system parameters

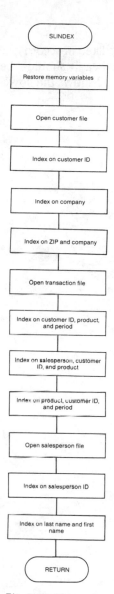

Fig. 5.10. The subroutine SLINDEX.

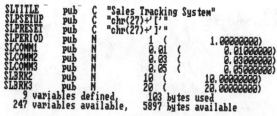

SLTITLE	pub	C	"Sales Tracking System"		
SLPSETUP	pub	C	"chr(27)+'['"		
SLPRESET	pub	C	"chr(27)+']'"		
SLPERIOD	pub	N	1	(	1.00000000)
SLCOMM1	pub	N	0.01	(	0.01000000)
SLCOMM2	pub	N	0.03	(	0.03000000)
SLCOMM3	pub	N	0.05	(	0.05000000)
SLBRK2	pub	N	10	(	10.00000000)
SLBRK3	pub	N	20	(	20.00000000)

```
     9 variables defined,    103 bytes used
   247 variables available,  5897 bytes available
```

Fig. 5.11. Contents of the system memory variable file, SLMEM.MEM.

needs to be changed. This program should be kept updated in accordance with the contents of SLMEM.MEM so that the file can be rebuilt easily should it be damaged during application development and testing. Figure 5.12 shows the flowchart for SLMEM.

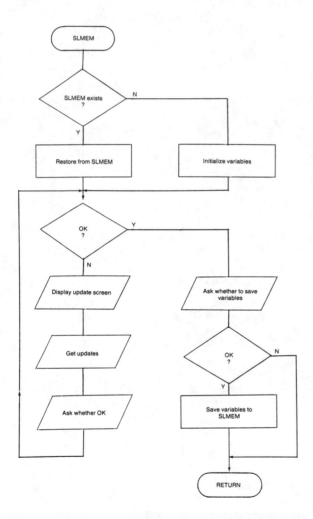

Fig. 5.12. Flowchart for program SLMEM.

To edit the system memory variables, the user chooses the fifth option on the System Maintenance menu (see the section "Creating a Menu System"). The program begins by using the FILE function to determine whether a file containing the memory variables currently exists (see listing 5.3).

If SLMEM.MEM is found, the program restores memory variables from the file, then pads the SLPSETUP and SLPRESET variables with spaces to 80 characters. Padding the variables enables the user to enter new printer setup and reset strings that are up to 80 characters in length regardless of the current contents of the two variables. If SLMEM.MEM is not found, the variables are initialized with default values. The program then calls subroutine BORDERS to display the edit screen (for a discussion of BORDERS, see the section "Designing a Consistent User Interface" in Chapter 3"). Next, several @ . . . SAY commands are used within a DO WHILE loop to display the current values for editing (see fig. 5.13).

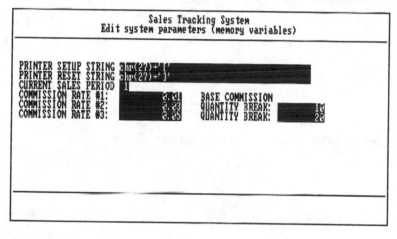

Fig. 5.13. Screen to edit system memory variables.

After editing the variables, the user is asked to verify that the changes are correct. If the user presses *N*, the program loops back through the editing process. After verifying that the changes are correct, the program trims trailing spaces from the variables SPPSETUP and SPPRESTOR and the user is prompted once again before the program stores the new values (see fig. 5.14). The new values then are stored, and the program ends.

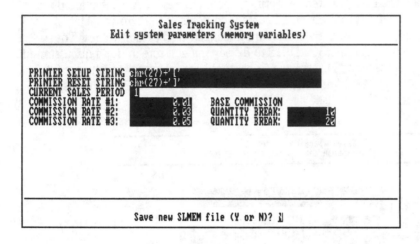

Fig. 5.14. Screen to verify storage of system memory variables.

Maintaining the Customer and Salesperson Files

The customer and salesperson files require programs for adding, changing, deleting, and reviewing records. The following sections describe the relevant programs and subroutines.

Adding and Updating Customer Records

The first option on the data-entry and -query menu enables the user to add or update customer information. Selecting this option loads the program SLCUSTFM. The program allows entry of several customer records at one time. The body of the SLCUSTFM program is a loop; each pass through the loop allows the user to enter or update one customer record. The loop is exited when the user leaves blank the value in CUST_ID. Figure 5.15 shows a flowchart for SLCUSTFM.

The program begins by calling the common subroutine SLOPEN to open the sales-tracking files (see listing 5.4.). Next, the main loop (DO WHILE .T.) is entered. The first statement in the loop is a call to the BORDERS subroutine, which clears the screen and displays a logo describing the operation being performed.

Within the main loop, the user is prompted first to enter a customer ID number (see fig. 5.16). The sales-tracking system identifies customers using a unique six-position alphanumeric ID number. The program then checks for a blank entry, which causes the program to exit the loop, close the databases, and end.

If the ID number is not blank, the SEEK command is used to look for the record in the file. If the record is found, the program determines whether that record has been deleted. If so, the user is given the option to recall the record and edit it. (Remember that "deleted" records are not actually removed from the database until the PACK command is used.) If the user presses N, a LOOP command transfers execution to the top of the loop, and the user again is prompted for an ID number. The user also has the option of returning to the first prompt if an incorrect ID number has been entered.

As a final check, the user is asked whether he or she wishes to proceed to enter or update this customer record. In figure 5.17, a record for MicroMedia Research has been found, and the user is asked to verify an update of this record. If the user does not want to enter or update the record, the program returns to the top of the loop and again prompts for an ID number.

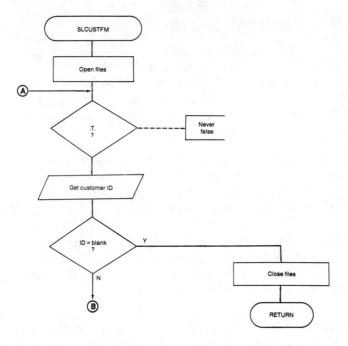

Fig. 5.15. Flowchart for SLCUSTFM.

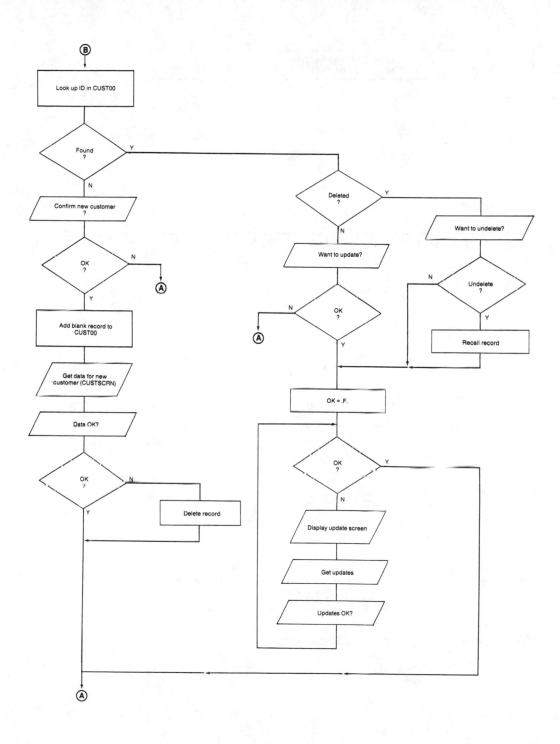

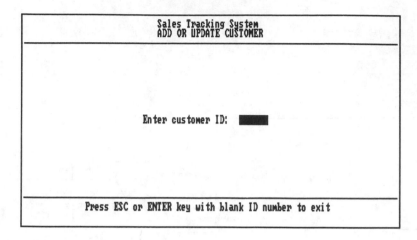

Fig. 5.16. Screen to enter customer ID.

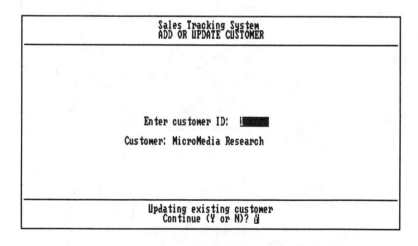

Fig. 5.17. User is prompted to verify customer update.

If a new customer record is being added, the user is informed and is prompted to indicate whether he or she wants to continue (see fig. 5.18). If so, a blank record is appended to the file and the subroutine CUSTSCRN (see listing 5.5) is called to

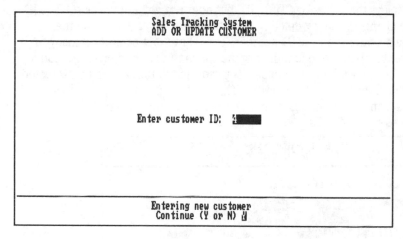

Fig. 5.18. User is prompted to verify creation of new customer record.

display a data-entry screen. CUSTSCRN begins by clearing the data area and message area of the screen. The remaining code for CUSTSCRN consists of a series of @ . . . SAY . . . GET commands to receive the data. Figure 5.19 shows the data-entry screen for adding a new record. When the customer information is entered, the program prompts the user to verify that the record is to be added to the database. If not, the record is deleted, and execution returns to the top of the loop.

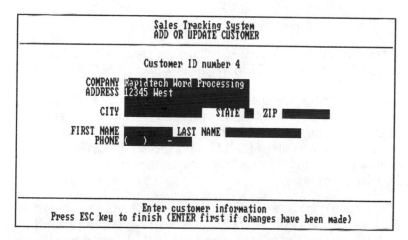

Fig. 5.19. Data-entry screen for new customer record.

If an existing asset is being updated, the current information is displayed using the data-entry screen produced by CUSTSCRN (see fig. 5.20). The user is allowed to change the contents of any displayed field except the ID number. (Notice that CUSTSCRN displays the value for CUST_ID, but does not get a new value.) The ID number can be changed only by deleting the existing record and entering the information again under the new ID number. The ID number cannot be changed directly because it is the unique identifier of the customer; allowing changes could result in duplicate ID numbers. The update is performed within a loop that is exited when the user says the changed data is OK. This verification gives the user a second chance to correct any typing errors without having to reenter the customer ID.

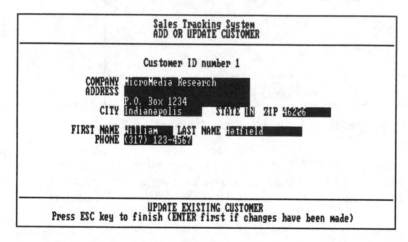

Fig. 5.20. Data-entry screen for updating customer record.

Querying Customer Records

The customer-query program (SLCUSTQY.PRG) allows the user to view but not update customer information. Figure 5.21 shows the flowchart for SLCUSTQY.PRG.

As with the add/update program, the query program is controlled by a DO WHILE .T. loop; the code within the loop allows the user to access as many customer records as desired and displays them one record at a time (see listing 5.6). The program begins by opening the files with a call to SLOPEN, using the SET DELETED ON command to restrict access to active records only, clearing the screen with BORDERS, and displaying the logo.

As with the add/update program, the user is then prompted for an ID number. If a blank ID is entered, the program exits the loop, closes the databases, and ends. If the ID number is not blank, the SEEK command is used to find the ID number in the customer file. If the ID number is not found, the program displays a warning message

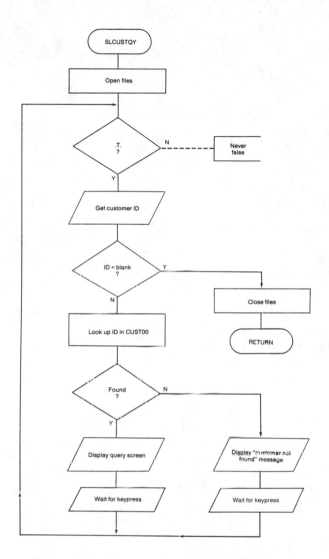

Fig. 5.21. Flowchart for the program SLCUSTQY.

(**Customer not found**), returns to the top of the loop, and prompts for another ID number.

When a correct ID has been entered, the information is displayed in the same format as with the add/update program (see fig. 5.19). SLCUSTQY calls the CUSTSCRN subroutine to display the data. The CLEAR GETS command following the call to CUSTSCRN clears all the entries @ . . . GET commands in CUSTSCRN, preventing the user from entering changes.

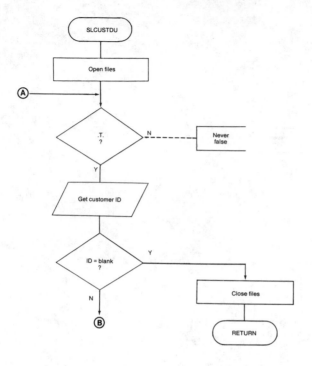

Fig. 5.22. Flowchart for the program SLCUSTDU.

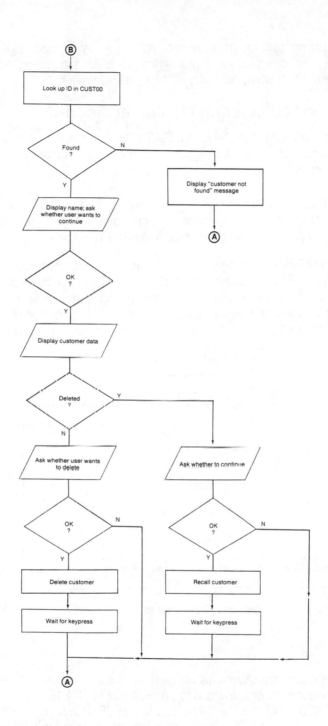

Next, a message reminds the user that the PrtScr key may be used to generate a printed copy of the screen image. The program pauses for a keypress; then execution returns to the top of the loop for entry of the next ID number.

Deleting and Undeleting Customer Records

The customer delete/undelete program, SLCUSTDU, allows the user to delete a customer record or, if the PACK program has not been run, to "undelete" a deleted record. The flowchart for SLCUSTDU is shown in figure 5.22.

Like the other on-line (data-entry and -query) programs, SLCUSTDU starts by opening files, clearing the screen, and displaying the appropriate logo (see listing 5.7). The main body of the program is a "do forever" loop (DO WHILE .T.).

After calling BORDERS, the program prompts the user for the customer ID number (see fig. 5.23). If the ID number is not left blank, the SEEK command is used to locate the record in the file. If the record is not found, an appropriate error message (**Customer not found**) is issued and the program returns to the top of the loop for the next ID. Leaving a blank at the customer ID prompt causes the program to exit the loop, close the databases, and end.

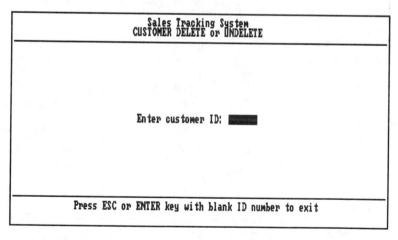

Fig. 5.23. Screen to enter customer ID number for the delete/undelete program.

If the record is found, the company name is displayed so that the user can verify it and indicate whether he or she wants to proceed (see fig. 5.24). If the user presses *Y* to continue, SLCUSTDU calls the subroutine CUSTSCRN to display the entire record (see fig. 5.25); a CLEAR GETS command prevents changes to the information.

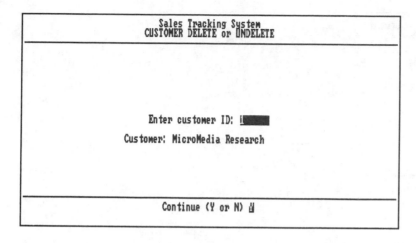

Fig. 5.24. User is prompted to verify continuation.

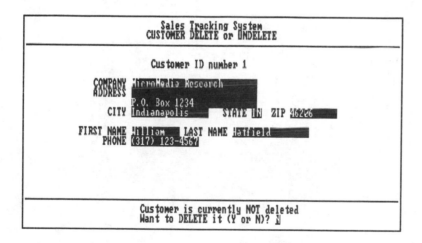

Fig. 5.25. Screen to indicate whether record is to be deleted.

The program then checks to see whether the record has already been deleted. In figure 5.25 the customer record for MicroMedia Research has not been deleted, as the prompt at the bottom of the screen indicates. If the record has not been deleted, the user is asked to verify that deletion is desired. If the user presses *Y* to indicate that he or she wants to delete the record, the program deletes the customer record and all associated sales transactions. If the user presses *N*, execution returns to the top of the loop for the next ID number.

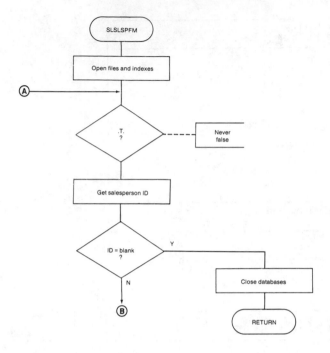

Fig. 5.26. Flowchart for the program SLSLSPFM.

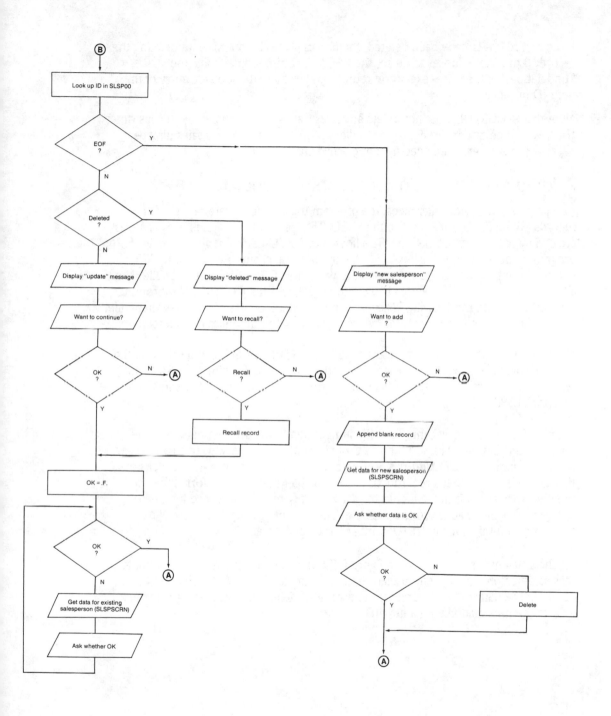

If the record has already been deleted, the user is given the option of undeleting the record. If the user chooses to do so, the RECALL command performs the "undeletion." Otherwise, execution returns to the top of the loop for entry of the next ID number.

Note that SLCUSTDU does not delete any sales transactions indexed by the customer ID. It would be disconcerting, to say the least, to have part of one's sales disappear because a customer is removed from the active customer list.

Adding and Updating Salesperson Records

Except for a few minor differences, the program to add and update salesperson records (SLSLSPFM) is identical to the SLCUSTFM program. In fact, SLSLSPFM was created by modifying SLCUSTFM. The flowchart for SLSLSPFM is shown in fig. 5.26; program code is shown in listing 5.8. The first of these changes was the SELECT command, which was altered to access the work area C for the salesperson file. Next, all references to CUST_ID were changed to SP_ID, and the CUSTSCRN subroutine was replaced with the SLSMSCRN subroutine to reflect the use of the salesperson file. Finally, all references to "customer" were replaced with references to "salesperson."

The subroutine SLSPSCRN is structured like CUSTSCRN. Both begin by clearing the data and message areas of the screen, and both contain a series of @ . . . SAY and @ . . . GET commands to accept data entries from the user. Listing 5.9 shows the code for SLSPSCRN.

A unique, six-position alphanumeric ID number identifies each salesperson in the sales-tracking system. The add/update program initially prompts for this ID number, as shown in figure 5.27. After the user enters the number, the program checks the database to see whether a record exists with this ID number and informs the user whether the record is in the file. In the screen in figure 5.28, a record for a new salesperson is being added to the database. The user has the option of going back to the first prompt if an incorrect ID number has been entered.

On the data-entry screen shown in figure 5.29, the user enters basic information for each salesperson. The only item that cannot be changed is the salesperson ID number. To change the ID number, the user must delete the salesperson record and reenter the information with a new ID number.

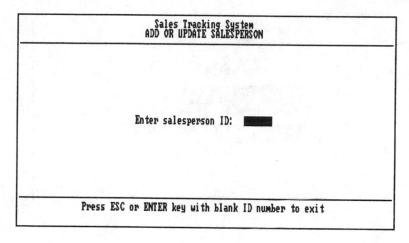

Fig. 5.27. Screen to enter salesperson ID number for add/update program.

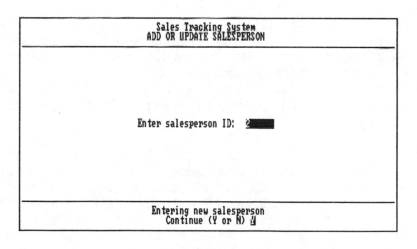

Fig. 5.28. User is prompted to verify addition of salesperson.

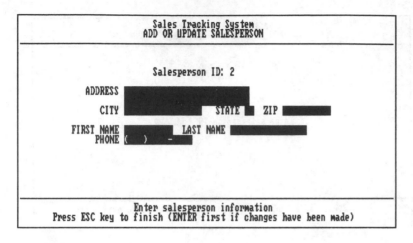

Fig. 5.29. Data-entry screen for updating salesperson information.

Querying Salesperson Records (SLSLSPQY)

The modular approach to program design has simplified greatly the coding of the data-entry and query programs. (For more on modular design, see Chapter 2, "Applications Development with dBASE III Plus.") The salesperson-query program (SLSLSPQY) was created in the same manner as the salesperson add/update program (SLSLSPFM). Both were adapted from similar programs for the customer file. The replacement of a key routine (SLSPSCRN for CUSTSCR) and modifications to reflect the file accessed were all that was required to convert SLCUSTQY to SLSLSPQY. The flowchart for SLSLSPQY is shown in figure 5.30; program code is shown in listing 5.10.

The salesperson-query screen is the fifth option available on the on-line functions menu. Selecting this option enables the user to view but not change the salesperson information. As with the salesperson add/update program, the first prompt is for the salesperson ID number. If an invalid ID number is entered, an error message is displayed and the user has a chance to reenter the ID number. When a correct ID number has been entered, the information is displayed using the same format as the add/update program (see fig. 5.29).

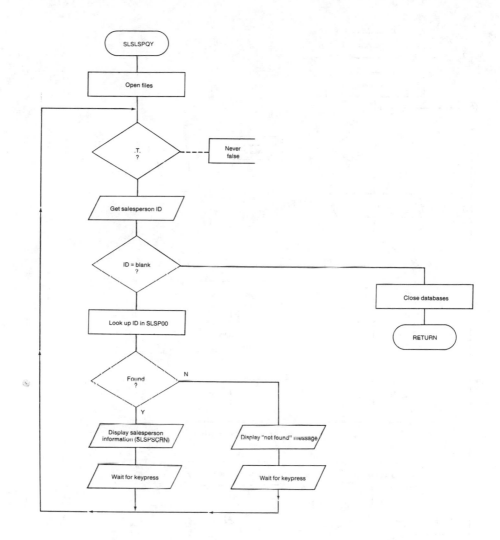

Fig. 5.30. Flowchart for the program SLSLSPQY.

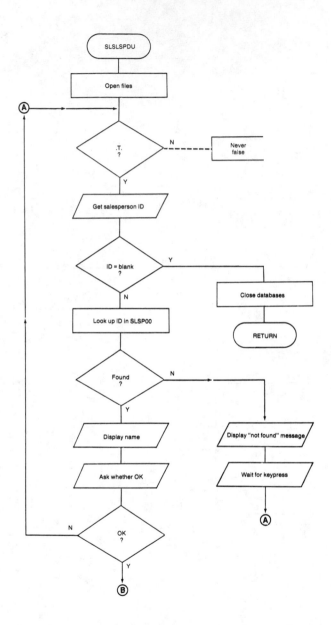

Fig. 5.31. Flowchart for SLSLSPDU.

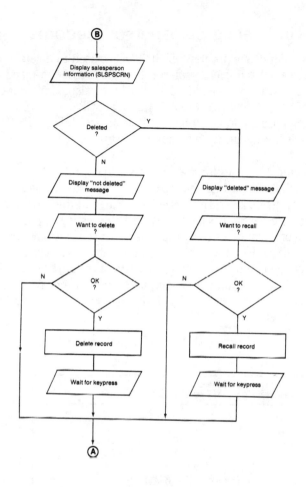

Deleting and Undeleting Salesperson Records

The salesperson delete/undelete program (SLSLSPDU) is used to delete a salesperson record, or to undelete a deleted salesperson record if the PACK command has not been issued since the record was deleted. SLSLSPDU was adapted from the SLCUSTDU program by replacing CUSTSCRN with SLSPSCRN, changing the work area to C, and making modifications to reflect the file accessed. Figure 5.31 shows a flowchart for SLSLSPDU; program code is shown in listing 5.11.

This program first prompts the user for the salesperson ID number (see fig. 5.32). The program then verifies that a record for that salesperson is on file. If the salesperson record is found, the last name is displayed (see fig. 5.33), and the user is asked to verify that the correct salesperson has been identified by pressing *Y*. If the correct salesperson has not been identified, the user presses *N* to return to the initial prompt. Once the proper record has been located, all the information is displayed, and the user is asked to verify deletion or undeletion. The screen in figure 5.34 displays the complete record for salesperson John Persistant, indicates that the record has not been deleted, and asks the user whether deletion is desired. If the user presses *Y*, the program will delete the record.

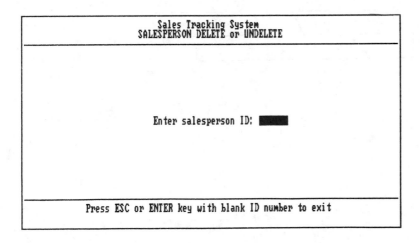

Fig. 5.32. Screen to enter salesperson ID number for delete/undelete program.

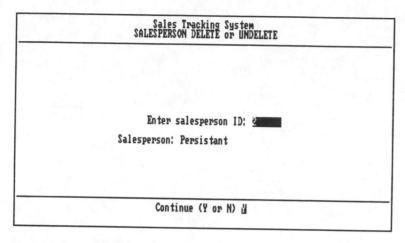

Fig. 5.33. Screen displays last name for salesperson and asks whether the user wants to continue.

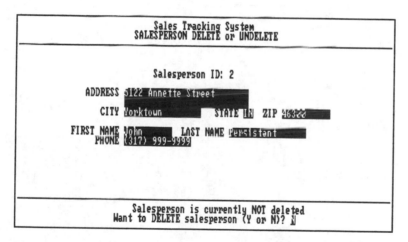

Fig. 5.34. Final screen to delete or undelete salesperson records.

Transaction Programs

The last of the on-line programs is a program to accept and record sales transactions. The flowchart for the transaction-entry program (SLTRANFM) is shown in figure 5.35. SLTRANFM begins by using SLOPEN to open the sales-tracking files, then uses the SELECT command to access the work area containing the transaction file (see listing 5.12).

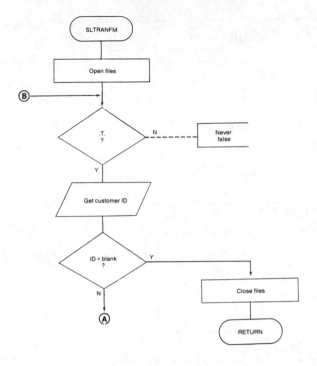

Fig. 5.35. Flowchart for the program SLTRANFM.

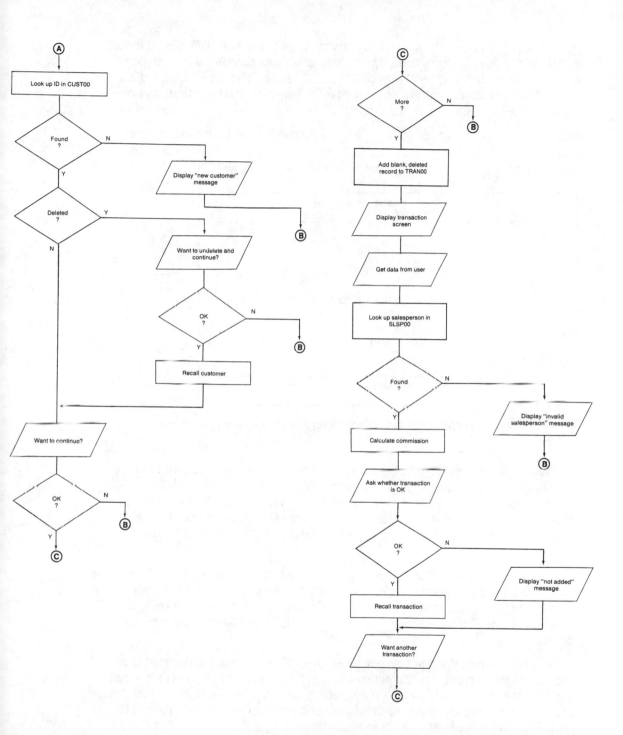

Note in listing 5.12 that the transaction-entry program uses nested DO WHILE loops to control the flow of transactions. The main loop handles all transaction operations except those related to entry of the actual transaction data. The inner loop handles entry of the transaction information, verifies the salesperson, computes commission, and adds the transaction to the file.

The outer loop begins by calling the BORDERS subroutine and prompting the user for a customer ID number (see fig. 5.36). As in the other programs, a blank response here causes the program to exit the loop, close the databases, and end.

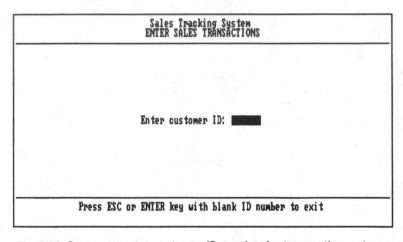

Fig. 5.36. Screen to enter customer ID number for transaction-entry program.

If a non-blank customer ID number is entered, the SEEK command is used to locate the number in the customer file. The program does this to ensure that the sale is being entered for a valid customer. If the number is not found in the file, an error message tells the user that first a record must be created in the customer file for all new customers. The program then returns to the top of the outer loop for entry of the next ID number.

If the customer record is found, the program checks to see whether it is a deleted record. If so, the user is given the option of recalling the customer and continuing. Pressing *Y* at this point undeletes the record. If the user does not want to recall the record, pressing *N* transfers execution to the top of the outer loop for the next ID number.

If the customer record has not been deleted (or if the record has been deleted, but the user chose to recall it), the program displays the name of the customer's company and asks the user to verify that this is the correct customer (see fig. 5.37). If the user presses *N*, the program returns to the top of the outer loop for entry of the next ID number. Otherwise, control passes to the inner loop.

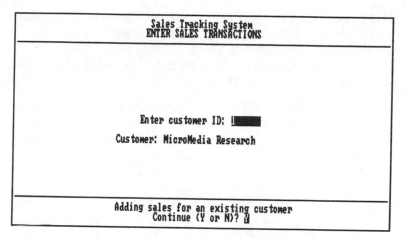

Fig. 5.37. Program displays customer name and asks whether the user wants to continue.

The inner loop appends a new, blank record to the transaction file to hold the new sales transaction. The new record is marked deleted until data entry is complete and the user accepts the new transaction. Then SLTRANFM calls the subroutine TRANSCRN to display a formatted screen on which the user fills in the sales information (see fig. 5.38). The data entered by the user includes the salesperson, product, quantity, price, and cost of the sale. Similar to CUSTSCRN and SLSMSCRN, TRANSCRN includes commands to clear the data-entry and message areas of the screen, followed by a series of @ . . . SAY and @ . . . GET commands to display the appropriate fields and accept data from the user (see listing 5.13).

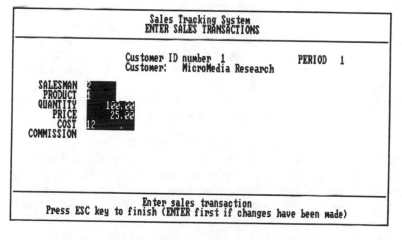

Fig. 5.38. Screen to enter sales-transaction information.

Once all data has been entered, SLTRANFM uses the SEEK command to check the salesperson file and verify that a valid salesperson ID has been entered. If not, the transaction is rejected, an error message is displayed, and the user is prompted to reenter the information. If the salesperson's ID is on file, the salesperson's last name is displayed as well as the commission amount for the sale.

The program uses the commission information contained in the system memory variables to calculate the commission for the sale. A base commission rate is maintained, as well as commissions for two higher "quantity breaks." The screen in figure 5.39 shows a commission of $125.00 for sales to MicroMedia Research by salesman John Persistant.

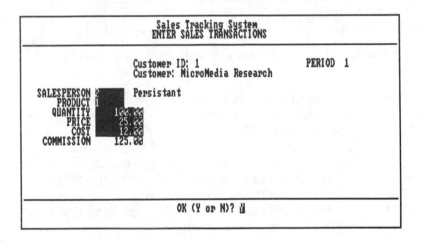

Fig. 5.39. User is asked to verify the sales-transaction data.

The prompt at the bottom of the screen in figure 5.39 allows the user to verify that the correct information has been entered. If the user presses *Y*, the transaction record is recalled and becomes an active sales-transaction record. If the user presses *N*, the transaction is left deleted, and the program returns to the top of the inner loop and again displays the data-entry screen shown in figure 5.38.

Once a transaction has been added, the user is asked whether he or she wants to to enter another sale for this customer. If entry of another sale is desired, the data-entry screen is displayed again. But if there are no more transactions to record for this customer, execution returns to the top of the outer loop, and the screen shown in figure 5.37 is displayed for entry of the next customer ID number.

Printing Reports

Having completed the on-line programs for the sales-tracking system, we now turn to the reporting function of the sales-tracking system. In the sections that follow, we look at programs that enable Fred Adams to produce reports showing information about customers, data on product sales, and commissions for salespersons.

Printing Customer Reports

The sales-tracking system produces three customer reports that differ only in their sort order. For each customer, the reports show company name, ID number, address, principal contact, and phone number. Figures 5.40, 5.41, and 5.42 show customer reports sorted by company name, ZIP code, and customer ID number, respectively.

A trick is used to fit more than 132 characters of information into a 132 character report line. The trick is to specify the company name as a control break. This causes the company name to be printed on a separate line from the rest of the record, making the record fit on a 132-line report.

```
Page No.     1
10/22/86

                                 Customer Master File Listing
                                    Sorted by Customer ID #


Cust.
ID      Address line 1          Address line 2       City          ST Zip    Last Name     First Name Phone #


** Company: MicroMedia Research
1                               P.O. Box 1234        Indianapolis  IN 46206 Hatfield       William   (317) 123-4567

** Company: R.F. Enterprises
2       123 West South Street                        Indianapolis  IN 46000 Brewer         Robert    (317) 234-5678

** Company: Computech
3       One Central Square                           Arlington Hts. IL 60050 Bitbanger     John      (312) 123-3214

** Company: Rapidtech Word Processing
4       12345 West Kennelworth                       Cereal City   MI 49200 Keyplucker     Harry     (616) 456-7890

** Company: Shoehorn Enterprises
5       1211 E. 5th St.                              Bradbury      MA 01234 Shoehorn       Ray       (111) 222-3333
```

Fig. 5.40. Customer report sorted by ID Number.

```
Page No.    1
10/22/86
                              Customer Master File Listing
                                 Sorted by Company Name


Cust                                                        First
ID #   Address line 1        Address line 2       City      ST Zip Code  Name      Last Name     Phone Number


** Company: Computech
3      One Central Square                         Arlington Hts.  IL 60050   John      Bitbanger     (312) 123-3214

** Company: MicroMedia Research
1                            P.O. Box 1234        Indianapolis    IN 46206   William   Hatfield      (317) 123-4567

** Company: R.F. Enterprises
2      123 West South Street                      Indianapolis    IN 46000   Robert    Brewer        (317) 234-5678

** Company: Rapidtech Word Processing
4      12345 West Kennelworth                     Cereal City     MI 49200   Harry     Keyplucker    (616) 456-7890

** Company: Shoehorn Enterprises
5      1211 E. 5th St.                            Bradbury        MA 01234   Ray       Shoehorn      (111) 222-3333
```

Fig. 5.41. Customer report sorted by company.

```
Page No.    1
10/22/86
                              Customer Master File Listing
                                 Sorted by Zip Code


Cust                                              First
ID #   Address line 1        Address line 2       City        ST Name     Last Name    Phone #


** Zip Code: 01234

* Company: Shoehorn Enterprises
5      1211 E. 5th St                             Bradbury    MA Ray      Shoehorn     (111) 222-3333

** Zip Code: 46000

* Company: R.F. Enterprises
2      123 West South Street                      Indianapolis  IN Robert   Brewer       (317) 234-5678

** Zip Code: 46206

* Company: MicroMedia Research
1                            P.O. Box 1234        Indianapolis  IN William  Hatfield     (317) 123-4567

** Zip Code: 49200

* Company: Rapidtech Word Processing
4      12345 West Kennelworth                     Cereal City   MI Harry    Keyplucker   (616) 456-7890

** Zip Code: 60050

* Company: Computech
3      One Central Square                         Arlington Hts.  IL John    Bitbanger    (312) 123-3214
```

Fig. 5.42. Customer report sorted by ZIP code.

The three different reports are used by Fred Adams for different purposes. The report by customer ID is used to match a customer name and address to a customer ID on other reports. The report by customer name is used to look up information about a customer from the customer name. Finally, the report by ZIP code is used in conjunction with promotional mailings, which are done by ZIP code.

The customer-report program (SLCUSTRP) begins by opening the files, clearing the screen, displaying the logo, and presenting the user with a list of sort orders for the report (see fig. 5.43). The report can be sorted by company, ZIP code, or customer ID number. The flowchart for SLCUSTRP is shown in figure 5.44; code is shown in listing 5.14.

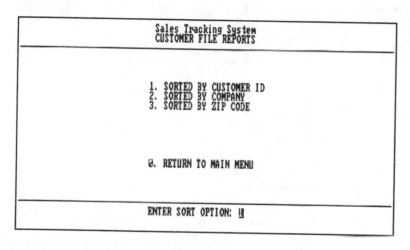

Fig. 5.43. Screen to select sort option for customer report.

After the user selects the sort option, a DO CASE structure is used to select the proper report. Within the DO CASE structure, a SET ORDER command uses the selected sort option to select the appropriate index file, the subroutine SETUP is called to set up the printer, and the REPORT FORM <filename> command produces the desired report. SETUP instructs the user to prepare the printer, pauses for a keypress, activates the printer, and sends the printer setup string (see listing 5.15 and fig. 5.45). When the report is printed, the program then closes the database files and ends.

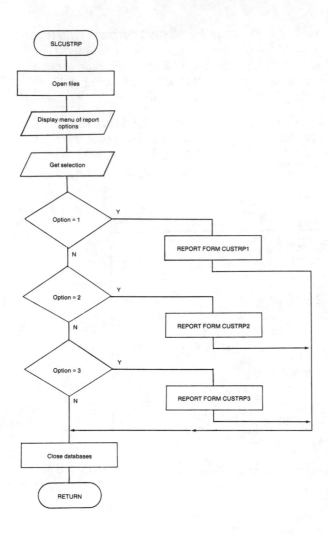

Fig. 5.44. Flowchart for the program SLCUSTRP.

The report definitions for the three reports are shown in figures 5.46, 5.47, and 5.48. They are almost identical except for the additional control-break specification in the ZIP code report.

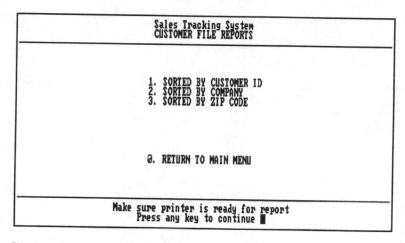

Fig. 5.45. User is prompted to ready the printer before printing a customer report.

```
Report definitions for report CUSTRP1.FRM

Page title:          Customer Master File Listing
                     Sorted by Customer ID #

Page width:     132
Left margin:      0

Group on expression      company
Group heading            Company:
Summary report only      No
Page eject after group   No
Sub-group on expression
Sub-group heading

COL  Contents      Heading                                      W  D Tot
---  --------      ------------------------------------------   -- -- ---
  1  Cust_id    ;;Cust.;ID                                       6
  2  addr1      ;;;Address line 1                               26
  3  addr2      ;;;Address line 2                               26
  4  city       ;;;City                                         16
  5  state      ;;;ST                                            2
  6  zip        ;;;Zip                                           5
  7  l_name     ;;;Last Name                                    16
  8  f_name     ;;;First Name                                   10
  9  phone      ;;;Phone #                                      14
```

Fig. 5.46. Definitions for report sorted by customer ID.

```
Report definitions for report CUSTRP2.FRM

Page title:            Customer Master File Listing
                       Sorted by Company Name

Page width:    132
Left margin:     0

Group on expression      company
Group heading            Company:
Summary report only      No
Page eject after group   No
Sub-group on expression
Sub-group heading

COL   Contents                   Heading              W  D Tot
---   ---------  ------------------------------------  -- -- ---
 1    Cust_id    ;;Cust.;ID                             6

 2    addr1      ;;;Address line 1                     26

 3    addr2      ;;;Address line 2                     26

 4    city       ;;;City                               16

 5    state      ;;;ST                                  2

 6    zip        ;;;Zip                                 5

 7    l_name     ;;;Last Name                          16

 8    f_name     ;;;First Name                         10

 9    phone      ;;;Phone #                            14
```

Fig. 5.47. Definitions for report sorted by company name.

```
Report definitions for report CUSTRP3.FRM

Page title:            Customer Master File Listing
                       Sorted by Zip Code

Page width:    132
Left margin:     0

Group on expression      zip
Group heading            Zip Code:
Summary report only      No
Page eject after group   No
Sub-group on expression  company
Sub-group heading        Company:

COL   Contents                   Heading              W  D Tot
---   ---------  ------------------------------------  -- -- ---
 1    Cust_id    ;;Cust.;ID                             6

 2    addr1      ;;;Address line 1                     26

 3    addr2      ;;;Address line 2                     26

 4    city       ;;;City                               16

 5    state      ;;;ST                                  2

 6    l_name     ;;;Last Name                          16

 7    f_name     ;;;First Name                         10

 8    phone      ;;;Phone #                            14
```

Fig. 5.48. Definitions for report sorted by ZIP code.

Printing Sales Reports

Sales reports are produced by the program SLTRANRP, which is similar to SLCUSTRP. The sales-reports program presents options for four separate reports: detailed product sales, summary product sales, detailed customer sales, and summary customer sales. Fred Adams can use these sales reports as a powerful marketing tool. For instance, when Fred's company introduces a new product or an enhancement to an existing one, Fred can use a list of customers who have purchased similar products to determine which customers would be likely to purchase the new product.

The detailed product-sales report shows the customer ID, quantity, unit price, sale amount, total cost, and gross profit by product (see fig. 5.49). The summary product-sales report shows quantity, unit price, sale amount, total cost, and gross profit by product as a single line (see fig. 5.50). The detailed customer-sales report shows the product ID number, quantity, unit price, sales amount, total cost, and gross profit by customer (see fig. 5.51). The summary customer-sales report shows the same information as a single line for each customer (see fig. 5.52).

```
Page No.     1
10/22/86

                        Sales Tracking System
                        Detail Product Sales



Cust                                              Gross
ID #     Quantity    Price   Sale amt  Tot Cost   Profit


** Product id: 1
  1         100.00   25.00    2500.00   1200.00   1300.00
  1           5.00   25.00     125.00     60.00     65.00
  2         100.00   25.00    2500.00   1200.00   1300.00
  5        1000.00   22.50   22500.00  12000.00  10500.00
** Subtotal **
           1205.00            27625.00  14460.00  13165.00


** Product id: 10
  2          35.00   75.00    2625.00   1050.00   1575.00
** Subtotal **
             35.00             2625.00   1050.00   1575.00


** Product id: 3
  1        1000.00    5.00    5000.00   3000.00   2000.00
** Subtotal **
           1000.00             5000.00   3000.00   2000.00


** Product id: 5
  1          11.00  200.00    2200.00    825.00   1375.00
** Subtotal **
             11.00             2200.00    825.00   1375.00
*** Total ***
           2251.00            37450.00  19335.00  18115.00
```

Fig. 5.49. Detailed product-sales report.

```
Page No.     1
10/22/86
                     Sales Tracking System
                     Product Sales (Summary)

Cust                                                   Gross
ID #       Quantity       Price  Sale amt     Cost     Profit


** Product ID: 1
** Subtotal **
            1205.00              27625.00  14460.00  13165.00

** Product ID: 10
** Subtotal **
              35.00               2625.00   1050.00   1575.00

** Product ID: 3
** Subtotal **
            1000.00               5000.00   3000.00   2000.00

** Product ID: 5
** Subtotal **
              11.00               2200.00    825.00   1375.00
*** Total ***
            2251.00              37450.00  19335.00  18115.00
```

Fig. 5.50. Summary product-sales report.

```
Page No.     1
10/22/86
                     Sales Tracking System
                     Customer Sales (Detail)

Prod                                                   Gross
ID #       Quantity       Price  Sale amt     Cost     Profit


** Customer: 1
 1          100.00       25.00    2500.00   1200.00   1300.00
 1            5.00       25.00     125.00     60.00     65.00
 3         1000.00        5.00    5000.00   3000.00   2000.00
 5           11.00      200.00    2200.00    825.00   1375.00
** Subtotal **
            1116.00               9825.00   5085.00   4740.00

** Customer: 2
 1          100.00       25.00    2500.00   1200.00   1300.00
10           35.00       75.00    2625.00   1050.00   1575.00
** Subtotal **
             135.00               5125.00   2250.00   2875.00

** Customer: 5
 1         1000.00       22.50   22500.00  12000.00  10500.00
** Subtotal **
            1000.00              22500.00  12000.00  10500.00
*** Total ***
            2251.00              37450.00  19335.00  18115.00
```

Fig. 5.51. Detailed customer-sales report.

```
Page No.     1
10/22/86

                        Sales Tracking System
                        Customer Sales (Summary)



Prod                                              Gross
ID #      Quantity    Price   Sale amt    Cost    Profit


** Customer: 1
** Subtotal **
            1116.00            9825.00   5085.00  4740.00

** Customer: 2
** Subtotal **
             135.00            5125.00   2250.00  2875.00

** Customer: 5
** Subtotal **
            1000.00           22500.00  12000.00 10500.00
*** Total ***
            2251.00           37450.00  19335.00 18115.00
```

Fig. 5.52. Summary customer-sales report.

The flowchart shown in figure 5.53 and the code provided in listing 5.16 indicate the similarity between SLTRANRP and SLCUSTRP. SLTRANRP begins by opening the files, clearing the screen, displaying the logo, and prompting the user to enter the sales period (see fig. 5.54). The current sales period is displayed as the default. Once the user has entered the desired sales period, the program displays the four report options: detail product sales, summary product sales, detail customer sales and summary customer sales (see fig. 5.55).

After the user selects the report option, SLTRANRP uses the same straight-line DO CASE structure as SLCUSTRP uses to produce the desired report. Within the DO CASE structure, the appropriate index file is selected, and the subroutine SETUP is called to set up the printer. SETUP instructs the user to prepare the printer (see fig. 5.56), pauses for a keypress, activates the printer, and sends the printer setup string to the printer.

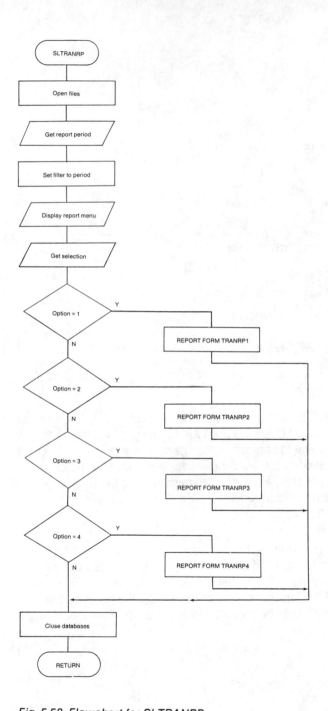

Fig. 5.53. Flowchart for SLTRANRP.

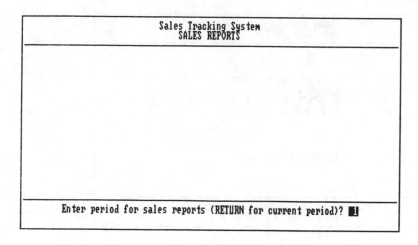

Fig. 5.54. User is prompted to enter period for sales reports.

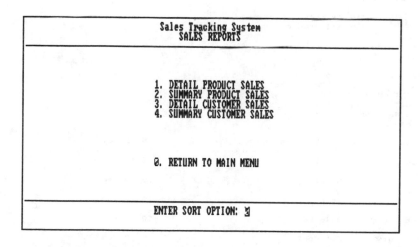

Fig. 5.55. Screen to choose sales-report option.

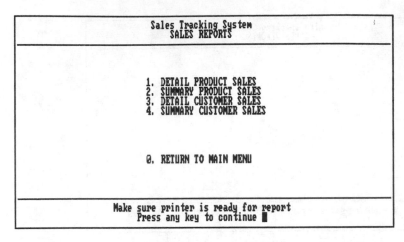

Fig. 5.56. User is prompted to ready the printer before printing a sales report.

The REPORT FORM <filename> command produces the report; figures 5.57 through 5.60 show the report definitions that are entered with MODIFY REPORT for these reports. After the report is printed, SLTRANRP resets the printer, closes the database files, and ends.

```
Report definitions for report TRANRP1.FRM

Page title:          Sales Tracking System
                     Detail Product Sales

Page width:     80
Left margin:     0

Group on expression       prod_id
Group heading             Product id:
Summary report only       No
Page eject after group    No
Sub-group on expression
Sub-group heading
```

COL	Contents	Heading	W	D	Tot
1	Cust_id	;;Cust;ID #	6		
2	qty	;;;Quantity	10	2	Yes
3	u_price	;;;Price	10	2	No
4	u_price * qty	;;;Sale amt	10	2	Yes
5	u_cost * qty	;;;Tot Cost	10	2	Yes
6	qty * (u_price-u_cost)	;;Gross;Profit	10	2	Yes

Fig. 5.57. Report definitions for product sales detail report.

```
Report definitions for report TRANRP2.FRM

Page title:            Sales Tracking System
                       Product Sales (Summary)

Page width:      80
Left margin:      0

Group on expression       prod_id
Group heading             Product id:
Summary report only       Yes
Page eject after group    No
Sub-group on expression
Sub-group heading
```

COL	Contents	Heading	W	D	Tot
1	Cust_id	;;Cust;ID #	6		
2	qty	;;;Quantity	10	2	Yes
3	u_price	;;;Price	10	2	No
4	u_price * qty	;;;Sale amt	10	2	Yes
5	u_cost * qty	;;;Tot Cost	10	2	Yes
6	qty * (u_price-u_cost)	;;Gross;Profit	10	2	Yes

Fig. 5.58. Report definitions for product sales summary report.

```
Report definitions for report TRANRP3.FRM

Page title:            Sales Tracking System
                       Customer Sales (Detail)

Page width:      80
Left margin:      0

Group on expression       cust_id
Group heading             Customer:
Summary report only       No
Page eject after group    No
Sub-group on expression
Sub-group heading
```

COL	Contents	Heading	W	D	Tot
1	prod_id	;;Prod;ID #	6		
2	qty	;;;Quantity	10	2	Yes
3	u_price	;;;Price	10	2	No
4	u_price * qty	;;;Sale amt	10	2	Yes
5	u_cost * qty	;;;Tot Cost	10	2	Yes
6	qty * (u_price-u_cost)	;;Gross;Profit	10	2	Yes

Fig. 5.59. Report definitions for customer sales detail report.

```
Report definitions for report TRANRP4.FRM

Page title:                 Sales Tracking System
                            Customer Sales (Summary)

Page width:      80
Left margin:      0

Group on expression         cust_id
Group heading               Customer:
Summary report only         Yes
Page eject after group      No
Sub-group on expression
Sub-group heading

COL   Contents                       Heading                     W   D  Tot
---   -------------      ------------------------------------    --  -- ---
 1    prod_id            ;;Prod;ID #                              6

 2    qty                ;;;Quantity                             10   2 Yes

 3    u_price            ;;;Price                                10   2 No

 4    u_price * qty      ;;;Sale amt                             10   2 Yes

 5    u_cost * qty       ;;;Tot Cost                             10   2 Yes

 6    qty *              ;;Gross;Profit                          10   2 Yes
      (u_price-u_cost)
```

Fig. 5.60. Report definitions for customer sales summary report.

Printing Commission Reports

The third printing capability of the sales-tracking system enables Fred Adams to document commissions for his sales staff. SLCOMMRP produces a detailed commission report and a summary commission report. The detailed commission report lists the customer, product, quantity, unit price, sale amount, and commission by salesperson for each sales transaction (see fig. 5.61). The summary commission report shows only the total sales amount and total commission by salesperson (see fig. 5.62).

These commission reports were generated using the dBASE Assistant to create the report forms. The Assistant allows quick creation of reports that access a single file. Reports of additional complexity could be programmed, but these reports supply the basic information required. (For more information on using the Assistant to create report forms, see "Printing Reports" in Chapter 3.)

```
Page No.     1
10/22/86
                          SALES TRACKING SYSTEM
                          DETAIL COMMISSION REPORT


PROD
ID #     QUANTITY     PRICE   SALE AMT COMMISSION


** SALESPERSON: 1

* CUSTOMER: 1
 5          11.00    200.00    2200.00       66.00
* Subsubtotal *
                               2200.00       66.00

* CUSTOMER: 2
 10         35.00     75.00    2625.00      131.25
* Subsubtotal *
                               2625.00      131.25

** Subtotal **
                               4825.00      197.25

** SALESPERSON: 2

* CUSTOMER: 1
 1         100.00     25.00    2500.00      125.00
 1           5.00     25.00     125.00        1.25
 3        1000.00      5.00    5000.00      250.00
* Subsubtotal *
                               7625.00      376.25


* CUSTOMER: 2
 1         100.00     25.00    2500.00      125.00
* Subsubtotal *
                               2500.00      125.00


* CUSTOMER: 5
 1        1000.00     22.50   22500.00     1125.00
* Subsubtotal *
                              22500.00     1125.00

** Subtotal **
                              32625.00     1626.25

*** Total ***
                              37450.00     1823.50
```

Fig. 5.61. Detailed commission report.

```
Page No.    1
10/22/86
                          SALES TRACKING SYSTEM
                          SUMMARY COMMISSION REPORT



PROD
ID #    QUANTITY    PRICE   SALE AMT COMMISSION


** SALESPERSON: 1

* CUSTOMER: 1
* Subsubtotal *
                            2200.00     66.00

* CUSTOMER: 2
* Subsubtotal *
                            2625.00    131.25
** Subtotal **
                            4825.00    197.25

** SALESPERSON: 2

* CUSTOMER: 1
* Subsubtotal *
                            7625.00    376.25

* CUSTOMER: 2
* Subsubtotal *
                            2500.00    125.00

* CUSTOMER: 5
* Subsubtotal *
                           22500.00   1125.00
** Subtotal **
                           32625.00   1626.25
*** Total ***
                           37450.00   1823.50
```

Fig. 5.62. Summary commission report.

The flowchart shown in figure 5.63 and the code provided in listing 5.17 indicate how similar SLCOMMRP is to SLCUSTRP and SLTRANRP. SLCOMMRP begins by opening the files, clearing the screen, displaying the logo, and prompting the user for the sales period (see fig. 5.64). The current sales period is displayed as the default. Once the user has entered the desired sales period, the program displays the two report options: detail commission report and summary commission report (see fig. 5.65).

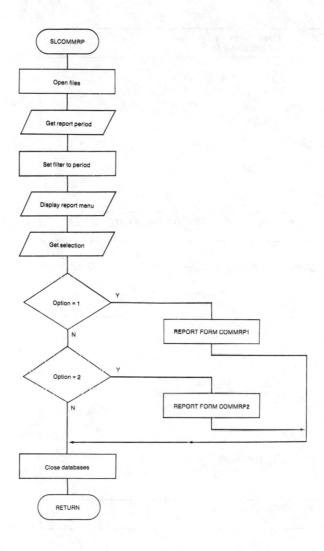

Fig. 5.63. Flowchart for the program SLCOMMRP.

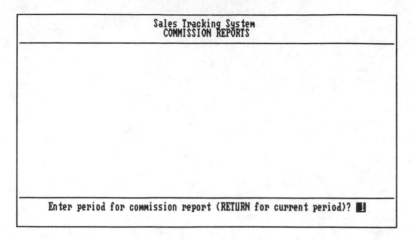

Fig. 5.64. User is prompted to enter sales period for commission report.

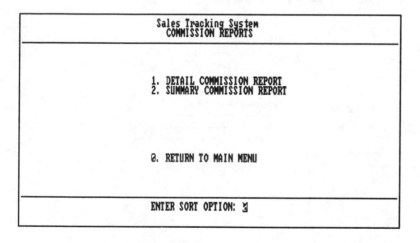

Fig. 5.65. Screen to select commission report option.

After the user selects the report option, SLCOMMRP uses the same straight-line DO CASE structure as is used by SLCUSTRP and SLTRANRP to produce the desired report. Within the DO CASE structure, a SET ORDER command selects the appropriate index file, and the subroutine SETUP is called to set up the printer. SETUP instructs the user to prepare the printer (see fig. 5.66), pauses for a keypress, activates the printer, and sends the printer setup string to the printer. The REPORT FORM <filename> command produces the desired report. Figure 5.67 shows the report

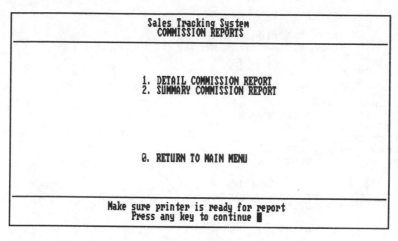

Fig. 5.66. User is prompted to set up the printer before printing the commission reports.

```
Report definitions for report COMMRP1.FRM

Page title:              SALES TRACKING SYSTEM
                         DETAIL COMMISSION REPORT

Page width:     80
Left margin:     6

Group on expression      SP_ID
Group heading            SALESPERSON:
Summary report only      No
Page eject after group   No
Sub-group on expression  CUST_ID
Sub-group heading        CUSTOMER:
```

COL	Contents	Heading	W	D	Tot
1	prod_id	;;PROD;ID #	6		
2	qty	;;;QUANTITY	10	2	No
3	u_price	;;;PRICE	10	2	No
4	u_price * qty	;;;SALE AMT	10	2	Yes
5	commission	;;;COMMISSION	10	2	Yes

Fig. 5.67. Report definition for detail commission report.

definition entered with MODIFY REPORT for the detail report, and figure 5.68 shows the report definitions for the summary report. After the report is printed, SLCOMMRP resets the printer, closes the database files, and ends.

```
Report definitions for report COMMRP2.FRM

Page title:           SALES TRACKING SYSTEM
                      SUMMARY COMMISSION REPORT

Page width:      80
Left margin:      6

Group on expression    SP_ID
Group heading          SALESPERSON:
Summary report only    Yes
Page eject after group No
Sub-group on expression CUST_ID
Sub-group heading      CUSTOMER:

COL   Contents                  Heading                     W  D Tot
---   -------------   ------------------------------------- -- -- ---
  1   prod_id         ;;PROD;ID #                            6
  2   qty             ;;;QUANTITY                           10  2 No
  3   u_price         ;;;PRICE                              10  2 No
  4   u_price * qty   ;;;SALE AMT                           10  2 Yes
  5   commission      ;;;COMMISSION                         10  2 Yes
```

Fig. 5.68. Report definition for summary commission report.

Maintaining the System

We have covered the portions of the sales-tracking system that allow the user to enter data and print reports. Now we turn to the maintenance programs needed to complete the system. Two utility programs, SLINDEX and SLMEM, were discussed previously. The utility programs that remain to be discussed allow the user to physically delete records marked for deletion by the on-line programs, back up data files on a hard disk to floppy disks, restore to the hard disk those data files backed up to floppy disks, and clear old sales transactions from the transactions file.

Packing the Database

The SLPACK program physically deletes records that have been flagged for deletion in the on-line programs. A flowchart is shown in figure 5.69. Until the database files have been packed, deleted records can be restored with the RECALL command. The SLPACK program should be used whenever many records have been deleted and disk space is scarce.

The program begins by opening the files, displaying the logo, and prompting the user to make certain that the files have been backed up (see listing 5.18). A series of @ . . . SAY commands displays a message on the screen after each file has been packed.

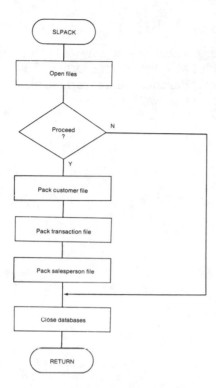

Fig. 5.69. Flowchart for the program SLPACK.

Backing Up Data to Floppy Disks (SLBACKUP)

The program SLBACKUP is used to copy data from the hard disk to floppy disks. The program uses the DOS BACKUP command to save the data files, index files, and the memory file to one or more formatted floppies (see listing 5.19). The program prompts the user to insert floppy disks as needed.

The SLBACKUP command uses the variable TARGET to identify the target drive. Use of a variable simplifies changing the designation of the target drive, if necessary. The macro substitution operator (&) is used to specify the target drive.

Restoring Data from Floppy Disks (SLRESTOR)

The SLRESTOR program uses the DOS RESTORE command to restore data to the hard disk from floppies created with SLBACKUP (see listing 5.20). SLRESTOR can be used to re-create data files when a user erases information, the hard disk crashes, or when it is necessary to move the application to another computer system. The program prompts the user to insert disks as needed.

Purging Old Sales Transactions (SLPURGE)

The last utility function needed for the sales-tracking system is a capability for purging old sales transactions from the transactions file. Otherwise, the sales transactions file would grow without limit. The SLPURGE program is designed to remove these old transactions. The code is provided in listing 5.21., and a flowchart is shown in figure 5.70.

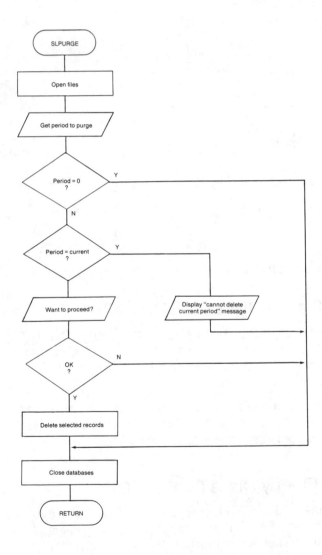

Fig. 5.70. Flowchart for the program SLPURGE.

SLPURGE opens the files and prompts the user for a sales period to purge (see fig. 5.71). If the user leaves the period value set to its initial value of zero, SLPURGE returns control to the caller. If the user enters a non-zero value, the program checks to make sure it is not the current period. If the user has entered the number of the current sales period, the program informs the user that current-period transactions cannot be deleted. Otherwise, SLPURGE prompts the user to verify that he or she wants to delete all sales transactions for the selected period. If not, the program ends. If the user verifies the operation, the program uses a DELETE command with a FOR qualifier to perform the deletion.

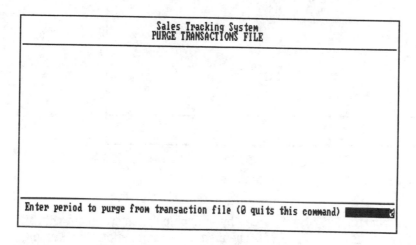

Fig. 5.71. Screen to specify the period to purge.

The message Working. . . is displayed as the program deletes the sales transactions for the selected period. After the selected periods have been purged, the user must run SLPACK from the system-maintenance menu to reclaim the file space.

Important note: *Should the user make a mistake and purge the wrong sales period, the data can be recovered by the consultant or a technical support person if the database files are not packed in the interim.*

Creating a Menu System

Although all the functions required for the sales-tracking system have been developed, we can hardly expect the user to remember what to do when he or she wishes to perform a certain function. We need a menu system to tie the sales-tracking system together and lead the user through the application.

The menu system developed for the sales-tracking system consists of a main menu and three submenus that correspond to the three main sections of the application: on-line functions, report printing, and system maintenance. Figure 5.72 shows the main menu.

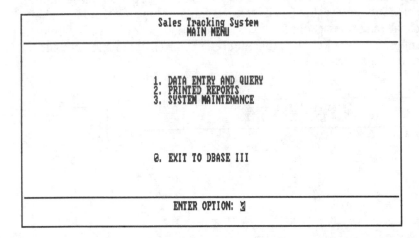

Fig. 5.72. Main menu for the sales-tracking system.

The main-menu program, SLSTRACK, begins by setting up the environment with a series of SET commands (see listing 5.22). The menu programs perform the task of setting the program environment before calling a program, and resetting the environment for interactive mode after the program ends. The primary changes in the environment before calling a program are to set TALK OFF, SAFETY OFF, and BELL OFF, and to make sure output is redirected to the screen from the printer.

A DO WHILE loop displays a menu screen, gets the desired option number from the user, and runs the corresponding program. Within the loop, a series of @ . . . SAY commands and an @ . . . GET command display the menu options: on-line functions, printed reports, and system maintenance. A straightforward DO CASE construction then calls the appropriate submenu program unless the user has entered a number other than 1, 2, or 3. In that case, the program prompts the user to verify that he or she wants to end the application. If so, the program ends.

The first option on the main menu leads to the data-entry and -query menu shown in figure 5.73. This menu provides access to the seven on-line options: adding or updating customer or salesperson data, querying customer and salesperson data, deleting or undeleting customer and salesperson records, and entering sales transactions.

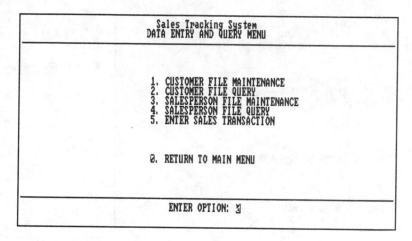

Fig. 5.73. Data-entry and -query menu.

Note that SLMENU1 is similar to SLSTRACK (see listing 5.23). SLMENU1 begins by clearing the screen. The main body of the program is a DO WHILE loop. Within the loop, a series of @ . . . SAY commands and an @ . . . GET command display the menu screen and present the user with the menu options. A straightforward DO CASE construction runs the correct program. Upon completion, the system returns to this menu for an additional choice. The user can select another function from this menu or return to the main system menu.

Selecting the second option on the main menu displays the report submenu shown in figure 5.74. The program SLMENU2 resembles SLSTRACK and SLMENU1. SLMENU2 begins by clearing the screen (see listing 5.24). Next, a DO WHILE loop displays the menu screen and gets the desired option number from the user. A straightforward DO CASE construct runs the correct program. Upon completion, the program displays this menu again for an additional choice. The user can select another function from this menu or return to the main system menu.

Selecting the third option on the main menu displays the system-maintenance menu shown in figure 5.75. The SLMENU3 program resembles SLSTRACK, SLMENU1, and SLMENU2. SLMENU3 begins by clearing the screen (see listing 5.25). Next, the code within a DO WHILE loop displays the menu screen, gets the desired option number from the user, and runs the corresponding program. Upon completion, the system returns to this menu for an additional choice. The user may select another function from this menu or return to the main system menu.

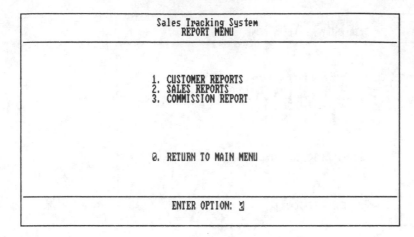

Fig. 5.74. Reports menu.

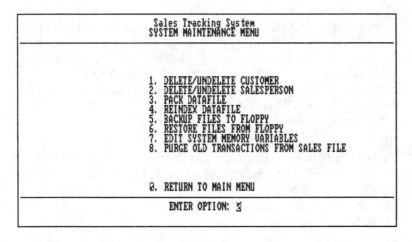

Fig. 5.75. System-maintenance menu.

Note that all of the menu choices available in the system could have been presented on one menu, and indeed many users may prefer the single-menu approach. The hierarchical arrangement shown here is used to illustrate the development of the system in functional groups.

Using Procedure Files

The final step in the development of the sales-tracking system is to test the programs and place the key routines in a procedure file. Although the programs were thoroughly tested as they were developed, you should thoroughly test the completed system before turning it over to a client.

Clients will appreciate the time you save them when you place often-used programs in a procedure file to speed execution. Recall from Chapter 2 that up to 32 routines can be placed in a procedure file. Because the sales-tracking system uses fewer routines than that, the routines have all been loaded into the procedure file. (For more on program testing and the use of procedure files, see Chapter 2, "Applications Development with dBASE III Plus.") In the main-menu program SLSTRACK (listing 5.22), notice the command SET PROCEDURE TO at the beginning and the command CLOSE PROCEDURE at the end.

Extensions to the System

A number of additions to the sales-tracking system would bring it closer to a complete order-management system. As mentioned earlier, the addition of a product master file would add the capability to report more detailed information about product sales. Linking a product master file and a bill-of-material file would allow tracking of subassemblies required to fulfill customer orders. Finally, an invoice program to generate an invoice for the sales transaction could be added easily, as could a packing-slip program to identify products sold for shipment.

Conclusion

The sales-tracking system presented here can keep track of sales for a small-to-medium-sized company. The system produces commission reports, sales-analysis reports, and customer lists for use in managing the sales function. With some expansion, this application could evolve into a complete-order management system including invoicing and shipping functions.

Listing 5.1. The subroutine SLOPEN.

```
***********************************************************
* SLOPEN - Open files for the Sales Tracking System     *
*               8/28/86                                  *
***********************************************************

SELECT A
USE cust00 INDEX cust01
SELECT B
USE tran00 INDEX tran01
SELECT C
USE slsp00 INDEX slsp01
RETURN
```

Listing 5.2. The subroutine SLINDEX.

```
*********************************************
* SLINDEX - REINDEX SALES TRACKING FILES *
*               8/31/86                   *
*********************************************
CLOSE DATABASES
CLEAR
RESTORE FROM slmem ADDITIVE
title= "RE-INDEX DATA FILES"

*Display logo
DO borders WITH sltitle,title
@ 12,35 SAY "Working ..."

*Index customer file
@ 13, 23 SAY 'Reindexing customer master file'
USE cust00
INDEX ON cust_id TO cust01                    && Index on ID #
INDEX ON company TO cust02                     && Index on company
INDEX ON zip+company TO cust03                 && Index on zip code & company

*Index data file
@ 14, 23 SAY 'Reindexing sales transaction file'
USE tran00
* Index on customer, product, & period
INDEX ON cust_id+prod_id+STR(period,2) TO tran01
* Index on salesperson, customer & product
INDEX ON sp_id+cust_id+prod_id TO tran02
* Index on product, customer & period
INDEX ON prod_id+cust_id+STR(period,2) TO tran03
* Index on period, product & customer
INDEX ON STR(period,2)+prod_id+cust_id TO tran04

*Index salesperson file
@ 15, 23 SAY 'Reindexing salesperson master file'
USE slsp00
INDEX ON sp_id TO slsp01                       && Index on ID #
INDEX ON s_lname+s_fname TO slsp02             && Index on last & first name

*Exit
CLOSE DATABASES
CLEAR
RETURN
```

Listing 5.3. The program SLMEM.

```
*************************************************************************
* SLMEM -          Define system parameters for Sales Tracking System *
*                  8/28/86                                             *
*************************************************************************
PRIVATE mok

*Restore existing or initialize to defaults
IF FILE("slmem.mem")
   RESTORE FROM slmem ADDITIVE                     && Restore memory variables
   slpsetup=SUBSTR(slpsetup+SPACE(80),1,80)        && pad printer setup string
   slpreset=SUBSTR(slpreset+SPACE(80),1,80)        && pad printer reset string
ELSE
   STORE 'Sales Tracking System' TO sltitle
   STORE SPACE(80) TO slpsetup
   STORE SPACE(80) TO slpreset
   STORE 1 TO slperiod
   STORE .01 TO slcomm1
   STORE .03 TO slcomm2
   STORE .05 TO slcomm3
   STORE 10 TO slbrk2
   STORE 20 TO slbrk3
ENDIF

* Display logo
title="Edit system parameters (memory variables)"
DO borders WITH sltitle,title

*Get new values
mok=.f.
DO WHILE .not.mok
   @  7,  2 SAY "PRINTER SETUP STRING" GET slpsetup PICTURE "@S40"
   @  8,  2 SAY "PRINTER RESET STRING" GET slpreset PICTURE "@S40"
   @  9,  2 SAY "CURRENT SALES PERIOD" GET slperiod PICTURE '99' RANGE 1,12
   @ 10,  2 SAY "COMMISSION RATE #1: " GET slcomm1
   @ 10, 40 SAY "BASE COMMISSION       "
   @ 11,  2 SAY "COMMISSION RATE #2: " GET slcomm2
   @ 11, 40 SAY "QUANTITY BREAK:" GET slbrk2
   @ 12,  2 SAY "COMMISSION RATE #3: " GET slcomm3
   @ 12, 40 SAY "QUANTITY BREAK:" GET slbrk3
   READ
   @ 22, 33 SAY "OK (Y or N)?" GET mok PICTURE "Y"
   READ
   @ 21, 1 CLEAR TO 22, 78
ENDDO

*Save new memory file
mok=.f.
@ 21, 1 CLEAR TO 22, 78
slpsetup=TRIM(slpsetup)
slpreset=TRIM(slpreset)
@ 22, 24 SAY "Save new SLMEM file (Y or N)?" GET mok PICTURE "Y"
READ
IF mok
   SAVE TO slmem ALL LIKE sl*
ENDIF

*tidy up and return
CLEAR
RETURN
```

Listing 5.4. The program SLCUSTFM.

```
**************************************************************
* SLCUSTFM - Customer file maintenance - Sales Tracking System *
*              8/28/86                                         *
**************************************************************

* Open files and set up
DO slopen                                   && Open files & primary indexes
SELECT A                                    && Select customer file
SET INDEX TO cust01,cust02,cust03           && Open all customer indexes
RESTORE FROM slmem ADDITIVE
title= "ADD OR UPDATE CUSTOMER"

*Main loop
DO WHILE .T.
   DO borders WITH sltitle,title            && Clear bottom of screen

   * Get ID number
   mid=SPACE(6)
   @ 12, 26 SAY "Enter customer ID: " GET mid
   @ 21, 14  SAY "Press ESC or ENTER key with blank ID number to exit"
   READ

   * Check for blank ID and exit
   IF mid=SPACE(6)
      EXIT
   ENDIF

   * Check if ID is on file.
   SEEK mid                                  && Check for ID on file
   @ 21, 1 CLEAR TO 22, 78                   && Clear status line
   IF EOF()                                  && NOT found

      * ID not found, ask user to confirm entering new customer
      @ 21, 29 SAY "Entering new customer"
      mok=.t.
      @ 22, 30 SAY "Continue (Y or N)" GET mok PICTURE "Y"
      READ
      IF .not.mok
         LOOP
      ENDIF

      *Append record for new customer. Get data
      APPEND BLANK
      REPLACE cust_id WITH mid
      DO custscrn
      @ 21, 27 SAY "Enter customer information"
      @ 22, 8 SAY "Press ESC key to finish (ENTER first if ";
        +"changes have been made)"
      READ

      * Verify entry
      @ 21, 1 CLEAR TO 22, 78                && Clear status lines
      mok=.f.
      @ 21, 30 SAY "Continue (Y or N)?" GET mok PICTURE 'Y'
      READ
```

```
     * If not ok, delete it
   IF .not.mok
      DELETE
      @ 21, 1 CLEAR TO 22, 78
      @ 21, 27 SAY "CUSTOMER NOT ADDED TO FILE"
      mok=" "
      @ 22, 24 SAY "Press any key to continue ..." GET mok
      READ
   ENDIF

ELSE                                  && salseperson found, check for deleted

   * Customer ID was found, check if it is deleted
   IF DELETED()

      * Customer is deleted. Ask if want to undelete
      @ 14, 22 SAY "Customer: "+company
      @ 21, 17 SAY "THIS CUSTOMER EXISTS, BUT HAS BEEN DELETED"
      mok=.f.
      @ 22, 17 SAY "Do you want to UNDELETE and continue (Y or N)?";
         GET mok PICTURE "Y"
      READ

      * If want to undelete, Recall, else return to top of data entry loop
      IF mok
         RECALL
      ELSE
         LOOP
      ENDIF

   ELSE

      * Customer not deleted. Ask if want to update
      @ 14, 22 SAY "Customer: "+company
      @ 21,  1 CLEAR TO 22, 78
      @ 21, 27 SAY "Updating existing customer"
      mok=.t.                                  && Verify update
      @ 22, 30 SAY "Continue (Y or N)?" GET mok PICTURE 'Y'
      READ

      * If don't want to update, return to top of data entry loop
      IF .not.mok
         LOOP
      ENDIF (not mok)

   ENDIF (deleted)

* Have existing, active customer ID, get changes & loop until ok
mok=.f.
DO WHILE .not.mok

   * Display update screen
   DO custscrn
   @ 21, 28 SAY "UPDATE EXISTING CUSTOMER"
   @ 22, 8 SAY "Press ESC key to finish (ENTER first if ";
         +"changes have been made)"
   READ
```

(Continued on next page.)

Listing 5.4, continued.

```
        * Ask user to verify changes
        @ 21, 1 CLEAR TO 22, 78
        @ 21, 33 SAY "OK (Y or N)?" GET mok PICTURE 'Y'
        READ
     ENDDO (not mok)

   ENDIF (eof)

*End of main loop
ENDDO (Do forever)

*tidy up and return
CLEAR
CLOSE DATABASES
RETURN
```

Listing 5.5. The subroutine CUSTSCRN.

```
**********************************************************************
* CUSTSCRN -    Display edit/update screen for customer data     *
*               8/28/86                                          *
**********************************************************************

@ 5, 1 CLEAR TO 19, 78
@ 21, 1 CLEAR TO 22, 78
@  6, 27 SAY "Customer ID number "+CUST_ID
@  8, 15 SAY "COMPANY" GET COMPANY
@  9, 15 SAY "ADDRESS" GET ADDR1
@ 10, 23 GET ADDR2
@ 11, 18 SAY "CITY" GET CITY
@ 11, 42 SAY "STATE" GET STATE PICTURE '@!'
@ 11, 52 SAY "ZIP" GET ZIP PICTURE '9999999999'
@ 13, 12 SAY "FIRST NAME" GET F_NAME
@ 13, 34 SAY "LAST NAME" GET L_NAME
@ 14, 17 SAY "PHONE" GET PHONE PICTURE "(999) 999-9999"

RETURN
```

Listing 5.6. The program SLCUSTQY.

```
********************************************************************
* SLCUSTQY - Customer file query for the Sales Tracking System *
*               8/28/86                                         *
********************************************************************

* Open files and set up
DO slopen                              && Open system files & primary indexes
SELECT A                               && Select customer master file
SET DELETED ON                         && Skip deleted records
RESTORE FROM slmem ADDITIVE
title= "CUSTOMER QUERY SCREEN"

*Main loop
DO WHILE .T.
  DO borders WITH sltitle,title              && Clear bottom of screen

  * Get ID number
  mid=SPACE(6)
  @ 12, 22 SAY "Enter customer ID: " GET mid
  @ 21, 14 SAY "Press ESC or ENTER key with blank ID number to exit"
  READ

  * Check for blank ID and exit
  IF mid=SPACE(6)
    EXIT
  ENDIF

  * Check if ID is on file, if so skip to update
  SEEK mid                                 && Check for ID on file
  @ 21, 1 CLEAR TO 22, 78                  && Clear status line
  IF EOF()                                 && NOT found
    @ 21, 31 SAY "Customer not found"
    mok=" "
    @ 22, 25 SAY "Press any key to continue" GET mok PICTURE "X"
    READ
    LOOP
  ENDIF

  * Have customer, display data
  DO custscrn
  CLEAR GETS

  * Pause until keypress
  @ 21, 21 SAY "Use the PRTSCR key to make a hardcopy"
  mok=" "
  @ 22,24 SAY "Press any key to continue ... " GET mok PICTURE "X"
  READ
*End of main loop
ENDDO

*tidy up and return
CLEAR
SET DELETED OFF
CLOSE DATABASES
option=-1
RETURN
```

Listing 5.7. The program SLCUSTDU.

```
*******************************************************************
* SLCUSTDU - Customer file delete/undelete - Sales Tracking     *
*             8/28/86                                            *
*******************************************************************

* Open files and set up
SET DELETED OFF
DO slopen                               && Open files & primary indexes
SELECT A                                && Select customer master file
RESTORE FROM slmem ADDITIVE
title= "CUSTOMER DELETE or UNDELETE"

*Main loop
DO WHILE .T.                            && Do forever
   DO borders WITH sltitle,title        && Clear bottom of screen

   * Get ID number
   mid=SPACE(6)
   @ 12, 27 SAY "Enter customer ID:" GET mid FUNCTION "!"
   @ 21, 14  SAY "Press ESC or ENTER key with blank ID number to exit"
   READ

   * Check for blank ID and exit
   IF mid=SPACE(6)
      EXIT                              && Exit from delete loop if blank
   ENDIF

   * Check if ID is on file. If not, return to top of loop
   SEEK mid                             && Check for ID in customer file
   @ 21, 1 SAY SPACE(77)                && Clear status line
   IF EOF()                             && If NOT found
      @ 21, 31 SAY "Customer not found"
      mok=" "                           && Display message & pause
      @ 22, 24 SAY "Press any key to continue ... " GET mok
      READ
      LOOP                              && Return to top of loop
   ENDIF (EOF)

   * Ask user to verify that he wants to continue with this customer
   mok=.t.
   @ 14, 22 SAY "Customer: "+company
   @ 21, 30 SAY "Continue (Y or N)" GET mok PICTURE "Y"
   READ
   IF .not.mok
      LOOP                              && If not, return to top of data entry loop
   ENDIF

   * Have customer, display data
   DO custscrn
   CLEAR GETS

   * Display delete/undelete message and process
   IF .not.DELETED()
```

```
        * Processing for non-deleted customer
        @ 21, 25 SAY "Customer is currently NOT deleted"
        mok=.F.
        @ 22, 25 SAY "Want to DELETE it (Y or N)?" GET mok PICTURE "Y"
        READ
        @ 21, 1 CLEAR TO 22, 78

        *If yes, perform delete
        IF mok

            * Perform deletion
            DELETE                                  && Delete from customer file
            @ 21, 13 SAY "Customer is now DELETED. Use this command ";
                    +"again to undelete"
            mok=" "
            @ 22, 25 SAY "Press any key to continue ... " GET mok PICTURE "X"
            READ
        ENDIF (mok)

    ELSE
        * Processing for deleted customer
        @ 21, 25 SAY "Customer is currently DELETED"
        mok=.F.
        @ 22, 22 SAY "Do you want to UNDELETE (Y or N)?" GET mok PICTURE "Y"
        READ
        @ 21, 1 CLEAR TO 22, 78
        *Perform undelete
        IF mok
            RECALL                          && Recall customer record
            @ 21, 13 SAY "Customer is now UNDELETED. Use this command ";
                    +"again to delete"
            mok=" "
            @ 22, 25 SAY "Press any key to continue ... " GET mok
            READ
        ENDIF (mok)

    ENDIF (not deleted)

*End of main loop
ENDDO (do forever)

*tidy up and return
CLEAR
CLOSE DATABASES
RETURN
```

Listing 5.8. The program SLSLSPFM.

```
********************************************************************
* SLSLSPFM - Salesperson file maintenance - Sales Tracking System *
*                 8/31/86                                          *
********************************************************************

* Open files and set up
DO slopen                              && Open system files & primary indexes
SELECT C                               && Select salesperson file
SET INDEX TO slsp01,slsp02             && Use all salesperson indexes
RESTORE FROM slmem ADDITIVE
title= "ADD OR UPDATE SALESPERSON"

*Main loop
DO WHILE .T.
   DO borders WITH sltitle,title            && Clear bottom of screen

   * Get ID number
   mid=SPACE(6)
   @ 12, 25 SAY "Enter salesperson ID: " GET mid
   @ 21, 14  SAY "Press ESC or ENTER key with blank ID number to exit"
   READ

   * Check for blank ID and exit
   IF mid=SPACE(6)
      EXIT
   ENDIF

   * Check if ID is on file.
   SEEK mid                                && Check for ID on file
   @ 21, 1 CLEAR TO 22, 78                 && Clear status line
   IF EOF()                                && NOT found

      * ID not found, ask user to confirm entering new salesperson
      @ 21, 28 SAY "Entering new salesperson"
      mok=.t.
      @ 22, 31 SAY "Continue (Y or N)" GET mok PICTURE "Y"
      READ
      IF .not.mok
        LOOP
      ENDIF

      *Append record for new salesperson. Get data
      APPEND BLANK
      REPLACE sp_id WITH mid
      DO slspscrn
      @ 21, 25 SAY "Enter salesperson information"
      @ 22, 8 SAY "Press ESC key to finish (ENTER first if changes ";
        +"have been made)"
      READ

      * Verify entry
      @ 21, 1 CLEAR TO 22, 78                      && Clear status lines
      mok=.f.
      @ 21, 30 SAY "Continue (Y or N)?" GET mok PICTURE 'Y'
      READ
```

```
   * If not ok, delete it
IF .not.mok
   DELETE
   @ 21, 1 CLEAR TO 22, 78
   @ 21, 25 SAY "SALESPERSON NOT ADDED TO FILE"
   mok=" "
   @ 22, 24 SAY "Press any key to continue ..." GET mok
   READ
ENDIF

ELSE                            && salesperson found, check for deleted

   * Salesperson ID was found, check if it is deleted
   IF DELETED()

      * Salesperson is deleted. Ask if want to undelete
      @ 14, 22 SAY "Salesperson: "+s_lname
      @ 21, 17 SAY "THIS SALESPERSON EXISTS, BUT HAS BEEN DELETED"
      mok=.f.
      @ 22, 17 SAY "Do you want to UNDELETE and continue (Y or N)?";
         GET mok PICTURE "Y"
      READ

      * If want to undelete, Recall, else return to top of data entry loop
      IF mok
         RECALL
      ELSE
         LOOP
      ENDIF

   ELSE

      * Salesperson not deleted. Ask if want to update
      @ 14, 22 SAY "Salesperson: "+s_lname
      @ 21,  1 CLEAR TO 22, 78
      @ 21, 25 SAY "Updating existing salesperson"
      mok=.t.                            && Verify update
      @ 22, 30 SAY "Continue (Y or N)?" GET mok PICTURE 'Y'
      READ

      * If don't want to update, return to top of data entry loop
      IF .not.mok
         LOOP
      ENDIF (not mok)

   ENDIF (deleted)

   * Have existing, active salesperson ID, get changes & loop until ok
   mok=.f.
   DO WHILE .not.mok

      * Display update screen
      DO slspscrn
      @ 21, 26 SAY "UPDATE EXISTING SALESPERSON"
      @ 22, 8 SAY "Press ESC key to finish (ENTER first if ";
            +"changes have been made)"
      READ
```

(Continued on next page.)

Listing 5.8, continued.

```
        * Ask user to verify changes
        @ 21, 1 CLEAR TO 22, 78
        @ 21, 33 SAY "OK (Y or N)?" GET mok PICTURE 'Y'
        READ
     ENDDO (not mok)

   ENDIF (eof)

*End of main loop
ENDDO (Do forever)

*tidy up and return

CLEAR
CLOSE DATABASES
RETURN
```

Listing 5.9. The subroutine SLSPSCRN.

```
********************************************************************
* SLSPSCRN -    Display data entry screen for salesperson data  *
*              8/31/86                                           *
********************************************************************

@ 5, 1 CLEAR TO 19, 78
@ 21, 1 CLEAR TO 22, 78

@  7, 29 SAY "Salesperson ID: "+sp_id
@  9, 15 SAY "ADDRESS" GET S_ADDR1
@ 10, 23 GET S_ADDR2
@ 11, 18 SAY "CITY" GET S_CITY
@ 11, 42 SAY "STATE" GET S_STATE PICTURE '@!'
@ 11, 52 SAY "ZIP" GET S_ZIP PICTURE '9999999999'
@ 13, 12 SAY "FIRST NAME" GET S_FNAME
@ 13, 35 SAY "LAST NAME" GET S_LNAME
@ 14, 17 SAY "PHONE" GET S_PHONE PICTURE "(999) 999-9999"

RETURN
```

Listing 5.10. The program SLSLSPQY.

```
***********************************************************************
* SLSLSPQY - Salesperson file query for the Sales Tracking System *
*             8/31/86                                             *
***********************************************************************

* Open files and set up
DO slopen                               && Open system files & primary indexes
SELECT C                                && Select salesperson master file
SET DELETED ON                          && Skip deleted records
RESTORE FROM slmem ADDITIVE
title= "SALESPERSON QUERY SCREEN"

*Main loop
DO WHILE .T.
   DO borders WITH sltitle,title          && Clear bottom of screen

   * Get ID number
   mid=SPACE(6)
   @ 12, 25 SAY "Enter salesperson ID:" GET mid
   @ 21, 15 SAY "Press ESC or ENTER key with blank ID number to exit"
   READ

   * Check for blank ID and exit
   IF mid=' '
     EXIT
   ENDIF

   * Check if ID is on file, if so skip to update
   SEEK mid                                && Check for ID on file
   @ 21, 1 CLEAR TO 22, 78                 && Clear status line
   IF EOF()                                && NOT found
     @ 21, 31 SAY "Salesperson not found"
     mok=" "
     @ 22, 25 SAY "Press any key to continue" GET mok
     READ
     LOOP
   ENDIF

   * Have salesperson, display data
   DO slspscrn
   CLEAR GETS

   * Pause until keypress
   @ 21, 21 SAY "Use the PRTSCR key to make a hardcopy"
   mok=" "
   @ 22, 24 SAY "Press any key to continue ... " GET mok
   READ
*End of main loop
ENDDO

*tidy up and return
CLEAR
SET DELETED OFF
CLOSE DATABASES
RETURN
```

Listing 5.11. The program SLSLSPDU.

```
******************************************************************
* SLSLSPDU - Salesperson file delete/undelete - Sales Tracking *
*              8/31/86                                          *
******************************************************************

* Open files and set up
SET DELETED OFF
DO slopen                               && Open files & indexes
SELECT C
RESTORE FROM slmem ADDITIVE
title="SALESPERSON DELETE or UNDELETE"

*Main loop
DO WHILE .T.
  DO borders WITH sltitle,title         && Clear bottom of screen

  * Get ID number
  mid=SPACE(6)
  @ 12, 28 SAY "Enter salesperson ID:" GET mid PICTURE "@!"
  @ 21, 14  SAY "Press ESC or ENTER key with blank ID number to exit"
  READ

  * Check for blank ID and exit
  IF mid=' '
    EXIT
  ENDIF

  * Check if ID is on file, if so skip to update
  SEEK mid                              && Check for ID on file
  @ 21, 1 SAY SPACE(78)                 && Clear status line
  IF EOF()                             &&  NOT found
    @ 21, 31 SAY "Salesperson not found"
    mok=" "
    @ 22, 24 SAY "Press any key to continue ... " GET mok
    READ                               &&  found, check for deleted
    LOOP
  ENDIF
    mok=.t.
    @ 14, 22 SAY "Salesperson: "+ s_lname
    @ 21, 30 SAY "Continue (Y or N)" GET mok PICTURE "Y"
    READ
    IF .not.mok
      LOOP
    ENDIF

  * Have salesperson, display data
  DO slspscrn
  CLEAR GETS
```

```
* Display delete/undelete message and process
IF .not.DELETED()
  @ 21, 25 SAY "Salesperson is currently NOT deleted"
  mok=.f.
  @ 22, 21 SAY "Want to DELETE salesperson (Y or N)?" GET mok PICTURE "Y"
  READ
  @ 21, 1 CLEAR TO 22, 78
  *Perform delete
  IF mok
    DELETE
    @ 21, 9 SAY "Salesperson is now DELETED. Use this command again to undelete"
    mok=" "
    @ 22, 25 SAY "Press any key to continue ... " GET mok
    READ

  ENDIF
ELSE
    @ 21, 27 SAY "Salesperson is currently DELETED"
    mok=.f.
    @ 22, 17 SAY "Do you want to UNDELETE salesperson (Y or N)?";
      GET mok PICTURE "Y"
    READ
    @ 21, 1 CLEAR TO 22, 78
    *Perform undelete
    IF mok
      RECALL
      @ 21, 9 SAY "Salesperson is now UNDELETED. Use this command ";
        +"again to delete"
      mok=" "
      @ 22, 25 SAY "Press any key to continue ... " GET mok
      READ
      ENDIF
    ENDIF
  *End of main loop
  ENDDO

  *tidy up and return
  CLEAR
  CLOSE DATABASES
  RETURN
```

Listing 5.12. The program SLTRANFM.

```
**********************************************************************
* SLTRANFM - Transaction file maint.  -  Sales Tracking System *
*              8/31/86                                          *
**********************************************************************

* Open files and set up
DO slopen                               && Open files & primary indexes
SELECT B                                && Select transaction file
SET INDEX TO tran01,tran02,tran03,tran04        && Open all trans. indexes
RESTORE FROM slmem ADDITIVE
title= "ENTER SALES TRANSACTIONS"

*Main loop
DO WHILE .T.                            && Do forever
   DO borders WITH sltitle,title        && Clear screen and display borders

   * Get ID number
   mid=SPACE(6)
   @ 12, 27 SAY "Enter customer ID:" GET mid
   @ 21, 14 SAY "Press ESC or ENTER key with blank ID number to exit"
   READ

   * Check for blank ID and exit
   IF mid=' '
      EXIT                      && Exit data entry loop if blank
   ENDIF

   * Check if ID is on file, if so skip to update
   SELECT A                             && Select customer file
   SEEK mid                             && Check for ID on file
   @ 21, 1 CLEAR TO 22, 78              && Clear status line
   IF EOF()                             &&  NOT found
      @ 21, 8 SAY "NEW CUSTOMER - Must set up customer prior to ";
        +"entering sales data"
      mok=" "
      @ 22, 26 SAY "Press any key to continue" GET mok
      READ
      LOOP                              && Return to top of data entry loop
   ELSE                                 &&  found, check for deleted

      * Found customer ID, check if deleted
      @ 14, 22 SAY "Customer: "+COMPANY
      IF DELETED()

         * If deleted, ask if want to undelete.
         @ 21, 19 SAY "THIS CUSTOMER EXISTS, BUT HAS BEEN DELETED"
         mok=.f.
         @ 22, 16 SAY "Do you want to UNDELETE and continue (Y or N)?";
              GET mok PICTURE "Y"
         READ
         @ 21, 1 CLEAR TO 22, 78

         * If want to undelete, recall. Else, return to top of data entry loop
         IF mok
            RECALL                      && Recall deleted customer
         ELSE
            LOOP
         ENDIF (mok)
```

```
      ENDIF (deleted)
      @ 21, 22 SAY "Adding sales for an existing customer"

   ENDIF (eof)
* Verify continuing
mok=.t.                                  && Verify update
@ 22, 30 SAY "Continue (Y or N)?" GET mok PICTURE 'Y'
READ
IF .not.mok
   LOOP
ENDIF

* Have customer ID, get data from user
@ 5, 1 CLEAR TO 19, 78                       && Clear used lines
@ 21, 1 CLEAR TO 22, 78
SELECT B                                     && Select transaction file
mcont=.t.


* Loop to enter transactions for this customer
DO WHILE mcont
   APPEND BLANK               && Append blank record for transaction
   DELETE                     && Record will be undeleted when accepted
   REPLACE cust_id WITH mid
   REPLACE period WITH slperiod
   comm=0
   DO transcrn
   @ 21, 28 SAY "Enter sales transaction"
   @ 22, 8  SAY "Press ESC key to finish (ENTER first if ";
     +"changes have been made)"
   READ
   @ 21, 1 CLEAR TO 22, 78

   *verify salesperson is on file
   SELECT C                                 && Select salesperson file
   SET DELETED ON                           && Skip deleted salespeople
   SEEK tran00->sp_id                       && Lookup salesperson id
   IF EOF()                                 && not on file, loop.
      @ 21, 1 CLEAR TO 22, 78
      @ 21, 20 SAY "INVALID SALESPERSON, RE-ENTER TRANSACTION"
      mok=" "
      @ 22, 20 SAY "Press any key to continue ..." GET mok
      READ
      SELECT B                              && Select transaction file
      SET DELETED OFF
      DELETE                                && Delete bad transaction
      EXIT                                  && Exit loop for this cust.
   ELSE
      @ 9, 24 SAY S_LNAME                   && Display salesperson name
      SELECT B                              && Select transaction file
      SET DELETED OFF
   ENDIF (EOF)

* Calculate commission based on sales quantity
DO CASE
   CASE qty > slbrk3
        comm=(qty*u_price*slcomm3)
   CASE qty > slbrk2
        comm=(qty*u_price*slcomm2)
   OTHERWISE
        comm=(qty*u_price*slcomm1)
ENDCASE
```

(Continued on next page.)

Listing 5.12, continued.

```
      * Update commission in new transaction
      REPLACE commission WITH comm

      * Verify entry
      @ 14, 16 SAY commission
      @ 21, 1 CLEAR TO 22, 78                    && Clear status lines
      mok=.t.
      @ 21, 33 SAY "OK (Y or N)?" GET mok PICTURE 'Y'
      READ

      * If ok, recall new entry
      IF .not.mok
         @ 21, 1 SAY SPACE(78)
         @ 21, 27 SAY "TRANSACTION NOT ADDED TO FILE"
         mok=" "
         @ 22, 28 SAY "Press any key to continue" GET mok
         READ
      ELSE
         RECALL                    && Activate new sales transaction
      ENDIF (.not.mok)

      *Another transaction?
      @ 21, 1 CLEAR TO 22, 78
      @ 21, 19 SAY "Another sale for this customer (Y or N)?";
         GET mcont PICTURE "Y"
      READ
   ENDDO (do while mcont

*End of main loop
ENDDO (do forever)

*tidy up and return
CLEAR
SET DELETED OFF
CLOSE DATABASES
RETURN
```

Listing 5.13. The subroutine TRANSCRN.

```
********************************************************************
* TRANSCRN -     Display data entry screen for sales transaction *
*                8/29/86                                          *
********************************************************************

@ 5, 1 CLEAR TO 19, 78
@  6, 24 SAY "Customer ID: "+cust_id
@  6, 60 SAY "PERIOD"
@  6, 67 SAY PERIOD PICTURE '99'
@  7, 24 SAY "Customer: "+CUSTOO->COMPANY
@  9,  4 SAY "SALESPERSON" GET SP_ID
@ 10,  4 SAY "    PRODUCT" GET PROD_ID
@ 11,  4 SAY "   QUANTITY" GET QTY
@ 12,  4 SAY "      PRICE" GET U_PRICE
@ 13,  4 SAY "       COST" GET U_COST
@ 14,  4 SAY " COMMISSION"

RETURN
```

Listing 5.14. The program SLCUSTRP.

```
************************************
* SLCUSTRP - Customer report driver *
*           8/31/86                  *
************************************

*Setup environment and open files
SET DELETED ON
DO slopen
SELECT A                                   && Select customer file
SET INDEX TO cust01,cust02,cust03          && Open all customer indexes
RESTORE FROM slmem ADDITIVE
title= "CUSTOMER FILE REPORTS"

* Display logo
DO borders WITH sltitle,title

* Display sort options
sortop=0
@  8, 28 SAY "1. SORTED BY CUSTOMER ID"
@  9, 28 SAY "2. SORTED BY COMPANY"
@ 10, 28 SAY "3. SORTED BY ZIP CODE"
@ 16, 28 SAY "0. RETURN TO MAIN MENU"
@ 21, 28 SAY "ENTER SORT OPTION:"
@ 21, 47 GET sortop PICTURE "9" RANGE 0,3
READ

DO CASE
  CASE sortop=1
    SET ORDER TO 1              && Report indexed by customer id
    DO setup
    REPORT FORM custrp1
  CASE sortop=2
    SET ORDER TO 2              && Report indexed by company
    DO setup
    REPORT FORM custrp2
  CASE sortop=3
    SET ORDER TO 3              && Report indexed by zip code
    DO setup
    REPORT FORM custrp3
ENDCASE

*Restore system defaults and exit
? &slpreset
SET CONSOLE ON
SET PRINT OFF
CLEAR
CLOSE DATABASES
RETURN
```

Listing 5.15. The subroutine SETUP.

```
**************************************
* SETUP   -   SETUP PRINTER          *
*             9/1/86                  *
**************************************

* Tell user to prepare printer
@ 21, 1 CLEAR TO 22, 78
mok=" "
@ 21, 21 SAY "Make sure printer is ready for report"
@ 22, 26 SAY "Press any key to continue" GET mok
READ
@ 21, 1 CLEAR TO 22, 78
@ 21, 36 SAY "WORKING ... "
SET PRINT ON
SET CONSOLE OFF
? &slpsetup

RETURN
```

Listing 5.16. The program SLTRANRP.

```
**************************************
* SLTRANRP - Sales report driver     *
*             8/31/86                 *
**************************************

*Setup environment and open files
SET DELETED ON
DO slopen                           && Open system files & indexes
SELECT B                            && Select transaction file
SET INDEX TO tran01,tran02,tran03,tran04  && Open all transaction indexes
RESTORE FROM slmem ADDITIVE
title= "SALES REPORTS"

* Display logo
DO borders WITH sltitle,title

*Get period for sales report
pperiod=slperiod
@ 21, 9 SAY "Enter period for sales reports (RETURN for current period)?";
  GET pperiod PICTURE '99' RANGE 1,12
READ
SET FILTER TO period=pperiod     && Select transactions for specified period
DO borders WITH sltitle,title

* Display sort options
sortop=0
@  8, 28 SAY "1. DETAIL PRODUCT SALES"
@  9, 28 SAY "2. SUMMARY PRODUCT SALES"
@ 10, 28 SAY "3. DETAIL CUSTOMER SALES"
@ 11, 28 SAY "4. SUMMARY CUSTOMER SALES"
@ 16, 28 SAY "0. RETURN TO MAIN MENU"
@ 21, 28 SAY "ENTER SORT OPTION:"
@ 21, 47 GET sortop PICTURE "9" RANGE 0,4
READ
```

```
* Do selected option
DO CASE
  CASE sortop=1
    SET ORDER TO 3                      && Report indexed by product
    DO setup
    REPORT FORM tranrp1
  CASE sortop=2
    SET ORDER TO 3                      && Report indexed by product
    DO setup
    REPORT FORM tranrp2
  CASE sortop=3
    SET ORDER TO 1                      && Report indexed by customer
    DO setup
    REPORT FORM tranrp3
  CASE sortop=4
    SET ORDER TO 1                      && Report indexed by customer
    DO setup
    REPORT FORM tranrp4
ENDCASE

*Restore system defaults and exit
? &slpreset
SET CONSOLE ON
SET PRINT OFF
SET ORDER TO 1                          && Restore default index
CLEAR
CLOSE DATABASES
RETURN
```

Listing 5.17. The program SLCOMMRP.

```
************************************
* SLCOMMRP - Commission reports    *
*            8/31/86               *
************************************

*Setup environment and open files
SET DELETED ON
DO slopen                            && Open files & primary indexes
SELECT B                             && Select transaction file
SET INDEX TO tran01,tran02,tran03,tran04    && Open all transaction indexes
SET ORDER TO 2                       && Use index by salesperson
RESTORE FROM slmem ADDITIVE
title= "COMMISSION REPORTS"

* Display logo
DO borders WITH sltitle,title

*Get period for commission reports
pperiod=slperiod
@ 21, 7 SAY "Enter period for commission report (RETURN for current period)?";
   GET pperiod PICTURE '99' RANGE 1,12
READ
SET FILTER TO period=pperiod
GO TOP
DO borders WITH sltitle,title

* Display options
repopt=0
@  8, 28 SAY "1. DETAIL COMMISSION REPORT"
@  9, 28 SAY "2. SUMMARY COMMISSION REPORT"
@ 16, 28 SAY "0. RETURN TO MAIN MENU"
@ 21, 28 SAY "ENTER SORT OPTION:" GET repopt PICTURE "9" RANGE 0,2
READ

DO CASE
  CASE repopt=1
    DO setup
    REPORT FORM commrp1
  CASE repopt=2
    DO setup
    REPORT FORM commrp2
ENDCASE

*Restore system defaults and exit
? &slpreset
SET CONSOLE ON
SET PRINT OFF
CLEAR
CLOSE DATABASES
RETURN
```

Listing 5.18. The program SLPACK.

```
************************************************************
* SLPACK - PACK delted records in the Sales Tracking Files   *
*          8/31/86                                            *
************************************************************

* Open files and set up
DO slopen                             && Open files
RESTORE FROM slmem ADDITIVE
title='Pack Deleted Records in Databases'

* Display logo
DO borders WITH sltitle,title
mok=.f.
@ 21, 21 SAY "Want to proceed with PACK (Y or N)?" GET mok PICTURE 'Y'
READ

IF mok
   * Delete customer records
   @ 8, 10 SAY "Deleting CUSTOMER records"
   SELECT A
   SET INDEX TO cust01,cust02,cust03      && Open all customer indexes
   PACK                                   && Pack file and indexes
   USE                                    && Close the 5 customer files

   * Delete transaction records
   @ 10, 10 SAY "Deleting SALES TRANSACTIONS"
   SELECT B
   SET INDEX TO tran01,tran02,tran03,tran04   && Open all transaction indexes
   PACK                                   && Pack file and indexes
   USE                                    && Close the 5 transaction files

   * Delete salesperson records
   @ 12, 10 SAY "Deleting SALESPERSON records"
   SELECT C
   SET INDEX TO slsp01,slsp02             && Open all salesperson indexes
   PACK                                   && Pack file and indexes
ENDIF (mok)

*tidy up and return
CLEAR
CLOSE DATABASES
RETURN
```

Listing 5.19. The program SLBACKUP.

```
*******************************************************************
* SLBACKUP -     Back up Sales Tracking System files             *
*               8/31/86                                          *
*******************************************************************
target="b:"                              && Target drive for backup
CLEAR
? "BACKUP Sales Tracking System Data Files"
?

* Ask user to verify backup command
mok=' '
DO WHILE UPPER(mok)#"Y".and.UPPER(mok)#"N"
   WAIT "Do you want to proceed with this command (Y or N)?" TO mok
   READ
ENDDO

* If answer is 'yes', do backup
IF UPPER(mok)="Y"
   files1="*.dbf"
   RUN BACKUP &files1 &target
   files2="*.ndx"
   RUN BACKUP &files2 &target/A
   files3="*.mem"
   RUN BACKUP &files3 &target/A
ENDIF

* Clear screen and return
CLEAR
RETURN
```

Listing 5.20. The program SLRESTOR.

```
*******************************************************************
* SLRESTOR -     RESTORE Sales Tracking System data from backup  *
*               8/31/86                                          *
*******************************************************************
* Display title
CLEAR
? "RESTORE Sales Tracking System Data from Backup"
?

* Ask user to verify restore command
mok=' '
DO WHILE UPPER(mok)#"Y".and.UPPER(mok)#"N"
   WAIT "Do you want to proceed with this command (Y or N)?" TO mok
ENDDO

* If answer is 'yes', do restore
IF UPPER(mok)="Y"
   source="b:"                       && Source drive for restore
   target="c:"                       && Target drive for restore
   files1=target+"*.*"
   RUN RESTORE &source &files1
ENDIF

* Clear screen and return
CLEAR
RETURN
```

Listing 5.21. The program SLPURGE.

```
*****************************************************************
* SLPURGE - Purge transactions file for a specified period *
*               8/31/86                                        *
*****************************************************************

*Setup environment and open files
SET DELETED ON
DO slopen
SELECT B
RESTORE FROM slmem ADDITIVE
title= "PURGE TRANSACTIONS FILE"

* Display logo
DO borders WITH sltitle,title

*Get period for sales report
pperiod=0
@ 21, 2 SAY "Enter period to purge from transaction file ";
        +"(0 quits this command)" GET pperiod RANGE 1,12
READ
@ 21, 1 SAY SPACE(78)

* Validate period
IF pperiod#0                              && Proceed if period # 0.

    *Check for period#current
    IF pperiod#slperiod

       *Ask user to verify file purge
       mok=.F.
       @ 12, 5 SAY 'CONTINUING WILL DELETE ALL SALES TRANSACTIONS FOR PERIOD ';
         +STR(pperiod,2)
       @ 21, 30 SAY "Confirm purge for period ";
         +STR(pperiod,2) GET mok PICTURE "Y"
       READ
       @ 12, 1 SAY SPACE(78)
       @ 21, 1 SAY SPACE(78)

       * if response is yes, proceed with delete
       IF mok
          @ 12, 35 SAY 'Working...'
          DELETE FOR period=pperiod
       ENDIF
    ELSE
       mok=' '
       @ 21, 20 SAY 'Cannot delete current period' GET mok
       READ
    ENDIF
ENDIF

*Restore system defaults and exit
CLEAR
CLOSE DATABASES
RETURN
```

Listing 5.22. The program SLSTRACK.

```
************************************
* SLSTRACK- Sales Tracking System *
*             8/29/86              *
************************************

*Setup environment
SET TALK OFF
SET SAFETY OFF
SET DEVICE TO SCREEN
SET PRINT OFF
* SET PROCEDURE TO slproc                   && Select procedure file
CLEAR ALL
RESTORE FROM slmem

*Main loop
option=-1
DO WHILE option#0

  * Display Logo
  option=0
  title="MAIN MENU"
  DO borders WITH sltitle,title

  * Display menu options
  @  8, 28 SAY "1. DATA ENTRY AND QUERY"
  @  9, 28 SAY "2. PRINTED REPORTS"
  @ 10, 28 SAY "3. SYSTEM MAINTENANCE"
  @ 16, 28 SAY "0. EXIT TO DBASE III"
  @ 21, 32 SAY "ENTER OPTION:" GET option PICTURE "9" RANGE 0,3
  READ

  * Do selected option
  DO CASE
    CASE option=1
      DO slmenu1                            && Online functions
    CASE option=2
      DO slmenu2                            && Report menu
    CASE option=3
      DO slmenu3                            && System maint. menu

    OTHERWISE                               && Verify prior to exit
      mok=.f.
      @ 22, 21 SAY "Do you really want to exit (Y or N)?" GET mok PICTURE "Y"
      READ
      option=IIF(mok,0,-1)                  && Reset option to -1 if "N"

  ENDCASE
*End of main loop
ENDDO (option#0)

*Restore system defaults and exit
SET TALK ON
SET SAFETY ON
SET PRINT OFF
SET DEVICE TO SCREEN
CLOSE PROCEDURE
CLEAR
RETURN
```

Listing 5.23. The program SLMENU1.

```
*****************************************
* SLMENU1 - Data Entry and Query menu   *
*              8/31/86                   *
*****************************************

PRIVATE option,title
CLEAR
RESTORE FROM slmem ADDITIVE

*Main loop
option=-1
DO WHILE option#0

   * Display logo
   title= "DATA ENTRY AND QUERY MENU"
   DO borders WITH sltitle,title

   * Display menu options
   option=0
   @  8, 28 SAY "1. CUSTOMER FILE MAINTENANCE"
   @  9, 28 SAY "2. CUSTOMER FILE QUERY"
   @ 10, 28 SAY "3. SALESPERSON FILE MAINTENANCE"
   @ 11, 28 SAY "4. SALESPERSON FILE QUERY"
   @ 12, 28 SAY "5. ENTER SALES TRANSACTION"
   @ 16, 28 SAY "0. RETURN TO MAIN MENU"
   @ 21, 32 SAY "ENTER OPTION:" GET option PICTURE "9" RANGE 0,5
   READ

   * Do selected option
   DO CASE
      CASE option=1
         DO slcustfm                         && customer file maintenance
      CASE option=2
         DO slcustqy                         && customer file query
      CASE option=3
         DO slslspfm                         && salesperson file maint.
      CASE option=4
         DO slslspqy                         && salesperson file query
      CASE option=5
         DO sltranfm                         && transaction entry
   ENDCASE

*End of main loop
ENDDO (option#0)

*Restore system defaults and exit
CLEAR
RETURN
```

Listing 5.24. The program SLMENU2.

```
***********************************
* SLMENU2 - Report menu          *
*          8/31/86               *
***********************************

PRIVATE title,option
CLEAR
RESTORE FROM slmem ADDITIVE

*Main loop
option=-1
DO WHILE option#0

   * Display logo
   title= "REPORT MENU"
   DO    ders WITH sltitle,title

   * Display menu options
   option=0
   @  8, 28 SAY "1. CUSTOMER REPORTS"
   @  9, 28 SAY "2. SALES REPORTS"
   @ 10, 28 SAY "3. COMMISSION REPORT"
   @ 16, 28 SAY "0. RETURN TO MAIN MENU"
   @ 21, 32 SAY "ENTER OPTION:" GET option PICTURE "9" RANGE 0,3
   READ

   * Do selected option
   DO CASE
     CASE option=1
       DO slcustrp                      && customer reports
     CASE option=2
       DO sltranrp                      && sales reports
     CASE option=3
       DO slcommrp                      && commission report
   ENDCASE

*End of main loop
ENDDO (option#0)

*Restore system defaults and exit
CLEAR
RETURN
```

Listing 5.25. The program SLMENU3.

```
**************************************
* SLMENU3 - System maintenance menu *
*            8/29/86                 *
**************************************

PRIVATE title,option
CLEAR
RESTORE FROM slmem ADDITIVE

*Main loop
option=-1
DO WHILE option#0

  * Display logo
  title= "SYSTEM MAINTENANCE MENU"
  DO borders WITH sltitle,title

  * Display menu options
  option=0
  @  8, 28 SAY "1. DELETE/UNDELETE CUSTOMER"
  @  9, 28 SAY "2. DELETE/UNDELETE SALESPERSON"
  @ 10, 28 SAY "3. PACK DATAFILE"
  @ 11, 28 SAY "4. REINDEX DATAFILE"
  @ 12, 28 SAY "5. BACKUP FILES TO FLOPPY"
  @ 13, 28 SAY "6. RESTORE FILES FROM FLOPPY"
  @ 14, 28 SAY "7. EDIT SYSTEM MEMORY VARIABLES"
  @ 15, 28 SAY "8. PURGE OLD TRANSACTIONS FROM SALES FILE"
  @ 19, 28 SAY "0. RETURN TO MAIN MENU"
  @ 21, 32 SAY "ENTER OPTION:" GET option PICTURE "9" RANGE 0,8
  READ

  * Do selected option
  DO CASE
    CASE option=1
      DO slcustdu                    && Customer delete/undelete
    CASE option=2
      DO slslspdu                    && Salesperson delete/undelete
    CASE option=3
      DO slpack                      && pack sales database
    CASE option=4
      DO slindex                     && reindex sales database
    CASE option=5
      DO slbackup                    && backup database to floppy
    CASE option=6
      DO slrestor                    && restore database from floppy
    CASE option=7
      DO slmem                       && edit memory variables
    CASE option=8
      DO slpurge                     && purge old transactions
  ENDCASE

*End of main loop
ENDDO (option#0)

*Restore system defaults and exit
CLEAR
RETURN
```

6

Fixed-Asset Manager

Smith and Jones Corporation is a medium-sized merchandising firm that has experienced good markets and healthy growth for the past few years. But controller Jim Jones has discovered that the manual ledger system used to record the company's fixed assets is no longer adequate. Corporate reorganization and the addition of new offices have made the job of keeping track of assets and figuring depreciation too complex for the old system.

What Jim needs is a computerized system that keeps track of all the company's assets and allows users to quickly retrieve information about an asset or to print a specified list of assets. Jim also wants the system to be able to compute depreciation using either the straight-line method or the declining-balance method to show book value. The depreciation calculation for income-tax purposes is currently handled separately, but Jim would like to be able to add this capability to his computerized system in the future.

Suppose that we've met with Jim, discussed his needs, and developed a fixed-asset tracking system in dBASE III Plus to meet those needs. This chapter takes you through all the stages involved in developing the application. You'll see how the system uses dBASE III Plus programs and subroutines to prepare the reports Jim Jones needs to chronicle his company's fixed assets and accumulated depreciation. Programs simplify data entry and database queries, making it possible for novice computer users to keep the fixed-asset list current. This chapter also covers important system utilities, a menu system that guides users through the application, and possible extensions to the system.

dBASE III Plus is ideal for Jim Jones's application because he can use the program in interactive mode to make *ad hoc* queries of the database. He doesn't need to develop new programs for this *ad hoc* analysis. And he will be able to expand the system's capabilities—to compute depreciation for income tax purposes, for example—when he is ready to do so.

Identifying the Purpose and Function of the System

The purpose of the fixed-asset tracking system is twofold:

- to record the description and location of each asset owned by the company
- to calculate depreciation on these assets for the financial statements

The system must perform these functions:

- accept asset data from the keyboard
- locate asset data in the fixed-asset file
- print reports about assets and depreciation
- delete asset data
- back up, restore, and maintain the data files

Defining File Structures

We've met with Jim Jones to determine what information he needs. The next step in developing the fixed-asset tracking system for the Smith and Jones Corporation is to design the data files. This application requires only one data file, FIXASSET, which contains one record for each physical asset. To accompany the FIXASSET data file, we'll need need six index files so that Jim Jones can print reports or view records in various orders (by ID number, type, location, and so on).

The structure of the fixed-asset file is shown in figure 6.1. The design of the fixed-asset tracking system assumes that each asset is assigned a unique ID number. This ID number is important because it is the simplest way to identify each asset in the system. The ID_NUMBER field in the FIXASSET data file is the primary key that is used to identify a particular asset when entering, updating, or deleting asset data.

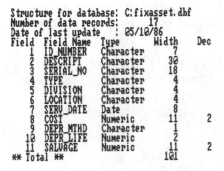

```
Structure for database: C:fixasset.dbf
Number of data records:      17
Date of last update   : 05/10/86
Field  Field Name  Type       Width  Dec
    1  ID_NUMBER   Character      7
    2  DESCRIPT    Character     30
    3  SERIAL_NO   Character     18
    4  TYPE        Character      4
    5  DIVISION    Character      4
    6  LOCATION    Character      4
    7  SERV_DATE   Date           8
    8  COST        Numeric       11    2
    9  DEPR_MTHD   Character      1
   10  DEPR_LIFE   Numeric        2
   11  SALVAGE     Numeric       11    2
** Total **                    101
```

Fig. 6.1. Structure of the file FIXASSET.DBF.

Many companies, including Smith and Jones Corporation, keep track of fixed assets by assigning each asset a unique ID number to distinguish that asset from others in the accounting system. Other companies may record serial numbers for those assets that have them, and use the description and location to identify those assets that do not have serial numbers. If the company that will use this application does not use an ID-number system to identify assets, then some other means must be found to uniquely identify each asset for entering, updating, and deleting data.

Because the first purpose of the fixed-asset tracking system is to record the description and location of each asset, the data file should contain additional information about the asset. The DESCRIPT, SERIAL_NO, TYPE, DIVISION, and LOCATION fields record descriptive information about the asset. The DESCRIPT and SERIAL_NO fields record a physical description of the asset. The TYPE field allows the asset to be classified by type. For example, desks and chairs might be TYPE="FURN". The DIVISION field indicates which division or accounting entity carries the asset on its books. Finally, the LOCATION field is a place to record the physical location of the asset.

The last five fields in the FIXASSET file support the second purpose of this application, which is to calculate depreciation for the fixed assets. These fields record the information necessary for computing book depreciation on either a straight-line or an accelerated basis. The SERV_DATE field records the date the asset was put in service. The COST, DEPR_MTHD, DEPR_LIFE, and SALVAGE fields record the remaining information necessary to determine depreciation.

All the fields are defined as character data type except for COST, DEPR_LIFE, and SALVAGE, which are numeric fields, and SERV_DATE, which is a date field. The ID_NUMBER field is defined as a character field so that it can hold ID numbers that include characters.

The field widths in figure 6.1 were selected with Jim Jones's needs in mind. If you alter them to fit your purposes, you'll need to change the PICTURE arguments to the @ . . . SAY . . . GET statements that generate the data-entry screen, the browse screens, and the printed reports. (The programs that create these screens and reports are discussed subsequently.)

Notice that no information about the actual amount of depreciation or depreciation rate is recorded in the file. Such information is difficult to keep current without recalculating it each time it is used. For example, suppose that the depreciation rate and the accumulated depreciation were stored in the file for each asset. If the update was run twice in one month, or if a month was skipped, the data stored in the file would no longer be current. In this system, the depreciation is recalculated each time it is displayed, and the values thereby are kept current.

Specifying the Function of Each Program

Figure 6.2 shows a block diagram of the fixed-assets tracking system. As previously mentioned, this application is designed to support entry, updating, and deletion of asset information; querying the database to isolate a record or a list of records meeting certain conditions; printing reports that show the assets and associated depreciation in several different ways; and performance of routine maintenance such as deleting assets, packing and reindexing the data file, backing up data to floppy disks, and restoring data from floppy disks.

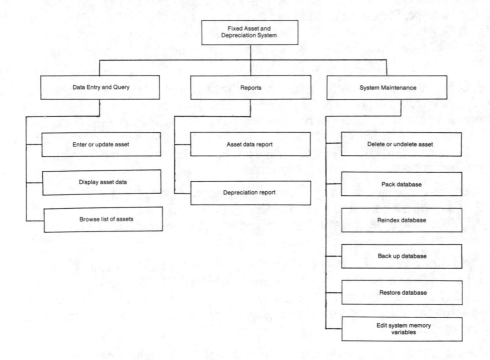

Fig. 6.2. Block diagram of the fixed-asset tracking system.

The system is modular: each function in figure 6.2 is performed by a separate program or subroutine. Subroutines perform functions that are common to more than one program, and the subroutines isolate complex portions of code from the main programs. Figure 6.3 shows an expanded block diagram of the fixed-asset system, including the subroutines called from each main routine. Figures 6.4 through 6.7 show the main menu and submenus of the system.

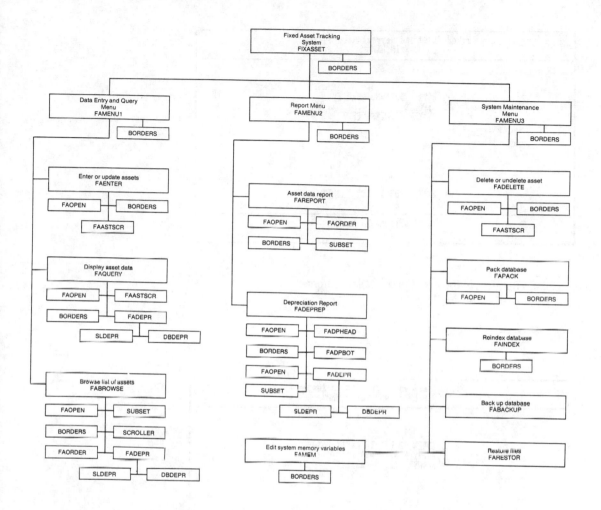

Fig. 6.3. Expanded block diagram of the fixed-asset system, showing subroutines.

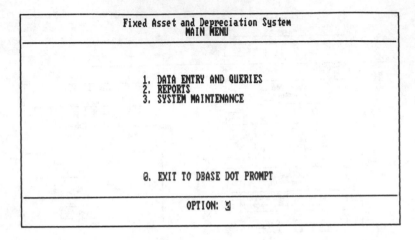

Fig. 6.4. The main menu of the fixed-asset system.

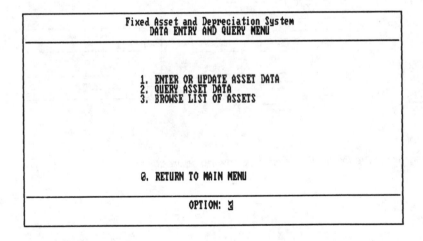

Fig. 6.5. The data-entry and -query menu.

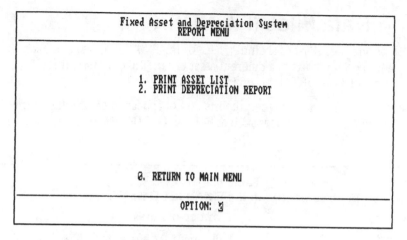

Fig. 6.6. The reports menu.

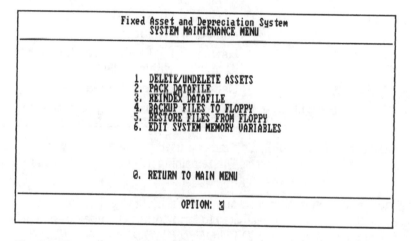

Fig. 6.7. The system-maintenance menu.

Developing the Programs

As the first step in developing the programs, we look at two maintenance programs, FAOPEN and FAINDEX. These programs set up and maintain the index files for the application. We then consider programs for entering data, querying the database, creating reports, performing various system-maintenance tasks, and creating a menu system to guide users through the application.

Indexing Data Files (FAINDEX)

The FAINDEX program establishes six index files for the FIXASSET data file. Each index file is used to print reports in a different asset order. Table 6.1 lists these indexes. The code for FAINDEX is shown in listing 6.1.

Listings are at the end of the chapter.

The database should be reindexed when reports do not appear to be printing in the proper order, or when error messages such as RECORD OUT OF RANGE appear during printing.

Table 6.1
Indexes Used with the FIXASSET Data File

Index Expression	Purpose of Index
ID_NUMBER	List assets by asset ID number. Used for data entry as well as reports.
TYPE+ID_NUMBER	List assets by type and ID number within type
LOCATION+ID_NUMBER	List assets by location and ID number within location
DIVISION+LOCATION +ID_NUMBER	List assets by division, location, and ID number within division
SERV_DATE	List assets by date placed in service
SERV_DATE+365*DEPR_LIFE	List assets by end of depreciable life

The primary index is on ID_NUMBER. This index is used by the data-entry and update programs to look up specific assets. The remaining five indexes are used to order the records for reports and browsing.

Several of the indexes combine more than one field. Each of these fields is of the *character* data type, and they are concatenated to form composite index keys. For example, the fourth index expression is *DIVISION+LOCATION+ID_NUMBER*. The key field consists of a 15-character field with DIVISION in the first four characters, LOCATION in the next four, and ID_NUMBER in the last seven. The purpose of the composite index is to order the data file on both primary and secondary keys.

Opening Data and Index Files (FAOPEN)

The FAOPEN subroutine, which opens the fixed-asset data file and the index files, is called at the start of each program. Because the programs in the system are designed to operate in a stand-alone mode to facilitate testing, each program calls this subroutine. Using a subroutine eliminates the necessity of including the code for these tasks in each program. Using a subroutine also simplifies modification of the system.

Adding or deleting an index file requires only a change to FAOPEN; from then on, all programs in the system open the database and use new indexes. The flowchart for FAOPEN is shown in figure 6.8. Code for this subroutine is provided in listing 6.2.

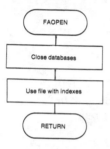

Fig. 6.8. Flowchart for the subroutine FAOPEN.

The FAOPEN and FAINDEX programs make it easier to modify and use indexes in the system. The index files are created with FAINDEX and opened with FAOPEN; changes to these subroutines affect the whole system. The only other changes that have to be made in the system when an index is changed are the specific SEEK or FIND commands that use the indexes.

Managing the System Memory File

Before we develop the main programs for the fixed asset tracking system, we need to set up a file to hold the system memory variables. And we'll need a program that allows users at Smith and Jones Corporation to edit these memory variables when the system is installed or when changes are needed.

The system memory file FAMEM.MEM holds five variables: FAPSETUP, FAPMARGIN, FAPRESET, FISCAL_YR, and FATITLE. These memory variables are used by the programs that print reports and calculate depreciation. FAPSETUP contains a printer setup string, such as a command to put your printer into compressed print mode or letter-quality print mode. That string is sent to the printer whenever a report is printed. FAPMARGIN specifies the left margin for reports. FISCAL_YR contains the ending date of the fiscal year. FATITLE contains the name of the system. FAPRESET contains a string to send to the printer after a report is completed to reset the printer to its default mode. Figure 6.9 shows the contents of the memory file.

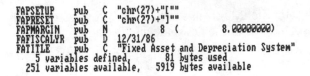

```
FAPSETUP    pub   C   "chr(27)+"["""
FAPRESET    pub   C   "chr(27)+"]"""
FAPMARGIN   pub   N           8  (         8.00000000)
FAFISCALYR  pub   D   12/31/86
FATITLE     pub   C   "Fixed Asset and Depreciation System"
    5 variables defined,        81 bytes used
  251 variables available,    5919 bytes available
```

Fig. 6.9. Contents of the file FAMEM.MEM.

The user chooses the Edit System Memory Variables option from the System
Maintenance Menu (see "Creating a Menu System") to change these system
parameters. Figure 6.10 shows the Edit System Memory Variables screen.

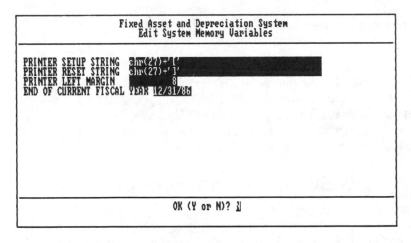

Fig. 6.10. Screen for changing the system memory variables.

The program FAMEM enables the user to edit the memory variables stored in
FAMEM.MEM. This program is used to adjust the fixed-asset tracking system when it
is installed, when a new printer is purchased, or when the fiscal year changes. Figure
6.11 shows the flowchart of the program. Code for the program is shown in
listing 6.3.

FAMEM is a straightforward program. First, the FILE function is used to determine
whether a file named FAMEM.MEM already exists. If so, the memory-variable values
are restored from that file and the FAPSETUP strings are padded with blanks to 80
characters. (When FAPSETUP and FAPRESET are stored to the file FAMEM.MEM,
trailing blanks are removed with the TRIM function.) If the file is not found, the title
is placed in FATITLE and the other variables are initialized with "dummy" values so
that the GET statements in the main loop will work properly.

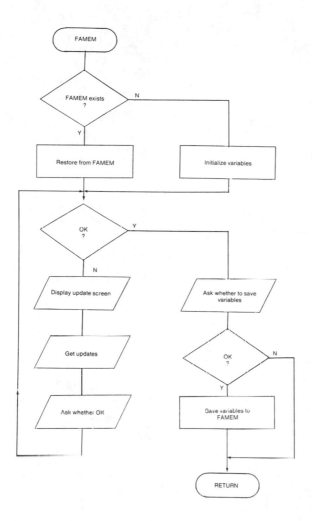

Fig. 6.11. Flowchart of the program FAMEM.

FAMEM calls the subroutine BORDERS, which is called by many of the programs in the fixed-asset tracking system. BORDERS clears the data and command areas of the screen and redraws the title and border. For a discussion and a listing of BORDERS, see the section "Designing a Consistent User Interface" in Chapter 3.

After the call to BORDERS, the main loop is executed. In this loop the current values of the memory variables are displayed, and the user's changes are entered. The loop is repeated until the user presses *Y* to confirm the entries.

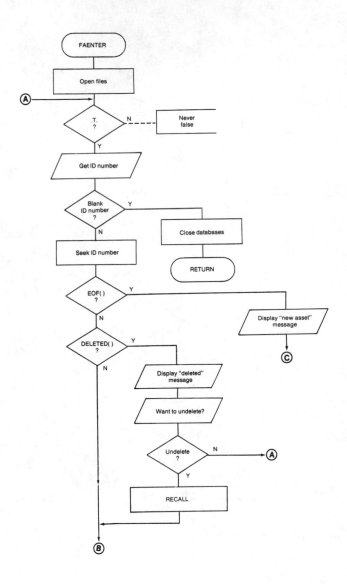

Fig. 6.12. Flowchart of the program FAENTER.

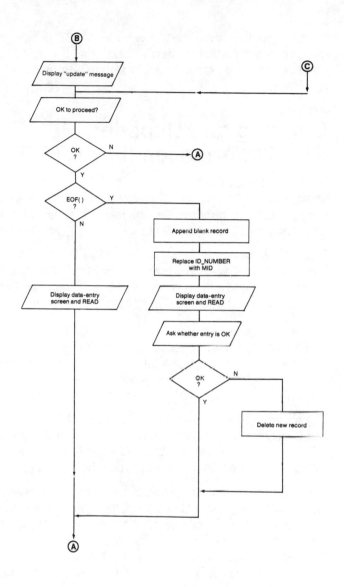

Then the program trims the blanks from FAPSETUP, and prompts the user for one more confirmation that the new values should be saved. FAMEM then saves the changes if the user presses *Y*, and execution returns to the main-menu program.

Entering and Updating Asset Information (FAENTER)

A single program, FAENTER, is used both to enter new asset information and to update existing information. The asset whose record is to be entered or updated must be specified by ID number. The program selects the enter or the update function, depending on whether the ID number that the user enters is found in the file.

Figure 6.12 shows a flowchart of FAENTER. This program is designed for entry or update of several asset records in one session. The body of the program is a loop that is exited only when the user enters a blank ID number. Each time through the loop the user can enter or update information on one asset.

The program does not use EDIT or APPEND, because those interactive commands give the user too much freedom to enter or change data without the verification and data checking that can be built into a custom data-entry program. Instead, FAENTER uses @ . . . SAY . . . GET commands and the APPEND BLANK command to allow data entry into the specified asset record.

The program code is shown in listing 6.4. FAENTER begins by opening the data file and displaying the logo on-screen. Then execution enters the main loop, which is a "do forever" loop controlled by a DO WHILE .T. command. An EXIT command transfers execution out of the loop when the user enters a blank ID number.

The data-entry and update program first requests the asset ID number, as shown in figure 6.13. If the user enters a blank ID number, then the loop is exited, the databases are closed, and execution returns to the calling program. If the ID number is not blank, the SEEK command is used to find a record containing the specified ID number. If no such record is found, the message *Entering New Asset* is displayed. If a record containing the ID number is found, the program then checks to see whether it has been deleted.

If the record with the specified asset ID number has been deleted, the user is asked whether the record should be "undeleted" (see fig. 6.14). If the record with the specified asset ID number has *not* been deleted, then the steps described in this paragraph are not performed. If the user presses *Y*, then the record is recalled and the update continues; if the user presses *N* or presses the Enter key to accept the N displayed on-screen, then execution transfers to the top of the loop for another ID number. This safety check prevents the user from entering a new active asset record with the same ID number as an existing deleted one.

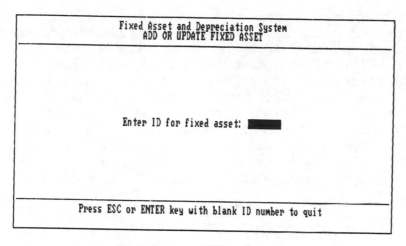

Fig. 6.13. Screen for entering asset ID number.

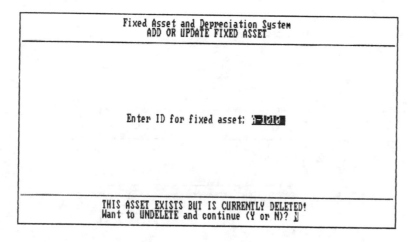

Fig. 6.14. Screen asking whether the user wants to undelete and continue.

If the specified asset is found and is not deleted, or if the user just undeleted it using the previous screen, then the message *Updating Existing Account* is displayed, and the program asks whether the user wants to proceed to enter or update this asset, as shown in figure 6.15. If the user does not want to proceed, execution returns to the top of the loop and the user can enter a new ID number. This final prompt gives the user a chance to correct the number if a mistake was made, such as choosing the wrong record to update.

If the record is being updated, the program calls the subroutine FAASTSCR to display the data-entry screen and accept the user's changes as in figure 6.16. When data entry is finished, execution returns to FAENTER. The user can change the contents of any field except ID_NUMBER. This field cannot be changed because it is the system's unique identification of the asset; allowing changes could result in duplicate ID numbers. To change the ID number of an asset, users must go to the System Maintenance menu and delete the asset's record, then reenter the asset information under a new ID number. Items the user can change, which are highlighted on the screen in figure 6.16, include the description, serial number, asset type, division and location of the asset, in-service date, cost, depreciation method, asset life, and salvage value. Figure 6.16 displays information about a Toyota Corolla owned by Smith and Jones Corporation.

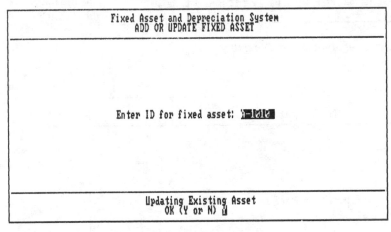

Fig. 6.15. Screen for confirming the asset ID.

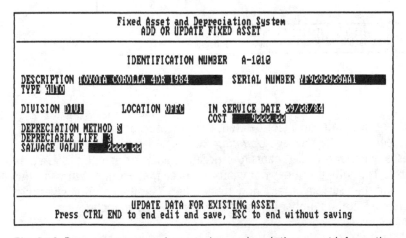

Fig. 6.16. Data-entry screen for entering and updating asset information.

If a new asset record is being added to the system, a blank record is appended to the file and the subroutine FAASTSCR is called. That subroutine displays the data-entry screen and accepts the user's input. When data entry is finished, execution returns to FAENTER, which verifies that the user wants to add this record to the database. If the user does not want to add this record, it is deleted. Execution then returns to the top of the loop. Figure 6.17 shows the data-entry screen for adding a new asset.

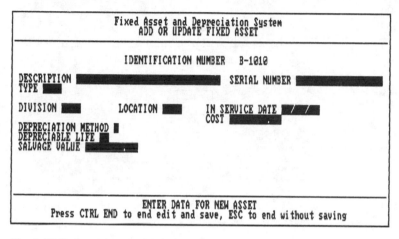

Fig. 6.17. Data-entry screen for adding a new asset.

The subroutine FAASTSCR creates the screen display shown in figure 6.17. The code for this subroutine is shown in listing 6.5. The FAASTSCR subroutine is a set of @ . . . SAY . . . GET commands that display the data for the current record in the asset database. FAASTSCR is used for both data entry and display of the asset information, and is called by other programs in the fixed-asset tracking system.

Querying the Database for Asset Information

The fixed-asset tracking system contains two programs for querying the database. The first program displays data for a single asset in a format similar to that of the data-entry screen shown in figure 6.17. The second program displays a list of assets, which the user can "browse" through to find a desired piece of information.

The Asset-Query Program (FAQUERY)

The asset-query program, FAQUERY, presents the data for an asset specified by ID number. The flowchart for FAQUERY is shown in figure 6.18. The body of the

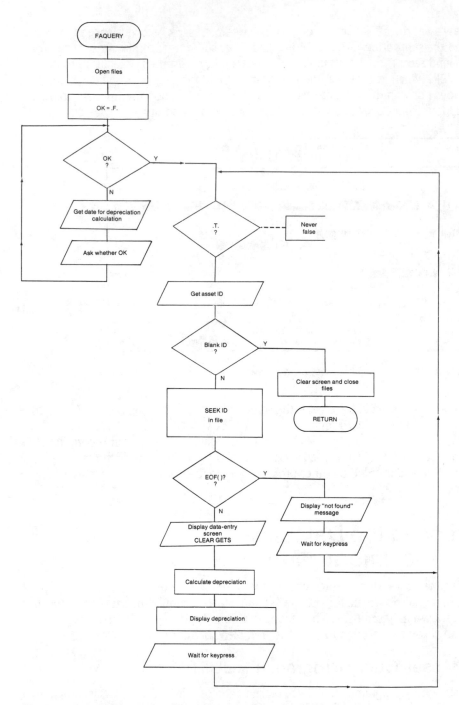

Fig. 6.18. Flowchart of the program FAQUERY.

program is a loop that accepts an asset ID number, and then displays the data for that asset. The loop is repeated until the user enters a blank asset ID number.

Program code for FAQUERY is shown in listing 6.6. The program calls FAOPEN, which opens the files; then FAQUERY displays the program logo at the top of the screen, and execution passes to the main loop.

The program first gets the asset ID number from the user. If the field is left blank, then the loop is exited, the program closes the data files, and execution returns to the calling program.

But if the ID number is not blank, a SEEK command is used to find a record containing the ID number. If the ID number is not found, then the warning message *ASSET NOT FOUND* is displayed, the program pauses for a keypress, and execution returns to the top of the loop for entry of a new ID number.

If the ID number is found, FAQUERY clears the data area and calls FAASTSCR to display the data contained in the file. Then FAQUERY calls subroutine FADEPR, which calculates depreciation for the asset, and the program displays the results (see fig. 6.19).

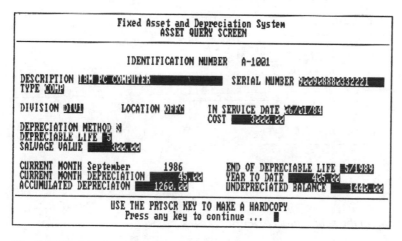

Fig. 6.19. Screen to query asset data.

Calculating Depreciation (FADEPR)

FADEPR calculates depreciation for the current asset on a specified date. The depreciation information that is displayed includes the date when the asset will be fully depreciated; the current month, year-to-date, and accumulated depreciation for the asset; and the balance remaining to be depreciated. This information is displayed at the bottom of the data area of the screen. For example, figure 6.19 shows information about an IBM PC owned by Smith and Jones Corporation.

The flowchart for FADEPR is shown in figure 6.20, and the code is shown in listing 6.7. FADEPR is also called by the browse-list-of-assets program and the depreciation-report program.

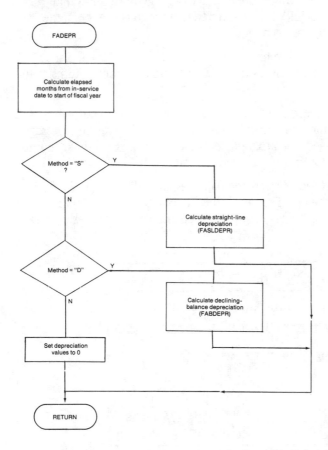

Fig. 6.20. Flowchart of the subroutine FADEPR.

FADEPR first calculates the number of months that have elapsed between the in-service date and the specified date, and the number of months between the start of the fiscal year and the specified date.

A DO CASE structure then is used to select the appropriate method for calculating depreciation; the method is selected according to the value in the field DEPR_MTHD, which is the depreciation-method flag for the asset. The program is currently set up to calculate straight-line depreciation and declining-balance depreciation, but it can be expanded to calculate depreciation by other methods as well.

Each calculation is a separate subroutine called from FADEPR. Straight-line depreciation is handled by the subroutine FASLDEPR. Declining-balance depreciation is handled by the subroutine FADBDEPR.

Calculating Straight-Line Depreciation (FASLDEPR)

The FASLDEPR subroutine calculates depreciation based on the cost, salvage value, the life of the asset, the number of months that have elapsed since the in-service date, and the number of months that have elapsed since the start of the fiscal year. The flowchart for the straight-line depreciation subroutine is shown in figure 6.21. Program code is shown in listing 6.8.

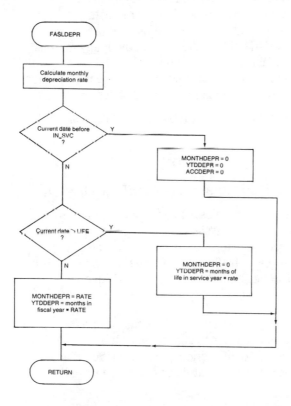

Fig. 6.21. Flowchart of the subroutine FASLDEPR.

Straight-line depreciation is calculated by dividing the amount to be depreciated (the cost minus the salvage value) by the life of the asset. Accumulated depreciation is this amount multiplied by the elapsed time. The year-to-date depreciation value is the monthly rate multiplied by the number of months since the start of the fiscal year.

The actual calculations are performed within a DO CASE structure that determines whether the current date is before the in-service date, after the end of the depreciable life, or within the depreciable life of the asset. The calculations are different for each of these cases.

If MTOT<1, then the current date is before the asset-acquisition date and all depreciation amounts are zero.

If MTOT>12∗LIFE, then the current date is after the end of the asset's depreciable life. In this case, the current-worth depreciation is zero and the accumulated depreciation is equal to the cost minus the salvage value. The year-to-date depreciation depends on whether the depreciable life ended after the start of the current fiscal year. The expression MTOT−12∗LIFE determines how many months have elapsed since the end of the depreciable life. The expression MAX(0,(MYTD−(MTOT−12∗LIFE))) subtracts that value from the number of months year-to-date in the fiscal year to determine the number of months of depreciation.

If neither of these two conditions applies, the asset is in the middle of its depreciable life, and the calculations are straightforward.

Calculating Declining-Balance Depreciation (FADBDEPR)

The FADBDEPR subroutine calculates depreciation based on the amount to be depreciated, the salvage value, the asset life, the acceleration factor, the number of months that have elapsed since the in-service date, and the number of months that have elapsed since the start of the fiscal year. The flowchart for the declining-balance depreciation subroutine is shown in figure 6.22. Program code is provided in listing 6.9.

The declining-balance calculation is more complicated than the straight-line calculation. The depreciation is calculated as a percentage rate times the undepreciated balance remaining at the start of the period. This calculation is an iterative one that must be repeated once for every year that has elapsed since the in-service date.

This subroutine calculates depreciation in the first year, based on the actual number of months following the in-service date. This is the convention used by Smith and Jones corporation for their financial statements. Many businesses use a half-year convention: assets purchased in the first six months of the year are depreciated for a full year, and assets purchased in the last six months are depreciated for a half year. The calculation

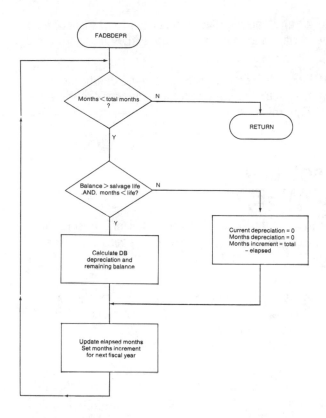

Fig. 6.22. Flowchart of the subroutine FADBDEPR.

of the number of months in the first fiscal year would have to be changed to accommodate this convention.

The subroutine first initializes the depreciation variables and calculates the number of months following startup in the first fiscal year. Next, the subroutine enters a loop to calculate the declining-balance depreciation in each fiscal year between the in-service date and the current date. The DO WHILE command at the top of the loop checks whether the end of the life has been reached. The code in the loop calculates declining-balance depreciation for one fiscal year at a time, from the first fiscal year through the specified date. This calculation is done by the IF clause of the IF statement. If the initial cost is depreciated to the salvage value or the end of the asset's depreciable life is reached, the loop is cut short by the ELSE clause of the IF statement.

The bottom of the loop contains two statements that update the months of depreciation already calculated (XM) and the number of months in the next fiscal year (XM1). The loop continues until the asset has been depreciated to its salvage value or to the end of its depreciable life, or until the specified number of months (specified by MTOT) is reached. After the depreciation loop is finished, the FADBDEPR subroutine returns control to the caller.

After control is returned to FADEPR, the program waits for a keystroke to indicate that the user is through looking at the current asset, and then goes back to the top of the loop to wait for a new asset ID number.

The Browse-Asset-List Program (FABROWSE)

The asset-by-asset query described in the preceding section is sufficient most of the time, but sometimes users need to browse through the assets in a particular order to find the desired information. The program for browsing the asset list, FABROWSE, is designed to accomplish this.

The FABROWSE program implements a full-screen browse capability for the fixed-assets database. Two browse screens display physical information and depreciation information for the list of assets. (These screens are described in detail under "Scrolling the Browse Screens.")

Our consideration of the FABROWSE program begins with a quick look at the code, followed by a consideration of subroutines FAORDER, FASUBSET, and SCROLLER. A flowchart of the browse-asset-list program is shown in figure 6.23. Program code is shown in listing 6.10.

The program begins by opening the files with FAOPEN and initializing data values for the browse. FABROWSE then gets the date for depreciation calculations from the user (fig. 6.24). FABROWSE next calls the subroutine FAORDER to set the browse order (that is, to select the active index file). FAORDER presents the user with a menu from which to choose a sort order for the records.

Then FABROWSE calls the subroutine FASUBSET, which begins by asking whether the user wants to select all the records in the database or a subset of the records. If the user wants a subset, the subroutine uses the MODIFY QUERY command to define the assets to be included in the browse list. A series of screens takes the user through the steps to filter the database.

After the database has been filtered, execution returns to the main program. FABROWSE enters a loop that displays the next browse screen and waits for the user to press a key. The code within the loop clears the screen and displays the heading for the current screen (the first or second browse screen). A nested loop displays a screen full of records. The data for the current screen (the first or second browse screen) is

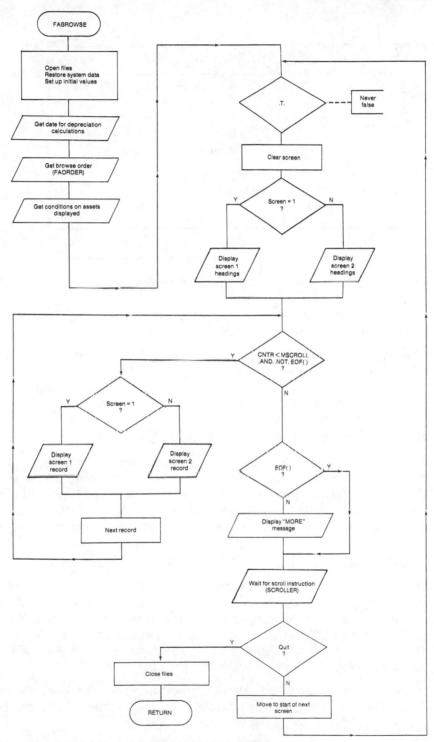

Fig. 6.23. Flowchart of the program FABROWSE.

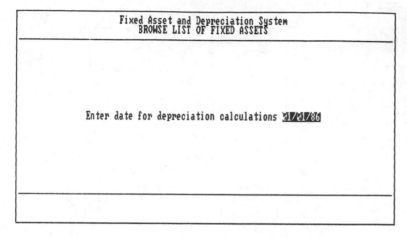

Fig. 6.24. Screen to enter date for depreciation calculations.

displayed record by record until the screen is full or the end of the file is reached. The browse screens are shown in figures 6.32 and 6.33.

After finishing the current screen display, the program calls subroutine SCROLLER, which accepts instructions to scroll the list up or down and to move between the first and second browse screens. If the user presses Esc, the program exits the loop, closes the files, and returns to the menu.

Setting the Browse Order (FAORDER)

The subroutine FAORDER presents the user with a menu for choosing the order of the assets (see fig. 6.25). (FAORDER is also called by the programs that print reports.) The user has seven choices, including the six index orders and the record-number order (no index). Table 6.2 explains the seven choices. Figure 6.26 shows the flowchart of the FAORDER subroutine, and program code is shown in listing 6.11.

Limiting the Browse to Specified Assets (FASUBSET)

The FASUBSET subroutine makes use of dBASE III Plus's powerful MODIFY QUERY command to allow the user to specify a subset of the asset records. The subroutine is very simple, first displaying a screen of instructions, and then performing the MODIFY QUERY command. The result is a sophisticated asset selection capability within the fixed-asset tracking system. Figure 6.27 shows a flowchart of the FASUBSET subroutine. Program code is shown in listing 6.12.

In the first screen displayed by FASUBSET, users are asked whether they want to display all assets starting with the first asset in the sorted order, or whether they want to limit the display to specified assets (see fig. 6.28).

Table 6.2
Setting the Order To Browse or Print Asset Records

Order By	Explanation
Record number	The sequence that the assets were entered into the file
ID number	List by asset ID number. Useful for looking up assets.
TYPE	List by type of asset and by ID number within type
LOCATION	List by location and by ID number within location
DIVISION	List by division, by location, and by ID number within division
In-service date	List by date placed in service
End date	List by end of depreciable life

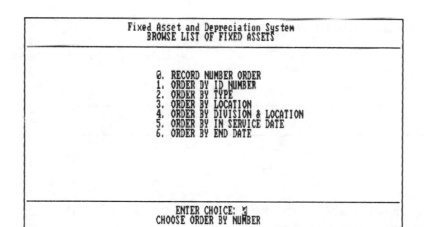

Fig. 6.25. The user can select one of seven sort orders to browse the list of assets.

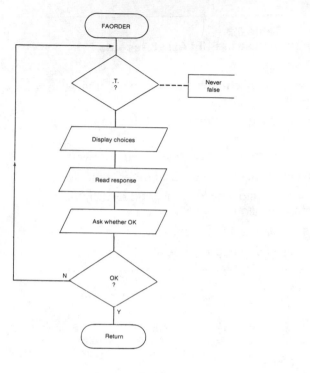

Fig. 6.26. Flowchart of the subroutine FAORDER.

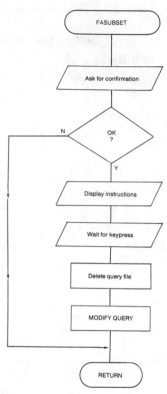

Fig. 6.27. Flowchart of the subroutine FASUBSET.

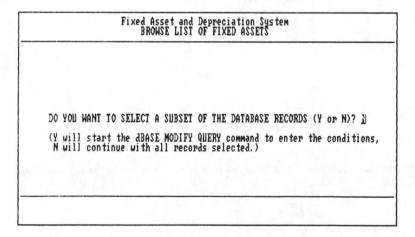

```
                Fixed Asset and Depreciation System
                     BROWSE LIST OF FIXED ASSETS
_____




    DO YOU WANT TO SELECT A SUBSET OF THE DATABASE RECORDS (Y or N)? N

    (Y will start the dBASE MODIFY QUERY command to enter the conditions,
    N will continue with all records selected.)




_____
```

Fig. 6.28. The user gets a chance to select the assets to display with the browse screens.

A user who chooses to limit the browse display to specified assets is presented with a screen of instructions (see fig. 6.29). If the user presses *Y* to continue, the dBASE interactive query building command is invoked to define the limits the user wants to place on the assets being displayed. This command is the most complex command that the user has to master in this system. Figure 6.30 shows the main screen for this command.

```
              Fixed Asset and Depreciation System
                   BROWSE LIST OF FIXED ASSETS

This command uses dBASE III Plus's built in MODIFY QUERY command to
build the filter. When the MODIFY QUERY screen appears, enter the filter
conditions in the space provided.

Building a query consists of four steps, repeated until the query is
complete. First, a field in the database is selected. Second, a logical
condition is specified for the field. Third, an expression is specified
to finish the condition placed on the selected field. Fourth, if another
condition is to be specified, the connection (.AND. or .OR.) between this
condition and the next is specified. These four steps are repeated once
for each condition to be placed on the data retrieval.

When finished defining the subset of assets to be displayed, be sure
to exit the interactive query command using the EXIT SAVE option. If the
abandon option is used to exit, the conditions will be discarded.

                    Press any key to continue ■
```

Fig. 6.29. Instructions on limiting the browse display to specified assets.

```
Set Filter          Nest         Display        Exit  9:48:13 PM

 Field Name
 Operator
 Constant/Expression
 Connect

 Line Number      1
```

Line	Field	Operator	Constant/Expression	Connect
1				
2				
3				
4				
5				
6				
7				

```
MODIFY QUERY    <C:> FASUBSET.QRY           Opt: 1/2
      Position selection bar - ↑↓.  Select - ↵.  Leave menu - ↔.
               Select a field name for the filter condition.
```

Fig. 6.30. The screen for selecting a subset of records for display by the browse program.

Building a query consists of four steps, repeated until the query is complete. First, a field in the database is selected. Second, a logical condition is specified for the field. Third, an expression is specified to finish the condition placed on the selected field. Fourth, if another condition is to be specified, the connection (.AND. or .OR.) between this condition and the next is specified. These four steps are repeated once for each condition to be placed on the data retrieval. Figure 6.31 shows the conditions required to retrieve data for assets owned by division 1 of Smith and Jones Corporation and located at the division office.

```
Set Filter              Nest           Display           Exit  09:58:28 PM
┌──────────────────────────────────────────────────────────┐
│ Field Name            LOCATION                             │
│ Operator              Matches                              │
│ Constant/Expression   "OFFC"                               │
│ Connect                                                    │
│                                                            │
│ Line Number           2                                    │
└──────────────────────────────────────────────────────────┘
```

Line	Field	Operator	Constant/Expression	Connect
1	DIVISION	Matches	"DIV1"	.AND.
2	LOCATION	Matches	"OFFC"	
3				
4				
5				
6				
7				

```
MODIFY QUERY     |<C:>|FASUBSET.QRY         |Opt: 4/5
         Position selection bar - ↑↓.  Select - ◄┘.  Leave menu - ↔.
           Select a logical connector for the filter condition.
```

Fig. 6.31. Conditions for selecting assets owned by division 1 and located at the office.

Scrolling the Browse Screens (SCROLLER)

The browse program "opens a window" on the selected list of assets. This window consists of two screens, shown in figures 6.32 and 6.33. The first screen displays information about the identification of the asset and its owner and physical location. This screen also shows the date when the asset was placed in service and the date when the asset will be fully depreciated. The second screen displays information concerning the asset's cost and depreciation. The ID number is displayed for identification, followed by the cost, salvage value, the depreciation method, the depreciable life, depreciation for the current month and the year-to-date, and accumulated depreciation.

```
┌─────────────────────────────────────────────────────────────────┐
│              Fixed Asset and Depreciation System                  │
│                BROWSE LIST OF FIXED ASSETS                        │
│                                                                   │
│ ID      DESCRIPT          SERIAL          TYPE DIV  LOC  IN SRVC END SRVC │
│ ─────────────────────────────────────────────────────────────── │
│ 1011-1  dBASE III Plus Sof 919191         SOFT CORP OFFC 03/01/86  2/1991 │
│ 123     Robot - R2D2      1234567890123   P&E  DIV2 PLT5 04/30/86  3/1994 │
│ 3434    Ledger book       11323           BOOK CORP OFFC 04/22/86  3/1988 │
│ A-1001  IBM PC COMPUTER   909908880332221 COMP DIV1 OFFC 06/01/84  5/1989 │
│ A-1004  17' rowboat & oars 1121           VHCL R&D  LAKE 04/08/86  3/1996 │
│ A-1010  TOYOTA COROLLA 4DR YF9090909AA1   AUTO DIV1 OFFC 09/08/84  8/1987 │
│ A-1100  Desk                              FURN DIV1 PLT1 01/30/82 12/1986 │
│ AJ-436  Machine Tool      aj-123-6116     MACH DIV1 PLT1 06/30/80  5/1988 │
│ B-0001  Pool Filter       1212121-9999    EQUP R&D  LAKE 06/01/81  5/1986 │
│ B-1010  Store Building                    BUIL SALE CHI  05/31/80  4/2010 │
│ B-77777 Forklift Truck    bd-98989898989  VHCL DIV2 PLT2 02/15/83  1/1988 │
│ C-1     File Cabinet      none            FURN CORP OFFC 01/01/60 12/1967 │
│ C-1010  Store Fixtures                    SALE SALE CHI  01/01/80 12/1984 │
│                                                                   │
│                          * MORE *                                 │
│ PRESS: ARROW KEYS, PGUP ,PGDN, ENTER, HOME (BOF), or END (EOF); ESC to quit │
└─────────────────────────────────────────────────────────────────┘
```

Fig. 6.32. *Browse display of asset identification and physical data.*

```
┌─────────────────────────────────────────────────────────────────┐
│          Fixed Asset and Depreciation System                      │
│            BROWSE LIST OF FIXED ASSETS     DEPR DATE 08/17/86     │
│                                                                   │
│ ID         COST      SALVAGE M LI START  MONTH DEPR  YTD DEPR   ACC DEPR │
│ ─────────────────────────────────────────────────────────────── │
│ 1011-1      695.00      0.00 S  5 03/86      11.58     69.50      69.50 │
│ 123     125345.69  12534.57 S  8 04/86    1175.12   5875.58    5875.58 │
│ 3434        13.95      0.00 S  2 04/86       0.58      2.91       2.91 │
│ A-1001    3000.00    300.00 S  5 06/84      45.00    360.00    1215.00 │
│ A-1004    1200.00    120.00 S 10 04/86       9.00     45.00      45.00 │
│ A-1010    9000.00   2000.00 S  3 09/84     194.44   1555.56    4666.67 │
│ A-1100    1500.00    150.00 S  5 01/82      22.50    180.00    1260.00 │
│ AJ-436   25400.00   2540.00 S  8 06/80     238.12   1905.00   17859.38 │
│ B-0001    5500.00      0.00 S  5 06/81       0.00    458.33    5500.00 │
│ B-1010  250000.00      0.00 D 30 05/80     779.15   6233.23   69236.17 │
│ B-77777  35000.00   5000.00 S  5 02/83     500.00   4000.00   21500.00 │
│ C-1        150.00      0.00 S  8 01/60       0.00      0.00     150.00 │
│ C-1010   10000.00      0.00 S  5 01/80       0.00      0.00   10000.00 │
│                                                                   │
│                          * MORE *                                 │
│ PRESS: ARROW KEYS, PGUP ,PGDN, ENTER, HOME (BOF), or END (EOF); ESC to quit │
└─────────────────────────────────────────────────────────────────┘
```

Fig. 6.33. *Browse display of asset depreciation data.*

The SCROLLER subroutine, which is called by the browse-asset-list program, accepts a keystroke from the user indicating the screen should be scrolled. The flowchart for the SCROLLER subroutine is shown in figure 6.34. Code for the subroutine is provided in listing 6.13.

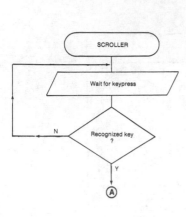

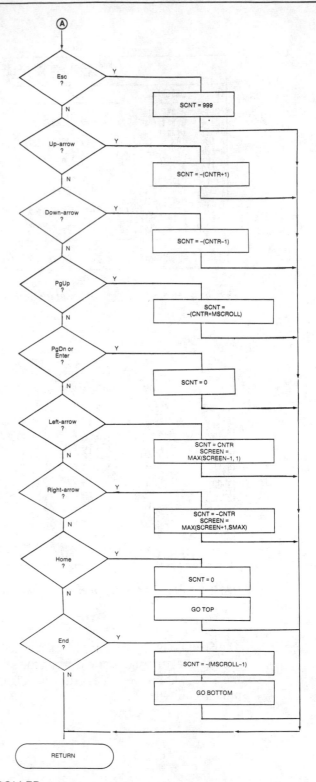

Fig. 6.34. Flowchart of the subroutine SCROLLER.

SCROLLER uses the INKEY command to read a keystroke from the user. The subroutine ignores all keystrokes except the arrow keys, PgUp, PgDn, Home, End, Enter, and Esc. These 10 keys, listed in table 6.3, are used to control the scrolling of the display through the list of records and the switching between the first and second browse screens. When the user presses any of these keys except for Esc, execution returns to the top of the screen-display loop, and the selected data screen is displayed. After accepting one of these ten keys, the subroutine uses a DO CASE statement to return the proper values to the main program.

Important note: *In some early versions of dBASE III Plus, the INKEY function apparently does not return the proper scan-code value for the left-arrow key. If that problem exists for your (or your client's) copy of dBASE III Plus, you will need to devise a work-around.*

SCROLLER returns to the calling program a value in SCNT indicating the number of records to skip forward or backward in the file before displaying the next screen. If the Esc key is pressed, indicating that the user wants to exit from the scrolling display, a value of 999 is returned. If the Home or End key is pressed, SCROLLER repositions the file pointer with a GO TOP or GO BOT command, then returns the value of SCNT needed to display one full screen at the beginning or end of the file. SCROLLER also returns a value in SCREEN indicating the screen to be used. The subroutine accepts left- and right-arrow commands to switch between multiple screens for the same records. A left arrow causes SCROLLER to decrement the value in SCREEN (with a minimum of one), and a right arrow causes SCROLLER to increment value in SCREEN (up to a specified maximum).

Table 6.3
Keys Used To Change the Browse Screens

Key	Function
←, →	Switch from the first screen to the second screen the same assets
↑, ↓	Scroll list of assets by one line up or down
PgUp	Display preceding full screen of assets
PgDn	Display next full screen of assets
Home	Display a screen starting at the beginning of the file
End	Display a screen at the end of the file
Enter	Same as PgDn
Esc	Close files and return to the Data Entry and Query menu

Figures 6.35 and 6.36 illustrate two scrolling techniques. Pressing the down-arrow key moves the display up one line on the screen and displays the next asset at the bottom of the display (see fig. 6.35). Pressing PgDn displays the next full screen of assets in the list (see fig. 6.36).

```
         Fixed Asset and Depreciation System
              BROWSE LIST OF FIXED ASSETS

 ID       DESCRIPT         SERIAL            TYPE DIV  LOC   IN SRVC END SRVC
 ───      ────────         ──────            ──── ───  ───   ─────── ────────
 123      Robot - R2D2     1234567890123     P&E  DIV2 PLT5  04/30/86  3/1994
 3434     Ledger book      11323             BOOK CORP OFFC  04/22/86  3/1988
 A-1001   IBM PC COMPUTER  900908880332221   COMP DIV1 OFFC  06/01/84  5/1989
 A-1004   17' rowboat & oars 1121            VHCL R&D  LAKE  04/08/86  3/1996
 A-1010   TOYOTA COROLLA 4DR YF9090909AA1    AUTO DIV1 OFFC  09/08/84  8/1987
 A-1100   Desk                               FURN DIV1 PLT1  01/30/82 12/1986
 AJ-436   Machine Tool     aj-123-6116       MACH DIV1 PLT1  06/30/80  5/1988
 B-0001   Pool Filter      1212121-9999      EQUP R&D  LAKE  06/01/81  5/1986
 B-1010   Store Building                     BUIL SALE CHI   05/31/80  4/2010
 B-77777  Forklift Truck   bd-98989898989    VHCL DIV2 PLT2  02/15/83  1/1988
 C-1      File Cabinet     none              FURN CORP OFFC  01/01/60 12/1967
 C-1010   Store Fixtures                     SALE SALE CHI   01/01/80 12/1984
 C-2      File Cabinet     none              FURN DIV1 OFFC  01/01/60 12/1967
                            * MORE *
 PRESS: ARROW KEYS, PGUP ,PGDN, ENTER, HOME (BOF), or END (EOF); ESC to quit
```

Fig. 6.35. Pressing the down-arrow key once displays the next record in the list of assets.

```
         Fixed Asset and Depreciation System
              BROWSE LIST OF FIXED ASSETS

 ID       DESCRIPT         SERIAL            TYPE DIV  LOC   IN SRVC END SRVC
 ───      ────────         ──────            ──── ───  ───   ─────── ────────
 C-3      File Cabinet     none              FURN DIV2 OFFC  01/01/60 12/1967
 KK-11    Typewriter       IBM-100100011001  EQUP DIV2 PLT5  01/01/83 12/1987
 KK-112   Copy Machine     112233445566      EQUP DIV2 PLT5  05/01/86  4/1991
 P-1001   Printer          EPSON FX185       COMP CORP OFFC  01/01/86 12/1990
 S-1001   Shelving                           FURN DIV1 PLT1  01/01/85 12/1994




 PRESS: ARROW KEYS, PGUP ,PGDN, ENTER, HOME (BOF), or END (EOF); ESC to quit
```

Fig. 6.36. Pressing PgDn displays the next full screen of assets in the list.

The display cannot move past the beginning or the end of the file. If a key is pressed that would move the display off the end of the file, the display stops at the beginning or end of the file. When finished with browsing, the user presses Esc to return to the Data Entry and Query menu.

A user who wants to produce a quick printout of any of the browse screens can use the PrtSc key. However, this method is only sufficient for *ad hoc* inquiries involving a few assets. In the next section, we look at Jim Jones's need for hard-copy lists of assets and management reports about assets and depreciation.

Printing Reports

The reporting component of the fixed-asset tracking system produces a variety of reports in two basic formats: a list showing all the information about each asset in the report, or a list showing just the depreciation for each asset. The variety in reporting possibilities comes from the ability to specify the sort order and select a subset of the records.

Printing Fixed-Asset Reports (FAREPORT)

The first report program, FAREPORT, generates a fixed-asset list in one of seven sort orders (see table 6.2). The printed report shows all the asset information contained in the file, plus one calculated item: the month and year of the end of the asset's depreciation life. The flowchart for the FAREPORT program is shown in figure 6.37. Program code is shown in listing 6.14.

The information in the report is printed out as a list with subtotals. Because the information for each asset comes from the current record in the FIXASSET file and no subroutines are required to calculate values, the dBASE report generator can be used to build the report formats. The desired report is then chosen by executing the appropriate REPORT FORM command in the FAREPORT program.

The program FAREPORT is all straight-line code with no loops. It prints one report and returns execution to the menu. The program begins by opening data files with FAOPEN, restoring the system memory variables from FAMEM, and displaying the logo on-screen.

Next, FAREPORT calls the subroutine FAORDER, which displays the screen in figure 6.38 and gets the desired sort order from the user. FAREPORT then calls FASUBSET, which prompts the user to indicate whether just a subset of the assets should be printed (see fig. 6.39). If so, the MODIFY QUERY command transfers execution to the dBASE interactive query facility so that the user can select the desired assets.

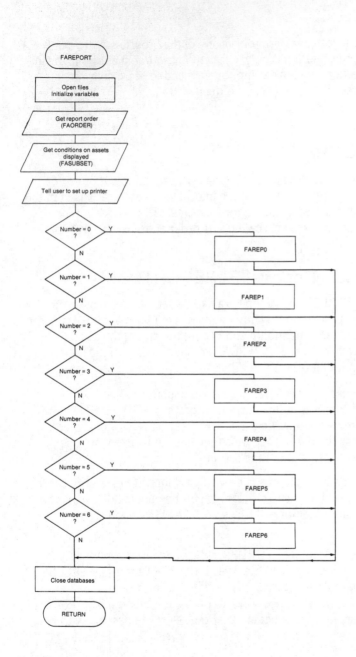

Fig. 6.37. Flowchart of the program FAREPORT.

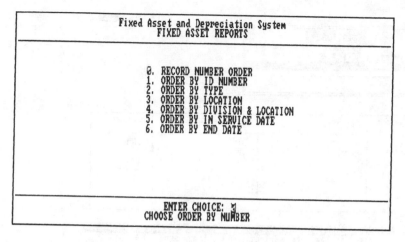

Fig. 6.38. Screen to let the user enter the report order for the asset list.

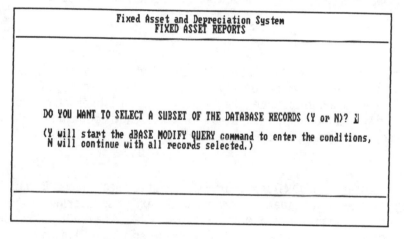

Fig. 6.39. Screen for selecting a subset of the asset records.

Filtering the database before printing is the same four-step process that is used to filter the database before browsing. This process includes specifying the field, the logical operator, the conditional constant or expression, and the logical connector (if any) between the current condition and the next one. Figure 6.40 shows the selection screen with the condition to select all division 1 assets at the division office.

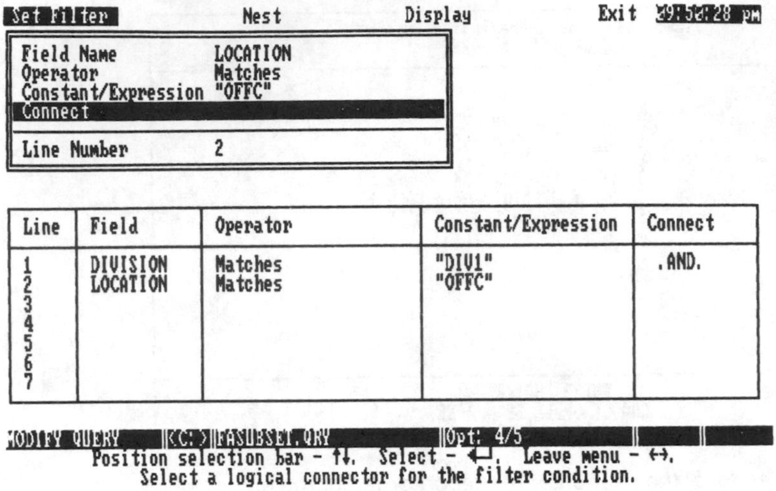

```
Set Filter           Nest          Display          Exit  09:58:28 pm
  Field Name         LOCATION
  Operator           Matches
  Constant/Expression "OFFC"
  Connect
  Line Number        2
```

Line	Field	Operator	Constant/Expression	Connect
1	DIVISION	Matches	"DIV1"	.AND.
2	LOCATION	Matches	"OFFC"	
3				
4				
5				
6				
7				

```
MODIFY QUERY      <C:> FASUBSET.QRY            Opt: 4/5
     Position selection bar - ↑↓.  Select - ◄┘.  Leave menu - ↔.
            Select a logical connector for the filter condition.
```

Fig. 6.40. The conditions for selecting assets owned by division 1 and located at the office.

After execution returns from FASUBSET, FAREPORT displays a message telling the user to turn on the printer and set it to the top of a page. After doing so, the user presses Y to tell the program to continue. The program prints the printer setup string restored from the system memory file and does a REPORT FORM command to print the selected report. After the report is finished, the program returns to the Report menu.

Note in listing 6.14 that FAREPORT uses a CASE statement to select a report form corresponding to the requested order. The reports for the fixed-asset tracking system have forms that differ in their titles, report breaks, and subtotals. As a result, a separate report format is needed for each desired report order, for a total of seven report formats.

Figures 6.41 through 6.47 give the report definitions for each of the seven report formats.

Report definitions for report FAREPO.FRM

Page title: Smith and Jones Corporation
                Fixed Asset Tracking System
                List of Fixed Assets

Page width: 132

Group on expression: -none-

COL	Contents	Heading	W	D	Tot
1	ID_number	;; ID;-------	7		
2	descript	;;DESCRIPTION ;------------------------------ (30 dashes)	30		
3	serial_no	;;SERIAL NUMBER ;------------------ (18 dashes)	18		
4	type	;ASSET; TYPE;-----	5		
5	serv_date	;IN-SERVICE; DATE;----------	10		
6	cost	; ORIGINAL; COST ;----------- (11 dashes)	11	2	Yes
7	salvage	; SALVAGE; VALUE ;----------- (11 dashes)	11	2	No
8	depr_mthd	;DEPR;METHOD;------	6		
9	depr_life	;DEPR.;LIFE;-----	5	0	No
10	STR(IIF(MONTH(serv_date)=1,12, MONTH(serv_date)-1),2) +'/'+SUBSTR(STR(YEAR(serv_date)+depr_life +IIF(month(serv_date)=1, -1,0),4),3,2)	;END OF;LIFE;------	6		

Fig. 6.41. Report format for record-number order.

Report definitions for report FAREP1.FRM

Page title: Smith and Jones Corporation
                 Fixed Asset Tracking System
                 Fixed Assets by ID Number

Page width: 132

Group on expression: -none-

COL	Contents	Heading	W	D	Tot
1	ID_number	;; ID;-------	7		
2	descript	;;DESCRIPTION ;------------------------------ (30 dashes)	30		
3	serial_no	;;SERIAL NUMBER ;------------------ (18 dashes)	18		
4	type	;ASSET; TYPE;-----	5		
5	serv_date	;IN-SERVICE; DATE;----------	10		
6	cost	; ORIGINAL; COST ;----------- (11 dashes)	11	2	Yes
7	salvage	; SALVAGE; VALUE ;----------- (11 dashes)	11	2	No
8	depr_mthd	;DEPR;METHOD;------	6		
9	depr_life	;DEPR.;LIFE;-----	5	0	No
10	STR(IIF(MONTH(serv_date)=1,12, MONTH(serv_date)-1),2) +'/'+SUBSTR(STR(YEAR(serv_date)+depr_life +IIF(month(serv_date)=1, -1,0),4),3,2)	;END OF;LIFE;------	6		

Fig. 6.42. Report format for ID-number order.

```
Report definitions for report FAREP2.FRM

Page title:     Smith and Jones Corporation
                Fixed Asset Tracking System
                Fixed Assets by Type
                ----------------------------

Page width:     132

Group on expression      type
Group heading            Asset Type:
Summary report only      No
Page eject after group   No
Sub-group on expression
Sub-group heading
```

COL	Contents	Heading	W	D	Tot
1	ID_number	;; ID;-------	7		
2	descript	;;DESCRIPTION ;------------------------------ (30 dashes)	30		
3	serial_no	;;SERIAL NUMBER ;------------------ (18 dashes)	18		
4	type	;ASSET; TYPE;-----	5		
5	serv_date	;IN-SERVICE; DATE;----------	10		
6	cost	; ORIGINAL; COST ;----------- (11 dashes)	11	2	Yes
7	salvage	; SALVAGE; VALUE ;----------- (11 dashes)	11	2	No
8	depr_mthd	;DEPR;METHOD;------	6		
9	depr_life	;DEPR.;LIFE;-----	5	0	No
10	STR(IIF(MONTH(serv_date)=1,12, MONTH(serv_date)-1),2) +'/'+SUBSTR(STR(YEAR(serv_date)+depr_life +IIF(month(serv_date)=1, -1,0),4),3,2)	;END OF;LIFE;------	6		

Fig. 6.43. Report format for order by type.

Report definitions for report FAREP3.FRM

```
Page title:       Smith and Jones Corporation
                  Fixed Asset Tracking System
                  Assets by Location
                  ----------------------------
```

Page width: 132

```
Group on expression      location
Group heading            Location:
Summary report only      No
Page eject after group   No
Sub-group on expression
Sub-group heading
```

COL	Contents	Heading	W	D	Tot
1	ID_number	;; ID;-------	7		
2	descript	;;DESCRIPTION ;------------------------------ (30 dashes)	30		
3	serial_no	;;SERIAL NUMBER ;------------------ (18 dashes)	18		
4	type	;ASSET; TYPE;-----	5		
5	serv_date	;IN-SERVICE; DATE ;---------- (10 dashes)	10		
6	cost	; ORIGINAL; COST ;----------- (11 dashes)	11	2	Yes
7	salvage	; SALVAGE; VALUE ;----------- (11 dashes)	11	2	No
8	depr_mthd	;DEPR;METHOD;------	6		
9	depr_life	;DEPR.;LIFE;-----	5	0	No
10	STR(IIF(MONTH(serv_date)=1,12, MONTH(serv_date)-1),2) +'/'+SUBSTR(STR(YEAR(serv_date)+depr_life +IIF(month(serv_date)=1, -1,0),4),3,2)	;END OF;LIFE;------	6		

Fig. 6.44. Report format for order by location.

Report definitions for report FAREP4.FRM

Page title: Fixed Asset Tracking System
                 List of Fixed Assets by Division
                 and Location

Page width: 132

Group on expression   division
Group heading   Division:
Summary report only   No
Page eject after group   No
Sub-group on expression location
Sub-group heading   Location:

COL	Contents	Heading	W	D	Tot
1	ID_number	;; ID;-------	7		
2	descript	;;DESCRIPTION ;------------------------------ (30 dashes)	30		
3	serial_no	;;SERIAL NUMBER ;------------------ (18 dashes)	18		
4	type	;ASSET; TYPE;-----	5		
5	serv_date	;IN-SERVICE; DATE ;---------- (10 dashes)	10		
6	cost	; ORIGINAL; COST ;----------- (11 dashes)	11	2	Yes
7	salvage	; SALVAGE; VALUE ;----------- (11 dashes)	11	2	No
8	depr_mthd	;DEPR;METHOD;------	6		
9	depr_life	;DEPR.;LIFE;-----	5	0	No
10	STR(IIF(MONTH(serv_date)=1,12, MONTH(serv_date)-1),2) +'/'+SUBSTR(STR(YEAR(serv_date)+depr_life +IIF(month(serv_date)=1, -1,0),4),3,2)	;END OF;LIFE;------	6		

Fig. 6.45. Report format for order by division and location.

Report definitions for report FAREP5.FRM

```
Page title:      Smith and Jones Corporation
                 Fixed Asset Tracking System
                 List of Fixed Assets by In Service Date
                 ----------------------------------------

Page width:      132

Group on expression      YEAR(serv_date)
Group heading            Year placed in service:
Summary report only      No
Page eject after group   No
Sub-group on expression
Sub-group heading
```

COL	Contents	Heading	W	D	Tot
1	ID_number	;; ID;-------	7		
2	descript	;;DESCRIPTION ;------------------------------ (30 dashes)	30		
3	serial_no	;;SERIAL NUMBER ;------------------ (18 dashes)	18		
4	type	;ASSET; TYPE;-----	5		
5	serv_date	;IN-SERVICE; DATE ;---------- (10 dashes)	10		
6	cost	; ORIGINAL; COST ;----------- (11 dashes)	11	2	Yes
7	salvage	; SALVAGE; VALUE ;----------- (11 dashes)	11	2	No
8	depr_mthd	;DEPR;METHOD;------	6		
9	depr_life	;DEPR.;LIFE;-----	5	0	No
10	STR(IIF(MONTH(serv_date)=1,12, MONTH(serv_date)-1),2) +'/'+SUBSTR(STR(YEAR(serv_date)+depr_life +IIF(month(serv_date)=1, -1,0),4),3,2)	;END OF;LIFE;------	6		

Fig. 6.46. Report format for order by in-service date.

```
Report definitions for report FAREP6.FRM

Page title:        Smith and Jones Corporation
                   Fixed Asset Tracking System
                   List of Assets by End of Life
                   ------------------------------

Page width:     132

Group on expression        YEAR(serv_date)+depr_life+
                           IIF(MONTH(serv_date)=1,-1,0)
Group heading              END OF ASSET LIFE:
Summary report only        No
Page eject after group     No
Sub-group on expression
Sub-group heading
```

COL	Contents	Heading	W	D	Tot
1	ID_number	;; ID;-------	7		
2	descript	;;DESCRIPTION ;------------------------------ (30 dashes)	30		
3	serial_no	;;SERIAL NUMBER ;------------------ (18 dashes)	18		
4	type	;ASSET; TYPE;-----	5		
5	serv_date	;IN-SERVICE; DATE ;---------- (10 dashes)	10		
6	cost	; ORIGINAL; COST ;----------- (11 dashes)	11	2	Yes
7	salvage	; SALVAGE; VALUE ;----------- (11 dashes)	11	2	No
8	depr_mthd	;DEPR;METHOD;------	6		
9	depr_life	;DEPR.;LIFE;-----	5	0	No
10	STR(IIF(MONTH(serv_date)=1,12, MONTH(serv_date)-1),2) +'/'+SUBSTR(STR(YEAR(serv_date)+depr_life +IIF(month(serv_date)=1, -1,0),4),3,2)	;END OF;LIFE;------	6		

Fig. 6.47. Report format for order by end date.

After printing the report, the program closes the data file and returns to the menu. Figure 6.48 shows a finished report listing fixed assets for Smith and Jones Corporation, sorted by division and location.

```
Page No.     1
10/27/86
                              Fixed Asset Tracking System
                             List of Fixed Assets by Division
                                   and Location
                             --------------------------------


                                             ASSET IN-SERVICE   ORIGINAL   SALVAGE DEPR  DEPR. END OF
   ID    DESCRIPTION             SERIAL NUMBER  TYPE    DATE       COST     VALUE METHOD  LIFE  LIFE
-------  ------------------------ ------------- ----- ---------- ---------- ----------- ------ ----- ------


** Division: CORP

* Location: OFFC
  1011-1  dBASE III Plus Software  919191       SOFT  03/01/86      695.00      0.00 S       5   2/91
  3434    Ledger book              11323        BOOK  04/22/86       13.95      0.00 S       2   3/88
  C-1     File Cabinet             none         FURN  01/01/60      150.00      0.00 S       8  12/67
  P-1001  Printer                  EPSON FX185  COMP  01/01/86      795.00    100.00 S       5  12/90
* Subsubtotal *
                                                                   1653.95
** Subtotal **
                                                                   1653.95


** Division: DIV1

* Location: OFFC
  A-1001  IBM PC COMPUTER          900908880332221 COMP  06/01/84    3000.00    300.00 S       5   5/89
  A-1010  TOYOTA COROLLA 4DR 1984  YF9090909AA1 AUTO  09/08/84    9000.00   2000.00 S       3   8/87
  C-2     File Cabinet             none         FURN  01/01/60      150.00      0.00 S       8  12/67
* Subsubtotal *
                                                                  12150.00

* Location: PLT1
  A-1100  Desk                                  FURN  01/30/82    1500.00    150.00 S       5  12/86
  AJ-436  Machine Tool             aj-123-6116  MACH  06/30/80   25400.00   2540.00 S       8   5/88
  S-1001  Shelving                              FURN  01/01/85    1000.00      0.00 S      10  12/94
* Subsubtotal *
                                                                  27900.00
** Subtotal **
                                                                  40050.00


** Division: DIV2

* Location: OFFC
  C-3     File Cabinet             none         FURN  01/01/60      150.00      0.00 S       8  12/67
* Subsubtotal *
                                                                    150.00


* Location: PLT2
  B-77777 Forklift Truck           bd-98989898989 VHCL  02/15/83   35000.00   5000.00 S       5   1/88
* Subsubtotal *
                                                                  35000.00

* Location: PLT5
  123     Robot - R2D2             1234567890123 P&E   04/30/86  125345.69  12534.57 S       8   3/94
  KK-11   Typewriter               IBM-10010011001 EQUP  01/01/83   1500.00      0.00 S       5  12/87
  KK-112  Copy Machine             112233445566 EQUP  05/01/86    3500.00      0.00 S       5   4/91
```

Fig. 6.48. Report listing fixed assets by division and location (page 1).

```
Page No.     2
10/27/86
                                    Fixed Asset Tracking System
                                    List of Fixed Assets by Division
                                           and Location
                                    --------------------------------


                                          ASSET IN-SERVICE    ORIGINAL    SALVAGE DEPR   DEPR.  END OF
   ID    DESCRIPTION                SERIAL NUMBER     TYPE    DATE           COST     VALUE METHOD  LIFE LIFE
-------  ---------------------      ------------------------ ----------  ----------- ----------- ------ ----- ------


* Subsubtotal *
                                                                        130345.69
** Subtotal **
                                                                        165495.69


** Division: R&D

* Location: LAKE
  A-1004  17' rowboat & oars       1121               VHCL  04/08/86       1200.00     120.00 S    10  3/96
  B-0001  Pool Filter              1212121-9999       EQUP  06/01/81       5500.00       0.00 S     5  5/86
* Subsubtotal *
                                                                          6700.00
** Subtotal **
                                                                          6700.00


** Division: SALE

* Location: CHI
  B-1010  Store Building                              BUIL  05/31/80     250000.00       0.00 D    30  4/10
  C-1010  Store Fixtures                              SALE  01/01/80      10000.00       0.00 S     5 12/84
* Subsubtotal *
                                                                        260000.00
** Subtotal **
                                                                        260000.00
*** Total ***
                                                                        473899.64
```

Fig. 6.48. Report listing fixed assets by division and location (page 2).

Printing Depreciation Reports

The second report program, FADEPREP, prints the asset's cost and salvage value, the depreciation for the current month and the year-to-date, and the depreciation accumulated since the asset was placed in service. The depreciation report can be sorted in any of seven ways, and the user can restrict the report to assets satisfying specified conditions.

Because FADEPREP prints values that are calculated by a subroutine, it cannot use the dBASE III Plus REPORT FORM command. Instead, the program simulates the REPORT FORM command, printing the items calculated by the depreciation subroutine with up to two levels of subtotals. Figure 6.49 shows the flowchart for the FADEPREP program. Program code is provided in listing 6.15.

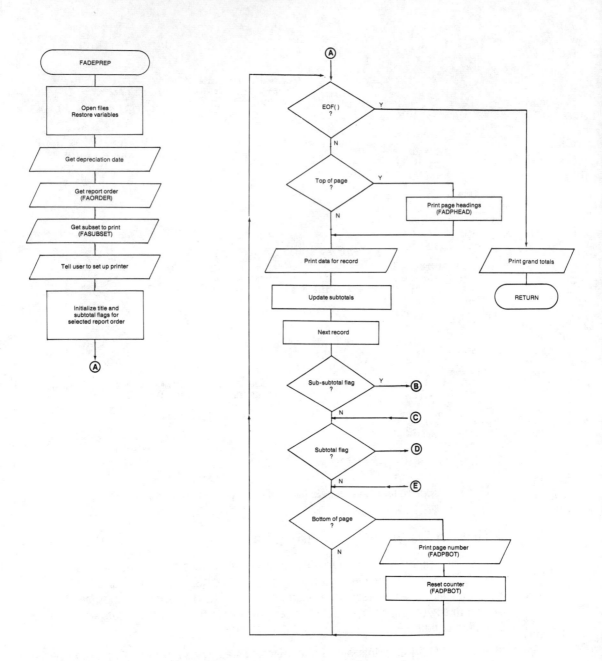

Fig. 6.49. Flowchart of the program FADEPREP.

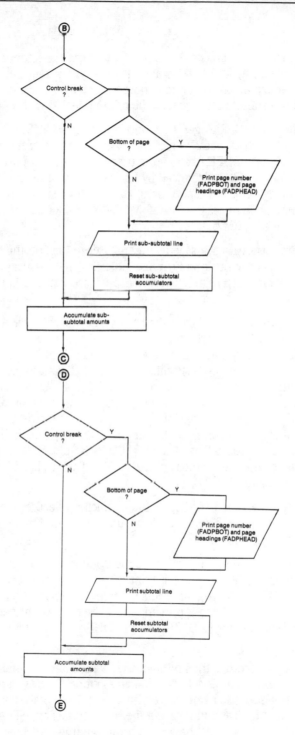

After the user selects the depreciation report option from the Reports menu, the program opens data files with FAOPEN and restores system memory variables from FAMEM. The user is then prompted to choose the report order and offered the option of selecting a subset of the assets to be printed, just as with FAREPORT.

The program calls FAORDER to get the report order and FASUBSET to get any conditions specifying which assets to include in the report. A screen similar to figure 6.38 is produced by FAORDER to allow the user to select the report order. Then a screen similar to figure 6.39 is produced by FASUBSET to allow the user to choose whether to print a depreciation report for all assets or for a subset. If the user wants to select a subset, FASUBSET uses the dBASE MODIFY QUERY command to specify the selection criteria, as in figure 6.40.

Next, the program displays a message telling the user to turn on the printer and set it to the top of a page, and waits for a keypress indicating that the user is ready to continue. The program then prints the printer setup string stored in the memory variable FAPSETUP.

A DO CASE structure is used to select the proper title and subtotal fields for the specified report order. Some of the reports, such as those in record-number and ID-number order, consist of simple lists of assets, with no subtotals. Others include up to two levels of subtotals. The title is specified by the TITLE variable. A first-level subtotal is enabled by setting the SFLAG variable to .T., and the SFIELD variable gives the field or dBASE expression to use for the control breaks. A control break occurs when the value of the specified field or expression changes from one record to the next. The STITLE variable gives the heading for the subtotal. Similarly, the SSFLAG variable specifies a sub-subtotal if set to true. The SSFIELD variable specifies the field or dBASE expression to use for the sub-subtotal control breaks. The SSTITLE variable gives the heading for the sub-subtotal.

The program then enters the main report loop, which is executed once for each asset to be included in the report. The asset information stored in the file is printed, then FADEPR is called to calculate depreciation.

Before printing an asset, the program checks the value in CNTR, which positions the line and is incremented after each line is printed. If the report is at the top of a page (CNTR=0), the FADPHEAD program prints the title and report headings, and sets CNTR to 12 so that the next line is printed where the body of the report begins. The program code for subroutines FADPBOT and FADHEAD is shown in listings 6.16 and 6.17, respectively.

The current database record is then printed, the totals, subtotals, and sub-subtotals are updated, and the next record is selected. Variables whose names start with "t" hold grand totals. Variables whose names start with "s" hold subtotals, and variables whose names start with "ss" hold sub-subtotals. If the sub-subtotal flag SSFLAG is set, the program checks for a sub-subtotal break. If a break is found, the sub-subtotal line is printed and the sub-subtotal counters are reset. The program first checks whether the sub-subtotal would print past the end of the page. If so, FADPBOT and FADPHEAD are executed before the line is printed. Regardless of whether a break was found, the current sub-subtotal field value is saved for comparison during the next iteration of the loop.

The sub-subtotal is used for reports with two control-break fields. For example, a report sorted by division and location will have a sub-subtotal for each location within a division, and a subtotal for each division. The occurrence of a new division will force a sub-subtotal for the location as well as a subtotal for the division, even though the same location may continue into the next division.

Note that the sub-subtotal is used for reports with two levels of control breaks, and the subtotal is used for reports with *either* one or two levels of breaks. For example, a report sorted by asset type will have a subtotal break at the end of each group of assets of the same type.

FADEPREP loops until end-of-file is reached, and then prints grand totals for the report. But if the program determines that the grand total would print past the end of a page, it calls the FADPBOT and FADPHEAD subroutines to move to the top of the next page before printing. Printing is complete when the program prints the page number at the bottom of this last page and ejects the page. The program then restores output to the screen, closes the databases, and returns.

Figures 6.50 through 6.52 illustrate several depreciation report examples produced with FADEPREP. Figure 6.50 shows a depreciation report for assets sorted by in-service date with subtotals for assets placed in service in each year. Figure 6.51 shows a depreciation report for assets sorted by ID number. Finally, figure 6.52 shows a depreciation report listing assets sorted by division, with subtotals for location and division.

Creating System-Maintenance Programs

The system-maintenance programs are utility programs necessary to complete the system. The number and type of system-maintenance programs varies from system to system. The fixed-asset tracking system contains six system-maintenance programs. Two of these programs, FAINDEX and FAMEM, have already been discussed. The system-maintenance programs discussed in this section perform the following functions:

- delete or undelete assets
- "pack" or compress the database to conserve disk space
- back up data files and index files to floppy disks
- restore data files and index files from floppy disks

```
                        SMITH AND JONES CORPORATION              Report Date: 10/27/86
                        FIXED ASSET TRACKING SYSTEM
                     DEPRECIATION REPORT BY IN SERVICE DATE
                         For September    1986
                     ----------------------------------------

ASSET                                   IN SERV.           DEPR  CURR MONTH      YTD  ACCUMULATED
  ID   DESCRIPTION            TYPE LOC DIV  DATE    COST   SALVAGE METH    DEPR      DEPR       DEPR
-------  --------------------  ---- ---- ---- -------- ----------- --------- ---- ----------- ----------- -----------
C-1     File Cabinet           FURN OFFC CORP 01/01/60   150.00     0.00  S      0.00       0.00    150.00
C-2     File Cabinet           FURN OFFC DIV1 01/01/60   150.00     0.00  S      0.00       0.00    150.00
C-3     File Cabinet           FURN OFFC DIV2 01/01/60   150.00     0.00  S      0.00       0.00    150.00

        *** SUBTOTAL FOR YEAR: 1960 ***                  450.00     0.00         0.00       0.00    450.00

C-1010  Store Fixtures         SALE CHI SALE 01/01/80  10000.00     0.00  S      0.00       0.00  10000.00
B-1010  Store Building         BUIL CHI SALE 05/31/80 250000.00     0.00  D    779.15    7012.38  80015.32
AJ-436  Machine Tool           MACH PLT1 DIV1 06/30/80  25400.00  2540.00  S    238.12    2143.12  18097.50

        *** SUBTOTAL FOR YEAR: 1980 ***               285400.00  2540.00      1017.27    9155.51 108112.82

B-0001  Pool Filter            EQUP LAKE R&D  06/01/81   5500.00     0.00  S      0.00     458.33   5500.00

        *** SUBTOTAL FOR YEAR: 1981 ***                 5500.00     0.00         0.00     458.33   5500.00

A-1100  Desk                   FURN PLT1 DIV1 01/30/82   1500.00   150.00  S     22.50     202.50   1282.50

        *** SUBTOTAL FOR YEAR: 1982 ***                 1500.00   150.00        22.50     202.50   1282.50

KK-11   Typewriter             EQUP PLT5 DIV2 01/01/83   1500.00     0.00  S     25.00     225.00   1125.00
B-77777 Forklift Truck         VHCL PLT2 DIV2 02/15/83  35000.00  5000.00  S    500.00    4500.00  22000.00

        *** SUBTOTAL FOR YEAR: 1983 ***                36500.00  5000.00       525.00    4725.00  23125.00

A-1001  IBM PC COMPUTER        COMP OFFC DIV1 06/01/84   3000.00   300.00  S     45.00     405.00   1260.00
A-1010  TOYOTA COROLLA 4DR 1984 AUTO OFFC DIV1 09/08/84  9000.00  2000.00  S    194.44    1750.00   4861.11

        *** SUBTOTAL FOR YEAR: 1984 ***                12000.00  2300.00       239.44    2155.00   6121.11

S-1001  Shelving               FURN PLT1 DIV1 01/01/85   1000.00     0.00  S      8.33      75.00    175.00

        *** SUBTOTAL FOR YEAR: 1985 ***                 1000.00     0.00         8.33      75.00    175.00

P-1001  Printer                COMP OFFC CORP 01/01/86    795.00   100.00  S     11.58     104.25    104.25
1011-1  dBASE III Plus Software SOFT OFFC CORP 03/01/86   695.00     0.00  S     11.58      81.08     81.08
A-1004  17' rowboat & oars     VHCL LAKE R&D  04/08/86   1200.00   120.00  S      9.00      54.00     54.00
3434    Ledger book            BOOK OFFC CORP 04/22/86     13.95     0.00  S      0.58       3.49      3.49
123     Robot - R2D2           P&E  PLT5 DIV2 04/30/86 125345.69 12534.57  S   1175.12    7050.70   7050.70
KK-112  Copy Machine           EQUP PLT5 DIV2 05/01/86   3500.00     0.00  S     58.33     291.67    291.67

        *** SUBTOTAL FOR YEAR: 1986 ***               131549.64 12754.57      1266.20    7585.18   7585.18

        GRAND TOTAL                                   473899.64 22744.57     24356.53  152351.62 298803.44




                               Page      1
```

Fig. 6.50. Depreciation report for assets sorted by in-service date.

```
                              SMITH AND JONES CORPORATION                    Report Date: 10/27/86
                              FIXED ASSET TRACKING SYSTEM
                             DEPRECIATION REPORT BY ID NUMBER
                                 For September     1986
                             ---------------------------------
```

ASSET ID	DESCRIPTION	TYPE	LOC	DIV	IN SERV. DATE	COST	SALVAGE	DEPR METH	CURR MONTH DEPR	YTD DEPR	ACCUMULATED DEPR
1011-1	dBASE III Plus Software	SOFT	OFFC	CORP	03/01/86	695.00	0.00	S	11.58	81.08	81.08
123	Robot - R2D2	P&E	PLT5	DIV2	04/30/86	125345.69	12534.57	S	1175.12	7050.70	7050.70
3434	Ledger book	BOOK	OFFC	CORP	04/22/86	13.95	0.00	S	0.58	3.49	3.49
A-1001	IBM PC COMPUTER	COMP	OFFC	DIV1	06/01/84	3000.00	300.00	S	45.00	405.00	1260.00
A-1004	17' rowboat & oars	VHCL	LAKE	R&D	04/08/86	1200.00	120.00	S	9.00	54.00	54.00
A-1010	TOYOTA COROLLA 4DR 1984	AUTO	OFFC	DIV1	09/08/84	9000.00	2000.00	S	194.44	1750.00	4861.11
A-1100	Desk	FURN	PLT1	DIV1	01/30/82	1500.00	150.00	S	22.50	202.50	1282.50
AJ-436	Machine Tool	MACH	PLT1	DIV1	06/30/80	25400.00	2540.00	S	238.12	2143.12	18097.50
B-0001	Pool Filter	EQUP	LAKE	R&D	06/01/81	5500.00	0.00	S	0.00	458.33	5500.00
B-1010	Store Building	BUIL	CHI	SALE	05/31/80	250000.00	0.00	D	779.15	7012.38	75515.32
B-77777	Forklift Truck	VHCL	PLT2	DIV2	02/15/83	35000.00	5000.00	S	500.00	4500.00	22000.00
C-1	File Cabinet	FURN	OFFC	CORP	01/01/60	150.00	0.00	S	0.00	0.00	150.00
C-1010	Store Fixtures	SALE	CHI	SALE	01/01/80	10000.00	0.00	S	0.00	0.00	10000.00
C-2	File Cabinet	FURN	OFFC	DIV1	01/01/60	150.00	0.00	S	0.00	0.00	150.00
C-3	File Cabinet	FURN	OFFC	DIV2	01/01/60	150.00	0.00	S	0.00	0.00	150.00
KK-11	Typewriter	EQUP	PLT5	DIV2	01/01/83	1500.00	0.00	S	25.00	225.00	1125.00
KK-112	Copy Machine	EQUP	PLT5	DIV2	05/01/86	3500.00	0.00	S	58.33	291.67	291.67
P-1001	Printer	COMP	OFFC	CORP	01/01/86	795.00	100.00	S	11.58	104.25	104.25
S-1001	Shelving	FURN	PLT1	DIV1	01/01/85	1000.00	0.00	S	8.33	75.00	175.00
	GRAND TOTAL					473899.64	22744.57		24356.53	147851.62	303303.44

Fig. 6.51. Depreciation report for assets sorted by ID number.

Deleting and Undeleting Assets

The delete-asset program, FADELETE, is considered a system-maintenance function in this application. In other systems, it might be more appropriate to put the delete command on a menu with the data-entry commands than on a menu with the system-maintenance commands. In this system, however, assets are deleted when they are retired from service or sold, which may be a long time after they are entered into the system. The program also allows assets that were entered under the wrong ID number to be removed so that they can be reentered correctly. And an undelete function enables users to restore an asset that has been deleted accidentally, provided the PACK command has not been run since the asset was deleted.

The flowchart for the FADELETE program is shown in figure 6.53. Program code is shown in listing 6.18.

```
                    SMITH AND JONES CORPORATION                 Report Date: 10/27/86
                    FIXED ASSET TRACKING SYSTEM
                  DEPRECIATION REPORT BY DIVISION
                      For September    1986
                  --------------------------------
```

ASSET ID	DESCRIPTION	TYPE	LOC	DIV	IN SERV. DATE	COST	SALVAGE	DEPR METH	CURR MONTH DEPR	YTD DEPR	ACCUMULATED DEPR
1011-1	dBASE III Plus Software	SOFT	OFFC	CORP	03/01/86	695.00	0.00	S	11.58	81.08	81.08
3434	Ledger book	BOOK	OFFC	CORP	04/22/86	13.95	0.00	S	0.58	3.49	3.49
C-1	File Cabinet	FURN	OFFC	CORP	01/01/60	150.00	0.00	S	0.00	0.00	150.00
P-1001	Printer	COMP	OFFC	CORP	01/01/86	795.00	100.00	S	11.58	104.25	104.25
	*** SUBTOTAL FOR LOCATION: OFFC ***					1653.95	100.00		23.75	188.82	338.82
	*** SUBTOTAL FOR DIVISION: CORP ***					1653.95	100.00		23.75	188.82	338.82
A-1001	IBM PC COMPUTER	COMP	OFFC	DIV1	06/01/84	3000.00	300.00	S	45.00	405.00	1260.00
A-1010	TOYOTA COROLLA 4DR 1984	AUTO	OFFC	DIV1	09/08/84	9000.00	2000.00	S	194.44	1750.00	4861.11
C-2	File Cabinet	FURN	OFFC	DIV1	01/01/60	150.00	0.00	S	0.00	0.00	150.00
	*** SUBTOTAL FOR LOCATION: OFFC ***					12150.00	2300.00		239.44	2155.00	6271.11
A-1100	Desk	FURN	PLT1	DIV1	01/30/82	1500.00	150.00	S	22.50	202.50	1282.50
AJ-436	Machine Tool	MACH	PLT1	DIV1	06/30/80	25400.00	2540.00	S	238.12	2143.12	18097.50
S-1001	Shelving	FURN	PLT1	DIV1	01/01/85	1000.00	0.00	S	8.33	75.00	175.00
	*** SUBTOTAL FOR LOCATION: PLT1 ***					27900.00	2690.00		268.96	2420.62	19555.00
	*** SUBTOTAL FOR DIVISION: DIV1 ***					40050.00	4990.00		508.40	4575.63	25826.11
C-3	File Cabinet	FURN	OFFC	DIV2	01/01/60	150.00	0.00	S	0.00	0.00	150.00
	*** SUBTOTAL FOR LOCATION: OFFC ***					150.00	0.00		0.00	0.00	150.00
B-77777	Forklift Truck	VHCL	PLT2	DIV2	02/15/83	35000.00	5000.00	S	500.00	4500.00	22000.00
	*** SUBTOTAL FOR LOCATION: PLT2 ***					35000.00	5000.00		500.00	4500.00	22000.00
123	Robot - R2D2	P&E	PLT5	DIV2	04/30/86	125345.69	12534.57	S	1175.12	7050.70	7050.70
KK-11	Typewriter	EQUP	PLT5	DIV2	01/01/83	1500.00	0.00	S	25.00	225.00	1125.00
KK-112	Copy Machine	EQUP	PLT5	DIV2	05/01/86	3500.00	0.00	S	58.33	291.67	291.67
	*** SUBTOTAL FOR LOCATION: PLT5 ***					130345.69	12534.57		1258.45	7567.36	8467.36
	*** SUBTOTAL FOR DIVISION: DIV2 ***					165495.69	17534.57		1758.45	12067.36	30617.36
A-1004	17' rowboat & oars	VHCL	LAKE	R&D	04/08/86	1200.00	120.00	S	9.00	54.00	54.00
8-0001	Pool Filter	EQUP	LAKE	R&D	06/01/81	5500.00	0.00	S	0.00	458.33	5500.00
	*** SUBTOTAL FOR LOCATION: LAKE ***					6700.00	120.00		9.00	512.33	5554.00

```
                              Page  1
```

Fig. 6.52. Depreciation report for assets sorted by division (page 1).

```
                              SMITH AND JONES CORPORATION              Report Date: 10/27/86
                              FIXED ASSET TRACKING SYSTEM
                              DEPRECIATION REPORT BY DIVISION
                                   For September    1986
                              --------------------------------


 ASSET                                          IN SERV.              DEPR  CURR MONTH        YTD ACCUMULATED
   ID   DESCRIPTION                TYPE LOC DIV  DATE        COST   SALVAGE METH       DEPR      DEPR       DEPR
 ------ -----------------------    ---- ---- --- -------- ----------- ------- ---- ----------- ---------- ----------
         *** SUBTOTAL FOR DIVISION: R&D  ***                6700.00  120.00            9.00     512.33    5554.00

 B-1010 Store Building             BUIL CHI  SALE 05/31/80 250000.00   0.00  D       779.15    7012.38   75515.32
 C-1010 Store Fixtures            SALE  CHI  SALE 01/01/80  10000.00   0.00  S         0.00       0.00   10000.00


         *** SUBTOTAL FOR LOCATION: CHI  ***               260000.00   0.00          779.15    7012.38   85515.32


         *** SUBTOTAL FOR DIVISION: SALE ***               260000.00   0.00          779.15    7012.38   85515.32


         GRAND TOTAL                                       473899.64 22744.57       24356.53  147851.62  303303.44




                                            Page        2
```

Fig. 6.52. Depreciation report for assets sorted by division (page 2).

FADELETE begins by opening the files with FAOPEN. Then the program enters a "do forever" loop that is executed once for each asset to be deleted or undeleted.

In the main loop, FADELETE first requests an asset ID from the user. Figure 6.54 shows the screen on which the user enters the ID number, which is A-1010 in this example.

If the ID number is blank, execution transfers out of the loop; this is the only way to exit the loop. If the user enters a nonblank ID number, the SEEK command is used to look for the ID number in the file. If the ID number is not found, an error message is displayed and the program pauses until the user presses any key to continue. Then the loop is repeated.

If the record containing the specified ID number is found, the user is prompted to verify the ID number. If the user does not verify the ID number, execution transfers to the top of the loop for a new ID number.

After the user enters and verifies the ID number, the program displays the asset data. FADELETE then asks whether the user wants to delete the asset (if it is not currently deleted) or to delete the asset (if it is currently deleted). Figure 6.55 shows an asset record for a Toyota Corolla owned by Smith and Jones Corporation. If the user in this example presses *Y*, the asset record will be deleted.

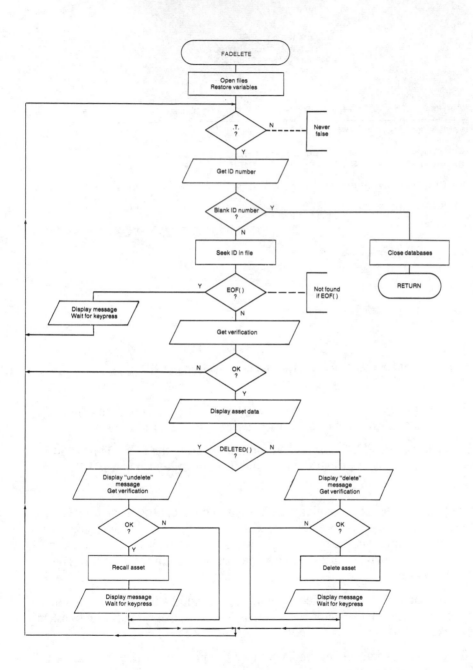

Fig. 6.53. Flowchart for the program FADELETE.

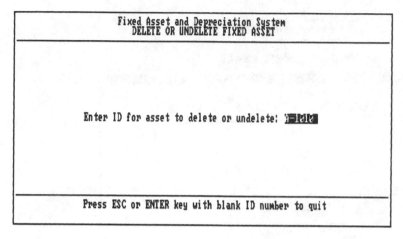

Fig. 6.54. Entering an ID number for the asset to be deleted or undeleted.

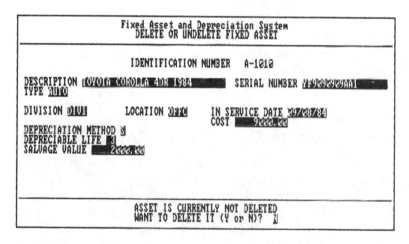

Fig. 6.55. Screen showing current asset selected for deletion.

If the asset is currently deleted, the program shows the screen in figure 6.56 and asks whether the user wants to undelete it. If the user presses *Y*, the asset is restored to active status in the file.

Finally, the program deletes or recalls the record and displays the appropriate message. After the user presses any key, the program returns to the top of the loop for another ID number.

When the loop is exited with a blank ID number, the program closes the data files and returns.

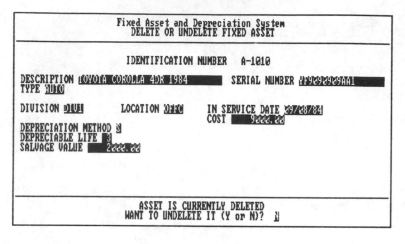

Fig. 6.56. The prompt for undeleting an asset record.

Packing the Database (FAPACK)

The pack-database program, FAPACK, compresses the database after many records have been added and deleted. This program should be used when disk space is short and there have been many deletions since the last time the program was run. The code for FAPACK is supplied in listing 6.19.

Backing Up the System to Floppy Disks (FABACKUP)

The FABACKUP program uses the DOS command BACKUP to save the data file, the index files, and the memory file to one or more formatted floppy disks. Users who operate the fixed-asset system on a computer with a hard disk will find this backup command essential. But to take full advantage of this feature, users must be aware of good backup procedures and know how to format floppy disks. The code for the FABACKUP program is provided in listing 6.20.

Restoring Data from Backup Floppy Disks

The last system-maintenance program, FARESTOR, enables users to restore all system data from backup files made with the FABACKUP command. This command would be used to restore the system after a hard-disk failure, for example, or to restore the system to its condition at a particular time, such as the end of the year.

Listing 6.21 shows the program code. Note that FARESTOR uses the DOS command RESTORE to restore the data from backup floppy disks. Like FABACKUP, FARESTOR uses dBASE's capability to run a DOS command from within a dBASE program. This capability gives you great flexibility when you need to perform a function that is not built into dBASE, such as the DOS backup functions used by these subroutines. If you choose not to use these subroutines, you can use a floppy disk backup program like FASTBACK. Or, if the user's hard disk has a tape backup drive, you can adapt the backup and restore programs presented here to use the tape drive for backup instead of floppy disks.

When users select the Restore Files from Floppy option from the System Maintenance menu, they are prompted to place the floppy disks for backup into the B drive. The program reads in the backup data and returns to the System Maintenance menu.

Creating a Menu System

The next stage in the development of the fixed-asset tracking system is to create the menus. This application uses a multiple-menu approach—a main menu with three subsidiary menus—to keep each menu simple. Figures 6.57 through 6.60 show the Main Menu, Data Entry and Query Menu, Report Menu, and System Maintenance Menu. Code for these menus is provided in listings 6.22 through 6.25.

The menu programs are straightforward. Information is displayed on the screen by means of @ . . . SAY commands, and the user's choice is read with an @ . . . GET command. Because a number is used to select the menu option, the user's choice is range-checked with the RANGE option of the @ . . . GET command.

The DO CASE structure at the bottom of each menu listing executes an option corresponding to a menu selection. Any selection from the main menu produces one of the submenus, but a selection from a submenu activates a program to perform the selected operation. The menu display and the DO CASE structure are contained in a loop that is repeated until the user selects option 0, the EXIT option.

The main-menu program, FIXASSET, is the entry point into the system. Part of its job therefore is to set the environment for the entire system. This task includes setting TALK and SAFETY off and making sure that PRINT is off.

The three subsidiary menu programs, FAMENU1, FAMENU2, and FAMENU3, directly call the programs that perform the major operations of the system. The first menu program groups together the data-entry and query functions. The second menu program controls the report functions. The third menu program contains system-maintenance functions like deleting assets, packing and reindexing the database, backing up the database, and changing system parameters.

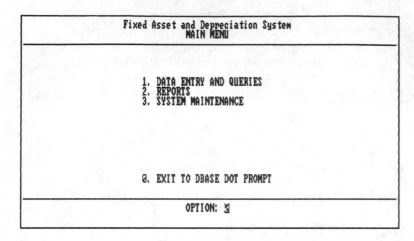

Fig. 6.57. The main menu.

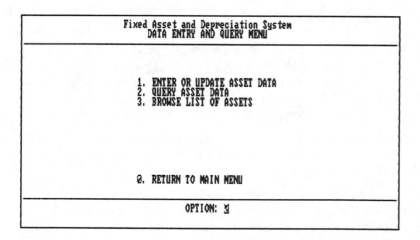

Fig. 6.58. The data entry and query menu.

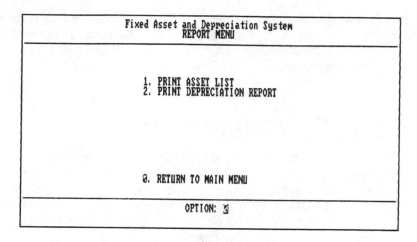

Fig. 6.59. The report menu.

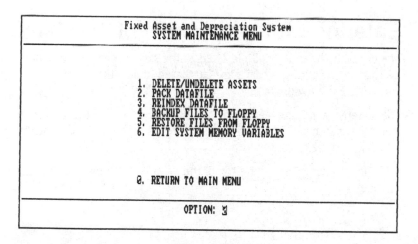

Fig. 6.60. The system-maintenance menu.

You may want to rearrange the menus to suit your customer's particular needs. One customer may prefer a single menu with all the system options in one place. Others may prefer a multiple-menu arrangement like the one designed here for the Smith and Jones Corporation.

Using Procedure Files

The last step in the development of the application is to place the key subroutines in a procedure file to speed execution. The most important subroutines in the fixed-asset tracking system to include in the procedure file are the depreciation subroutines FADEPR, FASLDEPR, and FADBDEPR. These subroutines are called for each asset displayed by the browse-asset-list program or printed by the depreciation-report program. For guidelines on using procedure files, see "Using Procedure Files" in Chapter 3.

Possible Extensions to the System

At least two extensions to the fixed-asset tracking system are possible. One simple extension involves making it easy to enter multiple assets of the same type into the system. Another extension adds additional methods of computing depreciation. You may find either extension quite useful, depending on the needs of your users.

Entering Multiple Assets of the Same Type

The capability to enter multiple assets of the same type is useful when several identical assets such as desks and chairs are purchased in quantity, but the system must keep track of them individually.

This extension is implemented by adding to the FAENTER program memory variables that store the entries from the last asset record entered. These entries serve as default values for the next asset record.

Add the following lines at the top of the FAENTER listing to define the memory variables:

```
PRIVATE mdescr, mserial, mtype, mdiv, mloc, mmthd, mserv,;
       mcost, mlife, msalv
STORE "" TO mdescr, mserial, mtype, mdiv, mloc, mmthd
STORE CTOD("  /  /  ") TO mserv
STORE 0 TO mcost, mlife, msalv
```

To set the default values of each new entry to those of the previous entry, insert the following command after the APPEND BLANK command:

```
REPLACE descript WITH mdescr, serial_no WITH mserial,type WITH mtype,;
       division WITH mdiv,;location WITH mloc, depr_mthd WITH mmthd,;
       serv_date WITH mserv, cost WITH mcost,depr_life WITH mlife,;
       salvage WITH msalvage
```

Finally, add the following block of code just after the user verification that the entry is acceptable. These commands assign the asset data in the current entry as defaults for the next entry:

```
IF mok
   mdescr=descript
   mserial=serial_no
   mtype=type
   mdiv=division
   mloc=location
   mmthd=depr_mthd
   mserv=serv_date
   mcost=cost
   mlife=depr_life
   msalvage=salvage
ENDIF
```

Adding Other Depreciation Methods

The fixed-asset tracking system is presented with calculations for two common depreciation methods implemented in subroutines. If you want to add other methods for computing depreciation, you need to write and test a subroutine to calculate the desired depreciation, and then add that subroutine's call to the DO CASE structure in the FADEPR subroutine.

Your depreciation subroutine should return the depreciation for the current month, the year-to-date depreciation for the current fiscal year, and the accumulated depreciation through the specified date. To keep your subroutine general, you should pass all inputs to the subroutine as parameters. The FADEPR subroutine passes the cost, salvage value, and the number of months between the in-service date and the specified date, and the number of months between the start of the fiscal year and the specified date, for use by the depreciation subroutines.

Important note: The two depreciation subroutines presented in this chapter are not used to compute tax depreciation for most assets. The tax law relating to depreciation is complex and at this writing (mid-1986) is expected to change. If you modify the application to handle tax depreciation, be sure to check with a tax accountant to determine the proper depreciation methods for each type of asset.

One type of depreciation that this fixed-asset tracking system cannot compute easily is units-of-production depreciation. To calculate this type of depreciation, you need to know the production history for an asset and must state the asset life in terms of total production instead of years.

Conclusion

The fixed-asset tracking system presented in this chapter can keep track of fixed assets and book-value depreciation for a small or medium-sized business. This application enables users to retrieve information about an asset quickly or print a specified list of assets. And by adding the appropriate depreciation methods, the fixed-asset tracking system could also be used to keep track of depreciation for tax purposes.

Listing 6.1. The program FAINDEX.

```
*****************************************
* FAINDEX - Reindex fixed asset file    *
*            10/23/86                    *
*****************************************

* Setup environment
CLOSE DATABASES
RESTORE FROM famem ADDITIVE
title='Reindex Fixed Asset Files'
DO borders WITH fatitle,title
USE fixasset

@  5, 20 SAY "Indexing fixed asset file ..."
@  6, 22 SAY "by ID"
INDEX ON id_number TO faid              && Index on id #
@  7, 22 SAY "by asset type and ID"
INDEX ON type+id_number TO fatype       && Index on type & id
@  8, 22 SAY "by location and ID"
INDEX ON location+id_number TO faloc    && Index on location & id
@  9, 22 SAY "by division, location, and ID"
INDEX ON division+location+id_number TO fadiv && Index on division, loc, & id
@ 10, 22 SAY "by in-service date"
INDEX ON serv_date TO fabegin           && Index on in service date
@ 11, 22 SAY "by end of depreciable life"
INDEX ON serv_date+365*depr_life-1 TO faend && Index on end of depreciable life
*                                                (Ignores leap years)

RETURN
```

Listing 6.2. The subroutine FAOPEN.

```
**********************************************************************
* FAOPEN - Open database and index files for Fixed Asset Manager *
*            8/17/86                                              *
**********************************************************************
CLOSE DATABASES
SELECT A
USE fixasset INDEX faid,fatype,faloc,fadiv,fabegin,faend
RETURN
```

Listing 6.3. The program FAMEM.

```
**************************************************
* FAMEM -         Define system parameters       *
*                 8/17/86                         *
**************************************************
PRIVATE mok

* Restore existing or initialize new entries, depending on whether file exists
IF FILE("famem.mem")
   RESTORE FROM famem ADDITIVE
   fapsetup=SUBSTR(fapsetup+SPACE(80),1,80)      && Pad w. blanks to 80 char.
   fapreset=SUBSTR(fapreset+SPACE(80),1,80)      && Pad w. blanks to 80 char.
ELSE
   STORE SPACE(80) TO fapsetup,fapreset
   STORE 8  TO fapmargin
   STORE CTOD("12/31/"+SUBSTR(LTRIM(STR(YEAR(DATE()))),3,2)) to fafiscalyr
   fatitle='Fixed Asset and Depreciation System'
ENDIF

* get new values
mok=.f.
DO borders WITH fatitle,"Edit System Memory Variables"
DO WHILE .not.mok
   @ 6, 2 SAY "PRINTER SETUP STRING " GET fapsetup FUNCTION "S40"
   @ 7, 2 SAY "PRINTER RESET STRING " GET fapreset FUNCTION "S40"
   @ 8, 2 SAY "PRINTER LEFT MARGIN  "  GET fapmargin RANGE 0,
   @ 9, 2 SAY "END OF CURRENT FISCAL YEAR" GET fafiscalyr
   READ
   @ 21,33 SAY "OK (Y or N)?" GET mok PICTURE "Y"
   READ
   @ 21, 1 CLEAR TO 22, 78
ENDDO

* Save new memory file
mok=.f.
fapsetup=TRIM(fapsetup)              && Remove trailing blanks from fapsetup
fapreset=TRIM(fapreset)             && Remove trailing blanks from fapreset
@ 6, 1 CLEAR TO 7, 78
@ 6, 2 SAY "PRINTER SETUP STRING " GET fapsetup FUNCTION "S40"
@ 7, 2 SAY "PRINTER RESET STRING " GET fapreset FUNCTION "S40"
CLEAR GETS
@ 21, 25 SAY "Save new FAMEM file (Y or N)" GET mok PICTURE "Y"
READ
IF mok
   SAVE TO famem ALL LIKE fa*
ENDIF

* Tidy up and return
CLEAR
RETURN
```

Listing 6.4. The program FAENTER.

```
***********************************************************************
* FAENTER - Enter or update asset in the Fixed Asset Management System *
*            8/17/86                                                  *
***********************************************************************

* Open files & set environment
DO faopen                               && Open fixed asset file and indexes
RESTORE FROM famem ADDITIVE             && Restore memory variables
mtitle="ADD OR UPDATE FIXED ASSET"

* Main loop.
DO WHILE .T.                        && DO forever
DO borders WITH fatitle,mtitle          && Display titles and borders

   * Get ID number
   mid=SPACE(7)
   @ 12, 23 SAY "Enter ID for fixed asset:" GET mid FUNCTION "!"
   @ 21, 14 SAY "Press ESC or ENTER key with blank ID number to quit"
   READ
   @ 21, 1 CLEAR TO 22, 78

   * Check for blank id. Exit DO FOREVER loop if so
   IF mid=SPACE(7)
      EXIT
   ENDIF

   * Check for id already in file. If exists & not deleted, skip rest of loop
   SEEK mid                             && Check for this ID in file

   IF EOF()            && New Asset
      @ 21, 31 SAY "Entering New Asset"

   ELSE                && Existing Asset

      *Check whether deleted. If so, give user chance to recall
      IF DELETED()
         @ 21, 18 SAY "THIS ASSET EXISTS BUT IS CURRENTLY DELETED!"
         mok=.f.
         @ 22, 18 SAY "Want to UNDELETE and continue (Y or N)?";
               GET mok PICTURE "Y"
         READ
         @ 21, 1 CLEAR TO 22, 78
         IF mok                 && If answer is yes, recall asset
            RECALL
         ELSE                   && Otherwise skip to end of DO FOREVER loop
            LOOP
         ENDIF
      ENDIF (deleted)

      @ 21, 29 SAY "Updating Existing Asset"

   ENDIF

   * Verify that user wants to enter/update data for this asset
   mok=.t.
   @ 22, 33 SAY "OK (Y or N)" GET mok PICTURE "Y"
   READ
   IF .not.mok                && If not OK, skip to end of DO FOREVER loop
      LOOP
   ENDIF
```

(Continued on next page.)

Listing 6.4, continued.

```
        @ 5, 1 CLEAR TO 19, 78
        @ 21, 1 CLEAR TO 22, 78

   * Check for end-of-file. If so, enter new asset. Else update existing asset
   IF EOF()

       *Have new asset. Append blank record and fill in asset ID
       APPEND BLANK                       && Append new record for asset
       REPLACE id_number WITH mid         && Fill in asset ID

       * Enter data for new asset
       @ 21, 28 SAY "ENTER DATA FOR NEW ASSET"
       DO faastscr                        && Display SAY's and GET's
       @ 22, 9   SAY "Press CTRL END to end edit and save, ";
                  +"ESC to end without saving"
       READ                               && Read GET's
       @ 21, 1 CLEAR TO 22, 78            && Clear status lines

       * Verify entry
       mok=.f.
       IF READKEY()#12                    && If user did not press ESC
          @ 21, 33 SAY "OK (Y or N)" GET mok PICTURE "Y"
          READ
       ENDIF

       * If entry not ok, delete it
       IF .not.mok        && Entry not ok
          REPLACE id_number WITH SPACE(7)
          DELETE                                    && Delete new record
          @ 21, 1 CLEAR TO 22, 78
          @ 21, 27 SAY "RECORD NOT ADDED TO FILE."      && Display message
          ans=' '
          @ 22, 20 SAY "Press any key to continue..." GET ans
          READ                                      && Wait for keypress
          @ 21, 1 CLEAR TO 22, 78
       ENDIF (entry not ok)

   * Otherwise, update data for existing asset
   ELSE
       @ 21, 25 SAY "UPDATE DATA FOR EXISTING ASSET"
       DO faastscr                        && Display SAY's and GET's
       @ 22, 9   SAY ;
          "Press CTRL END to end edit and save, ESC to end without saving"
       READ                               && Read GETs
   ENDIF (eof)

* End of main loop
ENDDO (DO FOREVER)

* Tidy up and return
CLEAR
SET DELETED OFF
CLOSE DATABASES
RETURN
```

Listing 6.5. The subroutine FAASTSCR.

```
**************************************************
* FAASTSCR -      Display data-entry screen      *
*                     8/17/86                     *
**************************************************

@  6, 24  SAY "IDENTIFICATION NUMBER"
@  6, 48  SAY  FIXASSET->ID_NUMBER  FUNCTION "!"
@  8,  2  SAY "DESCRIPTION" GET  FIXASSET->DESCRIPT
@  8, 46  SAY "SERIAL NUMBER" GET  FIXASSET->SERIAL_NO
@  9,  2  SAY "TYPE" GET  FIXASSET->TYPE  FUNCTION "!"
@ 11,  2  SAY "DIVISION" GET  FIXASSET->DIVISION  FUNCTION "!"
@ 11, 23  SAY "LOCATION" GET  FIXASSET->LOCATION  FUNCTION "!"
@ 11, 41  SAY "IN SERVICE DATE" GET  FIXASSET->SERV_DATE
@ 12, 41  SAY "COST" GET  FIXASSET->COST
@ 13,  2  SAY "DEPRECIATION METHOD" GET  FIXASSET->DEPR_MTHD  FUNCTION "!"
@ 14,  2  SAY "DEPRECIABLE LIFE" GET  FIXASSET->DEPR_LIFE
@ 15,  2  SAY "SALVAGE VALUE" GET  FIXASSET->SALVAGE  PICTURE "99999999.99"

RETURN
```

Listing 6.6. The program FAQUERY.

```
********************************************************************
* FAQUERY -      Look at asset including depreciation schedule    *
*                     8/17/86                                      *
********************************************************************

* Open files & set environment
DO faopen                            && Open fixed asset files and indexes
SET DELETED ON                       && Skip deleted records
RESTORE FROM famem ADDITIVE          && Restore system parameters
mdate=DATE()                         && Initialize today's date
mtitle="ASSET QUERY SCREEN"

* Get depr date
mok=.f.
DO WHILE .not.mok
   DO borders WITH fatitle,mtitle
   @ 12, 22  SAY "Enter date for depreciation ";
        GET mdate RANGE CTOD("1/1/01"),
   READ
   @ 21, 35  SAY "OK (Y or N)" GET mok PICTURE 'Y'
   READ
ENDDO

* Main loop.
DO WHILE .T.                              && DO FOREVER loop
   @ 5, 1 CLEAR TO 19, 78                 && Clear screen below logo
   @ 21, 1 CLEAR TO 22, 78

   * Get ID number
   mid=SPACE(7)
   @ 12, 24 SAY "Enter ID for fixed asset:" GET mid FUNCTION "!"
   @ 21, 13 SAY "Press ESC or ENTER key with blank ID number to quit"
   READ
   @ 21, 1 SAY SPACE(78)                 && Clear Status line
```

(Continued on next page.)

Listing 6.6, continued.

```
    * Check for blank id. Exit from DO FOREVER loop if so.
    IF mid=' '
      EXIT
    ENDIF

    * Check if id is in file. If not, skip rest of loop
    SEEK mid                            && Check for this ID in file
    IF EOF()                            && IF not found
      @ 21, 31 SAY "ASSET NOT FOUND"    && Warn user
      * Pause for keypress
      mok=" "
      @ 22,24 SAY "Press any key to continue ... " GET mok PICTURE "X"
      READ
      LOOP                              && And skip rest of loop
    ENDIF

    *  Have asset, Display account data
    @ 5, 1 CLEAR TO 19, 78                        && Clear screen below logo
    @ 21, 1 CLEAR TO 22, 78
    DO faastscr                         && Display file data for account
    CLEAR GETS                          && Make sure cannot change data!

    * Calculate depreciation for asset
    STORE 0 TO mcurr,mytd,maccum                  && Define depr. vars.
    DO fadepr WITH mdate,mcurr,mytd,maccum        && Call depr. subroutine

    * Calculate month and year that depreciation ends for this asset
    end_mnth=IIF(month(serv_date)=1,12,month(serv_date)-1)
    end_year=year(serv_date)+depr_life+IIF(month(serv_date)=1,-1,0)
    end_date=STR(end_mnth,2)+"/"+STR(end_year,4)

    * Calculate remaining undepreciated balance for asset
    mremain=cost-maccum-salvage

    * Display depreciation information for asset
    @  17,  2 SAY "CURRENT MONTH "+CMONTH(mdate)+" "+STR(YEAR(mdate))
    @  17, 45 SAY "END OF DEPRECIABLE LIFE" GET end_date
    @  18, 2  SAY "CURRENT MONTH DEPRECIATION" GET mcurr PICTURE "99999999.99"
    @  18, 45 SAY "YEAR TO DATE" GET mytd PICTURE "99999999.99"
    @  19, 2  SAY "ACCUMULATED DEPRECIATON" GET maccum PICTURE "99999999.99"
    @  19, 45 SAY "UNDEPRECIATED BALANCE" GET mremain PICTURE "99999999.99"
    CLEAR GETS                          && Don't want to READ these!
    @ 21,21 SAY "USE THE PRTSCR KEY TO MAKE A HARDCOPY"
    * Pause for keypress
    mok=" "
    @ 22,24 SAY "Press any key to continue ... " GET mok PICTURE "X"
    READ
* end of main loop
ENDDO

* tidy up and return
CLEAR
SET DELETED OFF
CLOSE DATABASES
RETURN
```

Listing 6.7. The program FADEPR.

```
************************************************************** ,***********
* FADEPR -        Calculate depreciation for specified date.          *
*                 Parameters are: mdate   - specified date input      *
*                                 mcurr   - returns depr for curr month *
*                                 mytd    - Returns YTD depr for year  *
*                                 maccum  - Returns accum depr thru curr *
*                 Also requires FAFISCALYR from system memory file     *
*                 Gets depreciation data from current FIXASSET record  *
*                 5/8/86                                               *
**************************************************************************
PARAMETERS mdate,mcurr,mytd,maccum
PRIVATE mmonths,curr_mnth

*Number of months since in-service date
mmonths=month(mdate)-month(serv_date)+;
        12*(year(mdate)-year(serv_date))+1
* Number of months YTD in current fiscal year
curr_mnth=MOD(MONTH(mdate)-MONTH(fafiscalyr)+11,12)+1

*Depreciation routine depends on depreciation method
DO CASE
    CASE depr_mthd$"Ss"                  && Straight line depr
        DO fasldepr WITH cost,salvage,depr_life,mmonths,curr_mnth,mcurr,;
            mytd,maccum

    CASE depr_mthd$"Dd"                  && 150% decl. bal. depr. for building
        DO fadbdepr WITH cost,salvage,depr_life,1.5,mmonths,;
            curr_mnth,mcurr,mytd,maccum

    OTHERWISE
        maccum=0
        mcurr=0
        mytd=0
ENDCASE

RETURN
```

Listing 6.8. The subroutine FASLDEPR.

```
*********************************************************************
* FASLDEPR -     Returns straight line depreciation amount        *
*                for the current month, year to date, and         *
*                accumulated depreciation.                        *
*                8/17/86                                          *
*********************************************************************
* PARAMETERS ARE:
*       cost     - cost of the asset
*       salvage  - salvage value
*       life     - life in years
*       mtot     - total months from start to current month
*       mytd     - number of months since start of fiscal year
*       monthdepr        - return current month depreciation
*       ytddepr          - return year to date depreciation
*       accumdepr        - return accumulated depreciation

PARAMETERS cost,salvage,life,mtot,mytd,monthdepr,ytddepr,accdepr
PRIVATE mdepr

*Calculate straight line monthly depreciation amount
mdepr=(cost-salvage)/(12*life)

DO CASE
    CASE mtot<1          && Current period before start of depreciable life
         monthdepr=0     && No depr before startup
         ytddepr=0
         accumdepr=0
    CASE mtot>12*life    && Current period after end of depreciable life
         monthdepr=0                                      && No current depr
         ytddepr=MAX(0,(mytd-(mtot-12*life)))*mdepr       && Months of depr YTD
         accdepr=cost-salvage              && Fully depreciated
    OTHERWISE                        && Current period within depreciable life
         monthdepr=mdepr             && Current depreciation
         ytddepr=MIN(mytd,mtot)*mdepr
         accdepr=mtot*mdepr
ENDCASE

RETURN
```

Listing 6.9. The subroutine FADBDEPR.

```
**************************************************************************
* FADBDEPR -    Returns declining-balance depr. amount for the current  *
*               month, year-to-date, and accumulated depreciation       *
*               8/17/86                                                  *
**************************************************************************
* PARAMETERS ARE:
*       cost      - amount to depreciate
*       salvage   - salvage value
*       life      - life in years
*       accel     - acceleration factor, i.e. 1.5 for 150% declining balance
*       mtot      - total months from start to current month
*       mytd      - number of months since start of fiscal year
*       monthdepr         - return current month depreciation
*       ytddepr           - return year to date depreciation
*       accumdepr         - return accumulated depreciation

PARAMETERS cost,salvage,life,accel,mtot,mytd,monthdepr,ytddepr,accdepr
PRIVATE mfirst,xm,balance,xm1

* Initialize Variables for depreciation loop
STORE 0 TO monthdepr,ytddepr,accumdepr   && zero the depreciation accumulators
balance=cost                             && beginning declining-balance amount
rate=accel/(12*life)                     && calc. depr. rate for decl. balance
xm=0                                     && accum. months of depreciation
xm1=MIN(mtot,MOD(mtot-mytd-1,12)+1)      && months of depr. in first fiscal year

* loop to calculate depreciation by year until current date
DO WHILE xm<mtot

    IF balance>salvage.and.xm<12*life      && More to depreciate

       *Calculate declining balance depr for year
       monthdepr=balance*rate      && depreciation rate this year
       ytddepr=MIN(xm1*monthdepr,balance-salvage)          && year to date depr
       accdepr=accdepr+ytddepr     && accumulated after current year
       balance=balance-ytddepr     && balance after current year

    ELSE                           && no more depreciation

       * After end of depreciation. Zero current depr. and terminate loop
       ytddepr=0
       monthdepr=0
       xm1=mtot-xm
    ENDIF

    *Setup for next pass through loop
    xm=xm+xm1                      && accumulated months to end of this year
    xm1=MIN(12,MIN(mtot-xm,12*life-xm)) && months depr in next fiscal year

ENDDO (depreciation loop)

RETURN
```

Listing 6.10. The program FABROWSE.

```
******************************************
* FABROWSE -     Browse fixed asset list *
*                 8/17/86                 *
******************************************

* Set environment and open files
SET DELETED ON
DO faopen
SELECT fixasset
RESTORE FROM famem ADDITIVE              && Restore system memory variables
smax=2                                   && Number of browse screens per record
mtitle="BROWSE LIST OF FIXED ASSETS"
DO borders WITH fatitle,mtitle

* Get date for depreciation calculations
mdate=DATE()
mok=.f.
DO WHILE .not.mok
   @ 12, 15 SAY "Enter date for depreciation calculations" GET mdate
   READ
   @ 21, 33 SAY "OK (Y or N)?" GET mok PICTURE "Y"
   READ
ENDDO
@ 5, 1 CLEAR TO 19, 78
@ 21, 1 CLEAR TO 22, 78

* Initial values before browse loop
scnt=0
screen=1
strow=7
endrow=20
mscroll=endrow-strow

* Get order of browse
no=0
DO faorder with no
DO borders WITH fatitle,mtitle

* Get filter for report
DO fasubset
DO borders WITH fatitle,mtitle

* Loop to browse through records and screen
DO WHILE .T.

   * Clear Screen
   @ 5, 1 CLEAR TO 19, 78
   @ 21, 1 CLEAR TO 22, 78

   * Display field headings
   DO CASE
      CASE screen=1
         @ 3, 60 SAY SPACE(18)
         @ 5, 1 SAY "ID      DESCRIPT         SERIAL              TYPE ";
                 +"DIV  LOC   IN SRVC END SRVC"
         @ 6, 1 SAY "------- ------------------ ------------------- ---- ";
                 +"---- ---- -------- --------"
      CASE screen=2
         @ 3, 60 SAY "DEPR DATE "+DTOC(mdate)
         @ 5, 1 SAY "ID              COST      SALVAGE M LI START ";
                 +"MONTH DEPR   YTD DEPR    ACC DEPR"
         @ 6, 1 SAY "------- ----------- ----------- - -- ----- ";
                 +"----------- ----------- -----------"
```

```
      ENDCASE

      * Display fields
      cntr=0
      DO WHILE cntr<mscroll.and..not.EOF()
         row=cntr+strow
         * display records on screen
         @ row,  1 SAY id_number
         IF screen=1
            @ row, 9 SAY descript PICTURE "XXXXXXXXXXXXXXXXXXX"
            @ row, 28 SAY serial_no
            @ row, 47 SAY type
            @ row, 52 SAY division
            @ row, 57 SAY location
            @ row, 62 SAY serv_date
            endmnth=IIF(MONTH(serv_date)=1,12,MONTH(serv_date)-1)
            endyr=YEAR(serv_date)+depr_life+IIF(MONTH(serv_date)=1,-1,0)
            @ row,  72 SAY STR(endmnth,2)+"/"+STR(endyr,4)
         ELSE (screen 2)
            @ row,  9 SAY cost
            @ row, 21 SAY salvage
            @ row, 33 SAY depr_mthd
            @ row, 35 SAY depr_life
            @ row, 38 SAY SUBSTR(DTOC(serv_date),1,2)+SUBSTR(DTOC(serv_date),6,3)
            STORE 0 to mcurr,mytd,maccum
            DO fadepr WITH mdate,mcurr,mytd,maccum
            @ row, 44 SAY mcurr PICTURE "99999999.99"
            @ row, 56 SAY mytd PICTURE "99999999.99"
            @ row, 68 SAY maccum PICTURE "99999999.99"
         ENDIF (screen 1)

         cntr=cntr+1
         SKIP
      ENDDO

      * Display MORE message
      IF .not.EOF()
         @ 21, 36 SAY "* MORE *"
      ENDIF

      * Wait for one of specified keys before continuing
      scnt=0
      DO scroller WITH scnt,cntr,mscroll,screen,smax
      * Check for exit condition (scnt=999)
      IF scnt=999
         EXIT
      ENDIF

      * Move to start of next screen
      SKIP scnt
      IF EOF()
         SKIP -1
      ENDIF

   ENDDO (Main loop)

   * Tidy up and return
   SET DELETED OFF
   CLOSE DATABASES
   CLEAR
   RETURN
```

Listing 6.11. The subroutine FAORDER.

```
*************************************************************************
* FAORDER -       Determine current file index and optional seek value  *
*                 8/17/86                                                *
*************************************************************************
PARAMETERS NO

DO WHILE .T.
    no=0
    @   7, 28 SAY "0. RECORD NUMBER ORDER"
    @   8, 28 SAY "1. ORDER BY ID NUMBER"
    @   9, 28 SAY "2. ORDER BY TYPE"
    @  10, 28 SAY "3. ORDER BY LOCATION"
    @  11, 28 SAY "4. ORDER BY DIVISION & LOCATION"
    @  12, 28 SAY "5. ORDER BY IN SERVICE DATE"
    @  13, 28 SAY "6. ORDER BY END DATE"
    @  21, 32 SAY "ENTER CHOICE:" GET no PICTURE "9" RANGE 0,6
    @  22, 28 SAY "CHOOSE ORDER BY NUMBER"
    READ
    @  22, 1 SAY SPACE(78)

    SET ORDER TO no
    GO TOP

    MOK=.f.
    @  22, 32 SAY "OK (Y or N)" GET MOK PICTURE "Y"
    READ
    @ 5,  1 CLEAR TO 19, 78
    @ 21, 1 CLEAR TO 22, 78
    IF MOK
        EXIT
    ENDIF
ENDDO

RETURN
```

Listing 6.12. The subroutine FASUBSET.

```
***********************************************************
* FASUBSET -     Accept limits on records in file        *
*                File must be opened first               *
*                Uses FACLS subroutine                   *
*                8/17/86                                  *
***********************************************************
SET FILTER TO
mok=.f.
@ 12, 7 SAY "DO YOU WANT TO SELECT A SUBSET OF THE DATABASE RECORDS (Y or N)?";
  GET mok PICTURE "Y"
@ 14, 7 SAY "(Y will start the dBASE MODIFY QUERY command to enter ";
       +"the conditions,"
@ 15, 7 SAY " N will continue with all records selected.)"
READ

IF mok
   @ 5, 1 CLEAR TO 19, 78                && Clear Screen
   mok=" "
   * Write Instructions
   @ 5, 2 SAY "This command uses dBASE III Plus's built in ";
       +"MODIFY QUERY command to"
   @ 6, 2 SAY "build the filter. When the MODIFY QUERY screen ";
       +"appears, enter the filter"
   @ 7, 2 SAY "conditions in the space provided."
   @ 9, 2 SAY "Building a query consists of four steps, repeated ";
       +"until the query is"
   @ 10, 2 SAY "complete. First, a field in the database is ";
       +"selected. Second, a logical"
   @ 11, 2 SAY "condition is specified for the field. Third, an ";
       +"expression is specified"
   @ 12, 2 SAY "to finish the condition placed on the selected ";
       +"field. Fourth, if another"
   @ 13, 2 SAY "condition is to be specified, the connection ";
       +"(.AND. or .OR.) between this"
   @ 14, 2 SAY "condition and the next is specified. These ";
       +"four steps are repeated once"
   @ 15, 2 SAY "for each condition to be placed on the data retrieval."
   @ 17, 2 SAY "When finished defining the subset of assets to be ";
       +"displayed, be sure"
   @ 18, 2 SAY "to exit the interactive query command using the ";
       +"EXIT SAVE option. If the"
   @ 19, 2 SAY "abandon option is used to exit, the conditions will ";
       +"be discarded."
   @ 21, 26 SAY "Press any key to continue" GET mok
   READ

   * Use dBASE III Plus modify query command to create filter
   DELETE FILE fasubset.qry
   MODIFY QUERY fasubset
   * move record pointer to engage query file
   GO TOP                 && Sets file pointer to first matching record in file.
ENDIF
RETURN
```

Listing 6.13. The subroutine SCROLLER.

```
****************************************************************************
* SCROLLER - Program to accept keystrokes from user to scroll the screen  *
*            PARAMETERS: SCNT    - returns vertical scroll amt to next screen *
*                        CNTR    - number of lines displayed on last screen  *
*                        MSCROLL - number of lines that fit on a screen      *
*                        SCREEN  - current screen number                     *
*                        SMAX    - maximum screen number                     *
*            9/10/86                                                       *
****************************************************************************
PARAMETERS scnt,cntr,mscroll,screen,smax
PRIVATE i

* Wait for one of specified keys
@ 22, 2 SAY "PRESS: ARROW KEYS, PgUp ,PgDn, Enter, Home (BOF), ";
        +"or End (EOF); Esc to quit"
i=0
SET ESCAPE OFF
DO WHILE .not.STR(i,2)$"13, 5,24,18, 3,27, 4,19, 1, 6"  && Valid keypresses
   i=INKEY()                                             && Read keypress
ENDDO
SET ESCAPE ON

* Reset record pointer and cumulative count based on key pressed
DO CASE
    CASE i=27           && ESC key
        * flag to Exit the display loop
        scnt=999

    CASE i=5            && UP arrow key
        * Move record pointer to one line above start
        scnt=-(cntr+1)

    CASE i=24           && DOWN arrow key
        * Move record pointer down one line
        scnt=-(cntr-1)

    CASE i=18           && PGUP key
        * Scroll up one screen
        scnt=-(cntr+mscroll)

    CASE i=3.or.i=13    && PGDN or ENTER key
        * Scroll down one screen
        scnt=0

    CASE i=19           && Left arrow key
        *move one screen left
        scnt=-cntr
        screen=MAX(screen-1,1)

    CASE i=4            && Right arrow key
        * move one screen right
        scnt=-cntr
        screen=MIN(screen+1,smax)

    CASE i=1            && HOME key
        * Move to beginning of filtered file
        scnt=0
        GO TOP
```

```
    CASE i=6                    && END key
        * Move to end of filtered file
        scnt=-(mscroll-1)
        GO BOTTOM
ENDCASE
RETURN
```

Listing 6.14. The program FAREPORT.

```
********************************************
* FAREPORT -        Print fixed asset list  *
*                   8/17/86                  *
********************************************

* Set environment and open files
SET DELETED ON
DO faopen
SELECT fixasset
mdate=DATE()
mtitle="FIXED ASSET REPORTS"
RESTORE FROM famem ADDITIVE      && Restore memory variables for this appl.

* Initial values before report loop
strow=7
endrow=55
lines=endrow-strow

* Get order of report
no=0
DO borders WITH fatitle,mtitle            && Display titles & border
DO faorder with no                        && Get report order
DO borders WITH fatitle,mtitle            && Display titles & border

* Get filter for report
DO fasubset                               && Get filter on database
DO borders WITH fatitle,mtitle            && Display titles & border

* Setup printer
mq=" "
@ 21, 14 SAY "Make sure printer is turned on and set at top of page"
@ 22, 25 SAY "Then press any key to continue" GET mq
READ
@ 21, 1 CLEAR TO 22, 78
@ 21,36  SAY "WORKING"                     && Clear Screen
SET PRINT ON
SET CONSOLE OFF
? &fapsetup

* Do Report Form based on index selected
DO CASE
    CASE no=0
        REPORT FORM farep0
```

(Continued on next page.)

Listing 6.14, continued.

```
    CASE no=1
        REPORT FORM farep1
    CASE no=2
        REPORT FORM farep2
    CASE no=3
        REPORT FORM farep3
    CASE no=4
        REPORT FORM farep4
    CASE no=5
        REPORT FORM farep5
    CASE no=6
        REPORT FORM farep6
ENDCASE

* Clean up and return
EJECT
? &fapreset
SET CONSOLE ON
SET PRINT OFF
SET FILTER TO
CLEAR
CLOSE DATABASES
RETURN
```

Listing 6.15. The program FADEPREP.

```
***************************************************
* FADEPREP -     Print depreciation schedule     *
*                  8/18/86                        *
***************************************************

* Set environment and open files
SET DEVICE TO SCREEN
SET DELETED ON
DO faopen
mdate=DATE()
mtitle="DEPRECIATION REPORTS"
RESTORE FROM famem ADDITIVE        && Restore memory variables for this appl.
pglen=55
DO borders WITH fatitle,mtitle

* Get depr date
mok=.f.
DO WHILE .not.mok
   @ 12, 26  SAY "Enter date for depreciation " GET mdate
   READ
   @ 22, 35  SAY "OK (Y or N)" GET mok PICTURE 'Y'
   READ
ENDDO
@ 5, 1 CLEAR TO 19, 78
@ 21, 1 CLEAR TO 22, 78
```

```
* Get record order for report
no=0
DO faorder with no                      && Get report order (index)
DO borders WITH fatitle,mtitle

* Get filter condition for report
DO fasubset                             && Select a subset of records to display
DO borders WITH fatitle,mtitle

* Setup printer
mq=" "
@ 21, 14 SAY "Make sure printer is turned on and set at top of page"
@ 22, 25 SAY "Then press any key to continue" GET mq
READ
DO borders WITH fatitle,mtitle
@ 21,36  SAY "WORKING"
SET PRINT ON
SET CONSOLE OFF
? &fapsetup                             && System printer setup string
SET CONSOLE ON
SET PRINT OFF
SET DEVICE TO PRINT
SET MARGIN TO fapmargin                 && System left margin

* Select title and subtotal fields for depr. report based on selected index
sflag=.F.
sfield="0"
stitle=""
ssflag=.F.
ssfield="0"
sstitle=""
DO CASE
   CASE no=0
        title="RECORD NUMBER"
   CASE no=1
        title="ID NUMBER"
   CASE no=2
        title="ASSET TYPE"
        sflag=.T.
        sfield="TYPE"
        stitle=title
   CASE no=3
        title="LOCATION"
        sflag=.T.
        sfield="LOCATION"
        stitle=title
   CASE no=4
        title="DIVISION"
        sflag=.T.
        sfield="DIVISION"
        stitle=title
        ssflag=.T.
        ssfield="LOCATION"
        sstitle=ssfield
```

(Continued on next page.)

Listing 6.15, continued.

```
    CASE no=5
         title="IN SERVICE DATE"
         sflag=.T.
         sfield="STR(YEAR(serv_date),4)"
         stitle="YEAR"
    CASE no=6
         title="END OF LIFE"
         sflag=.T.
         sfield="STR(YEAR(serv_date)+depr_life-IIF(MONTH(serv_date)=1,1,0),4)"
         stitle="YEAR"
ENDCASE
svalue=&sfield                    && Use macro to set svalue to first record
ssvalue=&ssfield                  && Use macro to set ssvalue to first record
pageno=1

*LOOP to print depreciation report
cntr=0
STORE 0 to sscost,sssalvage,sscurr,ssytd,ssaccum,scost,ssalvage,scurr,sytd,;
           saccum,tcost,tsalvage,tcurr,tytd,taccum
STORE 0 to mcurr,mytd,maccum
DO WHILE .NOT.EOF()

   * Top of page processing
   IF cntr=0
      DO fadphead WITH cntr,mdate        && Print title and headings
      incr=0
   ENDIF

   * Print next database record
   @ cntr,   0 SAY id_number
   @ cntr,   8 SAY descript
   @ cntr,  39 SAY type
   @ cntr,  44 SAY location
   @ cntr,  49 SAY division
   @ cntr,  54 SAY serv_date
   @ cntr,  63 SAY cost
   @ cntr,  75 SAY salvage
   @ cntr,  89 SAY depr_mthd
   DO fadepr  WITH mdate,mcurr,mytd,maccum
   @ cntr,  92 SAY mcurr PICTURE "99999999.99"
   @ cntr, 104 SAY mytd PICTURE "99999999.99"
   @ cntr, 116 SAY maccum PICTURE "99999999.99"
   cntr=cntr+1
   incr=1

   * Update subtotals and total
   tcost=tcost+cost
   tsalvage=tsalvage+salvage
   tcurr=tcurr+mcurr
   tytd=tytd+mytd
   taccum=taccum+maccum
   scost=scost+cost
   ssalvage=ssalvage+salvage
   scurr=scurr+mcurr
   sytd=sytd+mytd
   saccum=saccum+maccum
```

```
      sscost=sscost+cost
      sssalvage=sssalvage+salvage
      sscurr=sscurr+mcurr
      ssytd=ssytd+mytd
      ssaccum=ssaccum+maccum
      SKIP

    * Subsubtotal processing
    IF ssflag                             && Is there a subsubtotal?
       IF ssvalue#&ssfield..or.svalue#&sfield..or.EOF()   && Has break occurred?
          cntr=cntr+incr                             && Advance line count
          IF cntr>pglen                              && Need new page?
             DO fadpbot WITH pageno,cntr
             DO fadphead WITH cntr,mdate
          ENDIF
          @ cntr,   8  SAY "*** SUBTOTAL FOR &sstitle.: &ssvalue ***"
          @ cntr,  63  SAY sscost      PICTURE "99999999.99"
          @ cntr,  75  SAY sssalvage   PICTURE "99999999.99"
          @ cntr,  92  SAY sscurr      PICTURE "99999999.99"
          @ cntr, 104  SAY ssytd       PICTURE "99999999.99"
          @ cntr, 116  SAY ssaccum PICTURE "99999999.99"
          STORE 0 TO sscost,sssalvage,sscurr,ssytd,ssaccum
          cntr=cntr+2
          incr=0
       ENDIF
       ssvalue=&ssfield                      && Update stored field value
    ENDIF

    * Subtotal processing
    IF sflag                              && Is there a subtotal?
       IF svalue#&sfield..or.EOF()        && Control break reached?
          cntr=cntr+incr                  && Advance line count
          IF cntr>pglen                   && Need new page?
             DO fadpbot WITH pageno,cntr
             DO fadphead WITH cntr,mdate
          ENDIF
          @ cntr,   8  SAY "*** SUBTOTAL FOR &stitle.: &svalue ***"
          @ cntr,  63  SAY scost       PICTURE "99999999.99"
          @ cntr,  75  SAY ssalvage    PICTURE "99999999.99"
          @ cntr,  92  SAY scurr       PICTURE "99999999.99"
          @ cntr, 104  SAY sytd        PICTURE "99999999.99"
          @ cntr, 116  SAY saccum PICTURE "99999999.99"
          STORE 0 TO scost,ssalvage,scurr,sytd,saccum
          cntr=cntr+2
          incr=0
       ENDIF
       svalue=&sfield                        && Update stored field value
    ENDIF

    * Bottom of page processing
    IF cntr>pglen
       DO fadpbot WITH pageno,cntr
       incr=0
       ENDIF

    ENDDO
```

(Continued on next page.)

Listing 6.15, continued.

```
* Top of page processing
IF cntr=0
   DO fadphead WITH cntr,mdate            && Print title and headings
   incr=0
ENDIF

* Print grand totals
@ cntr,   7  SAY "GRAND TOTAL"
@ cntr,  63  SAY tcost      PICTURE "99999999.99"
@ cntr,  75  SAY tsalvage   PICTURE "99999999.99"
@ cntr,  92  SAY tytd       PICTURE "99999999.99"
@ cntr, 104  SAY taccum     PICTURE "99999999.99"
@ cntr, 116  SAY tcost-tsalvage-taccum  PICTURE "99999999.99"
@ pglen+5, 59 SAY "Page"
@ pglen+5, 64 SAY pageno
EJECT

* Clean up and return
SET PRINT ON
SET CONSOLE OFF
? &fapreset
SET CONSOLE ON
SET PRINT OFF
SET DEVICE TO SCREEN
SET DELETED OFF
CLEAR
CLOSE DATABASES
RETURN
```

Listing 6.16. The program FADPBOT.

```
**********************************************
* FADPBOT - Print page number and eject page *
*           8/18/86                          *
**********************************************
PARAMETERS pageno,cntr

@ pglen+5, 59 SAY "Page "
@ pglen+5, 64 SAY pageno PICTURE "99"
pageno=pageno+1
EJECT
cntr=0

RETURN
```

Listing 6.17. The subroutine FADPHEAD.

```
*************************************************************
* FADPHEAD - Print title and heading for depreciation report *
*          8/18/86                                          *
*************************************************************
PARAMETERS cntr,mdate
PRIVATE i,j
@  3,   49 SAY "SMITH AND JONES CORPORATION"
@  3,  106 SAY "Report Date:"
@  3,  119 SAY DATE()
@  4,   49 SAY "FIXED ASSET TRACKING SYSTEM"
@  5,  (101-LEN(title))/2 SAY "DEPRECIATION REPORT BY "+title
i=CMONTH(mdate)+" "+STR(YEAR(mdate))
@  6,   (126-len(i)-4)/2 SAY "For "+i
j=MAX(27,23+LEN(title))
@  7,  (126-j)/2 SAY REPLICATE("-",j)
@  9,   0 SAY " ASSET                                        ";
        +"IN SERV.                     DEPR  CURR MONTH      ";
        +"YTD ACCUMULATED"
@ 10,   0 SAY "  ID    DESCRIPTION                   TYPE LOC DIV   ";
        +"DATE          COST     SALVAGE METH      DEPR      ";
        +"DEPR      DEPR"
@ 11,   0 SAY "------- ------------------------------ ---- ---- ---- -------- ";
        +"----------- ----------- ---- ----------- ----------- -----------"
cntr=12
RETURN
```

Listing 6.18. The subroutine FADELETE.

```
***************************************************
* FADELETE -      Delete or undelete assets       *
*                 8/18/86                          *
***************************************************

* Open files & set environment
SET DELETED OFF
DO faopen                            && Open fixed asset files and indexes
RESTORE FROM famem ADDITIVE          && Restore memory variables
mtitle="DELETE OR UNDELETE FIXED ASSET"

* Main loop.
DO WHILE .T.
   DO borders WITH fatitle,mtitle

   * Get ID number
   mid=SPACE(7)
   @ 12, 15 SAY "Enter ID for asset to delete or undelete:";
       GET mid FUNCTION "!"
   @ 21, 15 SAY "Press ESC or ENTER key with blank ID number to quit"
   READ

   * Check for blank id
   IF mid=SPACE(7)
      EXIT
   ENDIF

   * Check if id is in file. zf not, warn user and skip rest of loop
   SEEK mid                          && Check for this ID in file
   @ 21, 1 CLEAR TO 22, 78           && Clear Status line
   IF EOF()                          && IF not found
      *ID not found, display error message and loop
      @ 21, 32 SAY "ASSET NOT FOUND!"
      mok=" "
      @ 22, 24 SAY "Press any key to continue ..." GET mok PICTURE "X"
      READ
      @ 21, 1 CLEAR TO 22, 78        && Clear Status line
      LOOP
   ELSE
      * ID found, ask user to verify id number
      mok=.t.
      @ 21, 33 SAY "OK (Y or N)" GET mok PICTURE "Y"
      READ
      IF .not.mok                    && Loop if user does not verify
         LOOP
      ENDIF
   ENDIF

   *  Have ID for asset, display data for user to review
   @ 5, 1 CLEAR TO 19, 78            && Clear display area
   @ 21, 1 CLEAR TO 22, 78           && Clear status line
   DO faastscr                       && Display SAYs and GETs
   CLEAR GETS                        && But don't read!
```

```
     * Display delete/undelete message, as appropriate. Get answer
     IF .not.DELETED()

        * If asset not deleted, ask user to verify delete
        @ 21, 25 SAY "ASSET IS CURRENTLY NOT DELETED"
        mok=.f.
        @ 22, 25 SAY "WANT TO DELETE IT (Y or N)? " GET mok PICTURE "Y"
        READ
        @ 21, 1 CLEAR TO 22, 78              && Clear Status line
        * If user verifies, perform deletion
        IF mok
           DELETE
           @ 21, 13 SAY "ASSET NOW DELETED. USE THIS COMMAND AGAIN TO UNDELETE"
           mok=" "
           @ 22, 25 SAY "Press any key to continue ... " GET mok PICTURE "X"
           READ
        ENDIF
     ELSE

        * If asset deleted, ask user to verify undelete
        @ 21, 27 SAY "ASSET IS CURRENTLY DELETED"
        mok=.f.
        @ 22, 24 SAY "WANT TO UNDELETE IT (Y or N)? " GET mok PICTURE "Y"
        READ
        @ 21, 1 CLEAR TO 22, 78              && Clear Status line

        * If user verifies, perform undeletion
        IF mok
           RECALL
           @ 21, 13 SAY "ASSET NOW RECALLED. USE THIS COMMAND AGAIN TO DELETE"
           mok=" "
           @ 22, 25 SAY "Press any key to continue ... " GET mok PICTURE "X"
           READ
        ENDIF
     ENDIF

* End of main loop
ENDDO

* Tidy up and return
CLEAR
CLOSE DATABASES
RETURN
```

Listing 6.19. The program FAPACK.

```
**********************************************************
* FAPACK -        PACK deleted records in data files    *
*                 8/18/86                                *
**********************************************************

* Open files
DO faopen
RESTORE FROM famem ADDITIVE
DO borders WITH fatitle,"Pack Files"

* Delete blank records in customer file and pack
@ 12,30 SAY "Packing FIXASSET file"
PACK

* Tidy up and return
CLEAR
CLOSE DATABASES
RETURN
```

Listing 6.20. The program FABACKUP.

```
********************************************************
* FABACKUP -     Back up Fixed Asset files       *
*                8/15/86                          *
********************************************************
target="b:"                              && Target drive for backup
CLEAR
? "BACKUP Fixed Asset and Depreciation System Data Files"
?

* Ask user to verify backup command
mok=' '
DO WHILE UPPER(mok)#"Y".and.UPPER(mok)#"N"
   WAIT "Do you want to proceed with this command (Y or N)?" TO mok
   READ
ENDDO

* If answer is 'yes', do backup
IF UPPER(mok)="Y"
   files1="*.dbf"
   RUN BACKUP &files1 &target
   files2="*.ndx"
   RUN BACKUP &files2 &target/A
   files3="*.mem"
   RUN BACKUP &files3 &target/A
ENDIF

* Clear screen and return
CLEAR
RETURN
```

Listing 6.21. The program FARESTOR.

```
***********************************************************************
* FARESTOR -    RESTORE Fixed Asset data files from backup         *
*               8/2/86                                              *
***********************************************************************
* Display title
CLEAR
? "RESTORE Fixed Asset and Depreciation System Data from Backup"
?

* Ask user to verify restore command
mok=' '
DO WHILE UPPER(mok)#"Y".and.UPPER(mok)#"N"
   WAIT "Do you want to proceed with this command (Y or N)?" TO mok
ENDDO

* If answer is 'yes', do restore
IF UPPER(mok)="Y"
   source="b:"                          && Source drive for restore
   target="c:"                          && Target drive for restore
   files1=target+"*.*"
   RUN RESTORE &source &files1
ENDIF

* Clear screen and return
CLEAR
RETURN
```

Listing 6.22. The program FIXASSET.

```
************************************************
* FIXASSET - Fixed asset management system *
*                8/17/86                       *
************************************************

* Setup environment
SET TALK OFF
SET SAFETY OFF
SET DEVICE TO SCREEN
SET PRINT OFF
CLEAR ALL

* Main loop
option=-1
DO WHILE option#0
CLOSE DATABASES

   * Display Menu
   option=0
   RESTORE FROM famem ADDITIVE   && Make sure system memory variables present
   DO borders WITH fatitle,"MAIN MENU"   && Display title and borders

   * Display menu options
   @  8, 26  SAY "1. DATA ENTRY AND QUERIES"
   @  9, 26  SAY "2. REPORTS"
   @ 10, 26  SAY "3. SYSTEM MAINTENANCE"
   @ 18, 26  SAY "0. EXIT TO DBASE DOT PROMPT"
   @ 21, 35  SAY "OPTION:" GET option PICTURE "9" RANGE 0,3
   READ

   * Do selected option
   DO CASE
      CASE option=1
         DO famenu1                           && Account maintenance
      CASE option=2
         DO famenu2                          && Data entry
      CASE option=3
         DO famenu3                          && Account status queries

      OTHERWISE                              && Confirm option=0 before leaving
         mok=.t.
         @ 22, 21 SAY "Do you really want to quit (Y or N)?";
               GET mok PICTURE "Y"
         READ
         option=IIF(mok,0,-1)    && Reset option to -1 if "N"
   ENDCASE
* End of main loop
ENDDO (option#0)

* Restore system defaults and exit
SET TALK ON
SET SAFETY ON
SET DEVICE TO SCREEN
SET PRINT OFF
CLEAR
RETURN
```

Listing 6.23. The program FAMENU1.

```
***********************************************************
* FAMENU1 -      Fixed asset entry and query menu        *
*               8/17/86                                   *
***********************************************************
PRIVATE option

* Main loop
option=-1
DO WHILE option#0

   * Display Menu
   option=0
   RESTORE FROM famem ADDITIVE  && Make sure system memory vars are present
   DO borders WITH fatitle,"DATA ENTRY AND QUERY MENU"  && Disp. title & borders

   * Display menu options
   @  8, 25  SAY "1. ENTER OR UPDATE ASSET DATA"
   @  9, 25  SAY "2. QUERY ASSET DATA"
   @ 10, 25  SAY "3. BROWSE LIST OF ASSETS"
   @ 18, 25  SAY "0. RETURN TO MAIN MENU"
   @ 21, 35  SAY "OPTION:" GET option PICTURE "9" RANGE 0,3
   READ

   * Do selected option
   DO CASE
      CASE option=1
           DO faenter                    && data entry/update
      CASE option=2
           DO faquery                    && asset data query
      CASE option=3
           DO fabrowse                   && browse list of assets
   ENDCASE
* End of main loop
ENDDO (option#0)

* Restore system defaults and exit
CLEAR
RETURN
```

Listing 6.24. The program FAMENU2.

```
*******************************************
* FAMENU2 -      Fixed asset report menu *
*                8/17/86                  *
*******************************************
PRIVATE option

* Main loop
option=-1
DO WHILE option#0

   * Display Menu
   option=0
   RESTORE FROM famem ADDITIVE  && Make sure system memory vars are present
   DO borders WITH fatitle,"REPORT MENU"        && Display title and borders

   * Display menu options
   @  8, 26  SAY "1. PRINT ASSET LIST"
   @  9, 26  SAY "2. PRINT DEPRECIATION REPORT"
   @ 18, 26  SAY "0. RETURN TO MAIN MENU"
   @ 21, 35  SAY "OPTION:" GET option PICTURE "9" RANGE 0,2
   READ

   * Do selected option
   DO CASE
      CASE option=1
         DO fareport                         && print asset list
      CASE option=2
         DO fadeprep                         && print depreciation report
   ENDCASE
* End of main loop
ENDDO (option#0)

* Restore system defaults and exit
CLEAR
RETURN
```

Listing 6.25. The program FAMENU3.

```
*************************************************************
* FAMENU3 -      Fixed asset system maintenance menu       *
*                8/17/86                                    *
*************************************************************
PRIVATE option

* Main loop
option=-1
DO WHILE option#0

    * Display Menu
    option=0
    RESTORE FROM famem ADDITIVE  && Make sure system memory vars are present
    DO borders WITH fatitle,"SYSTEM MAINTENANCE MENU"    && Disp. title & borders

    * Display menu options
    @  8, 25  SAY "1. DELETE/UNDELETE ASSETS"
    @  9, 25  SAY "2. PACK DATAFILE"
    @ 10, 25  SAY "3. REINDEX DATAFILE"
    @ 11, 25  SAY "4. BACKUP FILES TO FLOPPY"
    @ 12, 25  SAY "5. RESTORE FILES FROM FLOPPY"
    @ 13, 25  SAY "6. EDIT SYSTEM MEMORY VARIABLES"
    @ 18, 25  SAY "0. RETURN TO MAIN MENU"
    @ 21, 35  SAY "OPTION:" GET option PICTURE "9" RANGE 0,6
    READ

    * Do selected option
    DO CASE
        CASE option=1
            DO fadelete                && delete/undelete assets
        CASE option=2
            DO fapack                  && pack asset database
        CASE option=3
            DO faindex                 && reindex asset database
        CASE option=4
            DO fabackup                && back up datafiles to floppy
        CASE option=5
            DO farestor                && restore datafiles from floppy
        CASE option=6
            DO faedmem                 && edit system memory variables
    ENDCASE
* End of main loop
ENDDO (option#0)

* Restore system defaults and exit
CLEAR
RETURN
```

7

Customer-Account System

Quick and Clean Software had a thriving business designing applications with dBASE III Plus. Sales were brisk, and a number of customers had signed software-maintenance contracts. Quick and Clean Software decided it was time to develop a customer-account system. Such a system would help them track their customer accounts and could even be sold to clients later.

What Quick and Clean Software needed was a more-or-less traditional customer-account system with the addition of an automatic-billing provision for the maintenance contracts. Rather than choose a commercial package, which might require changing the way the company keeps records, Quick and Clean decided to create a custom application with dBASE. Quick and Clean Software also decided to develop the customer account system as a stand-alone application. However, the system was designed so that programs could be added to link the customer-account system to other modules of a computerized accounting system.

This chapter takes you through all the stages involved in developing the application. We consider the purpose and functions of the system, then describe the data and index files that need to be defined before the programs are developed. Next, we look at the programs and subroutines that enable the user to create and edit the system memory file; create and maintain customer-account records; post billings and payments; query the database; produce monthly statements and account histories, summaries, and lists; and perform a number of maintenance functions. Finally, we look at a menu system, the use of procedure files, and possible extensions to the system.

Before we begin our examination of the customer-account system, we need to consider two basic techniques for tracking customer accounts: the *ledger-card* system and the *open-invoice* system. Doing that will prepare us for the application and make it clear why Quick and Clean Software chose the ledger-card system.

Techniques for Managing Customer Accounts

Two basic systems for tracking customer accounts are the *ledger-card system* and the *open-invoice system*. With the ledger-card system, each transaction is posted to an account card and the balance is carried forward. With the open-invoice system each billing generates an open invoice and each payment is credited against that invoice.

The best approach for a particular business depends on whether the business needs to track payments against a specific invoice, or, like Quick and Clean Software, needs only to maintain an account history, a current balance, and a past-due balance. In general, if customers pay from the invoice, then the business will need to maintain the additional information to track payments against open invoices. If customers pay from monthly statements, then the ledger-card system is the system of choice.

The Ledger-Card System

The ledger-card system takes its name from the manual version of the system, which uses account-ledger cards that are updated by hand or by a posting machine. A customer-account application using the ledger-card system consists of two files: the customer-account master file and the transaction file. The relationships between the information in these files are shown in figure 7.1.

The customer-account master file contains necessary information about each customer, including the account number, name, address, account balance, credit limit, date of last statement, balance at last statement, and any other desired information.

If the customer-account master file is to be used for other purposes, such as sales tracking, then additional information may also be kept in the file. The application in this chapter includes a provision for automatic billing of a monthly fee. To facilitate automatic billing, information such as the automatic billing fee, billing ID number, and billing description must be stored in the customer master file.

The transaction file contains the information to be recorded about each customer transaction. This typically consists of account number, transaction date, transaction ID number, description, debit, credit, balance after the transaction, and any account-status flags needed for the application.

The Open-Invoice System

In the open-invoice system, payments are matched against invoices. The database consists of two files: the customer-account master file and the open-invoice file. The relationships between the customer file and the open-invoice file are shown schematically in figure 7.2.

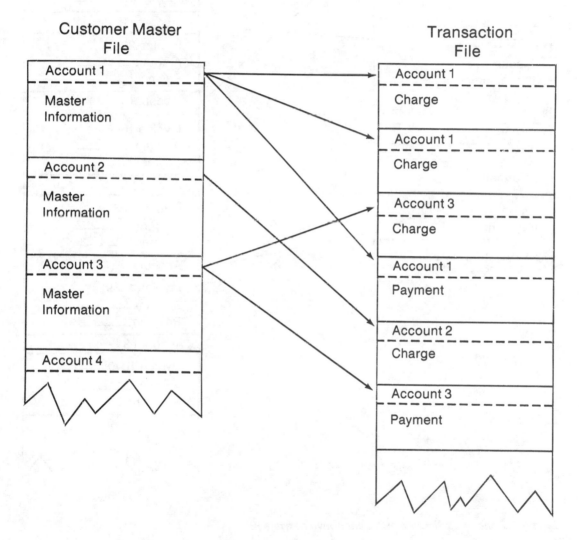

Fig. 7.1. Schematic diagram of the ledger-card system.

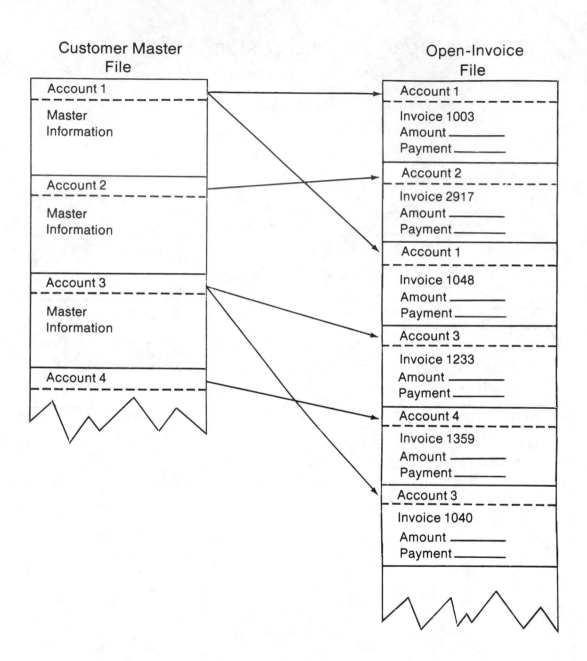

Fig. 7.2. Schematic diagram of the open-invoice system.

The customer-account master file contains necessary information about each customer, including the account number, name, address, account balance, credit limit, date of last statement, balance at last statement, and any other desired information. If the customer-account master file is used to generate invoices as well as track payments against invoices, the additional information required for invoicing would be kept in the customer-account master file as well as any information for other purposes, such as sales tracking.

The open-invoice file contains the information recorded about each open invoice. A typical open-invoice record might consist of account number, invoice number, invoice date, due date, discount date, description, gross amount, discount amount, amount paid, and any status flags needed for the application.

Choosing the Right System

After reviewing their billing practices, Quick and Clean settled on the ledger-card system. The company normally has an ongoing consulting relationship with its clients, and sends them monthly statements for services performed each month. Quick and Clean's business thus is different from that of a software or hardware retailer. For a retail business, it is more appropriate for a customer to be invoiced for each sale.

Identifying the Purpose and Functions of the System

After Quick and Clean Software chose the appropriate technique for managing its customer accounts, the next step was to identify clearly the purpose and functions of the application. The basic purpose of the customer-accounts system is to record customer charges and payments, automatic billings, and miscellaneous debits and credits against customer accounts. In addition, the system should generate monthly statements and management reports showing the status of each account and flagging accounts that have exceeded their credit limit or have past-due balances.

The customer-accounts system generates a monthly statement for customers that pay from statements. And the system computes automatic finance charges on past-due balances. But this system is not designed for automatically handling payment terms such as a 2-percent discount for payment within 10 days or the net amount in 30 days (2 percent 10, net 30), or for tracking payments made against specific invoices. These operations require the more complex open-invoice system described in the preceding section.

The customer-account system provides for creating, updating, and deleting a customer-account record; posting billings and payments; querying account status; printing customer statements and account-status reports; and maintaining the system. The system is intended for use by clerical workers with little or no dBASE knowledge, so all functions are accessed through a menu system. The following list summarizes the functions of the customer-account system:

- records billings, payments, and other debits and credits against an account
- performs automatic billing based on a fee that varies by client
- adds and deletes clients as they come and go
- allows on-line queries about the current account status and the account history
- prints account statements showing transactions, balance, overdue balance, and service charge
- prints an account history for each client that shows each transaction and the balance after the transaction
- prints an account summary for specified accounts
- prints a list of active customer accounts

In addition to these functions, there are provisions for removing old transactions from the files as well as backing up, restoring, reindexing, and recalculating the data files.

Defining the File Structures

The next step in developing the application is to design the data files and any necessary index files. Because the customer-account system uses the ledger-card approach, two data files are necessary: a customer file, containing one record per customer account, and a transaction file, containing one record for each charge or payment transaction against a customer account. The sections that follow describe these file structures in detail.

The two data files are indexed in several ways. The customer-master file is indexed by the customer's account number because the account number is the primary means of looking up a customer in the file. To include the capability to look up customers by name and by company, the file is also indexed on the name and company fields. The transaction file is indexed by a composite key made up of the customer ID, a flag indicating whether the transaction has been billed, and the transaction date. This index allows transactions to be retrieved by customer ID, in order by whether or not they have been billed, and by date for a given customer ID.

The Customer-Account File

The purpose of the customer-account file CACUST is to store pertinent information about each customer account (see fig. 7.3). The file contains one record for each customer with an open account.

```
Structure for database: C:cacust.dbf
Number of data records:        0
Date of last update    : 07/28/86
Field  Field Name   Type        Width  Dec
    1  CUST_ID      Character        6
    2  COMPANY      Character       26
    3  ADDR1        Character       26
    4  ADDR2        Character       26
    5  CITY         Character       16
    6  STATE        Character        2
    7  ZIP          Character       10
    8  F_NAME       Character       10
    9  L_NAME       Character       16
   10  PHONE        Character       14
   11  STATUS       Character        1
   12  BALANCE      Numeric         12    2
   13  CREDITLIM    Numeric         12    2
   14  AUTOBILL     Logical          1
   15  AUTOFEE      Numeric         12    2
   16  AUTODESCR    Character       30
   17  COMMENT      Character       60
   18  STMTDATE     Date             8
   19  STMTBAL      Numeric         12    2
** Total **                       301
```

Fig. 7.3. *The structure of the customer master file, CACUST.*

The CUST_ID field contains the customer ID number. The number in this key field links transactions to this account. Because Quick and Clean Consulting uses account numbers like *AM0001*, the account number is of the character data type.

The COMPANY, ADDR1, ADDR2, CITY, STATE, ZIP, F_NAME, L_NAME, and PHONE fields contain the name and address of the customer's company, and the customer's first name, last name, and phone number. This information is used for addressing customer statements; the customer's last name and the name of the company can also be used as alternate key fields for looking up account information.

The STATUS field is used to indicate the account's creditworthiness, which can be used to determine the payment terms and the treatment of past-due balances. The BALANCE field is updated each time a transaction is entered in the system. The CREDITLIM field is used to flag overextended accounts during screen inquiries and in the account-status reports.

The next three fields are used in the automatic-billing function. The AUTOBILL field contains a flag that indicates an automatic billing for the account. The AUTOFEE field contains the automatic-billing amount. The AUTODESCR field contains descriptive text that is entered in an automatic billing transaction.

The COMMENT field can be used to store any pertinent commentary on the account. The STMTDATE and STMTBAL fields record the date and statement balance of the last statement, respectively. This information is used to determine if the account has a past-due amount.

The Transaction File

The file CATRANS records individual transactions in the customer accounts (see fig. 7.4). The CUST_ID field contains the customer ID number, which links the transaction to an account in the customer file. This ID number field must be of the same length and data type as the corresponding field in the customer master; in both files, CUST_ID is of the character data type and has a width of 6 characters. The DATE field is used to print or look up transaction records in chronological order for each account number.

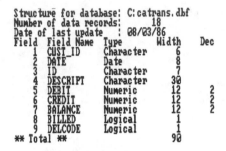

```
Structure for database: C:catrans.dbf
Number of data records:        18
Date of last update   : 08/03/86
Field  Field Name  Type       Width    Dec
    1  CUST_ID     Character      6
    2  DATE        Date           8
    3  ID          Character      7
    4  DESCRIPT    Character     30
    5  DEBIT       Numeric       12      2
    6  CREDIT      Numeric       12      2
    7  BALANCE     Numeric       12      2
    8  BILLED      Logical        1
    9  DELCODE     Logical        1
** Total **                     90
```

Fig. 7.4. The structure of the transaction file, CATRANS.

The next two fields contain a transaction ID number and a description, respectively. The ID field links the transaction to the originating document—that is, to the invoice number or the check number. The DESCRIPT field is a 30-character field that contains a description of the transaction for printing on the customer statement.

The DEBIT, CREDIT, and BALANCE fields record the transaction amount and the account balance after the current transaction. Users will normally fill in either the DEBIT or the CREDIT field, but not both. The BALANCE field is always filled in so that the program does not have to process all transactions recorded for an account every time a balance is to be displayed.

The last two fields are logical fields. The BILLED field indicates whether the transaction has been included in a customer statement. The DELCODE field is a flag that indicates whether the transaction should be recalled when the user is trying to recall transaction records for a deleted customer account. (See the discussions of the programs CACUADD and CACUDEL for further discussion.)

Index Files

The data files and their index files are listed in table 7.1. The customer-account file has three indexes, which allow selection of records by customer ID, by the name of the contact person, and by company name. Because the transaction file contains a list of transactions in chronological order by account, the file needs to be indexed by a combination of account number and transaction date. In addition, all billed transactions should be listed before all unbilled transactions for an account, even if this order differs from the chronological order. This is done by indexing on a dBASE expression that includes the account number, the BILLED flag, and the date.

Table 7.1
Indexes Used with Each Data File

Data File	Index Field	Index File	Indexed By
CACUST	CUST_ID	CACUACCT	Account ID number
	UPPER(l_name)+ UPPER(f_name)	CACUNAME	Name
	UPPER(company)	CACUCOMP	Company
CATRANS	cust_id+ IIF(billed,'B','N')+ DTOC(date)	CATRANS	Account ID number, billed flag, and ANSI date

The contents of the three fields must be converted to the character data type so that a valid indexing expression can be created. It is therefore necessary to convert the contents of the BILLED field from a logical value to a character value; hence the expression *IIF(billed, 'B', 'N')*. The contents of the date field are converted by means of the DTOC function. However, the standard dBASE American date format is MM/DD/YY, which does not sort the date in chronological order. The solution is to use the SET DATE ANSI command in the customer-accounts system whenever the transaction file is reindexed or written to. The ANSI date format is YY.MM.DD, which will support sorting in chronological order. (If the date were sorted in the default American format, then all January transactions would appear first in the sort, regardless of the year in which they occurred.)

Specifying the Function of Each Program

The data files provide a place to store information about customers and transactions. The next step in developing the application is to create a block diagram showing the programs needed for the system. This block diagram, which reflects the functions the system must perform, will serve as a "road map" during development of the system.

In the block diagram shown in figure 7.5, the customer-accounts system has been divided into functions dealing with data entry, reports and queries, and system maintenance. The system is built modularly, with each function performed by a separate program. Subroutines are used to perform functions that are common to more than one program, and to isolate complex portions of the code from the main programs. Figure 7.6 shows a block diagram including subroutines.

As the block diagram suggests, the customer-account system is designed to allow the user to add, update, delete, and undelete customer-account records; post billings and payments; review customer and transaction records; print customer statements and several types of account reports; and perform a wide range of maintenance functions. The maintenance functions support backing up, restoring, and reindexing the data files; recalculating account balances; purging old transactions from the files; and editing the system memory-variables file.

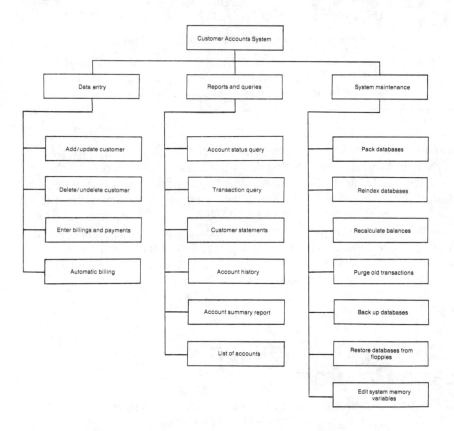

Fig. 7.5. Block diagram of the customer-accounts system.

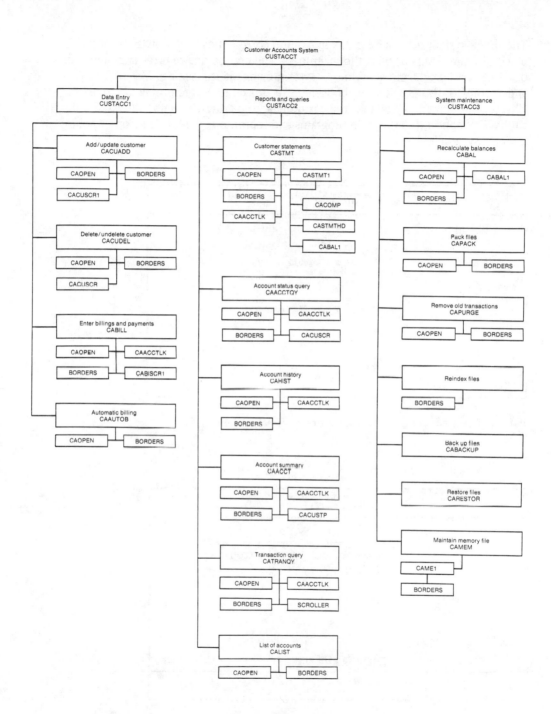

Fig. 7.6. Detailed block diagram with subroutines.

The menu system designed for this application corresponds to the divisions of the block diagram. Users begin at the main menu and choose one of three submenus for data entry, reporting and querying, or system maintenance (see figs. 7.7, 7.8, 7.9, and 7.10). Consistent with the "bottom-up" approach to programming described in Chapter 2, the menu system for the customer-accounts system is not discussed until after we've considered the main programs and subroutines (see the section "Creating a Menu System").

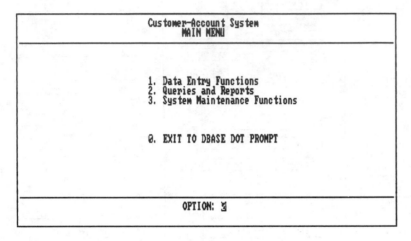

Fig. 7.7. The main menu of the customer-accounts system.

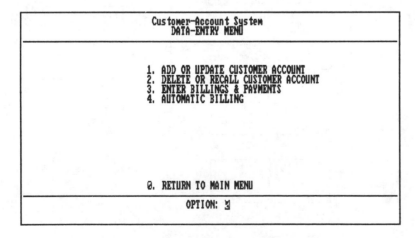

Fig. 7.8. The data-entry menu of the customer-accounts system.

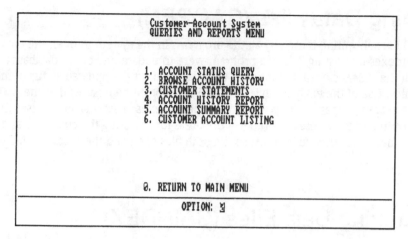

Fig. 7.9. The queries and reports menu of the customer-accounts system.

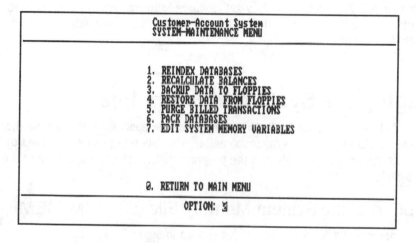

Fig. 7.10. The system-maintenance menu of the customer-accounts system.

Developing the Programs

The first step in developing the programs is to look at two utility programs: one to open the data files and another to reindex them if the indexes are clobbered during development and testing. We then consider programs for managing the system memory-variables file, entering and manipulating data, reviewing records, printing statements and reports, performing various maintenance functions, and generating menus.

Opening Data Files (CAOPEN)

The CAOPEN subroutine is used by all the programs in the system to open the data files and indexes (see listing 7.1). If a program were to update one of the databases without all the indexes open, the indexes would not reflect the updated status of the database files. Use of the easily modifiable CAOPEN subroutine ensures that the databases are always opened along with the proper indexes. This subroutine uses the SELECT command to choose the proper work areas for accessing the customer and transaction files. The subroutine returns with both files open and the customer file selected.

Listings are at the end of the chapter.

Reindexing Data Files (CAINDEX)

The subroutine CAINDEX reindexes all the data files in the system. Coding this subroutine at the beginning of the development process ensures that CAINDEX will be available to rebuild the indexes if they get clobbered during system development. The subroutine consists of a list of INDEX ON . . . commands that create the index files for each data file (see listing 7.2).

Managing the System Memory File

The last task before developing the main programs for the application is to set up the system memory file and write a program to edit it. The following sections discuss the contents of the system memory file and the program that enables the user to edit the memory variables.

Description of the System Memory File (CAMEM.MEM)

The system memory file, whose contents are shown in figure 7.11, holds 11 memory variables used by the programs in the customer-account system. The first four variables (CAPSETUP, CAPRESET, CAPAGELEN, CAPMARGIN) contain printer-setup and page-formatting information. The next four variables (CACOMPNAME, CAADDR1, CAADDR2, CAPHONE) are the name, address, and phone number of the Quick and Clean Software company. The next variable is the system title (CATITLE), which is used to format the user screens. The last two variables are the payment grace period (CAPERIOD) and the interest rate on overdue balances (CAINTEREST). The information in CAPERIOD and CAINTEREST is used in creating customer statements.

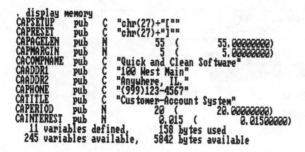

```
. display memory
CAPSETUP     pub   C   "chr(27)+"["" 
CAPRESET     pub   C   "chr(27)+"]"" 
CAPAGELEN    pub   N        55  (        55.00000000)
CAPMARGIN    pub   N         5  (         5.00000000)
CACOMPNAME   pub   C   "Quick and Clean Software"
CAADDR1      pub   C   "100 West Main"
CAADDR2      pub   C   "Anywhere, IL."
CAPHONE      pub   C   "(999)123-4567"
CATITLE      pub   C   "Customer-Account System"
CAPERIOD     pub   N        20  (        20.00000000)
CAINTEREST   pub   N     0.015  (         0.01500000)
    11 variables defined,      158 bytes used
   245 variables available,   5842 bytes available
```

Fig. 7.11. Contents of the system memory-variable file.

Program To Edit the System Memory File (CAMEM)

The program CAMEM enables the user to adjust the system memory variables when the system is installed, a new printer is purchased, or one of the system parameters needs to be changed. CAMEM.PRG should be modified in accordance with any changes or additions to CAMEM.MEM so that you can easily rebuild the memory file should it get clobbered during development or testing.

CAMEM begins by checking for existence of the file CAMEM.MEM (see listing 7.3). If CAMEM.MEM is found, the existing data is restored and the printer setup string and reset string are padded with blanks to a length of 80 characters. If CAMEM.MEM is not found, the memory variables are initialized by means of the STORE command.

Then the program enters a DO WHILE loop. The subroutine CAME1 is called to create an edit screen that displays the contents of CAMEM.MEM (see fig. 7.12). This subroutine consists of a series of @ . . . SAY . . . GET commands that display the contents of the variables (see listing 7.4). Because CAME1 is used to enter data as well as to view the data when no changes are desired, the subroutine does not contain a READ statement. But note that a READ command follows the first call to CAME1 in the listing for CAMEM. By contrast, a CLEAR GETS command follows the last call to CAME1, whose purpose is to display the variables for confirmation by the user.

After the user enters any desired changes and presses Esc or Enter, the program displays the system memory variables again and prompts the user to verify the changes. If the user presses *Y*, indicating that the changes are acceptable, the main loop is exited because variable MOK contains .T. But if the user presses *N*, he or she is prompted to indicate whether further changes are desired. If not, an EXIT command transfers control out of the loop.

If the user has confirmed the changes, the program uses the TRIM function to remove trailing blanks from the character strings, and calls CAME1 again to display

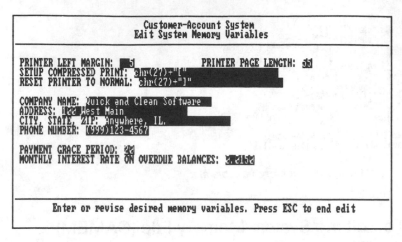

```
                        Customer-Account System
                      Edit System Memory Variables

PRINTER LEFT MARGIN: ▌5            PRINTER PAGE LENGTH: ▌5▌
SETUP COMPRESSED PRINT: chr(27)+"["
RESET PRINTER TO NORMAL: chr(27)+"]"

COMPANY NAME: Quick and Clean Software
ADDRESS: 123 West Main
CITY, STATE, ZIP: Anywhere, IL.
PHONE NUMBER: (999)123-4567

PAYMENT GRACE PERIOD: 2▌
MONTHLY INTEREST RATE ON OVERDUE BALANCES: ▌0.015▌

        Enter or revise desired memory variables. Press ESC to end edit
```

Fig. 7.12. Screen to edit the system memory variables.

the contents of the system memory file. A final prompt asks the user whether the edited memory variables should be saved to the file CAMEM.MEM. If the user presses *Y*, the edited variables are saved to CAMEM.MEM, the screen is cleared, and control is returned to the the calling program.

Entering Data

We now turn to the data-entry programs. First, we look at programs to add, update, delete, and undelete customer-account records. Then we consider programs to handle billings and payments.

Adding and Updating Customer Accounts (CACUADD)

The CACUADD program is used to add a new customer record to the customer master file or to update the information for an existing customer. A record for the customer account must be in the customer master file before transactions can be entered against the account. The flowchart for CACUADD is shown in figure 7.13.

The program begins by calling subroutine CAOPEN to open the database files and indexes (see listing 7.5). The body of CACUADD is a "do forever" loop (DO WHILE .T.) that gets an account number from the user, checks whether the account exists in the customer database, and allows the user to enter or update the customer data. If the account number is left blank, an EXIT command transfers control out of the loop.

Within the DO WHILE loop, the program gets an account ID number from the user. Then the program checks for the account ID number in the file CACUST. If the account is found but its record has been deleted, the program informs the user and asks whether he or she wants to continue. If the user wants to re-create the deleted account, the program selects CATRANS and sets the value in the DELCODE field to .T. for all records containing the account number. This marks all transactions for the account as "permanently" deleted so that they cannot be recalled by means of the delete/undelete program, CACUDEL. The program then initializes the data-entry variables for the new record. The customer-account record remains deleted until after the data entry is complete.

If the account is not found, the user is asked whether he or she wants to add the account, as shown in figure 7.14. If the user wants to add a record for the account, the program appends a blank record to the file CACUST and initializes the data-entry variables for the new record. The new record is left deleted until data entry is complete.

If the user presses *N* at the prompt for a deleted account or a new account, indicating that he or she does not want to proceed, a LOOP command is used to return execution to the top of the loop.

If the program finds an active account, the data-entry variables are initialized to the existing values. Subroutine CACUSCR1 then is called to display the full-screen data-entry form shown in figure 7.15. After the call to CACUSCR1, the READ command assigns the user's input to the variables. Listing 7.6 shows the code for CACUSCR1, which is a collection of @ . . . SAY . . . GET commands that display the data-entry screen.

The screen shown in figure 7.15 displays all the information for a new account with Adams Marketing. In this screen, everything but the account number can be changed. The only way the user can change an account number is to prepare a final statement for the account, delete the customer record, and then add the customer to the master file, using a new account number. All existing transactions are lost in the process of changing the account number, so users need to be careful to verify the correct account number when adding a new account to the system.

When the user is finished adding or editing the customer master record, he or she can save the changes by pressing Enter after the last entry on the page, or by pressing Esc, PgUp, or PgDn. If the user is adding this customer, the program switches to the file CATRANS.DBF and adds a beginning balance record for the customer.

After the edit is completed, the program returns to the top of the loop and prompts for another account number. The loop is exited by pressing Enter or Esc without entering an account number at the prompt **ENTER ACCOUNT TO ADD OR UPDATE (blank to exit)**. The program then exits the main loop, closes the databases, and returns control to the caller.

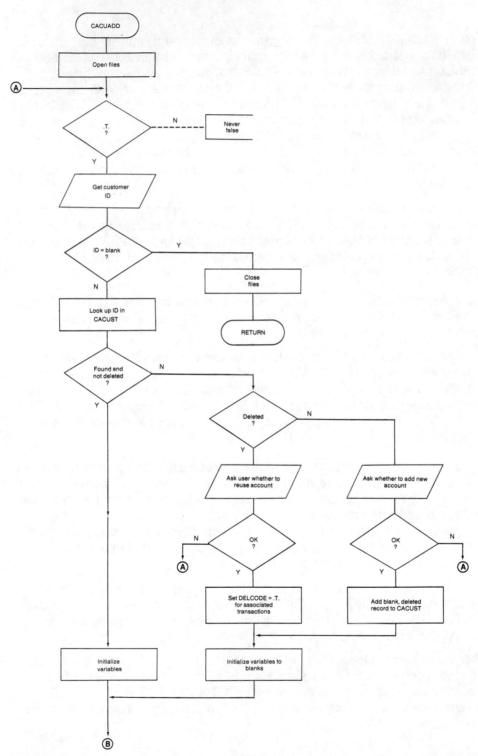

Fig. 7.13. Flowchart for the program CACUADD.

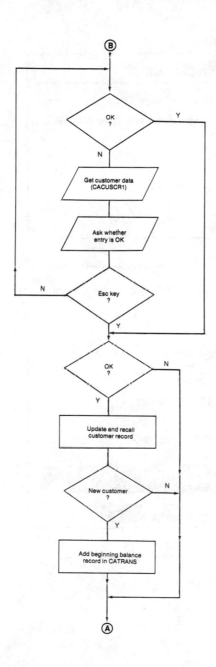

Ins

```
                    Customer-Account System
                  ADD OR UPDATE CUSTOMER ACCOUNT
─────────────────────────────────────────────────────────────

     ENTER ACCOUNT TO ADD OR UPDATE (blank to exit) AM0001

     Customer ID not found. Want to create new account (Y or N)? N




─────────────────────────────────────────────────────────────


```

Fig. 7.14. Entering an account number to add or update a customer record.

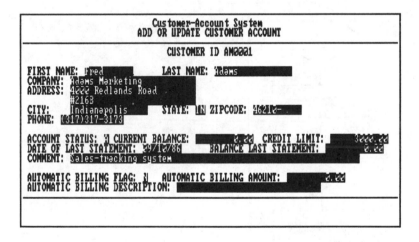

Fig. 7.15. Screen to add or update customer record.

Deleting or Undeleting Accounts (CACUDEL)

The program CACUDEL allows the user to delete the customer master record for an account, provided there have been no transactions entered for the account since the last statement. If transactions have been entered, the user has to run a final statement before deleting the account. The flowchart for CACUDEL is shown in figure 7.16.

This program can also be used to reactivate a deleted account if the database has not been packed since the account was deleted. The undelete option will restore all transactions for the account that are not flagged as deleted in the DELCODE field, and the balance will be restored as of the last statement before the deletion.

The program calls CAOPEN to open the files and indexes, then enters a "do forever" loop (DO WHILE .T.; see listing 7.7). The loop begins by getting from the user the number of the account to be deleted or undeleted. The screen for entering this number is similar to the add/update screen in figure 7.14. If the user leaves the account number blank, the loop is exited. If the user enters the number of an account that does not exist, an error message is displayed and a LOOP command transfers execution to the top of the loop for entry of another account number.

After the user enters a valid account ID number and verifies it, the program calls subroutine CACUSCR to display the contents of the customer master record for this account (see fig. 7.17). Recall that we entered a new account for Adams Marketing in the preceding section (see fig. 7.15). The screen in figure 7.17 shows the record for Adams Marketing after transactions have been entered against the account. Although similar to CACUSCR1, CACUSCR displays the data with @ . . . SAY commands only (see listing 7.8); no GET commands are used.

If the record has been deleted, the program prompts the user to indicate whether he or she wants to undelete the record. If this is desired, the RECALL command restores the record to active status. If the record is active, the program prompts the user to verify that he or she wants it deleted, then checks the transaction file for transactions entered since the last statement was generated for this account. If unbilled transactions are found, the program prompts the user to print a final statement first, and then returns to the top of the loop. Otherwise, the program asks the user to verify the account again, and then deletes the record.

The program loops back to the account-specification screen for another account until a blank account number is entered. The program then exits the loop, closes the databases, and returns control to the calling program.

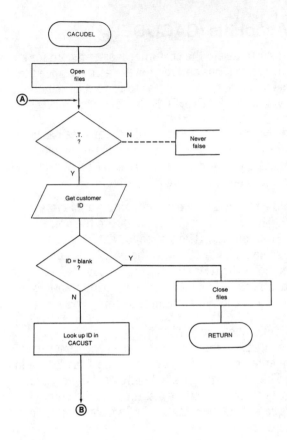

Fig. 7.16. Flowchart for the program CACUDEL.

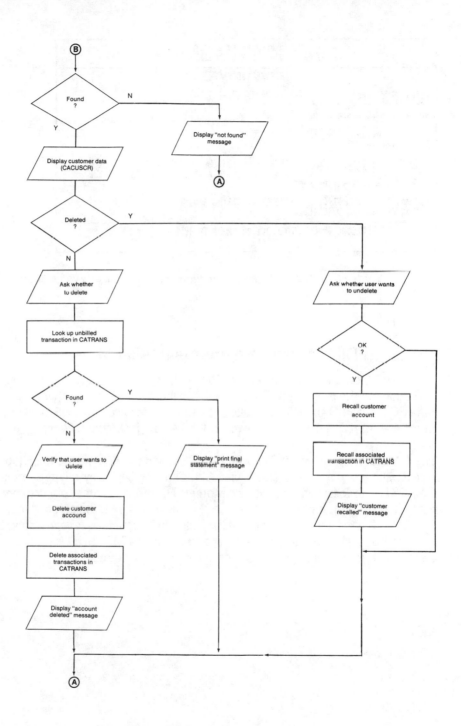

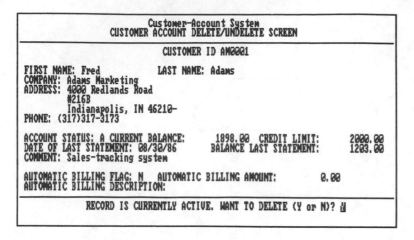

```
                    Customer-Account System
                CUSTOMER ACCOUNT DELETE/UNDELETE SCREEN

                        CUSTOMER ID AM0001

FIRST NAME: Fred              LAST NAME: Adams
COMPANY: Adams Marketing
ADDRESS: 4000 Redlands Road
         #216B
         Indianapolis, IN 46210-
PHONE: (317)317-3173

ACCOUNT STATUS: A CURRENT BALANCE:     1898.00  CREDIT LIMIT:    2000.00
DATE OF LAST STATEMENT: 08/30/86       BALANCE LAST STATEMENT:   1203.00
COMMENT: Sales-tracking system

AUTOMATIC BILLING FLAG: N   AUTOMATIC BILLING AMOUNT:       0.00
AUTOMATIC BILLING DESCRIPTION:

          RECORD IS CURRENTLY ACTIVE. WANT TO DELETE (Y or N)? N
```

Fig. 7.17. Screen to display account information and accept user's validation to delete record.

Entering Billings and Payments (CABILL)

The CABILL program supports entry of billings and payments against an account. The main body of the program is a loop to accept billings and payments. Subroutines CAACCTLK and CABISCR1 are called to find customer accounts and present a data-entry screen, respectively. The flowchart for CABILL is shown in figure 7.18.

The CABILL program opens files with CAOPEN, and then enters the main loop to accept billings and payments (see listing 7.9). The loop begins by calling subroutine CAACCTLK to locate an account by customer ID, company name, or customer name (CAACCTLK is discussed in the section that follows.) If the account specified in CAACCTLK does not exist in the CACUST file, the program issues a warning, and the loop is repeated for entry of a new account. The flag MFOUND is set by CAACCTLK to indicate whether or not the account was found.

But if the account is found in the file CACUST, the program enters a second loop to accept transactions for the account. The program creates a new empty transaction record, calls subroutine CABISCR1 to display a data-entry screen, and uses a READ command to accept the user's inputs. (CABISCR1 is described in the section "Subroutine To Display a Data-Entry Screen.") The new record is deleted immediately after it is appended to the file; the record is recalled when data entry is complete. (The record is left deleted until data entry is complete to prevent the possibility that a power glitch or a user error would leave an incomplete, active transaction in the transaction file.)

When input is completed, the program performs a simple data check to make sure that the user has not entered both a debit and a credit. If both have been entered, the user is warned with the message CAN'T ENTER BOTH A DEBIT AND A CREDIT. But if only a debit *or* a credit has been entered, the user is prompted to verify the entry. If the data is acceptable, the balance after the new transaction is computed and stored in both the transaction and the customer files. The blank transaction is not recalled if no debit or credit has been entered—if, in other words, the expression *debit#0.and.credit#0* evaluates as false.

The user is then asked whether another transaction for this account is desired. If so, control returns to the top of the transactions loop. The transaction data-entry screen is displayed again and the user can enter the next debit or credit. Otherwise, the program returns to the initial screen to enter the next account number. To exit, the user leaves the account number and name fields blank, and then presses Esc. An EXIT command transfers control out of the main loop if the account number is left blank.

Subroutine To Look Up an Account (CAACCTLK)

As mentioned previously, the subroutine CAACCTLK is used to find accounts by number or name. The flowchart for CAACCTLK is shown in figure 7.19; program code is provided in listing 7.10. CAACCTLK is also used by the account-status query program to find accounts by number or name. The subroutine begins by selecting the file CACUST; the body of the program is a data-entry loop. The code in the loop displays the lines shown in the center of the screen in figure 7.20.

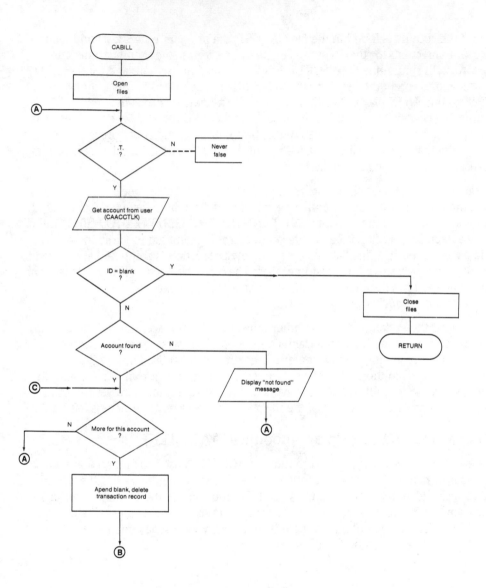

Fig. 7.18. Flowchart for the program CABILL.

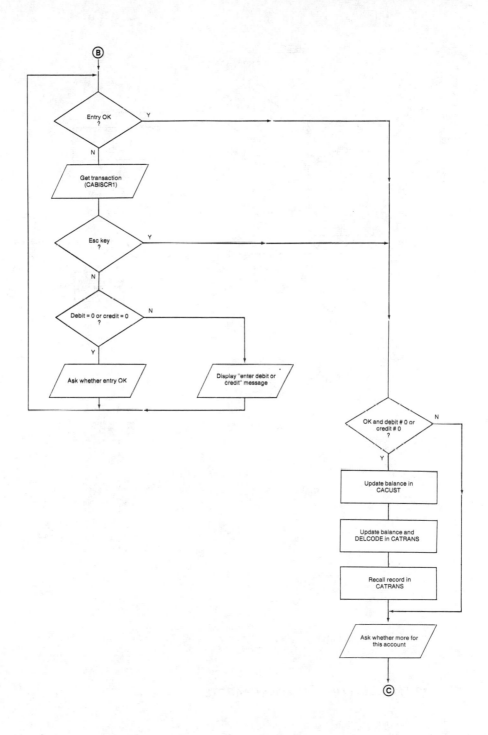

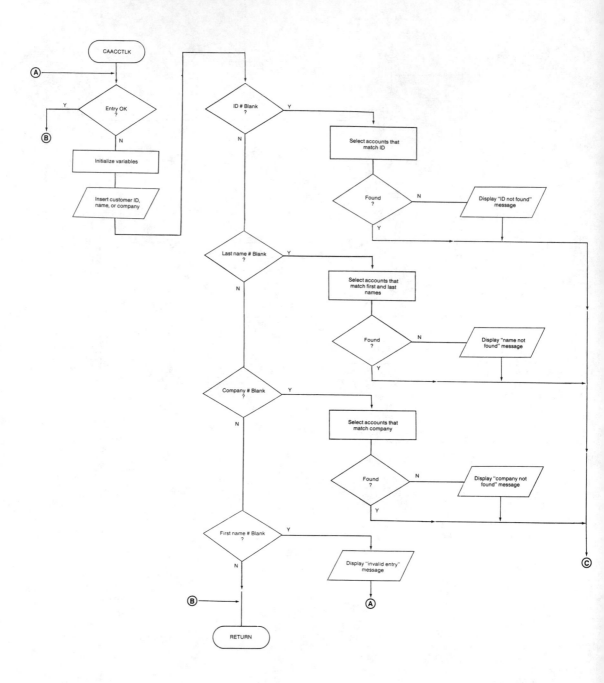

Fig. 7.19. Flowchart of the subroutine CAACCTLK.

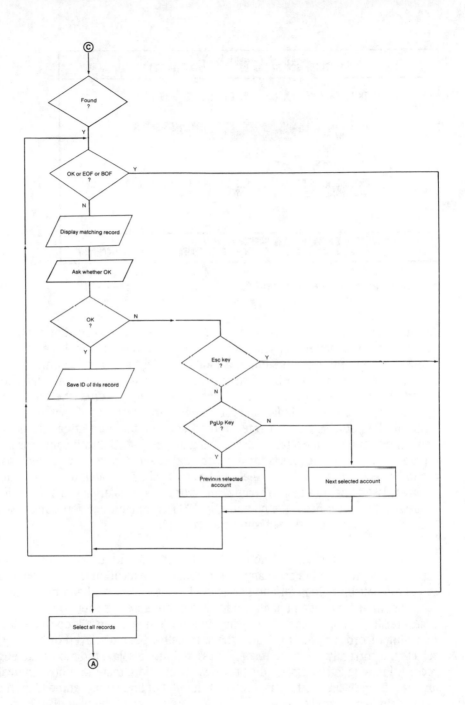

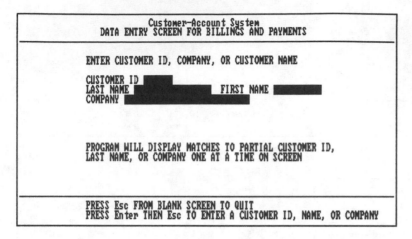

Fig. 7.20. Screen where user identifies account to charge or credit.

As indicated in figure 7.20, the user can specify the account by customer ID, by last name, or by company name. The user can enter whichever of the three items is most convenient. After the user has entered a full or partial customer ID number, contact name, or company name, a CASE structure is used to set the index and filter to select the matching records. If a customer ID number has been entered, the subroutine activates the customer ID index and sets the filter to select records with the indicated customer ID number. If a last name has been entered, the subroutine selects the name index and sets the filter to all matching names. If a company name has been entered, the subroutine selects the company index and sets the filter to records with the indicated company name. If the user has entered a first name but no account number, last name, or company name, an error message is displayed and the loop is repeated. If the user has made no entry, an EXIT command transfers control out of the data-entry loop, and the subroutine ends.

If an entry has been made and no matching record is found, the user is informed of that fact and prompted to press any key to continue; execution then transfers to the top of the data-entry loop for another entry. But if an entry has been made and the record pointer is not at end-of-file (and a match therefore has been found for the customer ID, name, or company name), the subroutine enters a loop to display the matching records one at a time until the last one has been displayed or the user selects the currently displayed record. Pressing Enter displays the next matching record. Pressing PgUp displays the previous match. Note that the subroutine will find an entry from its first characters; however, it will not find strings embedded in the name fields, or misspelled names. This is a consequence of the way dBASE compares matching strings in character fields with the command SET EXACT OFF in effect.

For each matching record found, the full customer ID, customer name, and company name are displayed for verification. Entry of the customer ID number shown in figure 7.21 causes the matching record for Johnson Typesetting to be found, as shown at the bottom of the screen. The user then is prompted to indicate whether the correct record has been found. If the user presses *Y*, the subroutine is exited and control returns to the calling program. Pressing Esc causes the browse loop to be exited; execution then transfers to the top of main loop, where a new set of selection criteria can be entered.

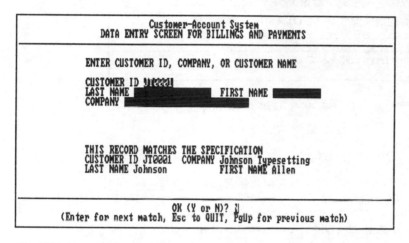

Fig. 7.21. Screen showing the selected record.

After the loop is exited, the subroutine clears the portions of the screen that it used and returns control to the calling program with the account number and a flag, OK, indicating whether the account number was found.

Subroutine To Display a Data-Entry Screen (CABISCR1)

The second subroutine used by CABILL (apart from CAOPEN and BORDERS, of course) is the screen-display subroutine CABISCR1 (see listing 7.11). CABISCR1 is merely a series of @ . . . SAY and @ . . . SAY . . . GET commands that display the data-entry screen shown in figure 7.22. As noted previously, a READ command following the call to CABISCR1 is used to accept entries from the user.

The transaction-entry screen in figure 7.21 displays the customer-account ID number, the customer's first and last names, the company name, and a transaction date. The user enters the transaction ID number, the transaction date (if the transaction date is not today's date), the description of the transaction, and the debit or the credit. In figure 7.22, no billings or payments have been entered for Johnson Typesetting.

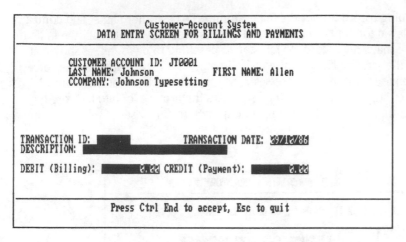

Fig. 7.22. Data-entry screen for billings and payments.

Billing Accounts Automatically (CAAUTOB)

The previous section described a manual approach to billing customer accounts. The customer-accounts system designed for Quick and Clean Software also includes a provision for billing accounts automatically. This capability reduces the workload for routine billings such as ongoing software-maintenance contracts.

The flowchart for the automatic-billing program CAAUTOB is shown in figure 7.23; program code is shown in listing 7.12. The program begins by opening the data files and asking the user to verify that he or she wants to proceed (see fig. 7.24). This initial verification is important because the program performs a major update of the transaction file.

After verifying, the user is then prompted for the automatic-billing date. The default is the current system date, but the user can change this to any date (see fig. 7.25).

After the date has been entered, the program displays the message WORKING . . . . The body of the program is a loop; the code within the loop processes each record in the customer file for which the automatic-billing flag is set. This process takes several minutes. For each automatic-billing account, the program switches to the transaction file and creates a billing transaction for that account. Then the program updates the account balance in the customer file, gets the next automatic-billing account in the customer file, and returns to the top of the loop. When the end of the customer file is reached, the program closes the databases and returns to the caller, the Data-Entry menu.

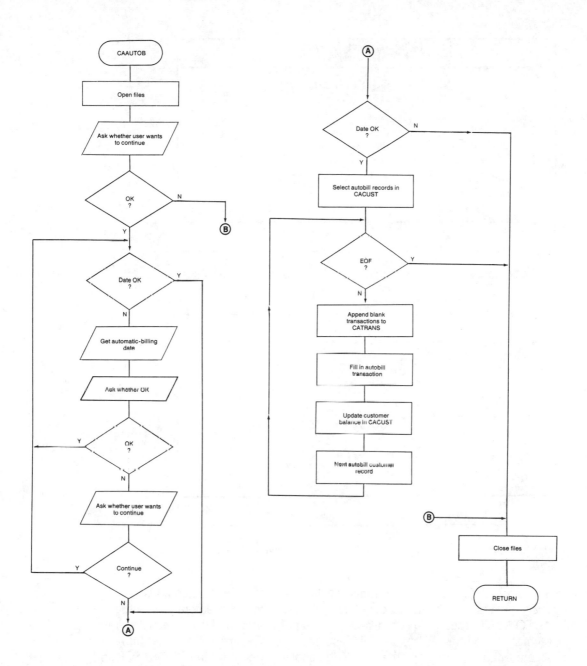

Fig. 7.23. Flowchart of the program CAAUTOB.

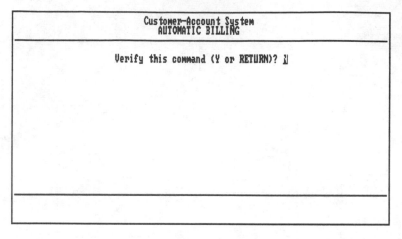

Fig. 7.24. Screen where user verifies the automatic-billing command.

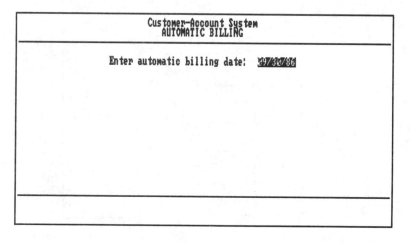

Fig. 7.25. Screen where user enters the automatic-billing date.

The process of generating an automatic billing transaction for an account is straightforward. First, the customer file is filtered so that only accounts with the AUTOBILL flag set set to .T. are active. Then the transaction file is selected and, for each active account, a blank record is appended. This record is filled in with the account number, date, and the description and amount from the AUTODESCR and AUTOFEE fields in the customer record. Then the balance is calculated and stored, and the BILLED and DELCODE flags are set to .F. Finally, the program switches back to the customer file and enters the new balance in the customer record.

Notice that the automatic billing program does not generate an invoice. In this system, the customer's statement is the invoice for the month's charges.

Querying the Database

The customer-accounts application contains programs that enable the user to review the status of customer accounts and browse the transaction records. Quick and Clean Software can review customer accounts for such information as current balance, credit limit, balance as of last statement, type of software package purchased, and the amount and reason for automatic billing, if applicable. The browse program makes it possible to review transaction records by account, giving Quick and Clean Software a quick look at payments, debits, and the outstanding balance. The sections that follow describe these system capabilities.

Determining the Status of an Account (CAACCTQY)

The program CAACCTQY is used to review the status of an account. Figure 7.26 shows the flowchart for the program. CAACCTQY calls CAOPEN to open files; then enters a "do forever" loop (DO WHILE .T.) to display account information (see listing 7.13).

The loop begins with a call to subroutine BORDERS to display the logo. Next, subroutine CAACCTLK is called so that the user can specify the account to browse by account number, company, or contact name (see fig. 7.27). CAACCTLK sets the variable OK to .T. if the specified account is found; for a full discussion of CAACCTLK, see the section "Entering Billings and Collections."

If the account is not found (signified by OK=.F.), the user is warned and the program calls CAACCTLK again for entry of a new account. If the user leaves the account-selection fields blank, the program exits the query loop and returns.

When the user has selected an account, CAACCTQY calls subroutine CACUSCR to display the contents of the customer master record (see fig. 7.28). This screen is similar to the screen in figure 7.15 for adding and updating customer records. CAACCTQY pauses for a keypress so that the user can read the account information, then loops back to the top of the "do forever" loop and waits for entry of another account ID. To exit the program, the user makes certain that the account-selection screen fields for account number, company, and last name are blank, then presses Esc.

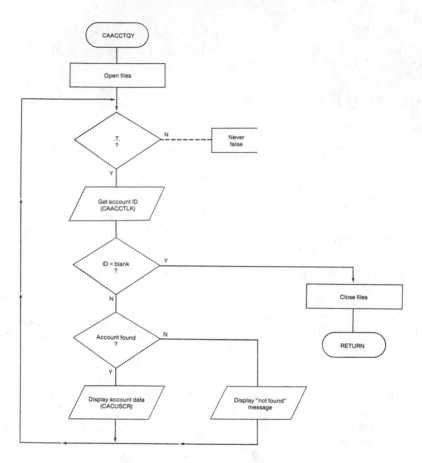

Fig. 7.26. Flowchart of the program CAACCTQY.

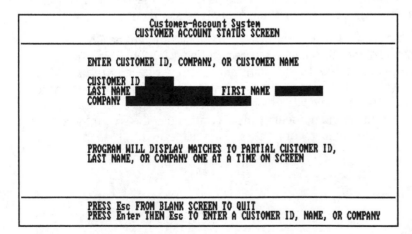

Fig. 7.27. Screen where user identifies the customer account to be reviewed.

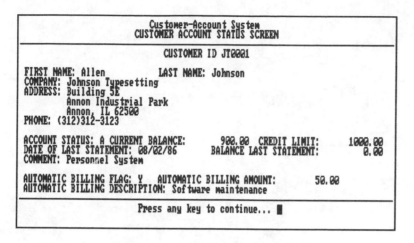

Fig. 7.28. Screen showing status of customer account.

Browsing Transactions (CATRANQY)

The browse-transactions program enables the user to review all the transactions for an account. CATRANQY begins by opening files with CAOPEN. The program then enters a "do forever" loop to display transactions for a selected customer account. The flowchart for CATRANQY is shown in figure 7.29; program code is provided in listing 7.14.

The loop begins by calling CAACCTLK to accept a customer ID number, customer name, or company name from the user. (CAACCTLK is discussed in the section "Entering Billings and Payments.") After the call to CAACCTLK, the program checks for a blank account number (MACCT = ' ') and exits the loop if the number is blank. Otherwise, the program displays the account number, first and last name, and current balance in the top half of the screen. Next, the program selects the transaction file (CATRANS) and sets a filter so that only records for the specified account will appear on-screen. The file pointer is positioned at the first record containing the account ID.

The program then enters a second "do forever" loop to display in the bottom half of the screen a chronological list of transactions for the account. In figure 7.30, all the transactions for Adams Marketing are displayed.

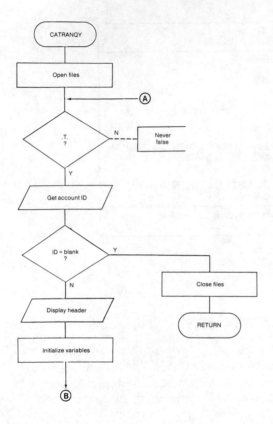

Fig. 7.29. Flowchart for the program CATRANQY.

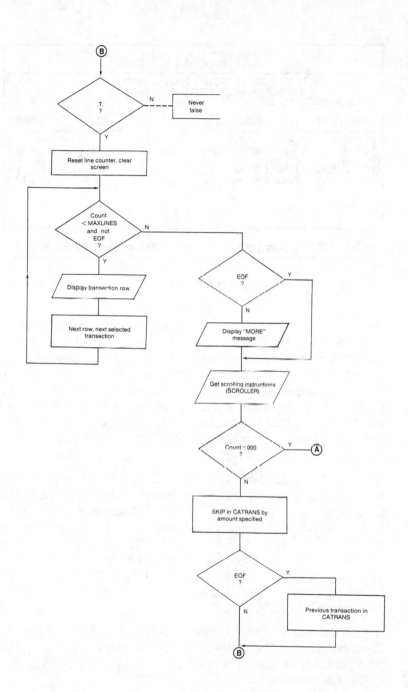

```
                        Customer-Account System
                      BROWSE TRANSACTIONS BY ACCOUNT

              CUSTOMER ID: AM0001 COMPANY: Adams Marketing
                    FIRST NAME: Fred        LAST NAME: Adams
 CURRENT BALANCE:        1898.00

   DATE       ID        DESCRIPT          DEBIT      CREDIT      BALANCE B

 08/02/86           OPENING BALANCE      1000.00       0.00     1000.00 Y
 08/04/86           Sales Tracking Progr 1000.00       0.00     2000.00 Y
 08/15/86           Payment                 0.00     800.00     1200.00 Y
 08/23/86  FINCHG    FINANCE CHARGE          3.00       0.00     1203.00 Y
 09/01/86           Modem and Remote Sof  695.00       0.00     1898.00 N




 PRESS: ARROW KEYS, PgUp ,PgDn, Enter, Home (BOF), or End (EOF); Esc to quit
```

Fig. 7.30. Screen to browse transactions.

The loop to display transactions begins by clearing the transaction-display area. Then a third-level DO WHILE loop displays the transactions in screen rows 11 through 19. Execution of this loop is controlled by the value in the variable CNTR and the result of the function EOF(); the loop repeats as long as CNTR is less than the number of lines allotted for display of transactions and the end of the filtered file has not been reached. When that loop is exited, the subroutine SCROLLER is called to read the user's keypress and to position the next screen display. The flowchart for SCROLLER is shown in figure 7.31; program code is presented in listing 7.15.

SCROLLER uses the INKEY function to read a keystroke from the user. A DO WHILE loop is repeated until the user presses one of the keys supported by the subroutine. Supported keys include the cursor-movement keys (arrow keys, PgUp, PgDn, Home, End), Enter, and Esc; the subroutine ignores all other keystrokes. The dBASE command SET ESCAPE OFF is executed before the loop to disable the Esc key's normal function. This allows the Esc key to be read by the INKEY function. Otherwise, pressing Esc during the INKEY loop would cause dBASE to interrupt program execution. After the loop, the Esc key is returned to its normal function with the command SET ESCAPE ON.

Important note: *In some early versions of dBASE III Plus, the INKEY function apparently does not return the proper scan-code value for the left-arrow key. If that problem exists for your (or your client's) copy of dBASE III Plus, you will need to devise a work-around.*

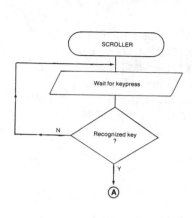

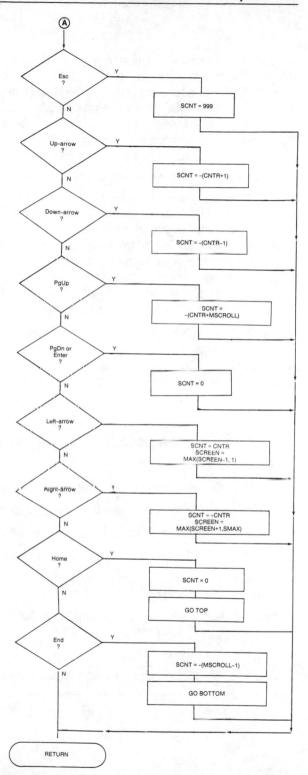

Fig. 7.31. Flowchart for the subroutine SCROLLER.

When the user presses a supported key, SCROLLER executes a DO CASE structure that sets the memory variable SCNT to the scroll count for the top of the next screen. The DO CASE structure sets SCNT to the correct value for the key that was pressed. That value indicates the number of lines to skip forward or backward in the file before displaying the next screen. In two cases (the Home and End keys), the subroutine also moves the record pointer. Otherwise, SCROLLER just returns the counter SCNT to the calling program, which adjusts the record pointer based on the count.

As indicated in figure 7.30, the user scrolls the account transactions by means of the up-arrow, down-arrow, PgUp, PgDn, Home, and End keys. The up-arrow and down-arrow keys scroll the transactions one line at a time. When the up-arrow key is pressed, the record pointer skips to a position one record before the start of the previous screen. The down-arrow key moves the record pointer to one line after the start of the previous screen. The PgUp and PgDn keys scroll the transactions one screen (11 lines) at a time. (Note that the Enter key performs the same function as the PgDn key.) The Home and End keys scroll to the first and last screens, respectively. The actions of the keys are summarized in table 7.2.

The SCROLLER subroutine is used in several other applications. In those applications, the ← and → keys are used to move between two or more screens showing data for the same records. In this transaction there is only one query screen, so the arrow keys merely display the same screen again.

Table 7.2
Keys Used To Change the Browse Screens

Key	Function
←, →	Redisplay current screen
↑, ↓	Scroll list of transactions by one line up or down
PgUp	Display preceding full screen of transactions
PgDn	Display next full screen of transactions
Home	Display a screen starting at the first transaction for this account
End	Display a screen including the last transaction for this account
Enter	Same as PgDn
Esc	Finish browsing transactions for this account

When the user presses Esc to exit from the browse screen, SCROLLER assigns the value 999 to memory variable SCNT. After the call to SCROLLER, CATRANQY tests SCNT for this value. If it is found, CATRANQY exits from the inner loop and returns to the top of the outer loop to get another account number, displaying the initial screen for account entry. To exit the main program, the user makes certain that the fields for account number, last name, and company are blank, then presses Esc.

Printing Reports

The customer-account system produces four types of reports: monthly statements, account histories, account summaries, and lists of accounts. The statements provide each customer with a monthly profile of his or her account as well as a summary. The reports for account histories, summaries, and lists enable Quick and Clean Software to monitor customer billings and payments. These four types of reports are discussed in detail in the sections that follow.

Printing Monthly Statements

The monthly-statement program CASTMT prints a customer statement for an account, as shown in figure 7.32. The statement shows an account balance as of the last statement, followed by all the transactions that have been posted during the month. Just below the list of transactions is a summary section that shows the beginning balance, the sum of the charges, the sum of the payments, and the ending balance. If the payments received by the due date are less than the beginning balance, a finance charge is shown; the charge is calculated as the monthly interest rate times the difference between the beginning balance and the payments received by the due date. The statement for Adams Marketing shown in figure 7.32 shows payments received by the due date that are less than the beginning balance, and a resulting finance charge of $3.00 for August, 1986.

The CASTMT program opens the files, then enters a "do forever" loop to get an account number from the user and print a statement for that account. The actual printing is done by the subroutine CASTMT1. Figure 7.33 shows the flowchart for CASTMT; program code is shown in listing 7.16.

The DO WHILE .T. loop begins by calling the CAACCTLK subroutine to get the account by customer ID number, customer name, or company name (for a detailed discussion of subroutine CAACCTLK, see the section "Entering Billings and Payments"). After the call to CAACCTLK, an IF clause tests for a blank account number. If found, the loop is exited.

```
                    Quick and Clean Software
                         100 West Main
                         Anywhere, IL.
                        (999)123-4567

                      ACCOUNT AM0001
              STATEMENT OF ACCOUNT AS OF 08/30/86

Fred Adams
Adams Marketing
4000 Redlands Road
#216B
Indianapolis, IN 46210-

   DATE   DESCRIPTION                CHARGES     PAYMENTS      BALANCE
   ------ ------------------------   ---------   ---------    ---------
   08/02/86 Previous balance                                  1,000.00
   08/04/86 Sales-tracking program   1,000.00                 2,000.00
   08/15/86 Payment                               -800.00     1,200.00
   08/23/86 FINANCE CHARGE               3.00                 1,203.00



   ACCOUNT SUMMARY
            Previous balance                                  1,000.00
            Payments before due date                           -800.00
                                                             ---------
            OVERDUE BALANCE                                     200.00

            FINANCE CHARGE                                        3.00
            Payments after due date                              0.00
            Current month charges                             1,000.00
                                                             ---------
            CURRENT BALANCE                                    1,203.00

   PLEASE PAY CURRENT BALANCE BY 09/20/86
```

Fig. 7.32. Customer statement printed by the monthly statement program.

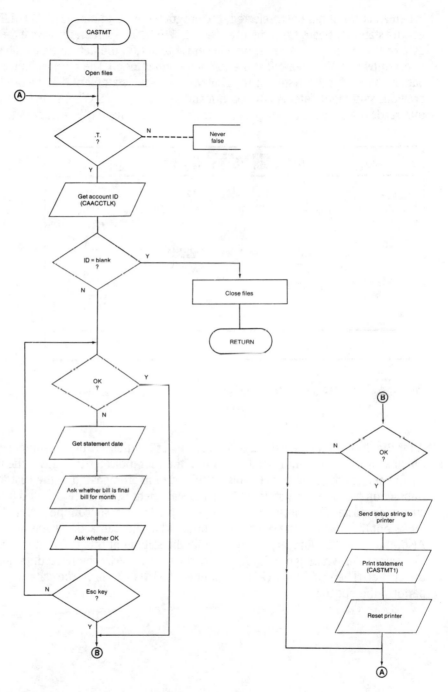

Fig. 7.33. Flowchart for the program CASTMT.

When an account has been selected, the program enters an inner DO WHILE loop to get the statement date from the user (see fig. 7.34). The screen displays either today's date or the last statement date, whichever is greater, as the default date. (This value is selected by the IIF statement at the top of the inner loop.) The purpose of using that date is to prevent the system from displaying a default statement date before the previous statement date. A range command in the @ . . . SAY . . . GET command that reads the statement date prevents the user from entering an earlier date.

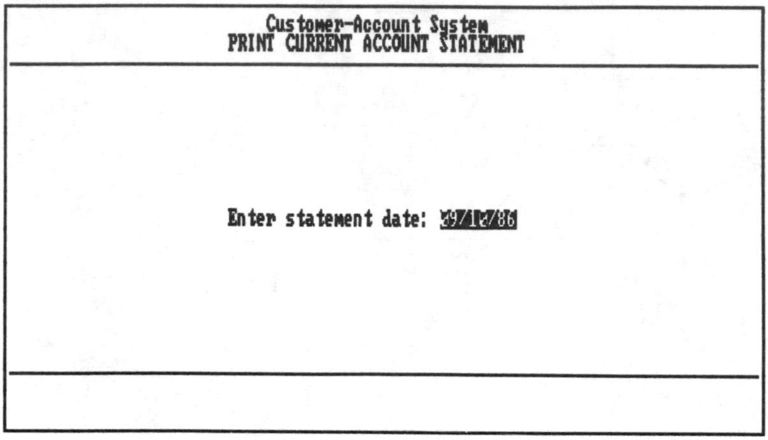

```
                    Customer-Account System
              PRINT CURRENT ACCOUNT STATEMENT



                  Enter statement date: 97/12/86
```

Fig. 7.34. Screen to get statement date.

After the user enters the date, a second screen asks whether the statement represents the final bill for the month (see fig. 7.35). If the user indicates that this is the final bill for the period, then the transactions for this account are updated in the customer transaction file, and the statement date and statement balance are updated in the customer master file (these updates are performed by the subroutine CASTMT1). If this is not the final bill, the statement is printed but the transaction file is not updated. Also, the word "preliminary" is included in the statement title to avoid confusion. The screen shown in figure 7.35 prompts the user to verify the procedure and set up the printer. Then CASTMT calls subroutine CASTMT1 to print the statement and perform the updates.

```
                              Ins
  ┌──────────────────────────────────────────────────────────────┐
  │                 Customer-Account System                        │
  │             PRINT CURRENT ACCOUNT STATEMENT                    │
  ├──────────────────────────────────────────────────────────────┤
  │                                                                │
  │                                                                │
  │                                                                │
  │                                                                │
  │          Enter statement date: 08/31/86                        │
  │                                                                │
  │          Final bill for month (Y or N): N                      │
  │                                                                │
  │                                                                │
  │                                                                │
  ├──────────────────────────────────────────────────────────────┤
  │                      OK (Y or N)? N                            │
  │          (If ok, setup printer before continuing)             │
  └──────────────────────────────────────────────────────────────┘
```

Fig. 7.35. Screen for indicating final bill.

The subroutine CASTMT1 calls subroutine CACOMP to print the company's name at the top of the page and subroutine CASTMTHD to print the customer's name and address and the report headings. Then CASTMT1 prints the balance from the last statement from the customer file. The flowchart for CASTMT1 is shown in figure 7.36. Program code for CASTMT1, CACOMP, and CASTMTHD is shown in listings 7.17, 7.18, and 7.19, respectively.

CACOMP and CASTMTHD include @ . . . SAY commands to print titles and headings for the report. CACOMP centers the company's name and address on the page. Figure 7.32 shows the name and address for Quick and Clean Software printed at the top of the page. Note the expression used to center the name and address. The name and address are printed starting at the margin plus half of the quantity of page width minus the length of the variable being printed. CASTMTHD centers the two title lines, but the widths of the titles are hard coded in the @ . . . SAY statements. CASTMTHD prints the customer's name and address, as well as the report headings; a series of IF statements is used to avoid printing blank lines in the customer name and address area. The subroutine also prints the word *PRELIMINARY* in the headings if the value of MFOUND is false. In figure 7.32, CASTMTHD has printed Fred Adams's name, the name and address of his company, and the column headings for the statement.

In the first line under the statement headings, CASTMT1 prints the balance from the last statement. Then the subroutine selects the transaction file (CATRANS.DBF) and filters the file for all unbilled transactions prior to the specified statement date for this account. Memory variables are initialized for total debits (charges), total credits (payments), any overdue balance, and the running balance.

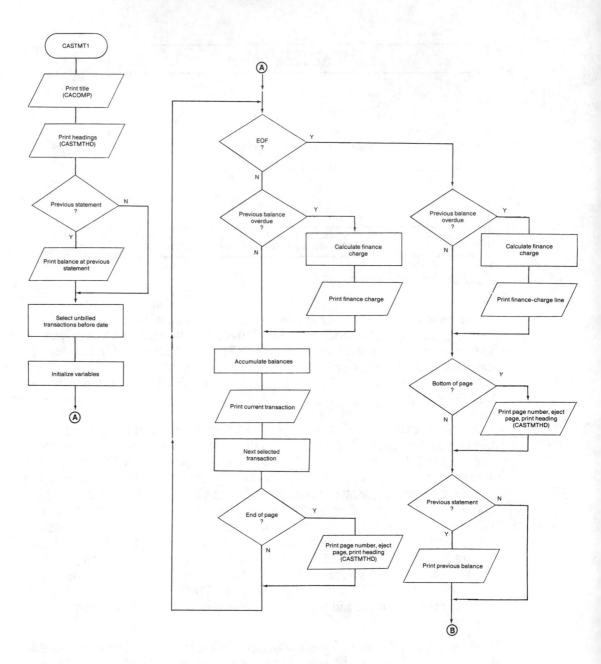

Fig. 7.36. Flowchart for the program CASTMT1.

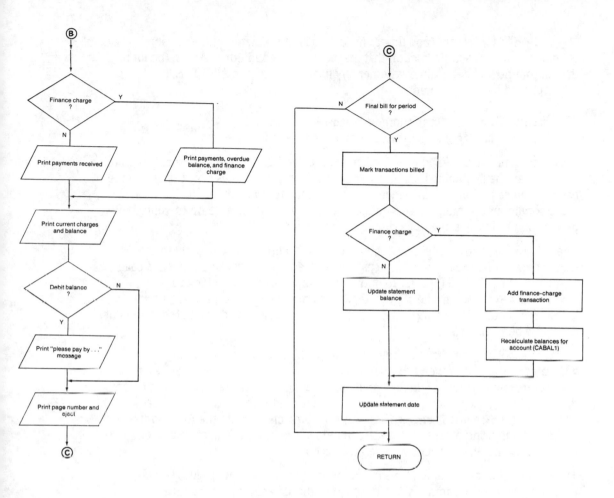

Next, CASTMT1 enters a loop that prints the body of the statement. The loop executes once for each transaction that meets the filter conditions. Within the loop, the subroutine first determines whether any finance charge is owed. This is accomplished by the statement

```
IF cacust->stmtbal>0.and.mcredit<cacust->stmtbal;
   .and.mdate>cacust->stmtdate+caperiod+1.and.finchg=0
```

This statement checks whether the balance is greater than zero, the payments to date are less than the beginning balance, the current transaction date is after the end of the payment grace period, and a finance charge has not already been calculated. If all of these conditions are met, the subroutine calculates a finance charge on the unpaid balance and prints it as a transaction on the statement.

The subroutine then updates its running balances and prints the currently selected transaction. When the bottom of the page is reached, the subroutine prints the page number, then calls CASTMTHD to print the headings for the following page. CASTMT1 next positions the file pointer at the next selected transaction, and the loop is repeated. The loop repeats until all unbilled transactions through the statement date have been printed.

Finally, the subroutine checks whether a finance-charge transaction should be generated at the end of the list of transactions. This occurs if the customer has not made complete payment of the beginning balance, but the last transaction was before the end of the grace period and the statement date is after the end of the grace period. In this case, the finance charge was not completed within the loop, so it is computed and printed here. In the statement in figure 7.32, a finance charge of $3.00 is printed on the line just below the last transaction.

The next section of the code prints the account summary. A new page is started, if necessary, before the summary is printed. After the statement is printed, the subroutine prints the page number on the last page.

If the statement is the final bill for the month, the unbilled transactions for the account are marked as billed. The unbilled transactions are marked by the statement

```
REPLACE billed WITH .T. WHILE .NOT. EOF()
```

This statement marks all transactions that meet the filter conditions still in effect from printing the statement—all transactions, that is, for the specified account up to the specified statement date. If a finance charge was calculated during statement printing, the subroutine generates a finance-charge transaction and calls subroutine CABAL1 to recalculate the transaction balances for the account.

The CABAL1 subroutine recalculates the balance for the specified account. Briefly, this subroutine contains a loop that keeps a running balance for the entire account and a separate balance for the billed transactions. Within the loop, the balance is recalculated for each transaction in CATRANS. When the loop ends, the subroutine uses the two running balances to update the current balance and the balance as of the last statement in CACUST. (For a complete discussion and listing for CABAL1, see the section "Recalculating Account Balances.")

Finally, the program updates the statement date and statement balance with the current values. Updating the balance is redundant if CABAL1 has just run, but it simplifies the program logic to update the balance in any case.

After finishing the statement and the updates, the CASTMT program returns to the top of its statement printing loop to accept another account number. To exit the program, the user first makes certain that the fields for account number, last name, and company are blank, then presses Esc. When the "do forever" loop is exited, the program closes the databases and returns.

Printing Account Histories

The account-history program prints a complete history of the transactions for a specified account, as shown in figure 7.37. Below the report title, the program prints the account ID number, the customer's name, the company name, the current balance, and the balance as of the last statement, followed by a list of all the transactions for this account that are recorded in the transaction file. When someone at Quick and Clean Software wants to clear out the transaction file, he or she would first print this report to create a permanent record of the activity for an account.

```
              CUSTOMER ACCOUNT STATUS                      08/03/86
              -----------------------                      16:35:02


ACCT # AM0001    NAME Fred Adams          COMPANY Adams Marketing
CURRENT BALANCE      1,898.00 LAST STMT DATE 08/30/86 LAST STMT BAL    1,203.00


 DATE    ID          DESCRIPT             DEBIT     CREDIT    BALANCE B
--------         --------------------   ---------  --------  ---------- - -
08/02/86         OPENING BALANCE         1,000.00     0.00   1,000.00 Y
08/04/86         Sales Tracking Program  1,000.00     0.00   2,000.00 Y
08/15/86         Payment                     0.00   800.00   1,200.00 Y
08/23/86 FINCHG  FINANCE CHARGE              3.00     0.00   1,203.00 Y
09/01/86         Modem and Remote Software 695.00     0.00   1,898.00 N
```

Fig. 7.37. Report showing history of transactions for an account.

The CAHIST program is quite straightforward. Briefly, the program opens files, and then enters a "do forever" loop to get an account ID and print the transaction history. The flowchart for CAHIST is shown in figure 7.38; program code is provided in listing 7.20.

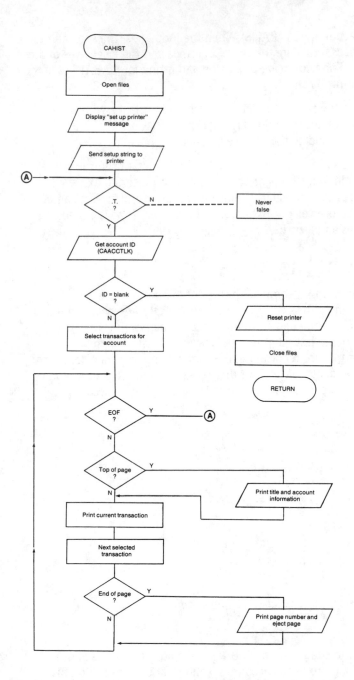

Fig. 7.38. Flowchart for the program CAHIST.

CAHIST prompts the user to set up the printer, sends a setup string to the printer, and enters a DO WHILE .T. loop to select and print account histories. The code in the loop selects the customer file (CACUST) and calls subroutine CAACCTLK so that the user can identify an account by account number, customer name, or company. When control is returned to CAHIST, the program tests for a blank account number. If one is found, the program exits the loop without printing a report.

After an account has been selected, the program selects the transaction file (CATRANS) and enters a nested loop that is controlled by the statement DO WHILE .NOT. EOF() to print the history for the selected account. This loop is repeated until the last transaction for the account has been printed.

The code in the inner loop consists of three sections. In the first section, the program checks the row counter to see whether the print head is at the top of a page. If so, a series of @ . . . SAY commands is used to print the title and headings.

In the second section of the loop, the running balance is calculated; then a series of @ . . . SAY commands prints a row on the report for the current transaction. Then a SKIP command moves the record pointer to the next transaction for printing. The transactions for the account are printed in the same order that they were entered. If they were not entered in strict chronological order, then the printed transaction list will not be in chronological order.

The third section of the loop is executed if the bottom of a page is reached or if the last transaction for the specified account has been printed. The program prints the page number, ejects the page, and resets the counter to the top of the next page.

After the account history for a particular account is printed, the program ejects the page and returns to the top of the main loop for another account-history report. To exit the program, the user first makes certain that the fields for account number and last name and company are blank, then presses Esc. The program exits the "do forever" loop, deactivates the printer and reactivates the console, closes the databases, and returns.

Printing Account Summaries

The account-summary report program, CAACCT, produces a hard-copy version of the information displayed by the program for reviewing the status of an account. This report summarizes the current information in the customer master record. Figure 7.39 shows the report generated by this program; the flowchart is shown in figure 7.40.

```
              Customer Account System        DATE: 08/03/86
            CUSTOMER ACCOUNT SUMMARY REPORT
               CUSTOMER ID: AM0001
            --------------------------------

        NAME: Fred Adams
        COMPANY: Adams Marketing
        ADDRESS:   40001 Redlands Road
                   #216B
                   Indianapolis, IN 46000-
        PHONE: (317)317-3173

ACCOUNT STATUS: A
CURRENT BALANCE:        1898.00 CREDIT LIMIT:      2000.00
COMMENT: Sales Tracking System

AUTOMATIC BILLING FLAG: N      AUTOMATIC BILLING AMOUNT:      0.00
AUTOMATIC BILLING DESCRIPTION:

DATE OF LAST STATEMENT: 08/30/86   BALANCE LAST STATEMENT:   1203.00
```

Fig. 7.39. An account-summary report.

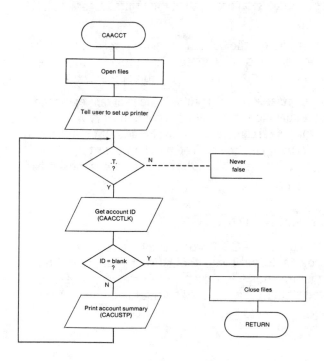

Fig. 7.40. Flowchart for the program CAACCT.

The program CAACCT begins by calling CAOPEN to open the files, then calls BORDERS to clear the screen and display borders and titles (see listing 7.21). The program then enters a "do forever" loop to print account-status reports for selected accounts. The loop begins with a call to CAACCTLK to get the account to print. If CAACCTLK returns with a blank account ID, no summary is printed and the loop is exited.

After the user verifies an account found with subroutine CAACCTLK, control returns to CAACCT. Then the subroutine CACUSTP is called. CACUSTP consists of @ . . . SAY commands that print the report page (see listing 7.22). After printing, the program ejects a page. The loop then is repeated for entry of another account. To return to the reports menu, the user first makes certain that the fields for account number, last name, and company are blank. The user then presses Esc, and an EXIT command transfers control out of the loop. CAACCT closes the databases and returns control to calling program, CUSTACCT2, which generates the queries and reports menu.

Printing Account Lists

The final report generated by the customer-account system is the list-of-accounts report. This report uses a tabular format to summarize the account data in the customer master file (see fig. 7.41). The report prints selected fields from the customer master file; a computed logical variable is used to flag accounts for which the balance exceeds the credit limit. Quick and Clean Software can use this report to document their accounts or scan the account list for problem accounts as well as marketing opportunities. The flowchart for CALIST is shown in figure 7.42.

Page No.   1
08/03/86

Customer Account System
Customer Account List

Cust. ID	Customer Name	Company Name	ST	Credit Limit	Balance	Over Lim.	Auto Bill Flag	Auto Bill Fee	Date of Last Statement	Statement Balance
AM0001	Fred Adams	Adams Marketing	A	2000.00	1898.00	N	N	0.00	08/30/86	1203.00
FU0001	Janet Jensen	First United Local Bank	A	10000.00	100.00	N	Y	100.00	08/02/86	0.00
JT0001	Allen Johnson	Johnson Typesetting	A	1000.00	800.00	N	Y	50.00	08/02/86	0.00
SJ0001	Jim Jones	Smith & Jones	A	2000.00	150.00	N	N	0.00	08/02/86	1000.00
*** Total ***					2948.00					2203.00

Fig. 7.41. Report showing list of accounts.

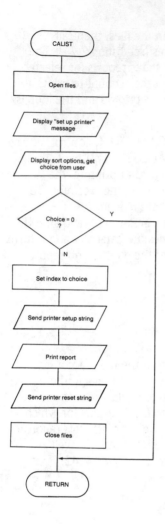

Fig. 7.42. Flowchart for the program CALIST.

CALIST opens the files and asks the user to indicate the sort order for the report (see listing 7.23). The report can be sorted and printed by account number, by customer name, or by company. After choosing the sort order, the user is prompted to set up the printer and then press any key. The program then prints the desired report and returns control to the calling program, CUSTACCT2, which produces the queries and reports menu. CALIST uses the REPORT FORM command to generate the actual report. The report definitions that are entered with MODIFY REPORT are shown in figure 7.43.

```
Report definitions for report CALIST.FRM

Page title:            Customer-Account System
                       Customer Account List
                       -----------------------

Page width:      132
Left margin:       0

Group on expression
Group heading
Summary report only      No
Page eject after group
Sub-group on expression
Sub-group heading

COL        Contents                 Heading             W   D Tot
---     ------------------  ----------------------------- --  -- ---
  1     cust_id             ;;Cust.;ID                    6
  2     TRIM(f_name)+       ;;Customer Name;             20
        " "+TRIM(l_name)    ---------------------
  3     company             ;;Company Name;
                            ---------------------         20
  4     status              ;;ST;--                       2
  5     creditlim           ;Credit;Limit;-----------    12
  6     balance             ;;Balance;------------       12   2 Yes
  7     IIF(balance>        ;Over;Lim.;----               4
        creditlim,'Y','N')
  8     IIF(autobill,'Y','N') Auto;Bill;Flag;----         4
  9     autofee             Auto;Bill;Fee;-----------    12
 10     stmtdate            Date of;Last;Statement;       9
                            ---------
 11     stmtbal             ;Statement;Balance;-----------12      YES
```

Fig. 7.43. Report definitions for CALIST.

Creating System-Maintenance Programs

The system-maintenance programs allow the user to perform maintenance functions without having to use interactive dBASE commands. We have already discussed programs for reindexing the database and maintaining the system memory-variables file. In this section we look at programs for packing the database, recalculating account balances, backing up and restoring data files, and removing old transactions from the files.

Packing the Database (CAPACK)

The CAPACK program permanently removes deleted accounts and transactions from the databases. Deleted records remain in a file and can be recalled to active status until the CAPACK program is run. To free up valuable disk space, users should periodically run CAPACK after purging the database of old transactions (see the section "Purging Old Transactions"). But note that packing can take several minutes.

CAPACK opens the files with CAOPEN and displays the screen borders and titles with BORDERS (see listing 7.24). Then the program prompts the user to verify the procedure. When this has been done, CAPACK packs the customer file (CACUST) and the transaction file (CATRANS). CAPACK closes the databases and returns to calling program CUSTACCT3, which creates the system maintenance menu.

Important note: Warn the user that deleted customer master and transaction records cannot be recovered after CAPACK is used.

Recalculating Account Balances (CABAL)

The program to recalculate account balances is included as a safety measure for users. As with CAINDEX, the user should never have to use CABAL during normal operations. CABAL might be needed, however, when someone has adjusted the transactions manually in interactive mode.

Important note: Be sure to tell the user to run CABAL after any manual adjustments are made.

CABAL opens files with CAOPEN, then calls BORDERS to display the screen borders and the title (see listing 7.25). The program prompts the user to verify the procedure, goes to the top of the customer master file, and enters a DO WHILE .NOT. EOF() loop to process each record in the customer master file, CACUST.

The program CABAL calls the subroutine CABAL1 to recalculate the balance for a specific account. (CABAL1 is also used by the subroutine CASTMT1 to recalculate account balances after posting a finance charge to the account.) CABAL1 begins by selecting all undeleted records for the specified account (see listing 7.26). Then the subroutine loops through each transaction record, calculating the new transaction balance and replacing the existing balance stored in the BALANCE field. CABAL1 keeps a running balance for the entire account and a separate balance for the billed transactions. The loop updates the running balance of all transactions for each transaction; it updates only the billed transaction balance for transactions with BILLED=.T. When the loop ends, the subroutine uses the accumulated transaction balance and the billed transaction balance to update the current balance and the balance as of the last statement in the customer master file.

Important note: An apparent bug in version 1.1 of dBASE III Plus may cause improper functioning of CABAL1 when that subroutine is called to print final statements. In such cases, the DO WHILE loop fails to terminate: the subroutine oscillates between two records and never reaches end-of-file. The problem apparently is related to the use of the REPLACE command. Carefully test this subroutine with your (or your client's) copy of dBASE III Plus to verify that the subroutine works properly.

Backing Up Data Files to Floppy Disks (CABACKUP)

The program CABACKUP uses the DOS BACKUP command to save the data files, index files, and memory file from a hard disk to one or more formatted floppy disks (see listing 7.27). The program prompts the user to insert floppy disks as needed. Urge the user to perform system backups regularly and to keep three sets of backup disks. Each time a backup is performed, the oldest backup set should be reused to make the new backup. The most recent backup should be maintained off site.

Restoring Data Files from Floppy Disks (CARESTOR)

The CARESTOR program enables users to restore all system data from backup files made with CABACKUP. You would use this command after a hardware failure or an accidental erasure of data. As with CABACKUP, this program prompts the user to insert disks as needed. CARESTOR can also be used to load data into another computer system.

CARESTOR begins by clearing the screen, presenting a title, and asking the user to confirm the procedure (see listing 7.28). Note that this subroutine uses the DOS RESTORE function to restore data from backup floppy disks. The CABACKUP and CARESTOR programs both use a memory variable and the & (macro substitution) operator to specify the target of the backup. This makes it easy to change the target drive ID from b: to another drive.

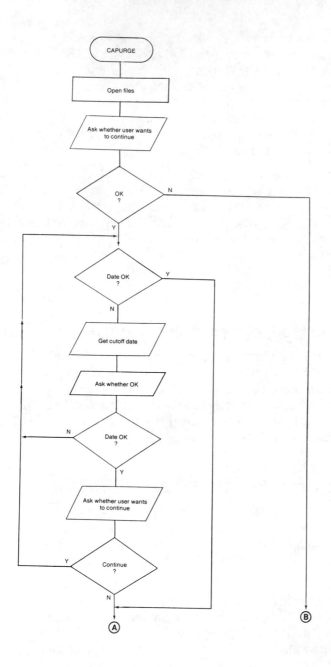

Fig. 7.44. Flowchart for the program CAPURGE.

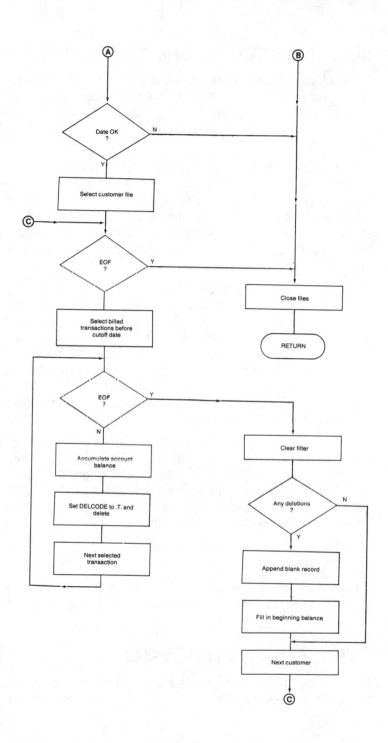

Purging Old Transactions (CAPURGE)

The last utility program for the customer-account system provides a method of purging old customer transactions from the transaction file. Otherwise, the file would grow without limit over time. The program CAPURGE purges billed customer transactions before a specified cutoff date. A flowchart for the program is shown in figure 7.44.

After opening the files with CAOPEN, CAPURGE prompts the user to confirm the procedure (see listing 7.29). The program then prompts the user to enter a cutoff date for the purge. The default cutoff date if 1/1/80, which is before any active transactions in Quick and Clean Software's customer account files. After the user enters the cutoff date, the program uses a DO WHILE loop to perform the deletions for each customer account. This loop is executed once for each active customer in the customer file.

An inner loop controlled by DO WHILE .NOT. EOF() deletes all the billed transactions for the currently selected account up to the cutoff date. The deleted transactions are selected by a SET FILTER command that selects all billed records for the current account before the cutoff date. The message `Working . . .` is displayed as the program deletes the customer transactions before the cutoff date. The inner loop calculates a running balance for the transactions being deleted, then deletes each record and marks it as permanently deleted by setting DELCODE to .T. This flag indicates to CACUADD and CACUDEL that the marked transactions are not to be recalled under any circumstances.

After the inner loop finishes, the program creates a new beginning balance transaction at the cutoff date and posts the running balance to that transaction. This balance is the net amount (DEBITS–CREDITS) for all the transactions that have been deleted by the inner loop. Then the program selects the customer file CACUST.DBF again and proceeds to the next customer. When finished, the program closes the databases and returns to the system-maintenance menu.

After the program has purged the records, the user must run the program CAPACK to reclaim the file space.

Important note: *Tell the user that if the wrong transactions are purged by mistake, the data can be recovered by the consultant if the database is not packed in the interim.*

Creating a Menu System

The next stage in the development of the customer-account system is to create the menus. To keep each menu simple, this application uses a multiple-menu approach with a main menu and three subsidiary menus. Figures 7.45 through 7.48 show the main menu, data-entry menu, queries and reports menu, and the system-maintenance menu, respectively. Note that the structure of this menu system mirrors the system block diagram shown in figure 7.5.

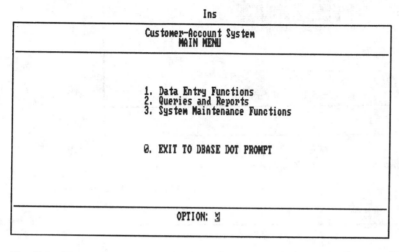

Fig. 7.45. The main menu.

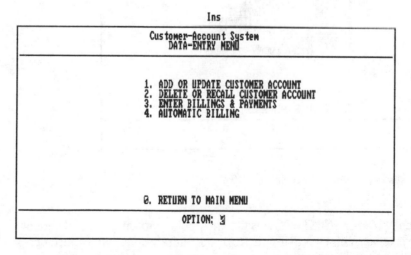

Fig. 7.46. The data-entry menu.

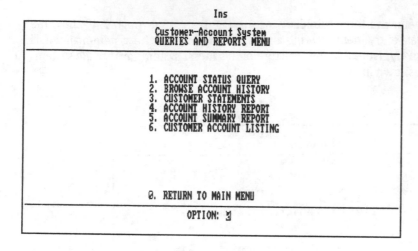

Fig. 7.47. The queries and reports menu.

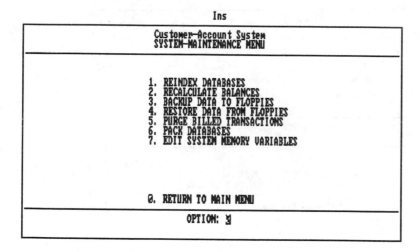

Fig. 7.48. The system-maintenance menu.

The main menu program, CUSTACCT, is the entry point into the system. Therefore, part of its job is to establish the environment for the entire system, which includes setting TALK and SAFETY off and making sure that the printer is off.

The three subsidiary menu programs, CUSTACCT1, CUSTACCT2, and CUSTACC3, call the programs that perform the major operations of the system. The first menu program groups together the data-entry functions. The second menu program controls the query and report functions. The third menu program gives access to system-maintenance functions like packing and reindexing the data files, purging old transactions, recalculating account balances, backing up the database, and changing system parameters.

Code for these straightforward programs is provided in listings 7.30 through 7.33. Information is displayed on the screen by means of @. . . SAY commands, and the user's choice is read with an @. . . GET command. Because a number is used to select the menu option, the user's choice is range-checked with the RANGE option of the @ . . . GET command.

The DO CASE structure at the bottom of each menu listing executes the option corresponding to the user's menu selection. Any selection from the main menu causes one of the submenu programs to be called, and a selection from a submenu activates a program to perform a particular function. The menu display and the DO CASE structure are contained in a DO WHILE loop that repeats the menu until the user selects option 0 to exit the system.

You may want to rearrange the menus to suit your customer's particular needs. One customer may prefer a single menu with all the system options in one place. Another may prefer a multiple-menu arrangement like the one created here for Quick and Clean Software.

Using Procedure Files

The final step in the development of the customer-account system is to place key routines in procedure files. Procedure files speed program execution by reducing the number of files accessed by the system. Clients will appreciate the time that procedure files will save them in running the application. Recall from Chapter 2 that up to 32 routines can be placed in a procedure file. (For more on the use of procedure files, see Chapter 2, "Applications Development with dBASE III Plus.")

Extensions to the System

A natural extension to the system would be a program to generate customer statements in batch mode so that the user would not have to enter every account number. A complementary enhancement would be to print statements for those customers that received their last statement a month or more ago. Then the bookkeeper could run the statement program routinely every day or week and it would automatically generate a statement for each customer once a month.

In another extension to the system, you could expand the automatic-billing concept to allow more than one automatic billing item per customer. This would be useful for Quick and Clean if its customers purchase software-maintenance contracts for more than one of Quick and Clean's products. Then an expanded automatic-billing function would allow Quick and Clean to list each software maintenance contract individually on a customer's statement. This could be done by adding a small database file that contains the account number, the automatic billing amount, an automatic-billing ID number, and the day of the month for the automatic-billing item. Then, when the automatic-billing program is run, it would create the automatic-billing transactions for each customer account on the dates indicated in the automatic-billing database file.

The most significant extension of this system would be to connect the customer-accounts system to other accounting modules to create an integrated accounts-receivable and ledger system. In this system, data would have to be entered only once. The mechanics of such a major step would depend on what packages you (or your client) are already using for entering orders and keeping a general ledger. If the other accounting packages are written in dBASE and run on the same PC, it shouldn't be too difficult to write additional programs to update the files in more than one system at the same time. Otherwise, you would have to transfer data in batch mode using report files or some other common file format. Chapter 9 provides details on how to link the fixed-asset manager, sales-tracking system, customer-accounts system, and general ledger.

The customer file in the customer-accounts system is very similar to the customer file in the sales-tracking system (see Chapter 5). These two systems are a natural combination, sharing a common file and some common data entries. However, the transaction file for the customer-accounts system would not necessarily contain the same information as the transaction file for the sales-tracking system. The sales-tracking file contains both cash and credit sales, whereas the customer-account system is only concerned with sales on account.

Conclusion

The customer-accounts system presented here can keep track of accounts receivable for a small- to medium-sized company. This system produces customer statements, account summaries, account histories, and various sorted lists showing customer-account balances. The system has a simple automatic-billing function for one automatic billing item per customer, but can be expanded to handle multiple items per customer. Although it is a stand-alone system, the customer-accounts system can be linked to accounting modules to create an integrated accounts-receivable and ledger system.

Listing 7.1. The subroutine CAOPEN.

```
****************************************************************
* CAOPEN - Open customer and transaction databases with indexes  *
*              9/11/86                                          *
****************************************************************

* Open databases with correct indexes. Return with customer selected.
CLOSE DATABASES
SELECT A
USE cacust INDEX cacuacct,cacuname,cacucomp
SELECT B
USE catrans INDEX catrans
SELECT cacust
RETURN
```

Listing 7.2. The program CAINDEX.

```
****************************************************************
* CAINDEX - Program to reindex all Customer Account data files  *
*              9/11/86                                          *
****************************************************************

* Setup environment
CLOSE DATABASES
RESTORE FROM camem ADDITIVE
title='Reindex Customer Account Files'
DO borders WITH catitle,title

*Index CUSTOMER file
USE cacust
@ 5, 20 SAY "Indexing customer file by customer ID"
INDEX ON cust_id TO cacuacct
@ 6, 20 SAY "Indexing customer file by customer name"
INDEX ON UPPER(l_name)+UPPER(f_name) TO cacuname
@ 7, 20 SAY "Indexing customer file by company"
INDEX ON UPPER(company) TO cacucomp

*Index transactions file
USE catrans
@ 8, 6 SAY "Indexing transactions file by customer ID, billing status, and date"
SET DATE ANSI
INDEX ON cust_id + IIF(billed,'B','N') + DTOC(date) TO catrans

*Return
CLEAR
SET DATE AMERICAN
CLOSE DATABASES
RETURN
```

Listing 7.3. The program CAMEM.

```
************************************************************************
* CAMEM   -       Define customer account system parameters       *
*                 9/9/86                                           *
************************************************************************

* Restore existing or initialize new entries, depending on whether file exists
IF FILE("camem.mem")
   RESTORE FROM camem ADDITIVE
   capsetup=SUBSTR(capsetup+SPACE(80),1,80)        && Pad to 80 chars with blanks
   capreset=SUBSTR(capreset+SPACE(80),1,80)        && Pad to 80 chars with blanks
   cacompname=SUBSTR(cacompname+SPACE(26),1,26)  && Pad company name to 26 chars
   caaddr1=SUBSTR(caaddr1+SPACE(26),1,26)          && Pad addr. line 1 to 26 chars
   caaddr2=SUBSTR(caaddr2+SPACE(26),1,26)          && Pad addr. line 2 to 26 chars
   caphone=SUBSTR(caphone+SPACE(13),1,13)          && Pad phone num. to 13 chars
ELSE
   STORE "Customer-Account System" TO catitle
   STORE SPACE(80) TO capsetup,capreset
   STORE 0 TO capmargin
   STORE 55 TO capagelen
   STORE SPACE(26) TO cacompname, caaddr1, caaddr2
   STORE SPACE(13) TO caphone
   STORE 30 TO caperiod
   STORE .015 TO cainterest
ENDIF

* get new values
mok=.F.
mok1=.F.
title= "Edit System Memory Variables"
DO WHILE .not.mok
   * Display data entry screen
   DO came1                && Display memory variable data entry screen
   @ 21, 9 SAY "Enter or revise desired memory variables. ";
        +"Press ESC to end edit"
   READ
   @ 21, 1 SAY SPACE(78)

   * Confirm edit.
   mok=.F.
   @ 21, 33 SAY "OK (Y or N)?" GET mok PICTURE "Y"
   READ
   IF .not. mok
      mok1=.T.
      @ 22, 20 SAY "Want to make further changes (Y or N)? ";
        GET mok1 PICTURE "Y"
      READ
      IF .not. mok1
         EXIT   && Quit loop with mok=.F.
      ENDIF
   ENDIF
ENDDO
```

```
* If ok, Save new memory file
IF mok
   capsetup=TRIM(capsetup)
   capreset=TRIM(capreset)
   cacompname=TRIM(cacompname)
   caaddr1=TRIM(caaddr1)
   caaddr2=TRIM(caaddr2)
   DO came1                             && Redisplay screen
   CLEAR GETS                           && but do not read
   mok=.T.
   @ 22,17 SAY "Save changes to new CAMEM file (Y or N) " GET mok PICTURE "Y"

    READ
    IF mok
       SAVE TO camem ALL LIKE ca*
    ENDIF
ENDIF

* Tidy up and return
CLEAR
RETURN
```

Listing 7.4. The subroutine CAME1.

```
*****************************************************************
* CAME1 -        Display memory variable data entry screen for  *
*                Customer Accounts System                       *
*                9/9/86                                         *
*****************************************************************

DO borders WITH catitle,"Edit System Memory Variables"
@  6,  2 SAY "PRINTER LEFT MARGIN:"  GET capmargin PICTURE "999" RANGE 0,132
@  6, 40 SAY "PRINTER PAGE LENGTH:" GET capagelen PICTURE "99" RANGE 1, 99
@  7,  2 SAY "SETUP COMPRESSED PRINT:" GET capsetup FUNCTION "S30"
@  8,  2 SAY "RESET PRINTER TO NORMAL:" GET capreset FUNCTION "S30"
@ 10,  2 SAY "COMPANY NAME:" GET cacompname
@ 11,  2 SAY "ADDRESS:" GET caaddr1
@ 12,  2 SAY "CITY, STATE, ZIP:" GET caaddr2
@ 13,  2 SAY "PHONE NUMBER:" GET caphone
@ 15,  2 SAY "PAYMENT GRACE PERIOD:" GET caperiod PICTURE '99'
@ 16,  2 SAY "MONTHLY INTEREST RATE ON OVERDUE BALANCES:" GET cainterest;
   PICTURE '9.9999'

RETURN
```

Listing 7.5. The program CACUADD.

```
************************************************************
* CACUADD - Add or update customer account record         *
*          9/10/86                                         *
************************************************************

* Setup environment
PRIVATE ok,mok,new,mbal

* Open files
DO caopen
RESTORE FROM camem ADDITIVE
mtitle='ADD OR UPDATE CUSTOMER ACCOUNT'

* Main loop.
DO WHILE .T.

    * get account number from user
    macct=SPACE(6)
    DO borders WITH catitle,mtitle
    @  6, 10  SAY "ENTER ACCOUNT TO ADD OR UPDATE (blank to exit)";
        GET macct PICTURE '!!!!!!'
    READ

    * Exit on blank customer ID
    IF macct=SPACE(6)
        EXIT
    ENDIF

    * Look for customer ID in file
    ok=.T.
    new=.F.
    SEEK macct

    * Check whether not found or found but deleted
    IF EOF().or.DELETED()          && If true, are ADDING new record

        IF DELETED()              && Customer acct. record exists but is deleted
            * If DELETED, warn user and ask if want to continue with add.
            mok=.F.
            @ 21, 4 SAY "This account is currently deleted. Want to continue ";
                    +"with ADD (Y or N)?" GET mok PICTURE 'Y'
            READ

            IF .not.mok            && If not ok, loop
                LOOP
            ELSE                   && If ok, prepare for ADD
                * If user wants to create anyway, mark all associated transactions
                * deleted, then recall account
                SELECT catrans
                SEEK macct
                REPLACE delcode WITH .T. WHILE cust_id=macct
                SELECT cacust
            ENDIF
```

```
   ELSE                          && Otherwise, no record found
      mok=.T.
      @ 8, 10 SAY 'Customer ID not found. Want to create new account ';
             +'(Y or N)?' GET mok PICTURE 'Y' && Verify add'n of new acct.
      READ
      IF .not.mok                    && If not verified, loop
         LOOP
      ELSE                           && Otherwise, create new record
         APPEND BLANK
         REPLACE cust_id WITH macct
         DELETE
      ENDIF
   ENDIF

   * In either case (DELETED or EOF), Initialize variables to blank
   STORE SPACE(60) TO mcomment
   STORE SPACE(30) TO mautodescr
   STORE SPACE(26) TO mcompany,maddr1,maddr2
   STORE SPACE(16) TO mcity,ml_name
   STORE SPACE(14) TO mphone
   STORE SPACE(10) TO mzip,mf_name
   STORE SPACE(2)  TO mstate
   STORE SPACE(1)  TO mstatus
   STORE 0 TO mbalance,mcreditlim,mautofee,mstmtbal
   STORE DATE() TO mstmtdate
   STORE .F. TO mautobill
   new=.T.

ELSE                          && Updating existing record
   * Initialize variables to values in file.
   macct=cust_id
   mcompany=company
   maddr1=addr1
   maddr2=addr2
   mcity=city
   mstate=state
   mzip=zip
   mf_name=f_name
   ml_name=l_name
   mphone=phone
   mstatus=status
   mbalance=balance
   mcreditlim=creditlim
   mautobill=autobill
   mautofee=autofee
   mautodescr=autodescr
   mcomment=comment
   mstmtdate=stmtdate
   mstmtbal=stmtbal
ENDIF
```

(Continued on next page.)

Listing 7.5, continued.

```
* Edit the record until ok
mok=.F.
DO WHILE .not. mok

   * Get data from user
   DO cacuscr1
   @ 22, 14 SAY 'Press Enter key before Esc if a change has been made'
   READ
   @ 21, 1 CLEAR TO 22, 78

   * Verify that data is ok
   @ 21, 26 SAY 'OK (Y or N) (Esc to quit)?' GET mok PICTURE 'Y'
   READ

   * Check for ESC key. Break out of loop if so.
   IF READKEY()=12
      EXIT
   ENDIF

ENDDO

IF mok                && ADD or UPDATE customer record if data entry was ok

   * If new customer, create new customer record.
   * Update record with user entries
   REPLACE company WITH mcompany,addr1 WITH maddr1,addr2 WITH maddr2,;
      city WITH mcity,state WITH mstate,zip WITH mzip,f_name WITH mf_name,;
      l_name WITH ml_name,phone WITH mphone,status WITH mstatus
   REPLACE balance WITH mbalance,creditlim WITH mcreditlim,autobill WITH;
      mautobill,autofee WITH mautofee,autodescr WITH mautodescr,comment WITH;
      mcomment,stmtdate WITH mstmtdate,stmtbal WITH mstmtbal
   RECALL             && And undelete record

   * If new customer, create beginning balance record in CATRANS file
   IF new
      SELECT catrans
      APPEND BLANK
      REPLACE cust_id WITH cacust->cust_id,date WITH DATE(),descript WITH;
        'OPENING BALANCE',debit WITH IIF(mbalance>0,mbalance,0),credit WITH;
        IIF (mbalance<0,-mbalance,0),balance WITH debit-credit,billed WITH;
        .T.,delcode WITH .F.
      SELECT cacust
   ENDIF new

ENDIF mok

ENDDO .T.               && end of main loop

* tidy up and return
CLEAR
CLOSE DATABASES
RETURN
```

Listing 7.6. The subroutine CACUSCR1.

```
***********************************************************
* CACUSCR1 -     Customer add/edit data entry screen     *
*               9/10/86                                   *
***********************************************************

DO borders WITH catitle,mtitle
@  5, 31  SAY "CUSTOMER ID "+macct
@  7,  2  SAY "FIRST NAME:" GET  mf_name
@  7, 30  SAY "LAST NAME:" GET ml_name
@  8,  2  SAY "COMPANY:" GET mcompany
@  9,  2  SAY "ADDRESS:" GET  maddr1
@ 10, 11  GET  maddr2
@ 11,  2  SAY "CITY:    " GET   mcity
@ 11, 30  SAY "STATE:" GET  mstate  FUNCTION "A!"
@ 11, 40  SAY "ZIPCODE:" GET mzip  PICTURE "99999-9999"
@ 12,  2  SAY "PHONE:" GET  mphone PICTURE "(999)999-9999"
@ 14,  2  SAY "ACCOUNT STATUS:" GET  mstatus  FUNCTION "!"
@ 14, 20  SAY "CURRENT BALANCE:" GET mbalance PICTURE '999999999.99'
@ 14, 51  SAY "CREDIT LIMIT:" GET mcreditlim PICTURE '999999999.99'
@ 15,  2  SAY "DATE OF LAST STATEMENT:" GET mstmtdate
@ 15, 40  SAY "BALANCE LAST STATEMENT:" GET mstmtbal PICTURE '999999999.99'
@ 16,  2  SAY "COMMENT:" GET mcomment
@ 18,  2  SAY "AUTOMATIC BILLING FLAG:" GET mautobill PICTURE "Y"
@ 18, 30  SAY "AUTOMATIC BILLING AMOUNT:" GET mautofee PICTURE '999999999.99'
@ 19,  2  SAY "AUTOMATIC BILLING DESCRIPTION:" GET mautodescr

RETURN
```

Listing 7.7. The program CACUDEL.

```
****************************************************************
* CACUDEL - Delete or undelete customer account record  *
*          9/11/86                                       *
****************************************************************

* Open files
DO caopen
RESTORE FROM camem ADDITIVE
mtitle="CUSTOMER ACCOUNT DELETE/UNDELETE SCREEN"

* Main loop.
DO WHILE .T.

   * get and verify account number
   DO borders WITH catitle,mtitle
   macct=SPACE(6)
   @  6, 10  SAY "ENTER ACCOUNT TO DELETE OR UNDELETE (blank to exit)";
      GET macct FUNCTION '!'
   READ

   * If account number is blank, exit
   IF macct=SPACE(6)
      EXIT
   ENDIF

   * Check that account exists. If not, loop back to start
   SEEK macct
   IF EOF()
      mok=' '
      @ 21,14 SAY "ACCOUNT DOES NOT EXIST. Press any key to continue" GET mok
      READ
      LOOP
   ENDIF                                         && .not.mfound

   * Display body of record
   DO cacuscr

   * Display deleted/undeleted status, request direction
   @ 21, 1 CLEAR TO 22, 78
   IF DELETED()

      * If record deleted, ask if want to recall.
      ok=.T.
      @ 21, 15 SAY "RECORD IS CURRENTLY DELETED. WANT TO UNDELETE (Y or N)?";
        GET ok PICTURE 'Y'
      READ
      IF ok
         RECALL
         SELECT catrans
         RECALL FOR cust_id=macct.and..not.delcode
         SELECT cacust
         mok=' '
         @ 22, 10 SAY "Customer has been recalled. Press any key to ";
                 +"continue..." GET mok
         READ
      ENDIF
      @ 21, 1 CLEAR TO 22, 78
   ELSE           && Not deleted
```

```
* If record active, ask if want to delete, then verify.
mok=.T.
@ 21, 15 SAY "RECORD IS CURRENTLY ACTIVE. WANT TO DELETE (Y or N)?";
   GET mok PICTURE 'Y'
READ
IF mok
    * Check for unbilled transactions in file
    SELECT catrans
    SET FILTER TO cust_id=macct.and..not.billed
    SET DELETED ON
    SEEK macct
    ok=IIF(EOF(),.T.,.F.)   && ok set false if unbilled record found
    SET FILTER TO
    SET DELETED OFF
    SELECT cacust

    * If no unbilled records found, continue with delete
    IF ok            && No unbilled records found in transaction file
       mok=.T.
       @ 22, 30 SAY "Are you sure (Y or N)?" GET mok PICTURE 'Y'
       READ
       @ 21, 1 CLEAR TO 22, 78
       IF mok
          DELETE
          SELECT catrans
          DELETE FOR cust_id=macct
          SELECT cacust
          mok=' '
          @ 21, 11 SAY "Customer has been deleted. Press any key ";
                   +"to continue..." get mok
          READ
       ENDIF
    ELSE             && Unbilled records in transaction file
       mok=' '
       @ 22, 2 SAY "Print final statement before deleting. Press ";
               +"any key to continue.";
          GET mok
          READ
          LOOP
    ENDIF ok
 ENDIF mok
ENDIF DELETED()

* end of main loop
ENDDO

* tidy up and return
CLEAR
CLOSE DATABASES
RETURN
```

Listing 7.8. The subroutine CACUSCR.

```
*******************************************************************
* CACUSCR -        Customer master file data display screen      *
*                  9/10/86                                        *
*******************************************************************

DO borders WITH catitle,mtitle
@  5, 31  SAY "CUSTOMER ID "+cust_id
@  7,  2  SAY "FIRST NAME: "+f_name
@  7, 30  SAY "LAST NAME: "+l_name
@  8,  2  SAY "COMPANY: "+company
@  9,  2  SAY "ADDRESS: "+addr1
@ 10, 11  SAY  addr2
@ 11, 11  SAY  TRIM(city)+', '+state+' '+zip
@ 12,  2  SAY "PHONE: "+phone
@ 14,  2  SAY "ACCOUNT STATUS: "+status
@ 14, 20  SAY "CURRENT BALANCE: "+STR(balance,12,2)
@ 14, 51  SAY "CREDIT LIMIT: "+STR(creditlim,12,2)
@ 15,  2  SAY "DATE OF LAST STATEMENT: "+DTOC(stmtdate)
@ 15, 41  SAY "BALANCE LAST STATEMENT: "+STR(stmtbal,12,2)
@ 16,  2  SAY "COMMENT: "+comment
@ 18,  2  SAY "AUTOMATIC BILLING FLAG:"
@ 18, 26  SAY  autobill PICTURE "Y"
@ 18, 30  SAY "AUTOMATIC BILLING AMOUNT: "+STR(autofee,12,2)
@ 19,  2  SAY "AUTOMATIC BILLING DESCRIPTION: "+autodescr

RETURN
```

Listing 7.9. The program CABILL.

```
************************************************************
* CABILL -       Enter billing or payment information    *
*               9/12/86                                  *
************************************************************

* Initialization & open data files
SET EXACT OFF                       && NO exact match on SEEK or FIND
SET DATE ANSI
DO caopen
RESTORE FROM camem ADDITIVE
mtitle= "DATA ENTRY SCREEN FOR BILLINGS AND PAYMENTS"

* Main loop
DO WHILE .T.

    * Read accountno, name, or company
    SELECT cacust
    DO borders WITH catitle,mtitle
    macct=SPACE(6)
    mfound=.F.
    DO caacctlk WITH macct,mfound

    * EXIT on blank account number
    IF macct=SPACE(6)
       EXIT
    ELSE

    * If account not found, display message and continue
    IF .not.mfound
       @ 12, 31 SAY "ACCOUNT NOT FOUND."
       @ 13, 11 SAY "YOU NEED TO SET IT UP BEFORE ENTERING BILLINGS OR PAYMENTS"
       mok=' '
       @ 21, 26 SAY "Press any key to continue..." GET mok
       READ
       LOOP
    ENDIF

    * Get billings or payments for this account
    more=.T.
    SELECT catrans                          && Use transactions file
    DO WHILE more

       * Append new, blank record, enter today's date
       @ 21, 1 CLEAR TO 22, 78
       SELECT catrans                       && Use transactions file
       APPEND BLANK
       REPLACE cust_id WITH macct, date WITH DATE(), billed WITH .F.,;
          delcode WITH .T.
       DELETE
```

(Continued on next page.)

Listing 7.9, continued.

```
* Use CABISCR1 subroutine for data entry
ok=.F.
DO WHILE .not.ok
   REPLACE debit WITH 0, credit WITH 0
   mdate=DATE()
   SET DATE AMERICAN
   DO cabiscr1                 && Display Say's and Get's
   @ 21, 21 SAY "Press Ctrl End to accept, Esc to quit"
   READ                        && Read Get's
   SET DATE ANSI
   REPLACE date WITH mdate       && date field must be replaced while
                                 && date is ansi for index to be updated
                                 && properly! mdate is read by cabiscr1.

       @ 21, 1 CLEAR TO 22, 78

       IF READKEY()=12                && If Esc key was pressed
          EXIT                        && Exit data entry loop
       ENDIF

       * Check data entered. If ok, prompt for acceptance
       IF debit#0 .and. credit#0
          mok=' '
          @ 21, 2 SAY "CAN'T ENTER BOTH A DEBIT AND A CREDIT. ";
             +"Any key to continue";
            GET mok
          READ
       ELSE
          ok=.T.
          @ 21, 33 SAY "OK (Y or N)? " GET ok PICTURE 'Y'
          READ
       ENDIF
   @ 21, 1 CLEAR TO 22, 78
   ENDDO .not.ok

   * If an amount was entered, update record
   IF ok.and.debit#0.or.credit#0
      SELECT cacust
      REPLACE balance WITH balance+catrans->debit-catrans->credit
      SELECT catrans
      REPLACE balance WITH cacust->balance, delcode WITH .F.
      RECALL                         && Activate finished transaction
   ENDIF

   * Ask about another transaction
   @ 21,13 SAY "Another transaction on this account (RETURN or N)? ";
      GET more PICTURE 'Y'
   READ
   ENDDO more

ENDDO .T.                            && End of loop on account

* Clean up and return
CLEAR
SET DATE AMERICAN
CLOSE DATABASES
RETURN
```

Listing 7.10. The subroutine CAACCTLK.

```
**********************************************************************
* CAACCTLK - Look up account by account number or  name           *
*                                                                 *
*           Called with customer database open with account &     *
*           and last name indexes, and logo & instructions in     *
*           top half of screen.                                   *
*                                                                 *
*           Returns macct & ok flag, sets CUSTOMER rec.           *
*           9/12/86                                               *
**********************************************************************
* Parameters
PARAMETERS macct,ok

* Initialization
SELECT cacust
ok=.F.

* Main loop to get & verify account number, company, or name
DO WHILE .not.ok
    @ 11, 1 CLEAR TO 19, 78
    @ 21, 1 CLEAR TO 22, 78
    macct=SPACE(6)
    mcomp=SPACE(26)
    mfirst=SPACE(10)
    mlast=SPACE(16)

    * Read customer id, company, or first and last name
    @ 6, 15  SAY "ENTER CUSTOMER ID, COMPANY, OR CUSTOMER NAME"
    @ 8, 15  SAY "CUSTOMER ID" GET macct FUNCTION '!'
    @ 9, 15  SAY "LAST NAME" GET mlast FUNCTION 'A!'
    @ 9, 43  SAY 'FIRST NAME' GET mfirst FUNCTION 'A!'
    @ 10, 15 SAY "COMPANY" GET mcomp FUNCTION '!'
    @ 15, 15 SAY 'PROGRAM WILL DISPLAY MATCHES TO PARTIAL CUSTOMER ID,'
    @ 16, 15 SAY 'LAST NAME, OR COMPANY ONE AT A TIME ON SCREEN'
    @ 21, 15 SAY "PRESS Esc FROM BLANK SCREEN TO QUIT"
    @ 22, 15 SAY "PRESS Enter THEN Esc TO ENTER A CUSTOMER ID, NAME, OR COMPANY"
    READ
    @ 11, 1 CLEAR TO 19, 78
    @ 21, 1 CLEAR TO 22, 78

    * determine which was entered, and look up in customer file
    DO CASE

        * Lookup customer ID
        CASE macct#' '                  && Look for non-blank customer ID
            SET ORDER TO 1              && If so, index is #1
            SET FILTER to cust_id=TRIM(macct)   && Select matching records
            SEEK TRIM(macct)                    && Find first match

            * Error if no matches found
            IF EOF()
               @ 21, 30 SAY "Customer ID not found."
            ENDIF
```

(Continued on next page.)

Listing 7.10, continued.

```
   * Lookup customer name
   CASE mlast#' '                        && Look for non-blank last name
       SET ORDER TO 2                     && If so, name index is #2
       IF mfirst#' '                      && Select matching records
          SET FILTER TO UPPER(f_name)=TRIM(mfirst);
              .and.UPPER(l_name)=TRIM(mlast) && Filter for first & last name
       ELSE
          SET FILTER TO UPPER(l_name)=TRIM(mlast) && Fltr for last name only
       ENDIF
       SEEK TRIM(mlast)                   && Find first match

       * Error if no matches found
       IF EOF()
          @ 21, 30 SAY "Customer Name not found."
       ENDIF

   CASE mcomp#' '                         && company name is not blank
       SET ORDER TO 3                     && company index is #3
       SET FILTER TO UPPER(company)=TRIM(mcomp)     && Select matching recs.
       SEEK TRIM(mcomp)                   && Find first match

       *Error if no matches found
       IF EOF()
          @ 21, 30 SAY "Company Name not found."
       ENDIF

   * Handle if wrong part of fields entered
   CASE mfirst#' '
       mok=' '
       @ 21, 12 SAY "Invalid search specification.  ";
         +"Press any key to continue" GET mok
       READ
       @ 21, 1 CLEAR TO 22, 78
       LOOP

   * No entry, EXIT data entry loop
   OTHERWISE                    && all fields are empty
       EXIT

ENDCASE

IF .not.EOF()                  && If a matching record was found

    * Browse matching database records
   DO WHILE .not.ok.and..not.EOF().and..not.BOF()

    * Display matching record.
    @ 15, 15  SAY "THIS RECORD MATCHES THE SPECIFICATION"
    @ 16, 15  SAY "CUSTOMER ID "+cust_id
    @ 16, 35  SAY "COMPANY "+company
    @ 17, 15  SAY "LAST NAME "+l_name
    @ 17, 43  SAY 'FIRST NAME '+f_name
    @ 21, 33  SAY "OK (Y or N)?" GET ok PICTURE 'Y'
    @ 22, 10  SAY '(Enter for next match, Esc to QUIT, ';
          +'PgUp for previous match)'
    READ

    * Check user response
    IF .not.ok              && If user does not accept
```

```
      *Check user's response with READKEY function
      i=READKEY()
      DO CASE
         CASE i=12                    && Esc key
            EXIT                      && Then EXIT
         CASE i=6                     && PGUP key
            SKIP -1                   && Then backup to last match
         OTHERWISE
            SKIP                      && Else, get next match
      ENDCASE
   ELSE                   && If user does accept
      macct=cust_id                   && Get complete customer id to return
            ENDIF .not.ok
         ENDDO                        && End of Browse loop

      ELSE                  && Record not found. Display message & wait
         mok=' '
         @ 22, 25 SAY 'Press any key to continue...' GET mok
         READ
      ENDIF .not.EOF()

      SET FILTER TO                   && Clear any set filter in the loop

   ENDDO && End of Main loop

   * Set index back to #1, reset filter, and return
   SET ORDER TO 1
   @ 5, 1 CLEAR TO 19, 78
   @ 21, 1 CLEAR TO 22, 78
   RETURN
```

Listing 7.11. The subroutine CABISCR1.

```
*********************************************************************
* CABISCR1 -     Data entry screen for billings and payments       *
*               9/12/86                                             *
*********************************************************************

@  6, 12  SAY "CUSTOMER ACCOUNT ID: "+cacust->cust_id
@  7, 12  SAY "LAST NAME: "+cacust->l_name
@  7, 42  SAY "FIRST NAME: "+cacust->f_name
@  8, 12  SAY "COMPANY: "+cacust->company
@ 14,  2  SAY "TRANSACTION ID:" GET catrans->id
@ 14, 36  SAY "TRANSACTION DATE:" GET mdate
@ 15,  2  SAY "DESCRIPTION:" GET catrans->descript
@ 17,  2  SAY "DEBIT (Billing):" GET catrans->debit
@ 17, 32  SAY "CREDIT (Payment):" GET catrans->credit

RETURN
```

Listing 7.12. The program CAAUTOB.

```
****************************************************************************
* CAAUTOB -      Automatic billing for customers with autobill flag set  *
*               9/10/86                                                   *
****************************************************************************

* open databases
DO caopen
RESTORE FROM camem ADDITIVE
mtitle= "AUTOMATIC BILLING"

* display logo
DO borders WITH catitle,mtitle

* Verify this command
ok=.F.
@ 6,22 SAY "Verify this command (Y or RETURN)?" GET ok PICTURE "y"
READ

* If ok to proceed, continue
IF ok

   * Get autobill date
   mdate=DATE()
   ok1=.F.
   DO WHILE .not.ok1
      @ 6,1 SAY SPACE(78)
      @ 6,20 SAY "Enter automatic billing date: " GET mdate
      READ
      @ 21, 33 SAY "OK (Y or N)? " GET ok1 PICTURE 'Y'
      READ
      * IF not ok, ask user if he wants to continue with this command
      IF .not.ok1
         mok=.T.
         @ 22, 26 SAY 'Want to continue (Y or N)?' GET mok PICTURE 'y'
         READ
         * If user does not want to continue, break out of date entry loop
         IF .not.mok
            EXIT
         ENDIF
      ENDIF
      @ 6, 1 CLEAR TO 19, 78
      @ 21, 1 CLEAR TO 22, 78
   ENDDO

   * If date entry was successfully completed, continue
   IF ok1

      * loop on all records in CUSTOMER file
      @ 12,35 SAY "WORKING..."
      SELECT cacust
      SET FILTER TO autobill              && Select automatic billing accounts
      GO TOP                             && First autobill account

      * Generate a transaction for each customer with autobill
      SET DATE ANSI      && Date must be set to ansi for correct catrans index.
      DO WHILE .not.EOF()
```

```
          * Select catrans file, append blank, and fill in fields
          SELECT catrans
          APPEND BLANK
          REPLACE cust_id WITH cacust->cust_id, date WITH mdate,;
                  id WITH "AUTOBIL",descript WITH cacust->autodescr,;
                  debit WITH cacust->autofee,credit WITH 0,;

                  balance WITH cacust->balance+debit-credit,billed WITH .F.,;
                  delcode WITH .F.

          * Return to cacust file, update balance
          SELECT cacust
          REPLACE balance WITH balance+catrans->debit-catrans->credit

          * next autobill account
          SKIP
       ENDDO
       SET DATE AMERICAN
    ENDIF ok1
ENDIF ok

CLEAR
CLOSE DATABASES
RETURN
```

Listing 7.13. The program CAACCTQY.

```
**************************************************
* CAACCTQY - Customer Account Status Screen     *
*              9/11/86                           *
**************************************************

* Set environment and open files
DO caopen
SELECT cacust
RESTORE FROM camem ADDITIVE
mtitle= "CUSTOMER ACCOUNT STATUS SCREEN"

DO WHILE .T.
   * Display logo
   DO borders WITH catitle,mtitle

   * Get account number to display
   macct=SPACE(6)
   ok=.F.
   DO caacctlk WITH macct,ok              && User can enter #, name, or co.

   * Exit if blank customer ID
   IF macct=' '
      EXIT
   ENDIF

   * If not found, display message and loop
   IF .not.ok
      mok=' '
      @ 21, 20 SAY "ACCOUNT NOT FOUND. Press any key to continue." GET mok
      READ
      LOOP
   ELSE

      * If found, display account on screen
      CLEAR
      DO cacuscr                    && Display record using display screen
      mok=' '
      @ 21, 26 SAY "Press any key to continue..." GET mok
      READ
   ENDIF
ENDDO

* Tidy up and return
CLEAR
CLOSE DATABASES
RETURN
```

Listing 7.14. The program CATRANQY.

```
**************************************************************
* CATRANQY -      Browse transactions for an account        *
*                   8/5/86                                   *
**************************************************************

* Set environment and open files
SET DELETED ON
DO caopen
SELECT cacust
SET RELATION TO cust_id into catrans
RESTORE FROM camem ADDITIVE
mtitle= "BROWSE TRANSACTIONS BY ACCOUNT"

DO WHILE .T.
   SELECT cacust

   * Display logo
   DO borders WITH catitle,mtitle

   * Get account to browse
   macct=SPACE(6)
   ok=.F.
   DO caacctlk WITH macct,ok

   * If macct=' ', exit
   IF macct=' '
      EXIT
   ENDIF

   * Display header
   @  5, 12 SAY "CUSTOMER ID: "+cust_id
   @  5, 32 SAY "COMPANY: "+company
   @  6, 15 SAY "FIRST NAME: "+f_name
   @  6, 38 SAY "LAST NAME: "+l_name
   @  7,  1 SAY "CURRENT BALANCE: "+STR(balance,12,2)
   @  9,  1 SAY "  DATE        ID           DESCRIPT                DEBIT        ";
       +"CREDIT        BALANCE B"
   @ 10,  1 TO  10, 78

   * Display next
   mcntr=11                             && First line of transaction display
   mscroll=9                            && Number of lines displayed
   scnt=0
   SELECT catrans
   SET FILTER TO cust_id=macct          && select transactions for account
   SEEK macct           && Find first record for account
   * Loop to display transactions for account
   DO WHILE .T.
      cntr=0
      @ 11, 1 CLEAR TO 19,78
```

(Continued on next page.)

Listing 7.14, continued.

```
* Loop to display screen lines
DO WHILE cntr<mscroll.and..not.EOF()
    @ cntr+mcntr,  1 SAY date
    @ cntr+mcntr, 10 SAY id
    @ cntr+mcntr, 18 SAY descript PICTURE "XXXXXXXXXXXXXXXXXXXX"
    @ cntr+mcntr, 39 SAY debit
    @ cntr+mcntr, 52 SAY credit
    @ cntr+mcntr, 65 SAY balance
    @ cntr+mcntr, 78 SAY billed PICTURE 'Y'
    cntr=cntr+1
    SKIP
ENDDO
        * Display MORE message
        IF .not.EOF()
            @ 21, 36 SAY "* MORE *"
        ENDIF

        * Wait for one of specified keys
        DO scroller WITH scnt,cntr,mscroll,1,1
        @ 21, 1 CLEAR TO 22, 78

        * break out of scroll loop if ESC key pressed
        IF scnt=999
            EXIT
        ENDIF

        * Position record pointer for next screen
        SKIP scnt

        * Handle if at end of file
        IF EOF()
            SKIP -1
        ENDIF

    ENDDO
ENDDO

* Tidy up and return
CLEAR
SET DELETED OFF
CLOSE DATABASES
RETURN
```

Listing 7.15. The subroutine SCROLLER.

```
*************************************************************************
* SCROLLER - Program to accept keystrokes from user to scroll the screen *
*               PARAMETERS: SCNT    - returns vertical scroll amt to next screen *
*                           CNTR    - number of lines displayed on last screen *
*                           MSCROLL - number of lines that fit on a screen *
*                           SCREEN  - current screen number         *
*                           SMAX    - maximum screen number         *
*               9/10/86                                             *
*************************************************************************
PARAMETERS scnt,cntr,mscroll,screen,smax
PRIVATE i

* Wait for one of specified keys
@ 22, 2 SAY "PRESS: ARROW KEYS, PgUp ,PgDn, Enter, Home (BOF), ";
        +"or End (EOF); Esc to quit"
i=0
SET ESCAPE OFF
DO WHILE .not.STR(i,2)$"13, 5,24,18, 3,27, 4,19, 1, 6"  && Valid keypresses
    i=INKEY()                                           && Read keypress
ENDDO
SET ESCAPE ON

* Reset record pointer and cumulative count based on key pressed
DO CASE
    CASE i=27           && ESC key
         * flag to Exit the display loop
         scnt=999

    CASE i=5            && UP arrow key
         * Move record pointer to one line above start
         scnt=-(cntr+1)

    CASE i=24           && DOWN arrow key
         * Move record pointer down one line
         scnt=-(cntr-1)

    CASE i=18           && PGUP key
         * Soroll up one screen
         scnt=-(cntr+mscroll)

    CASE i=3.or.i=13    && PGDN or ENTER key
         * Scroll down one screen
         scnt=0

    CASE i=19           && Left arrow key
         *move one screen left
         scnt=-cntr
         screen=MAX(screen-1,1)

    CASE i=4            && Right arrow key
         * move one screen right
         scnt=-cntr
         screen=MIN(screen+1,smax)

    CASE i=1            && HOME key
         * Move to beginning of filtered file
         scnt=0
         GO TOP
```

(Continued on next page.)

Listing 7.15, continued.

```
CASE i=6                 && END key
     * Move to end of filtered file
     scnt=-(mscroll-1)
     GO BOTTOM

ENDCASE
RETURN
```

Listing 7.16. The program CASTMT.

```
**********************************************************************
* CASTMT -        Print current month statement for an account    *
*                 9/11/86                                          *
**********************************************************************

* Set environment and open files
SET DATE AMERICAN
RESTORE FROM camem ADDITIVE                  && Get system memory variables
DO caopen                                    && Open customer and custacct files
mtitle= "PRINT CURRENT ACCOUNT STATEMENT"

DO WHILE .T.
   SELECT cacust

   * Display logo
   DO borders WITH catitle,mtitle

   * Get account to print
   macct=SPACE(6)
   ok=.F.
   DO caacctlk WITH macct,ok

   * If macct=' ', exit
   IF macct=' '
      EXIT
   ENDIF

   * Get statement date and trial or final bill
   mok=.F.
   DO WHILE .not.mok
      mdate=IIF(DATE()>cacust->stmtdate,DATE(),cacust->stmtdate)
      @ 12, 24 SAY "Enter statement date:" GET mdate;
        RANGE cacust->stmtdate,           && Cannot print stmt before last one
      READ
      mfinal=.F.
      @ 14, 24 SAY "Final bill for month (Y or N):" GET mfinal PICTURE "Y"
      READ
      @ 21, 33 SAY "OK (Y or N)?" GET mok PICTURE "Y"
      @ 22, 20 SAY "(If ok, setup printer before continuing)"
      READ
      @ 12, 1 CLEAR TO 19, 78
      @ 21, 1 CLEAR TO 22, 78
   ENDDO
```

```
      * Print statement for customer
      @ 12, 30 SAY "Printing statement..."
      SET PRINT ON
      SET CONSOLE OFF
      ? &capreset
      SET DEVICE TO PRINT
      DO castmt1 WITH macct,mdate,mfinal

      * Reset Printer & Console
      SET DEVICE TO SCREEN
      SET CONSOLE ON
      SET PRINT OFF
   ENDDO .T.

   * Tidy up and return
   CLOSE DATABASES
   SET DELETED OFF
   RETURN
```

Listing 7.17. The subroutine CASTMT1.

```
*********************************************************************
* CASTMT1 -      Print statement for currently selected customer.  *
*                Parameters are account number, date, and billing flag *
*                9/11/86                                            *
*********************************************************************

PARAMETERS macct,mdate,mfinal
PRIVATE pwidth,mpage,cntr,mdebit,mcredit,finchg

*Print title and headings
pwidth=80
mpage=1
cntr=0
finchg=0
DO cacomp with cntr,pwidth
DO castmthd WITH cntr,mfinal

* Print balance from last statement
IF DTOC(cacust->stmtdate)#' '
   @ cntr,capmargin SAY DTOC(cacust->stmtdate)+" Previous balance"
   @ cntr,capmargin+66 SAY cacust->stmtbal PICTURE "9,999,999.99"
   cntr=cntr+1
ENDIF

* Select transaction file, all unbilled records before cutoff date for customer
SELECT catrans
SET FILTER TO cust_id=macct.and..not.billed.and.date<=mdate
SET DELETED ON
GO TOP
SEEK macct

* Loop to print all unbilled transactions thru specified date for account
mdebit=0                       && Initialize total debits
mcredit=0                      && Initialize total credits
moverdue=0                     && Initialize overdue balance
mbal=cacust->stmtbal           && Initialize running balance

DO WHILE .not.EOF()            && Loop for each transaction that meets conds.
```

(Continued on next page.)

Listing 7.17, continued.

```
      * Check if finance charge
      IF cacust->stmtbal>0.and.mcredit<cacust->stmtbal.and.date>cacust->stmtdate+;
         caperiod+1.and.finchg=0     && If prev. balance not paid and overdue

         * Calculate finance charge and balances
         moverdue=cacust->stmtbal-mcredit
         finchg=cainterest*moverdue
         mbal=mbal+finchg
         mdebit=mdebit+finchg

         * Print finance charge line
         @ cntr, capmargin SAY cacust->stmtdate+caperiod+1
         @ cntr, capmargin+9 SAY "FINANCE CHARGE"
         @ cntr, capmargin+40 SAY finchg PICTURE "9,999,999.99"
         @ cntr, capmargin+66 SAY mbal PICTURE "9,999,999.99"
         cntr=cntr+1
      ENDIF

      * Print next transaction record
      mdebit=mdebit+debit
      mcredit=mcredit+credit
      mbal=mbal+debit-credit
      @ cntr, capmargin SAY date
      @ cntr, capmargin+9 SAY descript
      @ cntr, capmargin+40 SAY debit PICTURE "@Z 9,999,999.99"
      @ cntr, capmargin+53 SAY -credit PICTURE "@Z 9,999,999.99"
      @ cntr, capmargin+66 SAY mbal PICTURE "9,999,999.99"
      cntr=cntr+1

      * skip to next record. Eject page if necessary
      SKIP
      * Check for end of page
      IF cntr>capagelen
         @ capagelen+5, capmargin+(pwidth-10)/2 SAY "Page "+STR(mpage,2)
         mpage=mpage+1
         cntr=0
         DO castmthd WITH cntr,mfinal
      ENDIF
ENDDO

* Print finance charge after last transaction, if necessary
IF cacust->stmtbal>0.and.mcredit<cacust->stmtbal.and.mdate>cacust->stmtdate+;
   caperiod+1.and.finchg=0          && If prev. balance not paid and overdue

   * Calculate finance charge and balances
   moverdue=cacust->stmtbal-mcredit
   finchg=cainterest*moverdue
   mbal=mbal+finchg
   mdebit=mdebit+finchg

   * Print finance charge line
   @ cntr, capmargin SAY cacust->stmtdate+caperiod+1
   @ cntr, capmargin+9 SAY "FINANCE CHARGE"
   @ cntr, capmargin+40 SAY finchg PICTURE "9,999,999.99"
   @ cntr, capmargin+66 SAY mbal PICTURE "9,999,999.99"
   cntr=cntr+1
ENDIF
```

```
* Check for bottom of page
cntr=cntr+4
IF cntr+6>capagelen
    @ capagelen+5, capmargin+(pwidth-10)/2 SAY "Page "+STR(mpage,2)
    mpage=mpage+1
    cntr=0
    DO castmthd WITH cntr,mfinal
ENDIF

* Print account summary
@ cntr,capmargin SAY "ACCOUNT SUMMARY"
cntr=cntr+1
IF DTOC(cacust->stmtdate)#' '                          && If prev. balance
    @ cntr,capmargin+9 SAY "Previous balance"
    @ cntr,capmargin+66 SAY cacust->stmtbal PICTURE "9,999,999.99"
    cntr=cntr+1
ENDIF
IF moverdue>0                                          && If payments
    @ cntr,capmargin+9 SAY "Payments before due date"
    @ cntr,capmargin+66 SAY -(cacust->stmtbal-moverdue) PICTURE "9,999,999.99"
    @ cntr+1,    capmargin+66 SAY REPLICATE('-',12)
    @ cntr+2, capmargin+ 9 SAY "OVERDUE BALANCE"
    @ cntr+2, capmargin+66 SAY moverdue PICTURE "9,999,999.99"
    @ cntr+4, capmargin+ 9 SAY "FINANCE CHARGE"
    @ cntr+4, capmargin+66 SAY finchg PICTURE "9,999,999.99"
    @ cntr+5, capmargin+ 9 SAY "Payments after due date"
    @ cntr+5, capmargin+66 SAY -mcredit+(cacust->stmtbal-moverdue);
        PICTURE '9,999,999.99'
    cntr=cntr+6
ELSE
    @ cntr, capmargin+ 9 SAY "Payments received"
    @ cntr, capmargin+66 SAY -mcredit PICTURE '9,999,999.99'
    cntr=cntr+1
ENDIF
@ cntr,   capmargin+ 9 SAY "Current month charges"
@ cntr,   capmargin+66 SAY mdebit-finchg PICTURE "9,999,999.99"
@ cntr+1,capmargin+66 SAY REPLICATE("-",12)
@ cntr+2,capmargin+ 9 SAY "CURRENT BALANCE"
@ cntr+2,capmargin+66 SAY cacust->stmtbal+mdebit-mcredit PICTURE "9,999,999.99"
IF (cacust->stmtbal+mdebit-mcredit)>0                  && If current balance
    @ cntr+4,capmargin SAY "PLEASE PAY CURRENT BALANCE BY ";
        +DTOC(mdate+caperiod+1)
ENDIF

* Print page number at bottom of last page
@ capagelen+5, capmargin+(pwidth-10)/2 SAY "Page "+STR(mpage,2)
EJECT

* If final bill, update customer stmt bal and date
IF mfinal

    * Update status of all specified transactions to billed
    SET DATE ANSI
    SELECT catrans
    SEEK macct
    REPLACE billed WITH .T. WHILE .not.EOF()
    SET DATE AMERICAN
```

(Continued on next page.)

Listing 7.17, continued.

```
    * If there is a finance charge, add it to the transaction file
    IF finchg>0

        *Add finance charge transaction
        SELECT catrans
        SET DATE ANSI
        APPEND BLANK                && Add record to transaction file
        REPLACE cust_id WITH cacust->cust_id,date WITH;
            cacust->stmtdate+caperiod+1,ID with "FINCHG",descript WITH;
            "FINANCE CHARGE",debit WITH finchg,credit WITH 0,;
            billed WITH .T.,delcode WITH .F.
        SET DATE AMERICAN

        * Recalculate balances for account
        DO cabal1 WITH macct
    ELSE (no finance charge)

        * Update statement date and balance in customer file
        SELECT cacust
        REPLACE stmtbal WITH stmtbal+mdebit-mcredit
    ENDIF (finchg>0)
    SELECT cacust
    REPLACE stmtdate with mdate
ENDIF (mfinal)

SELECT catrans
SET FILTER TO               && Reset filter on transaction file
SET DELETED OFF

RETURN
```

Listing 7.18. The subroutine CACOMP.

```
*********************************************************************
* CACOMP -      Print company name and address centered on page *
*               9/11/86                                          *
*               Requires cntr and width parameters.             *
*********************************************************************

PARAMETERS cntr,width
* Get company name and address from sysparms
RESTORE FROM camem ADDITIVE
@ cntr,capmargin+(width-LEN(TRIM(cacompname)))/2 SAY cacompname
cntr=cntr+1
@ cntr,capmargin+(width-LEN(TRIM(caaddr1)))/2 SAY caaddr1
cntr=cntr+1
@ cntr,capmargin+(width-LEN(TRIM(caaddr2)))/2 SAY caaddr2
cntr=cntr+1
@ cntr,capmargin+(width-LEN(TRIM(caphone)))/2 SAY caphone
cntr=cntr+2

RETURN
```

Listing 7.19. The subroutine CASTMTHD.

```
**********************************************************************
* CASTMTHD - print customer name and header for customer statement *
*              9/11/86                                              *
*              Uses memory variables mdate,pwidth,pmargin          *
*              Uses parameters cntr,mfinal                         *
**********************************************************************
PARAMETERS cntr,mfinal

* Print title lines
cntr=IIF(cntr<1,1,cntr)                          && Initialize counter
@ cntr,capmargin+(pwidth-14)/2 SAY "ACCOUNT "+cacust->cust_id
IF mfinal
   @ cntr+1,capmargin+(pwidth-35)/2 SAY "STATEMENT OF ACCOUNT AS OF ";
      +DTOC(mdate)
ELSE
   @ cntr+1,capmargin+(pwidth-47)/2 SAY "PRELIMINARY STATEMENT OF ACCOUNT ";
      +"AS OF "+DTOC(mdate)
ENDIF
cntr=cntr+3

* Print customer name and address
IF cacust->l_name#' '            && Display customer name if non-blank
   @  cntr,capmargin SAY TRIM(cacust->f_name)+' '+cacust->l_name
   cntr=cntr+1
ENDIF
IF cacust->company#' '           && Display company if non-blank
   @  cntr,capmargin SAY cacust->company
   cntr=cntr+1
ENDIF
IF cacust->addr1#' '             && Display first address line if non-blank
   @  cntr,capmargin SAY cacust->addr1
   cntr=cntr+1
ENDIF
IF cacust->addr2#' '             && Display second address line if non-blank
   @  cntr,capmargin SAY cacust->addr2
   cntr=cntr+1
ENDIF
@  cntr,capmargin SAY TRIM(cacust->city)+", "+cacust->state+" "+cacust->zip
cntr=cntr+2

* Print statement column headings
@ cntr,capmargin SAY "  DATE      DESCRIPTION                         CHARGES";
   +"      PAYMENTS        BALANCE"
cntr=cntr+1
@ cntr,capmargin SAY "-------- ------------------------------ ------------";
   +" ------------ ------------"
cntr=cntr+1

RETURN
```

Listing 7.20. The program CAHIST.

```
************************************************************
* CAHIST -       Print all transactions for an account   *
*                9/11/86                                  *
************************************************************

* Set environment and open files
SET DELETED ON
DO caopen
RESTORE FROM camem ADDITIVE
mtitle= "PRINT ALL TRANSACTIONS FOR AN ACCOUNT"
DO borders WITH catitle,mtitle

*Wait for user to setup printer
mok= ' '
@ 21, 16 SAY 'Setup printer, then press any key to continue' GET mok
READ
@ 21, 1 CLEAR TO 22, 78
* Send setup string to printer
SET PRINT ON
SET CONSOLE OFF
? &capsetup
SET CONSOLE ON
SET PRINT OFF

* Main loop to print history cards
DO WHILE .T.
   SELECT cacust

   * Get account to print
   macct=SPACE(6)
   mfound=.F.
   DO caacctlk WITH macct,mfound

   * If macct=' ', exit
   IF macct=' '
      EXIT
   ENDIF

   * Print account history
   @ 12, 35 SAY "Working..."
   SET DEVICE TO PRINT
   mpage=capagelen                    && Page Length
   cntr=0                             && Initialize lines printed
   mbal=0                             && Initialize running balance
   mpageno=1                          && Initialize page number
   SELECT catrans                     && Select transaction file
   SET FILTER TO cust_id=macct        && Select transactions for account
   SEEK macct                         && Find first selected transaction

   * Loop to display transactions for account
   DO WHILE .not.EOF()
```

```
    * If top of page, print title, account information, headings
    IF cntr=0
       @  3, capmargin+33 SAY "CUSTOMER ACCOUNT STATUS"
       @  3, capmargin+80 SAY DATE()
       @  4, capmargin+33 SAY "------------------------"
       @  4, capmargin+80 SAY TIME()
       @  6, capmargin+ 0 SAY "ACCT #"
       @  6, capmargin+ 7 SAY cacust->cust_id
       @  6, capmargin+17 SAY "NAME"
       @  6, capmargin+22 SAY TRIM(cacust->f_name)+' '+cacust->l_name
       @  6, capmargin+48 SAY "COMPANY"
       @  6, capmargin+56 SAY cacust->company
       @  7, capmargin+ 0 SAY "CURRENT BALANCE"
       @  7, capmargin+17 SAY cacust->balance PICTURE '9,999,999.99'
       @  7, capmargin+30 SAY "LAST STMT DATE"
       @  7, capmargin+45 SAY cacust->stmtdate
       @  7, capmargin+54 SAY "LAST STMT BAL"
       @  7, capmargin+68 SAY cacust->stmtbal PICTURE '9,999,999.99'
       @  9, capmargin+ 0 SAY "  DATE        ID               DESCRIPT          ";
         +"      DEBIT       CREDIT        BALANCE B"
       @ 10, capmargin    SAY "-------- ------- -----------------------------";
         +" ------------ ------------ ------------ -"
       cntr=11
    ENDIF

    * Print next record
    mbal=mbal+debit-credit                  && Calculate running balance
    @ cntr, capmargin+0 SAY date
    @ cntr, capmargin+ 9 SAY id
    @ cntr, capmargin+17 SAY descript
    @ cntr, capmargin+48 SAY debit PICTURE '@Z 9,999,999.99'
    @ cntr, capmargin+61 SAY credit PICTURE '@Z 9,999,999.99'
    @ cntr, capmargin+74 SAY mbal PICTURE '9,999,999.99'
    @ cntr, capmargin+87 SAY billed PICTURE 'Y'
    cntr=cntr+1
    SKIP

    * If end of page, print page number and reset for top
    IF cntr>mpage.or.cust_id#macct
       @ mpage+5, capmargin+40 SAY "PAGE "+STR(mpageno,2)
       mpageno=mpageno+1
       cntr=0
    ENDIF
 ENDDO .not.EOF()

 * Return control to screen
 SET DEVICE TO SCREEN

ENDDO .T.

* Tidy up and return
CLEAR
SET PRINT ON
SET CONSOLE OFF
EJECT
? &capreset
SET CONSOLE ON
SET PRINT OFF
SET DELETED OFF
CLOSE DATABASES
RETURN
```

Listing 7.21. The program CAACCT.

```
************************************************
* CAACCT - Generate account summary printout  *
*              9/11/86                         *
************************************************

* Initialize and open databases
DO caopen
SELECT cacust
SET RELATION TO cust_id INTO catrans
mtitle= "PRINT ACCOUNT SUMMARY SHEET"

* Display logo and have user setup printer
DO borders WITH catitle,mtitle
mok=' '
@ 21, 17 SAY "Setup printer then press any key to continue" GET mok
READ

* Loop to get account number and print summary
DO WHILE .T.                              && Loop is exited with EXIT

    * Get account number
    macct=SPACE(6)
    mfound=.F.
    DO caacctlk WITH macct,mfound

    * EXIT if empty
    IF macct=' '
       EXIT
    ENDIF

    * Print account summary
    SET DEVICE TO PRINT
    DO cacustp
    EJECT
    SET DEVICE TO SCREEN
ENDDO

*Tidy up and return
CLEAR
CLOSE DATABASES
RETURN
```

Listing 7.22. The subroutine CACUSTP.

```
****************************************************
*  CACUSTP -         Print account summary page       *
*                    9/11/86                          *
****************************************************

@  2, capmargin+29   SAY  catitle
@  2, capmargin+64   SAY  "DATE: "+DTOC(DATE())
@  3, capmargin+25   SAY  "CUSTOMER-ACCOUNT SUMMARY REPORT"
@  4, capmargin+28   SAY  "CUSTOMER ID: "+cacust->cust_id
@  5, capmargin+25   SAY   REPLICATE("-",31)
@  7, capmargin+15   SAY  "NAME: "+TRIM(cacust->f_name)+' '+cacust->l_name
@  8, capmargin+15   SAY  "COMPANY: "+cacust->company
@  9, capmargin+15   SAY  "ADDRESS: "
@  9, capmargin+27   SAY   cacust->addr1
@ 10, capmargin+27   SAY   cacust->addr2
@ 11, capmargin+27   SAY    TRIM(cacust->city)+', '+;
         TRIM(cacust->state)+' '+cacust->zip
@ 12, capmargin+15   SAY  "PHONE: "+cacust->phone
@ 14, capmargin+ 0   SAY  "ACCOUNT STATUS: "+cacust->status
@ 15, capmargin+ 0   SAY  "CURRENT BALANCE: "+STR(cacust->balance,12,2)
@ 15, capmargin+30   SAY  "CREDIT LIMIT: "+STR(cacust->creditlim,12,2)
@ 16, capmargin+ 0   SAY  "COMMENT: "+cacust->comment
@ 18, capmargin+ 0   SAY  "AUTOMATIC BILLING FLAG:"
@ 18, capmargin+24   SAY   cacust->autobill PICTURE 'Y'
@ 18, capmargin+31   SAY  "AUTOMATIC BILLING AMOUNT: "+STR(cacust->autofee,12,2)
@ 19, capmargin+ 0   SAY  "AUTOMATIC BILLING DESCRIPTION: "+cacust->autodescr
@ 21, capmargin+ 0   SAY  "DATE OF LAST STATEMENT: "+ DTOC(cacust->stmtdate)
@ 21, capmargin+36   SAY  "BALANCE LAST STATEMENT: "+ STR(cacust->stmtbal,12,2)

RETURN
```

Listing 7.23. The program CALIST.

```
******************************************
* CALIST - Generate account list        *
*              9/11/86                   *
******************************************

* Initialize and open databases
DO caopen
SELECT cacust
RESTORE FROM camem ADDITIVE
mtitle= "PRINT ACCOUNT LISTING"
DO borders WITH catitle,mtitle

* Ask user which sort order
@ 6, 25 SAY "Select order of customer list:"
@ 8, 25 SAY '1. Account number order'
@ 9, 25 SAY '2. Last name, first name order'
@ 10, 25 SAY '3. Company name order'
msel=0
@ 21, 25 SAY 'Enter choice (0 to quit):' GET msel PICTURE '9' RANGE 0,3
READ
@ 21, 1 CLEAR TO 22, 78

*Do selection if not zero
IF msel#0
   SET ORDER TO msel

   * Wait for user to setup printer
   mok=' '
   @ 21, 24 SAY "Setup printer, then press any key to continue" GET mok
   READ
   @ 21, 1 CLEAR TO 22, 78

   * DO report
   SET PRINT ON
   SET CONSOLE OFF
   ? &capsetup
   REPORT FORM calist
   ? &capreset
   SET CONSOLE ON
   SET PRINT OFF
ENDIF

*Tidy up and return
CLEAR
CLOSE DATABASES
RETURN
```

Listing 7.24. The program CAPACK.

```
***************************************************************
* CAPACK -        PACK deleted records in data files        *
*                 9/11/86                                   *
***************************************************************

* Open files
DO caopen
RESTORE FROM camem ADDITIVE

* Ask user to verify command
DO borders WITH catitle,"PACK DATABASE FILES"
ok=.F.
@ 21, 24 SAY "Verify PACK command (Y or N)" GET ok PICTURE 'Y'
READ
@ 21, 1 CLEAR TO 22, 78

* If ok, pack files
IF ok
   @ 5, 1 SAY 'PACKING cacust FILE'
   SELECT cacust
   DELETE FOR cust_id=' '
   PACK
   @ 6, 1 SAY 'PACKING catrans FILE'
   SELECT catrans
   DELETE FOR cust_id=' '
   PACK
ENDIF

CLOSE DATABASES
RETURN
```

Listing 7.25. The program CABAL.

```
***************************************************************************
* CABAL -        Recalculate account balances from active transactions   *
*               9/12/86                                                   *
***************************************************************************

* Open files
SET DELETED ON
DO caopen
SELECT cacust
RESTORE FROM camem ADDITIVE
DO borders WITH catitle,'RECALCULATE ACCOUNT BALANCES'

* Ask user to verify command
ok=.F.
@ 21, 17 SAY "Verify RECALCULATE BALANCES command (Y or N)" GET ok PICTURE 'Y'
READ
@ 21, 1 CLEAR TO 22, 78

* If ok, recalculate balances
IF ok

   GO TOP                  && get to first account
   DO WHILE .not.EOF()  && loop for each account in customer master

      macct=cacust->cust_id
      @ 12, 19 SAY 'Recalculating balance for account: '+macct
      DO cabal1 WITH macct
      SELECT cacust
      SET DELETED ON
      SKIP

   ENDDO .not.EOF()

ENDIF ok

CLOSE DATABASES
SET DELETED OFF
RETURN
```

Listing 7.26. The subroutine CABAL1.

```
**************************************************************************
* CABAL1 -         Recalculate account balances for specified account   *
*                  9/11/86                                               *
**************************************************************************

PARAMETERS macct
PRIVATE mbal,mbbal

* Recalculate balances for billed transactions
SELECT catrans
SET DELETED ON
SET DATE ANSI
SET FILTER TO cust_id=macct
SEEK macct
mbal=0                      && Initialize account balance accumulator
mbbal=0                     && Initialize billed transactions balance accumulator
DO WHILE .not.EOF()         && Do for all transactions this account
   IF .not.(debit=0.and.credit=0)        && If valid transaction
      mbal=mbal+debit-credit                     && Accum. account balance
      mbbal=IIF(billed,mbbal+debit-credit,mbbal) && Accum. billed balance
      REPLACE balance WITH mbal           && Update balance this transaction
   ELSE                                   && If invalid transaction,
      REPLACE delcode WITH .T.                   && mark permanently deleted
      DELETE                                     && and delete
   ENDIF
   SKIP                            && Next trans. record
ENDDO

* Update balances in customer master
SELECT cacust
REPLACE stmtbal WITH mbbal                  && Update billed balance
REPLACE balance WITH mbal                   && Update curr. balance

SELECT catrans
SET DELETED OFF
SET DATE AMERICAN
SET FILTER TO
RETURN
```

Listing 7.27. The program CABACKUP.

```
******************************************************************************
* CABACKUP -    Back up Customer Account data files to backup device   *
*              8/2/86                                                   *
******************************************************************************
target="b:"                              && Target drive for backup
CLEAR
? "BACKUP Customer Account Data Files"
?

* Ask user to verify backup command
mok=' '
DO WHILE UPPER(mok)#'Y'.and.UPPER(mok)#'N'
   WAIT "Do you want to proceed with this command (Y or N)?" TO mok
ENDDO

* If answer is 'yes', do backup
IF UPPER(mok)="Y"
   files1="*.dbf"
   RUN BACKUP &files1 &target
   files2="*.ndx"
   RUN BACKUP &files2 &target/A
   files3="*.mem"
   RUN BACKUP &files3 &target/A
ENDIF

* Clear screen and return
CLEAR
RETURN
```

Listing 7.28. The program CARESTOR.

```
******************************************************************************
* CARESTOR -    RESTORE Customer Accounts data from backup device     *
*              8/2/86                                                   *
******************************************************************************
* Display title
CLEAR
? "RESTORE Customer Accounts Data from Backup"
?

* Ask user to verify restore command
mok=' '
DO WHILE UPPER(mok)#"Y".and.UPPER(mok)#"N"
   WAIT "Do you want to proceed with this command (Y or N)?" TO mok
ENDDO

* If answer is 'yes', do restore
IF UPPER(mok)="Y"
   source="b:"                           && Source drive for restore
   target="c:"
   files1=target+"*.*"
   RUN RESTORE &source &files1
ENDIF

* Clear screen and return
CLEAR
RETURN
```

Listing 7.29. The program CAPURGE.

```
********************************************************************
* CAPURGE - Purge old, billed transactions from transaction file  *
*            9/11/86                                               *
********************************************************************

* Set environment and open files
SET DELETED ON
RESTORE FROM camem ADDITIVE              && Get system memory variables
DO caopen                               && Open customer and custacct files
SELECT cacust
title= "PURGE TRANSACTIONS FILE"

* Display logo
DO borders WITH catitle,title

*Ask user to verify this command
ok=.F.
@ 12, 10 SAY "THIS COMMAND PURGES BILLED TRANSACTIONS BEFORE A CUTOFF DATE"
@ 21, 30 SAY 'Want to continue (Y or N)?' GET ok PICTURE 'y'
READ
@ 12, 1 CLEAR TO 13, 78
@ 21, 1 CLEAR TO 22, 78

IF ok                    && User has verified command
    * Get cutoff date
    mok=.F.
    DO WHILE .not.mok
        mdate=CTOD('1/1/80')
        @ 12, 20 SAY "Enter cutoff date:" GET mdate RANGE CTOD('1/1/80'),
        READ
        @ 21, 30 SAY "OK (Y or N)?" GET mok PICTURE "Y"
        READ
        * IF not ok, ask if want to continue
        IF .not.mok
            ok1=.t.
            @ 22, 30 SAY "Want to Continue (Y or N)?" GET ok1 PICTURE 'y'
            READ
            * Exit if don't want to continue
            IF .not.ok1
                EXIT
            ENDIF
        ENDIF
        @ 5, 1 CLEAR TO 19, 78
    ENDDO

    IF mok
        * Perform purge
        SET DATE ANSI            && Date must be ansi to preserve catrans index
        SELECT cacust
        GO TOP
        DO borders WITH catitle,title
        @ 12, 35 SAY "Working..."

        * Loop on all customer records
        DO WHILE .not.EOF()
```

(Continued on next page.)

Listing 7.29, continued.

```
         * Select billed transaction records for this customer through cutoff
         SELECT catrans
         SET FILTER TO cust_id=cacust->cust_id.and.date<=mdate.and.billed
         SEEK cacust->cust_id
         mbal=0                            && Account balance accumulator
         mdel=.f.                          && Flag marking if any records purged
         md=iif(mdate>cacust->stmtdate,cacust->stmtdate,mdate) && earliest of
                                           && statement date and cutoff date
        *Loop on each selected transaction
         DO WHILE .not.EOF()
            mbal=mbal+debit-credit         && Update account balance
            REPLACE delcode WITH .T.       && Mark record so programs won't recall
            DELETE                         && delete record
            mdel=.t.                && flag that have deleted at least one record
            SKIP
         ENDDO .not.EOF()
         SET FILTER TO

         * If any records were deleted, append new beginning balance record
         IF mdel
            APPEND BLANK
            REPLACE cust_id WITH cacust->cust_id, date WITH md,;
              descript WITH "Beginning Balance", debit WITH MAX(mbal,0),;
              credit WITH MAX(-mbal,0), balance with mbal, billed WITH .T.;
              delcode WITH .F.
         ENDIF

         * Get next account and loop
         SELECT cacust
         SKIP
      ENDDO .not.EOF()

   ENDIF mok
ENDIF ok

* Tidy up and return
CLOSE DATABASES
SET DATE AMERICAN
SET DELETED OFF
RETURN
```

Listing 7.30. The program CUSTACCT.

```
********************************************************
* CUSTACCT - Customer Account application main menu *
*               9/9/86                              *
********************************************************

* Setup environment
SET TALK OFF
SET SAFETY OFF
SET DEVICE TO SCREEN
SET PRINT OFF
SET DATE AMERICAN
CLOSE DATABASES
CLEAR ALL
RESTORE FROM camem

* Main loop
option=-1
DO WHILE option#0

    * Display Menu
    DO borders WITH catitle, "MAIN MENU"
    option=0
    @  8, 28   SAY "1. Data Entry Functions"
    @  9, 28   SAY "2. Queries and Reports"
    @ 10, 28   SAY "3. System Maintenance Functions"
    @ 14, 28   SAY "0. EXIT TO DBASE DOT PROMPT"
    @ 21, 35   SAY "OPTION:" GET option PICTURE "9" RANGE 0,3
    READ
    @ 21, 1 SAY SPACE(78)

    * Do selected option
    DO CASE
        CASE option=1
            DO custacc1                   && Data Entry Functions
        CASE option=2
            DO custacc2                   && Queries and Reports
        CASE option=3
            DO custacc3                   && System Maintenance

        OTHERWISE                         && Confirm option=0 before leaving
            mq=.T.
            @ 21, 20 SAY "Do you really want to quit (Y or N)?";
              GET mq PICTURE 'Y'
            READ
            option=IIF(mq,0,-1)           && Reset option to -1 if (N)o
    ENDCASE
* End of main loop
ENDDO (option#0)

* Restore system defaults and exit
SET TALK ON
SET SAFETY ON
SET DEVICE TO SCREEN
SET PRINT OFF
SET CONSOLE ON
CLEAR ALL
CLEAR
RETURN
```

Listing 7.31. The program CUSTACCT1.

```
**************************************************
* CUSTACC1 - Customer account Data Entry menu   *
*              9/9/86                            *
**************************************************

* Setup environment
PRIVATE mopt

* Main loop
mopt=-1
DO WHILE mopt#0

   * Display Menu
   mopt=0
   DO borders WITH catitle,"DATA-ENTRY MENU"
   @  7, 27  SAY "1. ADD OR UPDATE CUSTOMER ACCOUNT"
   @  8, 27  SAY "2. DELETE OR RECALL CUSTOMER ACCOUNT"
   @  9, 27  SAY "3. ENTER BILLINGS & PAYMENTS"
   @ 10, 27  SAY "4. AUTOMATIC BILLING"
   @ 19, 27  SAY "0. RETURN TO MAIN MENU"
   @ 21, 35  SAY "OPTION:" GET mopt PICTURE "9" RANGE 0,4
   READ
   @ 21, 1 SAY SPACE(78)

   * Do selected option
   DO CASE
      CASE mopt=1
           DO cacuadd                    && Add/Update account info
      CASE mopt=2
           DO cacudel                    && Delete account
      CASE mopt=3
           DO cabill                     && Billings and Payments
      CASE mopt=4
           DO caautob                    && Automatic Billing
   ENDCASE
* End of main loop
ENDDO (mopt#0)

* Restore system defaults and exit
CLEAR
RETURN
```

Listing 7.32. The program CUSTACC2.

```
***********************************************************
* CUSTACC2 - Customer Account Queries and Reports menu   *
*              9/9/86                                     *
***********************************************************

* Setup environment
PRIVATE mopt

* Main loop
mopt=-1
DO WHILE mopt#0

    * Display Menu
    mopt=0
    DO borders WITH catitle,"QUERIES AND REPORTS MENU"
    @  7, 27   SAY "1. ACCOUNT STATUS QUERY"
    @  8, 27   SAY "2. BROWSE ACCOUNT HISTORY"
    @  9, 27   SAY "3. CUSTOMER STATEMENTS"
    @ 10, 27   SAY "4. ACCOUNT HISTORY REPORT"
    @ 11, 27   SAY "5. ACCOUNT SUMMARY REPORT"
    @ 12, 27   SAY "6. CUSTOMER ACCOUNT LISTING"
    @ 19, 27   SAY "0. RETURN TO MAIN MENU"
    @ 21, 35   SAY "OPTION:" GET mopt PICTURE "9" RANGE 0,6
    READ
    @ 21, 1 SAY SPACE(78)

    * Do selected option
    DO CASE
       CASE mopt=1
          DO caacctqy                  && account status query
       CASE mopt=2
          DO catranqy                  && browse account history
       CASE mopt=3
          DO castmt                    && customer statements
       CASE mopt=4
          DO cahist                    && account history report
       CASE mopt=5
          DO caacct                    && account summary report
       CASE mopt=6
          DO calist                    && account listing
    ENDCASE
* End of main loop
ENDDO (mopt#0)

* Restore system defaults and exit
CLEAR
RETURN
```

Listing 7.33. The program CUSTACC3.

```
**********************************************************
* CUSTACC3 - Customer Account System Maintenance menu    *
*               9/9/86                                    *
**********************************************************

* Setup environment
PRIVATE mopt

* Main loop
mopt=-1
DO WHILE mopt#0

   * Display Menu
   mopt=0
   DO borders WITH catitle,"SYSTEM-MAINTENANCE MENU"
   @  7, 27  SAY "1. REINDEX DATABASES"
   @  8, 27  SAY "2. RECALCULATE BALANCES"
   @  9, 27  SAY "3. BACKUP DATA TO FLOPPIES"
   @ 10, 27  SAY "4. RESTORE DATA FROM FLOPPIES"
   @ 11, 27  SAY "5. PURGE BILLED TRANSACTIONS"
   @ 12, 27  SAY "6. PACK DATABASES"
   @ 13, 27  SAY "7. EDIT SYSTEM MEMORY VARIABLES"
   @ 19, 27  SAY "0. RETURN TO MAIN MENU"
   @ 21, 35  SAY "OPTION:" GET mopt PICTURE "9" RANGE 0,7
   READ
   @ 21, 1 SAY SPACE(78)

   * Do selected option
   DO CASE
      CASE mopt=1
         DO caindex                &&  reindex database files
      CASE mopt=2
         DO cabal                  &&  recalculate account balances
      CASE mopt=3
         DO cabackup               &&  backup data to floppies
      CASE mopt=4
         DO carestor               &&  restore data from floppies
      CASE mopt=5
         DO capurge                &&  purge billed transactions
      CASE mopt=6
         DO capack                 &&  pack database files
      CASE mopt=7
         DO camem                  &&  edit system memory variables
   ENDCASE
* End of main loop
ENDDO (mopt#0)

* Restore system defaults and exit
CLEAR
RETURN
```

8

General-Ledger and Financial-Reporting System

Jim Jones, controller of Smith and Jones Corporation, is ready to take another step toward computerizing his manual accounting system. You'll recall from Chapter 6 that we have already developed an application for managing the company's fixed assets. In this chapter we create a computerized general-ledger and financial-reporting system for Jim.

By choosing to develop Jim's system in dBASE III Plus, we will be able to tailor the system to his needs, and he will be able to modify the system when those needs change. dBASE III Plus will also give him the flexibility of an interactive query language, allowing him to work directly with the data files to prepare *ad hoc* reports that were not even considered when the system was set up.

Suppose that we have carefully examined Jim's manual accounting system and have arrived at the design for a full-featured computerized replacement. This chapter, which describes that replacement in detail, is divided into four sections. Section I, "Planning the System," begins with an overview of the entire system and takes you through the identification of the system's purpose and function, definition of file structures, and specification of program functions.

Section II presents some system utilities that are useful to have on hand during development of the application. It also presents programs for editing the system memory file; entering, updating, and deleting accounts; and printing the chart-of-accounts list.

Section III, "The General Ledger," takes you through the logic and design of the transaction-entry program and associated subroutines for the general ledger. Next, this section describes a program for producing reports that show journal entries, all transactions by account, and summaries of current account balances. A third program enables the user to close the general ledger and make necessary changes to the financial reporting ledger. Finally, a fourth program makes it possible to scan the general ledger for unbalanced transactions.

Section IV, "The Financial-Reporting Ledger and Financial Statements," describes programs and associated subroutines for entering budget data or last year's data from the keyboard, creating comparative and 12-month financial statements, and closing the year. Programs for system-maintenance tasks, such as backing up and restoring data files from floppy disks or tapes, are also presented.

In addition, Section IV explains how to tie other accounting packages into the general ledger so that transactions need to be entered into the computer only once. Other portions of a complete accounting system include payroll, order entry and inventory, accounts receivable, and accounts payable. Chapter 7, for example, presents an accounts receivable application as a stand-alone application.

Section I: Planning the System

In Section I, we discuss the stages of development for any system and proceed through these stages up to development of the programs for the General Ledger.

An Overview of the Entire System

The system we have developed for Jim Jones includes a general ledger and a financial-reporting ledger. The general ledger holds a detailed record of the current-period financial transactions, and the financial-reporting ledger holds the account balances at the end of each period. The general-ledger file is used for three purposes: to accept manual transaction entries, to collect summary entries from other accounting packages, and to prepare a general-ledger report showing the account balances at any time during the period. Jim's company prepares a monthly financial statement, so the system is set up for a monthly accounting period.

The role of the general ledger is to record and classify the financial transactions of Smith and Jones Corporation. The system is capable of handling a large number of transactions. As a single-user application, the general ledger can handle hundreds or thousands of transactions per accounting period and retrieve and summarize them by account. With appropriate changes to the programs, the general ledger can be used with the networking version of dBASE III Plus.

The financial-reporting ledger records year-to-date account balances at the end of each accounting period. The actual data is recorded in this file at the end of each accounting period when the general ledger is closed. The budget data is either entered from the keyboard or imported from a budget prepared with another software package. Finally, the year-end-close program automatically saves the current-year actual data as last year's actual data.

The financial-reporting ledger allows Jim Jones to prepare a comparative balance sheet, an income statement, and a flow-of-funds statement showing the current month and year-to-date results versus budget and last year's values. These statements can only be printed after the accounting period has been closed, although a trial balance can be obtained from the General Ledger at any time during the month.

The system supports both manual transaction entry and links to other computerized accounting modules so that data has to be entered only once. Because Jim sometimes needs several days to close his books at the end of the month, the general ledger will accept transactions for a new month before the books are closed on the old one. In fact, several months' data can be entered without closing the previous months, although the months must eventually be closed in sequence to prepare the financial reports.

Important note: The accounting system can be developed and tested on a computer with two floppy disk drives, but should be run on a computer with a hard disk drive. The volume of accounting transactions in all but the smallest companies will quickly exceed the capacity of a 360K floppy disk.

Identifying the Purpose and Function of the System

The first step in developing a system like the General-Ledger and Financial-Reporting System is to identify clearly its purpose and function. The purpose of the General-Ledger System is to record the financial transactions of Smith and Jones Corporation and to summarize those transactions by account at the end of the month.

The general ledger must be capable of accepting from the keyboard and validating double-entry bookkeeping data, maintaining an audit trail of accounting transactions, and printing a trial balance that summarizes the activity in each account during the month. Finally, the general ledger must feed the financial-reporting system. If there are other computerized accounting applications, then this general ledger should be able to pick up transactions from those other systems. The following list summarizes the functions of the general-ledger system:

- accepting double-entry bookkeeping transactions from the keyboard or another program

- verifying that all transactions balance before accepting them

- printing journal-entry reports to provide a record of transactions

- summarizing journal entries by account (Trial Balance)

- posting account balances to the Financial-Reporting Ledger at the end of the period

The purpose and function of the Financial-Reporting system also need to be identified. The purpose of the system is to accumulate the actual results for the year and to print financial statements comparing the current period to the budget and to last year's performance. The actual data is fed from the general ledger. The budget data must be entered from the keyboard or from another computer program. The following list summarizes the functions of the Financial-Reporting System:

- maintaining actual, budget, and last year's balances by period for each account

- accepting budget and last year's data from the keyboard or another program

- accepting data from General Ledger for actual balance

- printing financial statements for a specified month

- printing 12-month financials

- copying actual balance to last year's balance and clearing balances for actual and budget at end of year

Defining the File Structures

The data files needed for the General-Ledger and Financial-Reporting System include the general-ledger file, the financial-reporting ledger file, and the chart-of-accounts file. Each of these data files will have an accompanying index file. The sections that follow describe these data files in detail.

The General-Ledger File

The core of the accounting system is the general-ledger file. The accounting transactions for Smith and Jones Corporation are recorded serially in the general-ledger file as they occur. At the end of the accounting period, the transactions are summarized, posted to the Financial-Reporting Ledger, and cleared from the General Ledger, making room for the entries for a new accounting period.

An accounting transaction is recorded as two or more records in the general-ledger file: one record for each debit or credit. Any transaction may require entry of more than two records in the general-ledger file, depending on the number of accounts debited and credited.

Each record in the general-ledger file consists of eight fields. The general-ledger file records accounting transactions, and each record must contain certain information besides the account number and the debit or credit to provide an audit trail. The eight fields in the general-ledger file are shown in figure 8.1.

The first three fields hold information about the sequence and timing of a transaction. The TRANSACTNO field holds a transaction number that identifies the records making up a particular transaction. The DATE field holds the date of the transaction. The PERIOD field records the accounting period for the transaction, permitting the user to enter data for more than one accounting period at a time. The user can begin

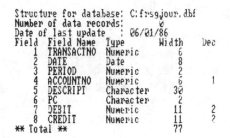

```
Structure for database: C:frsgjour.dbf
Number of data records:     0
Date of last update   : 06/01/86
Field  Field Name  Type       Width   Dec
   1   TRANSACTNO  Numeric        6
   2   DATE        Date           8
   3   PERIOD      Numeric        2
   4   ACCOUNTNO   Numeric        6      1
   5   DESCRIPT    Character     30
   6   PC          Character      2
   7   DEBIT       Numeric       11      2
   8   CREDIT      Numeric       11      2
** Total **                     77
```

Fig. 8.1. The structure of the general-ledger file, FRSGJOUR.

entering data for the next accounting period before closing out the current period. The fourth field, ACCOUNTNO, records the account number, which is the primary index for the file.

The DESCRIPT field provides space for a text description of the transaction. The PC field contains a posting code, which is used primarily to mark summary data posted to the General Ledger from other accounting systems.

The DEBIT and CREDIT fields hold the debit and credit amounts, respectively. Only one of these two fields is filled in any record. Providing space for both may seem redundant, but having the debits and credits in separate fields makes it easy to scan down a listing of the transactions and spot incorrectly entered items. In this era of cheap mass storage, such redundancy is worthwhile.

You can add or delete fields and adjust the size of the fields to meet your needs. The sizes shown were chosen to meet the specific needs of Smith and Jones Corporation. For example, the six-digit transaction number allows for 999,999 transactions before the numbers repeat. Most businesses will get through the year without duplicate transaction numbers. The 11-character debit and credit fields allow entry of amounts up to $99,999,999.99. The other fields were sized to fit the requirements of Smith and Jones Corporation and would apply to most small businesses.

You need to keep in mind two considerations about the sizes of records in the general ledger. First, you will want to be able to print each record on a single line in the General Journal report. Most printers can print at least 132 characters per line in one of their printing modes, so the 77-character record shown here meets the printing requirement.

The second consideration concerning record size is the amount of mass storage taken up by the general-ledger file and its associated indexes when it is full of accounting transactions. If each transaction requires two records and each record is 77 bytes long, then over 2,000 transactions will fit on a 360K floppy disk (ignoring the size of the index files).

The Financial-Reporting Ledger File

The financial-reporting ledger file is used to prepare comparative financial statements (balance sheet, income statement, and flow-of-funds statement). Each account has one record, which contains space for actual, budget, and last year's values for each accounting period. Figure 8.2 shows the structure of a file based on the monthly accounting period for Smith and Jones. If your application has significantly more than 12 accounting periods in a year, then another file structure might be necessary.

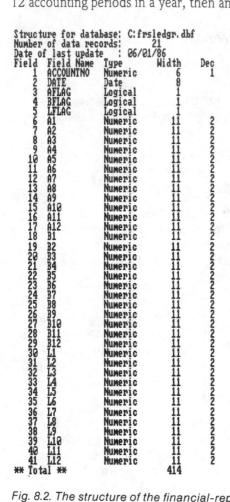

```
Structure for database: C:frsledgr.dbf
Number of data records:        21
Date of last update    : 06/01/86
Field  Field Name  Type      Width  Dec
    1  ACCOUNTNO   Numeric      6    1
    2  DATE        Date         8
    3  AFLAG       Logical      1
    4  BFLAG       Logical      1
    5  LFLAG       Logical      1
    6  A1          Numeric     11    2
    7  A2          Numeric     11    2
    8  A3          Numeric     11    2
    9  A4          Numeric     11    2
   10  A5          Numeric     11    2
   11  A6          Numeric     11    2
   12  A7          Numeric     11    2
   13  A8          Numeric     11    2
   14  A9          Numeric     11    2
   15  A10         Numeric     11    2
   16  A11         Numeric     11    2
   17  A12         Numeric     11    2
   18  B1          Numeric     11    2
   19  B2          Numeric     11    2
   20  B3          Numeric     11    2
   21  B4          Numeric     11    2
   22  B5          Numeric     11    2
   23  B6          Numeric     11    2
   24  B7          Numeric     11    2
   25  B8          Numeric     11    2
   26  B9          Numeric     11    2
   27  B10         Numeric     11    2
   28  B11         Numeric     11    2
   29  B12         Numeric     11    2
   30  L1          Numeric     11    2
   31  L2          Numeric     11    2
   32  L3          Numeric     11    2
   33  L4          Numeric     11    2
   34  L5          Numeric     11    2
   35  L6          Numeric     11    2
   36  L7          Numeric     11    2
   37  L8          Numeric     11    2
   38  L9          Numeric     11    2
   39  L10         Numeric     11    2
   40  L11         Numeric     11    2
   41  L12         Numeric     11    2
** Total **                  414
```

Fig. 8.2. The structure of the financial-reporting ledger file, FRSLEDGR.

The ACCOUNTNO field is the index field. Each record in the financial-reporting ledger is uniquely identified by its account number.

The AFLAG, BFLAG, and LFLAG fields contain logical values that indicate whether any data has been entered in the actual (AFLAG), budget (BFLAG), and last-year (LFLAG) sections of the record. These flags are used primarily to check whether a record can be deleted. The record should not be deleted if any of the three flags contains the value .T.

The actual data is entered in the 12 fields A1 through A12. This data is posted to the financial-reporting ledger by the program that closes the General Ledger at the end of each period. The data in the financial-reporting ledger is always one period behind because the data for the current period is still in the General Ledger. The account balances for the current period can be obtained from the general-ledger reports.

The budget data is entered in 12 fields named B1 through B12. This data can be entered from the keyboard, or you can add a program that imports the data from a file prepared with another software package. The year-end-close program erases the budget data to make room for the next year's budget data.

The last year's data is entered in 12 fields named L1 through L12. This data can be automatically entered by the year-end-close program or entered manually from the keyboard.

The financial-reporting ledger stores amounts as debit balances. An account with a debit balance will have a positive entry in the financial-reporting ledger; an account with a credit balance will have a negative entry in the financial-reporting ledger. Consequently, the asset and expense accounts will normally have positive balances, whereas liability, equity, and revenue accounts will normally have negative balances.

The Chart-of-Accounts File

The next file to identify is the chart-of-accounts file, which defines each account used in the accounting system as an asset, liability, equity, revenue, or expense account. The chart-of-accounts file is used during data entry to verify that an account exists so that the user does not enter data to a nonexistent account. The file is also used to format accounting reports. The reporting programs refer to the chart of accounts so that accounts of the same type can be grouped together.

Many accounting systems incorporate a chart of accounts partially or wholly in the code of the programs. This technique can improve the processing speed of the system, but it makes the system hard to debug, to adapt to another business, or to update as the requirements of the business expand over time. The system developed here for Smith and Jones Corporation maintains information about each account in the chart-of-accounts file, making it easier to debug the system during development, to add or update an account, or to completely revamp the chart of accounts.

This chart-of-accounts file contains four items for each account: the account number, the account name, the account type, and a noncash account flag (see fig. 8.3).

```
Structure for database: C:frsacct.dbf
Number of data records:      23
Date of last update   : 05/31/86
Field  Field Name  Type        Width    Dec
    1  ACCOUNTNO   Numeric         6       1
    2  NAME        Character      30
    3  TYPE        Character      11
    4  NONCASH     Logical         1
** Total **                      49
```

Fig. 8.3. The structure of the chart-of-accounts file, FRSACCT.

The data in the ACCOUNTNO field is the primary identification of an account. In this system, the identifier consists of a four-digit account number plus a single decimal digit to indicate subaccounts. The subaccounts provide for the future possibility of an additional level of subtotaling below the account number. The chart-of-accounts file is indexed by account number to make it easy for Jim Jones or another user to look up accounts by account number.

The NAME field holds the account name that the user wants printed on the reports. The system also displays the account names during data entry so that the user can verify the accounts to which data is being entered.

The chart of accounts also has a field for the account type. Smith and Jones Corporation's accounting system is typical of most small business accounting systems in that there are five account types: Assets, Liabilities, Equity, Revenues, and Expenses. Specifying the type for each account allows you to adapt a generic accounting system to a wide variety of businesses with different charts of accounts. The TYPE field holds the account type as it will be displayed on reports.

The last field in the chart-of-accounts file is a logical flag. A value of .T. in this field signifies an account that records noncash accounting transactions. The most common accounts in this category are Accumulated Depreciation and Depreciation Expense.

Index Files and File Limits

Each of the three data files in the General-Ledger and Financial-Reporting System has at least one index file. These index files are used for such purposes as searching the associated file or printing reports in a specified order. Table 8.1 shows the index files associated with each of the three database files.

In developing a system like the General-Ledger and Financial-Reporting System, you must keep in mind a serious constraint of dBASE III Plus: only 15 files can be open at one time. The 15-file limit includes open database files, indexes, the main program, and any procedure or program files called from the main program.

We can easily live within this constraint while developing the General-Ledger and Financial-Reporting System for Smith and Jones Corporation. However, we will also have to be careful when we link the General Ledger to other accounting systems to ensure that the 15-file limit is not exceeded while the systems are linked.

Table 8.1
Indexes Used with Each Data File

File	Index Field	Index Name	Indexed By
FRSGJOUR	ACCOUNTNO	FRSGACCT	Account number
	TRANSACTNO	FRSGTRAN	Transaction number
FRSLEDGR	ACCOUNTNO	FRSLACCT	Account number
FRSACCT	ACCOUNTNO	FRSAACCT	Account number

Specifying the Function of Each Program

The data files we've described provide places to store the information needed for this application. The next step in developing the system is to determine the "division of labor" between the programs by developing a block diagram of the system. We develop the block diagram by recalling the list of functions mentioned previously for the general-ledger and financial-reporting system. This block diagram serves as a road map during the development process. The block diagram will usually change as development proceeds, but an imperfect map at the outset is much better than none at all.

Figure 8.4 shows a block diagram of the General Ledger and Financial-Reporting System. The system has been divided into functions dealing with the general ledger, with financial reporting, and with system maintenance. These divisions will become the three submenus of the main menu.

The system is modular. Each function in figure 8.4 is performed by a separate program. Subroutines perform functions common to more than one program and isolate complex portions of code from the main programs.

Section II: Developing the Programs

Before we can develop the main programs for the General-Ledger and Financial-Reporting System, we must

- create two utility programs for the system index files

- set up the file that holds memory variables and the program that edits these variables

- develop programs to enter, update, delete, and print account information in the chart of accounts file

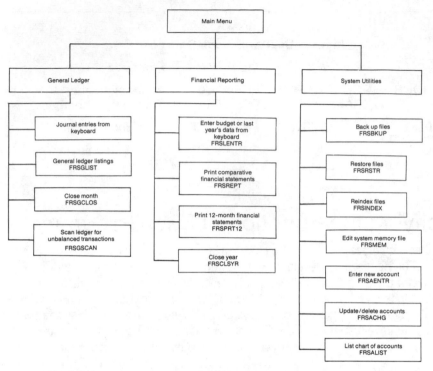

Fig. 8.4. Block diagram of the General-Ledger and Financial-Reporting System.

Creating Necessary Utility Programs

The first step in developing the programs for the application is to write the FRSINDEX program and the FRSOPEN subroutine. These programs will set up and maintain the index files while the system is being developed. The FRSINDEX program is one of the System Maintenance programs. It establishes all the indexes used by the General-Ledger and Financial-Reporting System. The FRSOPEN subroutine, which is called by every program in the system, opens the data files and associated index files.

Opening Data Files (FRSOPEN)

The FRSOPEN subroutine is a short dBASE routine that opens the three data files and four index files used in the application. Listing 8.1 shows the code for this subroutine. FRSOPEN is called by every system program that uses the database and the indexes. The purpose of this subroutine is to open all the files in a consistent manner in each program in the system. When you add or delete an index file, you only have to change FRSOPEN; then all programs in the system open the database with the new indexes.

Listings are at the end of the chapter.

Reindexing Data Files (FRSINDEX)

The FRSINDEX subroutine reindexes the data files in the General-Ledger and Financial-Reporting System. Index files can sometimes be destroyed or damaged during development or testing. The most common way to damage an index file is to write a new record to the database file when the index file is not open. Using the program FRSOPEN minimizes the likelihood of such an accident, but it can still happen; you should code this routine first so that it will be available if you ever have to rebuild the indexes.

Listing 8.2 shows the code for the FRSINDEX subroutine. The subroutine is merely a list of INDEX ON commands that create the index files for each data file.

Managing the System Memory File

Before you develop the main programs for the General-Ledger and Financial Reporting System, you need to set up a file to hold the system memory variables. And you will need a program that enables someone at Smith and Jones Corporation to edit these memory variables when the system is set up or when any changes need to be made.

Description of the System Memory File

The system memory file holds memory variables that are used by the programs in the General-Ledger and Financial-Reporting System. Figure 8.5 lists those memory variables.

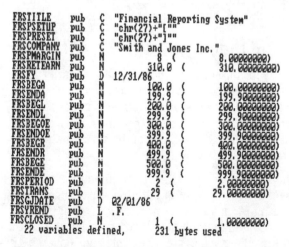

```
FRSTITLE     pub   C   "Financial Reporting System"
FRSPSETUP    pub   C   "chr(27)+"["" 
FRSPRESET    pub   C   "chr(27)+"]""
FRSCOMPANY   pub   C   "Smith and Jones Inc."
FRSPMARGIN   pub   N          8  (        8.00000000)
FRSRETEARN   pub   N        310.0 (      310.00000000)
FRSFY        pub   D   12/31/86
FRSBEGA      pub   N        100.0 (      100.00000000)
FRSENDA      pub   N        199.9 (      199.90000000)
FRSBEGL      pub   N        200.0 (      200.00000000)
FRSENDL      pub   N        299.9 (      299.90000000)
FRSBEGOE     pub   N        300.0 (      300.00000000)
FRSENDOE     pub   N        399.9 (      399.90000000)
FRSBEGR      pub   N        400.0 (      400.00000000)
FRSENDR      pub   N        499.9 (      499.90000000)
FRSBEGE      pub   N        500.0 (      500.00000000)
FRSENDE      pub   N        999.9 (      999.90000000)
FRSPERIOD    pub   N          2  (        2.00000000)
FRSTRANS     pub   N         29  (       29.00000000)
FRSGJDATE    pub   D   02/01/86
FRSYREND     pub   L   .F.
FRSCLOSED    pub   N          1  (        1.00000000)
     22 variables defined,    231 bytes used
```

Fig. 8.5. The contents of the system memory file, FRSMEM.

The first five variables are used in printing reports. They include the system title (FRSTITLE), the printer setup string for compressed print (FRSPSETUP), the printer setup string to restore the printer to normal print (FRSPRESET), the company title (FRSCOMPANY), and a numeric value for the left margin of printed reports (FRSPMARGIN). The values shown for FRSPSETUP and FRSPRESET are for a Toshiba printer. If this application will be used with another kind of printer, you will have to change the values.

The next variable, FRSRETEARN, holds the account number of the retained-earnings account. This account must be defined so that the system can close out the net margin to the retained-earnings account at the end of each month.

The 10 variables listed as FRSBEGA through FRSENDE define the beginning and the end of the account-number ranges for different types of accounts: assets, liabilities, equity, revenues, and expenses. These memory variables are used to validate account numbers during entry or updating of chart-of-accounts data. For each account range, the ending value must be greater than or equal to the beginning value, and the account ranges must not overlap.

The remaining memory variables include the current accounting period (FRSPERIOD), the next general-ledger transaction number (FRSTRANS), the date of the last close of the general ledger to the financial-reporting ledger (FRSGJDATE), a flag that is set when the general ledger is closed at the end of the 12th accounting period (FRSYREND), and the period number of the last period closed from the general ledger to the financial-reporting ledger (FRSCLOSED).

The system memory file may have only one or two entries at the beginning of a development project. For example, in this system the memory file started out containing only the system name and the printer setup string for compressed print. You can add more variables as needed during the development process.

Program to Edit the System Memory File (FRSMEM)

The program FRSMEM provides a way for Jim Jones or another user at Smith and Jones Corporation to adjust the system memory variables when the system is installed, a new printer is purchased, or one of the system parameters needs to be changed. You should modify this program whenever you change the contents of the system memory file so that you can easily change the values of the saved memory variables during development and testing.

The FRSMEM program retrieves the existing values of the system memory variables and displays the editing screen shown in figure 8.6. After entering any changes, the user ends the editing session by pressing Esc at any field or pressing Enter at the last field. Then the program verifies the account ranges. If the ranges are valid, the user is then prompted to indicate whether the edited values are acceptable and is offered another chance to edit the values.

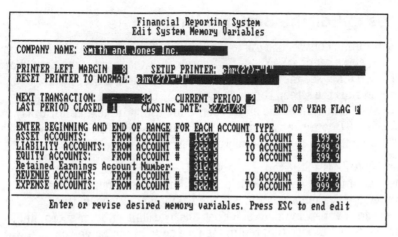

Fig. 8.6. A screen for editing the system memory variables

Listing 8.3 shows the code for the FRSMEM program, which is very straightforward. First, the existing data is retrieved. Then the program calls FRSME1, which displays the editing screen. After the editing is finished, the program calls FRSME2, which checks for range overlap. FRSME2, in turn, calls FRSATYPE to check individual range boundaries for overlap. FRSMEM then saves the edited memory variables back to the system memory file FRSMEM.MEM.

The FRSMEM program first uses the FILE function to determine if the file FRSMEM.MEM exists. If so, then the saved values are restored, the two printer-setup strings are padded with spaces to a length of 80 characters, and the company-name string is padded to 30 characters. The purpose of the padding is to enable the user to enter characters up to the specified number. The trailing spaces are removed with the TRIM function before these variables are stored. If the file FRSMEM.MEM does not exist, the memory variables are created.

Next, the program enters a loop in which the edit screen is displayed, account ranges (assets, liabilities, equity, revenues, and expenses) are checked for validity and lack of overlap, and the user is prompted to indicate whether to accept the edited variables. Execution transfers out of the loop when there are no errors and the user confirms the variables on screen, or when there *are* errors but the user does not want to do further editing. If the user confirms the variables, the loop ends with MOK="Y". If the user does not want to do further editing, the loop ends with MOK="N".

Finally, the program checks whether MOK="Y". If so, the user is prompted to indicate whether the edited variables should be saved to the system memory file. If the user says yes, the variables are saved. If MOK="N" or if the user says no, the program quits without saving the changes.

Subroutines to Edit the System Memory File

The FRSME1 subroutine consists of a call to the BORDERS subroutine, which sets up the display screen, and a set of @SAY . . . GET commands that display the data. (For a discussion of BORDERS, see the section "Designing a Consistent User Interface" in Chapter 3.) The result is the screen shown in figure 8.6. Listing 8.4 shows the code for FRSME1. You can either enter the entire subroutine using the text editor or lay out the @SAY . . . GET commands using dBASE III Plus's MODIFY SCREEN command and then enter the rest of the subroutine using the editor.

The subroutine FRSME2 is a little more complicated. FRSME2 checks for three types of errors in the account-range entries. First it checks for reversed ranges. Then it checks that the retained-earnings account is in the equity range. Finally, the subroutine checks for overlapping ranges. It does this by calling another subroutine, FRSATYPE, whose main purpose is to return the type code of the range containing an account number. FRSATYPE returns a blank type if the account number is in no range or in more than one range. FRSME2 calls the FRSATYPE subroutine eight times to check all possible combinations of overlapping ranges. (The FRSATYPE subroutine is discussed in the section "Entering New Accounts.") Listing 8.5 shows the code for subroutine FRSME2.

Maintaining the Chart of Accounts

At this point, we have created all three data files and have run FRSINDEX to set up the indexes. We have also set up the system memory variables with FRSMEM. Now we're ready to turn to the programs that define and modify account information in the chart-of-accounts file.

The following functions are needed for managing the chart-of-accounts file:

- entering new accounts
- updating account information
- deleting accounts
- printing a list of accounts

It is logical to group together the update and delete functions, because they both must check for data entered for that account before updating or deleting the account. Therefore, there are three chart-of-accounts programs: one program to enter new accounts (FRSAENTR), one to update or delete accounts (FRSACHG), and one to print a list of accounts (FRSALIST).

Entering New Accounts (FRSAENTR)

The program for entering a new account into the chart-of-accounts file (FRSAENTR) presents a data-entry screen on which a user at Smith and Jones Corporation can enter the number and name of a new account and indicate whether it is a cash-flow account. This data-entry screen is shown in figure 8.7.

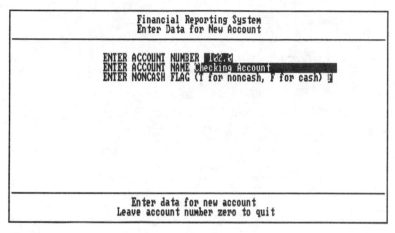

Fig. 8.7. A data-entry screen for entry of new-account information.

When the user enters an account number, the program checks for an existing account with this number. If the number is found, then the following error message is displayed:

Account number found in file .. Reenter

The program also determines whether the account number is within one of the defined ranges for types of account. If not, the following error message is displayed:

Account number is outside specified ranges .. Reenter

If there is no error, the account type is displayed and the user is asked OK (Y or N)? If the account type is OK, the account is added to the chart-of-accounts file. Then the program returns to the top of the data-entry loop, and the user can enter another account number. To exit the program, the user enters a value of zero for the account number. The program then asks the user whether a new chart-of-accounts listing should be printed; if so, the subroutine FRSALIS1 is called. Then the program ends.

The flowchart in figure 8.8 shows the logic of the FRSAENTR program. The program uses the subroutines FRSOPEN, BORDERS, and FRSATYPE. Code for the program is shown in listing 8.6.

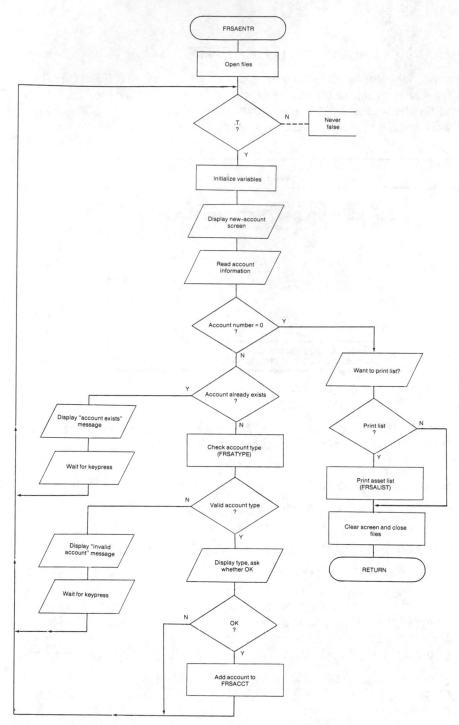

Fig. 8.8. Flowchart of the program FRSAENTR.

The program first calls FRSOPEN, which opens the system data files and indexes, and restores the system memory variables from FRSMEM.MEM. Then execution enters the main loop, leaving it only when the user enters a zero account number.

The main loop begins by initializing the account-number and account-name memory variables. Then the data-entry screen is displayed. After reading the data from the user, the program checks whether the account number already exists, and verifies that it is within one of the account ranges defined in the system memory variables. If not, the program enters a subloop that prompts the user to correct the account number. The loop is repeated until the user enters a valid new account number or a zero.

If a zero account number is entered, execution transfers out of the main loop. Otherwise, the program displays the account type (Asset, Liability, Equity, Revenue, or Expense) and asks the user if it is OK to add the new account to the chart-of-accounts file. If so, the program appends a blank record to the end of FRSACCT and fills its fields with account information from the user's input. Execution then returns to the top of the loop for another new-account entry.

When the main loop is exited, the program asks the user whether he or she wants a printed account list. If so, the program calls FRSALIST to print the list. Then the program clears the screen, closes the databases, and returns.

The FRSOPEN subroutine and the BORDERS subroutine have been discussed previously. FRSOPEN opens the data files and sets up the indexes, and BORDERS formats the data-entry screen. (The subroutine FRSALIST is discussed in the section "Printing a List of Accounts.")

The FRSATYPE subroutine has two purposes: it verifies that the account number falls within one of the defined account ranges, and it returns the corresponding account type. FRSATYPE uses a series of IF commands to check if the account number falls within each of the five ranges: Assets, Liabilities, Equity, Revenues, or Expenses. The program counts how many ranges the account number falls within. If the account number falls within exactly one range, the program returns the corresponding range type. Otherwise, the program returns a blank type, indicating an error. Listing 8.7 shows the FRSATYPE subroutine.

Updating and Deleting Accounts (FRSACHG)

The account-entry program, FRSAENTR, handles one necessary function of the General-Ledger and Financial-Reporting System: it permits the user to enter accounts into the chart of accounts. The next function that is needed is a program to modify or delete an account in the chart-of-accounts file. These functions are provided by the program FRSACHG and the subroutines FRSAUPD and FRSADEL.

The program FRSACHG gets the account number of the account to be modified or deleted, displays information about this account, and asks whether the user wants to

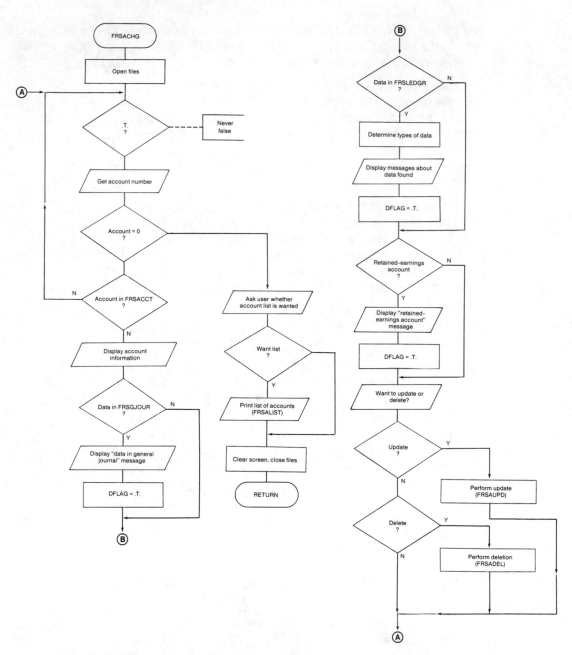

Fig. 8.9. Flowchart of the program FRSACHG.

modify or delete the account. If the user wants to modify the account, the program calls FRSAUPD to perform the update. If the user wants to delete the account, the program calls FRSADEL to perform the deletion.

The process of modifying or deleting account information is complicated if the files contain data for the account. If the account is being modified and the account number is changed, then all data entered against this account must be updated with the new account number. If the account is being deleted, then all data entered against this account must be transferred to another account. The FASAUPD and FASADEL subroutines take care of the necessary data transfers.

The FRSACHG program is the main program for modifying or deleting account information. The flowchart in figure 8.9 illustrates the logic of the program; the code is shown in listing 8.8.

The program begins by opening the data files and restoring memory variables from FRSMEM.MEM. Then the program enters the main loop. On each pass through the loop, the user enters the number of an account whose information is to be modified or deleted, and the program processes it. This loop is repeated until the user enters an account-number value of zero.

The main loop first presents a data-entry screen for the account number. This screen is shown in figure 8.10. After the user enters the account number, the program checks whether the number is zero. If so, the program exits the loop.

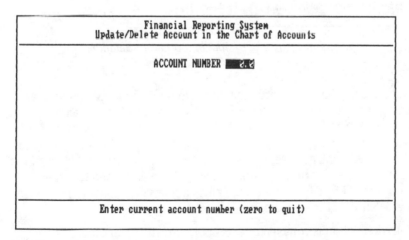

Fig. 8.10. The screen for entry of account numbers.

If the account number is not zero, the program checks to see if the account number is in the chart-of-accounts file. If the account number is not found, execution returns to the top of the loop for entry of another account number. If the account number is found, information about the account is retrieved and displayed. The program then checks for data that will need to be moved to a new account, and sets a flag indicating whether such data exists. Next, the program asks whether the user wants to update or delete the account information.

Figure 8.11 shows the Update/Delete screen after the account number for a Smith and Jones Corporation account has been entered. Notice the query at the bottom of the screen.

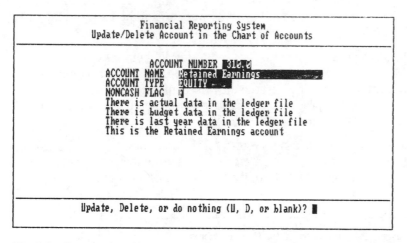

Fig. 8.11. Screen showing account data and prompt for update or deletion.

As mentioned previously, different subroutines are invoked depending on whether the user is modifying or deleting the account. If the user wants to update an account, the program calls the FRSAUPD subroutine. FRSAUPD accepts the user's updates, then calls FRSAUPD1 to handle the physical updating of the chart-of-accounts file and the data files. If the user wants to delete an account, the program calls the FRSADEL subroutine. FRSADEL accepts a new account number for the data, then calls the FRSADEL1 subroutine. FRSADEL1 handles the physical transfer of data to the new account and the deletion of the old account.

When the update or deletion is completed, execution returns to the program FRSACHG, and the main loop is repeated again for entry of the next account number.

After the program exits the main loop, a screen prompt asks whether the user wants a new chart of accounts printout:

Want to print a new chart-of-accounts listing (Y or N)?

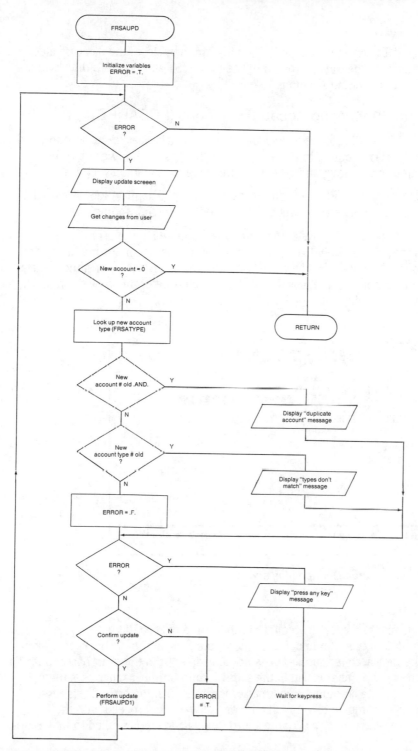

Fig. 8.12. Flowchart of the subroutine FRSAUPD.

If so, the FRSALIST subroutine is called. The program then closes the database files, and control returns to the calling program. (The FRSALIST subroutine is discussed in the section "Printing a List of Accounts.")

Accepting and Validating Account Changes (FRSAUPD)

The subroutine FRSAUPD accepts and validates the user's changes to the account, and calls the FRSAUPD1 subroutine to make the actual changes. The flowchart of the FRSAUPD subroutine is shown in figure 8.12; the code is shown in listing 8.9.

After initializing variables, FRSAUPD enters the main loop. The main loop is exited if the user enters a value of zero, or when the update is successfully completed.

The beginning of the loop displays a data-entry screen on which the user enters changes. This screen, shown in figure 8.13, is similar to the screen for modifying and deleting accounts. The user can enter a new account number, name, or noncash-flag value. The user cannot change the account type, which is determined by the range in which the account number falls.

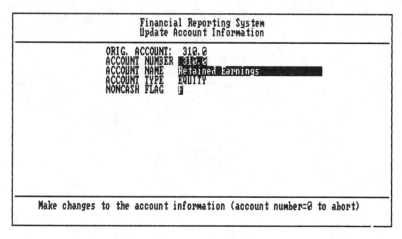

Fig. 8.13. Data-entry screen for updating accounts.

Next, the program checks for an account-number value of zero. If found, the main loop is exited. If the account number is not zero, the program then checks to make certain that the new account number does not already exist in the chart-of-accounts file and that the new number is within the same account-number range as is the old account number. If the account number passes these checks, the error flag is reset to .F. and the user is prompted to verify that he or she wants to proceed with the update. If the user wants to proceed, the subroutine FRSAUPD1 is called to make the changes. and FRSAUPD returns control to the calling program. If the account number does not pass these checks, the error flag remains set, an error message is displayed, and the program returns to the top of the loop for further changes.

Updating Accounts (FRSAUPD1)

If the user orders the program to proceed with the update, the subroutine FRSAUPD1 is called to perform the physical update of the account. Figure 8.14 shows a flowchart and listing 8.10 shows the code for the subroutine FRSAUPD1.

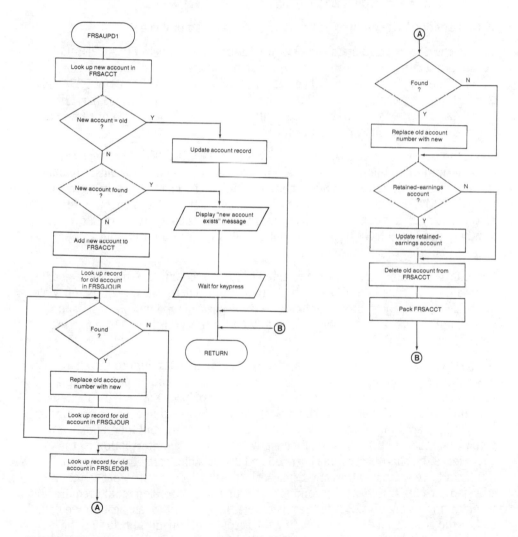

Fig. 8.14. Flowchart of the subroutine FRSAUPD1.

FRSAUPD1 updates the chart-of-accounts file and all the data files for the user's account modifications. First, the file FRSACCT is selected and the new account number is checked to see if the user changed the account number. If the account number was not changed, the subroutine updates the account record in the chart-of-accounts file. Execution then returns to FRSAUPD.

The process is more complicated if the account number has been changed. First, the subroutine looks up the new account in the chart-of-accounts file. If the new account number is not found, a blank record is appended and the new account data is entered. If the new account is found, an error message is issued:

`New account already exists. Cannot complete update.`

The user is instructed to press any key, and execution returns to FRSAUPD; the update is not completed. (The check for existence of the new account is a safety feature. The account has already been checked once by FRSAUPD before FRSAUPD1 is called. But you can't be too careful when updating a chart-of-accounts file. I have found that as systems are modified, such little safety features can prevent some nasty bugs from finding their way into the system.)

Next, the subroutine selects the general-ledger file (FRSGJOUR) and changes the old account number to the new account number for all journal entries against the old account. The subroutine then does the same thing in the financial-reporting ledger (FRSLEDGR). For each file, the subroutine loops until end-of-file is encountered. All records found that contain the old account number are updated with the new account number. The FRSLEDGR file should contain only one record for the old account number, but the loop is there just in case.

If the old account number was the retained-earnings account, the subroutine updates the memory variable FRSRETEARN and saves the change to the system memory file FRSMEM.MEM. The subroutine then selects the chart-of-accounts file again and deletes the old account number. Finally, a PACK command is issued to make the deletion permanent.

We have chosen to update the files by first adding the new account to the chart-of-accounts file, then making all changes in other data files, and finally deleting the old account. This method reduces the possibility of having stranded data items with no account in the chart of accounts. If we had chosen to update the account by changing the account number in the chart-of-accounts record and then updating the account numbers in the data files, then a power failure or an interruption by the user could leave the chart-of-accounts changed and the data files partially unchanged. The result could be journal entries and a financial-reporting ledger entry that cannot be accessed through the chart of accounts. Correcting such a problem could require—at a minimum—using dBASE in interactive mode. In a less critical application we could update the accounts file by just replacing the account information (including the account number) in the account record for the old account.

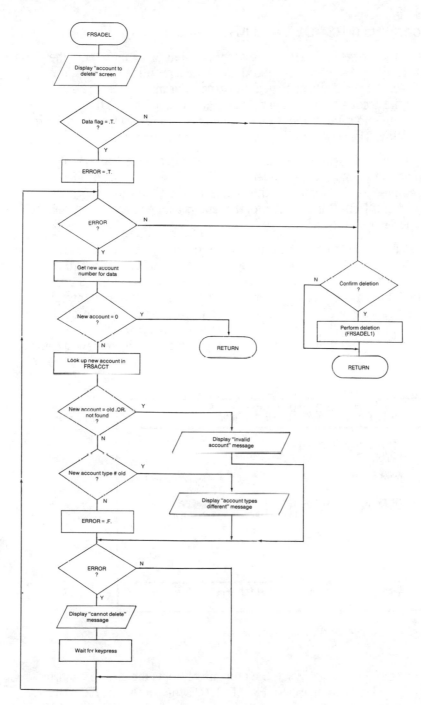

Fig. 8.15. Flowchart of the subroutine FRSADEL.

Deleting Accounts (FRSADEL and FRSADEL1)

If the user selects the Delete option from the Modify/Delete Account screen, the program FRSACHG calls the subroutine FRSADEL. That subroutine gets the new account number and, if necessary, also agets a new account number for the data recorded against the account that is being deleted. FRSADEL then calls the FRSADEL1 subroutine to perform the deletion. Figure 8.15 shows a flowchart for the FRSADEL subroutine. The code for this subroutine is shown in listing 8.11.

The FRSADEL subroutine begins by displaying information on the account to be deleted. Then the subroutine checks the data flag, DFLAG, which is set by FRSACHG if there is data entered for this account in the general-ledger file or the financial-reporting ledger file. If DFLAG is set, the program enters a loop to accept and validate a new account number for the data.

In the loop, the subroutine prompts the user to enter the new account number. Figure 8.16 shows the resulting data-entry screen. The program then checks the new account number for a zero value. If the number is zero, execution returns to FRSACHG. If the number is not zero, the program validates the new account number by verifying that it exists in the chart of accounts and that it has the same account type as the account that is being deleted. If the new account number is invalid, an error message is displayed and execution returns to the top of the loop. If the new account is valid, the loop is exited.

Fig. 8.16. Data-entry screen for deleting accounts.

Next, whether or not the data flag is set, the program prompts the user to confirm the deletion. If the deletion is confirmed, FRSADEL calls the subroutine FRSADEL1, which performs the actual deletion. Execution then returns to the caller, FRSACHG.

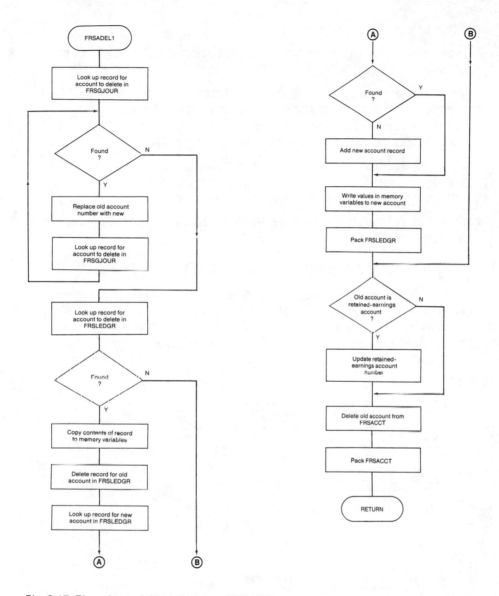

Fig. 8.17. Flowchart of the subroutine FRSADEL1.

The FRSADEL1 subroutine performs the physical deletion of the account from the files. Figure 8.17 shows a flowchart of the subroutine, and the code is shown in listing 8.12.

The deletion process consists of four steps:

1. Any journal entries for the old account are updated with the new account number.

2. The entry for the old account in the financial-reporting ledger file, FRSLEDGR, is added to the entry for the new account. If no financial-reporting ledger record exists for the new account, then one is created. After the new record is updated, the old record is deleted and the ledger file is packed.

3. If the old account is the retained-earnings account, the memory variable that contains the retained-earnings account number is updated with the new account number and saved to the system memory file.

4. Finally, the old account is deleted from the chart of accounts and the chart-of-accounts file is packed.

Printing a List of Accounts (FRSALIST)

The last program needed for managing the chart of accounts is a program to print the chart-of-accounts list. This program is kept simple through use of dBASE III Plus's report generator. The program opens files, pauses for the user to set up the printer, and prints the listing using the REPORT FORM command. The program prints the entire account list in account-number order. A sample printout is shown in figure 8.18.

```
                      Financial Reporting System
                      Chart of Accounts Listing

Account                             Account      Noncash
 Number  Account Name               Type         Flag
-------  --------------------------- -----------  -------

 100.0  Cash                        ASSETS       .F.
 104.0  Asset management account    ASSETS       .F.
 110.0  Accounts Receivable         ASSETS       .F.
 120.0  Inventory                   ASSETS       .F.
 130.0  Prepaid Expenses            ASSETS       .F.
 140.0  Fixed Assets                ASSETS       .F.
 141.0  Accumulated Depreciation    ASSETS       .T.
 150.0  Goodwill                    ASSETS       .T.
 190.0  Other Assets                ASSETS       .F.
 200.0  Accounts Payable            LIABILITIES  .F.
 210.0  Note Payable                LIABILITIES  .F.
 220.0  Deferred Taxes              LIABILITIES  .F.
 290.0  Other Liabilities           LIABILITIES  .F.
 300.0  Contributed Capital         EQUITY       .F.
 310.0  Retained Earnings           EQUITY       .F.
 320.0  Drawing account             EQUITY       .F.
 400.0  Sales                       REVENUES     .F.
 410.0  Other Income                REVENUES     .F.
 500.0  Cost of Sales               EXPENSES     .F.
 600.0  General Expenses            EXPENSES     .F.
 610.0  Wage Expense                EXPENSES     .F.
 620.0  Tax Expense - Except Income EXPENSES     .F.
 630.0  Depreciation Expense        EXPENSES     .T.
 700.0  General Overhead            EXPENSES     .F.
 710.0  Income Tax Expense          EXPENSES     .F.
```

Fig. 8.18. Sample chart-of-accounts printout.

The REPORT FORM command uses a report format set up with the MODIFY REPORT command. The MODIFY REPORT command is one of dBASE's full screen commands that allows the user to interactively create a report format. Figures 8.19 and 8.20 show the definitions for the report.

Important note: *You'll recall from Section I that the fifth stage in developing an application is testing the system. Before proceeding with Section III, enter some accounts in the chart-of-accounts. Doing so will enable you to test the General Ledger programs as you develop them.*

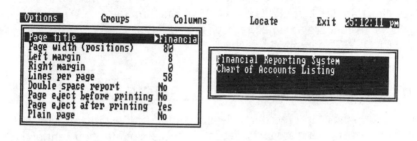

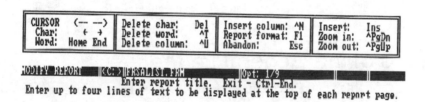

Fig. 8.19. The title and options screen for the report form FRSALIST.

```
Report definitions for report FRSALIST

Page title:      Financial Reporting System
                 Chart of Accounts Listing

Page width:    80
Left margin     8

Group on expression: -none-

COL    Contents                    Heading                W   D Tot
---   ------------------   -------------------------------  --  -- ---
 1    accountno           ;Account;Number;-------          7   1 No

 2    name                ;Account Name                    30    No
                          ;---------------------
                          --------- (30 dashes)

 3    type                ;Account;Type                    11    No
                          ;----------- (11 dashes)

 4    noncash             Noncash;Flag;-------             7     No
```

Fig. 8.20. Column definitions for report form FRSALIST.

The program code is shown in listing 8.13. First, the program calls FRSOPEN to open the data files, selects the chart-of-accounts file, and restores the system memory variables. Then the program displays a screen telling the user to set up the printer and press a key. After the user presses a key, the program resets the printer to normal mode and uses dBASE's REPORT FORM command to print the report, using the report-form file FRSALIST.FRM. Finally, the program closes files and ends.

Note that the program uses the SET PRINT ON and SET CONSOLE OFF commands to send the report to the printer. The output of REPORT FORM will appear on the screen if SET CONSOLE ON is in effect, and will not appear on the printer unless SET PRINT ON is in effect. In this way, REPORT FORM differs from the @ SAY . . . commands used for custom programmed reports; the output of @ SAY . . . is affected by the SET DEVICE command.

Section III: The General Ledger

In Section II, we set up the chart-of-accounts file and completed the programs for entering, modifying, and deleting accounts. Section III focuses on development of the general-ledger portion of the accounting system for Smith and Jones Corporation. In this section, we look at the programs that enable the general ledger to carry out its required functions.

Functions of the General Ledger

The General Ledger portion of the accounting system described here provides the following functions:

- allowing transaction entry from the keyboard and other systems
- printing reports of journal entries and trial balances
- closing the general ledger to the financial-reporting ledger at the end of the accounting period
- locating, printing, and deleting unbalanced transactions

This general ledger records the intended accounting period along with the data for each transaction so that the user can start entering data for a new period before closing out the old one. This method of recording accounting-period data gives the user more time to prepare closing entries at the end of the period. This extra time is particularly helpful at the end of the year, when Smith and Jones Corporation takes a physical inventory before closing the books on the last period.

The system keeps track of the current accounting period and the last period that was closed. If the user tries to close the current period and prior periods are still open, the user is instructed to close the prior periods first.

The reporting module can print a transaction list or a trial balance at any time during the month. Both the transaction list and the trial balance can include user-selected subsets of the general ledger. With this flexibility, the user can prepare analytical reports about the current period as well as the traditional journal-entry and trial-balance reports.

The closing module posts the account totals to the specified accounting period in the financial-reporting ledger, then deletes the transactions from the general ledger. An archive option lets the user accumulate transactions for prior accounting periods in a separate file. This option provides an on-line audit trail that supplements the paper audit trail represented by the journal-entry reports.

Another function provided by the general-ledger programs is the capability to scan the general-ledger files for unbalanced transactions and to print and delete any that are found.

Entering Transactions from the Keyboard

The transaction-entry program is one of the most complicated programs in this book. It must prevent entry of data against undefined accounts and entry of unbalanced transactions into the general ledger. This program and its subroutines implement a flexible, user-tolerant data-entry system for transactions entered into the general ledger from the keyboard.

The transaction-entry program uses a temporary transaction file to collect the user's entries. The general-ledger file is updated from the temporary file after all entries have been made and checked. This batch-posting technique ensures that the program will not stop with half a transaction entered in the ledger (unless an interruption occurs during the batch update at the end of data entry).

The program begins by prompting the user for the transaction's date, accounting period, description, and posting code. These items, which constitute the transaction-header information, are common to each journal entry for the transaction. On the initial data-entry screen shown in figure 8.21, a transaction header for advertising expenses at Smith and Jones Corporation has been entered.

After the user has entered and verified the date, period, description, and posting code (if any), the program puts up a second data-entry screen for the journal entries that make up the transaction (see fig. 8.22). As the user enters the journal entries one-by-one, the previous entries remain on-screen so that all the entries that make up the transaction can be seen, as in figure 8.23.

The program checks the account number for each journal entry. If the number is not acceptable, the user is prompted to reenter it. The program also checks that the user has entered either a debit or a credit but not both. If both have been entered, the user is instructed to enter only one or the other (see fig. 8.24).

```
                    Financial Reporting System
                  Enter Transaction in General Journal


Transaction #:     30      Date: 02/28/86     Acctg. Period:  2
Description: Advertising                      Posting Code:
```

Fig. 8.21. The data-entry screen for transaction-header information.

```
                    Financial Reporting System
                  Enter Transaction in General Journal


Transaction #:     30      Date: 02/28/86      Acctg. Period:  2
Description: Advertising                       Posting Code:

ACCT:  600.0    DEBIT:       1250.00    CREDIT:




Name: General Expenses            Type: EXPENSES    Balance =     1250.00
                            OK (Y or N)? Y
```

Fig. 8.22 Data-entry screen for journal entries.

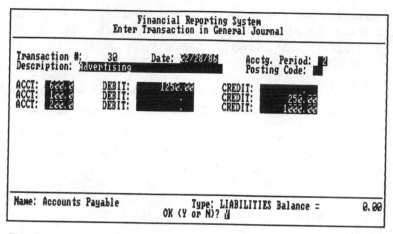

Fig. 8.23. Multiple journal entries on the transaction screen.

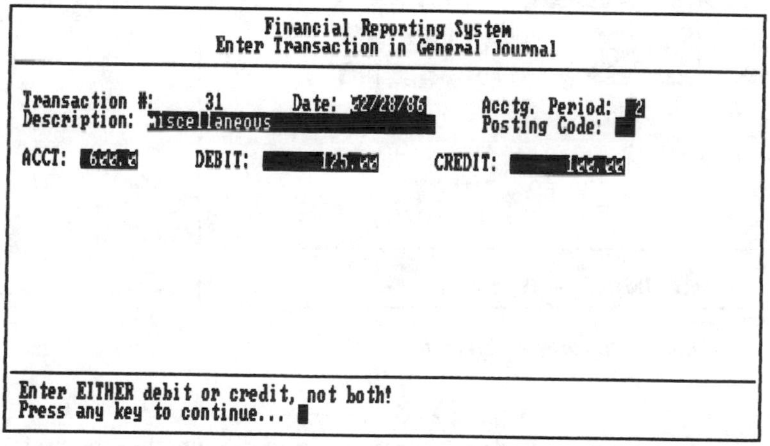

```
                    Financial Reporting System
                  Enter Transaction in General Journal

Transaction #:     31      Date: █2/28/86      Acctg. Period: █2
Description: ▓iscellaneous▓▓▓▓▓▓▓▓▓         Posting Code: █

ACCT: ▓6██.█▓   DEBIT: ▓▓▓▓▓▓125.██     CREDIT: ▓▓▓▓▓1██.██




Enter EITHER debit or credit, not both!
Press any key to continue... █
```

Fig. 8.24. Entry of both a debit and a credit is rejected.

After verifying the account number and the presence of either a debit entry or a credit entry, the program prompts the user to verify the journal entry before proceeding to the next one. In figure 8.22, the user is being prompted to verify entries for a transaction recording an advertising expenditure (see the prompt at the bottom of the screen). Note that there is a place to enter a posting code but that none has been entered. Smith and Jones Corporation has chosen to use the posting code field to record the origin of transactions entered automatically into the general ledger from other accounting systems.

When each journal entry has been verified and the balance of the transaction is zero, the user is asked whether he or she wants to accept the transaction (see fig. 8.25). By accepting a transaction, the user indicates that the last journal entry for that transaction has been made. If the user does not want to accept the transaction, another journal-entry line is displayed, and the record of journal entries for that transaction is kept open.

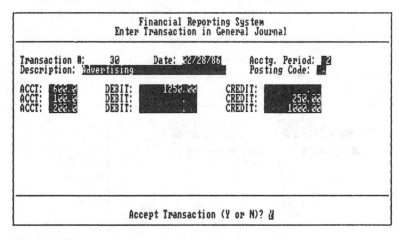

Fig. 8.25. The user is prompted to verify a transaction.

If the user presses *Y* to accept the transaction, the next prompt asks whether the user wants to enter another transaction. If the user chooses to enter additional transactions, the first transaction-entry screen is displayed again. If the user presses *N*, however, indicating that there are no more transactions to be entered, the program asks whether the user wants a list of the journal entries that have just been made. The program then updates the general ledger and, if a list of journal entries is desired, prints the list. Figure 8.26 shows a listing of journal entries for a transaction entered for February 28, 1986.

```
LISTING OF JOURNAL ENTRIES MADE ON 08/15/86
Page No.    1
08/15/86

                                    Smith and Jones Company
                                    Financial Reporting System
                                    General Journal Listing
                                    In Transaction Entry Order

Transaction          Accounting                            Post
   Number Date       Period Account Description            Code    DEBIT        CREDIT
---------- --------  ----------- ------- ------------------------------  ----  -----------  -----------


         30 02/28/86      2    600.0 Advertising                        1250.00        0.00
         30 02/28/86      2    100.0 Advertising                           0.00      250.00
         30 02/28/86      2    200.0 Advertising                           0.00     1000.00
*** Total ***

                                                                       1250.00     1250.00
```

Fig. 8.26. List of journal entries printed at the end of the data-entry program.

The Transaction-Entry Program (FRSGENTR)

The program that accomplishes all the general-ledger data-entry tasks, FRSGENTR, has three major sections. In the first section, files are opened and the temporary journal-entry data file is created. In the second section, the main loop, the user enters data for one or more transactions, using the first and second data-entry screens (see figs. 8.21 and 8.22). In the third section, the program appends the transaction journal entries from the temporary file to the general-ledger file, updates the transaction number in the system memory file, prints a journal-entry listing, and ends. Figure 8.27 shows a flowchart and listing 8.14 shows the code for the program FRSGENTR.

The program performs as much data checking and validation as possible to help forestall data-entry errors. For example, the accounting period is checked to make sure the user is not trying to enter data for a period that has already been closed. The program looks up account numbers in the chart-of-accounts file to make sure that no data is entered against a nonexistent account. Furthermore, a transaction entry is accepted only if it balances. And finally, by requiring that entries be confirmed, the program gives the user a chance to review the data before it is entered.

Let's take a look at the code for FRSGENTR (see listing 8.14). The program begins by opening the system data files and restoring the system memory variables from FRSMEM. Next, the program calls subroutine FRSGTEMP, which creates the temporary file that will hold the journal entries during data entry.

After the temporary file has been created, execution passes to the main section of the program, in which transaction-data entries are accepted. A "do forever" loop (DO WHILE .T.) is executed once for every transaction. The loop is exited when the user declines to enter another transaction.

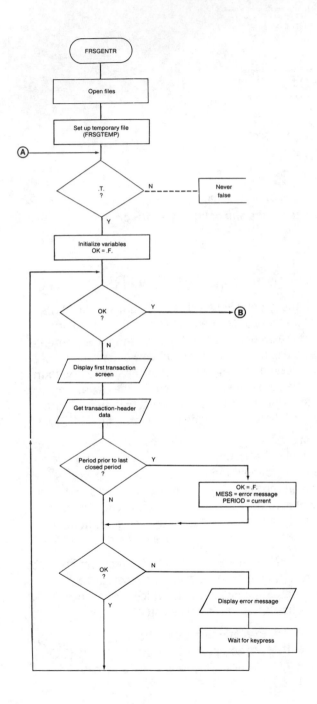

Fig. 8.27. Flowchart of the FRSGENTR program (part 1).

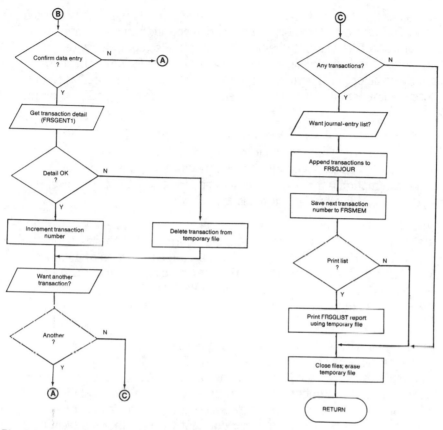

Fig. 8.27. Flowchart of the FRSGENTR program (part 2).

The first step is to display the first data-entry screen (fig. 8.21). On this screen the transaction number is displayed, and the user enters the transaction-header information. This step is performed within a second loop (DO WHILE .NOT. OK). The code within this loop accepts and also validates the data. If an invalid accounting-period number is entered, the loop repeats and the data-entry screen is displayed again. A message informs the user that the program cannot accept a transaction for a closed period.

The program checks the accounting period that the user specifies for the transaction by comparing the specified period with the last closed period, which is stored in the memory variable FRSCLOSED. This check prevents data from being entered into the general ledger for a period that has already been closed.

The algorithm used to check the accounting period must take into account the possibility of data entry for a new year before the preceding year is closed. The program does this by comparing the specified accounting period with the last closed period and a period six months before the last closed period. If the accounting period specified for an entry falls within this range, the entry is rejected. Otherwise, the entry is accepted. This flexibility allows the user to enter data for up to six periods into the next year before the previous year is closed. The user therefore has plenty of time to close the last period of the previous year, yet still is able to enter data for the new year.

Suppose, for example, that the last period closed is period 11, representing November, 1985; FRSCLOSED–6 therefore equals 5. If the user tries to enter a transaction for April 1985 (and MPERIOD therefore equals 4), the entry would be accepted. The assumption is that any entries into periods 1 through 5 are for the following year when the last period closed is 11.

After the user has filled in the transaction header and the data has been verified, the user is prompted to confirm the transaction-header information. If the user does not confirm the header, a LOOP command transfers execution to the top of the main loop, and the first data-entry screen (fig. 8.21) is presented again. But if the user confirms the header, the program calls subroutine FRSGENT1, which displays the second data-entry screen (see fig. 8.22) and accepts the entries for the current transaction.

If the journal entries balance and are accepted by the user, FRSGENT1 sets the flag variable OK to the value .T.; otherwise, the OK flag is set to .F. If the flag is true, the transaction number is incremented by one. If the flag is not true, the journal entries for the current transaction number are deleted. In either case, the user is then asked whether he or she wants to enter another transaction. If another transaction is desired, the main loop is repeated. If the user does not want another transaction, an EXIT command transfers execution out of the transaction data-entry loop. This is the only exit from the main loop.

The third major section of the program begins by asking the user whether a journal-entry printout is desired. The answer is saved in variable MOK. Then the program performs the general-ledger update. First, the PACK command is used to remove all deleted journal entries from the temporary file, TEMP.DBF. (Deleted entries are those that were rejected by either the program or the user during data entry.) Then the contents of the packed temporary file are appended to the general-ledger file. The system memory variables are saved to the file FRSMEM so that the updated transaction number is retained. The program asks the user about the listing before performing the update because the update can take some time to complete. The program performs the update before printing the report so that the program will not be aborted by a printer jam or some other problem before the update is complete.

When the update is done, the program prints the journal-entry listing if the user has requested one. Finally, the program closes the databases, erases the temporary file, and terminates. Erasing the temporary file at the end of the process has two benefits. First, it saves space on the user's disk drive. Second, if the temporary file is present in the system, this means that the program terminated abnormally. The consultant can check for existence of the temporary file to determine whether the problem occurred during data entry.

Subroutines Used by the Transaction Entry Program

The subroutines used by the FRSGENTR program are FRSOPEN, FRSGTEMP, FRSGENT1, and BORDERS. The program also uses the subroutine FRSGLIST.PRG and the report form FRSGLIST.FRM to print the optional journal-entry report. FRSOPEN and BORDERS are discussed in Section II of this chapter (see listing 8.1). See earlier comments in section II about BORDERS.

Opening the Temporary File for Journal Entries (FRSGTEMP)

The subroutine FRSGTEMP creates and opens the temporary file that holds the journal entries during entry of transaction data. The subroutine begins by deleting the file TEMP.DBF if it exists. Then the subroutine creates a new file TEMP.DBF by copying the structure of the general-ledger file. Finally, it opens the TEMP file in work area 9, which is chosen because this work area is normally the last one to be used. The code for FRSGTEMP is shown in listing 8.15.

Accepting Journal Entries for a Transaction (FRSGENT1)

The subroutine FRSGENT1 accepts journal entries for a transaction. This subroutine contains about half the total program code required for general-ledger data entry. FRSGENT1 puts up an open-ended data-entry screen for the journal entries (fig. 8.22). Journal entries are entered one by one on separate lines until the screen fills up. Then the screen is scrolled so that the last journal entry is at the top of the journal-entry area, and data entry continues. There is no limit to how many journal entries can be made for a single transaction. The flowchart for FRSGENT1 is shown in figure 8.28. Listing 8.16 shows the program code.

After variables are initialized, execution passes to the main loop (DO WHILE MORE), which is executed once for each journal entry. The loop is exited either when the user enters an account number of zero to abort data entry for the transaction, or when the transaction balances and the user has accepted the journal entries.

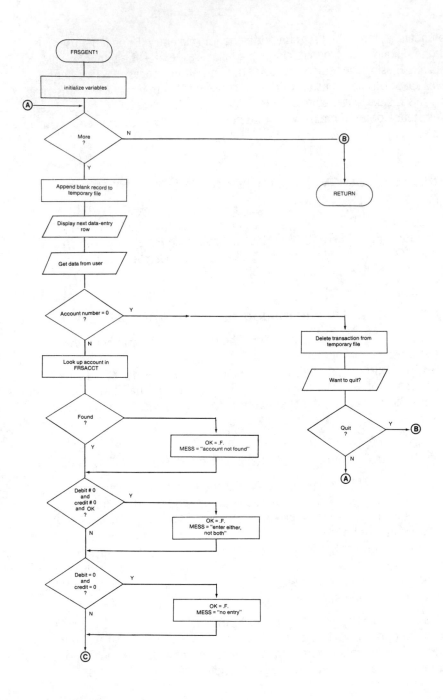

Fig. 8.28. Flowchart of the FRSGENT1 subroutine.

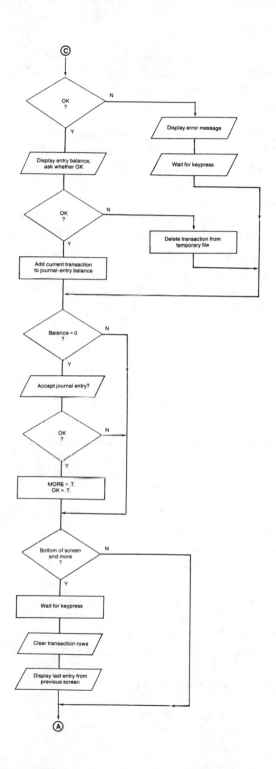

In the loop, a blank record is appended to the temporary file. Then the next journal-entry row in the data-entry screen (fig. 8.22) is displayed, and the user's input is read. The @ . . . GET statements that read the debit or credit amount have

RANGE 0,

clauses so that only positive or zero amounts are accepted. Next, the subroutine checks for an account number of zero. If the number is zero, the program asks the user if he or she wants to abandon data entry for this transaction. If the user does not want to abandon these transaction entries—because, for example, an account number of zero was entered by mistake—execution transfers to the top of the loop. If the number is not zero, the program verifies that the account number is listed in the chart of accounts and that the user has entered either a debit or a credit, but not both.

If an error is detected in the journal entry, an error message is displayed and the journal entry is deleted from the temporary file. Otherwise, the program displays the account name, account type, and transaction balance for this entry at the bottom of the screen, and asks the user whether the entry is acceptable. If the user presses Y to accept the entry, then the variables ESUM and BALANCE are updated and ROW is incremented. ESUM contains the total of all debits and credits for the transaction (not just this entry). ESUM is used within FRSGENT1 to check whether any valid journal entries have been made so far. BALANCE contains the balance for the transaction. ROW is used to position subsequent journal entries and to control "pagination" of the input screen. If the user presses N to reject the entry, the journal entry is deleted from the temporary file.

Next, the program checks for a balance of zero and for $ESUM>0$. If both conditions are met, the user is asked whether he or she wants to accept the transaction. If the user presses Y to accept the transaction, the MORE flag is set to .F. so that the loop will be exited normally at the bottom, and the OK flag is set to .T.

The last step in the loop is to check the value in ROW. If the MORE flag is true and value in ROW is greater than 18, then the journal-entry portion of the screen is cleared, and the last transaction entered is displayed on the first line of the journal-entry area. The subroutine accepts additional journal entries starting on the second line of the journal-entry area.

After the loop is exited, because the user either aborted the data entry or accepted the balanced transaction, execution returns to the calling program, FRSGENTR. The subroutine sets the value of the variable OK as a flag. The value of OK is .T. if the user accepted the transaction, and .F. if the user aborted the data entry.

Creating General-Ledger Reports

The general ledger can produce three reports that Jim Jones needs on a routine basis. The first is a journal-entry report, which can cover the entire contents of the general ledger or just a selected period. The second is a report showing all transactions by account. The third is a summary of current account balances; this report serves as a trial balance.

Figures 8.29, 8.30, and 8.31 show examples of each of these three reports. The journal-entry report in figure 8.29 shows all of Smith and Jones Corporation's transactions for the accounting period of February, 1986. The report in figure 8.30 categorizes the transactions by account for the same period and provides subtotals for each category. And the report in figure 8.31 summarizes the total debits, credits, and balances for each account.

```
TRANSACTIONS FOR ACCOUNTING PERIOD  2
Page No.    1
08/15/86
                                    Smith and Jones Company
                                    Financial Reporting System
                                    General Journal Listing
                                    In Transaction Entry Order

Transaction         Accounting                               Post
  Number Date       Period Account Description               Code    DEBIT      CREDIT
----------- --------  ------------ ------- --------------------------  ----  -----------  -----------


     19 02/01/86        2    200.0 Pay Bills                        20000.00      0.00
     19 02/01/86        2    100.0 Pay Bills                            0.00  20000.00
     20 02/01/86        2    100.0 Customer payments             10000.00      0.00
     20 02/01/86        2    110.0 Customer payments                 0.00  10000.00
     21 02/15/86        2    610.0 Payroll                       30000.00      0.00
     21 02/15/86        2    100.0 Payroll                           0.00  22500.00
     21 02/15/86        2    220.0 Payroll                           0.00   7500.00
     22 02/15/86        2    100.0 sales                         30000.00      0.00
     22 02/15/86        2    110.0 sales                         30000.00      0.00
     22 02/15/86        2    400.0 sales                             0.00  60000.00
     23 02/15/86        2    100.0 customer payments            10000.00      0.00
     23 02/15/86        2    110.0 customer payments                0.00  10000.00
     24 02/20/86        2    600.0 Advertising                   1250.00      0.00
     24 02/20/86        2    100.0 Advertising                       0.00   1250.00
     25 02/22/86        2    210.0 Loan Payment                 10000.00      0.00
     25 02/22/86        2    600.0 Loan Payment                  4000.00      0.00
     25 02/22/86        2    100.0 Loan Payment                      0.00  14000.00
     26 02/22/86        2    700.0 Utilities                     5000.00      0.00
     26 02/22/86        2    100.0 Utilities                         0.00   5000.00
     27 02/28/86        2    220.0 Sales Tax Payment            10000.00      0.00
     27 02/28/86        2    100.0 Sales Tax Payment                0.00  10000.00
     28 02/28/86        2    220.0 Income Tax Payment           20000.00      0.00
     28 02/28/86        2    100.0 Income Tax Payment               0.00  20000.00
     29 02/15/86        2    100.0 Cash on Hand          CR       1850.00      0.00
     29 02/15/86        2    500.0 Purchases             CR        250.00      0.00
     29 02/15/86        2    700.0 Miscellaneous         CR        100.00      0.00
     29 02/15/86        2    400.0 Sales                 CR          0.00   2050.00
     29 02/15/86        2    220.0 Sales Tax             CR          0.00    150.00
     30 02/28/86        2    600.0 Advertising                   1250.00      0.00
     30 02/28/86        2    100.0 Advertising                       0.00    250.00
     30 02/28/86        2    200.0 Advertising                       0.00   1000.00
*** Total ***

                                                                183700.00  183700.00
```

Fig. 8.29. Journal entry report.

```
TRANSACTIONS FOR ACCOUNTING PERIOD  2
Page No.    1
08/15/86
                                     Smith and Jones Company
                                     Financial Reporting System
                                     General Journal Listing
                                          By Account


Transaction Acctg                              Posting
   Number Period Date    Description            Code    DEBIT       CREDIT
----------- ------ -------- ------------------------------ ------- ----------- -----------


** Transactions for account:  100.0
        19     2 02/01/86 Pay Bills                                 0.00    20000.00
        20     2 02/01/86 Customer payments             10000.00        0.00
        21     2 02/15/86 Payroll                                   0.00    22500.00
        22     2 02/15/86 sales                         30000.00        0.00
        23     2 02/15/86 customer payments             10000.00        0.00
        24     2 02/20/86 Advertising                               0.00     1250.00
        25     2 02/22/86 Loan Payment                              0.00    14000.00
        26     2 02/22/86 Utilities                                 0.00     5000.00
        27     2 02/28/86 Sales Tax Payment                         0.00    10000.00
        28     2 02/28/86 Income Tax Payment                        0.00    20000.00
        29     2 02/15/86 Cash on Hand          CR       1850.00        0.00
        30     2 02/28/86 Advertising                               0.00      250.00
** Subtotal **
                                                        51850.00    93000.00


** Transactions for account:  110.0
        20     2 02/01/86 Customer payments                         0.00    10000.00
        22     2 02/15/86 sales                         30000.00        0.00
        23     2 02/15/86 customer payments                         0.00    10000.00
** Subtotal **
                                                        30000.00    20000.00


** Transactions for account:  200.0
        19     2 02/01/86 Pay Bills                     20000.00        0.00
        30     2 02/28/86 Advertising                               0.00     1000.00
** Subtotal **
                                                        20000.00     1000.00


** Transactions for account:  210.0
        25     2 02/22/86 Loan Payment                  10000.00        0.00
** Subtotal **
                                                        10000.00        0.00


** Transactions for account:  220.0
        21     2 02/15/86 Payroll                                   0.00     7500.00
        27     2 02/28/86 Sales Tax Payment             10000.00        0.00
        28     2 02/28/86 Income Tax Payment            20000.00        0.00
        29     2 02/15/86 Sales Tax             CR          0.00      150.00
** Subtotal **
                                                        30000.00     7650.00


** Transactions for account:  400.0
        22     2 02/15/86 sales                                     0.00    60000.00
        29     2 02/15/86 Sales                CR          0.00     2050.00
```

Fig. 8.30. Transactions by account report (page 1).

```
Page No.    2
08/15/86
                               Smith and Jones Company
                               Financial Reporting System
                               General Journal Listing
                                     By Account


Transaction  Acctg                            Posting
    Number Period Date    Description           Code     DEBIT      CREDIT
----------- ------ -------- ------------------------------ ------- ----------- -----------


** Subtotal **
                                                           0.00    62050.00


** Transactions for account:  500.0
        29      2 02/15/86 Purchases            CR        250.00       0.00
** Subtotal **
                                                         250.00       0.00


** Transactions for account:  600.0
        24      2 02/20/86 Advertising                   1250.00       0.00
        25      2 02/22/86 Loan Payment                  4000.00       0.00
        30      2 02/28/86 Advertising                   1250.00       0.00
** Subtotal **
                                                        6500.00       0.00


** Transactions for account:  610.0
        21      2 02/15/86 Payroll                      30000.00       0.00
** Subtotal **
                                                       30000.00       0.00


** Transactions for account:  700.0
        26      2 02/22/86 Utilities                     5000.00       0.00
        29      2 02/15/86 Miscellaneous        CR       100.00       0.00
** Subtotal **
                                                        5100.00       0.00

*** Total ***
                                                      183700.00   183700.00
```

Fig. 8.30. Transactions by account report (page 2).

```
TRANSACTIONS FOR ACCOUNTING PERIOD  2
Page No.     1
08/15/86
                                    Smith and Jones Company
                                    Financial Reporting System
                                    General Journal Listing
                                     Summary by Account

                          Total       Total      Debit
                          Debits      Credits    Balance
                        ----------- ----------- -----------


** Account  100.0
** Subtotal **
                        51850.00    93000.00   -41150.00

** Account  110.0
** Subtotal **
                        30000.00    20000.00    10000.00

** Account  200.0
** Subtotal **
                        20000.00     1000.00    19000.00

** Account  210.0
** Subtotal **
                        10000.00        0.00    10000.00

** Account  220.0
** Subtotal **
                        30000.00     7650.00    22350.00

** Account  400.0
** Subtotal **
                            0.00    62050.00   -62050.00

** Account  500.0
** Subtotal **
                          250.00        0.00      250.00

** Account  600.0
** Subtotal **
                         6500.00        0.00     6500.00

** Account  610.0
** Subtotal **
                        30000.00        0.00    30000.00

** Account  700.0
** Subtotal **
                         5100.00        0.00     5100.00
*** Total ***
                       183700.00   183700.00        0.00
```

Fig. 8.31. Account summary report.

These reports are generated by the program FRSGLIST. The coding of this program is made much simpler by the use of dBASE III Plus's MODIFY REPORT command to generate the report formats. The FRSGLIST program asks the user what kind of report is desired; the specified report is printed by means of the REPORT FORM command. This method avoids the necessity of writing code to print three different custom reports.

The flowchart for FRSGLIST is shown in figure 8.32 and the code in listing 8.17. The program begins by opening files and restoring the system memory variables. Then FRSGLIST calls the subroutine FRSGORDR, which asks the user for the desired report: transaction order, transactions by account, or summary by account. The code for FRSGORDR is shown in listing 8.18.

The subroutine FRSGORDR displays the screen shown in figure 8.33 and accepts the user's choice. FRSGORDR then verifies the choice and, using the SET ORDER command, sets the appropriate index as the primary index. Then execution returns to FRSGLIST.

After the kind of report has been selected, FRSGLIST displays a second data-entry screen, on which the user can specify the accounting period and a posting code to be printed or a posting code to be excluded (see fig. 8.34). If the user does not specify one of these, the report includes all posting codes. The program prints a report for a specified accounting period unless the accounting period is specified as zero, in which case the report includes all accounting periods.

The purpose of this second screen is to promote flexibility in the printing of general-ledger reports. The general ledger is designed to hold data for more than one period at a time, and the user must have some way of specifying the accounting period. On the other hand, sometimes it is necessary to get a listing of all the transactions in the ledger.

The second screen also allows the user to specify a posting code to be printed or excluded. Many times the user will want to list all transactions regardless of posting code. Other times, the user will want to exclude a posting code from the list. For example, the user may want to exclude closing transactions to get a general journal listing before closing entries. Or the user may want to print just the transactions with a certain posting code, such as cash-receipts entries posted automatically from the cash receipts system. If an accounting period or posting code is specified, the SET FILTER command is used to select the records from the file that meet these criteria.

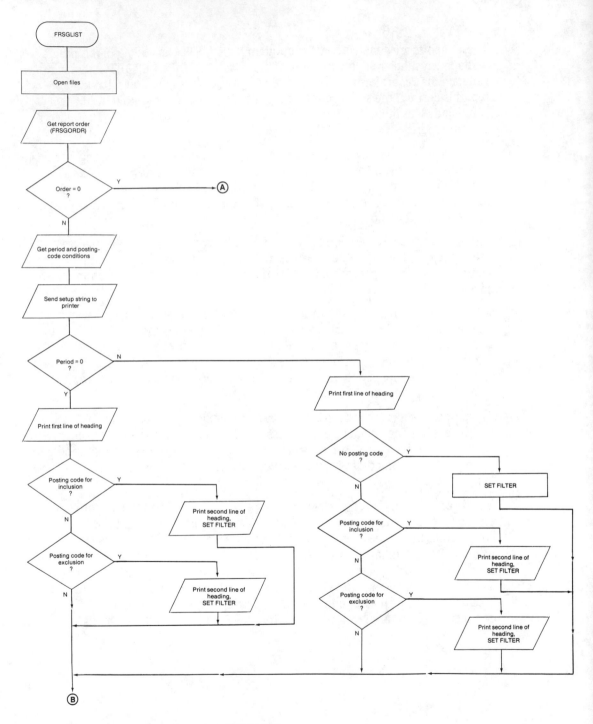

Fig. 8.32. Flowchart of the subroutine FRSGLIST.

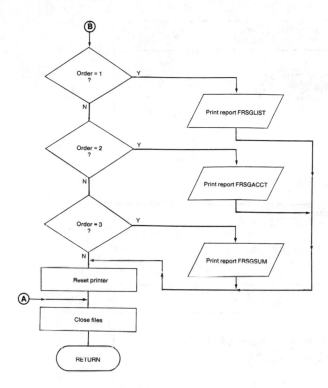

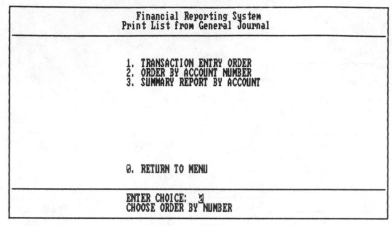

Fig. 8.33. Screen for selection of the report type.

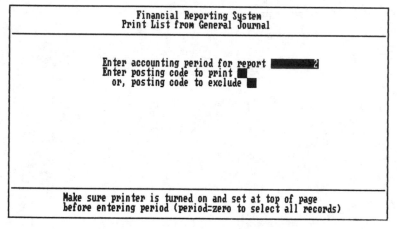

Fig. 8.34. Screen for selection of the accounting period and posting code.

After the user has specified the report, the period, and the posting codes, the report is printed. The program prints a heading and a date at the top of each report. Notice in listing 8.17 that the system memory variable FRSPMARGIN is passed as an argument to the SPACE function, so that the heading and date are aligned with the left margin of the report. When you set up the reports with MODIFY REPORT, be sure to use the same left margin as set in the system memory file.

Figures 8.35, 8.36, and 8.37 show the report definitions entered with MODIFY REPORT for each of the three types of general ledger report. The three reports are named FRSGLIST.FRM, FRSGACCT.FRM, and FRSGSUM.FRM. (The use of the MODIFY REPORT command is discussed in Chapter 3.)

```
Report definitions for report FRSGLIST

Page title:        Smith and Jones Corporation
                   Financial Reporting System
                   General Journal Listing
                   In Transaction Entry Order

Page width:        132
Left margin:         8
```

COL	Contents	Heading	W	Tot
1	transactno	Transaction;Number ;----------- (11 dashes)	11	No
2	date	;Date;--------	8	No
3	period	Accounting;Period ;-----------	11	No
4	accountno	;Account;-------	7	No
5	descript	;Description ;--------------------- --------- (30 dashes)	30	No
6	pc	Post;Code;----	4	No
7	debit	;Debit;-----------	11	Yes
8	credit	;Credit;-----------	11	Yes

Fig. 8.35. Report Definitions for listing in transaction order.

```
Report definitions for report FRSGACCT

Page title:        Smith and Jones Company
                   Financial Reporting System
                   General Journal Listing
                   By Account

Page width:            132
Left margin:             8
Group on expression:   accountno
Group heading:         Transactions for Account:
```

COL	Contents	Heading	W	Tot
1	transactno	Transaction;Number ;----------- (11 dashes)	11	No
2	period	Acctg;Period;------	6	No
3	date	;Date;--------	8	No
4	descript	;Description ;--------------------- --------- (30 dashes)	30	No
5	pc	Posting;Code;-------	7	No
6	debit	;Debit;-----------	11	Yes
7	credit	;Credit;-----------	11	Yes

Fig. 8.36. Report Definitions for listing by account.

```
Report definitions for report FRSGSUM

Page title:      Smith and Jones Company
                 Financial Reporting System
                 General Journal Listing
                 Summary by Account

Page width:          132
Left margin:           8

Group on expression:  accountno
Group heading:        Account
Summary report only:  Yes

COL      Contents                    Heading              W  Tot
---  --------------------  ------------------------------ -- ---
 1   debit                 ;Debit;-----------             41 Yes

 2   credit                Total;Credits                  11 Yes
                           ;----------- (11 dashes)

 3   debit-credit          Debit;Balance;                 11 Yes
                           ;----------- (11 dashes)
```

Fig. 8.37. Report Definitions for account summary report.

Closing the General Ledger

We have now developed programs to enter data into the general ledger and to print general-ledger reports by transaction or by account. Next we turn to the program that closes out the general ledger for the accounting period and posts the transaction totals to the appropriate accounts in the financial-reporting ledger. The general ledger is closed when all the regular and closing entries for the accounting period have been entered and it is time to prepare financial statements.

The General Ledger Close Program (FRSGCLOS)

The general-ledger close program, FRSGCLOS, is the connection between the general ledger, which contains business transactions for the current period, and the financial-reporting ledger, which contains actual, budget, and last year's account balances for each account. The functions of FRSGCLOS are

- summing the transaction amounts for the current period by account

- adding an account's current-period total to the previous-period balance to get the current-period balance into the financial reporting ledger file

- summing the revenue- and expense-account balances and using them to update the retained earnings account

- deleting the transactions that were posted to the financial-reporting ledger and updating the system memory variables for the last closed period, the current period, and the date the close program was last run

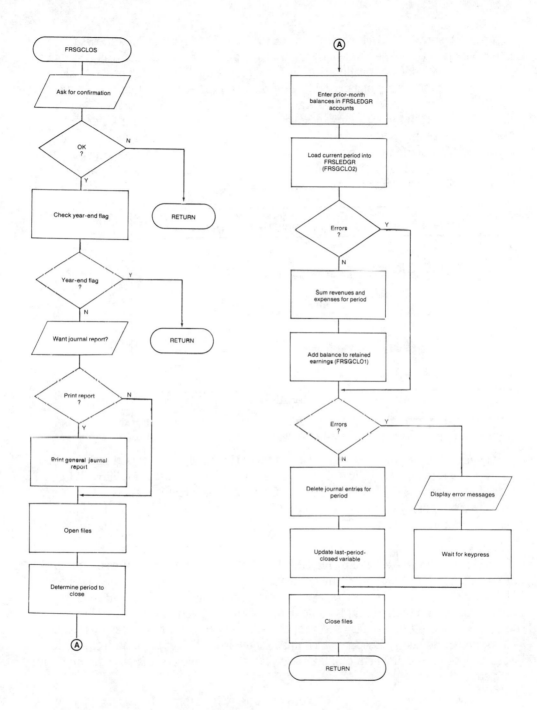

Fig. 8.38. Flowchart of the FRSGCLOS program.

Figure 8.38 shows a flowchart for the program FRSGCLOS; listing 8.19 shows the code. The program begins by asking the user to confirm that he or she really wants to use this command. Confirmation is important because the FRSGCLOS program closes the ledger for the accounting period. Figure 8.39 shows the screen that asks the user for confirmation. This screen was designed for Smith and Jones Corporation, but you may want to expand the warning message or even require that the user enter a password to continue with the close program. The screen we've designed for Smith and Jones Corporation directs the user to back up the data files *before* closing out the general ledger. (Section IV of this chapter discusses the utilities for maintaining the system, including a program for backing up data files.)

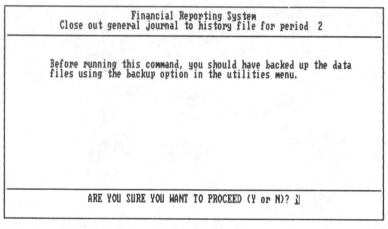

```
                    Financial Reporting System
          Close out general journal to history file for period  2


        Before running this command, you should have backed up the data
        files using the backup option in the utilities menu.












          ARE YOU SURE YOU WANT TO PROCEED (Y or N)? N
```

Fig. 8.39. User confirmation screen displayed by the FRSGCLOS program.

If the user confirms that he or she wants wants to proceed, the program asks whether the user wants a general-ledger listing before the closing is done. If so, FRSGCLOS calls the program FRSGLIST, which was discussed in the previous section. The user selects the report type and the accounting period; then FRSGLIST prints the report, and execution returns to FRSGCLOS.

Next, FRSGCLOS opens the system data files and restores the system memory variables (which are released by FRSGLIST). Then the program computes the period to be closed and defines the name of the current-month field for this period in the ledger file. The field name is stored in the memory variable FIELD1. Similarly, the name of the prior-period field is computed and stored in variable FIELD2. Then FRSGCLOS uses these variables to copy the account balances for the previous period into the period being closed, for each financial-reporting ledger account. If the period being closed is the first period of the fiscal year, the revenue and expense accounts are set equal to zero.

The copying is done with either one or two REPLACE commands, depending on whether or not the first period is being closed. If the first period is being closed, the prior-year balances are brought forward for the balance-sheet accounts, and the revenue and expense accounts are made equal to zero. If any other period is being closed, the previous balances are brought forward for all the accounts in the ledger. The field names are selected by using the *&* (macro substitution) operator to access the contents of memory variables FIELD1 and FIELD2, which contain the appropriate field names.

Next, the subroutine FRSGCLO2 is called. That subroutine sums the general-ledger transactions by account and posts the sum to the corresponding account and period in the financial-reporting ledger.

FRSGCLOS then uses the SUM function to sum the revenues and expenses for the month. The SUM function is applied to the financial-reporting ledger instead of the general-ledger file because there are generally far fewer records in the financial-reporting ledger. Working with the financial-reporting ledger therefore is generally faster. To calculate revenues less expenses for the current period, FRSGCLOS totals the current-period balance less the previous-period balance for each revenue and expense account. FRSGCLOS then calls the subroutine FRSGCLO1, which posts the revenues-less-expenses balance to the retained-earnings account balance.

FRSGCLOS is set up so that if an error occurs at any point in the closing process, the remainder of the process is skipped. An error occurs when an account number that is not in the chart-of-accounts file is entered in the general ledger. A flag records the occurrence of this error; the program checks the error flag before each successive operation.

Because the transactions are not deleted until the end of the closing process, the user can restart the process if an error occurs before the close program finishes and the transactions are deleted. The user merely has to restart the FRSCLOS program.

Finally, all records for the period just closed are deleted, and the general-ledger file is packed. The current period, the last period closed, and the date of the last close are updated and saved to the system memory file. If the period just closed is the final accounting period, then FRSYREND is set to the value .T. The program closes the databases, and returns.

Subroutines Used by the General Ledger Close Program

The close program uses the familiar FRSOPEN and BORDERS subroutines, plus two subroutines that perform parts of the posting: FRSGCLO1 and FRSGCLO2.

The subroutine FRSGCLO1 updates the corresponding financial-reporting ledger account and period with the general-ledger balance. This subroutine creates a new financial-reporting ledger account if the corresponding account does not exist in the financial-reporting ledger but is found in the chart-of-accounts file. The flowchart of FRSGCLO1 is shown in figure 8.40; the code is shown in listing 8.20.

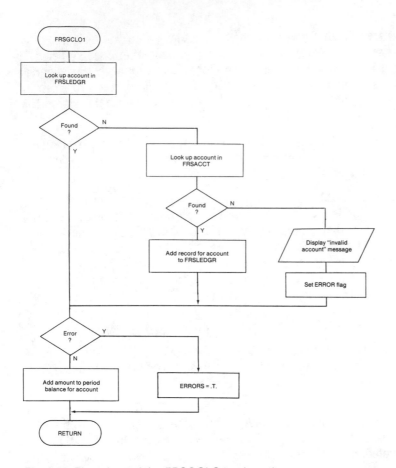

Fig. 8.40. Flowchart of the FRSGCLO1 subroutine.

When execution transfers to FRSGCLO1, the desired account number and the balance to be posted are stored in the memory variables MACCT and BALANCE. The subroutine has one parameter, ERRORS, which serves as an error flag. FRSGCLO1 begins by seeking in the financial-reporting ledger a record with the specified account number. If the record is found, the subroutine adds the balance to the specified period in the ledger account. Otherwise, the subroutine checks whether the account number exists in the chart-of-accounts file. If the number is not found in the chart-of-accounts file, an error message is displayed and the error flag is set. But if the account number is found in the chart-of-accounts file, a new ledger account is created and the subroutine adds the balance to the specified period. The field to be updated is specified by using the & (macro substitution) operator to access the contents of the memory variable FIELD1. (FIELD1 contains the field name of the actual field for the period being closed in the financial reporting ledger.)

The subroutine FRSGCLO2 accumulates the transactions in the general ledger by account and posts the balance for each account to the corresponding financial-reporting ledger account. The flowchart for the subroutine is shown in figure 8.41. Program code is shown in listing 8.21.

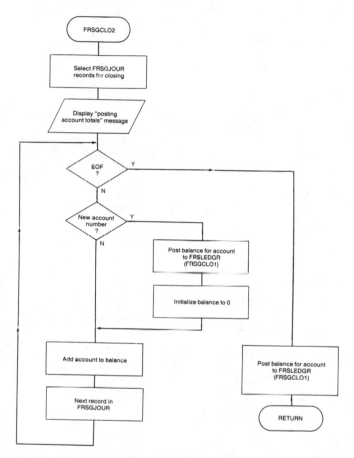

Fig. 8.41. Flowchart of the FRSGCLO2 subroutine.

When the subroutine begins, it selects the general-ledger file, which is indexed by account number and filtered to include only the transactions for the closing period. The main body of the subroutine is a loop that is executed once for each transaction in the filtered file.

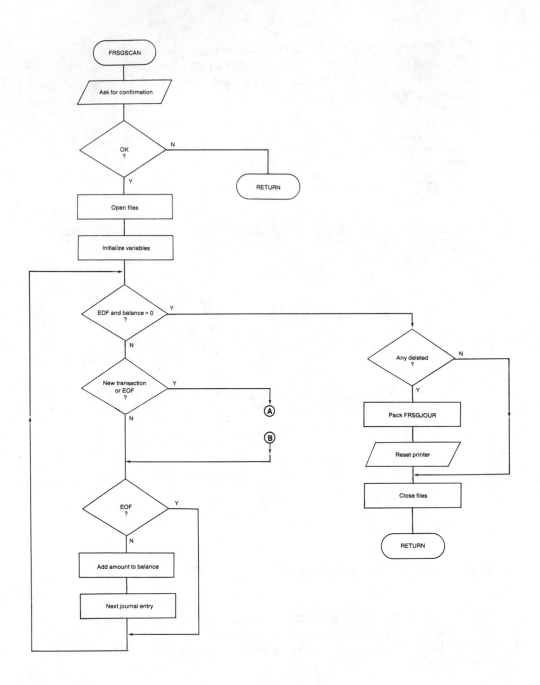

Fig. 8.42. Flowchart of the FRSGSCAN program (part 1).

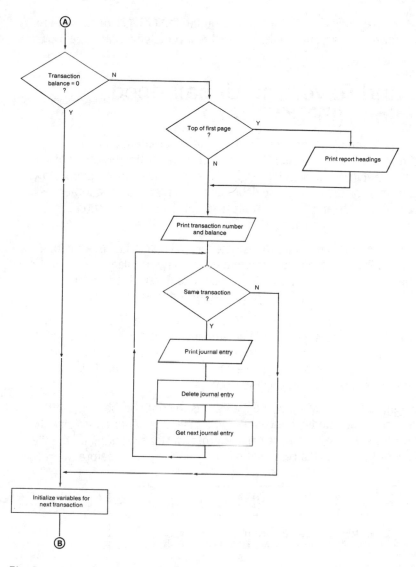

Fig. 8.42. Flowchart of the FRSGSCAN program (part 2).

Within the loop, the subroutine first checks for an account break, which occurs when the current transaction is for a different account than the previous. If a break has occurred, the subroutine calls FRSGCLO1 to post the balance, and resets the balance to zero for the new account. The remainder of the loop adds the debit balance for the current transaction to the account balance (the debit balance is the debit amount minus the credit amount), and skips to the next record.

After the loop is exited, FRSGCLO2 calls the subroutine FRSGCLO1 once more to post the balance for the last account to the financial-reporting ledger file. The program then ends.

Finding and Reversing Unbalanced Transactions (FRSGSCAN)

In developing an accounting system, you must pay particular attention to any problems that might arise. In this system, we must provide for the possibility of an unbalanced transaction in the general ledger. Because the data-entry program allows the user to enter only transactions whose debits and credits are equal, another program is needed to fix the general ledger file if an unbalanced transaction is somehow recorded in the general ledger.

The simplest approach is for a program to scan the general-ledger file looking for unbalanced transactions. The program prints and deletes any unbalanced transactions that it finds. The user can then examine the hard copy to determine the correct transactions and use the data-entry program to reenter those transactions.

Figure 8.42 shows a flowchart for the FRSGCAN program. Listing 8.22 shows the program code. FRSGCAN scans, prints, and deletes any unbalanced transactions that it finds. This program can take some time to run because it must index the general ledger by transaction before it can scan the file, and it must PACK the file if any unbalanced transactions are found during the scan.

The program begins by asking whether the user wants to continue (see fig. 8.43). Because this command can modify the general-ledger file, it is important to give the user a chance to cancel the command before the program starts working on the file. This screen gives the user the chance to quit or to set up the printer before the report starts.

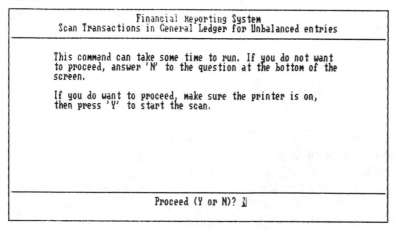

Fig. 8.43. Initial screen displayed by FRSGSCAN.

The program uses a loop to scan the file for unbalanced transactions. If the current record is for a new transaction, the program first checks whether the transaction sum for the last transaction was in balance. If the transaction sum for the previous transaction was not in balance, the program backs up the file to the first record for that transaction, then prints and deletes each record for the unbalanced transaction. Figure 8.44 shows a printed list of unbalanced transactions for Smith and Jones Corporation on June 17, 1986. Finally, the program resets the transaction counters for the next transaction.

```
LISTING OF UNBALANCED TRANSACTIONS FOUND ON 08/14/86


Transaction    29 Has a balance of     -1.00
  100.0      2  02/15/86  Cash on Hand            CR     185.00       0.00    *DELETED*
  500.0      2  02/15/86  Purchases               CR      25.00       0.00    *DELETED*
  700.0      2  02/15/86  Miscellaneous           CR       9.00       0.00    *DELETED*
  400.0      2  02/15/86  Sales                   CR       0.00     205.00    *DELETED*
  220.0      2  02/15/86  Sales Tax               CR       0.00      15.00    *DELETED*



*** FRSGJOUR FILE PACKED ***
```

Fig. 8.44. Printout of unbalanced transactions found and deleted from the general ledger.

The next step is to add the debit minus the credit to the transaction sum, and SKIP to the next record. Then execution returns to the top of the loop; the process is repeated until end-of-file is reached.

Then the program checks to see whether the transaction sum for the last transaction is zero. If the transaction sum is zero, the loop ends. But if the sum is not zero, the program makes one more pass through the loop to print and delete the last unbalanced transaction.

After the scanning loop is completed, the program checks a flag to see whether any unbalanced transactions were deleted. If so, the program packs the general-ledger file to permanently remove the deleted transactions. The program then resets the printer, closes the databases, and returns.

Section IV: The Financial Reporting Ledger, System Utilities, and Extensions to the System

In Section II, we looked at the development of programs for maintaining and managing Smith and Jones Corporation's data files and the chart of accounts. Section III focused on the programs, subroutines, and data-entry screens that enable Jim Jones to put the general ledger to full use. In Section IV, we look at the functions of the financial-reporting ledger. Those functions include entering budget data and last year's data from the keyboard, creating various financial statements, and closing the year. We then consider two important system-maintenance utilities, which support backing up and restoring the data files. Finally, we look briefly at the main menu and submenus that make this accounting system easy to use.

The Financial Reporting System

You'll recall that the financial-reporting ledger is used to record year-to-date account balances at the end of each accounting period. The actual data is recorded automatically in the financial reporting ledger when the general ledger is closed; the actual data from the general ledger is added to the account balances at the beginning of the accounting period to obtain the year-to-date actual balances at the end of each accounting period. The user enters budget data directly from the keyboard or imports this data from another software program. (See the section "Importing Budget Data.") A year-end closing program saves the current-year actual data as last year's actual data.

One of the most important functions of the financial-reporting system developed for Smith and Jones Corporation is to provide Jim Jones with three standard financial statements: a balance sheet, an income statement, and a flow-of-funds statement. These financial statements compare the financial results for the current period with the budget or with last year's results. Jim Jones can see at a glance the relationship between current and planned results, or current results and last year's.

Entering Budget or Last Year's Data from the Keyboard (FRSLDATA)

The first step in the development of the financial-reporting system is the program to enter data into the financial-reporting ledger. This program is used to enter the ledger data when the system is first installed and to make later entries or changes to the budget.

The program discussed here gives the user free access to all the financial-reporting ledger data. After the initial setup, however, the user should not normally be allowed to change last year's data or data for closed accounting periods. You may want therefore to create two versions of this program: one that works only on the budget data, and a second version that works on all data but whose use is restricted either by a password or by removal from the system when not needed. This will prevent the user from inadvertently changing actual or last year's data instead of budget data.

The purpose of this program is to allow the user to enter budget data and actual or last year's data for an entire year. The program must be able to accept data in three ways.

First, the program must accept direct entry of each period amount or of the account balance for each period. If the account is a revenue or expense account, the user will probably want to enter data as period amounts. If the account is a balance-sheet account, the user will probably want to enter the account balances at the end of each period. Figure 8.45 shows entry of period data for the Sales account at Smith and Jones Corporation. Figure 8.46 shows entry of end-of-period balances for the cash account.

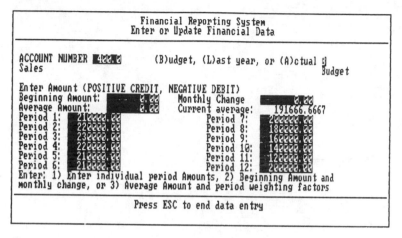

Fig. 8.45. Data-entry screen for direct entry of SALES data.

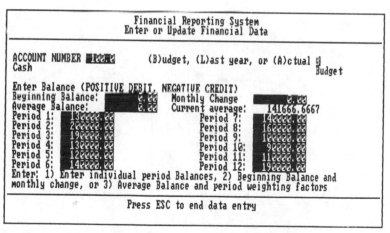

Fig. 8.46. Data-entry screen for direct entry of CASH data.

A second desired type of budget-data entry is the entry of a beginning balance or amount and a growth rate. The third and final type is entry of an average amount or balance and of period-weighting factors. This type of data entry is particularly useful for adjusting existing data up or down by a percentage.

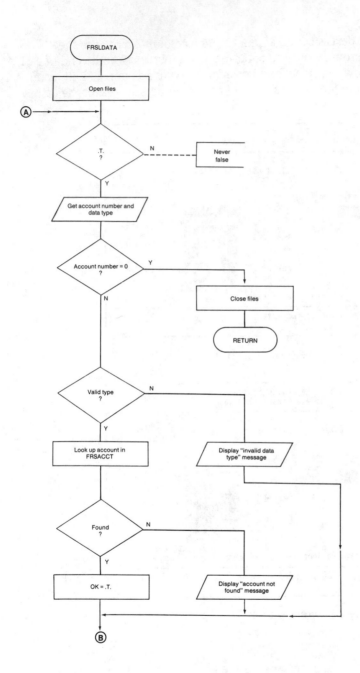

Fig. 8.47. Flowchart of the program FRSLDATA (part 1).

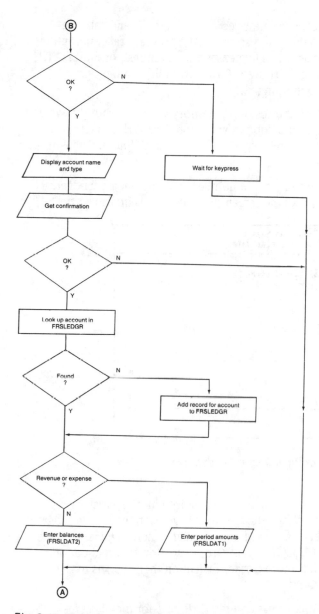

Fig. 8.47. Flowchart of the program FRSLDATA (part 2).

Let's turn now to a consideration of the program code. The keyboard entry program handles the three types of data entry described previously. The main program, FRSLDATA, gets the account number and type of the data to be entered or updated, validates the account and type, appends a new record if necessary, and calls the appropriate subroutine to accept data for the account. The program calls subroutine FRSLDAT1 for income-statement accounts (expenses and revenues), or FRSLDAT2 for balance-sheet accounts. Figure 8.47 shows a flowchart of the main program FRSLDATA; the code is presented in listing 8.23.

The program begins by opening files and restoring memory variables from the system memory file. Next the program enters a "do forever" loop (DO WHILE .T.), in which data is accepted from the user. The loop is repeated once for each line of data entered by the user.

The first step in data entry is to get the account number and type of data (budget, actual, or last-year). Figure 8.48 shows the screen that accepts this information.

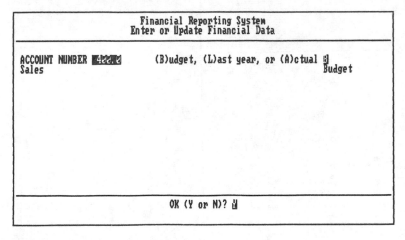

Fig. 8.48. Data-entry screen for account number and data type.

The user's entries of the account number and type are stored in two variables, MACCT and MTYPE, respectively. When these entries have been made, the program checks for an account number of zero. An account number of zero signifies that the user wishes to quit data entry. If MACCT equals zero, execution transfers out of the DO WHILE .T. loop, and the data files are closed. Execution then returns to the calling program.

Next, the program verifies that the user has entered *A*, *B*, or *L* for the data type (Actual, Budget, or Last-year), and verifies that the account number exists in the chart-of-accounts file, FRSACCT. If the account number is not found or if the user has not chosen a valid data type, then the program displays an error message, pauses until the user presses a key, and returns to the top of the loop. If the account number is found and the data type is valid, the program displays the account name and data type, then prompts the user to verify that information.

Such verifications have been incorporated into the programs to assure Jim Jones that his accounting data will be protected as much as possible from user error. Whenever it is possible to check the user's entries, the accounting programs do so.

The program then looks up the account in the financial-reporting ledger file. If FRSLEDGR does not have a record for this account, the program appends a blank record and fills in its account number and status flags. The three status flags—AFLAG, BFLAG, and LFLAG—are initially set to .F. to indicate that there is no actual, budget, or last-year data for this account.

The program then determines the account type, which is stored in the TYPE field of the chart-of-accounts file, and calls the appropriate data-entry subroutine based on the type. If the account type is *RE* or *EX* (REvenues or EXpenses), FRSLDATA calls the subroutine FRSLDAT1, which accepts amounts for each period (see fig. 8.45). If the account type is *AS*, *LI*, or *EQ* (ASsets, LIabilities, or EQuity), the program calls the subroutine FRSLDAT2, which accepts year-to-date balances for each period (see fig. 8.46). After the data-entry subroutine is finished, execution returns to the top of the loop for another pass.

Subroutines Used by the Keyboard Entry Program

The FRSLDATA program uses the usual FRSOPEN and BORDERS subroutines, plus two subroutines for the actual data entry, FRSLDAT1 and FRSLDAT2. FRSLDAT1 and FRSLDAT2 both call subroutine FRSLDAT3, which in turn calls FRSLDAT4.

The subroutines FRSLDAT1 and FRSLDAT2 are designed to set up and save the user's data entries for the account. The account data is stored in the ledger as debit balances. This format is convenient for manipulation by the computer, but it is not the easiest format for users to enter data into the ledger. FRSLDAT1 and FRSLDAT2 allow the user to enter data in a more familiar format.

A Subroutine for Entering Period Amounts (FRSLDAT1)

The subroutine FRSLDAT1 converts to monthly amounts the debit balances that the user normally thinks about as monthly amounts, like Revenues and Expenses. The subroutine translates the data currently in the ledger to monthly amounts, using the account type (as indicated in the chart-of-accounts file) to determine the sign of the data. Then FRSLDAT1 calls FRSLDAT3, which accepts the data entry for the account. After execution returns from FRSLDAT3, FRSLDAT1 converts the monthly amounts back to debit balances and stores them in the ledger.

With FRSLDAT1, the user enters the following string of monthly amounts for sales data:

    10000, 10000, 10000, 10000, . . . , 10000

Without FRSLDAT1, the user would instead enter balances:

−10000, −20000, −30000, −40000, . . . , −120000

The subroutine performs the task of adding monthly amounts to previous balances, enabling the user to enter the data in a more natural format. Figure 8.49 shows a flowchart of the subroutine FRSLDAT1. The program code is shown in listing 8.24.

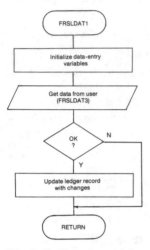

Fig. 8.49. Flowchart of the subroutine FRSLDAT1.

The code of the subroutine FRSLDAT1 is particularly obscure because of the heavy use of dBASE's macro-substitution operator (&). The subroutine first uses an IIF statement to determine the sign of the stored account balances (+ for debit accounts such as expenses, and − for credit accounts such as revenues). The sign is stored in the memory variable SIGN.

The subroutine then initializes the 12 memory variables (I1 through I12) that will be used for data entry in subroutine FRSLDAT3. The variables are initialized by formulas that use the macro substitutions of the SIGN variable and of the FIELD parameter, which is passed to the subroutine from FRSLDATA. For example, the memory variable I2 is defined by the expression

I2=LSIGN.(&FIELD.2−&FIELD.1)

Suppose that SIGN contains the value + and FIELD contains *A*. Then dBASE expands the macro expression

&SIGN.

into the value + and expands the macro expression

&FIELD.

into the value *A*. Next, dBASE evaluates the resulting expression, which is

I2=+(A2−A1)

After initializing the variables, the subroutine calls FRSLDAT3 to get the user's input. If this subroutine returns with the OK flag set to .T., the FRSLDAT1 subroutine replaces the year-to-date data in the ledger from the user's input. The macro-substitution operator is used to define both the field whose value is to be replaced and the sign of the data in the file (debit balance).

For example, if sign contains + and FIELD contains *A*, then dBASE expands the macros &FIELD. and &SIGN. in the expression:

&FIELD.1 with &SIGN.I1

into the expression *A1 with +I1*.

A Subroutine for Entering Period Balances (FRSLDAT2)

The subroutine FRSLDAT2 converts data that the user normally thinks of as account balances, such as assets, liabilities, and equity accounts, from and back to positive account balances in debit or credit accounts. The subroutine translates the debit balances in the financial-reporting ledger to either debit or credit balances, depending on the account type. Then the subroutine calls FRSLDAT3 to perform the actual data entry for the account. After FRSLDAT3 is completed, the subroutine converts the entered data back to debit balances in the ledger. Figure 8.50 shows a flowchart of the FRSLDAT2 subroutine. The program code is presented in listing 8.25.

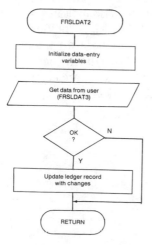

Fig. 8.50. Flowchart of the FRSLDAT2 subroutine.

FRSLDAT2 enables the user to enter balances as positive numbers, no matter whether the account is a debit or a credit account. For example, accounts payable is a credit account, so the balance carried in the financial-reporting ledger is negative. If the accounts-payable balance is $10,000 in each month, the financial-reporting ledger will contain this data:

   −10000, −10000, −10000, −10000, . . . , −10000

The FRSLDAT2 program translates these balances into positive numbers for the user. With FRSLDAT2, the user will see the accounts payable balances as follows:

   10000, 10000, 10000, 10000, . . . , 10000

FRSLDAT2 uses macro substitution to accomplish the translation from and back to debit balances, in a manner similar to FRSLDAT1.

A Versatile Data-Entry Subroutine (FRSLDAT3)

The subroutine FRSLDAT3 performs the data-entry task, allowing the user to enter data in any of the three ways discussed at the beginning of this section: direct entry, a beginning amount and a growth rate, or an average and period-weighting factors. Figure 8.51 shows a flowchart for the subroutine. Listing 8.26 presents the program code.

After initializing variables, FRSLDAT3 enters the main data-processing loop. This loop is executed once unless there are errors or the user does not accept the data that has been entered. In such a case, the loop is executed again.

First, the data-entry screen is displayed with the current data from the ledger, and the user enters the changes. Figure 8.52 shows an example of this data-entry screen from Smith and Jones Corporation's application. The screen displays the account (Sales) for which data is being entered and type of data (Budget). The screen also indicates whether amounts or balances are being entered, and whether the user is entering positive debits or positive credits. In the example from Smith and Jones Corporation, the user has entered period amounts and positive credits, as is shown by the line **Enter Balance (POSITIVE DEBIT, NEGATIVE CREDIT)**. If the user were entering amounts, the line would say **Enter Amount (POSITIVE DEBIT, NEGATIVE CREDIT)**.

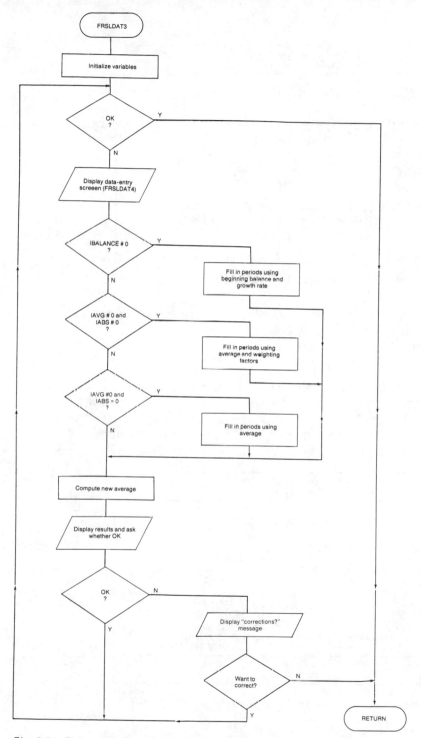

Fig. 8.51. Flowchart of the FRSLDAT3 subroutine.

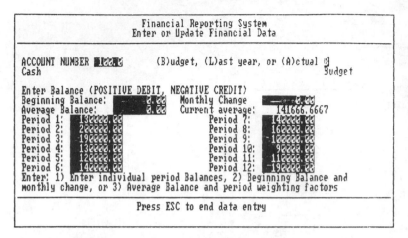

Fig. 8.52. Data-entry screen displayed by FRSLDAT3.

The data-entry portion of the screen includes a beginning amount (or balance), a growth rate (monthly change), an average amount (or balance), and 12 accounting-period amounts or balances. Depending on the type of data entry, the user fills in the appropriate portions of the screen.

For direct entry of data by accounting period, the user enters the period amounts and leaves empty the beginning amount, the monthly change, and the average amount (see fig. 8.52). To enter data as a beginning amount and monthly change, the user fills in the beginning-amount and monthly-change fields. From those entries, FRSLDAT3 calculates the monthly-amount data. An example is shown in figure 8.53.

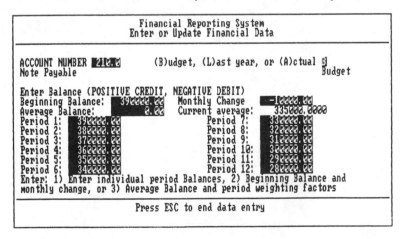

Fig. 8.53. Initial amount and monthly change screen.

To enter an average amount and weighting factors, the user leaves the beginning-amount and monthly-change fields blank, but fills in the average amount and individual periods. This data-entry capability is particularly useful for adjusting the data currently in the ledger by a percentage factor: the user just calculates what the new average is after the percentage adjustment and enters that value in the average field. Then FRSLDAT3 uses the current period amounts as the weighting factors and adjusts the data for each period in accordance with the new average. Figures 8.54 and 8.55 show the adjustment of the cash budget to obtain an average balance of $150,000.

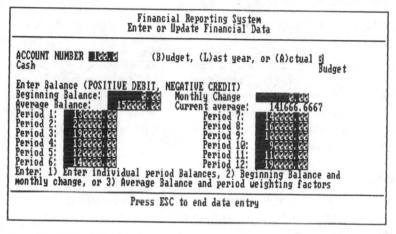

Fig. 8.54. Adjusting the existing amounts by changing the average amount.

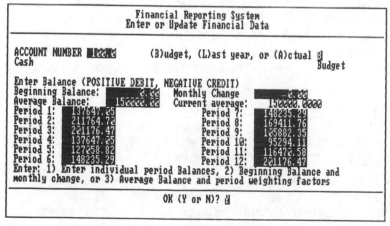

Fig. 8.55. Results of the cash budget adjustment.

After the user has entered changes in the data-entry screen, the subroutine checks for beginning-amount and average-amount entries. If a beginning amount has been entered, FRSLDAT3 calculates the monthly amounts from the beginning amount and monthly change.

If a beginning amount has not been entered but an average has, the program adjusts the period amounts so that they are consistent with the average. If the period amounts are all zero, the average is entered in each period. If the sum of the period amounts is negative, the period amounts are adjusted so that the absolute values of the period amounts are consistent with the average.

If neither a beginning amount nor an average has been entered, the period values are left as entered.

Finally, FRSLDAT3 redisplays the screen with the adjusted values and asks the user if the data is acceptable. If the user presses *Y*, execution transfers out of the main loop and returns to the calling program. But if the user presses *N*, he or she is asked whether corrections are desired. If so, execution transfers to the top of the loop. If the user does not want to make corrections, the subroutine sets an error flag, and execution returns to the calling program.

A Subroutine for Displaying the Data-Entry Screen (FRSLDAT4)

The final subroutine is FRSLDAT4. This subroutine, which is called by FRSLDAT3, consists of a series of @ SAY . . . GET commands that display the data-entry screen. The code is shown in listing 8.27.

Creating Comparative Financial Statements

Having looked at the programs and screens that allow the user to enter and update data in the financial ledger, we turn now to the programs that prepare the comparative financial statements. You'll recall that the purpose of the financial-reporting system is to prepare three standard financial statements: the balance sheet, the income statement, and the flow-of-funds statement. Jim Jones can use these comparative financial statements to assess Smith and Jones Corporation's performance over time.

The balance sheet presents the company's financial position at the end of an accounting period. It shows the company's assets balanced against the amounts it owes (liabilities) and the financial interest of the owners or stockholders (equity). The balance sheet presents the account balances from the ledger.

Figure 8.56 shows a balance sheet generated for Smith and Jones Corporation by the program presented here. There are several possible comparisons that can be presented with the current-period balances. The report in figure 8.56 shows the actual and budget balances for the current period, the balance at the beginning of the year, the difference between the current period and budget, and the difference between the current period and the beginning of the year.

Report Date: 08/16/86

Smith and Jones Inc.
Financial Reporting System
Balance Sheet as of 01/31/86

| | ---- Current Period ---- | | Beginning | ---- Actual Versus ---- | |
	Actual	Budget	of Year	Budget	Beg of Year
Assets					
Cash	108000.00	130000.00	100000.00	-22000.00	8000.00
Accounts Receivable	85000.00	72330.00	50000.00	12670.00	35000.00
Inventory	500000.00	500000.00	600000.00	0.00	-100000.00
Prepaid Expenses	30000.00	30000.00	30000.00	0.00	0.00
Fixed Assets	311500.00	300000.00	300000.00	11500.00	11500.00
Accumulated Depreciation	-108330.00	-108333.30	-100000.00	3.30	-8330.00
Other Assets	20000.00	20000.00	20000.00	0.00	0.00
Total Assets	946170.00	943996.70	1000000.00	2173.30	53830.00
Liabilities					
Accounts Payable	81500.00	81000.00	100000.00	500.00	-18500.00
Note Payable	390000.00	390000.00	400000.00	0.00	-10000.00
Deferred Taxes	60000.00	60000.00	100000.00	0.00	-40000.00
Other Liabilities	50000.00	51000.00	50000.00	-1000.00	0.00
Total Liabilities	581500.00	582000.00	650000.00	-500.00	-68500.00
Equity					
Contributed Capital	200000.00	200000.00	200000.00	0.00	0.00
Retained Earnings	164670.00	162000.00	150000.00	2670.00	14670.00
Total Equity	364670.00	362000.00	350000.00	2670.00	14670.00
Total Liabilities and Equity	946170.00	944000.00	1000000.00	2170.00	-53830.00

Fig. 8.56. Comparative balance sheet.

An income statement presents a firm's revenues and expenses for the period. The entries in the income statement are the changes in account balances between the beginning and the end of the current period (period revenues and expenses), or between the beginning of the year and the end of the current period (year-to- date revenues and expenses). Figure 8.57 shows an income statement for Smith and Jones Corporation. This report shows the current period next to the budget and the corresponding period last year, both on a current period and a year-to-date basis.

The flow-of-funds statement presents the change in the amount of cash employed in the business, showing where the cash came from and where it has been used. The report is broken down into two sections: Sources of Funds and Uses of Funds. Figure 8.58 shows a flow-of-funds statement for the Smith and Jones Corporation for the month ending January 31, 1986. The statement was produced by the programs subsequently discussed in this section.

Report Date: 08/16/86

Smith and Jones Inc.
Financial Reporting System
Income Statement for Month Ending 01/31/86

	----- Current Period -----			----- Year to Date -----		
	Actual	Budget	Last Year	Actual	Budget	Last Year

Revenues

Sales	220000.00	210000.00	0.00	220000.00	210000.00	0.00
Total Revenues	220000.00	210000.00	0.00	220000.00	210000.00	0.00

Expenses

Cost of Sales	100000.00	100000.00	0.00	100000.00	100000.00	0.00
General Expenses	12000.00	13000.00	0.00	12000.00	13000.00	0.00
Wage Expense	60000.00	60000.00	0.00	60000.00	60000.00	0.00
Tax Expense - Except Income	10000.00	10000.00	0.00	10000.00	10000.00	0.00
Depreciation Expense	8330.00	8333.30	0.00	8330.00	8333.30	0.00
General Overhead	5000.00	5000.00	0.00	5000.00	5000.00	0.00
Income Tax Expense	10000.00	10000.00	0.00	10000.00	10000.00	0.00
Total Expenses	205330.00	206333.30	0.00	205330.00	206333.30	0.00
Net Margin	14670.00	3666.70	0.00	14670.00	3666.70	0.00

Fig. 8.57. Income statement.

Report Date: 08/16/86

Smith and Jones Inc.
Financial Reporting System
Flow of Funds Statement for Month Ending 01/31/86

	----- Current Period -----			----- Year to Date -----		
	Actual	Budget	Last Year	Actual	Budget	Last Year

Sources of Funds

Accumulated Depreciation	8330.00	8333.30	-100000.00	8330.00	8333.30	-100000.00
Accounts Payable	-18500.00	-19000.00	-100000.00	-18500.00	-19000.00	-100000.00
Note Payable	-10000.00	-10000.00	-400000.00	-10000.00	-10000.00	-400000.00
Deferred Taxes	-40000.00	-40000.00	-100000.00	-40000.00	-40000.00	-100000.00
Other Liabilities	0.00	1000.00	-50000.00	0.00	1000.00	-50000.00
Contributed Capital	0.00	0.00	-200000.00	0.00	0.00	-200000.00
Retained Earnings	14670.00	12000.00	-150000.00	14670.00	12000.00	-150000.00
Total Sources of Funds	-45500.00	-47666.70	-1100000.00	-45500.00	-47666.70	-1100000.00

Uses of Funds

Cash	8000.00	30000.00	-100000.00	8000.00	30000.00	-100000.00
Accounts Receivable	35000.00	22330.00	-50000.00	35000.00	22330.00	-50000.00
Inventory	-100000.00	-100000.00	-600000.00	-100000.00	-100000.00	-600000.00
Prepaid Expenses	0.00	0.00	-30000.00	0.00	0.00	-30000.00
Fixed Assets	11500.00	0.00	-300000.00	11500.00	0.00	-300000.00
Other Assets	0.00	0.00	-20000.00	0.00	0.00	-20000.00
Total Uses of Funds	-45500.00	-47670.00	-1100000.00	-45500.00	-47670.00	-1100000.00

Fig. 8.58. Comparative flow-of-funds statement.

The firm's sources of funds are its creditors and stockholders. The amount each of those sources advances to the firm during the period is measured by the change in the balances of the liability and equity accounts. Consider the accounts-payable account, for example. The balance represents the amount the firm owes to suppliers for items purchased on credit. An increase in this balance during the period represents additional funds loaned to the company by its suppliers. A decrease during the period represents funds paid to the suppliers. Similarly, an increase in the equity accounts represents additional funds that the stockholders have invested in the company or undistributed earnings that the stockholders have chosen to leave invested in the company.

In addition to the changes in the liability and equity accounts, another item must be included to show a true picture of the firm's sources of funds. The equity accounts typically understate the amount of funds contributed by earnings retained in the business, because earnings are calculated net of expenses such as depreciation and goodwill that are not cash-flow items. To properly show the contribution of earnings to the sources of funds, we must add back any depreciation and goodwill expenses.

The firm uses funds to pay for assets. For example, the change in the fixed-assets balance represents the funds spent to acquire new buildings, machinery, or equipment during the period. The accounts-receivable balance represents the funds owed the firm by its customers. The uses-of-funds section shows the changes in the firm's asset accounts, excluding the non-cash accounts such as accumulated depreciation and goodwill that are shown in the sources-of-funds section.

The programs discussed here prepare a comparative flow-of-funds statement for the current-period actual, budget, and last year; and year-to-date actual, budget, and last year. These programs are disussed in the next section.

Programs to Create Comparative Financial Statements

The financial statements are prepared from the financial-reporting ledger by a system of eight programs and subroutines. Figure 8.59 shows a block diagram of the relationships between the eight programs. The main program, FRSREPT, prompts the user for the report(s) desired and accounting period. FRSREPT Then calls FRSBALSH for the balance sheet, FRSINCOM for the income statement, or FRSCASHF for the flow-of-funds statement. These programs, in turn, call the general-purpose report generator FRSRSECT to print individual sections of each report. FRSRSECT calls either FRSBHEAD, FRSIHEAD, or FRSCHEAD to print the appropriate heading for the report being printed.

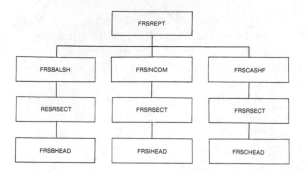

Fig. 8.59. Block diagram of the programs that prepare the financial statements.

The Main Program (FRSREPT)

The program FRSREPT is the main program for the system. It opens the files and presents the user with screens to select the report or reports to be printed and to select the accounting period. The screen for selecting reports is shown in figure 8.60. The second screen, for selecting the accounting period and the ending date for the accounting period, is shown in figure 8.61.

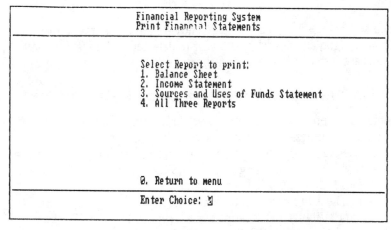

Fig. 8.60. Screen to specify which financial statements to print.

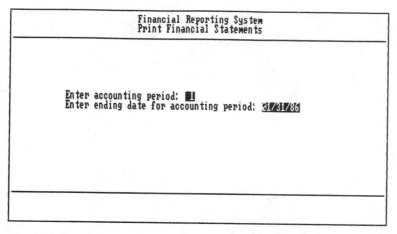

Fig. 8.61. Screen to specify the accounting period and ending date for the report.

After the user has specified the report(s) and accounting period, the program instructs the user to set up the printer; then the program calls the the subroutine that prepares the selected report. The report selection and printing is inside a "do forever" loop that returns to the report-specification screen after the report is printed. The loop is exited by entering a selection of zero at the report-specification screen. Figure 8.62 shows a flowchart of this program; listing 8.28 presents the code.

A Subroutine to Print the Balance Sheet (FRSBALSH)

The subroutine that FRSREPT calls to print the balance sheet is FRSBALSH. This subroutine sets up the report fields and calls FRSRSECT three times to print the assets, liabilities, and equity sections of the balance sheet. FRSBALSH also accumulates the total liabilities and the total equity values, which are returned by the FRSRSECT subroutine. After all three sections of the report are printed, FRSBALSH prints the total liabilities and equity at the end of the report. The flowchart of FRSBALSH is shown in figure 8.63; the program code is shown in listing 8.29.

This subroutine and the other two subroutines that call FRSRSECT employ some programming tricks to accomplish their purposes. The first of these tricks is the report-field definitions stored in memory variables that FRSBALSH passes to FRSRSECT. The second is the REPTHEAD variable, which FRSBALSH uses to pass the name of the balance-sheet header program to FRSRSECT. The third trick is the use of the SET FILTER command to define the balance-sheet report sections that are to be printed by FRSRSECT. The fourth is the use of the variable CREDIT as a logical flag to tell FRSRSECT whether an account is a debit account or a credit account. These tricks are discussed in the paragraphs that follow.

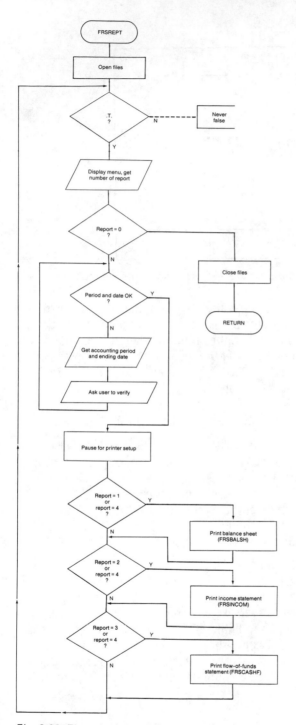

Fig. 8.62. Flowchart of FRSREPT program.

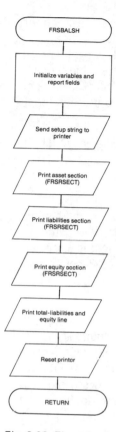

Fig. 8.63. Flowchart of subroutine FRSBALSH.

When I first developed this system, I wrote three completely separate report programs to print the balance-sheet, income-statement, and flow-of-funds reports. The purpose of employing these programming tricks is to allow one common subroutine, FRSRSECT, to print out all three types of reports, which are similar but not identical.

The report-field definitions at the top of the FRSBALSH listing define the fields that FRSRSECT will print for each selected account in the financial-reporting ledger. The field definitions FIELD1 through FIELD6 are character variables containing the names of fields in the FRSLEDGR file or dBASE expressions involving those field names. In FRSBALSH, for example, FIELD1 is defined by

FIELD1="A"+LTRIM(STR(MPER,2))

The memory variable MPER is set in FRSREPT. If MPER equals 1, then the value in the variable FIELD1 is the character string *A1*, which is the name of the field in the FRSLEDGR file containing the actual data for the first period. Similarly, FIELD5 is assigned the character string *A1–L12*, which expresses the difference between the actual data for the first period and last year's data for the 12th period in the FRSLEDGR file. The report fields for the budget report are: actual, budget, last year, actual-budget, and actual-last year. Note that FIELD6 is assigned the value *0* (the character zero, not the value). There are only five fields in the balance-sheet report, but the FRSRSECT program is set up for six fields. The sixth field must therefore be defined in FRSBALSH.

The memory variable REPTHEAD contains the character string *FRSBHEAD*. This is the name of the subroutine that prints the title and headings for the balance-sheet report. The subroutine FRSRSECT uses the variable REPTHEAD to determine the titles and headings to be printed.

FRSBALSH prints the balance sheet in three sections: assets, liabilities, and equity. The subroutine uses the SET FILTER command to select from FRSLEDGR only those account numbers that are in the selected section. This is done by setting a relation between the FRSLEDGR file and the FRSACCT file (done by FRSREPT before calling FRSBALSH), and by setting the filter to those records whose account number is defined to be of the correct type in FRSACCT.

FRSBALSH sets the CREDIT variable before each call to FRSRSECT. Asset accounts are debit accounts, so CREDIT is set to .F. for assets. Liability and equity accounts are credit accounts, so CREDIT is set to .T. for these report sections. FRSRSECT needs to know whether an account has a credit balance, because all balances in the FRSLEDGR file are debit balances, and FRSRSECT would otherwise print credit accounts such as liabilities and equity with negative debit balances. So if CREDIT is set to .T., FRSRSECT changes the sign of the values before printing them.

A Subroutine to Print the Income Statement (FRSINCOM)

The program that FRSREPT calls to print the income statement is FRSINCOM. This subroutine sets up the report fields and calls FRSRSECT twice to print the revenues and expenses sections of the income statement. It also accumulates the total revenues less the total expenses to get the net margin. FRSINCOM prints the net margin at the end of the report. The flowchart for FRSINCOM is shown in figure 8.64, and the program code is provided in listing 8.30.

The fields printed in the income statement are the current-period actual, budget, and last-year values, and the year-to-date values for these items. The three year-to-date fields are just the account balances for the corresponding fields in the FRSLEDGR file. The current-period values, however, are the difference between the account balances at the beginning of the period and at the end of the period. If the report is for the first accounting period, this value is just the account balance. Otherwise, it is the difference between the current-period amount and the last-period amount.

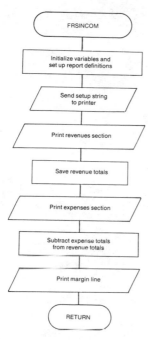

Fig. 8.64. Flowchart of FRSINCOM subroutine.

For example, if MPER is 2, then FIELD1 is defined to be the character string *A2–A1*. If MPER is 1, then FIELD1 is defined to be the character string *A1*. The other two current-period fields are defined similarly. In either case, the three year-to-date field definitions contain the field names in FRSLEDGR for the current accounting period.

The variable REPTHEAD is set to *FRSIHEAD* for the income statement. FRSIHEAD is the name of the program that prints the income-statement title and headings at the top of the page. The variable CREDIT is set to .T. for revenues and .F. for expenses.

A Subroutine to Print the Flow-of-Funds Statement (FRSCASHF)

The program that FRSREPT calls to print the flow-of-funds statement is FRSCASHF. This subroutine sets up the report fields and calls FRSRSECT twice to print the sources-of-funds and the uses-of-funds sections of the report. The flowchart for FRSCASHF is shown in figure 8.65. Listing 8.31 presents the program code.

The fields printed in the flow-of-funds statement are the actual, budget, and last-year funds flows for the current period and for the year to date. The three current-period fields are the differences between the account balances for the current period and the account balances for the previous period. The year-to-date values are the differences between the account balances in the current period and at the end of last year. If the

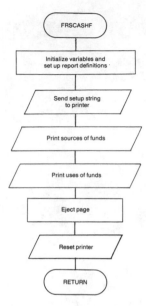

Fig. 8.65. Flowchart of the FRSCASHF subroutine.

report is for the first accounting period, the current-period amount equals the year-to-date amount; the report for Smith and Jones Corporation in figure 8.58 is an example. Otherwise, the current-period amount is the difference between the current-period amount and the last-period amount.

For example, if MPER is 2, then FIELD1 is defined to be the character string *A2–A1*. If MPER is 1, then field 1 is defined to be the character string *A1–L12*. The other two current-period fields are defined similarly. In either case, the year-to-date-actual field definitions (FIELD4–FIELD6) contain character strings defining the report field as the current period less the 12th period of last year.

The variable REPTHEAD is set to *FRSCHEAD* for the flow-of-funds statement. FRSCHEAD is the name of the program that prints the flow-of-funds statement title and headings at the top of the page. The variable CREDIT is set to .T. for sources of funds and .F. for uses of funds.

The filter commands for the flow-of-funds statement are more complex than for the other reports. The filter for the Sources of Funds is set to include liabilities and equity accounts that have the noncash flag in FRSACCT set to .F., plus the asset accounts that have the noncash flag set to .T. The filter for the Uses of Funds is set to include assets that have the noncash flag set to .F., plus any liability or equity accounts that have the noncash flag set to .T.

A Subroutine to Generate the Financial Statements (FRSRSECT)

The FRSRSECT subroutine is a general-purpose report generator used to generate the balance sheet, income statement, and flow-of-funds statement. FRSRSECT prints a line for each account that meets the filter conditions specified in the calling program, and prints a total line when end-of-file is encountered. The calling program specifies the contents of the report fields, the filter condition, the title and heading program called to print the top of a page, and whether the accounts being printed are debit accounts or credit accounts.

The flowchart of FRSRSECT is shown in figure 8.66. Listing 8.32 provides the program code. The subroutine begins by initializing the file and the memory variables that will accumulate the totals. Then execution passes to a loop, which is executed once for every account in the FRSLEDGR file that meets the filter conditions.

In the loop, the subroutine first checks if it is at the top of a new page (ROW=0). If so, the subroutine calls the program passed to it in the memory variable REPTHEAD. The called program will print the appropriate title and heading. The command DO &REPTHEAD calls the subroutine whose name is passed in the memory variable REPTHEAD. This command can be translated as, "DO the subroutine whose name is given by the character string stored in REPTHEAD."

Next, the subroutine calculates the contents of the six report fields using the field definitions set up in the calling program. Again, the subroutine uses the & (macro substitution) operator to use the contents of the variables FIELD1 through FIELD6 in dBASE expressions. If the CREDIT variable is true, the subroutine next changes the signs of the report fields. Finally, the subroutine prints either five or six report fields, depending on the setting of the variable FIELDS. The contents of the report fields are also added to the total variables.

If the report is at the bottom of the page, a page number is printed and the page is ejected. The variable ROW is set to zero so that the top-of-page section will print a new title and heading on the next pass through the loop.

At the bottom of the loop, a SKIP command is used to select the next record, and execution returns to the top of the loop.

When the loop is exited, the subroutine checks to see if the report is at the top of a new page. If so, the titles and headings are printed. Then the subroutine prints the summary total and returns.

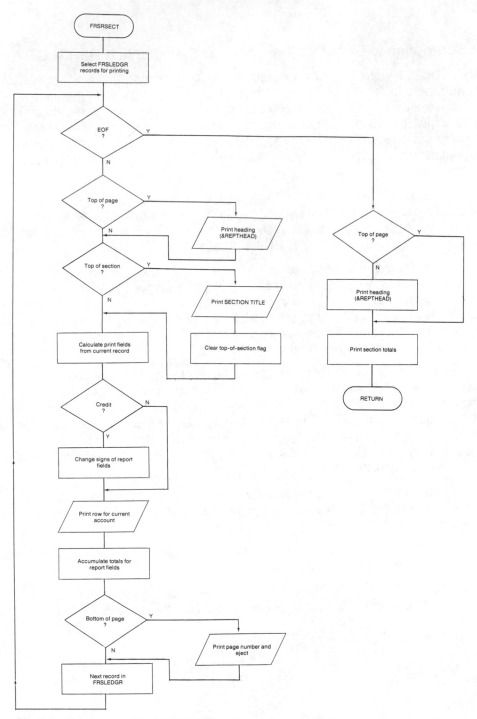

Fig. 8.66. Flowchart of the FRSRSECT subroutine.

Subroutines to Create Financial Report Headings

There are three heading subroutines, one for each financial statement report. The subroutine FRSBHEAD prints the headings for the balance sheet. The subroutine FRSIHEAD prints the headings for the income statement. And the subroutine FRSCHEAD prints the headings for the flow-of-funds statement. Each of these subroutines consists of @ . . . SAY commands, which display the headings, and a final command ROW=12, which sets the correct report row. Listings 8.33, 8.34, and 8.35 provide the program code for these subroutines.

Page No.   1
08/16/86

Smith and Jones Corporation
Financial Reporting System
Budgeted Balance Sheet

Acct Number Name	Period 1	Period 2	Period 3	Period 4	Period 5	Period 6	Period 7	Period 8	Period 9	Period 10	Period 11	Period 12
** ASSETS												
100.0 Cash	130000	200000	190000	130000	120000	140000	140000	160000	100000	90000	110000	190000
110.0 Accounts Receivable	72330	74670	57000	59330	58330	60670	53000	55330	54330	56670	59000	101330
120.0 Inventory	500000	450000	500000	500000	500000	500000	500000	500000	550000	550000	550000	450000
130.0 Prepaid Expenses	30000	30000	30000	30000	30000	30000	30000	30000	30000	30000	30000	30000
140.0 Fixed Assets	300000	300000	300000	300000	333333	333333	333333	333333	366667	366667	366667	366667
141.0 Accumulated Depreciation	-108333	-116667	-125000	-133333	-141666	-150000	-158333	-166666	-175000	-183333	-191666	-200000
190.0 Other Assets	20000	20000	20000	20000	20000	20000	20000	20000	20000	20000	20000	20000
** Subtotal **												
	943997	958003	972000	905997	919997	934004	918000	931997	945997	930004	944000	957997
** LIABILITIES												
200.0 Accounts Payable	-81000	-82000	-83000	-84000	-85000	-86000	-87000	-88000	-89000	-90000	-91000	-92000
210.0 Note Payable	-390000	-380000	-370000	-360000	-350000	-340000	-330000	-320000	-310000	-300000	-290000	-280000
220.0 Deferred Taxes	-60000	-70000	-80000	-10000	-20000	-30000	-10000	-20000	-30000	-10000	-20000	-30000
290.0 Other Liabilities	-51000	-52000	-53000	-54000	-55000	-56000	-57000	-58000	-59000	-60000	-61000	-62000
** Subtotal **												
	-582000	-584000	-586000	-508000	-510000	-512000	-484000	-486000	-488000	-460000	-462000	-464000
** EXPENSES												
500.0 Cost of Sales	100000	200000	300000	400000	500000	600000	700000	800000	900000	1000000	1100000	1200000
600.0 General Expenses	13000	26000	39000	52000	65000	78000	91000	104000	117000	130000	143000	156000
610.0 Wage Expense	60000	120000	180000	240000	300000	360000	420000	480000	540000	600000	660000	720000
620.0 Tax Expense - Except Income	10000	20000	30000	40000	50000	60000	70000	80000	90000	100000	110000	120000
630.0 Depreciation Expense	8333	16667	25000	33333	41666	50000	58333	66666	75000	83333	91666	100000
700.0 General Overhead	5000	10000	15000	20000	25000	30000	35000	40000	45000	50000	55000	60000
710.0 Income Tax Expense	10000	20000	30000	40000	50000	60000	70000	80000	90000	100000	110000	120000
** Subtotal **												
	206333	412667	619000	825333	1031666	1238000	1444333	1650666	1857000	2063333	2269666	2476000
*** Total ***												
	568330	786670	1005000	1223330	1441663	1660003	1878333	2096663	2314997	2533337	2751667	2969997

Fig. 8.67. Budgeted 12-month balance sheet for Smith and Jones Corporation.

Creating 12-month Financial Statements (FRSPRT12)

In addition to generating the comparative financial statements, Jim Jones will want to document the contents of the ledger file with 12-month financial statements. The programs discussed in this section prepare a balance sheet and an income statement for Smith and Jones Corporation to show the company's financial results for 12 months at a time. These statements can be prepared at any time from the current actual data, the budget data, or last year's actual data. Figure 8.67 shows the budgeted 12-month balance sheet for Smith and Jones Corporation. Figure 8.68 shows the budgeted 12-month income statement.

```
Page No.    1
08/16/86
                              Smith and Jones Corporation
                              Financial Reporting System
                               Budgeted P&L Statement

Acct         Period  Period  Period  Period  Period  Period  Period  Period  Period  Period  Period  Period
Number Name     1       2       3       4       5       6       7       8       9      10      11      12
------ ----------------  --------  --------  --------  --------  --------  --------  --------  --------  --------  --------  --------  --------


**  REVENUES
400.0 Sales      210000  220000  230000  220000  210000  210000  200000  180000  160000  140000  120000  200000
** Subtotal **
                 210000  220000  230000  220000  210000  210000  200000  180000  160000  140000  120000  200000


**  EXPENSES
500.0 Cost of Sales  -100000 -100000 -100000 -100000 -100000 -100000 -100000 -100000 -100000 -100000 -100000 -100000
600.0 General Expenses -13000  -13000  -13000  -13000  -13000  -13000  -13000  -13000  -13000  -13000  -13000  -13000
610.0 Wage Expense   -60000  -60000  -60000  -60000  -60000  -60000  -60000  -60000  -60000  -60000  -60000  -60000
620.0 Tax Expense -   -10000  -10000  -10000  -10000  -10000  -10000  -10000  -10000  -10000  -10000  -10000  -10000
      Except Income
630.0 Depreciation    -8333   -8333   -8333   -8333   -8333   -8333   -8333   -8333   -8333   -8333   -8333   -8333
      Expense
700.0 General Overhead -5000   -5000   -5000   -5000   -5000   -5000   -5000   -5000   -5000   -5000   -5000   -5000
710.0 Income Tax     -10000  -10000  -10000  -10000  -10000  -10000  -10000  -10000  -10000  -10000  -10000  -10000
      Expense
** Subtotal **
                 -206333 -206333 -206333 -206333 -206333 -206333 -206333 -206333 -206333 -206333 -206333 -206333

*** Total ***
                   3667   13667   23667   13667    3667    3667   -6333  -26333  -46333  -66333  -86333   -6333
```

Fig. 8.68. Budgeted 12-month income statement for Smith and Jones Corporation.

The FRSPRT12 program is kept simple by use of the MODIFY REPORT and REPORT FORM commands to produce the actual reports. The FRSPRT12 program gets the period and type of report from the user, sets up the printer, and then uses the REPORT FORM command to print the selected report. A flowchart of the FRSPRT12 program is shown in figure 8.69. Listing 8.36 presents the program code.

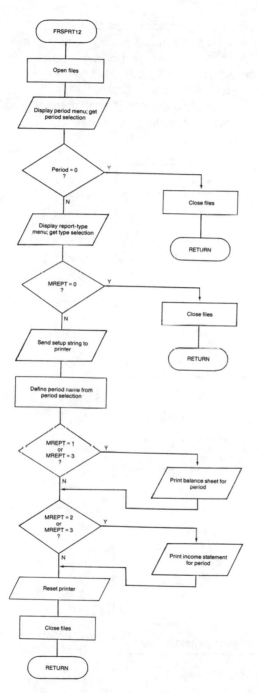

Fig. 8.69. Flowchart of the FRSPRT12 program.

Let's look closely at the program now. The FRSPRT12 program begins by opening files and restoring memory variables. Next it displays a screen (see fig. 8.70) on which the user selects the type of data to be printed: budget, last year, or this year (actual). After the user makes a selection, the program checks to see if a zero has been entered; the user quits the menu by entering *0*. If a zero has been entered, then the databases are closed, and execution returns to the calling program. The program then asks whether the user wants a balance sheet, income statement, or both (see fig. 8.71). Again, the program checks for a zero entry and returns if so.

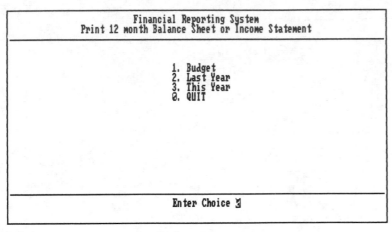

Fig. 8.70. Data-entry screen for data type in 12-month report.

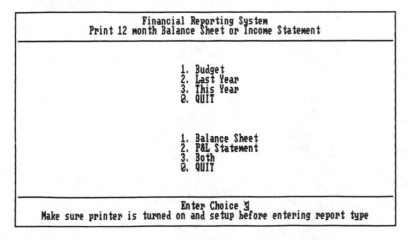

Fig. 8.71. Data-entry screen for report type in 12-month report.

After the user has specified the data and report type, the program sends the setup string to the printer and uses a DO CASE statement and the & (macro substitution) operator to construct the proper report name. This report is then called with a REPORT FORM command. For example, if the user has selected the budget report, then the memory variable MT contains the character string *bud*, and the statement

REPORT FORM frs&mt.bs

is expanded to the dBASE command

REPORT FORM frsbudbs

After the REPORT FORM command is finished, the program closes the databases and returns to the caller.

The use of the REPORT FORM command simplifies the programming required to produce a printed report. dBASE III Plus's MODIFY REPORT command is used to set up the title, headings, and report fields, and the program prints the report with the REPORT FORM command. The comparative financial statements discussed above required eight programs and some tricky programming to prepare three different reports. The 12-period reports discussed here require only one program to achieve the same result.

On the other hand, six report definitions must be created with MODIFY REPORT: FRSBUDBS, FRSBUDPL, FRSLYRBS, FRSLYRPL, FRSACTBS, and FRSACTPL. Figures 8.72 and 8.73 show the report definitions for the reports FRSBUDBS and FRSBUDPL, respectively. The other four reports use the same definitions with the titles changed accordingly and the field name changed from B1. . .B12 to A1. . .A12 or L1. . .L12. The profit-and-loss report uses expressions like −(b2−b1) to print a positive period amount for revenues and a negative period amount for expenses from the debit balances stored in the ledger.

The REPORT FORM command has limitations that prevent its use for the comparative financial statements. The REPORT FORM command can print a report with subtotals, as shown in the 12 month balance sheet and income statement. What it cannot do is switch the sign on specified accounts so that assets, liabilities, and equity accounts are all printed with positive balances in the balance sheet, and revenues and expenses are printed as positive numbers in the income statement. In general, you will not be able to use the REPORT FORM command to generate a report when the report must look "just so." The REPORT FORM command is primarily intended for internal reports that are not highly polished.

In addition, one report definition is needed for each different type and period of the report. Printing the comparative financial statements over a 12-month period would require 36 different reports defined with MODIFY REPORT. The 12-month statements require only six different report definitions to print a balance sheet and income statement for three different data types.

Report definitions for report FRSBUDBS

Page title: Smith and Jones Corporation
                 Financial Reporting System
                 Budgeted Balance Sheet

Page width: 132
Left margin   0

Group on expression: frsacct->type
Group heading: -none-

COL	Contents	Heading	W	D	Tot
1	accountno	Acct;Number;------	6	1	No
2	frsacct->name	;Name;-----------------	16		
3	b1	Period;1;--------	8	0	Yes
4	b2	Period;2;--------	8	0	Yes
5	b3	Period;3;--------	8	0	Yes
6	b4	Period;4;--------	8	0	Yes
7	b5	Period;5;--------	8	0	Yes
8	b6	Period;6;--------	8	0	Yes
9	b7	Period;7;--------	8	0	Yes
10	b8	Period;8;--------	8	0	Yes
11	b9	Period;9;--------	8	0	Yes
12	b10	Period;10;--------	8	0	Yes
13	b11	Period;11;--------	8	0	Yes
14	b12	Period;12;--------	8	0	Yes

Fig. 8.72. Report Definition for the FRSBUDBS report.

```
Report definitions for report FRSBUDPL

Page title:       Smith and Jones Corporation
                  Financial Reporting System
                  Budgeted P&L Statement

Page width:    132
Left margin      0

Group on expression: frsacct->type
Group heading:          -none-
```

COL	Contents	Heading	W	D	Tot
1	accountno	Acct;Number;------	6	1	No
2	frsacct->name	;Name;----------------	16		
3	-b1	Period;1;--------	8	0	Yes
4	-(b2-b1)	Period;2;--------	8	0	Yes
5	-(b3-b2)	Period;3;--------	8	0	Yes
6	-(b4-b3)	Period;4;--------	8	0	Yes
7	-(b5-b4)	Period;5;--------	8	0	Yes
8	-(b6-b5)	Period;6;--------	8	0	Yes
9	-(b7-b6)	Period;7;--------	8	0	Yes
10	-(b8-b7)	Period;8;--------	8	0	Yes
11	-(b9-b8)	Period;9;--------	8	0	Yes
12	-(b10-b9)	Period;10;--------	8	0	Yes
13	-(b11-b10)	Period;11;--------	8	0	Yes
14	-(b12-b11)	Period;12;--------	8	0	Yes

Fig. 8.73. Report Definition for the FRSBUDPL report.

Closing the Year

The final function of the financial-reporting ledger is accomplished by a program that cleans out the ledger file at the end of the year, making room for the next year's actual and budget data. The ledger file runs out of room after the twelfth period has been closed, and no periods for the new year can be closed until the ledger is reset with FRSCLSYR.

The program FRSCLSYR is very simple. It moves the actual data to the last-year section of the FRSLEDGR file, clears the budget and actual columns so that new data can be entered, and resets the system flags to enable the user to begin closing out periods in the new year to the FRSLEDGR file. Figure 8.74 shows a flowchart for the FRSCLSYR program. The program code is shown in listing 8.37.

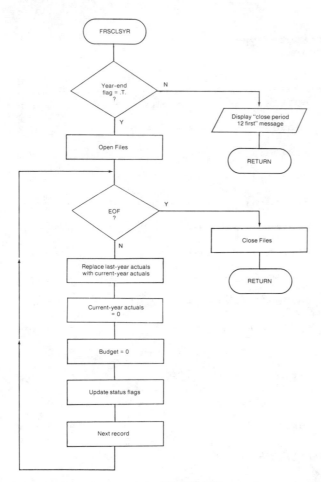

Fig. 8.74. Flowchart of the FRSCLSYR program.

System Maintenance Utilities

The only remaining programs needed for the General Ledger system are programs to back up and restore data files from floppy disk or tape. The backup and restore programs discussed here assume that your accounting system is running on a hard disk machine with no tape drive. The programs are set up to use the DOS BACKUP and RESTORE commands to save and restore the data files from floppy disk. The basic discussion of saving and restoring is in Chapter 3, "Tips and Techniques."

Backing Up Data Files (FRSBAKUP)

The code for the FRSBKUP program is shown in listing 8.38. This program uses the DOS BACKUP program to save the data to floppy disks. Three BACKUP commands are used to save the .dbf, .ndx, and .mem files. The second and third BACKUP commands have the /A option set so that they will not erase the data backed up by the first BACKUP command. Note that the program is set up to make it easy to change the target disk drive and the path to the accounting system files.

If the user's system has a tape drive, the tape drive's backup and restore commands can be substituted for the DOS commands.

Restoring Data Files (FRSRSTR)

The FRSRSTR program restores the accounting system to the state it was in when the backup disk was made. This program allows users to recover from their mistakes or from hardware problems. The code for FRSRSTR is shown in listing 8.39. The program consists of a single RESTORE command that restores the entire contents of the source disk(s) to the specified target directory. The source and target are stored in memory variables for easy updating.

The Menu System

The General-Ledger and Financial-Reporting System breaks down naturally into three sections: General Ledger, Financial Reports, and System Utilities. The main menu, shown in figure 8.75, is broken down into these three sections. Each section calls another menu, named FRSMENU1, FRSMENU2, or FRSMENU3. These three menus are shown in figures 8.76, 8.77, and 8.78. Program code for the main menu is shown in listing 8.40, and code for the three submenus is shown in listings 8.41, 8.42, and 8.43. These four menus provide a simple and effective user interface for the General-Ledger and Financial-Reporting System.

The menu programs are straightforward. Each program sets system parameters and restores memory variables, then enters its main menu loop. In this loop, each program displays the current options and prompts the user for a selection, then executes the appropriate subroutine. The main-menu program differs from the others, however, in that it sets dBASE parameters for the subsequent programs. These SET commands are enclosed in the main-menu loop so that the dBASE parameters are automatically reset each time execution returns to the loop. Upon exit from the main-menu loop, the main-menu program resets the dBASE parameters for interactive use.

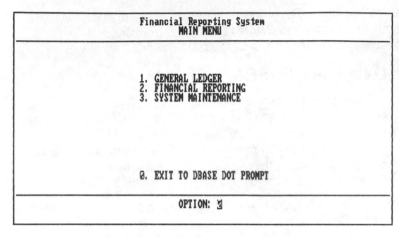

Fig. 8.75. Main menu of the General-Ledger and Financial-System.

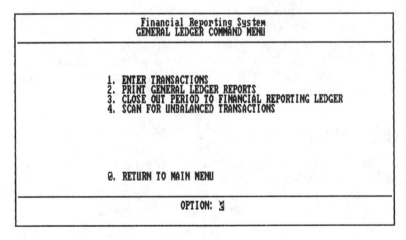

Fig. 8.76. The General Ledger menu.

Extensions to the General-Ledger and Financial-Reporting System

A computerized general ledger may not be very useful unless data can be easily imported into it from other computerized accounting modules. Jim Jones might want to feed transactions to his general ledger from a cash-receipts system, a cash-disbursements system, a payroll system, or a billing-and-accounts-receivable system.

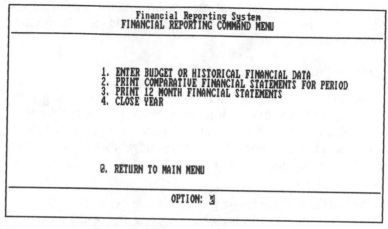

Fig. 8.77. The Financial Reporting menu.

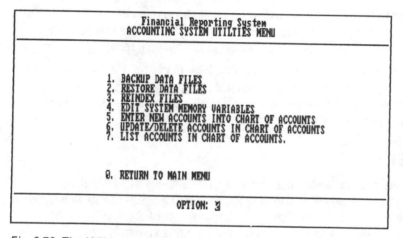

Fig. 8.78. The Utilities menu.

Connecting the General Ledger to Other Accounting Systems

If the other accounting modules are written in dBASE III Plus and use dBASE databases, then linking the general ledger and the other modules is relatively easy. It is important to set up the links so that they check the data before it is written into the general ledger. But beyond that, linking the modules is a matter of reading data from one dBASE database and writing it to another.

dBASE can read data directly from other software packages in a variety of formats, including 1-2-3 or Symphony worksheets, DIF or SYLK files, and report files written to disk. If the other accounting module can generate a report with the general ledger entries and save the report to disk, you will probably be able to load the data into the general ledger without reentering the data.

Importing Budget Data

An important component of financial analysis is the ability to enter and use budget data. You'll recall that Jim Jones uses budget information to create useful comparative financial statements for Smith and Jones Corporation. It's possible to use budget data created by another user with other software, but how this budget data is loaded into the General-Ledger and Financial-Reporting System depends on what software was used to prepare the budget data.

If the user prepares the budget using a software package that can write .DIF, .SLK, or .WKS files (that is, almost any commercially available budgeting or spreadsheet package for the IBM PC), then loading the budget data is a simple two-step process. The program to load the data first creates a temporary file and uses the APPEND FROM command to load the budget data into that file from the .DIF, .SLK, or .WKS file. Then the program opens the financial-reporting ledger database and posts the budget data to the corresponding account record in the financial-reporting ledger.

If the user prepares the budget with a software package that cannot write a file in one of the formats mentioned earlier, the data can still be imported if the budget program can save a report to disk. The budget data link is similar to the actual data link. See chapter 10 for an example of the process involved.

Conclusion

In this chapter, we have presented the core of a General-Ledger and Financial-Reporting System that is capable of handling the accounting needs of a small business. This is by far the most complex application in the book, primarily because of the multitude of checks and balances required in an accounting system.

We have presented this application as a stand-alone system. Chapter 9 will show how other accounting systems can easily be linked to the general ledger. The general ledger presented here provides the core for a larger accounting system containing several accounting modules that feed the general ledger as transactions are entered.

Listing 8.1. The subroutine FRSOPEN.

```
*********************************************************************************
*  FRSOPEN -      Open files for General Ledger and Financial Reporting    *
*                 Opens:  frsgjour - General Journal file                  *
*                         frsledgr - Financial reporting file, including   *
*                                    actual, budget, and last year         *
*                         frsacct  - Account master file                   *
*                 8/13/86                                                  *
*********************************************************************************

* Open general journal and financial reporting files (6 files)
CLOSE DATABASES
SELECT A
USE frsgjour INDEX frsgacct,frsgtran
SELECT B
USE frsledgr INDEX frslacct
SELECT C
USE frsacct INDEX frsaacct

RETURN
```

Listing 8.2. The subroutine FRSINDEX.

```
*******************************************************
*  FRSINDEX - Reindex Financial Statements Files *
*                  8/13/86                        *
*******************************************************

CLOSE DATABASES
@ 3, 1 SAY SPACE(78)
@ 5, 1 CLEAR TO 19, 78
@ 21, 1 CLEAR TO 22, 78
@ 12, 31 SAY "Indexing Files..."

*Index Financial Reporting Ledger
USE frsledgr
* index by account number
@ 14, 21 SAY "Financial Reporting Ledger by Account"
INDEX ON accountno TO frslacct

*Index General Ledger
USE frsgjour
* index by account number and transaction number
@ 14, 1 SAY SPACE(78)
@ 14, 27 SAY "General Ledger by Account"
INDEX ON accountno TO frsgacct
@ 14, 1 SAY SPACE(78)
@ 14, 22 SAY "General Ledger by Transaction Number"
INDEX ON transactno TO frsgtran

* Index Account Master File
USE frsacct
* index by account number
@ 14, 1 SAY SPACE(78)
@ 14, 26 SAY "Chart of Accounts by Account"
INDEX ON accountno TO frsaacct

RETURN
```

Listing 8.3. The program FRSMEM.

```
****************************************************
* FRSMEM  - Define Accounting System parameters   *
*               8/9/86                             *
****************************************************

* Restore existing or initialize new entries, depending on whether file exists
IF FILE("frsmem.mem")
   RESTORE FROM frsmem ADDITIVE
   frspsetup=SUBSTR(frspsetup+SPACE(80),1,80)    && Pad to 80 chars with blanks
   frspreset=SUBSTR(frspreset+SPACE(80),1,80)    && Pad to 80 chars with blanks
   frscompany=SUBSTR(frscompany+SPACE(30),1,30)  && Pad to 30 chars with blanks
ELSE
   STORE "Financial Reporting System" TO frstitle
   STORE SPACE(80) TO frspsetup,frspreset
   STORE SPACE(30) TO frscompany
   STORE 0 TO frspmargin,frsretearn,frsclosed
   STORE 0 TO frsbega,frsenda,frsbegl,frsendl,frsbegoe,frsendoe,;
              frsbegr,frsendr,frsbege,frsende
   STORE MONTH(DATE()) to frsperiod
   STORE 1 TO frstrans
   STORE DATE() TO frsgjdate
   STORE .F. to frsyrend
ENDIF

* get new values
mok=.f.
mok1=.f.
title= "Edit System Memory Variables"
DO WHILE .not.mok

   * Display data entry screen
   DO frsme1            && Display memory variable data entry screen
   @ 21, 9 SAY "Enter or revise desired memory variables. Press ESC to end edit"
   READ
   @ 21, 1 SAY SPACE(78)

   * Verify account ranges
   rangeok=.T.
   DO frsme2 WITH rangeok

   * If ranges ok, confirm edit. Else display error and ask about continuing
   mok=.f.
   IF rangeok
      @ 21, 35 SAY "OK (Y or N)? " GET mok PICTURE "Y"
      READ
   ELSE
      @ 21, 27 SAY "Error in account ranges"
   ENDIF

   * If mok # "Y"
   IF .not. mok
      mok1=.t.
      @ 22, 20 SAY "Want to make further changes (Y or N)? " GET mok1 PICTURE "Y"
      READ
      IF .not. mok1
         EXIT    && Quit loop with mok="N"
      ENDIF
   ENDIF
```

```
ENDDO

* If ok, Save new memory file
IF mok

    frspsetup=TRIM(frspsetup)
    frspreset=TRIM(frspreset)
    frscompany=TRIM(frscompany)
    DO frsme1                              && Redisplay screen
    CLEAR GETS                             && but do not read
    mok=.f.
    @ 22,17 SAY "Save changes to new FRSMEM file (Y or N) " GET mok PICTURE "Y"
    READ
    IF mok
       SAVE TO frsmem ALL LIKE frs*
    ENDIF
ENDIF

* Tidy up and return
CLEAR
RETURN
```

Listing 8.4. The subroutine FRSME1.

```
*********************************************************************
* FRSME1            - Display memory variable data entry screen for *
*                     Financial Reporting System                    *
*                     8/13/86                                        *
*********************************************************************

DO borders WITH frstitle,"Edit System Memory Variables"
@  5, 2 SAY "COMPANY NAME:" GET frscompany
@  7, 2 SAY "PRINTER LEFT MARGIN"  GET frspmargin PICTURE "999" RANGE 0,132
@  7,30 SAY "SETUP PRINTER:" GET frspsetup FUNCTION "S30"
@  8, 2 SAY "RESET PRINTER TO NORMAL:" GET frspreset FUNCTION "S30"
@ 10, 2 SAY "NEXT TRANSACTION:" GET frstrans
@ 10,35 SAY "CURRENT PERIOD" GET frsperiod PICTURE "99" RANGE 1,12
@ 11, 2 SAY "LAST PERIOD CLOSED" GET frsclosed PICTURE "99" RANGE 0,12
@ 11,28 SAY "CLOSING DATE:" GET frsgjdate
@ 11,56 SAY "END OF YEAR FLAG" GET frsyrend PICTURE "L"
@ 13, 2 SAY "ENTER BEGINNING AND END OF RANGE FOR EACH ACCOUNT TYPE"
@ 14, 2 SAY "ASSET ACCOUNTS:      FROM ACCOUNT # ";
        GET frsbega PICTURE "9999.9" RANGE 0,
@ 14,50 SAY "TO ACCOUNT # " GET frsenda PICTURE "9999.9" RANGE 0,
@ 15, 2 SAY "LIABILITY ACCOUNTS: FROM ACCOUNT # ";
        GET frsbegl PICTURE "9999.9" RANGE 0,
@ 15,50 SAY "TO ACCOUNT # " GET frsendl PICTURE "9999.9" RANGE 0,
@ 16, 2 SAY "EQUITY ACCOUNTS:     FROM ACCOUNT # ";
        GET frsbegoe PICTURE "9999.9" RANGE 0,
@ 16,50 SAY "TO ACCOUNT # " GET frsendoe PICTURE "9999.9" RANGE 0,
@ 17, 2 SAY "Retained Earnings Account Number:   ";
        GET frsretearn PICTURE "9999.9" RANGE 0,
@ 18, 2 SAY "REVENUE ACCOUNTS:    FROM ACCOUNT # ";
        GET frsbegr PICTURE "9999.9" RANGE 0,
@ 18,50 SAY "TO ACCOUNT # " GET frsendr PICTURE "9999.9" RANGE 0,
@ 19, 2 SAY "EXPENSE ACCOUNTS:    FROM ACCOUNT # ";
        GET frsbege PICTURE "9999.9" RANGE 0,
@ 19,50 SAY "TO ACCOUNT # " GET frsende PICTURE "9999.9" RANGE 0,

RETURN
```

Listing 8.5. The subroutine FRSME2.

```
***********************************************************************
*  FRSME2 - Check that account ranges have end >= beginning, no overlap, *
*           and that retained earnings account is in equity range       *
*           RETURNS ok=.T. if account ranges are ok.                    *
*                 8/15/86                                               *
***********************************************************************

PARAMETERS ok
PRIVATE acct,mok

@ 21, 1 SAY SPACE(78)
@ 21, 35 SAY "WORKING..."
* Verify that end >= beginning for each range
ok=frsenda>=frsbega.and.frsendl>=frsbegl.and.frsendoe>frsbegoe.and.;
   frsendr>=frsbegr.and.frsende>frsbege
* Verify that retained earnings account is an equity account
ok=ok.and.frsretearn>=frsbegoe.and.frsendoe>=frsretearn
* Verify that ranges do not overlap
mok=" "
acct=frsbega
DO frsatype WITH acct,mok
ok=ok.and.IIF(mok=" ",.F.,.T.)
acct=frsenda
DO frsatype WITH acct,mok
ok=ok.and.IIF(mok=" ",.F.,.T.)
acct=frsbegl
DO frsatype WITH acct,mok
ok=ok.and.IIF(mok=" ",.F.,.T.)
acct=frsendl
DO frsatype WITH acct,mok
ok=ok.and.IIF(mok=" ",.F.,.T.)
acct=frsbegoe
DO frsatype WITH acct,mok
ok=ok.and.IIF(mok=" ",.F.,.T.)
acct=frsendoe
DO frsatype WITH acct,mok
ok=ok.and.IIF(mok=" ",.F.,.T.)
acct=frsbegr
DO frsatype WITH acct,mok
ok=ok.and.IIF(mok=" ",.F.,.T.)
acct=frsendr
DO frsatype WITH acct,mok
ok=ok.and.IIF(mok=" ",.F.,.T.)

@ 21, 1 SAY SPACE(78)
RETURN
```

Listing 8.6. The program FRSAENTR.

```
*****************************************************
* FRSAENTR - Define a new account to the system    *
*                  8/13/86                          *
*****************************************************

PRIVATE mtitle,madd,macct,mname,mnonc,mtype,mans,ok

* Open files and initialize variables
DO frsopen          && Subroutine to open data files and indexes
RESTORE FROM frsmem ADDITIVE
mtitle="Enter Data for New Account"
madd=.f.

* Main data entry loop
DO WHILE .T.

   * Initialize Variables
   macct=0
   mname=SPACE(30)
   mnonc=.F.

   * Read data for new account
   DO borders WITH frstitle,mtitle          && Screen subroutine
   @ 6, 20 SAY "ENTER ACCOUNT NUMBER" GET macct PICTURE "9999.9" RANGE 0,
   @ 7, 20 SAY "ENTER ACCOUNT NAME" GET mname
   @ 8, 20 SAY "ENTER NONCASH FLAG (T for noncash, F for cash)" GET mnonc;
      PICTURE "L"
   @ 21, 26 SAY "Enter data for new account"
   @ 22, 23 SAY "Leave account number zero to quit"
   READ
   @ 21, 1 CLEAR TO 22, 78

   * Quit if account number is zero
   IF macct=0
      EXIT                  && Exit the data entry loop
   ENDIF

   * Check if account number already exists in chart of accounts
   mtype=" "
   SELECT frsacct                           && Select chart of accounts file
   SEEK macct                               && Position record pointer to account
   * Display message and loop if found in file
   IF .not.EOF()
      mans=' '
      @ 21, 2 SAY "This account already exists with the name: ";
         +UPPER(TRIM(name))
      @ 22, 25 SAY "Press any key to continue..." GET mans
      READ
      LOOP                  && Return to the top of the data entry loop
   ENDIF
```

(Continued on next page.)

Listing 8.6, continued.

```
* Check for valid account type.
DO frsatype WITH macct,mtype          && Subroutine to return account type
* If frsatype did not return a type, display message and loop.
IF mtype=" "
   mans= ' '
   @ 21, 2 SAY "Account number is outsde specified ranges .. Press any key";
      +" to continue" GET mans
   READ
   LOOP
ENDIF

* Display account type

   @ 9, 20 SAY "Account type: "+mtype

   * User verifies that account information is OK
   ok=.t.
   @ 22, 30 SAY "OK (Y or N)?" GET ok PICTURE "Y"
   READ
   @ 21 ,1 CLEAR TO 22, 78

   * If ok, entry is added to file
   IF ok
      APPEND BLANK
      REPLACE accountno WITH macct, name WITH mname, type WITH mtype,;
              noncash WITH mnonc
      madd=.t.
   ENDIF

ENDDO  (main data entry loop)

* If accounts were added, ask if want to print chart of accounts list
IF madd
   DO borders WITH frstitle,mtitle          && Screen subroutine
   ok=.t.
   @ 21, 11 SAY "Want to print a new Chart of Accounts listing (Y or N)?";
     GET ok PICTURE "Y"
   READ
   IF ok
      DO frsalist               && Subroutine to print chart of accounts list
   ENDIF ok
ENDIF madd

* Clear screen, close databases
CLEAR
CLOSE DATABASES

RETURN
```

Listing 8.7. The subroutine FRSATYPE.

```
*****************************************************************
* FRSATYPE -    Return account type for account number        *
*               Requires account number ranges to be public   *
*               variables                                      *
*               8/13/86                                        *
*****************************************************************

PARAMETERS acct,mtype
PRIVATE matches

* Determine whether account number is in an account number range
matches=0
mtype=" "
IF acct>=frsbega.and.acct<=frsenda
   mtype="ASSETS"
   matches=matches+1
ENDIF
IF acct>=frsbegl.and.acct<=frsendl
   mtype="LIABILITIES"
   matches=matches+1
ENDIF
IF acct>=frsbegoe.and.acct<=frsendoe
   mtype="EQUITY"
   matches=matches+1
ENDIF
IF acct>=frsbegr.and.acct<=frsendr
   mtype="REVENUES"
   matches=matches+1
ENDIF
IF acct>=frsbege.and.acct<=frsende
   mtype="EXPENSES"
   matches=matches+1
ENDIF

* Blank out type if more than one match was found
IF matches>1
   mtype=" "
ENDIF

RETURN
```

Listing 8.8. The program FRSACHG.

```
*****************************************************************************
* FRSACHG -     Update or delete an account in the chart of accounts      *
*               8/13/86                                                    *
*****************************************************************************

DO frsopen       && Subroutine to open data files and indexes
RESTORE FROM frsmem ADDITIVE
mtitle="Update/Delete Account in the Chart of Accounts"
```

(Continued on next page.)

Listing 8.8, continued.

```
DO WHILE .T.

   * Read data for new account
   macct=0
   DO borders WITH frstitle,mtitle        && Screen subroutine
   @ 6, 29 SAY "ACCOUNT NUMBER" GET macct PICTURE "9999.9" RANGE 0,
   @ 21, 18 SAY "Enter current account number (zero to quit)"
   READ
   @ 21, 1 CLEAR TO 22, 78

   * Quit if account number is zero
   IF macct=0
      EXIT
   ENDIF

   * Check if account number exists
   SELECT frsacct
   SEEK macct

   * If not, display message and go back to top of loop
   IF EOF()
      @ 21, 18 SAY "Account number not found in chart of accounts"
      ok=" "
      @ 22, 25 SAY "Press any key to continue..." GET ok PICTURE "X"
      READ
      LOOP
   ENDIF

   * Display account info on screen
   @ 7, 20 SAY "ACCOUNT NAME  " GET name
   @ 8, 20 SAY "ACCOUNT TYPE  " GET type
   @ 9, 20 SAY "NONCASH FLAG  " GET noncash
   CLEAR GETS
   row=10

   * Determine if there is data in the general journal
   SELECT frsgjour
   SEEK macct
   dflag=.F.
   IF .not.EOF()
      @ row, 20 SAY "There is data for this account in the general journal"
      row=row+1
      dflag=.T.
   ENDIF

   * Determine if there is data in the ledger
   SELECT frsledgr
   SEEK macct
   IF .not.EOF()
      dflag=.T.
      IF aflag
         @ row, 20 SAY "There is actual data in the ledger file"
         row=row+1
      ENDIF
      IF bflag
         @ row, 20 SAY "There is budget data in the ledger file"
         row=row+1
      ENDIF
      IF lflag
         @ row, 20 SAY "There is last year data in the ledger file"
         row=row+1
      ENDIF
   ENDIF
```

```
    * Check if this is the retained earnings account
    SELECT frsacct
    IF macct=frsretearn
        dflag=.T.
        @ row, 20 SAY "This is the Retained Earnings account"
    ENDIF

    * Ask if want to Update, Delete, or quit
    ans="x"
    DO WHILE ans#"U".and.ans#"D".and.ans#" "
        ans=" "
        @ 21, 15 SAY "Update, Delete, or do nothing (U, D, or blank)?";
            GET ans PICTURE "!"
        READ
    ENDDO
    @ 21, 1 CLEAR TO 22, 78

    * Perform update or delete
    DO CASE

        CASE ans="U"
            * Do account update
            DO frsaupd WITH macct

        CASE ans="D"
            * Do account delete
            DO frsadel WITH macct,dflag
    ENDCASE

ENDDO

* Ask if want to print chart of accounts list
DO borders WITH frstitle, mtitle                    && Screen subroutine
ok=.t.
@ 21, 11 SAY "Want to print a new Chart of Accounts listing (Y or N)?";
        GET ok PICTURE "Y"
READ
IF ok
    DO frsalist              && Subroutine to print chart of accounts list
ENDIF

* Clear screen, close databases
CLEAR
CLOSE DATABASES

RETURN
```

Listing 8.9. The subroutine FRSAUPD.

```
***************************************************************************
* FRSAUPD -       Update account information for specified account       *
*                 8/13/86                                                *
***************************************************************************
PARAMETERS macct
PRIVATE ok,oldacct,newacct,newname,oldtype,newtype,newcash,error

* Initialize variables
SELECT frsacct
SEEK macct
oldacct=accountno
newname=name
oldtype=type
newtype=" "
newcash=noncash
@ 3, 1 SAY SPACE(78)
@ 3, 27 SAY "Update Account Information"

* update loop
error=.T.
DO WHILE error

   * Prompt user to input changes
   newacct=accountno
   @ 5, 1 CLEAR TO 19, 78
   @ 5, 20 SAY "ORIG. ACCOUNT: "+ STR(oldacct,6,1)
   @ 6, 20 SAY "ACCOUNT NUMBER" GET newacct PICTURE "9999.9"
   @ 7, 20 SAY "ACCOUNT NAME  " GET newname
   @ 8, 20 SAY "ACCOUNT TYPE   "+oldtype
   @ 9, 20 SAY "NONCASH FLAG  " GET newcash PICTURE "L"
   @ 21, 6 SAY "Make changes to the account information ";
        +"(account number=0 to abort)"

   * Read user's entries. Exit the loop if account number is zero
   READ
   @ 21, 1 CLEAR TO 22, 78
   IF newacct=0
      EXIT
   ENDIF

   * Verify account number
   SEEK newacct
   DO frsatype WITH newacct,newtype
   DO CASE
      CASE (newacct#oldacct.and..not.EOF())
           @ 21, 22 SAY "DUPLICATE ACCOUNT NUMBER .. REENTER"
      CASE oldtype#newtype
           @ 21, 14 SAY "NEW ACCOUNT NOT SAME TYPE AS OLD ACCOUNT .. REENTER"
      OTHERWISE
           ERROR=.F.
   ENDCASE
```

```
      * If error found, display message and loop
      IF error
         ok=" "
         @ 22, 11 SAY "Press any key to continue..." GET ok PICTURE "X"
         READ
         LOOP
      ENDIF
      @ 21, 1 CLEAR TO 22, 78

      * Ok, ask whether user is sure
      ok=.f.
      @ 21, 13 SAY "Do you really want to perform this update (Y or N)?";
           GET ok PICTURE "Y"
      READ
      @ 21, 1 CLEAR TO 22, 78

      * If ok, perform update
      IF ok
         DO frsaupd1 WITH newacct,newname,newtype,newcash,oldacct
      ENDIF

ENDDO  (while error)

RETURN
```

Listing 8.10. The subroutine FRSAUPD1.

```
**********************************************************************
* FRSAUPD1 -     Perform physical file updates for FRSAUPD        *
*                8/13/86                                          *
**********************************************************************

PARAMETERS newacct,newname,newtype,newcash,oldacct
PRIVATE ok

* Select chart of accounts file
SELECT frsacct
SEEK newacct

* Check whether account number was changed
IF newacct=oldacct
   * If account number not changed, update record in chart of accounts
   REPLACE name WITH newname, type WITH newtype, noncash WITH newcash

ELSE
   *If account number changed, update chart of accounts and all data files
   IF EOF()
      * If end of file, append blank and enter new account information
      APPEND BLANK
      REPLACE accountno WITH newacct, name WITH newname, type WITH newtype,;
              noncash WITH newcash
```

(Continued on next page.)

Listing 8.10, continued.

```
    * update journal entries for old account
    SELECT frsgjour
    SEEK oldacct
    DO WHILE .not. EOF()
       REPLACE accountno WITH newacct
       SEEK oldacct
    ENDDO

    * update ledger file entry for old account
    SELECT frsledgr
    SEEK oldacct
    DO WHILE .not.EOF()
       REPLACE accountno WITH newacct
       SEEK oldacct
    ENDDO
    * Update retained earnings account number
    IF oldacct=frsretearn
       frsretearn=newacct
       SAVE ALL LIKE frs* TO frsmem
    ENDIF

    * delete old account and pack chart of accounts file
    SELECT frsacct
    SEEK oldacct
    DELETE
    PACK

ELSE (is not EOF)
    * Otherwise, an error has occurred. Display message and quit.
    ok=" "
    @ 21, 15 SAY "New account already exists. Cannot complete update."
    @ 22, 30 SAY "Press any key to continue..." GET ok
    READ
    @ 21, 1 CLEAR TO 22, 78

ENDIF (EOF)

ENDIF (newacct=oldacct)

RETURN
```

Listing 8.11. The subroutine FRSADEL.

```
**************************************************************************
* FRSADEL -      DELETE account information for specified account       *
*               8/13/86                                                 *
**************************************************************************

PARAMETERS macct,flag
PRIVATE oldtype,error,newacct,ok

* Display account number to delete
DO borders WITH frstitle,"Delete Account from Chart of Accounts"
SELECT frsacct
SEEK macct
@ 6, 20 SAY "ACCOUNT TO DELETE: "+ STR(macct,6,1)
@ 7, 20 SAY "ACCOUNT NAME        "+name
@ 8, 20 SAY "ACCOUNT TYPE        "+type
@ 9, 20 SAY "NONCASH FLAG"
@ 9, 40 SAY noncash
oldtype=type
newacct=0

* If data in other files, get and validate new account number
IF flag
   error=.T.
   DO WHILE error

      * Read new account number
      @ 12, 20 SAY "ENTER NEW ACCOUNT FOR ASSOCIATED DATA" GET newacct
      IF macct=frsretearn          &&Display additional info about ret earn.
         @ 13, 20 SAY "This will be the new retained earnings account"
         @ 21, 20 SAY "Leave account number zero to abort delete"

      ENDIF
      READ
      @ 21, 1 CLEAR TO 22, 78

      * return if account=0
      IF newacct=0
         RETURN
      ENDIF

      * Verify new account number
      SEEK newacct
      DO CASE
         CASE (newacct=macct.or.EOF())
            @ 21, 27 SAY "INVALID NEW ACCOUNT NUMBER."
         CASE oldtype#type
            @ 21, 16 SAY "NEW ACCOUNT NUMBER OUTSIDE CURRENT ACCOUNT RANGE"
         OTHERWISE
            error=.F.
      ENDCASE
```

(Continued on next page.)

Listing 8.11, continued.

```
        * If error found, display message and loop
        IF error
           ok=" "
           @ 22, 13 SAY "CANNOT DELETE ACCOUNT! Press any key to continue...";
                  GET ok PICTURE "X"
           READ
           LOOP
        ENDIF
        @ 21, 1 CLEAR TO 22, 78

    ENDDO    error

ENDIF flag (means that there is associated data for the account being deleted)

* Ok, ask user if he is sure
ok=.f.
@ 21, 13 SAY "Do you really want to delete this account (Y or N)?";
        GET ok PICTURE "Y"
READ
@ 21, 1 CLEAR TO 22, 78

* If ok, perform deletion
IF ok
    @ 21, 35 SAY "WORKING..."
    DO frsadel1 WITH macct,newacct          && Perform phys. reassignmt & deletion
ENDIF

RETURN
```

Listing 8.12. The subroutine FRSADEL1.

```
****************************************************************************
* FRSADEL1 -     Subroutine that performs physical relocation of data    *
*                and account deletion                                    *
*                8/13/86                                                 *
****************************************************************************

PARAMETERS oldacct,newacct
PRIVATE ma1,ma2,ma3,ma4,ma5,ma6,ma7,ma8,ma9,ma10
PRIVATE ma11,ma12,mb1,mb2,mb3,mb4,mb5,mb6,mb7,mb8,mb9,mb10,mb11,mb12
PRIVATE ml1,ml2,ml3,ml4,ml5,ml6,ml7,ml8,ml9,ml10,ml11,ml12,maflag,mbflag
PRIVATE mlflag,mdate

* update journal entries for old account to new account
SELECT frsgjour
SEEK oldacct
DO WHILE .not. EOF()
   REPLACE accountno WITH newacct
   SEEK oldacct
ENDDO

* Lookup data in the financial reporting ledger for the old account
SELECT frsledgr
SEEK oldacct
* If found, add data from old account to new account
IF .not.EOF()            &&Proceed if there is data for old account
   * save old account data to memory variables
   mdate=date
   maflag=aflag
   mbflag=bflag
   mlflag=lflag
   ma1=a1
   ma2=a2
   ma3=a3
   ma4=a4
   ma5=a5
   ma6=a6
   ma7=a7
   ma8=a8
   ma9=a9
   ma10=a10
   ma11=a11
   ma12=a12
   mb1=b1
   mb2=b2
   mb3=b3
   mb4=b4
   mb5=b5
   mb6=b6
   mb7=b7
   mb8=b8
   mb9=b9
   mb10=b10
   mb11=b11
   mb12=b12
   ml1=l1
   ml2=l2
   ml3=l3
   ml4=l4
```

(Continued on next page.)

Listing 8..12, continued.

```
    m15=15
    m16=16
    m17=17
    m18=18
    m19=19
    m110=110
    m111=111
    m112=112
    * Delete the old account
    DELETE
    * find the new account
    SEEK newacct
    * If no record for new account, add one.
    IF EOF()
        APPEND BLANK
        REPLACE accountno WITH newacct, aflag WITH .F., bflag WITH .F.,;
                lflag WITH .F., date WITH mdate
    ENDIF
    * add data to new account record
    IF mdate>date
        REPLACE date WITH MAX(date,mdate)
    ENDIF
    REPLACE aflag WITH aflag.or.maflag,;
            bflag WITH bflag.or.mbflag, lflag WITH lflag.or.mlflag
    REPLACE a1 WITH a1+ma1,a2  WITH a2 +ma2 ,a3  WITH a3 +ma3 ,a4  WITH a4 +ma4,;
            a5 WITH a5+ma5,a6  WITH a6 +ma6 ,a7  WITH a7 +ma7 ,a8  WITH a8 +ma8,;
            a9 WITH a9+ma9,a10 WITH a10+ma10,a11 WITH a11+ma11,a12 WITH a12+ma12
    REPLACE b1 WITH b1+mb1,b2  WITH b2 +mb2 ,b3  WITH b3 +mb3 ,b4  WITH b4 +mb4,;
            b5 WITH b5+mb5,b6  WITH b6 +mb6 ,b7  WITH b7 +mb7 ,b8  WITH b8 +mb8,;
            b9 WITH b9+mb9,b10 WITH b10+mb10,b11 WITH b11+mb11,b12 WITH b12+mb12
    REPLACE l1 WITH l1+ml1,l2  WITH l2 +ml2 ,l3  WITH l3 +ml3 ,l4  WITH l4 +ml4,;
            l5 WITH l5+ml5,l6  WITH l6 +ml6 ,l7  WITH l7 +ml7 ,l8  WITH l8 +ml8,;
            l9 WITH l9+ml9,l10 WITH l10+ml10,l11 WITH l11+ml11,l12 WITH l12+ml12
    PACK                              &&Remove old data record from ledger
ENDIF (data in ledger for old account number)

* Update retained earnings account number
IF oldacct=frsretearn
    frsretearn=newacct
    SAVE ALL LIKE frs* TO frsmem
ENDIF

* delete old account and pack chart of accounts file
SELECT frsacct
SEEK oldacct
DELETE
PACK

RETURN
```

Listing 8.13. The program FRSALIST.

```
************************************************
* FRSALIST - Print Chart of Acocunts list     *
*               8/13/86                        *
************************************************

* Set environment and open files
DO frsopen
SELECT frsacct
RESTORE FROM frsmem ADDITIVE
mtitle="Print Chart of Accounts"

* Pause for printer setup
DO borders with frstitle,mtitle
ok=" "
@ 21, 20 SAY "Setup printer and press any key to continue...";
        GET ok PICTURE "X"
READ

* select normal print
SET PRINT ON
SET CONSOLE OFF
? &frspreset

* Do Report Form
REPORT FORM frsalist

* Clean up and return
SET CONSOLE ON
SET PRINT OFF
CLEAR
CLOSE DATABASES
RETURN
```

Listing 8.14. The program FRSGENTR.

```
****************************************************************************
* FRSGENTR -    Make an entry in the General Journal from the keyboard  *
*                    8/14/86                                            *
****************************************************************************

* Open files & set environment
DO frsopen                && Open Financial Reporting System Files and Indexes
SELECT frsgjour
* Restore sytem memory variables
RESTORE FROM frsmem ADDITIVE
mtitle="Enter Transaction in General Journal"
mtrans=.F.

* Setup temporary file to hold data entry
DO frsgtemp      && Creates empty file with same structure
SELECT frsgjour

mdate=DATE()
mperiod=frsperiod
*Main loop - Accept transactions
DO WHILE .T.     && Loop is exited from within

   *Initialize variables
   STORE O TO balance,esum
   mdescr=SPACE(30)
   mdept=SPACE(4)
   mpc="   "

   * Get &verify common transaction data
   ok=.F.
   DO WHILE .not.ok
      DO borders WITH frstitle,mtitle   && Clear screen & display borders
      @ 6, 2  SAY "Transaction #: "+STR(frstrans,6)
      @ 6, 30  SAY "Date:" GET mdate;
         RANGE CTOD("1/2/80"),
      @ 6, 50  SAY "Acctg. Period:" GET mperiod PICTURE "99" RANGE 1,12
      @ 7, 2 SAY "Description:" GET mdescr
      @ 7, 50 SAY "Posting Code:" GET mpc PICTURE "!!"
      READ
      ok=.T.

      *Verify period
      IF (mperiod<=frsclosed.and.mperiod>frsclosed-6).and.mperiod#frsperiod
         ok=.F.
         mess="Cannot accept transction for closed period"
         mperiod=frsperiod
      ENDIF

      IF .not.ok
         mok=" "
         @ 21, 2 SAY mess
         @ 22, 2  SAY "Press any key to continue..." GET mok PICTURE "X"
         READ
      ENDIF

   ENDDO
```

```
    * Ask user to confirm transaction data
    mok=.t.
    @ 22,33 SAY "OK (Y or N)?" GET mok PICTURE "Y"
    READ
    @ 21, 1 CLEAR TO 22, 78
    IF .not.mok

       LOOP
    ENDIF

    * Get and verify transaction detail
    ok=.T.
    DO frsgent1 WITH mdate,mdescr,mpc,mperiod,ok

    * If transaction is ok, prepare for next & set flag. Else delete it.
    IF ok
       frstrans=frstrans+1
       mtrans=.T.
    ELSE
       DELETE FOR transactno=frstrans
    ENDIF

    *Inquire about another transaction
    @ 5, 1 CLEAR TO 19, 78
    @ 21, 1 CLEAR TO 22, 78
    mok=.t.
    @ 22, 21  SAY "Enter Another Transaction (Y or N)? " GET mok PICTURE "Y"
    READ
    IF .not.mok
       EXIT                    && Break out of loop if not yes.
    ENDIF

ENDDO                         && Get another transaction loop

* If any transactions were entered
IF mtrans                     && mtrans is true if any transactions were entered.

    * Ask if want a journal entry listing
    @ 5, 1 CLEAR TO 19, 78
    @ 21, 1 CLEAR TO 22, 78
    mok=.t.
    @ 21, 16 SAY "Do you want a journal entry listing (Y or N)?" GET mok PICTURE "Y"
    @ 22, 22 SAY "If so, setup printer and press enter."
    READ
    @ 21, 1 CLEAR TO 22, 78

    * Post transactions to general journal
    @ 21, 20 SAY "Posting transactions to General Journal"
    SELECT temp               && Select temporary file
    PACK                      && Remove deleted records from temp
    USE                       && Deselect temp for copy
    SELECT frsgjour
    APPEND FROM temp.dbf      && Copy transaction to frsgjour file
    SAVE TO frsmem ALL LIKE frs* && Save transaction count
```

(Continued on next page.)

Listing 8.14, continued.

```
* Print a journal entry listing if requested
IF mok

     * Print report
     USE temp
     GO TOP
     @ 21, 1 CLEAR TO 22, 78
     @ 21, 25 SAY "Printing journal entry listing"
     SET PRINT ON
     SET CONSOLE OFF
     ? &frspsetup                && Set compressed print
     ? SPACE(frspmargin)+"LISTING OF JOURNAL ENTRIES MADE ON "+DTOC(DATE())
     REPORT FORM frsglist

     * Reset console and printer
     ? &frspreset                && Set normal print
     SET CONSOLE ON
     SET PRINT OFF
  ENDIF (mok)

ENDIF (mtrans)

* tidy up and return
CLEAR
CLOSE DATABASES
ERASE temp.dbf                   && Delete temporary file

RETURN
```

Listing 8.15. The subroutine FRSGTEMP.

```
*************************************************************************
* FRSGTEMP -    Set up temporary file  for General Journal entries     *
*                 8/10/86                                              *
*************************************************************************

* Set up temporary file to hold data entry
IF FILE("temp.dbf")
   ERASE temp.dbf
ENDIF
COPY STRUCTURE TO temp
SELECT 9
USE temp

RETURN
```

Listing 8.16. The subroutine FRSGENT1.

```
**************************************************************************
* FRSGENT1 -     Get account entries for general journal transaction   *
*               8/14/86                                                 *
**************************************************************************

PARAMETERS mdate, mdescr, mpc, mperiod, ok
PRIVATE more, mok, mess, row, balance, esum

balance=0
esum=0
more=.T.
row=9
DO WHILE more    && Loop to read account entries

   * Next account entry
   SELECT temp
   APPEND BLANK
   REPLACE date WITH mdate, descript WITH mdescr, pc WITH mpc,;
           transactno WITH frstrans, period WITH mperiod
   @ row, 2 SAY "ACCT:" GET accountno PICTURE "9999.9" RANGE frsbega,frsende
   @ row, 20 SAY "DEBIT:" GET debit PICTURE "999999999.99" RANGE 0,
   @ row, 45 SAY "CREDIT:" GET credit PICTURE "999999999.99" RANGE 0,
   @ 21,57 SAY "Balance = "+STR(balance,12,2)
   @ 22, 10 SAY "Enter transaction item or zero account number to abort entry"
   READ
   @ 22, 1 SAY SPACE(78)

   * Check if account number is zero
   ok=.F.
   IF accountno=0
      DELETE
      mok=.t.
      @ 22, 21 SAY "ABANDON TRANSACTION ENTRY (Y or N)?" GET mok PICTURE "Y"
      READ
      IF mok
         EXIT
      ELSE
         LOOP
      ENDIF
   ENDIF

   * Verify that account exists
   ok=.T.
   SELECT frsacct
   SEEK temp->accountno
   IF EOF()
      ok=.F.
      mess="Account not found in Account Master"
   ENDIF
   SELECT temp

   * Verify that one number was entered
   IF debit#0.and.credit#0.and.ok
      ok=.F.
      mess="Enter EITHER debit or credit, not both!"
```

(Continued on next page.)

Listing 8.16, continued.

```
      ENDIF
      IF debit=0.and.credit=0
         ok=.F.
         mess="No entry for this account!"
      ENDIF

      * Verify that entry is ok
      @ 21, 1 CLEAR TO 22, 78

      IF ok
         @ 21, 2 SAY "Name: "+frsacct->name+" Type: "+frsacct->type
         @ 21,57 SAY "Balance = "+STR(balance+debit-credit,12,2)
         mok=.t.
         @ 22,33 SAY "OK (Y or N)?" GET mok PICTURE "Y"
         READ
         IF mok
            esum=esum+debit+credit
            balance=balance+debit-credit
            row=row+1
         ELSE
            DELETE
         ENDIF
      ELSE
         @ 21, 2 SAY mess
         mok=' '
         @ 22, 2  SAY "Press any key to continue..." GET mok
         READ
         @ row, 1 SAY SPACE(78)
         DELETE
      ENDIF

      @ 21, 1 CLEAR TO 22, 78

      * Check for balance=0
      IF ABS(balance)<.01.and.esum>0
         mok=.t.
         @ 22, 25 SAY "Accept Transaction (Y or N)?" GET mok PICTURE "Y"
         READ
         IF mok
            more=.F.
            ok=.T.
         ENDIF
      ENDIF

      * End of page processing
      IF row>18.and.more
         mok=" "
         @ 21, 27 SAY "Press any key to continue" GET mok
         READ
         @ 9, 1 CLEAR TO 19, 78
         @ 21, 1 CLEAR TO 22, 78
         row=9
         @ row, 2 SAY "ACCT:" GET accountno PICTURE "9999.9"
         @ row, 20 SAY "DEBIT:" GET debit PICTURE "999999999.99"
         @ row, 45 SAY "CREDIT:" GET credit PICTURE "999999999.99"
         CLEAR GETS
         row=10
      ENDIF

ENDDO              && Loop while more data for transaction

RETURN
```

Listing 8.17. The program FRSGLIST.

```
*****************************************
* FRSGLIST - Print General Journal list *
*              8/14/86                   *
*****************************************

PRIVATE mtitle,no,mperiod,pcdo,pcdont

* Set environment and open files
DO frsopen
SELECT frsgjour
RESTORE FROM frsmem ADDITIVE
mtitle="Print List from General Journal"


* Get order of report. Exit if none specified
DO borders with frstitle,mtitle
no=0
DO frsgordr with no
IF no#0

   * Get period and Setup printer
   mperiod=frsperiod
   pcdo="  "
   pcdont="  "
   DO borders with frstitle,mtitle
   @ 7, 20 SAY "Enter accounting period for report" GET mperiod RANGE 0,12
   @ 8, 20 SAY "Enter posting code to print" GET pcdo PICTURE "!!"
   @ 9, 20 SAY "  or, posting code to exclude" GET pcdont PICTURE "!!"
   @ 21, 12 SAY "Make sure printer is turned on and set at top of page"
   @ 22, 12 SAY "before entering period (period=zero to select all records)"
   READ
   @ 21, 1 CLEAR TO 22, 78
   @ 0, 0
   SET PRINT ON
   SET CONSOLE OFF
   ? &frspsetup
   EJECT

   * Set period and posting code criteria
   IF mperiod=0
      ? SPACE(frspmargin)+"ALL TRANSACTIONS FROM "+DTOC(frsgjdate+1)+" THRU ";
        +DTOC(date())
      DO CASE
         CASE pcdo#"  "
              ? SPACE(frspmargin)+"For posting code: "+pcdo
              SET FILTER TO pc=pcdo
         CASE pcdont#"  "
              ? SPACE(frspmargin)+"Excluding posting code: "+pcdont
              SET FILTER TO pc#pcdont
      ENDCASE
   ELSE
      ? SPACE(frspmargin)+"TRANSACTIONS FOR ACCOUNTING PERIOD "+STR(mperiod,2)
      DO CASE
         CASE pcdo="  ".and.pcdont="  "
              SET FILTER TO period=mperiod
         CASE pcdo#"  "
              ? SPACE(frspmargin)+"For posting code: "+pcdo
              SET FILTER TO pc=pcdo.and.period=mperiod
```

(Continued on next page.)

Listing 8.17, continued.

```
        CASE pcdont#"   "
              ? SPACE(frspmargin)+"Excluding posting code: "+pcdont
              SET FILTER TO pc#pcdont.and.period=mperiod
      ENDCASE
ENDIF
    * Print selected report form
    DO CASE
      CASE no=1
          * Journal Entry Report
          REPORT FORM frsglist
      CASE no=2
          * Transactions by account
          REPORT FORM frsgacct
      CASE no=3
          * Account summary report
          REPORT FORM frsgsum
    ENDCASE

    * Reset printer
    ? &frspreset
    SET CONSOLE ON
    SET PRINT OFF

ENDIF no#0       && End of IF statement

*Clear and return
CLEAR
CLOSE DATABASES
RETURN
```

Listing 8.18. The program FRSGORDR.

```
******************************************************************
* FRSGORDR - Determine current file index and optional seek value *
*           8/14/86                                               *
******************************************************************
PARAMETERS NO

DO WHILE .T.
   * Display choices to user
   no=0
   @  7, 25 SAY "1. TRANSACTION ENTRY ORDER"
   @  8, 25 SAY "2. ORDER BY ACCOUNT NUMBER"
   @  9, 25 SAY "3. SUMMARY REPORT BY ACCOUNT"
   @ 18, 25 SAY "0. RETURN TO MENU"
   @ 21, 25 SAY "ENTER CHOICE: " GET no PICTURE "9" RANGE 0,3
   @ 22, 25 SAY "CHOOSE ORDER BY NUMBER"

   * Read response
   READ
   @ 21, 1 CLEAR TO 22, 78

   * Have user verify response
   MOK=.t.
   IF no#0
      @ 22, 33 SAY "OK (Y or N)" GET MOK PICTURE "Y"
      READ
   ENDIF

   * If ok, set order and quit
   IF MOK
      * Set order.
      DO CASE
         * Order 0 is journal entry order. Order 1 is account order
         CASE no>0.and.no<=2
            SET ORDER TO no-1          && Define order as no-1
         * Summary is ordered by account
         CASE no=3
            SET ORDER TO 1             && Use index 1 for fourth option
      ENDCASE
      GO TOP
      EXIT
   ENDIF

ENDDO

RETURN
```

Listing 8.19. The program FRSGCLOS.

```
***************************************************************
* FRSGCLOS - Close out general journal to history file  *
*                   8/14/86                             *
***************************************************************


* Ask if user wants to proceed
RESTORE FROM frsmem ADDITIVE
closeper=MOD(frsclosed,12)+1
mtitle="Close out general journal to history file for period "+STR(closeper,2)
DO borders WITH frstitle,mtitle
mok=.f.
@ 7, 10 SAY "Before running this command, you should have backed up the data"
@ 8, 10 SAY "files using the backup option in the utilities menu."
@ 21,18 SAY "ARE YOU SURE YOU WANT TO PROCEED (Y or N)?" GET mok PICTURE "Y"
READ
@ 21, 1 CLEAR TO 22, 78
IF .not.mok
   CLEAR
   RETURN
ENDIF

* Check yearend flag. Return if set
IF frsyrend
   mok=" "
   @ 12, 2 SAY "CANNOT RUN GENERAL JOURNAL CLOSE UNTIL YEAREND HAS BEEN RUN"
   @ 21, 20 SAY "Press any key to return to menu..." GET mok PICTURE "X"
   READ
   CLEAR
   RETURN
ENDIF

* Ask about a general journal report
rept=.t.
@ 21, 20 SAY "Print General Journal report (Y or N)?" GET rept PICTURE "Y"
READ
@ 21, 1 CLEAR TO 22, 78
IF rept
   DO frsglist
   RESTORE FROM frsmem ADDITIVE
ENDIF

* Open files and restore memory variables.
DO frsopen
SELECT frsledgr
SET RELATION TO accountno INTO frsacct  && set lookup relation on account
SET EXACT OFF

* Determine period to close; store curr. month field name to var. FIELD1
closeper=MOD(frsclosed,12)+1
field1="A"+LTRIM(STR(closeper,2))

* Store previous period name to variable FIELD2 depending on whether it is
*          last year or not.
IF frsclosed=12
   field2="L"+LTRIM(STR(frsclosed,2))
ELSE
   field2="A"+LTRIM(STR(frsclosed,2))
ENDIF
row=7
```

```
* Preset current period account balances
DO borders WITH frstitle,mtitle
@ 21, 16 SAY "Entering prior month balances in ledger accounts"
SELECT frsledgr
GO TOP

* Post previous month balances (note exception for revenues and expenses
* at beginning of year
IF field1="A1"
   REPLACE A1 WITH 0, date WITH DATE();
        FOR frsacct->type="RE".or.frsacct->type="EX"
   REPLACE A1 WITH L12, date WITH DATE() FOR frsacct->type#"RE".and.;
        frsacct->type#"EX"
ELSE
   REPLACE ALL &field1. WITH &field2., date WITH DATE()
ENDIF

* load current period into ledger file from general journal
errors=.F.
DO frsgclo2 WITH errors

* Adjust retained earnings to reflect revenues and expenses
IF .not.errors
   @ 21, 1 CLEAR TO 22, 78
   @ 21, 22 SAY "Adjusting Retained Earnings account"

   * Sum revenue and expense changes for period (in ledger)
   SELECT frsledgr
   balance=0
   SET FILTER TO frsacct->type="RE".or.frsacct->type="EX"
   GO TOP
   IF field1="A1"
      * Beginning of year. Revenue & Expense balances start at zero
      SUM ALL A1 TO balance
   ELSE
      * Rest of year
      SUM ALL &field1.-&field2. TO balance
   ENDIF
   SET FILTER TO

   * Post balance to retained earnings account
   macct=frsretearn
   error=.F.
   DO frsgclo1 WITH error          && Add balance to ret earnings field
   errors=errors.or.error
ENDIF

* Delete journal entries for period just closed. Update memory variables
IF .not.errors
   * delete gjournal entries for accounting period
   @ 21, 1 CLEAR TO 22, 78
   @ 21, 13 SAY "Packing general journal and updating accounting period"
   SELECT frsgjour
   DELETE FOR period=closeper
   PACK
```

(Continued on next page.)

Listing 8.19, continued.

```
   * update accounting period
   frsgjdate=DATE()
   frsyrend=IIF(closeper=12,.T.,.F.)
   frsclosed=closeper
   frsperiod=IIF(frsperiod=closeper,MOD(frsperiod,12)+1,frsperiod)
   SAVE ALL LIKE frs* to frsmem

ELSE
   mok=" "
   @ row, 2 SAY "ERRORS ENCOUNTERED. GENERAL JOURNAL NOT CLOSED OUT TO LEDGER!"
   @ 21, 30 SAY "Press any key to continue..." GET mok PICTURE "X"
   READ
ENDIF

CLOSE DATABASES
CLEAR
RETURN
```

Listing 8.20. The subroutine FRSGCLO1.

```
**************************************************************************
* FRSGCLO1 - Post balance to ledger file. Create new record if necessary *
*               8/14/86                                                 *
**************************************************************************
PARAMETERS error

* select ledger file indexed by account
SELECT frsledgr

* seek record in ledger file with this account
SEEK macct
error=.F.
ok=.T.

* If none found, see if can create one
IF EOF()
   * Check for valid account number
   SELECT frsacct
   SEEK macct
   IF EOF()
      ok=.F.
      @ row, 2 SAY "INVALID ACCOUNT NUMBER IN GENERAL JOURNAL: "+STR(macct,6,1)
      row=row+1
   ENDIF
   SELECT frsledgr

   * If ok, create new record in ledger
   IF ok
      APPEND BLANK
      REPLACE accountno WITH macct,aflag WITH .T.,lflag WITH .F., bflag WITH .F.
   ENDIF
ENDIF

* Have valid record in ledger. Update ledger balance for period
IF ok
   REPLACE &field1. WITH &field1.+balance
ELSE
   error=.T.
ENDIF

RETURN
```

Listing 8.21. The subroutine FRSGCLO2.

```
**************************************************************************
* FRSGCLO2 - Load current period from general journal to the ledger file  *
*              8/14/86                                                     *
**************************************************************************

PARAMETERS errors
PRIVATE macct,balance

* Use frsgjour indexed by account number and department
SELECT frsgjour

* Load current period in history file from frsgjour totals
SET FILTER TO period=closeper
GO TOP
macct=accountno
errors=.F.
balance=0
@ 21, 1 SAY SPACE(78)
@ 21, 13 SAY "Posting general journal account totals to ledger file"
row=row+1
DO WHILE .not.EOF()

   * At account break, post account total to ledger
   IF macct<>accountno
      error=.F.
      DO frsgclo1 WITH error
      errors=errors.or.error
      balance=0
      SELECT frsgjour
      macct=accountno
   ENDIF

   * Add journal entry debit/credit to account balance
   balance=balance+debit-credit
   SKIP
ENDDO

* Post last account balance and return
error=.F.
DO frsgclo1 WITH error
errors=errors.or.error
SELECT frsgjour
SET FILTER TO              &&Reset filter for general ledger file

RETURN
```

Listing 8.22. The program FRSGSCAN.

```
**************************************************************************
* FRSGSCAN -    Check general ledger file for unbalanced transactions  *
*               8/14/86                                                 *
**************************************************************************

* Restore sytem memory variables
RESTORE FROM frsmem ADDITIVE
mtitle="Scan Transactions in General Ledger for Unbalanced entries"
DO borders WITH frstitle,mtitle

* Ask user if he wants to continue
mok=.F.
@ 6, 10 SAY "This command can take some time to run. If you do not want"
@ 7, 10 SAY "to proceed, answer 'N' to the question at the bottom of the"
@ 8, 10 SAY "screen."
@ 10, 10 SAY "If you do want to proceed, make sure the printer is on,"
@ 11, 10 SAY "then press 'Y' to start the scan."
@ 21, 31 SAY "Proceed (Y or N)?" GET mok PICTURE "Y"
READ
IF .not.mok
   RETURN
ENDIF

* Open files. Use frsgjour indexed by transactno
DO borders WITH frstitle,mtitle
DO frsopen              && Open Financial Reporting System Files and Indexes
SELECT frsgjour
SET ORDER TO 2
GO TOP

*Initialize variables and printer for general ledger scan
tsum=0
tno=0
row=0
tfirst=RECNO()
anydel=.F.
anyprint=.f.
@ 12, 12 SAY "SCANNING GENERAL LEDGER FILE FOR UNBALANCED TRANSACTIONS"

*Main loop - scan transactions
SET DEVICE TO PRINT
DO WHILE .not.EOF().or.tsum#0

   *Check for new transaction
   IF transactno#tno.or.EOF()

      * If old transaction was unbalanced
      IF tsum#0
```

```
        * Print heading, if necessary
        IF row=0
           SET PRINT ON
           SET CONSOLE OFF
           ? &frspsetup                    && Set compressed print
           EJECT
           ? SPACE(frspmargin)+"LISTING OF UNBALANCED TRANSACTIONS FOUND ON ";
             +DTOC(DATE())
           SET CONSOLE ON
           SET PRINT OFF
           row=5
           anyprint=.T.
        ENDIF
        * Save pointer to last record for transaction and goto first record
        tlast=RECNO()
        GOTO RECORD tfirst

        * Print offending transaction
        @ row, frspmargin SAY "Transaction "+STR(transactno,6)+;
          " Has a balance of "+STR(tsum,11,2)
        row=IIF(row<=55,row+1,5)

        *Print and delete offending journal entries
        DO WHILE RECNO()#tlast
           @ row,frspmargin SAY accountno
           @ row,frspmargin+13 SAY period
           @ row, frspmargin+17 SAY date
           @ row, frspmargin+27 SAY descript
           @ row, frspmargin+60 SAY pc
           @ row, frspmargin+65 SAY debit
           @ row, frspmargin+78 SAY credit
           DELETE
           @ row, frspmargin+95 SAY "*DELETED*"
           anydel=.T.
           row=IIF(row<=55,row+1,5)
           skip
        ENDDO
        row=IIF(row<=55,row+1,5)

     ENDIF tsum#0

     * Reset parameters
     tfirst=RECNO()
     tsum=0
     tno=transactno
   ENDIF transactno#tno.or.EOF()

   * Update balance and skip to next record
   IF .not.EOF()
      tsum=tsum+debit-credit
      SKIP
   ENDIF
ENDDO .not.EOF().or.tsum#0

SET DEVICE TO SCREEN
@ 12, 1 SAY SPACE(78)
```

(Continued on next page.)

Listing 8.22, continued.

```
* If any transactions were deleted, pack general ledger
IF anydel
   @ 12, 26 SAY "PACKING GENERAL LEDGER FILE"
   DO FRSOPEN
   SELECT frsgjour
   PACK
   SET DEVICE TO PRINT
   @ row+2, frspmargin SAY "*** FRSGJOUR FILE PACKED ***"
   SET DEVICE TO SCREEN
   anyprint=.T.
ENDIF

* Reset console and printer
IF anyprint               && If anything was printed
   SET PRINT ON
   SET CONSOLE OFF
   ? &frspreset           && Set normal print
   SET CONSOLE ON
   SET PRINT OFF
ENDIF

* tidy up and return
CLEAR
CLOSE DATABASES
RETURN
```

Listing 8.23. The program FRSLDATA.

```
*************************************************************
* FRSLDATA -    Enter or update data in ledger file      *
*                 8/15/86                                 *
*************************************************************

* Open files & memory variables
DO frsopen
SELECT frsledgr
RESTORE FROM frsmem ADDITIVE
mtype=" "

* Main loop
DO WHILE .T.
   DO borders WITH frstitle,"Enter or Update Financial Data"
   macct=0
   mdept="      "
   @ 6, 2 SAY "ACCOUNT NUMBER" GET macct PICTURE "9999.9"
   @ 6, 30 SAY "(B)udget, (L)ast year, or (A)ctual" GET mtype PICTURE "!"
   @ 22, 11 SAY "ESC or ENTER with account number = zero to quit"
   READ
   @ 21, 1 CLEAR TO 22, 78

   * Check for exit condition
   IF macct=0
      EXIT
   ENDIF
```

```
      * Check account and type
      ok=.F.
      IF mtype$"LBA"
         SELECT frsacct
         SEEK macct
         IF .not.EOF()
            ok=.T.
         ELSE
            @ 21, 20 SAY "Account not found in Account Master File"
         ENDIF
      ELSE
         mtype=" "
         @ 21, 31 SAY "Invalid data type!"
      ENDIF

      * If not ok, skip back to beginning of loop
      IF .not.ok
         mok=" "
         @ 22, 25 SAY "Press any key to continue..." GET mok PICTURE "X"
         READ
         LOOP
      ENDIF
      SELECT frsledgr

      * Display account name and ask if ok
      @ 7, 2 SAY frsacct->name
      DO CASE
         CASE mtype="B"
            @ 7, 65 SAY "Budget"
         CASE mtype="L"
            @ 7, 65 SAY "Last Year"
         CASE mtype="A"
            @ 7, 65 SAY "Actual"
      ENDCASE
      mok=.T.
      @ 21, 33 SAY "OK (Y or N)?" GET mok PICTURE "Y"
      READ
      IF .not.mok
         LOOP
      ENDIF
      @ 21, 1 CLEAR TO 22, 78

      * Position ledger file to correct record. Append one if necessary
      SEEK macct
      IF EOF()
         APPEND BLANK
         REPLACE accountno WITH macct,aflag WITH .F.,bflag WITH .F.,lflag WITH .F.
      ENDIF

      * Display data entry screen
      IF UPPER(frsacct->type)="RE".or.UPPER(frsacct->type)="EX"
         * Period data entry
         DO frsldat1 WITH mtype
      ELSE
         * YTD Balance data entry
         DO frsldat2 WITH mtype
      ENDIF

   ENDDO

   CLOSE DATABASES
   CLEAR
   RETURN
```

Listing 8.24. The subroutine FRSLDAT1.

```
***************************************************************************
* FRSLDAT1 -     Data entry for monthly data (Revenues or Expenses)    *
*                8/11/86                                                *
***************************************************************************

PARAMETERS field

*Initialize data entry variables
sign=IIF(UPPER(frsacct->type)="EX","+","-")
i1=&sign.(&field.1)
i2=&sign.(&field.2-&field.1)
i3=&sign.(&field.3-&field.2)
i4=&sign.(&field.4-&field.3)
i5=&sign.(&field.5-&field.4)
i6=&sign.(&field.6-&field.5)
i7=&sign.(&field.7-&field.6)
i8=&sign.(&field.8-&field.7)
i9=&sign.(&field.9-&field.8)
i10=&sign.(&field.10-&field.9)
i11=&sign.(&field.11-&field.10)
i12=&sign.(&field.12-&field.11)

* Get data from user
ok=.F.
DO frsldat3 WITH "Amount",ok

*If ok, update record
IF ok
   REPLACE &field.1 WITH &sign.i1, &field.2 WITH &field.1&sign.i2,;
      &field.3 WITH &field.2&sign.i3, &field.4 WITH &field.3&sign.i4,;
      &field.5 WITH &field.4&sign.i5, &field.6 WITH &field.5&sign.i6
   REPLACE &field.7 WITH &field.6&sign.i7, &field.8 WITH &field.7&sign.i8,;
      &field.9 WITH &field.8&sign.i9, &field.10 WITH &field.9&sign.i10,;
      &field.11 WITH &field.10&sign.i11, &field.12 WITH &field.11&sign.i12
   REPLACE &field.flag WITH .T.
ENDIF

RETURN
```

Listing 8.25. The subroutine FRSLDAT2.

```
***************************************************
* FRSLDAT2 -      Data entry for account balances *
*                 data                            *
*                 8/15/86                         *
***************************************************

PARAMETER field

*Initialize data entry variables
sign=IIF(UPPER(frsacct->type)="AS".or.UPPER(frsacct->type)="EX","+","-")
i1=&sign.&field.1
i2=&sign.&field.2
i3=&sign.&field.3
i4=&sign.&field.4
i5=&sign.&field.5
i6=&sign.&field.6
i7=&sign.&field.7
i8=&sign.&field.8
i9=&sign.&field.9
i10=&sign.&field.10
i11=&sign.&field.11
i12=&sign.&field.12

* Get data from user
ok=.F.
DO frsldat3 WITH "Balance",ok

*If ok, update record
IF ok
   REPLACE &field.1 WITH &sign.i1, &field.2 WITH &sign.i2,;
        &field.3 WITH &sign.i3, &field.4 WITH &sign.i4,;
        &field.5 WITH &sign.i5, &field.6 WITH &sign.i6,;
        &field.7 WITH &sign.i7, &field.8 WITH &sign.i8,;
        &field.9 WITH &sign.i9
   REPLACE &field.10 WITH &sign.i10, &field.11 WITH &sign.i11,;
        &field.12 WITH &sign.i12, &field.flag WITH .T.
ENDIF

RETURN
```

Listing 8.26. The subroutine FRSLDAT3.

```
****************************************************************************
* FRSLDAT3 -      Accept data for account balances or period amounts    *
*                 data                                                   *
*                 8/15/86                                                *
****************************************************************************

PARAMETERS title3,ok

ok=.F.
ibalance=0
iavg=0
igrow=0
* loop until ok or loop exited from inside
DO WHILE .not.ok

   * Display data entry screen
   iaverage=(i1+i2+i3+i4+i5+i6+i7+i8+i9+i10+i11+i12)/12
   IF sign="+"
       @ 9, 2 SAY "Enter &title3. (POSITIVE DEBIT, NEGATIVE CREDIT)"
   ELSE
       @ 9, 2 SAY "Enter &title3. (POSITIVE CREDIT, NEGATIVE DEBIT)"
   ENDIF
   @ 10, 2 SAY "Beginning &title3.:" GET ibalance PICTURE "99999999.99"
   @ 10,35 SAY "Monthly Change  " GET igrow PICTURE "99999999.99"
   @ 11, 2 SAY "Average &title3.:  " GET iavg PICTURE "99999999.99"
   DO frsldat4
   @ 18, 2 SAY "Enter: 1) Enter individual period &title3.s, ;
2) Beginning &title3. and"
   @ 19, 2 SAY "monthly change, or 3) Average &title3. and period ;
weighting factors"
   @ 21, 26 SAY "Press ESC to end data entry"
   READ
   @ 21, 1 CLEAR TO 22, 78
   iabs=(ABS(i1)+ABS(i2)+ABS(i3)+ABS(i4)+ABS(i5)+ABS(i6)+ABS(i7)+ABS(i8)+;
        ABS(i9)+ABS(i10)+ABS(i11)+ABS(i12))/12

   * Process periods depending on values of ibalance, iavg, and iaverage
   DO CASE
       * If beginning balance/amount <> 0
       * Fill in periods from beginning balance/amount and growth rate
       CASE ibalance<>0
             i1=ibalance
             i2=i1+igrow
             i3=i2+igrow
             i4=i3+igrow
             i5=i4+igrow
             i6=i5+igrow
             i7=i6+igrow
             i8=i7+igrow
             i9=i8+igrow
             i10=i9+igrow
             i11=i10+igrow
             i12=i11+igrow
```

```
     * Average balance/amount <>0 and periods contain data.
     * Calculate period bals./amts from avg. bal/amt and weighting factors
     CASE iavg<>0 .and. iabs<>0
          * Calculate period balances/amounts
          i1=i1*iavg/iabs
          i2=i2*iavg/iabs
          i3=i3*iavg/iabs
          i4=i4*iavg/iabs
          i5=i5*iavg/iabs
          i6=i6*iavg/iabs
          i7=i7*iavg/iabs
          i8=i8*iavg/iabs
          i9=i9*iavg/iabs
          i10=i10*iavg/iabs
          i11=i11*iavg/iabs
          i12=i12*iavg/iabs

     * Average balance/amount <> 0 and no data in periods
     CASE iavg<>0 .and. iabs=0
          STORE iavg TO i1,i2,i3,i4,i5,i6,i7,i8,i9,i10,i11,i12

  ENDCASE

  iaverage=(i1+i2+i3+i4+i5+i6+i7+i8+i9+i10+i11+i12)/12

  *Display results and ask if ok
  @ 11, 2 SAY "Average &title3.:   " GET iavg PICTURE "99999999.99"
  DO frsldat4
  CLEAR GETS
  ok=.T.
  @ 21, 33 SAY "OK (Y or N)?" GET ok PICTURE "Y"
  READ
  @ 21, 1 CLEAR TO 22, 78
  IF .not.ok
     mok=.T.
     @ 22, 22 SAY "Want to make corrections (Y or N)?" GET mok PICTURE "Y"
     READ
     @ 21, 1 CLEAR TO 22, 78
     IF .not.mok
        EXIT
     ENDIF
  ENDIF

ENDDO

RETUPN
```

Listing 8.27. The subroutine FRSLDAT4.

```
**********************************************************
* FRSLDAT4 -     Ledger file account data entry screen  *
*               8/15/86                                  *
**********************************************************

* Print data entry screen
@ 11, 35 SAY "Current average:   "+STR(iaverage,13,4)
@ 12,  2 SAY "Period 1:" GET i1 PICTURE "99999999.99"
@ 13,  2 SAY "Period 2:" GET i2 PICTURE "99999999.99"
@ 14,  2 SAY "Period 3:" GET i3 PICTURE "99999999.99"
@ 15,  2 SAY "Period 4:" GET i4 PICTURE "99999999.99"
@ 16,  2 SAY "Period 5:" GET i5 PICTURE "99999999.99"
@ 17,  2 SAY "Period 6:" GET i6 PICTURE "99999999.99"
@ 12, 41 SAY "Period 7: " GET i7 PICTURE "99999999.99"
@ 13, 41 SAY "Period 8: " GET i8 PICTURE "99999999.99"
@ 14, 41 SAY "Period 9: " GET i9 PICTURE "99999999.99"
@ 15, 41 SAY "Period 10:" GET i10 PICTURE "99999999.99"
@ 16, 41 SAY "Period 11:" GET i11 PICTURE "99999999.99"
@ 17, 41 SAY "Period 12:" GET i12 PICTURE "99999999.99"


RETURN
```

Listing 8.28. The program FRSREPT.

```
**********************************************************************
* FRSREPT -      Print financial statements for specified period *
*               8/15/86                                          *
**********************************************************************

* Open files and restore memory variables
DO frsopen
SELECT frsledgr
SET RELATION TO accountno INTO frsacct
RESTORE FROM frsmem ADDITIVE
mtitle="Print Financial Statements"

* Main loop
DO WHILE .T.

   * Ask what kind of report
   mok=.F.
   DO WHILE .not. mok
      mrept=0
      DO borders WITH frstitle,mtitle
      @ 7, 28 SAY "Select Report to print:"
      @ 8, 28 SAY "1. Balance Sheet"
      @ 9, 28 SAY "2. Income Statement"
      @ 10, 28 SAY "3. Sources and Uses of Funds Statement"
      @ 11, 28 SAY "4. All Three Reports"
      @ 19, 28 SAY "0. Return to menu"
      @ 21, 28 SAY "Enter Choice:" GET mrept PICTURE "9" RANGE 0,4
      READ

      mok=.T.
      IF mrept#0
         @ 22, 28 SAY "OK (Y or N)?" GET mok PICTURE "Y"
         READ
      ENDIF
   ENDDO
```

```
     * Exit if option 0 selected
     IF mrept=0
        EXIT
     ENDIF

     * Specify period and (optionally) date
     mok=.F.
     DO WHILE .not.mok
        mper=frsperiod-1
        mdate=frsgjdate
        DO borders WITH frstitle,mtitle
        @ 10, 12 SAY "Enter accounting period:" GET mper PICTURE "99"
        @ 11, 12 SAY "Enter ending date for accounting period:" GET mdate
        READ
        mok=.T.
        @ 21, 33 SAY "OK (Y or N)?" GET mok PICTURE "Y"
        READ
     ENDDO

     * Set printer
     @ 5, 1 CLEAR TO 19, 78
     @ 21, 1 CLEAR TO 22, 78
     mok=" "
     @ 21, 16 SAY "Setup printer then press any key to continue...";
           GET mok PICTURE "X"
     READ
     @ 21, 1 SAY SPACE(78)
     @ 12, 35 SAY "WORKING..."

     * Print reports
     IF mrept=1.or.mrept=4
        DO frsbalsh
     ENDIF
     IF mrept=2.or.mrept=4
        DO frsincom
     ENDIF
     IF mrept=3.or.mrept=4
        DO frscashf
     ENDIF

  ENDDO

  * Close files and return
  CLOSE DATABASES
  CLEAR
  RETURN
```

Listing 8.29. The subroutine FRSBALSH.

```
**************************************************
* FRSBALSH -     Print balance sheet report     *
*               6/13/86                          *
**************************************************

*Set variables
row=0
page=1
pagelen=55
width=92
* Report field definitions
fields=5
field1="A"+LTRIM(STR(mper,2))    && current period actual
field2="B"+LTRIM(STR(mper,2))    && current period budget
field3="L12"                     && balance at end of previous year
field4=field1+"-"+field2         && actual less budget
field5=field1+"-L12"             && actual less yearend
field6="0"                       && field not used in this rept (cannot be null)
STORE 0 TO tot1,tot2,tot3,tot4,tot5,tot6

*Set printer
SET PRINT ON
SET CONSOLE OFF
? &frspsetup
SET CONSOLE ON
SET PRINT OFF
@ 0, 0
SET DEVICE TO PRINT

* Print assets section
repthead="frsbhead"
section="Assets"
credit=.F.
SET FILTER TO UPPER(frsacct->type)="AS"
DO frsrsect WITH tot1,tot2,tot3,tot4,tot5,tot6

* Print liabilities section
section="Liabilities"
credit=.T.
row=IIF(row<>0,row+1,row)
SET FILTER TO UPPER(frsacct->type)="LI"
DO frsrsect WITH tot1,tot2,tot3,tot4,tot5,tot6
le1=tot1
le2=tot2
le3=tot3
le4=tot4
le5=tot5

* Print equity section
section="Equity"
credit=.T.
row=IIF(row<>0,row+1,row)
SET FILTER TO UPPER(frsacct->type)="EQ"
DO frsrsect WITH tot1,tot2,tot3,tot4,tot5,tot6
le1=tot1+le1
le2=tot2+le2
le3=tot3+le3
le4=tot4+le4
le5=tot5+le5
```

```
* Print total liabilities and equity line and eject last page
row=IIF(row<>0,row+2,row)
@ row, frspmargin SAY "Total Liabilities and Equity"
@ row, frspmargin+31 SAY le1 PICTURE "99999999.99"
@ row, frspmargin+43 SAY le2 PICTURE "99999999.99"
@ row, frspmargin+55 SAY le3 PICTURE "99999999.99"
@ row, frspmargin+70 SAY le4 PICTURE "99999999.99"
@ row, frspmargin+82 SAY le5 PICTURE "99999999.99"
row=row+1
@ row, frspmargin+31 SAY "=========== =========== ===========     ===========";
                       +" ==========="
@ pagelen+5, frspmargin+width/2 SAY "PAGE "+STR(page,2)
EJECT

*reset printer and return
SET DEVICE TO SCREEN
SET PRINT ON
SET CONSOLE OFF
? &frspreset
SET CONSOLE ON
SET PRINT OFF

RETURN
```

Listing 8.30. The subroutine FRSINCOM.

```
**************************************************
* FRSINCOM -    Print Income Statement report   *
*              6/13/86                           *
**************************************************

*Set variables
row=0
page=1
pagelen=55
width=104
* Report field definitions
fields=6
field4="A"+LTRIM(STR(mper,2))              && Actual year to date
field5="B"+LTRIM(STR(mper,2))              && Budget year to date
field6="L"+LTRIM(STR(mper,2))              && Last Year year-to-date
IF mper=1
   field1=field4
   field2=field5
   field3=field6
ELSE
   field1=field4+"-A"+LTRIM(STR(mper-1,2))     && Actual for period
   field2=field5+"-B"+LTRIM(STR(mper-1,2))     && Budget for period
   field3=field6+"-L"+LTRIM(STR(mper-1,2))     && Last Year for period
ENDIF
STORE 0 TO tot1,tot2,tot3,tot4,tot5,tot6
```

(Continued on next page.)

Listing 8.30, continued.

```
*Set printer
SET PRINT ON
SET CONSOLE OFF
? &frspsetup
SET CONSOLE ON
SET PRINT OFF
@ 0, 0
SET DEVICE TO PRINT

* Print Revenues section
repthead="frsihead"
section="Revenues"
credit=.T.
SET FILTER TO UPPER(frsacct->type)="RE"
DO frsrsect WITH tot1,tot2,tot3,tot4,tot5,tot6
le1=tot1
le2=tot2
le3=tot3
le4=tot4
le5=tot5
le6=tot6

* Print Expenses section
section="Expenses"
credit=.F.
row=IIF(row<>0,row+1,row)
SET FILTER TO UPPER(frsacct->type)="EX"
DO frsrsect WITH tot1,tot2,tot3,tot4,tot5,tot6
le1=le1-tot1
le2=le2-tot2
le3=le3-tot3
le4=le4-tot4
le5=le5-tot5
le6=le6-tot6

* Print total liabilities and equity line and eject last page
row=IIF(row<>0,row+2,row)
@ row, frspmargin SAY "Net Margin"
@ row, frspmargin+31 SAY le1 PICTURE "99999999.99"
@ row, frspmargin+43 SAY le2 PICTURE "99999999.99"
@ row, frspmargin+55 SAY le3 PICTURE "99999999.99"
@ row, frspmargin+70 SAY le4 PICTURE "99999999.99"
@ row, frspmargin+82 SAY le5 PICTURE "99999999.99"
@ row, frspmargin+94 SAY le6 PICTURE "99999999.99"
row=row+1
@ row, frspmargin+31 SAY "=========== =========== ===========    ===========";
                     +" =========== ==========="
@ pagelen+5, frspmargin+width/2 SAY "PAGE "+STR(page,2)
EJECT

*reset printer and return
SET DEVICE TO SCREEN
SET PRINT ON
SET CONSOLE OFF
? &frspreset
SET CONSOLE ON
SET PRINT OFF
RETURN
```

Listing 8.31. The subroutine FRSCASHF.

```
****************************************************
* FRSCASHF -      Print flow of funds report      *
*                 6/13/86                          *
****************************************************

*Set variables
row=0
page=1
pagelen=55
width=104
* Report field definitions
fields=6
field4="A"+LTRIM(STR(mper,2))+"-L12"              && Actual year-to-date
field5="B"+LTRIM(STR(mper,2))+"-L12"              && Budget year-to-date
field6="L"+LTRIM(STR(mper,2))+"-L12"              && Last year year-to-date
IF mper=1
    field1="A"+LTRIM(STR(mper,2))+"-L12"          && Actual for period
    field2="B"+LTRIM(STR(mper,2))+"-L12"          && Budget for period
    field3="L"+LTRIM(STR(mper,2))+"-L12"          && Last year for period
ELSE
    field1="A"+LTRIM(STR(mper,2))+"-A"+LTRIM(STR(mper-1,2))
    field2="A"+LTRIM(STR(mper,2))+"-B"+LTRIM(STR(mper-1,2))
    field3="A"+LTRIM(STR(mper,2))+"-L"+LTRIM(STR(mper-1,2))
ENDIF
STORE 0 TO tot1,tot2,tot3,tot4,tot5,tot6

*Set printer
SET PRINT ON
SET CONSOLE OFF
? &frspsetup
SET CONSOLE ON
SET PRINT OFF
@ 0, 0
SET DEVICE TO PRINT

*PRINT SOURCES OF FUNDS
section="Sources of Funds"
credit=.T.
repthead="frschead"
* set filter to cash liabilities & equity, and noncash assets
SET FILTER TO ((UPPER(frsacct->type)="LI".or.UPPER(frsacct->type)="EQ").and.;
    .not.frsacct->noncash).or.(UPPER(frsacct->type)="AS".and.frsacct->noncash)
DO frsrsect WITH tot1,tot2,tot3,tot4,tot5,tot6

* PRINT USES OF FUNDS
STORE 0 TO sact,sbud,syact,sybud
section="Uses of Funds"
credit=.F.
* Set filter to cash assets, and noncash liabilities & equity
SET FILTER TO ((UPPER(frsacct->type)="AS").and..not.frsacct->noncash).or.;
        ((UPPER(frsacct->type)="LI".or.UPPER(frsacct->type)="EQ").and.;
        frsacct->noncash)
DO frsrsect WITH tot1,tot2,tot3,tot4,tot5,tot6

* Print last page break
@ pagelen+5, frspmargin+(width-7)/2 SAY "PAGE "+STR(page,2)
EJECT
```

(Continued on next page.)

Listing 8.31, continued.

```
*reset printer and return
SET DEVICE TO SCREEN
SET PRINT ON
SET CONSOLE OFF
? &frspreset
SET CONSOLE ON
SET PRINT OFF

RETURN
```

Listing 8.32. The subroutine FRSRSECT.

```
***********************************************************************
* FRSRSECT -    Loop to print a section of a balance sheet,     *
*               income statement, or flow of funds report       *
*               8/15/86                                          *
***********************************************************************

PARAMETERS tot1,tot2,tot3,tot4,tot5,tot6

* Initialize file and variables
GO TOP
top=.T.
STORE 0 TO tot1,tot2,tot3,tot4,tot5,tot6

*report printing loop
DO WHILE .not. EOF()

    * If new page, print header
    IF row=0
       DO &repthead
    ENDIF

    * If top of section, print title
    IF top
       @ row, frspmargin SAY section
       row=row+1
       @ row, frspmargin SAY "-------------------------------"
       row=row+1
       top=.F.
    ENDIF

    * Calculate account data to print on current line
    f1=&field1
    f2=&field2
    f3=&field3
    f4=&field4
    f5=&field5
    f6=&field6

    * If account has a credit balance, convert ledger amount to positive credit.
    IF credit
        f1=-f1
        f2=-f2
        f3=-f3
        f4=-f4
        f5=-f5
        f6=-f6
    ENDIF
```

```
* Print account info
@ row, frspmargin SAY frsacct->name
@ row, frspmargin+31 SAY f1 PICTURE "99999999.99"
@ row, frspmargin+43 SAY f2 PICTURE "99999999.99"
@ row, frspmargin+55 SAY f3 PICTURE "99999999.99"
@ row, frspmargin+70 SAY f4 PICTURE "99999999.99"
@ row, frspmargin+82 SAY f5 PICTURE "99999999.99"
IF fields>5
    @ row, frspmargin+94 SAY f6 PICTURE "99999999.99"
ENDIF
row=row+1

* Accumulate section totals
tot1=tot1+f1
tot2=tot2+f2
tot3=tot3+f3
tot4=tot4+f4
tot5=tot5+f5
tot6=tot6+f6

* If bottom of page, eject
IF row>pagelen
    @ pagelen+5, faspmargin+width/2 SAY "PAGE "+STR(page,2)
    EJECT
    page=page+1
    row=0
ENDIF

* get next record from ledger
    SKIP
ENDDO

* If new page, print header
IF row=0
    DO &repthead
ENDIF

* Print section totals
@ row, frspmargin+31 SAY "----------- ----------- -----------     -----------";
                        +" -----------"
IF fields>5
    @ row, frspmargin+94 SAY "-----------"
ENDIF

row=row+1
@ row, frspmargin SAY "Total "+section
@ row, frspmargin+31 SAY tot1 PICTURE "99999999.99"
@ row, frspmargin+43 SAY tot2 PICTURE "99999999.99"
@ row, frspmargin+55 SAY tot3 PICTURE "99999999.99"
@ row, frspmargin+70 SAY tot4 PICTURE "99999999.99"
@ row, frspmargin+82 SAY tot5 PICTURE "99999999.99"
IF fields>5
    @ row, frspmargin+94 SAY tot6 PICTURE "99999999.99"
ENDIF
row=row+1
@ row, frspmargin+31 SAY "=========== =========== ===========     ===========";
                        +" ==========="
IF fields>5
    @ row, frspmargin+94 SAY "==========="
row=row+2

RETURN
```

Listing 8.33. The subroutine FRSBHEAD.

```
*********************************************************************
* FRSBHEAD -     Print title and heading for Balance Sheet       *
*               6/13/86                                          *
*********************************************************************

@  1, frspmargin+width-20 SAY "Report Date:"
@  1, frspmargin+width-7 SAY DATE()
@  3, frspmargin+(width-LEN(frscompany))/2 SAY frscompany
@  4, frspmargin+(width-LEN(frstitle))/2 SAY frstitle
@  5, frspmargin+(width-28)/2 SAY "Balance Sheet as of "+DTOC(mdate)
@  8,  frspmargin SAY "                            ---- Current Period ";
       +"---   Beginning    ---- Actual Versus ----"
@  9,  frspmargin SAY "                                     Actual      ";
       +"Budget     of Year         Budget Beg of Year"
@ 10,  frspmargin SAY "                              ----------- ";
       +"----------- -----------    ----------- -----------"
row=12
RETURN
```

Listing 8.34. The subroutine FRSIHEAD.

```
*********************************************************************
* FRSIHEAD -     Print title and heading for income statement report *
*               6/13/86                                          *
*********************************************************************

@  1, frspmargin+width-20 SAY "Report Date:"
@  1, frspmargin+width-7 SAY DATE()
@  3, frspmargin+(width-LEN(frscompany))/2 SAY frscompany
@  4, frspmargin+(width-LEN(frstitle))/2 SAY frstitle
@  5, frspmargin+(width-43)/2 SAY "Income Statement for Month Ending ";
        +DTOC(mdate)
@  8,  8 SAY "                         --------- Current Period ";
       +"----------   ----------- Year to Date ----------"
@  9,  8 SAY "                              Actual     Budget    ";
       +"Last Year      Actual     Budget   Last Year"
@ 10,  8 SAY "                         ----------- ----------- ";
       +"-----------   ----------- ----------- -----------"

row=12
RETURN
```

Listing 8.35. The subroutine FRSCHEAD.

```
***********************************************************************
* FRSCHEAD -      Print title and heading for flow of funds report   *
*                 6/13/86                                             *
***********************************************************************

@  1, frspmargin+width-20 SAY "Report Date:"
@  1, frspmargin+width-7 SAY DATE()
@  3, frspmargin+(width-LEN(frscompany))/2 SAY frscompany
@  4, frspmargin+(width-LEN(frstitle))/2 SAY frstitle
@  5, frspmargin+(width-49)/2 SAY "Flow of Funds Statement for Month Ending ";
      +DTOC(mdate)
@  8,  8 SAY "                                  --------- Current Period ";
      +"----------      ----------- Year to Date ----------"
@  9,  8 SAY "                                    Actual      Budget    ";
      +"Last Year          Actual      Budget    Last Year"
@ 10,  8 SAY "                                  ----------- ----------- ";
      +"----------      ----------- ----------- ----------"

row=12
RETURN
```

Listing 8.36. The program FRSPRT12.

```
***********************************************************************
* FRSPRT12 -      Print 12 month balance sheet or P&L statement     *
*                 8/15/86                                            *
***********************************************************************

* Open files
DO frsopen
SELECT frsledgr
SET RELATION TO accountno INTO frsacct
RESTORE FROM frsmem ADDITIVE
mtitle="Print 12 month Balance Sheet or Income Statement"

* Read period to print
DO borders WITH frstitle,mtitle
mtype=0
@ 7, 35 SAY "1. Budget"
@ 8, 35 SAY "2. Last Year"
@ 9, 35 SAY "3. This Year"
@ 10, 35 SAY "0. QUIT"
@ 21, 35 SAY "Enter Choice" GET mtype PICTURE "9" RANGE 0,3
READ
@ 21, 1 CLEAR TO 22, 78

* Quit if choice=0
IF mtype=0
   CLOSE DATABASES
   CLEAR
   RETURN
ENDIF
```

(Continued on next page.)

Listing 8.36, continued.

```
* Read type(s) of report
mrept=0
@ 14, 35 SAY "1. Balance Sheet"
@ 15, 35 SAY "2. P&L Statement"
@ 16, 35 SAY "3. Both"
@ 17, 35 SAY "0. QUIT"
@ 21, 35 SAY "Enter Choice" GET mrept PICTURE "9" RANGE 0,3
@ 22,  6 SAY "Make sure printer is turned on and setup before ";
        +"entering report type"
READ
@ 21, 1 CLEAR TO 22, 78

* Quit if choice=0
IF mrept=0
   CLOSE DATABASES
   CLEAR
   RETURN
ENDIF

* Setup printer
@ 5, 1 CLEAR TO 19, 78
@ 12, 35 SAY "WORKING..."
SET PRINT ON
SET CONSOLE OFF
? &frspsetup

* Do Report Form
DO CASE
   CASE mtype=1
        mt="bud"
   CASE mtype=2
        mt="lyr"
   CASE mtype=3
        mt="cur"
ENDCASE
IF mrept=1.or.mrept=3
   SET FILTER TO UPPER(frsacct->type)="AS".or.UPPER(frsacct->type)="LI";
      .or.UPPER(frsacct->type)="EX"
   REPORT FORM frs&mt.bs
ENDIF
IF mrept=2.or.mrept=3
   SET FILTER TO UPPER(frsacct->type)="RE".or.UPPER(frsacct->type)="EX"
   REPORT FORM frs&mt.pl
ENDIF

* Clean up and return
? &frspreset
SET CONSOLE ON
SET PRINT OFF
CLEAR
CLOSE DATABASES
RETURN
```

Listing 8.37. The program FRSCLSYR.

```
*****************************************************************************
* FRSCLSYR -    Close out current accounting year. Move current year   *
*               data to last year. Zero out budget.                    *
*               8/15/86                                                 *
*****************************************************************************

* Check close flag
RESTORE FROM frsmem ADDITIVE
mtitle="Close Year"
DO borders with frstitle,mtitle
* Quit if close flag not set
IF frsyrend
   @ 12, 35 SAY "WORKING..."
ELSE
   mok=" "
   @ 21, 20 SAY "Cannot run yearend close until period 12 closed!"
   @ 22, 20 SAY "Press any key to continue..." GET mok
   READ
   CLEAR
   RETURN
ENDIF

* Open files
DO frsopen

* Zero out budget, move actuals to last year
SELECT frsledgr
GO TOP
DO WHILE .not.EOF()

   *Update last year actuals
   REPLACE l1 WITH a1, l2 WITH a2, l3 WITH a3, l4 WITH a4, l5 WITH a5,;
      l6 WITH a6, l7 WITH a7, l8 WITH a8, l9 WITH a9, l10 WITH a10,;
      l11 WITH a11, l12 WITH a12

   * Zero current year actual
   REPLACE a1 WITH 0, a2 WITH 0, a3 WITH 0, a4 WITH 0, a5 WITH 0, a6 WITH 0,;
      a7 WITH 0, a8 WITH 0, a9 WITH 0, a10 WITH 0, a11 WITH 0, a12 WITH 0

   * Zero budget
   REPLACE b1 WITH 0, b2 WITH 0, b3 WITH 0, b4 WITH 0, b5 WITH 0, b6 WITH 0,;
      b7 WITH 0, b8 WITH 0, b9 WITH 0, b10 WITH 0, b11 WITH 0, b12 WITH 0

   * Update status flags and skip to next ledger record
   REPLACE aflag WITH .F., bflag WITH .F., lflag WITH .T.
   SKIP
ENDDO

* Reset accounting period and yearend flag
frsyrend=.F.
frsperiod=1
SAVE TO frsmem ALL LIKE frs*

* Tidy up and return
CLOSE DATABASES
CLEAR
RETURN
```

Listing 8.38. The program FRSBKUP.

```
*************************************************************************
* FRSBKUP -      Back up Financial Reporting System files         *
*               8/15/86                                           *
*************************************************************************
target="b:"                              && Target drive for backup
CLEAR
? "BACKUP Financial Reporting System Data Files"
?

* Ask user to verify backup command
mok=' '
DO WHILE UPPER(mok)#"Y".and.UPPER(mok)#"N"
   WAIT "Do you want to proceed with this command (Y or N)?" TO mok
   READ
ENDDO

* If answer is yes, do backup
IF UPPER(mok)="Y"
   files1="*.dbf"
   RUN BACKUP &files1 &target
   files2="*.ndx"
   RUN BACKUP &files2 &target/A
   files3="*.mem"
   RUN BACKUP &files3 &target/A
ENDIF

* Clear screen and return
CLEAR
RETURN
```

Listing 8.39. The program FRSRSTR.

```
*************************************************************************
* FRSRSTR -      RESTORE Financial Reporting System data from backup    *
*               8/2/86                                                  *
*************************************************************************
* Display title
CLEAR
? "RESTORE Financial Reporting System Data from Backup"
?

* Ask user to verify restore command
mok=' '
DO WHILE UPPER(mok)#"Y".and.UPPER(mok)#"N"
   WAIT "Do you want to proceed with this command (Y or N)?" TO mok
ENDDO

* If answer is 'yes', do restore
IF UPPER(mok)="Y"
   source="b:"                          && Source drive for restore
   target="c:"                          && Target drive for restore
   files1=target+"*.*"
   RUN RESTORE &source &files1
ENDIF

* Clear screen and return
CLEAR
RETURN
```

Listing 8.40. The program FRSMAIN.

```
*****************************************************************************
* FRSMAIN - Main menu for General-Ledger and Financial-Reporting System *
*            8/13/86                                                     *
*****************************************************************************


CLEAR ALL
RESTORE FROM frsmem
option=-1

* Main loop
DO WHILE option#0
   * Setup environment
   SET TALK OFF
   SET SAFETY OFF
   SET DEVICE TO SCREEN
   SET PRINT OFF
   SET DELETED OFF
   CLOSE DATABASES

   * Display Menu
   option=0
   * Display logo
   CLEAR
   DO borders WITH frstitle,"MAIN MENU"

   * Display menu options
   @  8, 27  SAY "1. GENERAL LEDGER"
   @  9, 27  SAY "2. FINANCIAL REPORTING"
   @ 10, 27  SAY "3. SYSTEM MAINTENANCE"
   @ 18, 27  SAY "0. EXIT TO DBASE DOT PROMPT"
   @ 21, 35  SAY "OPTION:" GET option PICTURE "9" RANGE 0,3
   READ

   * Do selected option
   DO CASE
      CASE option=1
         DO frsmenu1            && General Ledger
      CASE option=2
         DO frsmenu2            && Financial Reporting
      CASE option=3
         DO frsmenu3            && System Maintenance

      OTHERWISE                 && Confirm option=0 before leaving
         mok=.f.
         @ 22, 21 SAY "Do you really want to quit (Y or N)?";
              GET mok PICTURE "Y"
         READ
         option=IIF(.not.mok,-1,0)    && Reset option to -1 if false
   ENDCASE
* End of main loop
ENDDO (option#0)
```

(Continued on next page.)

Listing 8.40, continued.

```
* Restore system defaults and exit
SET TALK ON
SET SAFETY ON
SET PRINT OFF
SET DEVICE TO SCREEN
CLEAR ALL
CLEAR
RETURN
```

Listing 8.41. The program FRSMENU1.

```
******************************************.******
* FRSMENU1 - General Ledger command menu        *
*            8/13/86                             *
*************************************************
PRIVATE option

* Main loop
option=-1
DO WHILE option#0

   * Display Menu
   option=0
   * Display logo
   DO borders WITH frstitle,"GENERAL LEDGER COMMAND MENU"

   * Display menu options
   @  8, 20  SAY "1. ENTER TRANSACTIONS"
   @  9, 20  SAY "2. PRINT GENERAL LEDGER REPORTS"
   @ 10, 20  SAY "3. CLOSE OUT PERIOD TO FINANCIAL REPORTING LEDGER"
   @ 11, 20  SAY "4. SCAN FOR UNBALANCED TRANSACTIONS"
   @ 18, 20  SAY "0. RETURN TO MAIN MENU"
   @ 21, 35  SAY "OPTION:" GET option PICTURE "9" RANGE 0,4
   READ

   * Do selected option
   DO CASE
      CASE option=1
           DO frsgentr          && Data entry/update
      CASE option=2
           DO frsglist          && Asset data query
      CASE option=3
           DO frsgclos          && Browse list of assets
      CASE option=4
           DO frsgscan          && Check for unbalanced transactions
   ENDCASE
* End of main loop
ENDDO (option#0)

* Restore system defaults and exit
CLEAR
RETURN
```

Listing 8.42. The program FRSMENU2.

```
**************************************************************
* FRSMENU2 -     Financial Reporting command menu         *
*               8/13/86                                    *
**************************************************************
PRIVATE option

* Main loop
option=-1
DO WHILE option#0

    * Display Menu
    option=0
    * Display logo
    DO borders WITH frstitle,"FINANCIAL REPORTING COMMAND MENU"

    * Display menu options
    @  8, 20   SAY "1. ENTER BUDGET OR HISTORICAL FINANCIAL DATA"
    @  9, 20   SAY "2. PRINT COMPARATIVE FINANCIAL STATEMENTS FOR PERIOD"
    @ 10, 20   SAY "3. PRINT 12 MONTH FINANCIAL STATEMENTS"
    @ 11, 20   SAY "4. CLOSE YEAR"
    @ 18, 20   SAY "0. RETURN TO MAIN MENU"
    @ 21, 35   SAY "OPTION:" GET option PICTURE "9" RANGE 0,4
    READ

    * Do selected option
    DO CASE
       CASE option=1
            DO frsldata  && Ledger data entry/update
       CASE option=2
            DO frsrept   && Print financial statements
       CASE option=3
            DO frsprt12  && Print 12 month statements
       CASE option=4
            DO frsclsyr  && Check for unbalanced transactions
    ENDCASE
* End of main loop
ENDDO (option#0)

* Return
CLEAR
RETURN
```

Listing 8.43. The program FRSMENU3.

```
**********************************************************
* FRSMENU3 -     Accounting System utilities menu        *
*               8/15/86                                   *
**********************************************************
PRIVATE option

* Main loop
option=-1
DO WHILE option#0

   * Display Menu
   option=0
   * Display logo
   DO borders WITH frstitle,"ACCOUNTING SYSTEM UTILTIES MENU"

   * Display menu options
   @  8, 20   SAY "1. BACKUP DATA FILES"
   @  9, 20   SAY "2. RESTORE DATA FILES"
   @ 10, 20   SAY "3. REINDEX FILES"
   @ 11, 20   SAY "4. EDIT SYSTEM MEMORY VARIABLES"
   @ 12, 20   SAY "5. ENTER NEW ACCOUNTS INTO CHART OF ACCOUNTS"
   @ 13, 20   SAY "6. UPDATE/DELETE ACCOUNTS IN CHART OF ACCOUNTS"
   @ 14, 20   SAY "7. LIST ACCOUNTS IN CHART OF ACCOUNTS."
   @ 18, 20   SAY "0. RETURN TO MAIN MENU"
   @ 21, 35   SAY "OPTION:" GET option PICTURE "9" RANGE 0,7
   READ

   * Do selected option
   DO CASE
      CASE option=1
           DO frsbkup
      CASE option=2
           DO frsrstr
      CASE option=3
           DO frsindex
      CASE option=4
           DO frsmem
      CASE option=5
           DO frsaentr
      CASE option=6
           DO frsachg
      CASE option=7
           DO frsalist
   ENDCASE
* End of main loop
ENDDO (option#0)

* Return
CLEAR
RETURN
```

9

Linking Stand-Alone Applications

In Chapters 4 through 8 we looked at five business applications developed with dBASE III Plus. Although each of these applications can be used in stand-alone mode, you would probably want to connect related applications to maximize their usefulness. dBASE III Plus applications can be linked to each other or to other applications not written in dBASE III Plus. By linking applications, you eliminate the extra labor, expense, and potential for error involved when the same data needed by two separate systems is entered twice, or when the output of one system must be reentered as input for another system.

Four of the five applications in this book can be linked to form part of an accounting system: the fixed-asset system, the sales-tracking system, the customer-accounts system, and the general-ledger and financial-reporting system. The remaining application—the personnel system—is basically a stand-alone application that doesn't have much in common with the four accounting-related applications.

This chapter begins with an overview of four basic methods for linking applications. First, you see how three of these methods are used to link the accounting-related applications in this book. Then you see how the fourth method enables you to link one of the accounting-related applications with a non-dBASE application.

Methods of Linking Applications

dBASE III Plus applications can be linked to each other and to non-dBASE applications in four ways. First, applications can sometimes share data files. For example, the sales-tracking system and the customer-accounts system each have a customer master file that contains the customer's name and address. This customer file can be modified so that both programs can share it.

Second, applications can be linked by means of common data-entry programs. Consider again the applications for sales-tracking and customer-accounts. Sales are always recorded in the sales-tracking database; credit sales are recorded as receivables in the customer-accounts system. These systems can be linked by means of data-entry programs to eliminate repetition of sales-data entry.

Third, applications can be linked by means of programs that summarize and transfer data from one application to another. This method is the most common technique for connecting systems originally designed to be independent. For example, you can use the output of the fixed-asset system, the sales-tracking system, and the customer-accounts system to update periodically (daily, weekly, or at the end of each accounting period) the general-ledger accounts for depreciation, sales, cost of sales, and customer payments.

Table 9.1 summarizes the three ways of linking the dBASE applications for sales tracking, customer accounts, fixed assets, and general ledger, and suggests the most appropriate technique for each link.

Table 9.1

Possible Links between the Four Accounting-Related Applications

Shared Data	Method(s)	Applications
Customer data	Common database file	Sales Tracking and Customer Accounts
Sales data	Common data-entry program	Sales Tracking and Customer Accounts
	Program to summarize and transfer sales totals	Sales Tracking to General Ledger
Accounts-receivable data	Program to summarize and transfer accounts-receivable totals	Customer Accounts to General Ledger
Fixed-asset data	Program to summarize and transfer fixed-asset additions, retirements, and depreciation	Fixed Asset to General Ledger

Fourth, a dBASE application can be linked to a non-dBASE application by means of a dBASE program that reads the output from the non-dBASE application and converts the output into dBASE file format. For example, you could update the general ledger from a report generated by Lotus 1-2-3.

Using Common Database Files

The sales-tracking system and the customer-accounts system both require a file to store information about customers. If you operate the two applications independently, you need to keep both customer files current, enter the same data twice, and be alert to any disparities between the two customer files. Linking these two systems with a common file saves time and effort, ensures fewer data-entry errors, and avoids the problem of data disparities.

If you are installing the sales-tracking system and the customer-accounts system for the same business, you don't need a separate customer file for each application. It makes more sense to have one customer file that records the information required by both systems than to have separate files.

Before discussing the structure of a shared customer file, we need to look at the individual files. The structure of the customer file (CUST00.DBF) for the sales-tracking system is shown in figure 9.1. The customer data required by the sales-tracking system includes the customer account number, the company name and address, and the name and phone number of the the customer contact (the person who places the orders).

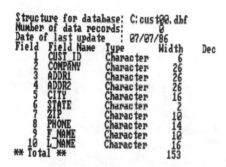

```
Structure for database: C:cust00.dbf
Number of data records:        0
Date of last update   : 07/07/86
Field  Field Name  Type       Width    Dec
    1   CUST_ID     Character      6
    2   COMPANY     Character     26
    3   ADDR1       Character     26
    4   ADDR2       Character     26
    5   CITY        Character     16
    6   STATE       Character      2
    7   ZIP         Character     10
    8   PHONE       Character     14
    9   F_NAME      Character     10
   10   L_NAME      Character     16
** Total **                     153
```

Fig. 9.1. Structure of the customer file used in the sales-tracking system.

The structure of the customer file (CACUST.DBF) for the customer-account system is shown in figure 9.2. The data required by the customer-account system includes the account number, the name and billing address, and account status information.

A combined customer file would consolidate the data requirements of both systems. Because the first 10 fields in both customer files contain the same information— account number, name, address, and phone—we can use the file for the customer-account system (CACUST.DBF) as the combined customer file. The nine additional fields in CACUST.DBF contain account status and billing information that is used exclusively by the customer-account system.

```
Structure for database: C:catrans.dbf
Number of data records:      18
Date of last update   : 08/03/86
Field  Field Name  Type        Width   Dec
    1  CUST_ID     Character       6
    2  DATE        Date            8
    3  ID          Character       7
    4  DESCRIPT    Character      30
    5  DEBIT       Numeric        12     2
    6  CREDIT      Numeric        12     2
    7  BALANCE     Numeric        12     2
    8  BILLED      Logical         1
    9  DELCODE     Logical         1
** Total **                       90
```

Fig. 9.2. Structure of the customer file used in the customer accounts system.

The use of a shared customer file requires some changes in each system. First, you must make the customer file available to both systems. If you place both systems and the combined customer file in the same DOS subdirectory, both systems will automatically have access to the file. If you place the customer file in a subdirectory not occupied by one of the systems, you should add a dBASE command SET PATH to the main menu program or the file-opening program for that system and indicate the subdirectory containing the shared file.

Suppose that the sales-tracking application is in subdirectory C:\SALES, the customer-accounts system is the subdirectory C:\CUSTACCT, and the customer file is in the customer account subdirectory. The command

SET PATH TO C:\CUSTACCT

should be placed either in the initialization section of main-menu program SLSTRACK or in file-opening program SLSOPEN.

In addition, make sure that the programs in the two systems refer to the same customer file name and the same variable names for variables from the customer file. In the systems presented in this book, program and database file names all begin with a two-letter abbreviation of the system name. To reflect the new name of the common customer file, you need to change in each system any references to the customer file that are of the form

ALIAS->VARIABLE

If the customer file is called CACUST, the programs in the sales-tracking system must be changed to reference this name instead of CUST00, which is used in the sales-tracking system. For example, the command

@ 7,24 SAY "Customer: "+CUST00–>COMPANY

would become

@ 7,24 SAY "Customer: "+CACUST–>COMPANY

in the program TRANSCRN.

Finally, you need only one set of data-entry and update programs for the common customer file. The common data-entry and update programs can be called from both systems once the SET PATH command has been used to identify the location of the files.

Using Common Data-Entry Programs

In the preceding section, we looked at how a common file can be used to link the customer-account system with the sales-tracking system. These two applications can be linked also with a common data-entry program. Because both applications use sales data, a common data-entry program for sales data could update the files in both systems. Such a data-entry program might use a screen like the one shown in figure 9.3.

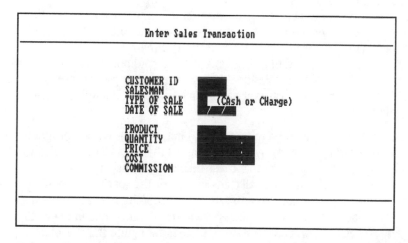

Fig. 9.3. Combined data-entry screen for sales tracking and customer accounts.

Although similar to the sales-transaction data-entry screen in the sales-tracking application, this screen allows the user to enter the sale date and identify the type of sale (cash or charge). The associated data-entry program would post the same information to the sales-tracking file: customer ID number, salesperson, product, period, quantity, unit price, unit cost, and commission for each item sold.

For credit sales, the data-entry program accumulates the total amount of the items sold to the customer and adds a new transaction in the customer-accounts file. The total amount is entered as a debit transaction in the customer accounts transaction file; then the new balance is used to update the customer file.

The data-entry program could also update the appropriate general-ledger accounts at the time a sale is entered. However, this would result in a large number of general journal entries that duplicate the detail already kept in the sales-tracking system and the customer-accounts system. Therefore, you would probably want to set up the system to periodically post the sales totals to the general ledger from the sales-tracking system, the accounts receivable from the customer-accounts system, and the cash-receipts totals from the company's cash-receipts system. (The latter is not one of the systems discussed in this book.) The use of a program to process the data in one system and prepare input to another system—the third method of linking systems—is discussed in the following section.

Using Programs To Summarize and Transfer Data Between Systems

The third method of linking systems involves the use of dBASE programs to summarize and transfer data between systems. This method is appropriate when the data entered into the receiving system is a summary or is calculated from the detail data in the sending system. For example, you could use this method to post depreciation from the fixed-asset system to the general ledger, to post sales and cost of sales to the general ledger from the sales-tracking system, and to post accounts receivable (including both sales and customer payments) to the general ledger from the customer-accounts system.

The transfer of data can be accomplished in two ways. First, you can write a program that processes the data from the sending system and inputs that data to the receiving system. An example would be a program that reads the customer-accounts transaction file (CATRANS.DBF) and sums all transactions for the specified period. Then the program writes a general journal entry for the sum of the transactions. This technique is most appropriate for smaller businesses where the same person operates the sending system as well as the receiving system. Orchestrating the transfer of data is not a problem in such situations.

The second way to accomplish the data transfer is to have two programs and an intermediate file. The first program processes the data in the sending system. Instead of transferring the data directly to the receiving system, the program writes the summary data to an intermediate file. You could incorporate such a program into a month-end close sequence without worrying about whether the other system is ready to receive the data. The second program reads the intermediate file and generates the necessary transactions in the receiving system. This program can be run

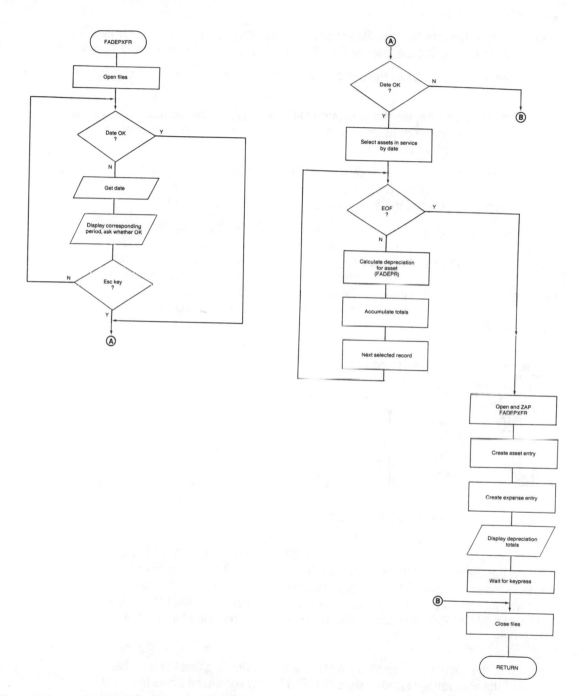

Fig. 9.4. Flowchart for the program FADEPXFR.

at any time after the intermediate file has been generated. You can include safety flags in the code to ensure that the intermediate file is read only once after it is created.

Here's how the second way to transfer data would work with the fixed-asset system and the general ledger:

- On the cutoff date, the first program would be run from the fixed-asset system to generate an intermediate database file containing the depreciation ledger entries for the month.

- When it is time to enter depreciation into the general ledger, the user would run the second program, which picks up the contents of the intermediate file and generates the required general journal entries.

Let's look at a program for the fixed-asset system to calculate monthly depreciation for all assets that are in service on a specified date. The flowchart for FADEPXFR is shown in figure 9.4. Briefly, FADEPXFR gets the depreciation date from the user, calculates depreciation on assets, creates journal entries, and displays depreciation totals. FADEPXFR uses the database file FADEPXFR.DBF to hold the journal entries. Note that FADEPXFR.DBF has the same structure as the general-ledger file FRSGJOUR.DBF (see fig. 9.5).

```
Structure for database: C:fadepxfr.dbf
Number of data records:      0
Date of last update   : 08/20/86
Field  Field Name  Type      Width  Dec
    1  TRANSACTNO  Numeric       6
    2  DATE        Date          8
    3  PERIOD      Numeric       2
    4  ACCOUNTNO   Numeric       6     1
    5  DESCRIPT    Character    30
    6  PC          Character     2
    7  DEBIT       Numeric      11     2
    8  CREDIT      Numeric      11     2
** Total **                    77
```

Fig. 9.5. Structure of the file FADEPXFR.DB.

After opening files with a call to FAOPEN, FADEPXFR enters a DO WHILE loop and prompts the user to enter the depreciation date (see listing 9.1). The data-entry screen is shown in figure 9.6. The program accepts the date entry and displays the corresponding accounting period. If the user verifies the date, the OK flag is set to true and FADEPXFR continues. Otherwise, the loop is repeated for entry of a new date.

The rest of the code is executed only if MOK is true, indicating that the user has accepted the accounting period. If so, a SET FILTER TO command filters the fixed-asset file (FIXASSET.DBF) to exclude any assets placed in service after the specified date (MDATE). This step allows the user to calculate depreciation for a specified period but still enter assets for the following period.

Next, the program enters a DO WHILE .NOT.EOF ( ) loop that calls subroutine FADEPR to calculate the depreciation for each qualifying asset. (For more on subroutine FADEPR, see Chapter 6, "Fixed-Asset Manager.") After the depreciation is calculated, FADEPXFR selects the last work area (9), opens the file FADEPXFR.DBF, and uses the ZAP command to clear the file before writing to it. Then the program writes the debit-ledger entry for depreciation expense and the credit-ledger entry for the depreciation asset account. The two depreciation journal entries written by FADEPXFR are shown in figure 9.7.

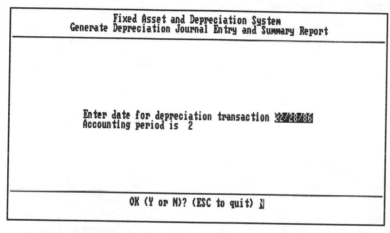

Fig. 9.6. Screen to enter the depreciation date.

```
Record#  TRANSACTNO DATE    PERIOD ACCOUNTNO DESCRIPT            PC
         DEBIT     CREDIT
      1            02/28/86    2     141.0 depreciation expense  FA
       0.00   1915.81
      2            02/28/86    2     600.0 depreciation expense  FA
    1915.81       0.00
```

Fig. 9.7. Depreciation journal entries written to FADEPXFR.DBF by program FADEPXFR.

Finally, FADEPXFR displays the depreciation totals and pauses (see fig. 9.8). The user is prompted to press the PrtSc key if a hard-copy summary is desired. To quit this screen, the user presses any key. The program then closes the database files and returns control to the calling program, which would be one of the menu programs in the fixed-asset system. (Note that FADEPXFR uses the memory variable FATITLE, which is stored in the fixed-asset system memory file. To run FADEPXFR as a stand-alone program, you will need to add a line assigning an appropriate value to FATITLE.)

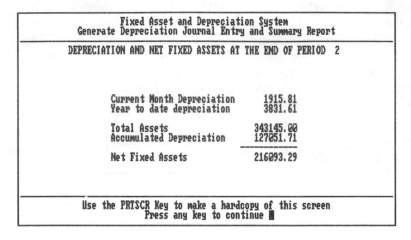

```
                  Fixed Asset and Depreciation System
            Generate Depreciation Journal Entry and Summary Report

        DEPRECIATION AND NET FIXED ASSETS AT THE END OF PERIOD  2



             Current Month Depreciation      1915.81
             Year to date depreciation        3831.61

             Total Assets                   343145.00
             Accumulated Depreciation       127051.71
                                            ----------
             Net Fixed Assets               216093.29



         Use the PRTSCR Key to make a hardcopy of this screen
                    Press any key to continue ▮
```

Fig. 9.8. Screen showing depreciation and net assets at the end of the specified accounting period.

The receiving program, FRSGDEPR, is added to the general-ledger system. This program reads and validates each journal entry from file FADEPXFR.DBF in the fixed-assets system. If the journal entry is validated, the program prompts the user to approve the posting of these entries to the general ledger. If the user approves, the program appends the journal entries to the general ledger file and prints an optional journal-entry report. The flowchart for FRSGDEPR is shown in figure 9.9.

FRSGDEPR begins by opening the files, selecting the general-ledger file (FRSGJOUR.DBF), and prompting the user to confirm that he or she wants to proceed (see listing 9.2). If the user wants to continue, FRSGDEPR uses the command

    SET PATH TO c:\dbase\applib\fa

to set the path to the directory of the fixed-assets system. The program selects the last work area (9) and opens the file FADEPXFR.DBF.

Then FRSGDEPR enters a DO WHILE loop to scan the entries in FADEPXFR.DBF to verify that they make up a valid ledger entry. The program checks each record for a valid account number, verifies that there is either a debit or a credit (but not both), and sums the entries to verify that the transaction balances. Appropriate error messages are displayed if the program detects any problems.

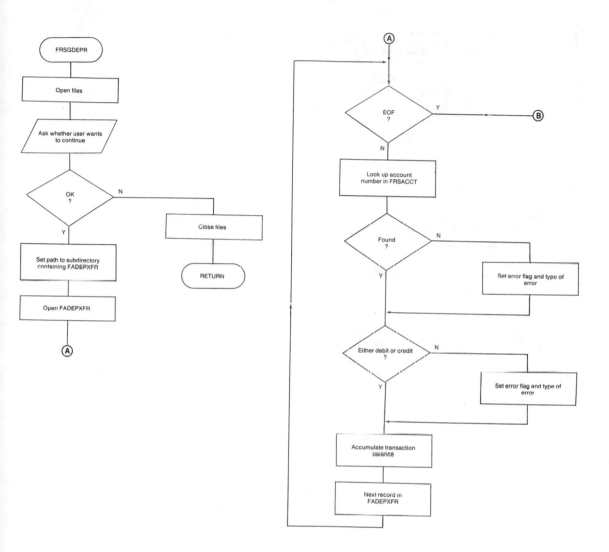

Fig. 9.9. Flowchart for the program FRSGDEPR.

After the program has finished checking the entries in FADEPXFR.DBF, the program displays a summary screen as shown in figure 9.10. Any errors found by FRSGDEPR are indicated at the bottom of this screen. If no errors were found, the message NO ERRORS DETECTED is displayed, and the reader presses any key to continue.

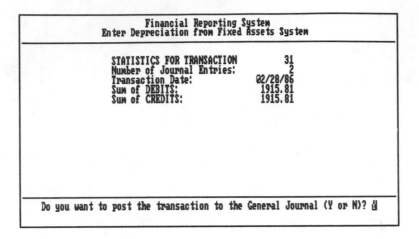

Fig. 9.10. Summary screen for depreciation ledger entries.

If no errors were detected, the program prompts the user to indicate whether he or she wants to post this entry to the general ledger and whether a journal-entry listing is desired. If the user wants to do the posting, FRSGDEPR appends the transactions from the FADEPXFR.DBF file to the general ledger file, FRSGJOUR.DBF. If the user specifies a journal-entry report, a report similar to the one in figure 9.11 for Smith and Jones Corporation is printed.

```
LISTING OF DEPRECIATION JOURNAL ENTRIES FOR 02/28/86
Page No.    1
08/20/86
                                     Smith and Jones Company
                                     Financial Reporting System
                                     General Journal Listing
                                     In Transaction Entry Order


Transaction        Accounting                             Post
   Number Date     Period Account Description             Code    DEBIT        CREDIT
----------- -------- ----------- ------- -------------------------------- ---- ------------ -----------


        31 02/28/86      2   141.0 depreciation expense    FA      0:00       1915.81
        31 02/28/86      2   600.0 depreciation expense    FA   1915.81          0.00
*** Total ***
                                                               1915.81       1915.81
```

Fig. 9.11. Depreciation journal-entry report.

Finally, FRSGDEPR uses the ZAP command to erase the contents of the
FADEPXFR.DBF file to prevent it from being posted a second time. Then the program
closes files and returns control to the calling program.

Using a Program To Read Data From a Non-dBASE System

To demonstrate the fourth method of linking applications, we look at how entries are
posted to the general ledger from a cash receipts report generated by Lotus 1-2-3.
This report is saved to disk as a .PRN file. Figure 9.12 shows the report that is read
into the general ledger. This cash-receipts report for Smith and Jones Corporation
shows five journal entries for cash transactions on February 15, 1986.

```
               Cash Receipts Journal Entry Report
                          For 2/15/86


Account Description           Debit   Credit
------- -----------------     ------- -------
    100 Cash on Hand          185.00
    500 Purchases              25.00
    700 Miscellaneous          i0.00
    400 Sales                          205.00
    220 Sales Tax                       15.00
                             -------  -------
         Total                220.00   220.00
```

Fig. 9.12. Cash-receipts journal entry to read into the general ledger.

The cash-receipts report is read into the general ledger by a dBASE III Plus program
designed to read fields from this particular report. dBASE III Plus can directly read
delimited ASCII files into a database file, but the report in figure 9.12 contains
extraneous information that must be filtered out. We must also check the data to be
sure the transaction is balanced before the data is entered into the general ledger.

Important note: *You should set up a separate program for each different
accounting report that you read into the journal. A separate program for each
different report helps to document exactly what is being done to read each set of
journal entries.*

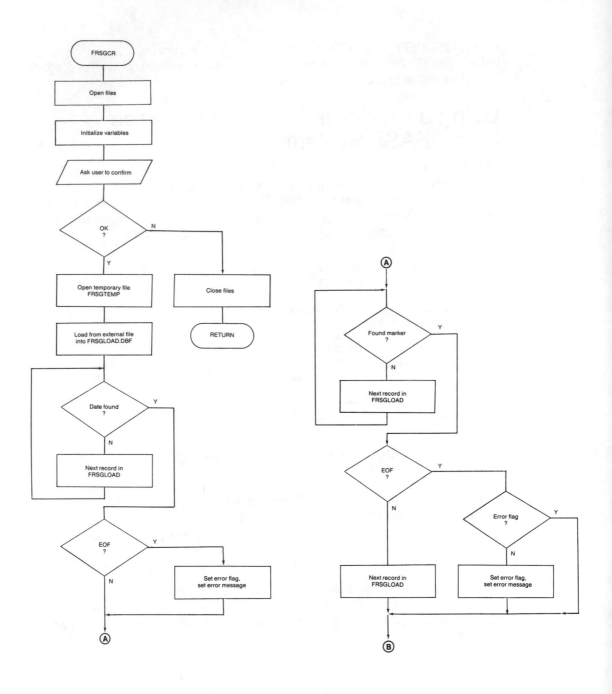

Fig. 9.13. Flowchart of the program FRSGCR.

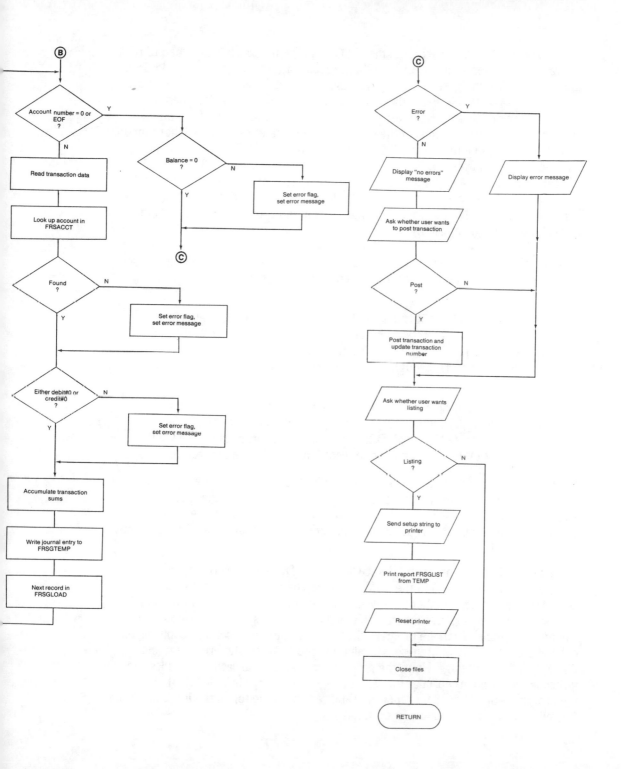

Figure 9.13 shows the flowchart of the FRSGCR program, which is designed to read the cash-receipts report into dBASE. FRSGCR reads cash-receipt journal entries from the report shown in figure 9.12. Briefly, FRSGCR first reads each line of the report into FRSGLOAD.DBF, a special database with one 132-character field. Then the program uses dBASE string functions to extract the journal-entry information contained in the four columns of the report. The remainder of the FRSGCR program treats the extracted journal entry information exactly as FRSGENTR treats data entered from the keyboard. (For more on FRSGENTR, see Chapter 8, "General-Ledger and Financial-Reporting System.") The program checks the validity of each account and verifies that the transaction is balanced before any data is written to the general ledger. Finally, the program produces a journal-entry report and posts the transaction to the general ledger.

To use FRSGCR, you need to create database file FRSGLOAD.DBF. This file contains a single field, BUFFER, that is defined as a character type with a length of 132 characters.

As noted previously, FRSGCR is designed to read the report in figure 9.12. The program processes the transaction journal entries by reading the account from columns 6 through 12, the description from columns 14 through 29, the debit amount from columns 31 through 39, and the credit amount from columns 41 through 49.

The program begins by opening the files and asking whether the user wants to continue (see listing 9.3). If the user wants to proceed, FRSGCR creates the temporary journal entry file TEMP.DBF and reads the report lines into the buffer database, FRSGLOAD.DBF, creating one record in the database for each report line.

Next, the program scans the buffer line by line for the transaction date, which always starts in position 36 in the report line. If the date is found, the program proceeds to look for a marker indicating that the first transaction is on the next line. The marker in this report (see fig. 9.12) is the dashed line under the account heading in columns 6 through 12 of the report line.

If the date and marker are found, FRSGCR enters a DO WHILE loop that processes the remainder of the file until end of file is reached or the program encounters a zero or blank account number field. Within the loop, the program reads the journal entry account number, description, debit, and credit from specified positions in the current report line. Then the program checks the account number and confirms the debit and credit. If either of these is invalid, the program sets the error flags and displays an error message. Next, the program updates the transaction statistics and writes the journal-entry data to the temporary journal entry file TEMP.DBF. Finally, the program skips to the next report line and returns to the top of the loop. Errors are flagged, but the loop continues executing.

When the loop is exited, FRSGCR checks for a non-zero transaction balance and sets the error flags if it finds one. The program displays a screen showing the transaction statistics and any error flag that was set, and asks whether the user wants to print a journal-entry report (see fig. 9.14).

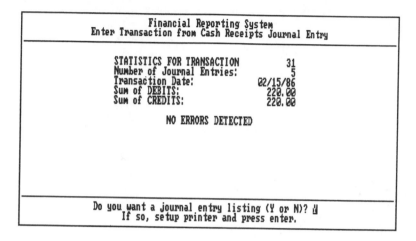

```
                    Financial Reporting System
             Enter Transaction from Cash Receipts Journal Entry


               STATISTICS FOR TRANSACTION          31
               Number of Journal Entries:           5
               Transaction Date:               02/15/86
               Sum of DEBITS:                    220.00
               Sum of CREDITS:                   220.00

                    NO ERRORS DETECTED





             Do you want a journal entry listing (Y or N)? N
                   If so, setup printer and press enter.
```

Fig. 9.14. Screen produced by FRSGCR to display transaction statistics.

If no errors have occurred, the program asks the user whether the transaction should be posted to the general ledger, and does so if the user presses Y in response to the prompt. The program then checks whether the user asked for a journal-entry report and prints the report if so. A journal-entry report printed for the cash-receipts entry of figure 9.12 is shown in figure 9.15.

Finally, FRSGCR uses the ZAP command to remove all records from buffer database FRSGLOAD.DBF and deletes the temporary journal entry file TEMP.DBF.

The program FRSGCR is designed to read one specific report format. However, with minor revisions, the program can read journal-entry data from most reports in which all the data for each journal entry is on one line with a fixed format.

Conclusion

The applications for sales tracking, customer accounts, fixed assets, and general ledger are more useful if they are integrated where appropriate. Linked together, they form part of a business-accounting system. This chapter has shown you how to link these four stand-alone accounting applications. You've seen also how to link one of these applications to an application not written in dBASE III Plus.

```
LISTING OF CASH RECEIPTS JOURNAL ENTRIES FOR 02/15/86
Page No.    1
08/21/86
                                       Smith and Jones Company
                                       Financial Reporting System
                                       General Journal Listing
                                       In Transaction Entry Order


Transaction          Accounting                              Post
    Number Date      Period Account Description              Code    DEBIT      CREDIT
----------- --------  ----------- ------- -------------------------------  ---- ------------ ------------


        32 02/15/86       2     100.0 Cash on Hand           CR      185.00       0.00
        32 02/15/86       2     500.0 Purchases              CR       25.00       0.00
        32 02/15/86       2     700.0 Miscellaneous          CR       10.00       0.00
        32 02/15/86       2     400.0 Sales                  CR        0.00     205.00
        32 02/15/86       2     220.0 Sales Tax              CR        0.00      15.00
*** Total ***
                                                                    220.00     220.00
```

Fig. 9.15. The general journal entry report for the cash-receipts journal entry.

At a minimum, however, you'll probably need additional systems to handle cash receipts, cash disbursements, and accounts payable. You can follow the techniques presented in this book and use dBASE III Plus to develop these additional applications, or you can write dBASE III programs to connect non-dBASE accounting modules to the general ledger.

Listing 9.1. The program FADEPXFR.

```
*****************************************************************************
* FADEPXFR -     calculate depreciation and transfer to General Ledger  *
*               8/19/86                                                  *
*****************************************************************************

* Set environment and open files
SET DELETED ON
DO faopen
RESTORE FROM famem ADDITIVE      && Restore memory variables for this appl.
mdate=date()
mtitle="Generate Depreciation Journal Entry and Summary Report"
DO borders WITH fatitle,mtitle

* Get depr date
mok=.f.
DO WHILE .not.mok
   @ 12, 16  SAY "Enter date for depreciation transaction" GET mdate
   READ
   mperiod=MOD(MONTH(mdate)-MONTH(fafiscalyr)-1,12)+1 && Determine acctg period
   @ 13, 16 SAY "Accounting period is "+STR(mperiod,2)
   @ 21, 26  SAY "OK (Y or N)? (ESC to quit)" GET mok PICTURE 'Y'
   READ
   IF readkey()=12        && If ESC key pressed
     EXIT                 && Break out of loop with mok=.f.
   ENDIF
ENDDO
@ 5, 1 CLEAR TO 19, 78
@ 21, 1 CLEAR TO 22, 78

IF mok          && Do remainder only if mok=.T.

   * Set up for depreciation loop
   STORE 0 TO tcurr,tytd,taccum,tcost,mcurr,mytd,maccum
   @ 12, 35 SAY "Working..."
   SET FILTER TO serv_date<=mdate
   GO TOP

   *LOOP to calculate depreciation
   DO WHILE .NOT.EOF()

      DO fadepr  WITH mdate,mcurr,mytd,maccum
      tcurr=tcurr+mcurr
      tytd=tytd+mytd
      taccum=taccum+maccum
      tcost=tcost+cost
      SKIP

   ENDDO

   * Create and open depreciation transfer file
   SELECT 9                        && Next to last work area avoids conflicts
   USE fadepxfr                    && Open depr transfer file
   ZAP                             && And clear it out
```

(Continued on next page.)

Listing 9.1, continued.

```
* Asset half of journal entry
APPEND BLANK
REPLACE date WITH mdate, period WITH mperiod, accountno WITH 141.0,;
   descript WITH "depreciation expense", pc WITH "FA", debit with 0,;
   credit WITH tcurr

* Expense half of journal entry
APPEND BLANK
REPLACE date WITH mdate, period WITH mperiod, accountno WITH 600.0,;
      descript WITH "depreciation expense", pc WITH "FA", debit with tcurr,;
      credit WITH 0

   * Display totals
   @ 5, 1 CLEAR TO 19, 78
   @ 5, 11 SAY "DEPRECIATION AND NET FIXED ASSETS AT THE END OF PERIOD ";
     +STR(mperiod,2)
   @ 10, 20  SAY "Current Month Depreciation "+STR(tcurr,12,2)
   @ 11, 20  SAY "Year to date depreciation  "+STR(tytd,12,2)
   @ 13, 20  SAY "Total Assets               "+STR(tcost,12,2)
   @ 14, 20  SAY "Accumulated Depreciation   "+STR(taccum,12,2)
   tnet=tcost-taccum
   @ 15, 20  SAY "                           ------------"
   @ 16, 20  SAY "Net Fixed Assets           "+STR(tnet,12,2)
   CLEAR GETS
   @ 21, 14  SAY "Use the PRTSCR Key to make a hardcopy of this screen"
   ans=' '
   @ 22, 27  SAY "Press any key to continue" GET ans
   READ

ENDIF (mok)

* Clean up and return
SET DELETED OFF
CLEAR
CLOSE DATABASES
RETURN
```

Listing 9.2. The program FRSGDEPR.

```
*************************************************************************
* FRSGDEPR -     Make an entry for depreciation in the General Ledger   *
*                from The Fixed Assets System                           *
*                8/20/86                                                *
*************************************************************************

* Open files & set environment
DO frsopen                      && Open Financial Reporting System Files and Indexes
SELECT frsgjour

* Restore sytem memory variables
RESTORE FROM frsmem ADDITIVE
title="Enter Depreciation from Fixed Assets System"
DO BORDERS WITH frstitle,title

* Make sure user wants to do this
mok=.f.
@ 21, 22 SAY "Do you want to continue (Y or N)?" GET mok PICTURE "Y"
READ
IF .not.mok
   CLOSE DATABASES
   CLEAR
   RETURN
ENDIF
@ 21, 1 SAY SPACE(78)

*Open file containing depreciation journal entries
SET PATH TO c:\dbase\applib\fa          && Path to file being read
SELECT 9                                && Last work area to avoid conflicts
USE fadepxfr

* Process depreciation journal entry file to check for valid entry
GO TOP                                          && First record in temp file
ok=.t.                                          && Begin by assuming data ok
error=' '
STORE 0 TO number,md,mc,mbal
DO WHILE .not.EOF()                             && Process each record in file

   *Check account number
   SELECT frsacct
   SEEK fadepxfr->accountno
   IF EOF()                                     && If account not found
      ok=.f.
      error="Invalid account number: "+STR(fadepxfr->accountno,6,1)
   ENDIF

   * Confirm that there is one nonzero number
   SELECT fadepxfr
   IF .not.((debit>0.and.credit=0).or.(debit=0.and.credit>0))
      ok=.F.
      error="Journal entry with bad debit or credit for acct: ";
         +STR(accountno,6,1)
   ENDIF
```

(Continued on next page.)

Listing 9.2, continued.

```
    * Add transactno
    REPLACE transactno WITH frstrans

    * Accumulate transaction statistics
    mdate=date
    number=number+1
    md=md+debit
    mc=mc+credit
    mbal=mbal+debit-credit

    * Next entry
    SKIP

ENDDO

* Check Balance
IF ABS(mbal)>.005
    ok=.F.
    error="Out of Balance"
ENDIF

* Ask if want a journal entry listing and want to post
DO borders with frstitle, title
@ 6, 20 SAY "STATISTICS FOR TRANSACTION "+STR(frstrans,11)
@ 7, 20 SAY "Number of Journal Entries: "+STR(number,11)
@ 8, 20 SAY "Transaction Date:            "+DTOC(mdate)
@ 9, 20 SAY "Sum of DEBITS:               "+STR(md,11,2)
@ 10, 20 SAY "Sum of CREDITS:             "+STR(mc,11,2)
IF .not.ok
    @ 12, (73-LEN(error))/2 SAY "ERROR: "+error
ELSE
    @ 12, 31 SAY "NO ERRORS DETECTED"
ENDIF

* Pause for user to read screen
ans= ' '
@ 21, 26 SAY "Press any key to continue" GET ans
READ
@ 21, 1 CLEAR TO 22, 78
@ 12, 1 SAY SPACE(78)

* Post transactions to general journal
IF ok
    * Ask about posting transaction
    mok1=.T.
    @ 21, 5 SAY "Do you want to post the transaction to the General Journal ";
        +"(Y or N)?" GET mok1 PICTURE "Y"
    READ
    @ 21, 1 SAY SPACE(78)

    * Ask about a journal entry listing
    mok2=.t.
    @ 21, 20 SAY "Do you want a journal entry listing (Y or N)?";
        GET mok2 PICTURE 'Y'
    @ 22, 20 SAY "If so, setup printer before entering Y"
    READ
    @ 21, 1 CLEAR TO 22, 78
```

```
* Post transaction to general ledger
IF mok1
   @ 12, 20 SAY "Posting transactions to General Journal"
   SELECT fadepxfr                       && Select depreciation file
   USE                                   && Deselect before copy
   SELECT frsgjour
   APPEND FROM fadepxfr                  && Copy transaction to frsgjour file
   frstrans=frstrans+1
   SAVE TO frsmem ALL LIKE frs*          && Save transaction count
ENDIF

* Print a journal entry listing if requested
IF mok2
   CLOSE DATABASES

   USE fadepxfr
   @ 12, 1 SAY SPACE(78)
   @ 12, 25 SAY "Printing journal entry listing"
   SET PRINT ON
   SET CONSOLE OFF
   ? &frspsetup                && Set compressed print
   ? SPACE(frspmargin)+"LISTING OF DEPRECIATION JOURNAL ENTRIES FOR ";
      +DTOC(mdate)
   REPORT FORM frsglist
   ? &frspreset                && Set normal print
   SET CONSOLE ON
   SET PRINT OFF
ENDIF

ENDIF

* tidy up and return
CLEAR
USE fadepxfr
ZAP
CLOSE DATABASES                       && Delete depreciation transactions
RETURN
```

Listing 9.3. The program FRSGCR.

```
**************************************************************************
* FRSGCR -       Make an entry in the general ledger from the cash     *
*                receipts journal entry                                *
*                8/15/86                                               *
**************************************************************************

* Open files & set environment
DO frsopen             && Open financial reporting system files and indexes
SELECT frsgjour

* Restore sytem memory variables
RESTORE FROM frsmem ADDITIVE
title="Enter Transaction from Cash Receipts Journal Entry"
DO BORDERS WITH frstitle,title
markst=6                  && Marker definition -  Start Column
marker='-------'         &&                              marker text
marklen=LEN(marker)      &&                              marker length
acctst=6          && Start of account field in report
acctlen=7         && Length of account field
descst=14         && Start of description field in report
desclen=16        && Length of description field
drst=31           && Start of debit field in report
drlen=9           && Length of debit field
crst=41           && Start of credit field in report
crlen=9           && Length of credit field
datest=36         && Start of transaction date field

* Make sure user wants to do this
mok=.f.
@ 21, 22 SAY "Do you want to continue (Y or N)?" GET mok PICTURE "Y"
READ
IF .not.mok
   CLOSE DATABASES
   RETURN
ENDIF
@ 21, 1 SAY SPACE(78)

* Setup temporary file to hold data entry
@ 12, 34 SAY "Opening files"
DO frsgtemp     && Creates empty file with same structure as general ledger

* Open external transfer database and load cash receipts report
SELECT 8
USE frsgload
ZAP
APPEND FROM cashr.prn SDF
GO TOP
ok=.T.
```

```
*Find date for transaction being imported
@ 12, 1 SAY SPACE(78)
@ 12, 20 SAY "Reading and checking Cash Receipts data"
DO WHILE CTOD(SUBSTR(buffer,datest,8))=CTOD("").and..not.EOF()
   SKIP
ENDDO
mdate=CTOD(SUBSTR(buffer,datest,8))
mper=frsperiod
IF EOF()
   ok=.F.
   error="End of file encountered while looking for date"
ENDIF

*Find first journal entry for transaction

DO WHILE SUBSTR(buffer,markst,marklen)#marker.and..not.EOF()
   SKIP
ENDDO
IF .not.EOF()
   SKIP
ELSE
   IF ok
      ok=.F.
      error="End of file encountered while looking for first transaction"
   ENDIF
ENDIF

* Loop to process transaction journal entries
STORE 0 TO mbal,mc,md,number
DO WHILE VAL(SUBSTR(buffer,acctst,acctlen))#0.and..not.EOF()
   * Read transaction data
   macct=VAL(SUBSTR(buffer,acctst,acctlen))      && Read accountno field
   mdescr=SUBSTR(buffer,descst,desclen)          && Read descript field
   mdebit=VAL(SUBSTR(buffer,drst,drlen))         && Read debit field
   mcredit=VAL(SUBSTR(buffer,crst,crlen))        && Read credit field

   * Confirm account
   SELECT frsacct
   SEEK macct
   IF EOF()
      ok=.F.
      error="Invalid account number: "+STR(macct,6,1)
   ENDIF

   * Confirm that there is one nonzero number
   IF .not.((mdebit>0.and.mcredit=0).or.(mdebit=0.and.mcredit>0))
      ok=.F.
      error="Journal entry with bad debit or credit for acct: "+STR(macct,6,1)
   ENDIF

   * Accumulate transaction statistics
   number=number+1
   md=md+mdebit
   mc=mc+mcredit
   mbal=mbal+mdebit-mcredit
```

(Continued on next page.)

Listing 9.3, continued.

```
    * Write to temporary journal entry file
    SELECT temp
    APPEND BLANK
    REPLACE accountno WITH macct, date WITH mdate, period WITH frsperiod,;
            descript WITH mdescr, pc WITH "CR", transactno WITH frstrans,;
            debit WITH mdebit, credit WITH mcredit

    SELECT frsgload
    SKIP

ENDDO                           && READ next journal entry loop

* Check Balance
IF ABS(mbal)>.005
    ok=.F.
    error="Out of Balance"
ENDIF

* Ask if want a journal entry listing and want to post
DO borders with frstitle, title
@ 6, 20 SAY "STATISTICS FOR TRANSACTION "+STR(frstrans,11)
@ 7, 20 SAY "Number of Journal Entries: "+STR(number,11)
@ 8, 20 SAY "Transaction Date:          "+DTOC(mdate)
@ 9, 20 SAY "Sum of DEBITS:             "+STR(md,11,2)
@ 10, 20 SAY "Sum of CREDITS:           "+STR(mc,11,2)
IF .not.ok
    @ 12, (73-LEN(error))/2 SAY "ERROR: "+error
ELSE
    @ 12, 31 SAY "NO ERRORS DETECTED"
ENDIF
mok=.T.
@ 21, 16 SAY "Do you want a journal entry listing (Y or N)?";
        GET mok PICTURE "Y"
@ 22, 22 SAY "If so, setup printer and press enter."
READ
@ 21, 1 SAY SPACE(78)
@ 22, 1 SAY SPACE(78)
@ 12, 1 SAY SPACE(78)

* Post transactions to general journal
IF ok
    mok1=.T.
    @ 21, 5 SAY "Do you want to post the transaction to ";
                +"the General Journal (Y or N)?" GET mok1 PICTURE "Y"
    READ
    @ 21, 1 SAY SPACE(78)
    IF mok1
       @ 12, 20 SAY "Posting transactions to General Journal"
       SELECT temp                      && Select temporary file
       USE                              && Deselect temp for copy
       SELECT frsgjour
       APPEND FROM temp.dbf             && Copy transaction to frsgjour file
       frstrans=frstrans+1
       SAVE TO frsmem ALL LIKE frs*     && Save transaction count
    ENDIF
```

```
* Print a journal entry listing if requested
IF mok

    * Print report
    CLOSE DATABASES
    USE temp
    @ 12, 1 SAY SPACE(78)
    @ 12, 25 SAY "Printing journal entry listing"
    SET PRINT ON
    SET CONSOLE OFF
    ? &frspsetup            && Set compressed print
    ? SPACE(frspmargin)+"LISTING OF CASH RECEIPTS JOURNAL ENTRIES FOR ";
        +DTOC(mdate)
    REPORT FORM frsglist

    * Reset console and printer
    ? &frspreset            && Set normal print
    SET CONSOLE ON
    SET PRINT OFF
ENDIF

* tidy up and return
CLEAR
CLOSE DATABASES
USE frsgload
ZAP
CLOSE DATABASES
ERASE temp.dbf                      && Delete temporary file
RETURN
```

Index

R

More Computer Knowledge from Que

Que Order Line: **1-800-428-5331**

All prices subject to change without notice.

MORE COMPUTER KNOWLEDGE FROM QUE

dBASE III Plus Handbook, 2nd Edition
by George T. Chou, Ph.D.

A complete, easy-to-understand guide to dBASE III Plus commands and features. The handbook provides full discussion of basic and advanced operations for displaying and editing data. Numerous examples of databases show the options for handling, sorting, summarizing, and indexing data. The book explains error messages in detail and offers tips on how to avoid errors when you create files and enter data. For both newcomers to dBASE III and former dBASE III users, the *dBASE III Plus Handbook* will help you manage your office or business more efficiently.

Using NetWare
by Michael Durr and Bill Lawrence

Novell's NetWare software supports networking equipment from such manufacturers as IBM, Corvus Systems, 3Com Corporation, and Novell. Que's *Using NetWare* addresses NetWare as a self-contained program in networking and as a guide to the networking environment. The book sums up many capabilities and resources to the personal computer user: hard disk storage, communication among personal computers, and a variety of printer options. This book also shows how to use these new capabilities. Other features discussed are sharing and protecting data, user commands, and electronic mail.

dBASE III Advanced Programming
by Joseph-David Carrabis

Experienced dBASE users and other programmers will find this book an excellent guide to tight, fast, and efficient programming. This book is divided into three sections: advanced programming techniques, turnkey systems with dBASE III, and business applications. The book emphasizes how to speed up dBASE programs and how programs written in assembly, BASIC, Pascal, or C language can be adapted to run with dBASE III applications. For those who want to learn and write the best programs, *dBASE III Advanced Programming* is an excellent choice.

Managing Your Hard Disk
by Don Berliner

Que's *Managing Your Hard Disk* introduces innovative techniques to bring the hard disk to peak performance. Storing and retrieving "libraries" of information is simple when the reader follows the book's easy-to-understand instructions. Learning how to use programs that usually won't run on a hard disk, activating "menu programs," and backing up data also are included in this information-packed book. *Managing Your Hard Disk* may well be the best thing that's happened to hard disk convertees.

Mail to: Que Corporation • P. O. Box 50507 • Indianapolis, IN 46250

Item	Title	Price	Quantity	Extension
68	dBASE III Plus Handbook, 2nd Edition	$19.95		
183	Using NetWare	$24.95		
194	dBASE III Advanced Programming	$22.95		
67	Managing Your Hard Disk	$19.95		
	Book Subtotal			
	Shipping & Handling ($2.50 per item)			
	Indiana Residents Add 5% Sales Tax			
	GRAND TOTAL			

Method of Payment:

☐ Check ☐ VISA ☐ MasterCard ☐ American Express

Card Number _____ Exp. Date _____

Cardholder's Name _____

Ship to _____

Address _____

City _____ State _____ ZIP _____

If you can't wait, call **1-800-428-5331** and order TODAY.

All prices subject to change without notice.

dBASEapp-8611

FOLD HERE

Place
Stamp
Here

Que Corporation
P. O. Box 50507
Indianapolis, IN 46250

REGISTER YOUR COPY OF
dBASE III PLUS APPLICATIONS LIBRARY

Register your copy of *dBASE III Plus Applications Library* and receive information about Que's newest products relating to databases. Complete this registration card and return it to Que Corporation, P.O. Box 50507, Indianapolis, IN 46250.

Name _____

Company _____ Title _____

Address _____

City _____ State _____ ZIP _____

Phone _____

Where did you buy your copy of *dBASE III Plus Applications Library*?

_____

How do you plan to use the programs in this book?

_____

_____

_____

What other kinds of publications about dBASE III Plus would you be interested in?

_____

_____

Which operating system do you use? _____

THANK YOU!

dBASEapp-8611

FOLD HERE

Place
Stamp
Here

Que Corporation
P. O. Box 50507
Indianapolis, IN 46250

save yourself hours of time with . . .

dBASE III Plus Applications
Library Disk

$39.95

The entire code for the applications in the *dBASE III Plus Applications Library* has been placed on this companion disk to save you hours of programming. Containing over 10,000 lines of tested code, this disk enables you to run your application much sooner and makes it easy to modify the code to suit your own needs.

Avoid the delay and inconvenience of manual entry, while you ensure that each line of code is accurate. Use the order blank below to order your *dBASE III Plus Applications Library* disk today. For more information, call a Que representative at 1-800-428-5331.

Mail to: Que Corporation • P.O. Box 50507 • Indianapolis, IN 46250

Please send _____ copy(ies) of *dBASE III Plus Applications Library* disk(s), #233, at $39.95 each.

Subtotal	$ _____
Shipping & handling ($2.50 per item)	$ _____
Indiana residents add 5% sales tax	$ _____
TOTAL	$ _____

Method of Payment:

☐ Check ☐ VISA ☐ MasterCard ☐ American Express

Card Number _____ Expiration Date _____

Cardholder's Name _____

Ship To _____

Address _____

City _____ State _____ ZIP _____

In a hurry? Call **1-800-428-5331** and order TODAY.

dBASEapp-8611

FOLD HERE

‾‾‾‾‾‾‾‾‾‾‾‾‾‾‾‾‾‾‾‾‾‾‾‾‾‾‾

‾‾‾‾‾‾‾‾‾‾‾‾‾‾‾‾‾‾‾‾‾‾‾‾‾‾‾

‾‾‾‾‾‾‾‾‾‾‾‾‾‾‾‾‾‾‾‾‾‾‾‾‾‾‾

‾‾‾‾‾‾‾‾‾‾‾‾‾‾‾‾‾‾‾‾‾‾‾‾‾‾‾

Place
Stamp
Here

Que Corporation
P. O. Box 50507
Indianapolis, IN 46250

FOLD HERE

Que Corporation
P. O. Box 50507
Indianapolis, IN 46250